Contents

Notes on contributors

Shawkat Alam is Professor of Law and Director of the Centre for Environmental Law at Macquarie University, Australia. His research and teaching explore the relationship between international law, international environmental law and international trade and sustainable development. Professor Alam holds an LLB (Hons) from Rajshahi University, Bangladesh, an LLM from Dhaka University, Bangladesh, and a PhD from Macquarie University. He has recently co-edited *International Environmental Law and the Global South* (Cambridge University Press, 2015), *International Trade Law and the WTO* (Federation Press, 2013) and *Routledge Handbook of International Environmental Law* (Routledge, 2012) and has authored several other books and scholarly articles. Professor Alam is a member of the IUCN Academy of Environmental Law and is engaged in its Teaching and Capacity Building Committee.

Rebecca Bates is a Lecturer in Environmental Law at Queen Mary College, University of London, UK. Dr Bates holds a PhD from the University of Sydney, examining the governance of privatised water markets in both domestic and international contexts. Her area of research has focused on international environmental law with a particular interest in international water law and governance.

Upendra Baxi is Professor of Law in Development Emeritus at University of Warwick, UK. He was previously President of the Indian Society of International Law, Honorary Director of Research at the Indian Law Institute and served as Vice-Chancellor at the University of South Gujarat, India, and the University of Delhi, India. Professor Baxi holds LLM degrees from the University of Bombay, India, and the University of California, Berkeley, USA. Professor Baxi has also been awarded a Doctorate in Juristic Sciences from University of California, Berkeley.

Jahid Hossain Bhuiyan teaches law at Northern University, Bangladesh, and was a visiting scholar at the University of Oxford, UK; Cardiff University, UK; Emory University, USA; University of British Columbia, Canada and Abo Akademi University, Finland. He holds a PhD in law from the

University of Queensland, Australia, and an LLM from Vrije Universiteit Brussel, Belgium. He has recently co-edited *International Trade Law and the WTO* (Federation Press, 2013), *An Introduction to International Refugee Law* (Brill, Martinus Nijhoff Publishers, 2013), *Globalization, International Law, and Human Rights* (Oxford University Press, 2012) and *Routledge Handbook of International Environmental Law* (Routledge, 2012), amongst other scholarly articles and texts.

Jürgen Bröhmer is Professor and Dean of Law at Murdoch University, Australia. Professor Bröhmer is a world leading expert in German constitutional law, European law and public international law with an emphasis on human rights and state immunity issues. He has authored numerous monographs, chapters and articles on public international, constitutional and European Union law and holds a PhD from Saarland University, Germany.

Philippe Cullet is Professor of International and Environmental Law at the School of Oriental and African Studies (SOAS), University of London and a Senior Visiting Fellow at the Centre for Policy Research in New Delhi. His main areas of interest include environmental law, natural resources, human rights and the socio-economic aspects of intellectual property. His latest book (with S. Koonan eds) is *Water Law in India – An Introduction to Legal Instruments* (Oxford University Press, 2nd edition, 2017).

Onita Das is Senior Lecturer at the University of the West of England, Bristol, UK, where her primary research area focuses on sustainable development, environmental protection during armed conflict and land grabbing. She was a visiting fellow at the Lauterpacht Centre for International Law, Cambridge University and is Head of Environmental Law Research at the University of the West of England. Dr Das is also a member of the Global Network on Human Rights and the Environment (GNHRE).

Mariel Dimsey is an international commercial and investment arbitration specialist currently practicing in Hong Kong. Her previous roles include practicing at leading international law firms in Germany and working at the Secretariat of the ICC International Court of Arbitration in Paris. Dr Dimsey holds an LLM from the University of Cologne, Germany, and has a doctorate in law (*summa cum laude*) from the University of Basel, Switzerland. She has taught international arbitration and international commercial law at the University of Bonn and University of Frankfurt, Germany.

Sarah Down is a PhD candidate at the Australian National University, Australia, where she is undertaking research on Māori mineral rights. She holds a LLB (1st class Hons) and a BA from the University of Canterbury, New Zealand, and has developed an extensive body of work at the Ngāi Tahu Research Centre, University of Canterbury and the National Aboriginal and Torres Strait Islander Legal Services (NATSILS), Australia.

Andrew Erueti (Ati Hau Nui A Paparanga, Nga Ruahinerangi) is a Senior Lecturer at the Faculty of Law, University of Auckland, New Zealand. Formerly the indigenous rights adviser for Amnesty International, he now teaches and researches in indigenous rights law and holds a PhD from the University of Toronto, Canada. He is the lead investigator of a Nga Pae o te Maramatanga; New Zealand's Māori Centre of Research Excellence project entitled: *Māori Engagement in New Zealand's Extractive Industry: Innovative Legal Solutions.*

Ilaria Espa is a Senior Research Fellow and Lecturer at the World Trade Institute (WTI) and the University of Milan. Her expertise explores the trade law implications of climate, energy and commodities policies, as well as the law governing the sustainable management of natural resources. Dr Espa was formerly awarded a Marie Curie Fellowship by the European Commission, holds a PhD from Bocconi University, Italy, and an MA from Luiss University, Italy. She has recently authored *Export Restrictions on Critical Minerals and Metals: Testing the Adequacy of WTO Disciplines* (Cambridge University Press, 2015) and has co-edited *International Trade in Sustainable Electricity: Regulatory Challenges in International Economic Law* (Cambridge University Press, 2017).

Abdullah Al Faruque is Professor of Law at the University of Chittagong, Bangladesh and Visiting Fellow for the Centre for Environmental Law, Macquarie University, Australia. Professor Faruque holds a PhD from Dundee University, UK, and was former Dean and Head of Chittagong Law School, Bangladesh. He has published numerous books including *Petroleum Contracts: Stability and Risk Management in Development Countries* (Bangladesh Institute of Law and International Affairs, 2011) and *International Human Rights Law: Protection Mechanisms and Contemporary Issues* (New Warsi, 2012), amongst other scholarly publications.

Michael Faure is Professor at Maastricht University, the Netherlands, and Academic Director of the Maastricht European Institute for Transnational Legal Research (METRO). He has published extensively in the areas of environmental criminal law, tort, insurance and economic analysis of accident law, and also serves as a Professor of Comparative Private Law and Economics at Erasmus University, Netherlands. He is Programme Director of the European Doctorate in Law and Economics (EDLE) and holds over 30 years' experience at the Antwerp Bar.

Paolo Galizzi is Clinical Professor of Law and Faculty Director of the Sustainable Development Legal Initiative (SDLI) and Corporate Social Responsibility (CSR) programme at the Leitner Center for International Law and Justice at Fordham Law School, USA. Professor Galizzi is an expert on multinational corporations and international human rights law, environmental law and sustainable development. He has led numerous legal research, capacity building and CSR projects in partnership with public and private stakeholders in sub-Saharan Africa, Latin America and Southeast Asia.

Beatriz Garcia is a Lecturer at Western Sydney University, Australia. Dr Garcia holds an LLM and a PhD from the Graduate Institute of International and Development Studies, Geneva, Switzerland. Dr Garcia has worked on several projects with the United Nations Conference on Trade and Development and other UN agencies; the Australian Centre for Climate and Environmental Law, University of Sydney, Australia; the Brazilian Government; as well as several NGOs. She is author of chapters in *Regional Environmental Law: Transregional Comparative Lessons in Pursuit of Sustainable Development* (Edward Elgar, 2015), and *Law, Tropical Forests and Carbon: The Case of REDD+* (Cambridge University Press, 2013) and has written *The Amazon from an International Law Perspective* (Cambridge University Press, 2011).

Kamal Hossain (Barrister) is a Senior Advocate of the Supreme Court of Bangladesh. Dr Hossain was Minister of Law (1972–73), Minister of Petroleum and Minerals (1973–75) and Minister of Foreign Affairs (1973–75) for the Government of Bangladesh. He was a member of the UN Compensation Commission for two terms (1994–96 and 1999–2005) and was Chairman of two of its Panels. He was also the UN Special Rapporteur on the Human Rights Situation in Afghanistan from 1999–2003. He is a member, Panel of Arbitrators, ICSID and served as Chair and Member of a number of international arbitral tribunals (ICC, ICSID and UNCITRAL). He was appointed as a Judge ad hoc by Malaysia for the International Tribunal of the Law of the Sea in the case *Malaysia v Singapore* (2003), a Member of International Law of the Sea Annex VII Tribunal in the same case, and also in the case of *Guyana v Suriname* (2005–2007). Dr Hossain is currently Vice Chairman of the International Law Association (London), Chairman of both the Bangladesh Legal Aid and Services Trust (BLAST) and the South Asian Institute of Advanced Legal and Human Rights Studies (SAILS), Honorary Fellow of the Institute of Mineral and Petroleum Law, University of Dundee, and Advisory Council Member for Transparency International.

Phuong Le is a PhD candidate at the University of the West of England, Bristol, UK. Ms Le's research focuses on the fields of international investment law and sustainable development in agricultural sectors from developing countries. She holds an LLM in International Trade Law from the University of the West of England, UK, and an LLB from Ho Chi Minh City University, Vietnam. She holds previous experience in trade and investment, having served as the Deputy Head of the Investment Promotion Division (Dong Thap Province) in Vietnam.

Feja Lesniewska is a Senior Fellow at the School of Oriental and African Studies (SOAS), University of London, UK. Dr Lesniewska's research focuses on climate change law, sustainable development, energy, ecosystems law and international law. She has undertaken fieldwork in West Africa, East Asia and Russia on a range of forest related issues including the illegal timber trade, community tenure rights and climate change. She has worked as a consultant publishing work with leading NGOs on forest related law and policy. She co-founded the Law, Environment and Development Centre at SOAS and is a member of the Centre's *Law Environment and Development (LEAD) Journal* Editorial Board.

Elizabeth Maruma Mrema is Director, Environmental Law Division of the United Nations Environment Programme (UNEP). She has worked with the UNEP for almost two decades. From July 2009 until January 2013, she was the Executive Secretary of the UNEP/Secretariat of the Convention on the Conservation of Migratory Species of Wild Animals (CMS), Acting Executive Secretary of the UNEP/ASCOBANS and Interim Executive Secretary of the UNEP/Gorilla Agreement all based in Bonn, Germany. Since January 2013, she has been the Deputy Director and Coordinator, Operations and Programme Delivery Branch in the Division of Environmental Policy Implementation (DEPI).

Elena Merino Blanco is an Associate Professor of International Economic Law at the University of the West of England, Bristol, UK. Professor Blanco holds law degrees from three different countries and worked in practice on international arbitration and litigation, and as a consultant on Spanish law. Her research focuses on distributional justice and access to natural resources, international investment law, environmental justice, corruption, bribery and good governance and litigation against corporate actors.

Jona Razzaque is Professor of Environmental Law at the University of the West of England, Bristol, UK. Professor Razzaque holds an LLM from Kings College London, UK, and a PhD from Queen Mary College, University of London, UK. Her expertise lies in the relationship between human rights and the environment, including participatory rights and environmental justice. Professor Razzaque has recently co-edited *Biodiversity and Nature Protection Law* (Edward Elgar, 2017), *International Environmental Law and the Global South* (Cambridge University Press, 2015) and *Natural Resources and the Green Economy* (Brill, 2012). Professor Razzaque has also published *Environmental Governance in Europe and Asia* (Routledge, 2012), *Globalisation and Natural Resources Law* (Edward Elgar, 2011) and *Public Interest Environmental Litigation in India, Pakistan and Bangladesh* (Kluwer, 2004).

Benjamin J. Richardson is a scholar of environmental law who holds a joint professorial appointment with the University of Tasmania's (UTAS) Faculty of Law and the Institute for Marine and Antarctic Studies. After completing his undergraduate studies in law and political science at Macquarie University and his PhD at the Australian National University, Professor Richardson worked abroad for over 18 years in law faculties in New Zealand, Canada and the UK. Prior to joining UTAS in July 2014, Professor Richardson was at the University of British Columbia where he held the Canada Research Chair in Environmental Law and Sustainability and was Director of the Centre for Law and the Environment. Earlier, from 2003–10, he was a Professor at Osgoode Hall Law School of York University, and before then a Senior Lecturer at the law faculties of the University of Manchester (1999–2002) and at the University of Auckland (1996–99). Prior to working in academia, Professor Richardson had stints in policy and consultancy roles for the New South Wales National Parks and Wildlife Service in Sydney and the IUCN (International Union for Conservation of Nature) in Kathmandu and Nairobi.

Jacinta Ruru (Raukawa and Ngati Ranginui) is Professor of Law at the University of Otago, New Zealand and is Co-Director of Nga Pae o te Maramatanga; New Zealand's Māori Centre of Research Excellence. Her research explores indigenous' legal interests to own, manage and govern land and water resources, and has co-authored *Discovering Indigenous Lands* (Oxford University Press, 2010). Professor Ruru is editor of the *Resource Management Journal*, *Resource Management Theory & Practice*, and consultative editor for the *Māori Law Review*.

Priscilla Schwartz is Senior Lecturer and Director of the Energy and Natural Resources Law Programme at the School of Business and Law, University of East London. She is also the Deputy Chair of the African International Economic Law Network, Mandela Institute, Johannesburg, South Africa. She holds a PhD and LLM from the University of London, Queen Mary and Kings College respectively; and a BA and LLB (Hons) from the University of Sierra Leone, Fourah Bay College. Her current research interest is in legal and policy aspects of the sustainability of mining and oil and gas activities in Africa, and the regulatory dynamics surrounding energy governance. She has published widely in the field. She is currently working on several projects with the OHCHR Right to Development section, including on devising educational tools for operationalising the 2016 sustainable development goals on energy access. Priscilla is also a lawyer with over 20 years' experience, working with governments, companies and international institutions on energy, mining, and natural resources regulatory issues in developing countries.

Adam Simpson is Senior Lecturer at the University of South Australia, Australia, and Director of the Centre for Peace and Security. Dr Simpson's research adopts a critical perspective on development and environmental politics in Southeast Asia. He has published numerous works including *Energy, Governance and Security in Thailand and Myanmar (Burma): A Critical Approach to Environmental Politics in the South* (NIAS Press, 2014) and is lead editor of the *Routledge Handbook of Contemporary Myanmar* (2018).

Emily Smith Ewing is Executive Director of the Corporate Social Responsibility (CSR) program at the Leitner Center for International Law and Justice at Fordham Law School, USA, where she is also a Senior Fellow and Adjunct Professor of Law. Her expertise includes CSR, business and human rights, business and the environment, labour rights and corporate accountability. Professor Smith Ewing has extensive experience working with both the private and public sectors on collaborative initiatives.

List of acronyms and abbreviations

3TG	tin, tantalum, tungsten and gold
AAAA	Addis Ababa Action Agenda
AAU	Assigned Amount Unit
ACR	American Carbon Registry
AMC	advance market commitment
ANP	National Agency of Petroleum, Natural Gas and Biofuels
APA	Ad Hoc Working Group on the Paris Agreement
AUD	Australian dollar
AUSFTA	Australia–United States Free Trade Agreement
BASD	Business Action for Sustainable Development
BIT	bilateral investment treaty
BP	British Petroleum
CBD	Convention on Biological Diversity
CCB	Climate, Community and Biodiversity
CDM	Clean Development Mechanism
CEDAW	Convention on the Elimination of All Forms of Discrimination against Women
CER	Certified Emission Reduction
CERDS	Charter of Economic Rights and Duties of States
CETA	Comprehensive Economic and Trade Agreement
CFP	core financing principle
CIEL	Center for International Environmental Law
CITES	Convention on International Trade in Endangered Species
CMA	Crown Minerals Act
CMA1	First Conference of the Parties serving as the Meeting of the Parties to the Paris Agreement
CO_2	carbon dioxide
COMEST	World Commission on the Ethics of Scientific Knowledge and Technology
COP	Conference of the Parties
CPC	Central Product Classification
CRC	Convention on the Rights of the Child

CSO	civil society organisation
CSR	corporate social responsibility
DfID	Department for International Development
DR-CAFTA	Dominican Republic–Central America–United States Free Trade Agreement
DRC	Democratic Republic of Congo
DSU	Dispute Settlement Understanding
ECHR	European Convention on Human Rights
ECJ	European Court of Justice
ECT	Energy Charter Treaty
EEZ	Exclusive Economic Zone
EEZ Act	Exclusive Economic Zone and Continental Shelf (Environmental Effects) Act 2012 (NZ)
EGAS	Egyptian Natural Gas Holding Company
EGPC	Egyptian General Petroleum Corporation
EHS Guidelines	World Bank Group Environmental, Health and Safety Guidelines
EIA	environmental impact assessment
EIC	East India Company
EITI	Extractive Industry Transparency Initiative
EMG	East Mediterranean Gas Company
ENAP	Empresa Nacional del Petroleo
EP	Equator Principle
EPC	energy performance contracting
EPFI	Equator Principles financial institution
ERU	emission reduction unit
ESC	energy service company
ESG	environmental, social and governance
ESIA	environment and social impacts assessment
ESMP	environment and social management plan
ETS	emissions trading scheme
EU	European Union
EU-ETS	European Union Emissions Trading System
EY	Ernst & Young
FAO	Food and Agriculture Organization of the United Nations
FARDC	Armed Forced of the Democratic Republic of Congo
FCPF	Forest Carbon Partnership Facility
FDI	foreign direct investment
FDLR	Democratic Forces for the Liberation of Rwanda
FET	fair and equitable treatment
FIP	Forest Investment Programme
FLEGT	Forest Law Enforcement, Governance and Trade
FNLA	Frente Nacional para Libertação de Angola
FPIC	Free, Prior and Informed Consent

FTA	free trade agreement
GA	General Assembly
GATS	General Agreement on Trade in Services
GATT	General Agreement on Tariffs and Trade
GBEP	Global Bioenergy Partnership
GDP	gross domestic product
GEF	Global Environmental Facility
GHG	greenhouse gas
GIF	Global Infrastructure Facility
GIS	Geographic Information System
GLR	Great Lakes Region
GoE	Group of Experts
GRI	Global Reporting Initiative
GVC	global value chain
GWP	Global Water Partnership
HRC	Human Rights Committee
IBRD	International Bank for Reconstruction and Development
ICC	International Chamber of Commerce
ICC Charter	International Chamber of Commerce Business Charter for Sustainable Development
ICCPR	International Covenant on Civil and Political Rights
ICESCR	International Covenant on Economic, Social and Cultural Rights
ICGLR	International Conference for the Great Lakes Region
ICJ	International Court of Justice
ICMM	International Council on Mining and Metals
ICSID	International Centre for Settlement of Investment Disputes
IDA	International Development Association
IEC	Israel Electric Corporation
IFAD	International Fund for Agricultural Development
IFC	International Finance Corporation
IFM	improved forest management
IIA	international investment agreement
IISD	International Institute for Sustainable Development
ILA	International Law Association
ILC	International Law Commission
IMF	International Monetary Fund
INDC	Intended Nationally Determined Contribution
INECE	International Network on Environmental Compliance and Enforcement
IOC	international oil company
IP	indigenous people
IPCC	Intergovernmental Panel on Climate Change
IRMA	Initiative for Responsible Mining Assurance

ISDS	investor–state dispute settlement
ISO	International Organization for Standardization
ITMO	internationally transferred mitigation outcomes
IUCN	International Union for the Conservation of Nature
JI	Joint Implementation
JPOI	Johannesburg Plan of Implementation
KAFTA	Korea–Australia Free Trade Agreement
LIC	lower-income country
LULUCF	land use, land use change and forestry
MATA	Myanmar Alliance for Transparency and Accountability
MDB	multilateral development bank
MDRI-CESD	Myanmar Development Resources Institute's Centre for Economic and Social Development
MEA	multilateral environmental agreement
MEITI	Myanmar Extractive Industry Transparency Initiative
MFN	most favoured nation
MIGA	Multilateral Investment Guarantee Agency
MNC	multinational corporation
MPLA	Movimento Popular de Libertação de Angola
MPRDA	Mineral and Petroleum Resources Development Act
MSG	Multi-Stakeholder Group
MSME	medium and small–medium enterprise
$MtCO_2e$	million tonnes of carbon dioxide equivalent
NAAEC	North American Agreement on Environmental Cooperation
NAFTA	North American Free Trade Agreement
NCP	National Contact Point
NDC	Nationally Determined Contribution
NGO	non-governmental organisation
NIEO	new international economic order
NLD	National League for Democracy
NNPC	Nigerian National Petroleum Company
NOC	national oil company
NRDB	national and regional development bank
NZ ETS	New Zealand Emissions Trading Scheme
ODA	official development assistance
OECD	Organisation for Economic Co-operation and Development
OP	Operational Policy
OPEC	Organization of the Petroleum Exporting Countries
OTC	over-the-counter
PCA	Permanent Court of Arbitration
PDC	project development company
PDD	project design document
Pemex	Petróleos Mexicanos

PFC	project finance company
PMfD	pull mechanisms for development
POC	private oil company
PoE	panel of experts
PP	precautionary principle
PPP	public–private partnership
PRG	partial risk guarantee
PSNR	Permanent Sovereignty over Natural Resources
PTPA	US–Peru Trade Promotion Agreement
PWYP	Publish What You Pay
RCM	Regional Certification Mechanism
RED	Renewable Energy Directive
REDD	Reducing Emissions from Deforestation and Forest Degradation
RINR	Regional Initiative against the Illegal Exploitation of Natural Resources
Rio+20	United Nations Conference on Sustainable Development
RIT	regional investment treaty
RMA	Resource Management Act
RSB	Roundtable on Sustainable Biomaterials
SD	sustainable development
SDG	Sustainable Development Goal
SDM	Sustainable Development Mechanism
SE4All	Sustainable Energy for All
SEC	Securities and Exchange Commission
SIA	sustainability impact assessment/social impact assessment
SOE	state owned enterprise
SPDC	Shell Petroleum Development Corporation
SPV	special purpose vehicle
SWF	sovereign wealth fund
TFEU	Treaty on the Functioning of the European Union
TPP	Trans-Pacific Partnership
TPPA	Trans-Pacific Partnership Agreement
TREM	trade-related environmental measure
TRIM	trade-related investment measure
TTIP	Transatlantic Trade and Investment Partnership
UAE	United Arab Emirates
UN	United Nations
UN-PNSR	United Nations General Assembly Resolution on Permanent Sovereignty over Natural Resources
UNAC	United Nations Convention against Corruption
UNCCD	United Nations Convention on Combating Desertification
UNCED	United Nations Conference on Environment and Development

UNCITRAL	United Nations Commission on International Trade Law
UNCLOS	United Nations Convention on the Law of the Sea
UNCTAD	United Nations Conference on Trade and Development
UNDD	United Nations Due Diligence Guidelines
UNDRIP	United Nations Declaration on Indigenous Peoples' Rights
UNEP	United Nations Environmental Programme
UNESCO	United Nations Educational, Scientific and Cultural Organization
UNFCCC	United Nations Framework Convention on Climate Change
UNGA	United Nations General Assembly
UNGC	United Nations Global Compact
UNGPs	United Nations Guiding Principles on Business and Human Rights
UNITA	União Nacional para a Indêpendencia Total de Angola
UNSC	United Nations Security Council
VCS	Voluntary Carbon Standard/Verified Carbon Standard
VGGT	Voluntary Guidelines on the Responsible Governance of Tenure of Land, Fisheries and Forests in the Context of National Food Security
VOC	Vereenigde Oost-Indische Compagnie
WCED	World Commission on Environment and Development
WEF	World Economic Forum
WSSD	World Summit on Sustainable Development
WTO	World Trade Organization
YPF	Yacimientos Petrolíferos Fiscales
YPFB	Yacimientos Petrolíferos Fiscales Bolivianos

Acknowledgements

We are very thankful to Olivia Manley from Routledge for the support from the inception through to the completion of the book. We would like to thank all the experts who contributed in this book with commitment and enthusiasm. Our sincere thanks also go to Samuel Voller for his diligent and thorough editorial assistance.

We would like to extend our special thanks to Ms Elizabeth Maruma Mrema, Dr Kamal Hossain, Professor Philippe Cullet and Professor Benjamin Richardson for their willingness, enthusiasm and endorsement of the book.

Shawkat Alam would like to thank Macquarie University for granting him a sabbatical to complete this project. Shawkat Alam also extends his special thanks to friends and colleagues of the Centre for Environmental Law for their suggestions, sustained interest and moral support throughout the project.

Jahid Hossain Bhuiyan is thankful to the Department of Law, Northern University, Bangladesh for giving him considerable professional freedom in undertaking this project.

Jona Razzaque wishes to thank the Faculty of Business and Law and the Department of Law of the University of the West of England for providing research time to edit the manuscript.

The law and policy developments throughout this book are reflected as they were on 31 March 2017.

Preface

Historically, resource abundant nations have been plagued with issues concerning poor environmental, social and economic outcomes that are often dubbed as the 'resource curse'. Despite an abundance of natural resources which can facilitate development, weak governance and institutional capacity have often resulted in inequitable economic growth at the expense of local communities and the environment. However, with the rise of developing countries as new sites for global investment, coupled with the many natural resources that provide developing countries with comparative advantages, there is renewed impetus to explore how natural resource investment and its supporting legislative and policy frameworks can contribute to more sustainable outcomes in developing countries.

In addition, there is growing consensus that a traditional view of excluding natural resource use in favour of improving environmental objectives does not fully address the development concerns of the Global South, such as the need to alleviate poverty. With the recognition of the revised Sustainable Development Goals to include stronger investment in developing countries as a key mechanism to deliver sustainable development, the issue turns to how developing countries can utilise their natural resources effectively to attract foreign investment, without sacrificing long term goals of improving environmental performance and equitable economic growth.

International Natural Resources Law, Investment and Sustainability provides a clear and concise insight into the relationship between the institutions that govern foreign investment, sustainable development and the rules and regulations that administer natural resources. From the outset, the purpose of this book is not to provide a single narrative regarding the relationship between natural resource law, investment and sustainable development. Rather, this book embraces the expertise of several leading experts to explore different perspectives in how investment and natural resources come together to achieve sustainable development in developing countries.

Despite varying perspectives, it is clear that several themes are central in considering the linkages between natural resources, investment and sustainability. Specifically, transparency, good governance and citizen empowerment are vital conditions which encourage positive social, economic and environmental outcomes for developing countries. In addition, this book provides new insights into key concepts which underpin international law, including sovereign rights and state responsibility principles. It is clear from this book that in the attempt to reconcile these concepts and principles from separate legal regimes, complex policy questions emerge whereby it is difficult to attain mutually beneficial or succinct outcomes. This book explores how countries prioritise their policy objectives to achieve their notion of sustainable natural resource use, which is strongly influenced by power imbalances which inform North–South cooperation, as well as South–South cooperation in the international investment regime.

We hope that you will find this book informative and that it contributes to your understanding of the latest issues concerning international investment law, sustainable development and natural resource law. It is exciting to live in times where new linkages and relationships that can contribute to sustainable development are explored, as well as the maturing of sustainable development debate into specific contexts and perspectives from key participants and policy communities. Whether much needed reform, both internationally and domestically, occurs of the legal and policy frameworks which support international investment in natural resources only time will tell, however its success will depend upon the work of many different actors and perspectives for many years to come.

Introduction

Shawkat Alam, Jahid Hossain Bhuiyan and Jona Razzaque

The basis for human continuation in a modern society relies on the sustainable use and exploitation of natural resources. However, the question of sustainable use inevitably raises the issue of how competing interests might be balanced between resource-rich countries, keen to conserve their natural resources even while they exploit them, and resource-hungry nations desirous of investing in natural resources extraction and importation. It is now accepted that the unsustainable extraction and export of natural resources can drive economic growth, but can also ultimately lead to increased poverty and conflict. This link between resource abundance, poor governance, corruption and deteriorating social, environmental and economic outcomes, dubbed the 'resource curse',[1] is a central theme of this book. The shift of economic power toward developing countries such as Brazil, India, China, South Africa, along with growing South–South cooperation, have provided renewed impetus for reassessing the legitimacy and efficacy of the international regulation of natural resources and whether this balance between interests has been sufficiently achieved, both under international instruments and within domestic legislative and policy frameworks.

The diversity of perspectives contained within this book demonstrates that there is no one-size-fits-all approach to achieving sustainability in the natural resources sector. Nevertheless, an overarching argument of the discussions within these pages is that transparency, good governance and citizen empowerment are central to transforming resource–investment–sustainability dynamics, especially for developing countries. The aim of this book is to provide a background to the law governing natural resources and to explore the relationship of natural resources law with key concepts such as sustainable development, sovereign rights and state responsibility principles, all of which are now central to international law. The book's chapters examine the existing legal structures for conserving, preserving, using and extracting natural resources at an international level, and also discuss the inter-linkage between investment and international natural resources law.

1 For instance, by R. Auty in *Sustaining Development in Mineral Economies: The Resource Curse Thesis* (Routledge, 1993).

The various analyses explore the contribution of non-state actors, including the World Bank and private multinational companies, to the utilisation of natural resources, and also consider the responsibility of these and other key players for their effective conservation.

Part I addresses the problematic relationship between natural resources law and investment law. The chapters in this section deal with the question of how a state's development needs and its reliance on the exploitation of its natural resources for economic growth can be consistent with its duty to regulate and protect natural resources for the benefit of both present and future generations.

Shawkat Alam, Md Jahid Hossain Bhuiyan and Jona Razzaque argue that sustainable development and growth can be achieved by governments, but only through careful management of natural resources. The authors argue that foreign investment is, perhaps paradoxically, increasingly perceived as a precondition for sustainable development. Such a view is not without its controversy, given that investment laws have tended to favour foreign investors at the expense of local community interests. However, if the positive effects of foreign investment on communities and the environment are optimised, while the negative effects are simultaneously mitigated, Sustainable Development Goals are brought closer. Indeed, as long as the activities of foreign investors are oriented in the direction of the maximisation of profit instead of the promotion of sustainable development, social and environmental wellbeing in developing countries is compromised. The authors therefore argue that if the focus of investment in natural resources is shifted to include growing recognition of the environmental and social aspects of sustainability together with the typical preoccupation with economic development and growth, international investment law may continue to evolve so as to encompass the objectives of sustainability.

Upendra Baxi views the role of states as critical to the development of a sustainable approach to investment. Sustainable development has been given a meaningful theoretical footing for reforms and developments in leading international legal instruments, such as the United Nations Declaration on the Permanent Sovereignty over Natural Resources (PSNR). However, as Baxi notes, the authority of states to exploit their natural resources, as allowed by that instrument, does not mean that inequitable 'plunder' by those in power within states is permitted by the PSNR. Nor does it allow states to act in the interests of their own development whilst adversely affecting the environment of other states. Accordingly, Baxi proposes that a similar norm or standard extends to the context of foreign investment, prohibiting states from acting at the behest and on behalf of multinational corporations (MNCs) without consideration of the communities affected by natural resources investment and exploitation. Awareness of constraints on the use of natural resources, as well as opportunities for acknowledgement of how they might be wisely used, provide the means by which both individuals and the community might approach a balance between development and conservation.

Md Jahid Hossain Bhuiyan takes up the discussion of the PSNR to trace the evolution of the principle in the context of the investment regime. He also examines resolutions of the United Nations General Assembly for their expression of the nature of shared sovereignty over natural resources between state and people and for their impact on investment regulations. He demonstrates that a peoples' right to PSNR was recognised in the initial stages of the concept's development, but that the PSNR concept subsequently transformed to be progressively considered an aspect of state sovereignty. Although states have the right to use and exploit their natural resources for the sake of national development and for the benefit of their citizens, the right is accorded to the state on the understanding that it commits to exercise it for the wellbeing of the people. Consistent with the possession of a right is the power or freedom not to exercise that right. However, in circumstances where a state chooses not to exercise its right to exploit natural resources, that decision must also be made for the people's wellbeing.

A common theme, running through Bhuiyan's chapter and the two preceding papers in this section, is that international environmental instruments impose restrictions on the sovereign right of a state to use and exploit its natural resources. Meanwhile, sustainable development is both facilitated and impacted by any restriction similarly imposed on foreign investment in those natural resources.

Part II takes this examination of international instruments further, by focusing on the protection of natural resources against the state's desire for foreign investment and investors' interest in being indemnified against any change in the regulatory climate. The chapters treat this issue from a variety of perspectives, from the obligations arising from investment treaties to their treatment in arbitration, and from the self-regulation of corporations to the political role of states in the extraction of natural resources, thus reflecting the multifaceted nature of the issue of sustainable development.

Ilaria Espa explores how key principles of the growing international law of sustainable development have been incorporated into the World Trade Organization (WTO) legal regime. The chapter identifies the current WTO rules pertinent to natural resources management and examines the link between such rules and the principle of sustainable development, as reflected in the Preamble of the WTO Agreement and in contemporary WTO jurisprudence. She argues that policies intended to sustainably manage the pace of natural resources extraction appear likely to be consistent with WTO rules, falling within the ambit of the conservation exception in Article XX(g) of the General Agreement on Tariffs and Trade (GATT). She further argues that measures having a sustainable *economic* development objective, such as supply management, by contrast go against WTO principles, falling within the range of policies to be 'sacrificed' so as to facilitate fair and foreseeable access to natural resources.

Shawkat Alam explores the natural resources and investment nexus through the complex relationship between international investment agreements (IIAs), regional investment treaties (RITs) and bilateral investment treaties (BITs), and considers the capacity of these instruments to regulate natural resource protection. He argues that the existing RITs and BITs framework lacks several significant features crucial for achieving equitable natural resource management for developing countries, among them measures for ensuring transparency and public participation. Soft law instruments, such as the International Finance Corporation Sustainability Framework and Environmental and Social Performance Standards, are viewed as playing a vital role in addressing these shortcomings, but will not suffice on their own. Any necessary reform entails the implementation of measures for monitoring and reporting on foreign firm performance. Corporate social responsibility (CSR) entails an obligation to directly address the environmental and social impacts of firms' investments. Furthermore, environmental and social impact assessment is critical for building the institutional capacity of host states and for inspiring better-informed decision-making. Alam proposes that such measures be incorporated within the provisions of IIAs in order to provide for a stable regulatory system capable of addressing the need for investor certainty, whilst achieving the fair and equitable management of natural resources.

Mariel Dimsey shows that many challenges now exist in the arbitration of disputes concerning natural resources. She argues that at the centre of the challenges are competing interests: the foreign investor's interest in having its investment realised according to the contract and the underlying BIT, the state's interests in obtaining the required technology and simultaneously appeasing the local inhabitants, and also the third person's or *amici curiae*'s interests, which are frequently claimed to represent the 'public interest'. She notes that, to date, arbitral tribunals are generally reluctant to prescribe a clear 'pecking order' of priority of interests, and argues that more courage should be exercised by arbitral tribunals in addressing this complex interaction of interests through appropriate inclusion of third person participation in tribunal proceedings. Furthermore, the increasing acknowledgment of a state's right to regulate investment in natural resources, both in academic discourse and in the language of recent BITs, may help in empowering arbitral tribunals to address the question of which interests should be allowed more priority in natural resources disputes. Dimsey argues for the adoption of new and innovative approaches that reconcile competing rights in a way appropriate to the particular circumstances of a case. This will likely consist not of favouring one set of interests over another, but of undertaking a balancing exercise which would seek to respect the diverse objectives of foreign investment projects that have 'public interest' implications.

Taking up the notion of competing interests, Jurgen Brohmer argues that the term 'resource nationalism' is strictly political and without any legal meaning. He analyses the legality for expropriations and measures of equivalent effect in the resources sector under international law and demonstrates that the legal framework for the management of natural resources is mainly governed by domestic law, and entirely unaffected by 'resource nationalism'. The policies followed by states concerning their natural resources are for the states themselves to determine. He further argues that expropriation or nationalisation is not illegal but necessitates certain safeguards and these safeguards are mostly the same as those laid down by customary international law. He argues that a public policy interest in nationalising natural resources would not, therefore, legitimise expropriations.

Leaving aside the role of the state to focus on the investor, Paolo Galizzi and Emily Smith Ewing emphasise the advantages of a CSR approach to natural resource protection and examine three facets of MNC regulation: international soft law instruments, voluntary industry initiatives and the role of other non-state actors, such as international organisations, non-governmental organisations (NGOs) and individuals. While domestic law in both home and host states might be the principal means of regulating MNCs, these legal frameworks are often weak and insufficient for effectively regulating MNCs, in that they lack enforcement mechanisms and thus fail to stem widespread corruption. New legislation informed by CSR, by contrast, offers the opportunity for the strengthening of CSR principles and for encouraging self-regulation by MNCs, while also allowing for robust accountability where CSR standards are not met. Given existing patterns of the worldwide use and consumption of natural resources, the international community needs to reinforce and strengthen CSR as well as regulate MNCs, particularly in circumstances where traditional legal channels fall short of doing so.

Continuing the book's examination of the practices of MNCs, Elena Blanco examines the relationship of MNCs with home and host states in the conduct of resource extraction. The chapter looks at the early extractive imperial companies from a North–South angle and views the colonial plunder's lasting legacy in the context of the evolving politics of resource extraction from the decolonisation period to the advent of globalisation, and most recently, with the development and growth of postcolonial South–South investment. With a focus on oil and on state-owned enterprises, the author provides an overview of the expansion of natural resource extraction companies, the simultaneous growth of the Global South as an economic power and the subsequent development of South–South investment. Given the tendency for resource extraction companies to impose a high toll, in the form of environmental destruction and human rights violations, on the states where they operate, Blanco concludes that a commitment to responsible growth requires clearer, faster and more effective mechanisms of accountability, regardless of whether extraction companies are private or state-owned.

Part III considers changing dynamics across the broad spectrum of investment regimes and their wide-ranging impacts. The chapters in this section focus particularly on the way in which investment practices are increasingly constrained and informed by matters important to the public interest, whether this is the sustainable provision of ecosystem services, genuine consultation with indigenous communities or the 'greening' of markets so as to favour investment projects with environmentally and socially responsible objectives.

In her examination of the issues encompassing water, investment and the sustainable use of water resources, Rebecca Bates focuses on water privatisation, one of the most significant trends in the water sector over the last 50 years, and its link with the General Agreement on Trade in Services (GATS). Though sustainability, as a concept, has the ability to integrate environmental, economic and practical aspects, such as infrastructure and capacity, within one operational model, the challenge remains as to how to balance these factors so as to ensure the ecosystem's capacity to continue delivering adequate services. The naturally monopolistic character of the water market and its inclination towards long term investment suggests that planning is an important component in achieving this objective. Meanwhile, Bates argues that investment treaties, including the GATS, and their ability to open markets to new providers, generate an extra layer of uncertainty within an already challenging sector, necessitating the re-examination of these treaties by the WTO with a view to supporting the long-standing and sustainable provision of water services.

Jona Razzaque and Phuong Le continue the consideration of the sustainable management of natural resources important to the developing world by focusing on agricultural investment and the relevant legal safeguards existing in investment contracts as well as under national legal regimes. The authors argue that the responsibility of the state, to provide adequate legal tools and market incentives so as to ensure sustainability, needs to be balanced against the liability of investors when public interests are endangered. With different forms of agricultural investment contracts applying across jurisdictions, this balancing act is a difficult task. A well designed and well implemented contract may protect the livelihoods of the local people and environments affected by the investment project, if the investment regime takes into account wider concerns of human rights or environmental sustainability. The chapter concludes that the sustainability agenda requires the state to include effective legal safeguards in national laws and the authors argue for better incentive mechanisms as well as collaborative business practices in order to reduce governance gaps. It follows that the pursuit of liberalisation in agricultural foreign direct investment (FDI) must not come at the cost of overarching public interest matters.

Abdullah Al Faruque continues this line of reasoning by applying it to the evolving social and human rights aspects and trends in mineral extraction in developing states. He argues that an appreciation of human rights and social concerns by extraction companies is a precondition for a sustainable community and company relationship in areas where mineral extraction is undertaken. Therefore, human rights and social and environmental issues should be considered in the planning and implementation of mineral projects so as to enhance a stable relationship between the host communities and extraction companies, especially on the part of those which are operating in areas that are environmentally sensitive and socially fragile. Developing a robust community relations programme at the beginning of a project and integrating social policy into companies' decision-making are among strategies that may assist the success of a project on both social and environmental grounds. In implementing such objectives, a balance needs to be struck between the need for mineral extraction for the acceleration of economic and social development, and the need for any such project to address societal concerns. In this sense, the legislative and policy framework of the host government must include measures for addressing human rights matters and social impacts whilst also providing for consultation and the equitable distribution of revenue among affected communities.

The Māori people of New Zealand are among the indigenous communities affected by investment in natural resources, and Andre Erueti, Sarah Down and Jacinta Ruru adopt this case study in order to examine how the current legal structure and the regulation of mining activities recognise indigenous interests. The UN Declaration on the Rights of Indigenous Peoples and the United Nations Guiding Principles on Business and Human Rights provide an international perspective on how those interests should be incorporated within the mining investment regime. The authors propose reform compatible with these instruments and discuss the various models that may be adopted with that end in mind. In comparison to many other states, New Zealand has a robust regulatory framework for environmental regulation and the regulation of the extractive industry, one that includes protections for Māori interests. However, in some respects, the existing regulations do not meet international standards, with tribes having an insignificant role in the management of minerals in their traditional lands. The problem is compounded by a dearth of clear direction from government with respect to recognition of the indigenous rights of tribes by companies. Meanwhile, however, recent innovations in co-management provide some guidance for achieving a more equitable model for the exploitation of New Zealand's mineral wealth.

Adopting a different focus on the roles and responsibilities of the investment regime, Priscilla Schwartz examines the international financing framework through evaluations of the Addis Ababa Action Agenda on financing for development (AAAA)/CFP) from the perspective of energy sustainability, and the role of multilateral development banks (MDBs) as an indispensable catalyst in addressing the goals of SE4All. She argues that energy finance is consistently associated with broader goals such as climate change and development. In pursuing these objectives, financing strategies aim to mitigate climate risks and reduce poverty, whilst also addressing the need to provide inclusive energy commercialisation for small-to-medium and medium sized enterprises. In light of this more sustainable approach to energy financing, energy policy planners, Schwartz argues, will need to address the challenge of balancing competing interests but without overlooking energy policy necessities.

Continuing with a focus on the international investment regime and its recently shifting emphasis to more sustainable markets, Beatriz Garcia examines the way in which carbon market mechanisms operate and also how these may evolve following the 21st Conference of the Parties (COP21) in Paris. She argues that one of the key challenges after Paris is to ensure the environmental integrity of the market mechanisms under the UN system, through robust accounting rules, transparency, rigorous verification and through compliance with the requirements of the United Nations Framework Convention on Climate Change (UNFCCC). Given that the parties to the UNFCCC are extremely heterogeneous, developing these mechanisms may prove challenging. With these concerns in mind, Garcia asks whether carbon offset projects and emission trading schemes have been fruitful market devices for the reduction of emissions, the conservation and enhancement of carbon sinks, and the protection of natural resources. She argues that forest carbon projects are generally more likely to be successful in states which have clear land ownership and carbon rights policies and also the economic and political stability to attract investment, among other measures to strengthen governance and prevent corruption. Nevertheless, such projects face many obstacles in developing states, including uncertainty over land ownership, possible land disputes, corruption and poor governance.

Feja Lesniewska offers a different perspective on the impact of natural resources investment on vulnerable communities in her consideration of modern biofuels. She notes that modern biofuels are offered as a sustainable, low-carbon alternative to substitute hydrocarbons in the electricity and transport sectors. However, increased modern biofuels demand across developing and emerging states, driven by climate change mitigation strategies and energy security issues, is resulting in adverse social, environmental and economic impacts. Impoverished rural communities and minority groups, including indigenous peoples, experience the bulk of the adverse impacts in biofuel producing states, which are typically least developed countries. The chapter examines whether current initiatives under voluntary standards and European Union regulations are sufficient to advance sustainability and overcome the social and environmental challenges presented by modern biofuels. Lesniewska argues for an integrated approach to designing and implementing sustainability standards, such that climate change is mitigated, energy poverty is reduced and global energy security is increased.

Finally, in **Part IV,** the focus of the book narrows to consider the problems of conflict and corruption that arise from a failure to implement sustainable investment law and policy. There is consensus across these chapters for the proposition that liability falls not only to the investor, but also to the state, for social and environmental problems resulting from inadequate regulation of natural resources exploitation. However, the situation is far from hopeless, with all three authors suggesting viable possibilities for reform.

Using the Democratic Republic of Congo (DRC) as a case study, Onita Das explores the relationship between natural resources and conflict. Noting new challenges in the extractive industries concerned with 'conflict minerals', especially in the Eastern DRC, Das argues that legislative measures to address the issue of trade in conflict minerals cannot be dealt with independently, especially as natural resources are never the only cause of conflicts. The adverse impacts and the complexities involved in the mineral-conflict situation in the DRC, as well as in other conflict prone areas, warrant a more holistic approach by the international community and companies investing in these contested resources. Existing legislative measures should therefore be adapted so as to integrate such principles as equity, public participation and good governance. The development of such measures could mean a more comprehensive approach to sustainable investment in the mineral resources sector, one which is not only targeted at curbing conflict but which is also directed at better supporting the millions reliant on the mineral sector for their development needs.

Considering further the potentially negative consequences of natural resources investment in least developed countries, Adam Simpson examines the impact of corruption on the natural resources sector in the South and, with a particular focus on Myanmar, assesses the role of the Extractive Industries Transparency Initiative (EITI) in alleviating this problem. Although Myanmar is yet to be evaluated against the EITI Standard 2016, Simpson notes that the country has made noticeable improvements in meeting EITI requirements for transparency and civil society engagement. He argues that the establishment of a legal framework supportive of the requirements of the EITI would play an important role in formalising transparency norms. Attempts at reducing the opportunities for corruption, through the implementation of the EITI, face the same obstacles that impede other attempts at effective governance in Myanmar. However, the EITI offers a model of civil society engagement through the Multi-Stakeholder Group (MSG). If the MSG were to be adopted by Myanmar's new National League for Democracy (NLD) government, its civil society engagement model could be replicated across other aspects of the country's resource governance, and could thus help to reduce opportunities for corruption in the natural resources sector.

Taking up the thread of improvements to governance in the natural resources sector, Michael Faure emphasises the role of the criminal law in the conservation and preservation of natural resources at different levels of governance. He argues that the protection of natural resources, which needs to be aimed at restoring the natural environment and preventing future harm, may necessitate different sanctions to those of traditional fines and imprisonment. With respect to the implementation and enforcement of criminal laws aimed at the protection of the natural environment, practical problems may be overcome by the prioritisation by governments of natural resources law, as well as by increasing the capacity of enforcement agencies and introducing more severe sanctions. In addition, since many transgressions are often transboundary, the significance of international cooperation and networking is critical to the effectiveness of any new sanctioning system for criminal activity in connection with natural resources exploitation.

Our aims in compiling this book were to allow opportunity for the analysis of the interactions between natural resources governance and investment law, to explore international jurisprudence in relation to investment and sustainability, to provide a balanced account of the efforts by countries to regulate investment in their natural resources and to examine recent developments in determining liability for any breach of standards introduced to protect natural resources and the communities dependent on them. By exploring these crosscutting legal issues, we hope to provide the reader with a foundation from which to develop a critical appreciation of natural resources law and investment agreements and an understanding of their nexus with the broader field of international law. Given the richness and depth of the discussions offered here, we trust that these aims have been satisfied.

Part I

Natural resources law and investment law

Interactions

Foreword

Elizabeth Maruma Mrema

Natural resources are essential to sustaining people's livelihoods, safeguarding peace and security and promoting economic development, yet they are being rapidly overexploited. Forests are under threat from illegal logging and trade. Fish stocks continue to be depleted. The illegal trade in wildlife is hastening the extinction of flora and fauna, and destabilizing ecosystems. And the illegal extraction and trade in minerals is fueling many conflicts in the poorest of countries and stifling economic development. The sound governance of natural resources is one of our most effective means of addressing the illegal and unsustainable use of natural capital, promoting inclusive economic growth and ensuring peace and security. It is international natural resources law that provides the foundation upon which sound and effective governance can be exercised.

This timely publication presents a much needed analysis of the principles that underpin the sustainable utilization of natural resources and adds momentum to UN Environment's work on the establishment of just and legal frameworks to support the sustainable use of natural resources across borders. *International Natural Resources Law, Investment and Sustainability* examines the existing legal structures for conserving, preserving, using and extracting natural resources at an international level and provides examples of how to balance social, economic and environmental priorities in an investment context.

We know that human beings are entirely dependent on what our environment provides in order to survive and thrive. This interdependence is being increasingly recognised in courts of law around the world where the relationship between biodiversity loss and human rights is coming under closer scrutiny. The illegal and unsustainable exploitation of natural resources – from water theft and artisanal mining, to deforestation and pollution – affects people's livelihoods, health and security: in short, it jeopardises their enjoyment of a range of human rights.

That is why the development and application of sustainable international natural resources law and international investment law is so integral to protecting human rights and to achieving the Sustainable Development Goals. Without them, the balance between economic, social, cultural and environmental priorities in an investment context cannot be achieved. The responsibility to ensure a sustainable earth for future generations not only rests with international organisations, governments and environmental human rights defenders, but on the shoulders of the business community whose interests can threaten the wellbeing of those relying on natural resources for their survival.

This book covers many critical social and environmental issues relating to investment in natural resources law for sustainable decision-making at international, regional and national levels. It addresses the key considerations that must be met for investment regimes to harmonise economic, social, cultural and environmental priorities. I hope that the book becomes a central reference for strong and effective governance of natural resources – including the enhancement of the rights of the most vulnerable groups – in the use of natural resources.

1 International natural resources law and sustainable investment

Principles and practices

Shawkat Alam, Jahid Hossain Bhuiyan and Jona Razzaque

Introduction

Natural resources are important for both developing and developed countries given their significant contribution to economic activity.[1] States need to use and manage natural resources carefully to achieve sustainable development. Sustainable use and management of natural resources are also necessary to reduce the potential for resource depletion and environmental degradation. The International Union for the Conservation of Nature (IUCN) in its report *World Conservation Strategy* provides three fundamental objectives in relation to development and environmental limits:

(a) to maintain essential ecological processes and life-support systems (such as soil regeneration and protection, the recycling of nutrients, and the cleaning of waters) on which human survival and development depend;
(b) to preserve genetic diversity; and
(c) to ensure the sustainable utilization of species and ecosystems (notably fish and other wildlife, forests and grazing lands), which support millions of rural communities as well as major industries.[2]

Increased foreign investment in the natural resources sector of developing countries plays an important role in promoting sustainable development, especially in countries that are heavily reliant on natural resources for

1 'Natural resources are actual or potential sources of wealth that occur in a natural state, such as timber, water, fertile land, wildlife, minerals, metals, stones, and hydrocarbons. A natural resource qualifies as a renewable resource if it is replenished by natural processes at a rate comparable to its rate of consumption by humans or other users. A natural resource is considered non-renewable when it exists in a fixed amount, or when it cannot be regenerated on a scale comparative to its consumption'. United Nations Environmental Programme 2009, *From Conflict to Peacebuilding – The Role of Natural Resources and the Environment Policy Paper No. 1*, UNEP, 7

2 IUCN, *World Conservation Strategy*, Gland, Switzerland, 1980

economic growth and wellbeing. Sustainability has become a vital component in contemporary management of natural resources by governments. Within the resource sectors, international bodies such as the World Bank, World Economic Forum (WEF) and the UN are working with national governments to establish programmes intended to help increase environmental standards as well as develop sustainability. New businesses are being urged to become increasingly sustainable in their practices through policy development and regulatory reform, as well as subsidies. Globally, economically disadvantaged communities rely on natural resources, where these are readily available, as vitally important to their prospects of development. The economic benefits to be derived from natural resources are equally important to indigenous communities and smallholder individuals. In recognition of the need for an increase in the living standards of these communities, international development efforts are accordingly directed with this aim.[3]

Recent developments indicate that various low or middle-income countries have shown interest in attracting foreign investment in projects such as petroleum, mining, food and other commodities, including rubber.[4] The investment resulting from economic liberalisation in resource-rich host countries has enhanced communication and transport systems in those countries and has gone some way to supplying the rising demand for agricultural, mineral and energy products, particularly in those countries new to the influence of international investment. Within sub-Saharan Africa alone, approximately US$64 billion in foreign investment flows were largely attributed to the natural resource sector.[5]

Sustainable development and growth can be attained by governments through careful management and regulation of natural resources.[6] Historically, there is a high cost associated with mismanagement of natural resources, leading typically to social, environmental and economic damage, including corruption. Given that domestic governments are responsible for natural resources within their countries' borders, they must ensure that these natural resources are regulated appropriately for the benefit and future prosperity of present and future generations. It is also the responsibility of the relevant extractive industries to manage an effective and transparent system

3 Marta Maretich, 'Sustainability Drives Impact Investment in Natural Resources' <http://maximpactblog.com/sustainability-drives-impact-investment-in-natural-resources/> accessed 21 January 2017

4 Lorenzo Cotula, *Investment Contracts and Sustainable Development: How to Make Contracts for Fairer and More Sustainable Natural Resource Investments* (International Institute for Environment and Development, 2010) 1

5 Ibid

6 Technical Report for the Post-2015 Development Agenda, *Harnessing Natural Resources for Sustainable Development: Challenges and Solutions* 18 September 2013, Report of the SDSN Thematic Group 10 on the Good Governance of Extractive and Land Resources <unsdsn.org/wp-content/uploads/2014/02/TG10-Final-Report.pdf> accessed 28 February 2017

for the exploitation and production from forest holdings, agricultural land, hydrocarbon resources and minerals. Such an initiative would help foster inclusive as well as sustainable economic development.[7]

The value in pursuing sustainable development was recognised in the Stockholm Declaration on the Human Environment, adopted at the 1972 UN Conference on the Human Environment,[8] which states '[m]an is both creature and moulder of his environment, which gives him physical sustenance and affords him the opportunity for intellectual, moral, social and spiritual growth'.[9] Consequently, '[t]he natural growth of population continuously presents problems for the preservation of the environment, and adequate policies and measures should be adopted, as appropriate, to face these problems'.[10] Again, recognising the intrinsic importance of economic development to the capacity for increased environmental protection, the Declaration acknowledges that '[e]conomic and social development is essential for ensuring a favourable living and working environment for man and for creating conditions on earth … essential for the improvement of the quality of life'.[11] Meanwhile, it was accepted that the onus was on host states to ensure that economic growth arising from investment in natural resources occurred in the context of appropriate measures taken for the protection of those resources and the environment impacted by their exploitation, but that these should not be excessively restrictive. Accordingly, the Declaration also states that '[t]he environmental policies of all States should enhance and not adversely affect the present or future development potential of developing countries, nor should they hamper the attainment of better living conditions for all'.[12]

Sustainable development has received worldwide attention following the publication of the report *Our Common Future*, known as the Brundtland Report, by the World Commission on Environment and Development (WCED) in 1987. The report defined sustainable development as 'development that meets the needs of the present without compromising the ability of future generations to meet their own needs'.[13] It explained sustainable development in the following terms, as: 'a process of change in which the exploitation of resources, the direction of investments, the orientation of technological development, and institutional change are all in harmony and

7 Ibid
8 Stockholm Declaration on the Human Environment, UN Doc A/CONF.48/14 and Corr. 1 (1972)
9 Section 1, ibid
10 Section 5, ibid
11 Principle 8, ibid
12 Principle 11, ibid
13 Chapter II, Article 1, World Commission on Environment and Development, *Our Common Future: Report of the World Commission on Environment and Development* [Brundtland Report 1987] <www.un-documents.net/wced-ocf.htm> accessed 27 February 2017

enhance both current and future potential to meet human needs and aspirations'.[14] A crucial component of sustainable development defined in this way is the inclusion of the concept of 'needs', both those of the present and also future generations. In emphasising this concept, the WCED acknowledged that the vital requirements of the majority of individuals over the world, in both developed and developing states, are in danger of not being met in an adequate manner, where these needs are ignored in the pursuit of the economic benefits arising from natural resource exploitation and investment.[15]

A little over a decade after the Brundtland Report, at the World Summit on Sustainable Development (WSSD) in Johannesburg, South Africa, in 2002, Summit President and President of South Africa Thabo Mbeki acknowledged the increasing global importance of sustainable development throughout both the developed and developing world:

> In the last 30 years, the torch of sustainable development has travelled from Europe, to the Americas, through Asia, and now burns in Africa. After a protracted journey, it has arrived in the continent that is the cradle of humanity. The fact that we have convened at this cradle of humanity, emphasises the obligation we all face to respond with all seriousness and with a sense of urgency to adopt a meaningful Johannesburg Plan of implementation, in the interests of all humanity and our common planet.[16]

Role of international law in promoting the sustainable use of natural resources

In the context of growing global appreciation of sustainability, the International Law Association (ILA) Committee on the Legal Aspects of Sustainable Development drafted the New Delhi Declaration of Principles of International Law on Sustainable Development. The Declaration recognises that 'sustainable development is now widely accepted as a global objective and that the concept has been amply recognized in various international and national legal instruments, including treaty law and jurisprudence at international and national level'.[17] It emphasises that 'sustainable development … should be integrated into all relevant fields of policy' in order to realise its goals and identifies seven principles in the field of sustainable development

14 Chapter II, Article 15, ibid

15 Christina Voigt, *Sustainable Development as a Principle of International Law: Resolving Conflicts between Climate Measures and WTO Law* (Martinus Nijhoff Publishers, 2009) 14

16 <www.un.org/events/wssd/statements/openingsaE.htm> accessed 25 February 2017

17 International Law Association, *New Delhi Declaration on the Principles of International Law Related to Sustainable Development* (ILA, 2002).

that are considered 'instrumental in pursing the objective of sustainable development in an effective way'.[18]

The first of these principles, echoing those already long established in UN General Assembly (UNGA) Resolution 1803, or the United Nations Declaration on the Permanent Sovereignty over Natural Resources, stipulates that it is the duty of states to ensure sustainable use of natural resources. The New Delhi Declaration takes the concept of permanent sovereignty over natural resources and its inherent duties further, by providing that 'all States have the sovereign right to manage their own resources … and the responsibility to ensure that activities within their jurisdiction or control do not cause significant damage to the environment of other States'.[19]

Second, the Declaration prioritises equity and broadens this concept to include 'both *inter-generational equity* (the right to future generations to enjoy a fair level of the common patrimony) and *intra-generational equity* (the right of all peoples within the current generation of fair access to the current generation's entitlement to the Earth's natural resources)'.[20] Third, the Declaration recognises that the principle of common but differentiated responsibilities imposes an additional duty on states 'to co-operate in the achievement of global sustainable development and the protection of the environment'.[21] The polluter-pays principle gives effect to these latter two objectives of equity and cooperation toward a common goal.[22] Fourth, a precautionary approach to human health, natural resources and ecosystems is upheld as a principle encouraging the efforts of 'States, international organizations and the civil society, particularly the scientific and business communities, to avoid human activity which may cause significant harm to human health, natural resources or ecosystems, including in the light of scientific uncertainty'.[23]

The Declaration also expresses the intrinsic importance of the method of governance to the achievement of sustainable development goals and foresees a role for international law in informing governance practices and structures. The fifth principle, pertaining to public participation and access to information and justice, is justified as 'essential to sustainable development and good governance in that it is a condition for responsive, transparent and accountable governments',[24] while good governance, the sixth principle, is 'essential to the progressive development and codification of international law relating to sustainable development'.[25] Finally, the seventh principle of integration and interrelationship 'reflects the interdependence of social,

18 Ibid, Preamble
19 Ibid, para 1.1
20 Ibid, para 2.1
21 Ibid, para 3.1
22 Ibid
23 Ibid, para 4.1
24 Ibid, para 5.1
25 Ibid, para 6.1

economic, financial, environmental and human rights aspects of principles and rules of international law relating to sustainable development as well as of the interdependence of the needs of current and future generations of humankind'.[26] The principles enshrined in the New Delhi Declaration suggest that domestic regulation of natural resources exploitation should be informed by international law if sustainability is to be achievable.

International environmental law has emerged as a framework for determining appropriate means for the regulation of natural resources. The Brundtland Report advocated a fundamental and radical transformation of policy and law to incorporate the ideals of sustainable development and to ensure the recognition of intergenerational needs and concerns. Reflecting and incorporating these concerns, the sustainable use of natural resources is defined in Article 2 of the 1992 Convention on Biological Diversity as the '[u]se of components of biological diversity in a way and at a rate that does not lead to the long-term decline of biological diversity, thereby maintaining its potential to meet the needs and aspirations of present and future generations'. More recently, Schrijver and Cordonier-Segger, in a 2016 draft report for the ILA, set out the means by which the rules and practices of international law may be directly applied to the sustainable management of natural resources by states.[27]

In growing recognition of the potentially destructive impact of trade on natural resources, multilateral environmental agreements (MEAs) have incorporated trade-related environmental measures (TREMs) that intended to restrict or regulate the environmental consequences of trade and investment on these resources.[28] However, there remain some doubts as to how these measures, imposed by signatory states within the context of global trade, may withstand any challenge from international investors.[29] The interests of the investor have typically been upheld in disputes concerning state-imposed environmental measures that have been brought to the World

26 Ibid, para 7.1

27 Nicolas J. Schrijver and Marie-Claire Cordonier-Segger, 'Sustainable Natural Resource Management for Development: Final Draft, First Report of the Committee' (Draft Report, International Law Association, Committee for the Role of International Law in Sustainable Natural Resource Management for Development, 2016) 3–38

28 For discussion, see Margareta Timbur, 'Multilateral environmental agreements and the trade measures incorporated in these agreements' (Working Paper 4(2), CES, 2012). Pursuant to its obligations under such agreements, Australia, for instance, has incorporated TREMs into domestic legislation ratifying the Convention on Trade in Endangered Species and the Montreal Protocol on the Protection of the Ozone Layer: Rohan Hardcastle, 'Australian GATT-Inconsistent Trade Measures under Multilateral Environmental Agreements' (1998) 15(3) *Environmental and Planning Law Journal* 199, 201–204

29 A concern explored by Aditi Mathur and Siddharth Dang in 'Multilateral Environmental Agreements versus World Trade Organization System: A Comprehensive Study' (2009) 1(3) *American Journal of Economics and Business Administration* 219, 221–223

Trade Organization's (WTO) Dispute Settlement Body.[30] Such a tendency has led to the conclusion that the WTO is, as a body dedicated to the promotion of trade, ill-equipped to deal with the validity of TREMs under its own rules, even where these are introduced in compliance with MEA requirements.[31] Though there has long been a call for the legitimacy of environmental concerns to be more solidly recognised within the General Agreement on Tariffs and Trade (GATT) regime,[32] WTO negotiations have frequently foundered on the question of how this might be achieved on an equitable basis without hindering the access of resource-rich, developing countries to the benefits from global trade and investment in their natural resources. TREMs, such as eco-labelling, may nevertheless hold some promise for overcoming the reluctance of countries to engage in increased environmental regulation where this may impact on trade.[33]

The alignment of domestic trade policy with a state's obligations under international environmental law instruments may contribute to protect precious natural resources.[34] A corresponding benefit of linking trade and investment policy with environmental regulation is the increased prospect of economic growth and a rise in the standard of living for those states willing to implement reform. In the context of the global problem of climate change, for instance, the introduction of trade policy measures such as clean energy subsidies and the transfer of climate-friendly technologies in fulfilment of international climate change commitments has, commentators suggest, the capacity to not only enable the more efficient use of natural resources within a lower emission economy, but also may augment growth and development through the exchange of climate-friendly goods and services.[35]

30 As discussed by Nidhi Singh, 'Trade Related Environmental Measures in Multilateral Environmental Agreements and the WTO: Irreconcilable Differences?' (2009) 1(3) *American Journal of Economics and Business Administration* 251, 255

31 As argued recently by Umair Ghori in 'An Epic Mess: "Exhaustible Natural Resources" and the Future of Export Restraints after the *China – Rare Earths* Decision' (2015) 16(2) *Melbourne Journal of International Law* 398–431

32 See, for instance, Chris Wold, 'Multilateral Environmental Agreements and the GATT: Conflict and Resolution?' (1996) 26(3) *Environmental Law* 841, 910–915

33 See Aaron Cosbey et al., 'Environmental Goods and Services Negotiations at the WTO: Lessons from multilateral environmental agreements and ecolabels for breaking the impasse' (Working Paper, IISD, March 2010) 34–38

34 Mike Muller and Christophe Bellmann, 'Trade and Water: How Might Trade Policy Contribute to Sustainable Water Management?' (Issue Paper, ICTSD, 13 October 2016) 14–37

35 Sonja Hawkins, 'Use Trade Policy to Achieve the Benefits of Low Emissions Development' (Brief for LEDS in Practice Series, ICTSD, 28 June 2016); Kasturi Das and Kaushik Bandyopadhyay, 'Climate Change and Clean Energy in the 2030 Agenda: What Role for the Trade System?' (Think Piece, ICTSD, 26 October 2016) 6–12. See also Heleen de Coninck et al., 'International Technology-Orientated Agreements to Address Climate Change' (2008) 36(1) *Energy Policy* 335

Sustainable development is also acknowledged in the Preamble to the Agreement Establishing the World Trade Organization,[36] which makes reference to its members:

> allowing for the optimal use of the world's resources in accordance with the objective of the sustainable development, seeking both to protect and preserve the environment and to enhance the means for doing so in a manner consistent with their respective needs and concerns at different levels of economic development.[37]

The WTO Appellate Tribunal in the matter of *United States – Import Prohibition of Certain Shrimp and Shrimp Products* has also stated that sustainable development, as mentioned in the Preamble to the WTO Agreement, showed that 'the signatories to that Agreement were, in 1994, fully aware of the importance and legitimacy of environmental protection as a goal of national and international policy' and that this preambular recognition 'informs not only the *General Agreement on Tariffs and Trade* (GATT), but also the other covered agreements of the *WTO Agreement*'.[38] In this case, the Appellate Body examined the definition of 'exhaustible natural resources' as mentioned in Article XX(g) of the GATT, and determined that the broad scope of the Article legitimised measures introduced by domestic governments to protect renewable natural resources from over-exploitation:

> Given the recent acknowledgement by the international community of the importance of concerted bilateral or multilateral action to protect living natural resources, and recalling the explicit recognition by the WTO Members of the objective of sustainable development in the preamble of the WTO Agreement, we believe it is too late in the day to suppose that Article XX(g) of the GATT 1994 may be read as referring only to the conservation of exhaustible mineral or other non-living natural resources. Moreover, two adopted GATT 1947 panel reports previously found fish to be an 'exhaustible natural resource' within the meaning of Article XX(g). We hold that, in line with the principle of effectiveness in treaty interpretation, measures to conserve exhaustible natural resources, whether living or non-living, may fall within Article XX(g).[39]

36 Adopted on 15 April 1994 at Marrakesh, entry into force on 1 January 1995
37 Preamble to the WTO Agreement
38 *United States – Import Prohibition of Certain Shrimp and Shrimp Products*, Report of the Appellate Body, Doc WT/DS58/AB/R, Geneva, WTO, 12 October 1998; para 129, italics in original
39 Ibid, para 131

As Werge notes, the exceptions available under Article XX(b) and (g) of the GATT constitute the only means by which TREMs might be rescued from being deemed a violation of WTO rules.[40] Furthermore, as Ghori illustrates with reference to the *China – Rare Earths* decision, the meaning of 'exhaustible natural resources' under GATT Article XX(g) is unclear and provides no direction to developing countries on how to impose WTO compliant restrictions on exports with the aim of conserving their natural resources.[41]

Indeed, as an alternative to trade measures which seeks purely to impose restrictions or bans on the exploitation of natural resources, MEAs may act constructively as a means by which technology transfer is enabled and public investment encouraged, as a way of building the capacity within developing countries to protect against the 'resource curse' and prevent over-exploitation of natural resources.[42] Yet even though capacity building has evolved to become part of what Drumbl describes as the international environmental consensus,[43] often forming the basis upon which developing countries have committed to MEAs, the achievement of capacity building is contingent on the encouragement and effectiveness of public–private partnerships (PPPs) which are most frequently expressed through investment agreements. The Organisation for Economic Co-operation and Development (OECD) recognises the role MEAs can play in offering stimulation for investment, but also warns that contribution from private investors to environmental causes in the public interest will only occur if the goals of MEAs are consistent with private financial objectives, such as profit, efficiency and competitiveness.[44]

Thus, the goals of international environmental law and the way in which these are implemented by states may fundamentally conflict with a state's obligations to foreign investors. Foreign investment in the exploitation of a country's natural resources raises significant issues of access, control and distribution that have the potential to give rise to conflict, or at least, inconsistency between the international legal regimes which apply to natural resource management. The Declaration on Permanent Sovereignty over Natural Resources sought to clarify the basis upon which natural resources could be shared and exploited between states, by providing for a host state's control over the environmental policies and regimes it introduces in order to

40 Thomas Werge, 'Environmental Standards under the Peru FTA: A Template for the WTO?' (2010) 23(1) *Georgetown International Environmental Law Review* 71, 85

41 Ghori, above n 31, 408–414

42 See, for example, Dr Eric Neumayer, 'Multilateral Environmental Agreements, Trade and Development: Issues and Policy Options Concerning Compliance and Enforcement' (Report, Consumer and Unity Trust Society Jaipur, India) 37–41

43 Mark Drumbl, 'Does Sharing Know its Limits? Thoughts on implementing International Environmental Agreements: A Review of National Environmental Policies, a Comparative Study of Capacity Building' (1999) 18 *Virginia Environmental Law Journal* 281, 282

44 OECD, *Multilateral Environmental Agreements and Private Investment: Business Contribution towards Addressing Global Environmental Problems* (OECD, 2005) 5–6

regulate and encourage the sustainable use and consumption of its own natural resources. It has long been a subject of discussion that the objectives of international environmental law which rely on a state's implementation, and the imperatives informing international investment law which facilitate an investor's access to a state's natural resources, are two historically separate legal regimes, the interaction of which is complex and often problematic.[45] As Jorge Vinuales notes, a host state and a foreign investor may of course share the objective of wishing to capitalize on that state's natural resources, but this may be ultimately to the detriment of public welfare if the environmental and social pillars of sustainable development are ignored in pursuit of economic priorities.[46]

Investment in natural resources and the promotion of sustainable development

Foreign investment is increasingly viewed as having the potential to promote sustainable development. The 1992 United Nations Conference on Environment and Development (UNCED) produced Agenda 21, which declares:

> Investment is critical to the ability of developing countries to achieve needed economic growth to improve the welfare of their populations and to meet their basic needs in a sustainable manner, all without deteriorating or depleting the resource base that underpins development. Sustainable development requires increased investment, for which domestic and external financial resources are needed. Foreign private investment and the return of flight capital, which depend on a healthy investment climate, are an important source of financial resources.[47]

Later in 2002, the heads of state and government at the United Nations International Conference on Financing for Development in 2002 adopted the Monterrey Consensus,[48] which suggests in the following terms, a nexus between sustainable development and the provision of a favourable investment environment:

45 See, for example, Konrad von Moltke, *International Environmental Management, Trade Regimes and Sustainability* (IISD, 2001) 33–36

46 See Jorge Vinuales, 'International Investment Law and Natural Resource Governance' in Elisa Morgera and Kati Kulovesj, *Research Handbook on International Law and Natural Resources* (Edward Elgar, 2016) 2

47 Agenda 21: Programme of Action for Sustainable Development, Report of the UNCED. UN GAOR, 46th Sessions, Agenda Item 21, UN Doc A/Conf.151/6/Rev.1 (1992), para 2.23

48 Monterrey Consensus of the International Conference on Financing for Development of 22 March 2002 as recommended for endorsement by the General Assembly of the UN (A/CONF/198/11, chapter 1, resolution 1, annex)

> To attract and enhance inflows of productive capital, countries need to continue their efforts to achieve a transparent, stable and predictable investment climate, with proper contract enforcement and respect for property rights, embedded in sound macroeconomic policies and institutions that allow businesses, both domestic and international, to operate efficiently and profitably and with maximum development impact.[49]

The link between foreign investment and sustainable development is also emphasised in the 2009 G8 Leaders' Declaration on Responsible Leadership for a Sustainable Future.[50] The Declaration states that capital flows, including foreign direct investments (FDIs), are 'an important source of financing and a driver of economic growth and integration'.[51] It stresses 'an open, receptive climate for foreign investment, especially in emerging and in developing countries' for favourable FDI.[52] The Declaration evinced that the G8 leaders were '[c]onscious of the contemporary role played by governments and the private sector in reaching a sustainable growth', prompting them to 'call for enhanced efforts to ... promote responsible business practices'.[53]

The relationship between foreign investment and sustainable development is also evident in the United Nations Conference on Trade and Development (UNCTAD) *2014 World Investment Report*, with Ban Ki-moon, then UN Secretary-General, noting that 'after a decline in 2012 global foreign direct investment, flows rose by 9 per cent in 2013, with growth expected to continue in the years to come'.[54] His conclusion is emphatic with respect to the contribution of FDI to sustainability:

> This demonstrates the great potential of international investment, along with other financial resources, to help reach the goals of a post-2015 agenda for sustainable development. Transnational corporations can support this effort by creating decent jobs, generating exports, promoting rights, respecting the environment, encouraging local content, paying fair taxes and transferring capital, technology and business contracts to spur development.[55]

49 Para 21

50 G8 Leaders' Declaration: Responsible Leadership for a Sustainable Future (2009), <www.g8italia2009.it/static/G8_Allegato/G8_Declaration_08_07_09_final,0.pdf> accessed 19 February 2017

51 Ibid, para 49

52 Ibid

53 Ibid, para 53

54 Ban Ki-moon, 'Preface' in UNCTAD, *World Investment Report 2014. Investing in the SDGs: An Action Plan*, iii, <http://unctad.org/en/pages/PublicationWebflyer.aspx?publicationid=937> accessed 19 February 2017

55 Ibid

The International Institute for Sustainable Development (IISD), an NGO based in Canada, echoes these statements, asserting that '[w]ithout investment, sustainable development is impossible. Well planned, high quality foreign investment in developed and developing countries can help make current economic practices more sustainable'.[56]

An incentive underlying the ratification of MEAs by developing countries lies in the fact that such international agreements (e.g., biodiversity, land, chemicals and hazardous waste) have the potential to facilitate access by signatories to export markets and other benefits.[57] Similarly, as Condon notes, the inclusion of MEAs in international investment treaties may make trade liberalisation more attractive to potential host states that might otherwise be afflicted by the 'resource curse', by offering an ostensible guarantee that the protection of natural resources will remain a shared concern of the parties to any such investment agreement.[58] Certainly, the growing proliferation of bilateral investment treaties (BITs) and regional investment treaties (RITs) means that countries are becoming increasingly inter-dependent as a result of global investment, warranting greater agreement between state parties on measures to protect natural resources for the benefit of both exporting and importing economies.[59] Indeed, the incorporation of environmental conditions and standards in a global foreign investment agreement has been proposed as a means of ensuring the achievement of both trade and environmental objectives.[60]

Nevertheless, it is essential to also recognise the potential drawbacks of FDI in natural resources. This is particularly the case in circumstances where the host state may relinquish control over natural resources to secure FDI or fail to regulate factors arising from FDI that could negatively influence the environment, and detrimentally impact the local population and their living conditions. It should be acknowledged that some ventures, such as those pertaining to minerals and oil extraction, bear a high risk of extensive damage to the environment, to local population health and to traditional living conditions. Hence, it is vital to establish a balance between the positive and negative aspects of FDI, so as to mitigate as much as possible any detrimental consequences. In practical terms, this is only possible if the respective host

56 <www.iisd.org/project/working-parliamentarians-africa-investment-policies> accessed 19 February 2017

57 See the arguments of Peter Egger et al., 'Trade and Investment Liberalization as Determinants of Multilateral Environmental Agreement Membership' (2011) 18(6) *International Tax and Public Finance* 605–633

58 Madison Condon, 'The Integration of Environmental Law into International Investment Treaties and Trade Agreements: Negotiation Process and the Legalization of Commitments' (2015) 33 *Virginia Environmental Law Journal* 102, 119–121

59 Egger et al., supra n 57, 612–614.

60 See Martin Benjamin, 'An Environmental Remedy to Paralyzed Negotiations for a Multilateral Foreign Direct Investment Agreement' (2007) 1 *Golden Gate University Environmental Law Review* 209, 238–243

state implements appropriate regulation. It also depends on the attitude taken by foreign investment companies and by their home states, as well as the international system at large.[61]

The UNGA Resolution 1803[62] declared, unequivocally, that '[t]he right of peoples and nations to permanent sovereignty over their natural wealth must be exercised in the interest of their national development and of the well-being of the people of the State concerned'. The Declaration on Permanent Sovereignty over Natural Resources offers basic rules concerning the treatment of foreign investors and proportionate sharing on any profit derived from the exploration, development and disposition of natural resources.[63] In cases where the state chooses to nationalise, expropriate or requisition natural resources, customary international law, as encapsulated in the Declaration, suggests that exploitation of natural resources must be limited in order to protect the public interest, and goes so far as to recommend compensation be payable in accordance with national legislation, where the public interest is adversely affected. The rules put forward by the Resolution reveal the legacy of a historical struggle between private interests in property and wealth generation and a growing sense of the public interest, and the evolution of this tension into the underlying principle that the sovereign rights of national governments, including the right to exploit their countries' natural resources, must be exercised in the interest of national development and public wellbeing. Though international law recognises the sovereignty of national governments over their natural resources, international investment law ensures protection to foreign investors against economic loss as a result of actions taken by domestic governments in the national interest. These protections might be described as falling broadly into protection from discriminatory measures, the right to redress in cases of expropriation and the protection afforded to an investor's legitimate expectations.[64]

Discriminatory measures, national treatment and MFN principles

National treatment and most favoured nation (MFN) principles afford protection from the imposition of natural resource management measures by a state where these may have a discriminatory effect.[65] Domestic environmental regulation may easily fall foul of these protections where an investor's interests are impacted by a state's attempt to limit exploitation or extraction

61 Stephan W. Schill, 'International Investment Law as International Development Law' in Andrea K. Bjorklund (ed.), *Yearbook on International Investment Law & Policy 2012–2013* (Oxford University Press, 2014), 327, 331

62 Paragraphs 3, 4, 6 and 8. General Assembly Resolution 1803 (XVII) of 14 December 1962, 'Permanent sovereignty over natural resources', <www.ohchr.org/Documents/ProfessionalInterest/resources.pdf>

63 See Chapters 2 (Baxi) and 3 (Bhuiyan) in this book

64 See Chapters 2 (Baxi), 3 (Bhuiyan) and 5 (Alam) in this book

65 See Chapter 5 (Alam) in this book

of its natural resources, resulting in the threat of investor–state dispute settlement (ISDS) arbitration, so as to enforce the terms of an international investment agreement (IIA). One way in which the reach of these protective principles might be limited is by inclusion, within the BIT itself, of clauses restricting ISDS arbitration in the interests of environmental protection. Whitsitt, however, describes the problematic deployment of MFN standards by investors in order to overcome such restrictions.[66] Arbitration tribunals are thus caught between, on the one hand, granting primacy to an investor's procedural rights and the need for stability in natural resource projects, and on the other, recognising state consent to an investment treaty as fundamental to the concept of state sovereignty over natural resources. Their ambivalence to date is indicative of the difficulties encountered in approaching such a fraught issue.

The demand for compensation for expropriation

Where investors are impacted by regulatory change, and this amounts to expropriation of a natural resource that would otherwise have been available for use, compensation is typically expected.[67] Though Waelde and Kolo have suggested that environmental regulation introduced for the legitimate purpose of protecting natural resources from over-exploitation is unlikely to be challengeable by investors,[68] the significant implications of the prospect of ISDS for developing countries mean regulatory chill is a foreseeable consequence.[69]

Legitimate expectations of investors and FET

A key principle of international investment law, fair and equitable treatment (FET) requires that a host state avoid subjecting a foreign investor to arbitrary, discriminatory or fraudulent treatment, or treatment that would constitute a lack of due process or a denial of justice. Where FET is invoked, the risk for host states, in situations where natural resources require measures for their protection from over-exploitation, is that any regulation can be subject to challenge.[70] Indeed, Vinuales suggests that the inherent structure of international investment law lends itself to an overemphasis on the protection of the investor's legitimate expectations over and above a state's interest in protection of its natural resources.

66 Elizabeth Whitsitt, 'Application of Most-Favoured-Nation Clauses to the Dispute Settlement Provisions of Bilateral Investment Treaties: An Assessment of the Jurisprudence' (2009) 27 *Journal of Energy and Natural Resources* 527, 528

67 As discussed later, in Chapter 5 (Alam)

68 See Thomas Waelde and Abba Kolo, 'Environmental Regulation, Investment Protection and "Regulatory Taking" in International Law' (2001) 50(4) *International and Comparative Law Quarterly* 811, 843–848

69 See Chapter 5 (Alam) in this book.

70 Vinuales, supra n 46, 8

Though diverse and broad reaching in the economic, social, environmental and cultural consequences it produces for host states, FDI lacks a unified and definitive multilateral treaty text or a single over-arching international institution informing and regulating its practices.[71] The development of international investment law is influenced by the proliferation of BITs, free trade agreements (FTAs), national law, customary international law, institutionally generated law[72] and the jurisprudence of international investment tribunals.[73] Though the WTO has evinced an increasing and influential interest in the impacts of FDI[74] and the World Bank deals with natural resource related investments,[75] universal endorsement of the principles that should ideally govern FDI remains lacking. In spite of the prevalence of standards such as 'national treatment' or 'fair and equitable treatment', it is difficult to consider the network of investment agreements as a single system or as coherent regime of harmonious rules. Because of growing diversity among countries' BITs, 'countries and firms have to operate within an increasingly complicated framework of multi-layered and multi-faceted investment rules with overlapping obligations and commitments, and also with gaps'.[76] In addition, different dispute settlement systems operating under various rules[77] have led to fragmentation within the investment regime with inconsistent

71 David Collins, 'A New Role for the WTO in International Investment Law: Public Interest in the Post Neoliberal Period' (2010) 25(1) *Connecticut Journal of International Law* 1

72 A number of relevant General Assembly Resolutions and other soft law efforts e.g. OECD's Guidelines for Multilateral Enterprises, the OECD's Code of Capital Movements also play a role. See Chapter 8 (Galizzi and Ewing) in this book

73 See generally, Jeswald W. Salacuse, *The Law of Investment Treaties* (Oxford University Press, 2010); M. Sornarajah, *The International Law of Foreign Investment* (3rd edn, Cambridge University Press, 2010); Jose E. Alvarez, Karl P. Sauvant, Kamil Ahmed and Gabriela del P. Vizcaino, *The Evolving International Investment Regime: Expectation, Realities, Options* (Oxford University Press, 2011); Jose E. Alvarez, *The Public International Law Regime Governing International Investment* (Ail-Pocket – Hague Academy of International Law, 2011). Rudolf Dolzer and Christoph Schreuer, *Principles of Investment Law* (2nd edn, Oxford University Press, 2008); Andrew Newcombe and Lluis Paradell, *The Law and Practice of Investment Treaties* (Kluwer, 2008)

74 The WTO's agreements for example, the Trade-Related Investment Measures (TRIMs), Services Agreement (GATS), and Trade-Related Aspects of Intellectual Property (TRIPS) are relevant. See Chapter 4 (Espa) in this book

75 World Bank, Projects and Programs on environment and natural resource management, <www.worldbank.org/en/topic/environment/projects> accessed 22 March 2017

76 UNCTAD, Recent Development in Investor-State Dispute Settlement IIA MONITOR No. 2 (2005), <http://unctad.org/en/docs/webiteiit20051_en.pdf> accessed 22 March 2017

77 The World Bank International Centre for the Settlement of Investment Disputes (ICSID) and other arbitral mechanisms, such as UNCITRAL. Karl P. Sauvant, 'The Regulatory Framework for Investment: Where Are We Headed?' in Ravi Ramamurti and Niron Hashai (eds), *The Future of Foreign Direct Investment and the Multinational Enterprise* (Research in Global Strategic Management, Volume 15, Emerald Group Publishing Limited, 2011) 407–433

arbitral decisions.[78] Such inconsistency can result from different interpretation of laws and facts by different tribunals,[79] or conflicting views of tribunals concerning the comparable treaty provisions in different treaties.[80]

Though the principles expressed in the UN Declaration on the Permanent Sovereignty over Natural Resources arguably constitute international customary law, as Ng'ambi points out,[81] the body of international jurisprudence on investment disputes supports the proposition that states are bound under international investment law to protect investors from the impacts of their regulation. Given the threat posed, particularly to developing countries, by ISDS arbitration, and the bias toward the investor which some perceive is betrayed by the principles of international investment law, Vinuales recommends reform to the system of ISDS arbitration in order to redress the balance in favour of state sovereignty so as to afford increased protection to natural resources.[82] Others, such as Matveev, are more optimistic, and consider that the ISDS system has evolved so as to offer protection to the investor without compromising state sovereignty. Nevertheless, Matveev recommends that developing states, those most prone to the 'resource curse', be supported to conduct thorough regulatory impact assessments prior to concluding IIAs.[83]

Challenges posed by sustainable investment in the natural resource sector

Certainly, foreign investors take huge risks when investing project capital in countries with inadequate legal protection. However, in these circumstances, the dual level of protection afforded to investors, by way of accepted international standards as well as access to international arbitration tribunals, reflects the tendency for investor interests to be prioritised, even at the expense of host countries. The comparative lack of protection

78 Jose E. Alvarez (2011), supra, n 73

79 Stephan W. Schill, 'International Investment Law and the Host State's Power to Handle Economic Crises' (2007) 24 *Journal of International Arbitration*, 265. Schill cites *CMS v Argentina* and *LG&E v Argentina* where the tribunals reached different conclusions in applying the US–Argentine BIT. *CMS Gas Transmission Company v Argentine Republic.* (ICSID Case No. ARB/01/8). *LG&E Energy Corp., LG&E Capital Corp. and LG&E International Inc. v The Argentine Republic*, ICSID Case No. ARB/02/1 (Decision on Liability) (3 October 2006)

80 Judith Gill and others, 'Contractual Claims and Bilateral Investment Treaties: A Comparative Review of the SGS Cases' (2004) 21 *Journal of International Arbitration* 397. *SGS Société Générale de Surveillance v Republic of the Philippines*, ICSID Case No. ARB/02/6 (Dec on Jurisdiction) (29 Jan 2004)

81 Sangwani Patrick Ng'ambi, *Resource Nationalism in International Investment Law* (Routledge, 2016) 50

82 Vinuales, supra, n 46

83 The complexity of the task of reform in this area is explored in Chapter 5 (Alam) in this book

afforded to host countries becomes more problematic if the host country is also a developing country with weak legal infrastructure. While host countries compete to attract investments, unequal bargaining power between host states and foreign investors may lead to the 'race to the bottom' with respect to the minimisation of legal regulations.[84] In the absence of effective domestic regulation, the challenge is how to make foreign investors respect environmental and human rights, including the rights to a healthy environment and food, and the rights of existing users of land, water and other resources.

The following discussion explores how investments in the natural resource sector have evolved over the years to meet this challenge, with a focus on the changes in the investment practices, the protection of public interest, transparency, sustainable investment and the developing notion of a green economy.

Emphasis on resource-seeking investment

Foreign investment may be aimed at taking advantage of the low cost of production in a host country (efficiency seeking), investing in a new large domestic market (market seeking) or exploiting a natural resource available in the host country (resource seeking).[85] Agricultural investments, for instance, are primarily resource-seeking investments as these investments involve land acquisition with an impact on land and water rights.[86] From the perspective of a capital-exporting country, BITs provide a significant incentive to investors for capturing market share and exploiting the opportunities offered in host countries.[87] The capital-exporting country may seek a new market of substantial size and per capita income, with the prospect of cheap labour and market growth. In the natural resource sector, investment generally takes place when resource-abundant countries lack the capital, technical skills or infrastructure required to extract raw materials or sell them to the market. The proliferation of resource-seeking investment, for example, in the construction of pipelines, water privatisation, agriculture and mining, has been one of the most important determinants of FDI to date. However, whereas the dominant motive of investment remains resource seeking,

84 Kevin R. Gray, 'Foreign Direct Investment and Environmental Impacts – Is the Debate Over?' (2002) 11(3) *RECIEL* 306, 308 <www.worldtradelaw.net/articles/grayfdi.pdf> accessed 22 March 2017

85 J.H. Dunning 'Re-evaluating the Benefits of FDI' in John H. Dunning (ed.), *Global Capitalism, FDI and Competitiveness: The Selected Essays of John H. Dunning*, Volume II (Edward Elgar, 2002) 223

86 See Chapter 11 (Razzaque and Le) in this book. Also see: Carin Smaller and Howard Mann, 'A Thirst for Distant Lands: Foreign Investment in Agricultural Land and Water', May 2009, International Institute for Sustainable Development <www.iisd.org/pdf/2009/thirst_for_distant_lands.pdf> accessed on 19 March 2017

87 M. Sornarajah, supra, n 73

market-seeking motivations also constitute a significant contribution to the local economy of a host country.[88]

Even when the motive to invest in developing countries is primarily resource seeking, the social complexities of FDI are inescapable. The lack of consistency in the respective legal system of a host country, bureaucracy, corruption and problems in establishing clear ownership rights are some of the biggest concerns for investors, along with political and economic instability and lack of physical infrastructure. At the same time, there is now an increasing expectation that the home states of multinational corporations (MNCs) should have control over the activities of their MNCs operating overseas.[89] The expectation is apparent in guidelines which require measures to be taken to promote the flow of FDI into developing countries, as well as measures to ensure that MNCs do not act to the detriment of host developing countries.[90]

At the same time, in circumstances whereby developing countries are also involved in investing in the natural resource extraction taking place in another developing country, many of these investor countries[91] see themselves not only as *host* countries but also as *home* countries.[92] Developing countries (such as China, Russia, Brazil, India) have increasingly become capital exporters whereas developed countries (such as the US, Singapore, Chile) have simultaneously become capital importers.[93] The integration of these new global players in the global FDI market has given rise to the question of whether state-controlled entities should pursue non-commercial objectives when investing abroad.[94] The broader implication of this development is that a number of developed countries that previously sought a stringent international investment regime are now seeking greater flexibility and more policy space to be able to change policies and enshrine this approach in their national regulatory frameworks and investment agreements.

88 John H. Dunning, *Multinational Enterprises and the Global Economy* (Addison Wesley, 1993) 56

89 UNCTAD, World Investment Report 2012 <http://unctad.org/en/PublicationsLibrary/wir2012_embargoed_en.pdf> accessed 17 February 2017. UN Human Rights Council, Guiding Principles on Business and Human Rights (2008) <https://business-humanrights.org/sites/default/files/reports-and-materials/Ruggie-report-7-Apr-2008.pdf> accessed on 19 March 2017

90 M. Sornarajah, supra n 73

91 Outstanding emerging markets are Brazil, Russia, India and China (the BRICs) and Chile, Mexico, Egypt, South Africa, Malaysia, the Republic of Korea, Singapore and Thailand

92 UNCTAD (2012), supra n 89

93 Wenshua Shan, 'From "North–South Divide" to "Public–Private Debate": Revival of the Calvo Doctrine and the Changing Landscape in International Investment Law' (2007) 27 *Northwestern Journal of International Law and Business* 631; Zachary Elkins, Andrew T. Guzman and Beth Simmons, 'Competing for Capital: The Diffusion of Bilateral Investment Treaties, 1960–2000' (2008) *University of Illinois Law Review* 265

94 See Chapter 9 (Blanco) in this book

From economic efficiency to public interest?

FDI attracts considerable public attention as it may interfere with the host states' power to regulate for the public interest,[95] or 'those outcomes best serving the long-run survival and well being of a social collective construed as a "public"'.[96] Notwithstanding the prominence of public interest considerations in the UNGA Resolution 1803, any interest based purely on human rights or environmental considerations may not be able to compete with strongly organised private (or public) economic interests. Part of this is due to the isolation of international investment law from public interest concerns, such as those dealing with the environment, human rights and social development.

While there is a growing interplay between international investment law and other competing areas of international law, such as international environmental law, international human rights law, corporate social responsibility and good corporate governance, almost all IIAs focus only on investment protections at the expense of many other societal values and international norms.[97] The general tendency of arbitral tribunals not to adequately address or balance private interests with the public interest contributes to this tendency.[98] It is questionable whether private arbitral tribunals are appropriate forums for addressing issues of public importance, such as public access to water or energy.[99] The concern is especially acute in the context of ISDS, which requires investment tribunals to review state legislation and decisions made by state's judicial and administrative authorities.[100] Thus, the risk in disputes where environmental concerns are raised is that investment issues fail to be considered through a sustainable development lens.[101] Indeed, in recent years, there is a rising realisation that the main objective of IIAs is to

95 Thomas Polland, *Legal Framework for the Admission of FDI* (Eleven International Publishing 2006) 16–18; Smaller and Mann, supra n 86

96 Barry Bozeman, *Public Values and Public Interest: Counterbalancing Economic Individualism* (Georgetown University Press 2007) 12

97 Surya P. Subedi, *International Investment Law: Reconciling Policy and Principle* (Hart Publishing, 2008) 167–169

98 Jan Wouters and Nicolas Hachez, 'The Institutionalisation of Investment Arbitration and Sustainable Development' in Marie-Claire Cordonier Segger, Markus W Gehring and Andrew Newcombe (eds), *Sustainable Development in World Investment Law* (Wolters Kluwer, 2011) 611

99 Ibid

100 Marie-Claire Cordonier Segger and Avidan Kent, 'Promoting Sustainable Investment through International Law' in Marie-Claire Cordonier Segger, Markus W Gehring, and Andrew Newcombe (eds), *Sustainable Development in World Investment Law* (Wolters Kluwer 2011) 771–792

101 Graham Mayeda, 'International Investment Agreements between Developed and Developing Countries: Dancing with the Devil? A Case Commentary on the Vivendi, Sempra and Enron Awards' (2009) 4 (2) *McGill International Journal of Sustainable Development Law and Policy* 129

protect foreign investors against political and economic risks in the host country, regardless of the intentions and priorities of domestic legislatures and governments, a situation deemed by many to be unsatisfactory.[102]

In response to this problem, the International Centre for Settlement for Investment Disputes (ICSID) Arbitration Panel in the *Suez/Vivendi* case, a dispute which centred upon the water distribution and sewage systems of a large metropolitan area, explicitly accepted the relevance of 'public interest' considerations, including those pertaining to human rights.[103] However, this statement was made in the response to requests for amicus participation, with the Panel omitting any reference to the relevance of human rights in the tribunal's awards.[104]

In both *Aguas del Tunari v Bolivia* and *Vivendi v Argentina*, the tribunals did not directly address human rights concerns.[105] In the *SAUR v Argentina* case, the tribunal agreed that, although human rights and investment treaties operate at different levels, human rights provisions were relevant factors going to the tribunal's decision.[106] In the *Azurix* case, Argentina claimed that there was a conflict between the investment treaty and the protection of consumers' rights and argued that consumers' public interests should prevail over the private interest of service providers. However, the tribunal did not consider the matter.[107] These cases highlight the fact that arbitral tribunals, despite acknowledging the intrinsic 'public interest' element of investment agreements, ultimately continue to sideline the human rights dimension of foreign investments.

From confidentiality to transparency?

Until recently, investment arbitration was regarded as a private matter between two disputing parties. However, the proliferation of investment cases is producing much wider implications that go beyond traditional commercial considerations. There is a concern that ISDS may lead to trade-offs being concluded between the environmental and social interests of the

102 Surya P Subedi, *International Investment Law: Reconciling Policy and Principle* (Hart Publishing, 2008)

103 *Suez, Sociedad General de Aguas de Barcelona, S.A. and Vivendi Universal, S.A. v Argentina*, ICSID Case No. ARB/03/19, Order in Response to a Petition for Transparency and Participation as Amicus Curiae dated 19 May 2005, paras 19, 20 <www.italaw.com/cases/1057> accessed 17 February 2017

104 Similarly, see: *Biwater v Tanzania*, Procedural Order No. 5, of 2 February 2007, para 52

105 *Aguas del Tunari S.A. v Bolivia*, ICSID Case No. ARB/02/3; *Compañiá de Aguas del Aconquija S.A. and Vivendi Universal S.A. v Argentina*, ICSID Case No. ARB/97/3

106 *SAUR International SA v Argentina*, ICSID Case No. ARB.04/4. Decision on jurisdiction and liability, of 6 June 2012

107 The Tribunal stated that 'the matter has not been fully argued and the Tribunal fails to understand the incompatibility in the specifics of the instant case'. *Azurix Corp v The Argentine Republic*, ICSID Case No. ARB/01/12, Award of 14 July 2006, para 261

host states' citizens and the economic rights of the investor.[108] One of the current trends in investment arbitration, directed at solving this problem, is the participation of *amicus curiae*, or friends of the court. Because of the difference in nature between commercial disputes and investment disputes, with the latter testing the limits of national sovereignty over natural resources, there is a need for greater legitimacy and public participation.[109] The involvement of non-litigating parties, mainly NGOs and civil society groups, in arbitral proceedings means the public interest is granted increased scope in investment-related proceedings, in what represents a gain for sustainable development.[110] Nevertheless, issues of commercial confidentiality and privacy, the potential for delay and the associated increase in costs for litigants, along with the potential politicisation of *amicus* participation, all constitute factors which may inhibit the widespread adoption of this approach in ISDS.[111]

Sustainable development may be promoted through measures intended to encourage transparency and accountability in the management of FDI in natural resources. Increased transparency and access to information in the arbitral tribunals can be achieved through greater access to documents and public access to the arbitral proceedings, whether through *amicus* participation or public hearings. Indeed, proper disclosure of documents and information is vital for better participation. The United Nations Commission on International Trade Law (UNCITRAL) Rules on Transparency establishes the general principle that documents relating to the arbitration must be made available to the public, which can be achieved by uploading documents into the UNCITRAL Transparency Registry.[112] However, the existence of a special provision to protect the interests of the parties and the integrity of the arbitral process, by not making confidential or protected information available to the public, can be relied upon to prevent proper disclosure.[113] Once the respondent state receives the notice of arbitration, either the state or the investor must send a copy of the notice of arbitration to the '*repository*' under the Transparency Rules.[114] The UNCITRAL

108 Graham Mayeda, 'Sustainable International Investment Agreements: Challenges and Solutions for Developing Countries' in Marie-Claire Cordonier Segger, Markus W. Gehring and Andrew Newcombe (eds), *Sustainable Development in World Investment Law* (Wolters Kluwer 2011) 535

109 See Chapter 6 (Dimsey) in this book

110 Eugenia Levine, '*Amicus Curiae* in International Investment Arbitration: The Implications of an Increase in Third-Party Participation' (2012) 29 (1) *Berkeley Journal of International Law* 200

111 Ibid

112 Article 3 UNCITRAL Transparency Rules (2013) <www.uncitral.org/pdf/english/texts/arbitration/arb-rules-2013/UNCITRAL-Arbitration-Rules-2013-e.pdf> accessed 19 March 2017

113 Ibid. Article 7 Transparency Rules

114 The '*repository*' is the Transparency Registry operated by UNCITRAL. <www.uncitral.org/transparency-registry/> accessed 22 March 2017

amendment indicates some scope for the ICSID in relation to broadening access to documents and information.

The ICSID Arbitration Rule 32(2) offers limited access to the tribunal to those not involved in proceedings, but only with the consent of the parties:[115]

> *Unless either party objects*, the Tribunal, after consultation with the Secretary-General, *may allow other persons*, besides the parties, their agents, counsel and advocates, witnesses and experts during their testimony, and officers of the Tribunal, to attend or observe all or part of the hearings, subject to appropriate logistical arrangements. The Tribunal shall for such cases establish procedures for the protection of proprietary or privileged information.

Moreover, Article 37(2) of the ICSID Arbitration Rules provides that:

> *After consulting both parties*, the Tribunal *may allow a person* or entity that is not a party to the dispute (in this Rule called the 'non-disputing party) to file a written submission with the Tribunal regarding a matter within the scope of the dispute.

ICSID cases in which *amicus* briefs were submitted demonstrate that these provisions do not confer any rights on the non-party and that participation is strictly subject to the discretion of the parties and the tribunal.[116] Similar provisions can be found in the UNCITRAL Transparency Rules,[117] which uphold the tribunal's discretion as to whether to allow such submissions. Nevertheless, the UNCITRAL Rules provide for open public hearings,[118] leaving it open to the ICSID to adopt this approach in any particular case. In addition, North American Free Trade Agreement (NAFTA) countries (i.e. Canada, US and Mexico) have agreed that investor–state hearings should be

115 International Centre for Settlement of Investment Disputes (ICSID) Arbitration Rules, amended in 2006 <https://icsid.worldbank.org/en/Documents/resources/2006%20CRR_English-final.pdf 9> accessed 17 March 2017, emphasis added

116 *Methanex Corp. v United States of America*; *Biwater Gauff (Tanzania) Ltd v United Republic of Tanzania*, ICSID Case No. ARB/05/22 and *Suez, Sociedad General de Aguas de Barcelona, S.A. and Vivendi Universal, S.A. v Argentine Republic*, ICSID Case No. ARB/03/19. See Chapter 6 (Dimsey) of this book

117 Article 4 of the Transparency Rules allow a person that is not a disputing party to make written submissions with respect to a matter within the scope of the dispute. Article 5 allows a person that is a non-disputing party to the concerned treaty to make submissions with respect to a matter within the scope of the dispute or with respect to issues of treaty interpretation. The Transparency Rules were adopted in 2013 and came into effect on 1 April 2014. Supra, n 112

118 Ibid. Article 6 of UNCITRAL Transparency Rules (2013)

open to the public.[119] Article 29(2) of the 2012 US Model Bilateral Investment Treaty also provides for 'hearings open to the public'.[120]

From profit maximisation to sustainable investment?

With the increasing recognition of the importance of international human rights and environmental law to business and investment,[121] the challenge for international investment law is how to reconcile the economic imperatives of FDI with the goals of sustainable development.[122] Regulatory chill may be a consequence of the threat of heavy compensation claims, in the event of degradation and the financial burden these pose to the foreign investor. The multi-layered aspect of the investment regime, which is governed both by domestic law and the requirements of any applicable investment agreement, may bring about significant impacts, and not all of them negative, in many host states, particularly where there is insufficient or unclear domestic law concerning land rights, water rights, pollution controls for intensive agriculture, human health and worker protection.[123]

Optimising the positive effects of FDI for communities and the environment, while simultaneously mitigating the negative effects, is important for the achievement of sustainable development. The main purpose of sustainable investment is to provide equitable benefits to all stakeholders in a holistic manner by ensuring economic development, social inclusion and environmental sustainability. From an economic angle, sustainable development provides the ideal conditions for FDI by contributing to trade liberalisation and market access, and by creating the conditions for the encouragement of foreign investment flows.[124] At the same time, effective

119 The US and Canada announced their intention to consent to open public hearings. Department of Foreign Affairs and International Trade News Release No. 152, NAFTA Commission Joint Statement (7 October 2003). Mexico announced its support for open hearings in investor–state disputes following the 2004 NAFTA Commission Meeting. NAFTA Free Trade Commission Joint Statement, Decade of Achievement (16 July 2004)

120 Treaty between the Government of the United States of America and the Government of [Country] Concerning the Encouragement and Reciprocal Protection of Investment (2012), available at <https://ustr.gov/sites/default/files/BIT%20text%20for%20ACIEP%20Meeting.pdf>

121 For example UN Sustainable Development Goals (2015) <www.un.org/sustainabledevelopment/sustainable-development-goals/> accessed 22 March 2017. UN Guiding Principles on Business and Human Rights (2011) <www.ohchr.org/Documents/Publications/GuidingPrinciplesBusinessHR_EN.pdf> accessed 22 March 2017. Equator Principles (2013) <www.equator-principles.com/resources/equator_principles_III.pdf> accessed 22 March 2017

122 See chapters in Part 3 of this book, for example the chapters by Bates, Razzaque and Le, Faruque, Lesniewska and Erueti et al.

123 Smaller and Mann, supra n 86

124 J. Anthony Vanduzer, Penelope Simons and Graham Mayeda, *Integrating Sustainable Development into International Investment Agreements – A Guide for Developing Country Negotiators* (Commonwealth Secretariat, 2013)

sustainable development policies can protect the environment for the present and future generations, and promote equitable development to reduce poverty and improve the health of populations. However, foreign investors operating within the host state may fail to respect indigenous peoples' rights in the decision-making process, provide adequate working conditions or pay adequate wages, or may become complicit in corruption involving government agencies.[125] Although FDI has the potential to aid economic development in developing countries, it does not always ensure positive development outcomes because the activities of foreign investors are primarily oriented towards the maximisation of profit and not the promotion of socially responsible investment[126] or sustainable development.

Revised model BITs of some countries have been updated in such a way as to better reflect public interest considerations. As developing countries have increasingly become major investors and have increasingly entered into BITs with one another, and developed countries have shifted focus to become capital importers, several countries, including the US, Canada, Japan and some Latin American states, have reformed their approach to BITs.[127] Hence, the 2012 US Model BIT[128] added two provisions regarding environmental and labour standards in order to offer increased protection of these matters and to expand the regulatory mandate of host states. These amendments can be seen as an important signal of the willingness of home states to pursue a more balanced BIT, one that seeks to reconcile the objectives of foreign investment and sustainable development.[129] It is notable that many BITs, such as the Japan–Papua New Guinea BIT and the Colombia–Japan BIT, have been concluded with provision being made for matters conducive to sustainable development.[130]

The 1993 NAFTA between the US, Canada and Mexico intends to 'increase substantially the investment opportunities in the territories of the Parties',[131] and 'in a manner consistent with environmental protection and conservation', while promoting 'sustainable development' and contributing

125 Ibid. See Chapter 13 (Erueti et al.) and 18 (Simpson) in this book

126 Benjamin J Richardson, *Socially Responsible Investment Law: Regulating the Unseen Polluters* (Oxford 2008)

127 Wenshua Shan, 'From 'North–South Divide' to 'Public–Private Debate': Revival of the Calvo Doctrine and the Changing Landscape in International Investment Law' (2007) 27 *Northwestern Journal of International Law & Business* 631

128 Articles 12 and 13. Treaty between the United States of America and the Government of [Country] Concerning the Encouragement and Reciprocal Protection of Investment, 2004 <www.bilaterals.org/spip.php?article137> accessed 22 March 2017; and Treaty between the Government of the United States of America and the Government of [Country] Concerning the Encouragement and Reciprocal Protection of Investment, 2012 <https://ustr.gov/sites/default/files/BIT%20text%20for%20ACIEP%20 Meeting.pdf> accessed 22 March 2017

129 UNCTAD (2012), supra n 89

130 Ibid, 90

131 NAFTA, Introduction, Article 102(1)(c)

to 'the harmonious development and expansion of world trade'.[132] The Agreement also provides that '[t]he Parties recognize that it is inappropriate to encourage investment by relaxing domestic health, safety or environmental measures'.[133] Furthermore, the Agreement states that in the event of an inconsistency between the NAFTA and certain environmental agreements, such as the 1973 Convention on International Trade in Endangered Species of Wild Fauna and Flora, the latter shall prevail.[134]

Nevertheless, the inclusion of environmental provisions within RITs and BITs remains typically minimal,[135] even if some authors observe growing interest in the negotiation of conditions within IIAs which limit the extent to which states may derogate from environmental commitments and even impose measures for enforcement.[136] The 2009 US–Peru Trade Promotion Agreement (PTPA), for instance, incorporates a series of MEAs directly into the trade context and enforces environmental laws through a series of mechanisms, including dispute settlement. However, as Werge notes, the controversial implementation of the environmental provisions of PTPA, and the violence that occurred as a result in Bagua between the indigenous communities of Peru and government officials, highlight the problem with rushed adoption of strong environmental rules in order to satisfy an investment agenda.[137] States which seek to impose their own domestic measures, conversely, risk opposition by foreign investors seeking the stability and protection afforded by the standards upheld under international investment law.[138] As Nikiema argues, if well formulated and applied, state-imposed performance requirements on foreign investments can be effective tools for maximising the economic, environmental and social benefits of foreign investments. However, the recent and growing trend of prohibiting the inclusion of performance requirements in BITs impairs the ability of states to use these tools in order to prevent over-exploitation of their own resources.[139]

The green economy and investment

Grounded in the Rio+20 outcome, the green economy is an alternative economic model for achieving the Sustainable Development Goals

132 Ibid, Preamble
133 Ibid, Article 1114(2)
134 Ibid, Article 104(1)
135 See Chapter 5 (Alam), section 3.1, in this book
136 As discussed by Gerda van Roozedaal, 'The Inclusion of Environmental Concerns in US Trade Agreements' (2009) 18(3) *Environmental Politics* 431, 431
137 As discussed by Werge, above n 40, 83
138 These are elucidated in Chapter 5 (Alam) in this book. A useful and thorough overview of these standards is also provided by Surya P. Subedi in *International Investment Law* (2nd edn, Hart 2012)
139 Suzy H. Nikiema, 'Performance Requirements in Investment Treaties' (Best Practices Paper, IISD, December 2014) 3–7

(SDGs).[140] A green economy can be defined as 'one that results in improved human well-being and social equity, while significantly reducing environmental risks and ecological scarcities'.[141] It is promoted as a means for linking the economic, environmental and social considerations of sustainable development in such a manner that long-term economic development is achieved by investing in environmentally friendly and socially equitable solutions.[142] As the UN Environment Programme's (UNEP) post-2015 briefing note states:

> Giving a proper value to natural capital and ecosystem services, protecting, restoring and enhancing natural assets, ensuring equitable access to natural resources and sustainably-derived basic services, promoting green and innovative fiscal policies and investments, and tracking progress through new indicators should be part of the drive towards eradicating poverty irreversibly through smart, sustainable and inclusive growth.[143]

A green economy is not intended to replace sustainable development, and the implementation of a green economy must be consistent with the principles identified in the Rio Declaration on Environment and Development[144] and the Johannesburg Declaration on Sustainable Development.[145] These include justice, dignity, social inclusion, good governance and accountability, resilience and inter- and intra-generational equity.[146]

On the one hand, the notion of a green economy recognises the economic and social value of the environment and promotes conservation, as well as the rights of members of communities to enjoy their livelihoods and their basic amenities (water, food, housing, etc.). It encourages adequate investment (both public and private), incentives (e.g. subsidies, access to credit or tax breaks) and technology transfer to promote environmentally sound ecosystem services. On the other hand, many argue that the green economy is an instrument for the advancement of corporate interests, as it emphasises markets and businesses as a solution to environmental and economic

140 United Nations Sustainable Development Goals (2015) <www.un.org/sustainabledevelopment/sustainable-development-goals/> accessed 17 March 2017

141 UNEP, Towards a Green Economy: Pathways to Sustainable Development and Poverty Eradication, A Synthesis for Policy Makers (UNEP, 2011) <http://web.unep.org/greeneconomy/sites/unep.org.greeneconomy/files/publications/ger/GER_synthesis_en.pdf> accessed 17 March 2017

142 UNECE, What does Green Economy mean? <www.unece.org/sustainable-development/green-economy/what-does-green-economy-mean.html> accessed 19 January 2017

143 UNEP, Eradicating Poverty through an Inclusive Green Economy (United Nations Environment Programme, 2015)

144 Rio de Janeiro, 13 June 1992, UN Doc A/CONF.151/26 (vol. I); 31 ILM 874 (1992)

145 Johannesburg, 4 September 2002, UN Doc A/CONF. 199/20), Resolution 1, Annex

146 UN General Assembly, *Resolution Adopted by the General Assembly: The Future We Want,* 27 July 2012, UN Doc A/RES/66/288, paras. 15–18

problems.[147] Valuation of natural resources (such as forests and water) remains one of the pressing concerns, as preferences are given to market-based instruments such as taxes, permits or payment schemes (e.g. forest certification or payment for forest or water ecosystem services).[148] Failure to factor environmental imperatives into economic incentives can result in long-term constraints on future economic opportunities and will have a detrimental effect on efforts to alleviate poverty or increase food and energy security.[149] Developing countries remain particularly concerned about the unjustified protectionism, economic restructuring and conditionality that may be encouraged by any measures introduced in order to support the development of a green economy.[150] Developing countries' concerns regarding the application of a green economy model within the context of sustainable development highlight the distrust between developed and the developing countries in relation to the rhetoric and reality of the idea of a green economy.[151]

There are several ways in which sustainable investment may be promoted so as to contribute to the growth of a green economy. These may include stakeholder involvement in the early stages of investment policy conceptualisation, economic diversification, strategic planning to bring sustainable development policies and plans into the mainstream, green taxation and incentives granted to investors in order to promote technology development and transfer.[152] The UN has acknowledged that private finance will need to complement public financing of green projects if sustainable development goals are to be achieved. Ensuring access for all to affordable, reliable, sustainable and modern energy, for example, will require a considerable amount of private investment. As Albino argues, in a green economy, 'growth should be driven by public and private investments that reduce

147 Friends of the Earth International, 'Reclaim the UN from Corporate Capture', 1 June 2012, <www.foei.org> accessed 17 March 2017

148 See Chapters 15 (Garcia) and 16 (Lesniewska) in this book

149 William Mark Adams, *The Future of Sustainability: Re-thinking Environment and Development in the Twenty First Century* (International Union for Conservation of Nature, 2006), 12–13. Jerneja Penca, 'Green Economy and Environmental Law: A Mismatch and Why Bother?' in Vasilka Sancin (ed.), *International Environmental Law: Contemporary Concerns and Challenges*, Papers presented at the First Contemporary Challenges of International Environmental law Conference, Ljubljana, 28–29 June, 2012, 388–396

150 UNCTAD, 'The Green Economy: Trade and Sustainable Development Implications' (2011), 9–12 <https://sustainabledevelopment.un.org/content/documents/ 8211UNCTAD-Report-EGM-on-Green-Economy-background2.pdf> accessed 22 March 2017

151 Shawkat Alam and Jona Razzaque, 'Sustainable Development versus Green Economy: The Way Forward?' in Shawkat Alam, Sumudu Attapattu, Carmen G. Gonzalez and Jona Razzaque (eds), *International Environmental law and the Global South* (Cambridge University Press, 2015) 609–623

152 Nadine Smith, Anna Halton and Janet Strachan, *Transitioning to a Green Economy: Political Economy of Approaches in Small States* (Routledge, 2016)

carbon emissions and pollution, enhance energy and resource efficiency, and prevent the loss of biodiversity and ecosystem services'.[153] The greater role of the private investment to achieve SDGs is reaffirmed in the Addis Ababa Action Agenda[154] that underscores the importance of aligning private investment with the development of infrastructure for energy, transport, water and sanitation. Investors have the financial clout to significantly influence policy makers' adoption of public policies in support of sustainable development goals. According to a UNEP report on the financing of a global green economy, investors may even lead by example: 'Governments should involve the private sector in establishing clear, stable and coherent policy and regulatory frameworks to facilitate the integration of ESG (environmental, social and governance) issues into financial and investment decisions'.[155]

While investment incentives can play a crucial role in triggering the transition to a low-carbon green economy,[156] the emphasis placed on leadership by the private sector also means private investors attain an increased level of influence in natural resource governance. That being the case, the prospect of increased fairness or justice within a green economy remains uncertain. Much would depend on how natural resources are to be effectively managed by a combination of economic instruments, such as financial incentives, voluntary agreements and fiscal measures, and public governance tools and regulatory approaches, such as environmental impact assessment, taxation and the provision of information to the public about development projects.[157] While the concept of the green economy places emphasis on public policies and regulatory frameworks for offering the right incentives to investors,[158] the concern nevertheless persists that 'privatised development' will not be equipped to promote sustainable development or protect the public interest.[159] Any model which turns to the promotion of market instruments,

153 Vito Albino, 'Green Economy' in Paolo Taticchi, Paolo Carbone and Vito Albino (eds), *Corporate Sustainability* (Springer, 2013) 11

154 See Chapter 14 (Schwartz) in this book. Addis Ababa Action Agenda of the Third International Conference on Financing for Development (Addis Ababa Action Agenda), 17 August 2015, A/Res/69/313, <http://undocs.org/A/RES/69/313> accessed 17 March 2017

155 UNEP, Finance: Supporting the transition to a global green economy, 589 <http://web.unep.org/greeneconomy/sites/unep.org.greeneconomy/files/field/image/15.0_finance.pdf> accessed 22 March 2017

156 Ibid

157 Greenpeace, A Just and Fair Green Economy (June 2012) <www.greenpeace.org/canada/earthsummit/> accessed 22 March 2017

158 UNEP, Enabling Conditions: Supporting the Transition to a Global Green Economy <https://web.unep.org/greeneconomy/sites/unep.org.greeneconomy/files/field/image/14.0_enablingconditions_0.pdf> accessed 22 March 2017

159 Oxfam, Rich countries provide a poor outcome at Addis Financing for Development Conference (15 July 2015) <www.oxfam.org/en/pressroom/reactions/rich-countries-provide-poor-outcome-addis-financing-development-conference-oxfam> accessed 22 March 2017

economic incentives and subsidies in pursuit of sustainable development goals runs the risk of supplanting the state's primary role in the protection of poor and marginalised communities and the natural resources on which they depend for their living. Public concerns which lack commercial value – such as land tenure, forest management and water access – are potentially endangered by a model which channels government resources into markets and consumer-based incentives as a means of achieving broad social and environmental wellbeing.

Conclusion

With increasing recognition of the environmental and social pillars of sustainable development growing alongside the typical preoccupation with economic growth and development, international investment law may well be in the process of evolving to encompass the goals of sustainability, such that economic and non-economic objectives, including environmental protection, may not always be in conflict with each other.[160] Although some attempts are made to incorporate public policy objectives, including environmental conservation, into IIAs and BITs, such references are rare and in many instances negligible. Thus, the subordination of peoples' rights in the investment agreements fosters legitimacy concerns.[161]

The legitimacy crisis is apparent at the national level where government agencies allow unhindered exploitation of natural resources to generate economic growth. Recognition of peoples' rights in the domestic legal framework remains either inadequate or not enforced, and access to national remedies is particularly weak. While developing countries' policy to attract foreign investment may create a chill to regulate in the public interest, it is not easy to measure or assess the effects of such regulatory chill. In any case, the protection granted to foreign investors needs to be proportionate against the duty to protect people's rights. To create such a balance between the protection of investment risks and the regulatory space to guarantee the peoples' rights is daunting. As private law guides ISDS, affected peoples or communities have no standing or extremely limited opportunities to participate. *Amicus* submissions are inadequate and discretionary. Merely opening the dispute settlement process, for example, through open hearings, appellate reviews and access to information will not eliminate all legitimacy concerns.

The interplay of laws guiding investor responsibility, investment incentives and voluntary standards and initiatives is increasingly influencing investment

160 Lone Wandahl Mouyal, *International Investment Law and the Right to Regulate: A Human Rights Perspective* (Routledge, 2016) 80

161 Human Rights Council, Report of the Special Rapporteur on the rights of indigenous peoples, A/HRC/33/42, 11 August 2016

decisions. In the neoliberal society, the ideological shift from the 'statist' approach underscores the need to involve private sectors to incorporate sustainable development objectives in their investment practices and take responsibility for assessing the human rights risks associated with their investments. Whether such 'new generation'[162] investment policies would promote sustainable development or turn out to be a new generation of risks to people and communities – only time will tell.

162 UNCTAD, Investment Policy Framework for Sustainable Development (2015) <http://investmentpolicyhub.unctad.org/Upload/Documents/Investment%20Policy%20Framework%20for%20Sustainable%20Development%202015.pdf> accessed 18 March 2017

2 Sovereign rights, state obligations and natural resources

Upendra Baxi

Introduction

The recently concluded Paris Agreement concerning climate change has been hailed as both 'progressive' and 'regressive':[1] some even question the efficacy of a climate change treaty, in which the voluntary character of treaty

1 On December 12, 2015, 195 countries arrived at the final 12-page document of the Paris Agreement (the fuller title being the Paris Agreement under the United Nations Framework Convention on Climate Change) to reduce emissions as part of the method for reducing global warming: United Nations Framework Convention on Climate Change, *Adoption of the Paris Agreement: Report of the Conference of the Parties on its twenty-first session, held in Paris from 30 November to 13 December 2015* (FCCC/CP/2015/L.9/Rev.1). The members agreed to reduce their carbon output 'as soon as possible' and to do their best to keep global warming 'to well below 2 degrees C.' Already, 187 nations had submitted, well before the Conference, detailed national plans for how they will contain the rise in greenhouse gas emissions (core commitments of the Paris deal). This 'ambitious and balanced' scheme (in the words of French foreign minister Laurent Fabius, the plan was a 'historic turning point' in the goal of reducing global warming. The Agreement will not become binding on its member states until 55 parties who produce over 55 per cent of the world's greenhouse gas have ratified the Agreement.

Each country that ratifies the agreement will be required to set a voluntary target for emission reduction, though it remains to be seen whether some countries, especially the United States, will agree to do so, in the light of – in the words of US Secretary of State John Kerry – 'a victory for all of the planet and for future generations,' and – in the words of President Obama – 'We have set a course here. The world has come together around an agreement that will empower us to chart a new path for our planet, a smart and responsible path, a sustainable path'. See A. Doyle and B. Lewis, 'With Landmark Climate Accord, World Marks Turn from Fossil Fuels', *Reuters* (December 13, 2015) <www.reuters.com/article/us-climatechange-summit-idUSKBN0TV04L20151213> accessed 8 April 2016.

For discussion of the criticisms of the Paris Agreement raised by many environmental and climate change proponent NGOs, and others, see Erik Lindberg, 'To Paris and Beyond: Climate and Freedom' (*Resilience*, 27 January 2016) <www.resilience.org/stories/2016-01-27/to-paris-and-beyond-climate-and-freedom/> accessed 10 March 2016; Brian Tokar, 'Inside the Paris Climate Agreement: Hope or Hype?' (*Counterpunch*, 30 December 2015) <www.counterpunch.org/2015/12/30/ inside-the-paris-climate-agreement-hope-or-hype/> accessed 14 January 2017. No doubt the fine print of this deal will be subjected to further critical analyses in the near future

commitments, the dependence of these on 'Intended Nationally Determined Contributions' (INDCs), the relative absence of third party enforcement and the precarious place afforded to the principle of 'common but differentiated responsibility' together suggest the treaty's inadequacy as a means of addressing issues of inequity posed by this particular global environmental problem.[2] Furthermore, the situation of island states threatened by rising sea levels and facing possible future disappearance compounds the challenges posed to state sovereignty by climate change.[3] New theoretical approaches to climate change justice are now emerging.[4] At the same time, the United Nations Conference in Human Environment in 1972 led to the establishment of the UN Environmental Programme (UNEP). UNEP adopted large-scale monitoring of 'Our Only Earth' via three significant institutional devices known as Earthwatch – 'environmental assessment', 'environmental management' and 'supporting measures' – marking a watershed moment for contemporary global environmental jurisprudence and action.[5]

The notion of intergenerational justice emerged as early as 1987 when the Brundtland Report gave currency to the conception of sustainable development. The concept extended the idea of intergenerational justice to entire economies and societies; it said that development is sustainable when it 'meets the needs of the present without compromising the ability of future

2 Drawing on field work in Tuvalu, Kiribati and Bangladesh, and maintaining a distinction between 'legal' and 'political' benefits, McAdam 'queries the utility – and, importantly, the policy consequences – of pinning "solutions" to climate change-related displacement on a multilateral instrument, in light of the likely nature of movement, the desires of communities affected by it, and the fact that a treaty will not, without wide ratification and implementation, "solve" the humanitarian issues': J. McAdam and B. Saul, 'An Insecure Climate for Human Security? Climate-Induced Displacement and International Law' in A. Edwards and C. Ferstman (eds), *Human Security and Non-Citizens: Law, Policy and International Affairs* (Cambridge University Press 2010) 357

3 Maxine Burkett in 'Chaos Theory and the Justice Paradox' (1993) 35 *William & Mary Law Review* 329, has focused on the notion of a 'justice paradox' devised and developed by R.E. Scott, which broadly consists in the fact that 'we aspire to a just society that satisfies the essential conditions of both Present and Future Justice, and yet we live in a world that often forces us to choose between one or the other' (at 330). See also here, 'A Justice Paradox: Climate Change, Small Island States and the Absence of International Legal Remedy', in S. Alam, S. Atapattu, C.G. Gonzalez and J. Razzaque (eds), *International Environmental Law and the Global South* (Cambridge University Press 2015) 435–450; and M.B. Gerrard and G.E. Wannier (eds), *Threatened Island Nations: Legal Implications of Rising Seas and a Changing Climate* (Cambridge University Press 2013)

4 Upendra Baxi, 'Towards A Climate Change Justice Theory?' (2016) 7(1) *Journal of Human Rights and the Environment*, 7

5 See for this model of action of international governance, B. Gosovic, *The Quest for World Environmental Cooperation: The Case of Global Environment Monitoring System* (Routledge 1992); Phillipe Sands (ed.), *Greening International Law* (Earthscan 1993); Bharat Desai, *Internationalising International Environmental Law* (Transnational Publishers 2004); Bharat Desai, 'UNEP: A Global Environmental Authority?' (2006) 36(3–4) *Environmental Policy and Law* 137

generations to meet their own needs'.[6] The Report, probably, deployed the concept of future generations nebulously as not imposing obligations of any species or planetary loyalty as would be entailed in the Anthropocene era now upon us.[7]

Yet, in many ways the Bruntland Report changed the vocabulary of global governance, as testified by the emergence of the right of states and peoples to development.[8] This right to development is evident in the UN Millennium Development Goals accompanied by a Plan of Action,[9] and now the recently declared UN Sustainable Development Goals.[10] In this sense, the Report's

6 See World Commission for Environment and Development, *Our Common Future* (Oxford University Press 1987) ('Brundtland Report') 41

7 See, for a general account, Naomi Klein, *This Changes Everything: Capitalism versus Climate* (Allen Lane/Penguin 2014). Fostering activist knowledge, legality, justice and solidarity among suffering and struggling peoples of the earth is especially important and this work admirably also conveys a vivid description of tactics pursued by neoliberal markets and governments, especially job blackmail, 'desperation' as means to predation and 'total control'. See Chapters 12 and 13 for some wise activist and sage counsel. See her highly popular, and assiduously accurate, work *The Shock Doctrine: The Rise of Disaster Capitalism* (Metropolitan Books 2007). In her 2014 work, Naomi Klein comes close to describing the uses of law as a 'tactic' foreshadowed by Michel Foucault. On this point, see Allan Hunt and George Wickham, *Foucault and Law: Towards a Sociology of Law as Governance* (Pluto Press 1994); Antony Beck, 'Foucault and Law: The Collapse of Law's Empire' (1996) 16(3) *Oxford Journal of Legal Studies* 489. See also, v Tadros, 'Between Governance and Discipline: The Law and Michel Foucault' (1998) 18 *Oxford Journal of Legal Studies* 75

8 See Chapter 4 of Upendra Baxi, *Human Rights in a Posthuman World: Critical Essays* (Oxford University Press 2007)

9 The eight Millennium Development Goals and Programme of Action, which extend from halving extreme poverty rates to halting the spread of HIV/AIDS and providing universal primary education, all form a blueprint agreed to by all the world's countries and leading development institutions. They are said by the UN to have 'galvanized unprecedented efforts to meet the needs of the world's poorest'. See, however, Upendra Baxi, 'A Report for All Seasons? Small Notes towards Reading the Larger Freedom' in C. Raj Kumar and D.K. Srivastava (eds), *Human Rights and Development: Law, Policy and Governance* (Butterworth Lexis/Nexis 2006) 504–508. See also, Philip Alston, 'Ships Passing by the Night: The Current State of Human Rights and Development Discourse Seen through the Lens of Millennial Development Goals' (2005) 27(3) *Human Rights Quarterly* 755. Incidentally, I have always maintained the need to speak of 'impoverishment' rather than 'poverty'. 'Impoverishment' directs attention to the fact that people are constantly made 'poor' by willed performances of public policy measures and choice. See, for some further elaboration, my Introduction to Upendra Baxi (ed.) *Law and Poverty: Critical Essays* (N.M. Tripathi 1989) and see further, M.E. Saloman, *Global Responsibility for Human Rights: World Poverty and the Development of International Law* (Oxford University Press 2007)

10 See, for an early exposition, Bruce Jenks, 'From an MDG World to an SDG/GPG World: Why the United Nations Should Embrace the Concept of Global Public Goods' (2015) Development Dialogue Paper No. 15 <www.daghammarskjold.se/wp-content/uploads/2015/10/DD-Paper-no-15.pdf> accessed 14 January 2017; Derek Osborn, Amy Cutter and Farooq Ullah, 'Universal Sustainable Development Goals: Understanding the Transformational Challenge for Developed Countries' (Stakeholder Forum, May 2015) <https://sustainabledevelopment.un.org/content/documents/1684SF_-_SDG_Universality_Report_-_May_2015.pdf> accessed 14 January 2017; Markus Loewe,

rather general summons for 'sustainability' – as environmental protection with economic growth, governance with human rights and development with justice – ushered in (what is today called) a global change theory.

Environmental and ecological discourse, with a specific international law and governance discursivity and normativity of its own, has emerged. But, we all live in a world where the forces of 'creative destruction'[11] seem to triumph over, or at least coexist with, the named benefits of 'market civilisation'[12] or of 'creative capitalism'.[13] If earlier forms of industrial capital accumulation were destructive, the post-Fordism mode[14] is presented as the creative phase of global capital. Understandably, many things happen in this combined and uneven growth of capitalism, better known as contradictions of late capitalism.[15] We engage here the discursive events created by the motto, methods and means of 'sustainable development' and multinational corporate social responsibility.[16] It looks coincidental, and even amazing, but is true that these notions developed almost simultaneously, each reinforcing each other.[17]

If sustainable development brought with it the rise of environmental jurisprudence[18] and the 'greening' of international law, we now see the

'Post 2015: How to Reconcile the Millennium Development Goals (MDGs) and the Sustainable Development Goals (SDGs)?' (German Development Institute, Briefing Paper 18, 2012) <https://post2015.files.wordpress.com/2013/01/loewe-2012-post-2015-mdgs-and-sdgs-english.pdf> accessed 14 January 2017

11 For an interesting extension of Schumpeterian insights, see W.J. Baumol, R.E. Litan and C.J. Schramm, *Good Capitalism, Bad Capitalism, and the Economics of Growth and Prosperity* (Yale University Press 2007)

12 S. Gill, 'Globalization, Market Civilisation, and Disciplinary Neoliberalism' (1995) 24 *Millennium* 399; S. Gill and D. Law, 'Global Hegemony and the Structural Power of Capital' (1989) 33(4) *International Studies Quarterly* 475. See also n 15 *infra*

13 See, for differing perspectives, M. Lewitt, *The Death of Capital: How Creative Policy Can Restore Stability* (John Wiley & Sons 2010); G. Dumneil and D. Levy, *The Crisis of Neoliberalism* (Harvard University Press 2013)

14 H. Braverman, *Labor and Monopoly Capital: The Degradation of Work in the Twentieth Century* (Monthly Review Press 1974); Fredric Jameson, *Postmodernism, or the Cultural Logic of Late Capitalism* (Verso 1991); David Gartman, 'Postmodernism; Or, The Cultural Logic of Post-Fordism?' (1998) 39(1) *The Sociological Quarterly* 119; Linda McDowell, 'Life without Father Ford: The New Gender Order of post-Fordism' (1991) 16 *Transactions of the Institute of British Geographers* 400; A. Amin (ed.), *Postfordism: A Reader* (Oxford 1994).

15 D. Harvey, *Seventeen Contradictions and the End of Capitalism* (Oxford University Press 2015); C. Leys, *Total Capitalism: Market Politics, Market State* (Three Essays Collective 2008); A. Supiot, *The Spirit of Philadelphia: Social Justice vs. the Total Market* ((Saskia Brown tr, Verso 2012)

16 U. Baxi, 'Human Rights Responsibility of Multinational Corporations, Political Ecology of Injustice: Learning from Bhopal Thirty Plus?' (2016) 1 *Business and Human Rights Journal* 21

17 The conspiracy theorist would see a design – a design of late capitalism in the making

18 See G. Walker, *Environmental Justice: Concepts, Evidence and Politics* (Routledge 2012); R. Holifield, M. Potter and G. Walker (eds), *Spaces of Environmental Justice* (Wiley-Blackwell 2010); David Schlosberg, *Defining Environmental Justice: Theories, Movements, and Nature* (Oxford University Press 2007); and, in a different vein, A. Philippopoulos

movement of justice – theorising in the context of the Anthropocene epoch now upon us.[19]

Thinking about development involves thinking about the dialectics of *Vikas* (Development) and *Vinash* (Destruction).[20] No development without destruction is the motto of all societies which develop – whether on capitalist or socialist or social movement or any other path. The sustainable development secular theologies also try to attain a balance between institutions of economic development and environmental friendliness.[21] Creative destruction was thus coded into sustainable development and the subsequent decoding of it by environmental movements and the law proved to be a Herculean task; even when pluralisms of the non-state law and social movement captured an alternative imagery of sustainable development, the monism of the state law ultimately prevails.[22] To utter a Baxi-moron (akin to an oxymoron) one can think of sustainable development talk as inviting one to engage in unsustainable thought; one ought not merely to think out of

(ed.), *Law and Ecology: New Environmental Foundations* (Taylor & Francis 2011). See also note 20, *infra* and Baxi, 'Towards a Climate Change Justice Theory?' (n 4)

19 See, in addition to literature cited in Baxi, 'Towards a Climate Change Justice Theory?' (n 4), M. Bourban, 'Climate Change, Human Rights and the Problem of Motivation' (2014) 1(1) *De Ethica A Journal of Philosophical, Theological and Applied Ethics* 37; D. Jamieson, 'Duties to the Distant: Aid, Assistance, and Intervention in the Developing World' (2005) 9 *The Journal of Ethics* 151

20 Shankar Guha Nyogi, an activist trade union leader in Madhya Pradesh, who was murdered, wrote in Hindi a whole book of essays on this thematic. See Anil Sadgopal and Syam Bhadur Namra (eds), *Sangarsgh aur Nirman: Shankar Guha Niyogi aur un Ke Nayae Bharat Ka Nirman* (Rajkamal Prakshan 1993)

21 See, for critical perspectives, D. Shelton, 'Legitimate and Necessary: Adjudicating Human Rights Violations Related to Activities Causing Environmental Harm or Risk' (2015) 6(2) *Journal of Human Rights and the Environment* 139; A. Philippopoulos-Mihalopoulos, *Absent Environments: Theorising Environmental Law and the City* (Routledge-Cavendish 2007). But see, for a celebrationist perspective, Voula Meg, *Sustainable Development, Energy and the City: A Civilisation of Visions and Actions* (Springer 2005). See also, D. Schlosberg, 'Reconceiving Environmental Justice: Global Movements and Political Theories' (2004) 13(3) *Environmental Politics* 517; N.C. Carre, 'Environmental Justice and Hydraulic Fracturing: The Ascendancy of Grassroots Populism in Policy Determination' (2012) 4(1) *Journal of Social Change* 1

22 Sam Adelman reinforced a general truth about environmental law of tropical forests and biodiversity preservation measures when he observed: 'that existing legal regimes are limited, contradictory and contain much unenforceable "soft" law … There is a clear mismatch between environmental and climate science and the structures and institutions of international environmental governance. Most international environmental regimes are predicated upon the assumption that environmental changes are linear and gradual and do not deal easily with complex risks and strong uncertainty. The precautionary principle, which stipulates that we should err on the side of caution where scientific evidence is inconclusive, is widely embraced but regularly disregarded … Environmental governance regimes are slow to gestate and generally lead to agreements around the lowest common denominators'. See Sam Adelman, 'REDD+: Tropical Forests and Climate Change: A Critique of Green Governmentality' (2015) 11(2) *International Journal of Law in Context* 195

the box but even to smash the box. How is that to be done? Although we have discussed the decoding of creative destruction in the concept of sustainable development in the last three decades, this idea has provided an important theoretical basis for reforms and developments in key international legal instruments such as the Permanent Sovereignty over Natural Resources (PSNR) Declaration, and the precautionary principle, which this chapter will now consider.

The PSNR Declaration

The landmark UN Declaration of PSNR is the first child in the normative progeny of decolonisation of international law, relations and organisation. Once anticolonial struggles in recent history grasped a truth it partly created: many of the problems created by colonial worlds will disappear with the need for colonialism and although new ones will take the place of the old, Third Worldism will always be marked by a genuine, if problematic, quest for justice.[23] The PSNR is certainly one instance of de-provincialising[24] European hegemony over norms and standards of international law: in one of the first post-Westphalian moves, we are able to espy a move away from 'a European-oriented law towards a truly universal law'.[25] The contexts of the adoption were very different than now; but it can be safely said that all these mark a passage of the Declaration into international law.[26]

23 See, for this resistant yet roseate consciousness of which Third Worldism persists as a state of global social consciousness, Upendra Baxi, 'Some Newly Emergent Geographies of Injustice: Boundaries and Borders in International Law' (2016) 23(1) *Indiana Journal of Global Legal Studies* 15

24 See, D. Chakrabarty, *Provincializing Europe: Postcolonial Thought and Historical Difference* (Princeton University Press 2007)

25 B.V.A. Rolling, *International Law in an Expanded World* (Djambatan 1960) 73; C.G. Weeramantry, *Universalising International Law* (Martinus Nijhoff 2004) 105; G. Abi-Saab, 'Permanent Sovereignty over Natural Resources and Economic Activities' in Mohamed Bedjaoui (ed.), *International Law: Achievements and Prospects* (UNESCO and Martinus Nijhof 1991) 597–617

26 See, B.H. Weston, 'The Charter of Economic Rights and Duties of States and the Deprivation of Foreign-Owned Wealth' (1961) 75(3) *The American Journal of International Law* 437; N. Schrijver, 'Permanent Sovereignty over Natural Resources versus Common Heritage of Mankind – Contradictory or Complementary Principles of International Economic Law' in P. de Waart et al. (eds), *International Law and Development* (Martinus Nijhoff 1998) 87–101; E. Guntrip, 'The Common Heritage of Mankind: An Adequate Regime for Managing the Deep Seabed?' (2003) 4(2) *Melbourne Journal of International Law* 376; S.K. Chatterjee, 'The Charter of Economic Rights and Duties of States – An Evaluation after 15 Years' (1991) 40(3) *International and Comparative Law Quarterly* 669; C.J. Fromherz, 'Indigenous Peoples' Courts: Egalitarian Juridical Pluralism, Self-Determination, and the United Nations Declaration on the Rights of Indigenous Peoples' (2008) 156 *University of Pennsylvania Law Review* 1341

The PSNR declares eight principles.[27] A careful look at the PSNR definitely reveals that while on the one hand 'mutual respect of States [is] based on their sovereign equality' (Principle 5), the PSNR is, on the other hand, to be exercised only for 'the interest of their national development and of the well-being of the people of the State concerned' (Principle 1). However, the Declaration forbids 'Impairment, for any reason, of that State's sovereignty

27 *United Nations Declaration on the Permanent Sovereignty over Natural* Resources, GA Res 1803 (XVII), UNGAOR, 17th sess, 1194th plen mtg, UN Doc A/5217 (14 December 1962). It declares that:

> 1. The right of peoples and nations to permanent sovereignty over their natural wealth and resources must be exercised in the interest of their national development and of the well-being of the people of the State concerned.
> 2. The exploration, development and disposition of such resources, as well as the import of the foreign capital required for these purposes, should be in conformity with the rules and conditions which the peoples and nations freely consider to be necessary or desirable with regard to the authorization, restriction or prohibition of such activities.
> 3. In cases where authorization is granted, the capital imported and the earnings on that capital shall be governed by the terms thereof, by the national legislation in force, and by international law. The profits derived must be shared in the proportions freely agreed upon, in each case, between the investors and the recipient State, due care being taken to ensure that there is no impairment, for any reason, of that State's sovereignty over its natural wealth and resources.
> 4. Nationalization, expropriation or requisitioning shall be based on grounds or reasons of public utility, security or the national interest which are recognized as overriding purely individual or private interests, both domestic and foreign. In such cases the owner shall be paid appropriate compensation, in accordance with the rules in force in the State taking such measures in the exercise of its sovereignty and in accordance with international law. In any case where the question of compensation gives rise to a controversy, the national jurisdiction of the State taking such measures shall be exhausted. However, upon agreement by sovereign States and other parties concerned, settlement of the dispute should be made through arbitration or international adjudication.
> 5. The free and beneficial exercise of the sovereignty of peoples and nations over their natural resources must be furthered by the mutual respect of States based on their sovereign equality.
> 6. International co-operation for the economic development of developing countries, whether in the form of public or private capital investments, exchange of goods and services, technical assistance, or exchange of scientific information, shall be such as to further their independent national development and shall be based upon respect for their sovereignty over their natural wealth and resources.
> 7. Violation of the rights of peoples and nations to sovereignty over their natural wealth and resources is contrary to the spirit and principles of the Charter of the United Nations and hinders the development of international co-operation and the maintenance of peace.
> 8. Foreign investment agreements freely entered into by or between sovereign States shall be observed in good faith; States and international organizations shall strictly and conscientiously respect the sovereignty of peoples and nations over their natural wealth and resources in accordance with the Charter and the principles set forth in the present resolution.

over its natural wealth and resources' (Principle 3). And the catch-all Principle 8 obligation attaches to all: 'States and international organizations shall strictly and conscientiously respect the sovereignty of peoples and nations over their natural wealth and resources in accordance with the Charter and the principles set forth in the present resolution'. Even though the missing links are the obligations of multinational corporations, finance capital and managerial neoliberals, the defiance of these Principles is a 'violation' of 'the rights of peoples and nations to sovereignty over their natural wealth and resources ... contrary to the spirit and principles of the Charter of the United Nations' and a process and outcome that 'hinders the development of international co-operation and the maintenance of peace' (Principle 8). Closely read, the PSNR, at least now, can be said to establish core human and environmental rights (sustainable rights) for states as well as non-states, especially for market and economic actors.

Despite the fact that it may be open to other interpretations now, at the time of its adoption (and for a very long time indeed) the PSNR had been variously and numerously noted as an integral aspect of struggle for decolonisation of international law.[28] In a basic sense, it gave economic and social meaning to the ideal of self-determination, and as Sundhya Pahuja has demonstrated, the 'bare sovereignty' of state enshrined in the PSNR also entailed an 'imaginative appeal of international law' and its 'putative secularity'.[29] At the same time, this 'openness' to a will to law-saying jurisdiction installed a 'transcendent positioning of development' and the reproduction of the 'West as world'.[30] There is, indeed, much evidence that the PSNR did not arrest subservience to, or even enslavement of, models of development produced by international financial institutions. The paradoxical symbolic character of the PNSR thus remains particularly noteworthy. It symbolises a complex and contradictory unity of the postcolonial intent.

Even so, the PSNR does not make it normatively clear whether natural resources belong to the state or its people or the entire humankind. Nor does it explicate whether it states collective or individual 'moral' rights or legal enlistments of persons and what is called the 'corporate legal humanity'.[31] And the question of justification of principles thus declared remains, especially of Principle 4 (denationalisation) with which the PSNR Declaration as a whole stands equated.

The concern with whom the PSNR belongs depends on the identification of component rights, as its meaningless to talk about PSNR in the abstract. Chris Armstrong (following Elinor Ostrom's distinction of five different

28 S. Pahuja, *Decolonizing International Law: Development, Economic Growth, and the Politics of Universality* (Cambridge University Press 2011)

29 Ibid 112–113

30 Ibid 115–160

31 A. Grear, *Redirecting Human Rights: Facing the Challenge of Corporate Legal Humanity* (Palgrave Macmillan 2010)

property rights)[32] valuably suggests that six kinds of property rights exist in general or the PSNR rights.[33] These rights overall lack as yet any justification for the belief or assertion that 'natural resources' belong to the 'people' for many reasons. The category of peoples is itself polysemic: existentially there only are people concerned with the pursuit and satisfaction of their own short-term interests. There are, as Benhabib long pointed out, the 'generalized' and 'concrete' others.[34] How does one attend to the diverse peoples via the unity of the abstract and general conception of a 'people'? Under what precise conditions can a modern 'state' be said to necessarily personify the interests of people at large? And under what conditions may (some) people be justly opposed to the state? Put it another way, under what conditions and circumstances may the acts of insurgent reason be made and accepted?

Issues as deep as these constantly develop in putting the PSNR conceptions to work. The plunder and predation, cruel devastation and the tendency of some states and ruling elites have, for example, converted some PSNR sovereign rights as a 'resource curse' which needs to be combated in a struggle to avoid global injustice.[35] Thomas Pogge has been among the foremost to maintain global justice principles for authoritarian or rapacious rulers[36] and Leif Wenar has a Pogge-like proposal for a 'Clean Hands Fund',[37] whether or not

32 E. Ostrom, 'Private and Common Property Rights' in B. Bouckaert and G. De Geest (eds), *Encyclopaedia of Law and Economics: Vol. II Civil Law and Economics* (Edward Elgar 2000) 332–379

33 C. Armstrong, 'Against "Permanent Sovereignty" over Natural Resources' (2015) 14(2) *Politics, Philosophy & Economics* 129. These include: (1) *Access*: 'right to interact with a resource and to enjoy "nonsubtractive" benefits from it'; (2.) *Withdrawal*: 'right to obtain and indeed to remove resource units for one's own use'; (3) *Management*: 'right to regulate use patterns and to transform a resource by making improvements to it'; (4) *Exclusion*: 'right to determine who can access and withdraw a resource'; (5) *Alienation*: 'right to sell a resource, or moving up a level, the right to sell management and exclusion rights' and (6) *Derive Income*: 'right to obtain proceeds from the sale of a resource, or to extract some other form of income from it'

34 S. Benhabib, *Situating the Self: Gender, Community and Postmodernism in Contemporary Ethics* (Routledge 1992) Ch. 5. See also D. Young, 'Claims for Recognition and the Generalized Other: The Reasonable Person and Judgment in Criminal Law' (2008) 23(1–2) *Canadian Journal of Law and Society* 15

35 L. Wenar, 'Property Rights and the Resource Curse' (2008) 36 *Philosophy & Public Affairs* 2. Wenar deals with the resource curse that 'afflicts many countries that derive a large portion of their national income from exporting high-value extractive resources such as oil, natural gas, and diamonds. Less developed countries that gain a large portion of their national incomes from these extractive resources are subject to three overlapping "curses." They are more prone to authoritarian governments, they are at a higher risk for civil conflict, and they exhibit lower rates of growth. Several causal pathways explain these surprising correlations between natural resources and national misery': ibid 3

36 T. Pogge, *World Poverty and Human Rights* (Polity 2008); Thomas Pogge (ed.), *Freedom from Poverty as a Human Right (Who Owes What to the Very Poor?)* (Oxford University Press 2007). See also Upendra Baxi, 'International Development, Global Impoverishment and Human Rights' in S. Scott Sheeran and Sir N. Rodley (eds), *Routledge Handbook of International Human Rights Law* (Routlege 2013) 594–614

37 See note 35 *supra*

this finds an eventual acceptance. But there are strong reasons to read the PSNR as precisely forbidding the conversion of people's resources into a ruler's personal ones this way. Whether or not we can settle the theoretical question of peoples versus state ownership of natural resources, there is full pragmatic merit in saying that 'plunder' by the rulers or constitutional elites is not an aspect of the PSNR. And the same norm or standard may be said to extend when it is shown that the state elites act on the behest and behalf of multinational corporations and communities of direct foreign investment (certainly to the point of the 'host' state becoming a state held hostage).

States of sustainability

The discourse on sustainable development (SD) has further integrated the earlier PSNR contexts, yet it curiously also reiterates its norms and principles, particularly the 'development' and the 'well-beings' of the peoples. And yet SD discourse has gone beyond. This contradictory unity is, of course, understandable when we take into full account the deradicalisation of both the concepts. Revolutionary looking, these concepts are in substance (and operation) both trade-related and free market-development friendly.

There are many notable features of the Bruntland Report, some of which are of continuing relevance even today. For example, Annex 1 to *Our Common Future* provides a Summary of Proposed Legal Principles for Environmental Protection and Sustainable Development Adopted by the WCED Experts Group on Environmental Law. Principles 1–3 of the Annex declare respectively that 'All human beings have the fundamental right to an environment adequate for their health and wellbeing', 'States shall conserve and use the environment and natural resources for the benefit of present and future generations' and 'States shall maintain ecosystems and ecological processes essential for the functioning of the biosphere, shall preserve biological diversity, and shall observe the principle of optimum sustainable yield in the use of living natural resources and ecosystems'. Read with later enunciations at Rio and within the UN system, arguably these principles have become binding customary precepts or as evidence of the practice of civilised nations and some maintain that in the Anthropocene era there exists a right to sustainable development.[38]

38 There is at least consensus towards the collusion that the PP has become an 'emergent' norm of customary international law. On a careful examination of international state practice, it stands concluded that: 'If present trends continue, the precautionary principle could become the fundamental principle of environmental protection policy and law at the international, regional, and local levels': James Cameron and Juli Abouchar, 'The Precautionary Principle: A Fundamental Principle of Law and Policy for the Protection of the Global Environment' (1991) 14(1) *Boston College International and Comparative Law Review* 1. See also Virginie Barra, 'Sustainable Development in International Law: Nature and Operation of an Evolutive Legal Norm' (2012) 23(2) *European Journal of International Law* 377

Similarly, wise is the insistence that while the 'accumulation of knowledge and the development of technology can enhance the carrying capacity of the resource base', there exist some 'ultimate limits', and sustainability requires that long before these are reached, the world must ensure equitable access to the constrained resource and reorient technological efforts to relieve the presumption.[39] Equally wise – momentous at the time of this utterance but now household wisdom – is the insistence on interlinkage between development and environment.[40]

As a concept, SD is rather vast and often unwieldy as it relates to such diverse fields as agriculture, biodiversity, industry, city, urbanisation, rivers, water, mountains, fisheries, animals, endangered species, natural and human made disasters, toxic and hazardous wastes, degradation/pollution and 'atmospheric justice', among others. Rights, obligations and legal regimes vary in addition to evasion and enforcement in each sector. Each demands a separate science and policy domain knowledge: one impact of SD is a proliferation of disciplines and subdisciplines and the other is multidisciplinarity of natural and human scientific understandings. There is no unified field called sustainable development and it is a good thing too![41]

However, the concept demands some understanding of the social fact of finitude of all natural resources, even when there exists a holistic regard for economics and environment. This fact demands an awareness of constraints as well as opportunities for wise use of natural resources provides an essential tool for both individuals and the community through a balanced approach between development and conservation. However, the task of fashioning concepts of sustainability remains formidable. This stands highlighted by the career and vicissitudes of two conceptions: the notions of 'carrying capacity'[42] and 'ecological footprint'.[43]

39 Brundtland Report (n 6) 42

40 The Brundtland Report reaffirms the connection between an approach to development that takes account of the effects of development efforts and a corresponding change in the quality of economic growth and development, with both economic and social development to be considered as 'mutually reinforcing': Brundtland Report (n 6) 49

41 The statement references Stanley Fish, *There's No Such Thing as Free Speech: And It's a Good Thing, Too* (2nd edn, Oxford University Press 1995)

42 Garrett Hardin posed overpopulation as a collective action problem befalling unregulated commons. He has tracked the 'ethical implications' of carrying capacity. Contingent upon environmental conditions of scarcity, morality cannot escape this condition. The moral prohibition against killing the innocent, for example, is not absolute but relative to time, manner and circumstance: factors such optimum herd size often determine whether killing is to be considered a moral wrong. See G. Hardin, 'The Tragedy of the Commons', (1968) 162 *Science* 1243. See also G. Hardin, 'Lifeboat Ethics: The Case against Helping the Poor', (1974) *Psychology Today* 38–43, 124–26; Garrett Hardin, 'The Ethical Implications of Carrying Capacity', in G. Hardin and J. Baden (eds), *Managing the Commons* (W.H. Freeman 1977) 112–125. See also, for the notion of 'phantom' carrying capacity, W. Catton, *Overshoot: The Ecological Basis of Revolutionary Change* (University of Illinois Press 1980).

43 This concept was specifically developed by W.E. Rees and M. Wackernagel in 'Ecological

The precautionary principle

Considered as a cornerstone of environmental protection and SD, the precautionary principle (PP) was enshrined under Principle 15 of the Rio Declaration. It proclaimed that:

> In order to protect the environment, the precautionary approach shall be widely applied by States according to their capabilities. Where there are threats of serious or irreversible damage, lack of full scientific certainty shall not be used as a reason for postponing cost effective measures to prevent environmental degradation.

The acceptance of PP at Rio, and since, has been made possible only because of its overall indeterminacy. The PP is to be applied by states 'according to their capabilities'; it is applicable only when 'threats of serious or irreversible damage' emerge. Even so, these must be accompanied by the 'lack of full scientific certainty'; and appropriate measures be taken when these are 'cost effective'. And yet the PP has been reiterated several times to the point of being held as a soft law. As many commentators have noted, much is left to sovereign states or supranational bodies and the community of adjudicators to define the precise ambit of PP. Besides, there exist about 14 definitions which make a general conclusion about the PP an affair of brave souls.[44] It has been said of the EU operations of PP that: 'The precautionary principle may well be the most innovative, pervasive, and significant new concept in environmental policy over the past quarter century. It may also be the most reckless, arbitrary, and ill-advised'. However, it remains to be said vehemently that an open-ended conception is necessary for such a diverse field as environmental protection and degradation. Further, while some believe that it is a part of the regime of international customary law, others articulate merely a hope that someday this soft law will become hard, at least as a rule of international customary law.[45]

Footprints and Appropriated Carrying Capacity: Measuring the Natural Capital Requirements of the Human Economy' in A.M. Jansson, M. Hammer, C. Folke and R. Costanza (eds) *Investing in Natural Capital: The Ecological Economics Approach to Sustainability* (Island Press 1994); W.E. Rees, 'Consuming the Earth: The Biophysics of Sustainability' (1999) 29(1) *Ecological Economics* 23–27

44 D. Vander Zwaagm, 'The Precautionary Principle in Environmental Law and Policy: Elusive Rhetoric and First Embraces' (1999) 8 *Journal of Environmental Law & Practice* 355; and see UNESCO, *The Precautionary Principle, World Commission on the Ethics of Scientific Knowledge and Technology (COMSET)* (UNESCO 2005) ('the COMSET Report')

45 See, particularly Agne Sirinskiene, 'The Status of Precautionary Principle: Moving Towards a Rule of Customary Law' (2009) 4(118) *Jurisprudencija/Jurisprudence* 349; A.W. Harris, 'Derogating the Precautionary Principle' (2008) 19 *Villanova Environmental Law Journal* 1; Lucas Bergkamp, 'Biotech Food and the Precautionary Principle under EU and WTO Law', <www.researchgate.net/publication/228125560> (2011)

Much concern has also been expressed about the collapse of the preventive nature from the precautionary approach. The difference between the two is not easily stated; in terms of historic evolution, the preventive approach probably arose out of concern for transboundary harm and indeed to that extent became an aspect of customary international law. Conceptually, it remains to be argued that the PP deals with environmental integrity as an end and not as a means to any other end. Shall one then say that there is no difference in law and jurisprudence between PP and that the preventive approach stands thus subsumed by PP?[46]

Finally (for the present purposes at least), the distinction between an ethical and moral perspective and a legal perspective needs to be maintained. The United Nations Educational, Scientific and Cultural Organization's (UNESCO) report entitled *The Precautionary Principle, World Commission on the Ethics of Scientific Knowledge and Technology* (COMEST) has recently formulated the latter thus: 'When human activities may lead to morally unacceptable harm that is scientifically plausible but uncertain, actions shall be taken to avoid or diminish that harm'. Morally unacceptable harm, as per this hypothesis, comprises any of the following: 'harm to humans or the environment that is threatening to human life', or 'health, or serious and effectively irreversible', or 'inequitable to present or future generations' or 'imposed without adequate consideration of the human rights of those affected'.[47]

This is a very sophisticated ethical version of what may be called the 'harm theory'. The ethical principle outlined here extends to the entire communities of harm-doers, whether these are states, governments, markets or other non-state actors. What lawyers call *mens rea* (the element of intention – the culpable or guilty mind) is as highlighted *actus reus* (that conduct which lies in attempt, omission or commission of an act). Morally unacceptable harm is carefully defined as 'threatening', 'irreversible', 'inequitable' or as not taking into account a 'moral right to have a say'. While the horizon of expectation thus created may not be ignored, difficulties surround this moral 'right to have a say'. State practice remains ambivalent concerning this right and in any case, if the ethical principle itself allows the availability of this right, then appropriate state parties remain entitled to deny this right in certain matters. The question then arises as to the conditions in which these moral rights become defeasible. Of course, the COMEST is entirely right about the ways of passage of moral rights into legal rights: in a hermeneutical legal situation while the PP 'provides a rational framework for managing uncertain risks', it 'is not a decision algorithm and thus cannot guarantee consistency between

46 Arie Trouwborst, 'Prevention, Precaution, Logic and Law: The Relationship between the Precautionary Principle and the Preventative Principle in International Law and Associated Questions' (2009) 2(2) *Erasmus Law Review* 105

47 UNESCO, COMSET Report (n 45), Chapter 3. See also Baxi, 'Towards a Climate Change Justice Theory?' (n 4) 15–31

cases'. Nor may interpretive plurality gestated by different 'facts, uncertainties, circumstances', argumentation and 'decision-maker' which generate 'the element of judgement ... be eliminated'.

The principles of law 'constitute important tools for crystallization of new concepts and values' and a 'strength of the PP being a principle is its open-endedness and flexibility, which creates a possibility and an incentive for social learning'; vastly varying 'areas of application and different legal frameworks which may lead to more specific guidance and regulations'. However, as already noted, how far have rules imposing obligations in international law emerged, distinct from approaches, standards, principles and measures. It may be in the future that the 'repeated use of State practice and consistent *opinio juris* are likely to transform the PP into a customary relevant and cannot be disregarded by the countries in the international order, nor by legislators, policy makers and courts in the internal sphere'. For the present, 'precautionary measures should in any case be judged transparently on a case-by-case basis, and be subjected to scrutiny from many parties ...'[48]

The complex and contradictory interaction between legal (*lex lata*) and ethical dimensions (*de lege feranda*) thus plays an important part in progressive codification of environmental and climate justice. Yet, we should be mindful of precaution against PP sounded by Professor Cass Sunstein that the PP is dangerous 'not because it leads in bad directions, but because, read for all that it is worth, it leads in no direction at all. The principle threatens to be paralyzing, forbidding regulation, inaction, and every step in between'.[49]

State obligations

While much has been written on the subject in general, the question of obligations to environmental international law has mainly been confined to the domains of state responsibility. Private international law is not considered as an integral aspect of environmental law as such doctrines like *forum non conveniens*, the choice of law, the proper law of contracts and torts, and problems associated with the enforcement of a foreign judgment are scarcely considered. But a preliminary listing of environmental obligation includes whole categories of enormous obligations. We may ask therefore not merely what obligation states owe each other but also what is environmentally owed to significant others: the peoples of planet earth, peoples as citizens, excluded peoples (such as victims of violent social apartheid – marginalised women, stigmatised peoples living with disability, First Nations peoples, impoverished

48 All quotations, in the previous as well as this paragraph, are from the COMSET Report at section 2:2. The Report advances and celebrates a 'precautionary culture' as providing contexts for the determination of the scope of legal principles and regimes

49 C.R. Sunstein, 'Beyond the Precautionary Principle' (2003) 151 *University of Pennsylvania Law Review* 1003

people, street children and the girl child). We also further ask – and this is a main concern of climate change justice approaches – about intergenerational justice and duties to distant others. How far these obligations extend to international humanitarian law and the law of armed conflicts are important questions. How does this bear upon the PSNR Declaration? One may say that any decision of sovereignty in the sphere of environment affects the other nations and even the earth system as a whole. Even decisions of defence production and preparation, decisions to put 'boots on the ground' in foreign countries and territories, the actual conduct of warfare, and the aftermath of armed conflict in establishing a new normal state of affairs, need to be more carefully explored in studies of modern and contemporary environmental international law. What part the PSNR and precautionary principles in particular, and the doctrines of sustainable development in general, may play looms large as an important problem.

The implications of saying that state sovereignty is not illimitable or unlimited are worth pursuing. After all, not unlimited is the norm that a state is sovereign to organise its own resources, endowments and development. Inter-borders as well transboundary concerns (and now in the Anthropocene, some emerging standards of planetary loyalty) are also very pertinent. States are not so sovereign to organise their own development so as to manifestly adversely affect the environment of other states.

Principle 2 of the Rio Declaration says as much when it emphasises the 'good neighbourliness' concept which sets some limits to the sovereignty of a state with an obligation to prevent harm to the environment of other states. 'Equitable basis' doctrine offers some scope for accommodation for the conflicting interests of neighbouring states and results in the draft Convention on the Prevention of Transboundary Harm from Hazardous Activities, 2001, prepared by the International Law Commission (ILC). The Convention applies to all activities within a state that expose, cause and induce transboundary and environmental harm to other states; risks, in this context, may be posed by the possibility of disastrous accidents, such as industrial air pollution, natural watersheds or international watercourses. The ILC reflects Principle 2 of the Rio Declaration, and urges interstate cooperation, with an obligation to ensure that no hazardous activities are undertaken without a prior impact assessment and authorisation by the state in which it is to be conducted.

Conclusion

The questions of obligations to environmental international law have mainly been confined to the domains of state responsibility, though much has been written on the subject.[50] What precise obligations of interstate conduct and

50 See the important work of P. Birnie and A. Boyle, *International Law and the Environment* (2nd edn, Oxford University Press 2002); S. Cohen, *The Resilience of the State. Democracy*

behaviour have been prescribed by the PSNR Declaration? How has its reiteration in subsequent treaties and declarations crystallised in binding norms of international law? Has it served any of its major aspirations or purposes even as an approach, conception or standard of international relations? As noted earlier, these latter terms express a difference that does matter, but similar questions certainly surround the PSNR and its subsequent evolution.[51]

Sovereignty is Janus-faced: it looks both as a community of peoples and as a community of states. The statement that a state is sovereign merits full recognition in the theory of the law of peoples as well as states to organise their own development.[52] But this Principle does not (as noted) confer any immunity as well as impunity on any entity so as to adversely affect the environment of other states. While no one either in theory or practice denies the importance of *ex ante* legal regimes preventing environmental degradation and promoting ecological integrity, there is enormous scope for exploring the question of how far their enunciation and subsequent progress towards realisation of these aims are shackled by the complexities and contradictions of multilevel global *realpolitik*. For example, the 2015 United Nations General Assembly Resolution Basic Principles on Sovereign Debt Restructuring Processes, which prescribe nine approved principles for promoting the conception of 'sustainable debt',[53] tells us little about the future of SD, or even of the efficaciousness of environmental clearance,[54] even when some interesting ways ahead for this regime are also proposed.[55]

and the Challenge of Globalization (Jonathan Derric tr, Hurst 2003); M.C. Segger and A. Khalfan, *Sustainable Development Law. Principles, Practices and Prospects* (Oxford University Press 2004); P. Wetterstein, *Harm to the Environment: The Right to Compensation and the Assessment of Damages* (Oxford University Press 1997). See also, J.M. Harris, T.A. Wise, K.P. Gallagher and N.R. Goodwin (eds), *A Survey of Sustainable Development: Social and Economic Dimensions* (Island Press 2011)

51 Agne Sirinskiene (n 46) carefully notes most of state and scholarly usages of these terms to conclude that: 'Nevertheless, it seems that doubts about the precautionary principle being a "principle" are more common to Anglo-Saxon tradition. The European Union (EU) law does not draw a clear difference between "principle", "approach", and "measures"; these terms are used in parallel to define the same principle and there is nothing to suggest that these three terms cannot be used interchangeably. The European Commission in Communication On the Precautionary Principle also does not differentiate among these terms and recognizes the precautionary principle as a fully-fledged and general principle of international law or, as already discussed, even as a general customary rule of international law': at 353–355

52 See note 35, *supra* whereby the situation of a 'resource curse' needs to be imaginatively linked with the notion of sustainable debt

53 *United Nations Declaration on the Basic Principles on Sovereign Debt Restructuring Processes*, GA Res 69/139, UN GAOR, 69th sess, UN Doc A/RES/69/139 (10 September 2015)

54 Michael Faurec, 'Effectiveness of Environmental Law: What Does the Evidence Tell Us?' (2012) 36(2) *William & Mary Environmental Law & Policy Review* 293

55 D. Schoenbrod and R. Stewart (eds), *Breaking the Logjam: Environmental Protection that Will Work* (Yale University Press 2012); L. Paddock et al. (eds), *Compliance and Enforcement in Environmental Law: Toward More Effective Implementation* (Edward Elgar 2012)

There is no doubt, overall, that the PSNR principles, and in turn their normative progeny, have impacted on many a normative international law regime[56] and have densely populated international law. One may mention here, for example, the UN instruments such as the International Law concerning Friendly Relations and Co-operation among States in accordance with the Charter of the United Nations (1970), the Right of States and Peoples for Development (1985), the right and responsibility to protect, the Millennium Development Goals now replaced by the Sustainable Development Goals, the Declaration of Basic Principles of Justice for Victims of Crime and Abuse of Power (1985) and the Right and Responsibility of Individuals, Groups and Organs of Society to Promote and Protect Universally Recognized Human Rights and Fundamental Freedoms (1998). To these, we must add the two UN events that occurred in 2015: the recently concluded Paris Agreement on Climate Change and somewhat ambivalently the nine UN 'basic principles' for sovereign debt restructuring.

When we collate all these, and human rights, principles and approaches, we have what Francis Deng and his associates describe as the notion of *sovereignty as responsibility*[57] – a notion perhaps fully anticipated and even accepted by the PSNR.[58] The notion of course presents a contradictory unity which must also be appreciated as move from a regime of international law of cooperation and coexistence to a regime of competitive globalisation.[59] All forms of international ordering introduce their own contradictions and conflicts. We may have travelled away in these days of hyper-competitive forms of life from Wolfgang Friedman's roseate optimism about the potential of progress of international law,[60] yet may we still not maintain that 'optimism of will' amidst our dream talks and nightmares about the future?[61]

56 For this fecund notion, see, Robert Keohane and David Victor, 'The Regime Complex for Climate Change' (2011) 9(1) *Perspectives on Politics* 7

57 Frances M. Deng et al., *Sovereignty as Responsibility: Conflict Management in Africa* (Brookings Institution Press 1996); see also, A. Etzioni, 'Sovereignty as Responsibility' (2006) *Orbis* 71

58 There is certainly scope for saying that the PSNR *invented* the concept of the law of peoples. Articles 1, 5 and 7 explicitly refer to this and conjoin it with sovereignty of states. The latter is understandable in the first flush of postcoloniality (or more accurately and aptly in the early neocolonial times, where the national states were thought to personify the nation-peoples

59 See, A.L. Herbert, 'Cooperation in International Relations: A Comparison of Keohane, Haas and Franck' (1996) 14 *Berkeley Journal of International Law* 222

60 See Wolfgang Friedman's magisterial study, *The Changing Structure of International Law* (Stevens 1964)

61 Pierre-Marie Dupuy, 'International Law: Torn between Coexistence, Cooperation and Globalization: General Conclusions' (1998) 9 *European Journal of International Law* 278

3 Evolution of the permanent sovereignty over natural resources in the context of the investment regime

Jahid Hossain Bhuiyan

Introduction

A major principle of international law following the establishment of the United Nations pertained to the 'permanent sovereignty over natural resources' (PSNR). This principle calls for the creation of exclusive sovereignty of states over natural resources in those areas where sovereign rights can be exercised.[1] States have the right to use and exploit their natural resources for the purpose of national development and for the welfare of their citizens.[2] The right is conferred on the state on the condition that it undertakes to use that right for the benefit of the people. The purpose of this principle was mainly to assist developing countries within the global economy.[3] However, the objective remained unattained. Developing nations continued to face economic troubles and were unable to merge into the international economic system.[4]

One of the contributing factors for this phenomenon was that decision makers of developing states felt that PSNR was actually giving them ownership of the resources of the country, leading to the belief that they had the authority to use national wealth. In different countries across the globe, kleptocratic rulers, such as General Sani Abacha of Nigeria, have stolen money from their countries, leading to a decrease in economic development.[5] So the

1 Nico J. Schrijver, 'Permanent Sovereignty over Natural Resources versus the Common Heritage of Mankind', in Paul de Waart, Paul Peters and Erik Denters (eds), *International Law and Development* (vol I, Martinus Nijhoff Publishers, 1988) 87

2 *Right to Exploit Freely Natural Wealth and* Resources, GA Res 626 (VII), UN GAOR, 7th sess, 411th plen mtg, UN Doc A/RES/626(VII) (21 December 1952) preamble; *Permanent Sovereignty over Natural Resources*, GA Res 1803 (XVII), 17th sess, 119th plen mtg, UN Doc A/RES/1803(XVII) (14 December 1962) para 1 ('1803 Resolution')

3 Leo-Felix Lee, 'Sovereignty Over, Ownership of, and Access to Natural Resources' in A. F. Munir Maniruzzaman and others (eds), *International Sustainable Development Law* (vol II, Eolss Publishers, 2010) 51, 68

4 Emeka Duruigbo, 'Permanent Sovereignty and Peoples' Ownership of Natural Resources in International Law' (2006) 38 *George Washington International Law Review* 33, 35

5 Ibid

problem remains that states assert their right to resources without accepting that they have a duty to use those resources for the benefit of their peoples.

A country that has ample natural resources is believed to be a blessed one. For example, Saudi Arabia and Norway are considered to be wealthy nations as they are world leaders in the production of oil and gas. An economy benefits greatly from a consistent flow of money from natural resources. In industrialized countries, a significant role is played by natural resources. For example, the US and France are world leaders in the export of agricultural goods.[6] However, in the past few years, the existence of natural resources in a country is sometimes considered to be a curse.[7] Because every country wants to have abundant natural resources, countries are sometimes tempted to appropriate the resources of other countries in border regions or in international regions that are not governed by any state.[8] Hence, various states have indulged in wars for acquiring natural resources, resulting in damaging effects for civilians and the environment.[9] The invasion of Kuwait by Iraq in 1990 and of the Democratic Republic of Congo by Uganda in the late 1990s are two examples of wars being instigated *inter alia* to capture natural resources. Furthermore, the economic worth of natural resources gives rise to internal disagreements over power by rebel forces fighting to overthrow a legitimate government, such as in the case of the conflict over 'blood diamonds' in Liberia and Sierra Leone.[10] Therefore, natural resources are sometimes considered a resource curse.[11]

Certain natural resources are reserved for the corporation of the nations or for those sectors which are controlled by the government. However, to

6 Stephane Garelli, *Top Class Competitors: How Nations, Firms and Individuals Succeed in the New World of Competitiveness* (John Wiley & Sons, 2006) 9

7 Nico J. Schrijver, 'Permanent Sovereignty over Natural Resources' in Rudiger Wolfrum (ed.), *Max Planck Encyclopedia of Public International Law* para 17 <http://opil.ouplaw.com/view/10.1093/law:epil/9780199231690/law-9780199231690-e1442?prd=EPIL> accessed 27 February 2017. Schrijiver notes that not one of the newly industrialised countries acquired success on the basis of their natural resources

8 But appropriation by neighbouring countries is not the only problem. A country where natural resources are the sole or predominant source of national income and those resources are owned by the state or a ruling elite, e.g., Saudi Arabia, Venezuela, concentrates power in the hands of the ruling elite. See Toyin Falola and Ann Genova, *The Politics of the Global Oil Industry: An Introduction* (Praeger Publishers, 2009). Thus the ruling elite has the power/freedom to use those resources for their own benefit rather than the benefit of the people

9 Nico Schrijver, *Development without Destruction: The UN and Global Resource Management* (Indiana University Press, 2010) 158

10 Schrijver, 'Permanent Sovereignty over Natural Resources' (n 7) para 17

11 '"Resource curse" refers to the fact that countries with large primary exports, such as natural resources, often, but not always, grow more slowly than countries that do not have such resources'. Rhuks Ako and Nilopar Uddin, 'Good Governance and Resource Management in Africa', in Francis N. Botchway (ed.), *Natural Resource Investment and Africa's Development* (Edward Elgar, 2011) 21, 25

make sure the sector operates efficiently, foreign company alliances have been formed. Foreign companies have the capital and technology required for natural resources exploitation and exploration. The interests of multinational companies in carrying out activities in the natural resources sector must be protected and the international law on foreign investment should be focused upon. During the 1990s, it was accepted that foreign investors' interest was to be protected in accordance with the idea of liberalisation. However, mainly due to the global economic crisis and the failure of neoliberal policies, the trend has been reversed. In places like Latin America, governments were regaining control of their natural resources in order to carry out the desired development.[12]

This chapter traces the development of the principle of PSNR in the context of the international investment regime. The genesis of the principle may be traced back to the concept of sovereignty and self-determination. The principle of PSNR has been incorporated in a number of resolutions of the United Nations General Assembly, including Resolution 1803. This chapter will examine these resolutions and the nature of shared sovereignty on natural resources between state and people. It will also examine the impact of these resolutions on investment regulations. The chapter will then examine how environmental instruments are imposing certain restrictions on the sovereignty of the state. Finally, it will further examine the legal status of the principle of PSNR.

Evolution of the PSNR principle

The roots: Permanent sovereignty and the right to self-determination of peoples

Colonization is characterized by an imbalance of power and wealth. By contrast, international law provided political self-determination rights to foreign colonial territories in their entirety.[13] Following the Iranian nationalization of the Anglo Iranian Oil Company in 1952, the United Nations General Assembly (UNGA) Resolution 626 (VII) was presented on 21 December 1952. Uruguay then presented a Draft Resolution in which member states were called upon to recognise every country's right to 'nationalize and freely exploit' its natural wealth as a critical aspect of

12 M. Sornarajah, *The International Law on Foreign Investment* (3rd edn, Cambridge University Press, 2010) 41. The Australian federal government's failed attempt to introduce a mining tax circa 2010

13 The purpose of the UN Charter as per Article 1(2) is 'to develop friendly relations among nations based on respect for the principle of equal rights and self-determination of peoples'. In addition, Article 55 pertaining to economic and social cooperation reiterated self-determination. Thus, obligations were accepted by the UN member states for attaining economic self-determination. The term 'pledge' mentioned in Article 56 additionally strengthens these assumed obligations

economic independence.[14] Resolution 626 is still referred to as the 'nationalization' resolution,[15] even though in the ultimate document the term 'nationalize and freely exploit' was substituted with 'freely use and exploit'.[16] It was asserted in Resolution 626 that *peoples'* right to make use of and exploit 'their natural wealth and resources is inherent in their sovereignty'. It was recommended in this Resolution that all member states should have the freedom to exercise their right 'to use and exploit their natural wealth and resources'.

The PSNR principle continued to develop, not just as part of international arguments with respect to the political right of colonized peoples to self-determination, but also with respect to the development of human rights. It was determined by the UNGA through the Resolution 545 (VI) of 5 February 1952 that the draft covenants – the International Covenant on Civil and Political Rights (ICCPR) and the International Covenant on Economic, Social and Cultural Rights (ICESCR) – would incorporate an Article pertaining to the right of peoples with respect to political and economic self-determination.[17] The intensity of the arguments became more severe when Chile suggested on 16 April 1952 that a paragraph would be incorporated which particularly mentioned '[t]he right of the peoples to self-determination shall also include permanent sovereignty over their natural wealth and resources'.[18] It was also asserted in this paragraph that people should not be prevented from using their personal methods of sustenance under any circumstances, in case there are other states that put a claim to any of those rights.[19] Schrijver notes that this suggestion led to a debate on subtle problems such as the definition of 'sovereignty', the legal position of self-determination in international law and the concept of people's rights in contrast to rights of states, the validity of treaties, contracts and concession agreements, etc.[20]

All capital-exporting (Western) delegations such as the UK were not in favour of including the phrase 'permanent sovereignty' in the self-determination discussion in the draft covenants. It was argued by these countries that the concept of permanent sovereignty was threatening, as it

14 *Draft Resolution – Uruguay – Economic Development of Under-Developed Countries*, 2nd comm, 7th sess, Agenda Item 25, UN Docs A/C.2/L.165 and Corr. 1–3 (5 November 1952) preamble para 5

15 Nico Schrijver, *Sovereignty over Natural Resources: Balancing Rights and Duties* (Cambridge University Press, 1997) 41–49

16 UN GAOR, 7th sess, 411th plen mtg, UN Doc A/PV.411 (21 December 1952) para 1

17 Schrijver, *Sovereignty over Natural Resources* (n 15) 49. The ICCPR and ICESCR were adopted in 1966. The right to self-determination of all peoples is evidently recognised in Article 1 of the ICCPR and ICESCR

18 Schrijver, *Sovereignty over Natural Resources* (n 15) 49

19 Ibid

20 Ibid 49

may allow appropriation and confiscation of property owned by foreigners.[21] By contrast, the delegations of capital-importing (developing) countries such as Afghanistan were of the view that the concept of self-determination essentially involved the concept that a nation or peoples should control their own natural resources.[22] It was claimed by these countries that the recognition of permanent sovereignty did not call for sanction of abuses, nor was it to dissuade foreign investment. Rather, its intention was to protect the economic and political independence of underdeveloped countries from being misused by foreign investors.[23]

On 12 January 1952, UNGA Resolution 523 (VI) was adopted, pertaining to *integrated economic development and commercial agreements*, which stated that underdeveloped countries were free to decide the attainment of their economic development plans, keeping in view their national interests, and also the expansion of the world economy.[24] In addition, it is stressed in Resolution 523 that commercial agreements shall not include 'economic or political conditions violating the sovereign right of the underdeveloped countries', such as the right to decide their own means of attaining economic development.[25]

In 1960, the process of decolonization was advanced significantly. As the liberation movements became more intense, it was proclaimed by the UN that there should be a quick and unconditional end to colonialism. For this to occur, the Special Committee on Decolonization should be tasked with supervision of this whole procedure.[26]

The right to self-determination was recognised in the UN Declaration on the Granting of Independence to Colonial Countries and Peoples (UNGA Resolution 1514 (XV)) of 14 December 1960 and also in other subsequent instruments as a significant principle concerning the disintegration of the colonial system. This Declaration considered the self-determination right as being all peoples' freedom to decide their political standing and 'their economic, social and cultural development'.[27] There were arguments against the 'inter-war' concept, which stated that insufficient political, economic or

21 Ndiva Kofele-Kale, *The International Law of Responsibility for Economic Crimes: Holding State Officials Individually Liable for Acts of Fraudulent Enrichment* (Routledge, 2016) 84–85

22 Ibid 85

23 Ibid

24 *Integrated Economic Development and Commercial Agreements*, GA Res 523 (VI), UN GAOR, 6th sess, 360th plen mtg, UN Doc A/RES/523(VI) (12 January 1952) preamble, para 1

25 Ibid para 1(b), preamble

26 Andrzej Jakubowski, *State Succession in Cultural Property* (Oxford University Press, 2015) 119

27 *Declaration on the Granting of Independence to Colonial Countries and Peoples*, GA Res 1514 (XV), UN GAOR, 15th sess, 947th plen mtg, UN Doc A/RES/1514(XV) (14 December 1960) Art 2

social readiness could explain the delay in independence.[28] Self-determination turned into a legal principle, which obliged previous colonial powers to defer to the will of colonized peoples.[29]

Furthermore, a special status was granted to the questionable territories, which then became legal at the international level.[30] It is asserted by Pereira and Gough that the Declaration on the Granting of Independence to Colonial Countries and Peoples as well as the Declaration on Principles of International Law concerning Friendly Relations and Co-operation among States in accordance with the Charter of the United Nations (UNGA Resolution 2625 (XXV)) of 24 October 1970) extended the idea of self-determination to much more than colonialism.[31] This happened due to the recognition of a people's right of secession when a state does not conduct itself according to the principle of equal rights and self-determination of peoples, or in circumstances where a state does not have any government that is representative of the entire population living in that region, without any discrimination on the basis of race, creed or colour.[32] The rights of a state have to be understood as subject to its duties to the people for whom the state governs.

This extended version of the principle of self-determination was at first not accepted readily by the International Court of Justice (ICJ) due to the ICJ's view of colonialism as a sacred trust, as is evident in its advisory opinion of 1971, Legal Consequences for States of the Continued Presence of South Africa in Namibia (South West Africa) notwithstanding Security Council Resolution 276 (1970),[33] and also in its advisory opinion of 1975, Western Sahara.[34] However, in its advisory opinion of 2010, which pertained to the declaration of independence by Kosovo,[35] the ICJ expressed the view that general international law or the practice of the Security Council did not contain any prohibition on unilateral declarations of independence.[36] The

28 Jakubowski (n 26) 119

29 Ibid. One may question whether the absence of a colonial power equates to self-determination by a people. Perhaps, in some cases, it resulted in a local elite exercising power over the colonial power. Further questions may arise if there is not a unified will shared by the two powers under these circumstances

30 Ibid

31 Ricardo Pereira and Orla Gough, 'Permanent Sovereignty over Natural Resources in the 21st Century: Natural Resource Governance and the Right to Self-Determination of Indigenous Peoples under International Law' (2013) 14 *Melbourne Journal of International Law* 451, 465

32 GA Res 2625 (XXV), UN GAOR, 15th sess, 1883rd plen mtg, Agenda Item 85, UN Doc A/RES/25/2625 (24 October 1970) preamble; Pereira and Gough (n 31) 465

33 *Legal Consequences for States of the Continued Presence of South Africa in Namibia (South West Africa) notwithstanding Security Council Resolution 276 (1970) (Advisory Opinion)* [1971] ICJ Rep 16, 31 para 52

34 *Western Sahara (Advisory Opinion)* [1975] ICJ Rep 12, 33 para 59 ('Western Sahara')

35 *Accordance with International Law of the Unilateral Declaration of Independence in Respect of Kosovo (Advisory Opinion)* [2010] ICJ Rep 403 ('Kosovo Advisory Opinion')

36 Ibid 437 para 81; Pereira and Gough (n 31) 465–466

ICJ mentioned that '[d]uring the second half of the twentieth century, the international law of self-determination developed in such a way as to create a right to independence for the peoples of non-self-governing territories and peoples subject to alien subjugation, domination and exploitation'.[37] In Kosovo, there was a minority group (ethnic Serbs) who felt threatened by the majority group's decision to secede from Yugoslavia.[38] The case of Kosovo illustrates the problem with unilateral declarations of independence where a minority group has a close attachment to the entity which is being seceded from.

Pereira and Gough argue that the sovereign ownership of natural resources is questioned if the local communities or indigenous groups claim resource rights, individually or in a group.[39] The claims may cause issues with natural resource sector economic operators.[40] The PSNR was formed during the postcolonial era, when developing countries claimed sovereignty over their natural resources on a legal basis. In present times, a wide purpose has been attributed to permanent sovereignty and this may be used to legitimise the claims of non-state actors and communities. Such claims would define the usage and ownership rights regarding the natural resources within a country.[41] Hence, according to Pereira and Gough, the right to permanent sovereignty is not limited to the postcolonial period but it is used as a strong basis upon which individuals or communities may challenge the decision of a government to allow foreign corporations' exploration and exploitation of a country's natural resources. This, however, may not prove to be advantageous.[42] Pereira and Gough continue that the traditional Westphalian concept of sovereignty informs the notion of sovereignty at international law, a concept which may no longer be so relevant since international law is continuously evolving. There is constant development in international law from a state-centred focus to non-state actors having participation rights in terms of decision making and being granted access to justice.[43]

The 1962 Declaration on PSNR and the subsequent years: Focusing on foreign investment

After World War II, there was an increase in conflicts as postcolonial developing countries, especially in Africa and Asia, started claiming rights for sovereignty over natural resources.[44] Many developing countries started

37 *Kosovo Advisory Opinion* [2010] ICJ Rep 403, 436 para 79
38 See Neal G. Jesse and Kristen P. Williams, *Identity and Institutions: Conflict Reduction in Divided Societies* (State University of New York, 2005) 11
39 Pereira and Gough (n 31) 453
40 Ibid
41 Ibid
42 Ibid
43 Ibid 453–454
44 Ibid 455

debating the validity of concession agreements that had been entered into between governments and foreign investors, or that were enforced during the colonial era for exploring and exploiting natural resources. Such concession agreements were mainly one-sided and were inclined towards foreign investors, giving rise to disagreements.[45]

The Commission on Permanent Sovereignty over Natural Resources, comprising nine members, was set up in 1958 with the aim of carrying out a complete survey of the fundamental elements of the right to self-determination, along with recommendations for making it more powerful.[46] Based on the Commission's report, Permanent Sovereignty over Natural Resources was adopted by the General Assembly in Resolution 1803 (XVII) on 14 December 1962. Keeping in view the fact that foreign direct investment (FDI) is unavoidable in developing states, every state (including these developing states) is given the right by the Resolution to have full sovereignty over its economic activities, and this affirms each state's right to look after the foreign investment that takes place within its national boundaries. Freedom was also awarded to governments to ensure a constructive environment for foreign investors.[47] Resolution 1803 strengthens the concept of permanent sovereignty. According to Paragraph 1 of Resolution 1803, it is the right of both peoples and nations to exercise PSNR, and this right must be exercised for the purpose of attaining national development and the welfare of the people of the state in question.[48]

45 Ibid

46 *Recommendations Concerning International Respect for the Right of Peoples and Nations to Self-Determination* GA Res 1314 (XIII), UN GAOR, 13th sess, 788th plen mtg, UN Doc A/RES/1314(XIII) (12 December 1958)

47 During the 1960s and 1970s, a 'confidence crisis' took place, since many developing states were expropriating or nationalizing foreign investments in accordance with their understanding of sovereignty. Within emerging markets, FDI was jeopardized, since investors were discouraged by such an unpredictable and unforeseen political environment. Developing states required foreign investment to make sure their markets experienced growth and expansion. They also wanted long-term development of the economic advantages which were expected to eventually positively affect the political climate. However, potential investors were unwilling to carry out any business until their investments were sufficiently protected. Investors had lost their confidence in the foreign markets, a situation which was subsequently rectified by the 1803 Resolution, UN Doc A/RES/1803(XVII) and the 1974 *Charter of Economic Rights and Duties of States,* GA Res 3281 (XXIX), UN GAOR, 29th sess, 2315th plen mtg, Agenda Item 48, UN Doc A/Res/29/3281 (12 December 1974) ('CERDS'): Andreas R. Ziegler and Louis-Philippe Gratton, 'Investment Insurance' in Peter Muchlinski, Federico Ortino and Christoph Schreuer (eds), *The Oxford Handbook of International Investment Law* (Oxford University Press, 2008) 524, 527–528

48 Nico J. Schrijver asserts that as the decolonization process moves forward, emphasis on the right of 'peoples' to PSNR and the link with 'self-determination' declined. He also asserts that, with the exception of certain particular resolutions regarding the right of particular peoples, especially those 'under foreign occupation, colonial domination or apartheid', the general resolutions on the PSNR following those of 1962 are increasingly focused on states as the subject of the right to PSNR. This can be discerned in the Declaration on the Progressive Development of Principles of Public International Law

Sovereignty of indigenous people over their natural resources is acknowledged in the present times by the international law, particularly the UN Declaration of the Rights of Indigenous Peoples 2007.

When states nationalize, expropriate or relinquish natural wealth and resources, this obligation becomes enforceable.[49] Paragraphs 2, 3, 6, 7 and 8 of Resolution 1803, when read simultaneously, stress the dominance of the PSNR over host state obligations with respect to foreign investors and investment activities. The goal of these paragraphs is to prevent the issues that may emerge from investors' expectations of investment protection, such as any reduction in value or acquisition of these investments according to the application of regulatory sovereignty by capital-importing nations. For instance, Paragraph 2 of Resolution 1803 calls for creating a balance between the concerns of foreign capital investors and those of the host state, so as to expand '[t]he exploration, development and disposition' of natural resources by a host state whilst safeguarding the exercise of regulatory sovereignty by host states with respect to PSNR.[50]

Paragraph 4 of Resolution 1803 asserts that the basis for nationalization, expropriation or requisition shall be 'public utility, security or the national interest', subject to payment of 'appropriate compensation'. It also states that when a question of compensation leads to a controversy, then 'the national jurisdiction of the State taking measures shall be exhausted'. In addition, it provides the likelihood of moving towards arbitration or international settlement in the event of a dispute.

This shows the possibility of reconciling investor protection with the national standard presented by the Calvo doctrine, as first articulated by the Argentinian jurist Carlos Calvo (1822–1906).[51] The doctrine called on

relating to a New International Economic Order (Seoul Declaration) 1986 of the International Law Association where no reference to the 'people's right' is made in its Paragraph 5 on PSNR: Schrijver, 'Permanent Sovereignty over Natural Resources versus the Common Heritage of Mankind' (n 1) 89. Pereira and Gough state that there are powerful reasons for people to have the right to permanent sovereignty. The recognition of the peoples' right to PSNR is significant from a practical perspective in the sense that it could, undoubtedly, create the grounds for protesting against the government's decision to provide power to multinational companies to exploit natural resources within a state. Pursuant to 'the peoples' right', governments would have the power to use natural resources for the benefit of the entire population: Pereira and Gough (n 31) 460. It may be argued that there is a higher obligation with respect to indigenous peoples since 'their physical and cultural survival' has an unavoidable relationship with connection to their traditional lands and natural resources. See *Saramaka People v Suriname (Preliminary Objections, Merits, Reparations and Costs)* (Inter-American Court of Human Rights, Ser C No. 172, 28 November 2007) para 122

49 Daniella Dam-de Jong, *International Law and Governance of Natural Resources in Conflict and Post-Conflict Situations* (Cambridge University Press, 2015) 37

50 Pedro J. Martinez-Fraga and C. Ryan Reetz, *Public Purpose in International Law: Rethinking Regulatory Sovereignty in the Global Era* (Cambridge University Press, 2015) 308

51 Elena Merino Blanco and Jona Razzaque, *Globalisation and Natural Resources Law: Challenges, Key Issues and Perspectives* (Edward Elgar Publishing, 2011) 72

foreign governments to avoid becoming involved in conflicts regarding treatment of aliens' property so as to stop what was known as the 'gunboat diplomacy' that governed foreign investment in that period. The doctrine recognises that expropriation needs should be fulfilled by fair compensation, not on the ground that it is a global obligation, but because the obligation stems from domestic law and constitutional provisions.[52]

It is vital to give up diplomatic protection of the foreign investor which, according to international law, is the state's right and not the individual's.[53] Developing countries were in favour of the Calvo doctrine. Since Resolution 1803 backs the Calvo doctrine ('appropriate' compensation) in contrast with the Hull Formula ('adequate, effective and prompt' compensation), there exists an adverse effect on foreign investment in natural resources sectors. 'Adequate, effective and prompt' compensation is to be attained by investors in cases where host states nationalize, expropriate or relinquish their natural resource investments. In Paragraph 7 of Resolution 1803, it is asserted that any breach of the PSNR principle is against 'the spirit and principles of the Charter of the United Nations' and creates obstructions to the establishment of international cooperation and peace. It was asserted by Dam-de Jong that even though this provision was initially intended to protect developing nations from foreign investors exploiting their natural resources on an unequal basis, it is also questionably appropriate in situations in which foreign nations plunder another state's natural resources, as has occurred (and is still occurring to some extent) in the Democratic Republic of Congo.[54]

Lastly, Paragraph 8 of Resolution 1803 provides that those foreign investment agreements that are freely entered into by sovereign states shall be adhered to in good faith. The sovereignty of peoples and nations over their natural wealth and resources shall be stringently and diligently respected by states and international organizations, as per the Charter and the principles contained in Resolution 1803.

Resolution 2158 (XXI) of 6 December 1966 on Permanent Sovereignty over Natural Resources asserts that the principle of PSNR should be safeguarded and that developing countries should be able to benefit from the effective and strategic use of resources. Martinez-Fraga and Reetz argue that the attempt to safeguard the application and use of PSNR, especially in terms

52 Ibid

53 Ibid. In present times, most of the international investment agreements (IIAs) follow the standard of 'adequate, effective and prompt' compensation (called the Hull Formula, after the US Secretary of State Cordell Hull who developed it in 1938). This formula was backed by nearly all developed, capital-exporting states. The Hull Formula is usually relied upon by developed countries that want to empower their foreign investors by raising the compensation needed for expropriation and other interventions by foreign countries: David Collins, *An Introduction to International Investment Law* (Cambridge University Press, 2017) 188

54 Dam-de Jong (n 49) 37–38

of 'foreign capital', essentially depends on the supervision of foreign investment by host state governments and in the interests of developing states.[55] There is clear reference to the need to offer 'government supervision over the activity of foreign capital' to make certain that it is utilized for the purpose of national development. However, no statements are provided regarding the obligations of the host state 'to safeguard' foreign investments.[56] Also, it is confirmed in Resolution 2158 'that the exploitation of natural resources in each country shall always be conducted in accordance with its national laws and regulations'.[57]

Following Resolution 1803, the spirit of cooperation came to be replaced by a powerful conflict over natural resources. Various developing states faced investment problems, leading to the establishment of a new international economic order (NIEO).[58] This led to the commencement of the North–South discussion throughout the 1970s. During this time, there was intense pressure over the price of raw materials coupled with erratic fluctuations in the global monetary mechanism and exchange rates. Oil prices increased by four times in 1974 in a span of a few months. Developed nations showed concerns about protecting their goods. The global economy faced a downturn and the political environment of developing states became threatening, which led to a decline in foreign investment in natural resource schemes. This was an ideal time for discussions between the North and South. The General Assembly convened in special sessions for two years consecutively, on the initiative of Algeria. Different texts were published in this tense environment, such as a Declaration on the Establishment of the New International Economic Order (NIEO Declaration) on 1 May 1974 and the Charter of Economic Rights and Duties of States (CERDS) on 10 December 1974.[59]

It is strongly affirmed in the NIEO Declaration that the basis of the new economic order should be complete adherence to the permanent sovereignty of each state over its natural resources and economic activities.[60] It is also affirmed in the NIEO Declaration that for the safeguard of these resources, each state has the right to effectively control them and their exploitation in a way that is appropriate for the circumstances, which also includes the right

55 Martinez-Fraga and Reetz (n 50) 310

56 *Permanent Sovereignty over Natural Resources*, GA Res 2158 (XXI), 21st sess, 1478th plen mtg, UN Doc A/RES/2158(XXI) (25 November 1966) ('Resolution 2158'), in pertinent part

57 Ibid

58 *Declaration on the Establishment of a New International Order* GA Res 3201 (S-VI), 6th special sess, 2229th plen mtg, Agenda Item 7, UN Doc A/RES/S-6/3201 (1 May 1974) ('NIEO Declaration')

59 Marie-Claude Smouts, 'The General Assembly: Grandeur and Decadence' in Paul Taylor and A.J.R. Groom (eds), *The United Nations at the Millennium: The Principal Organs* (Continuum, 2000) 21, 45–46; Schrijver, *Sovereignty over Natural Resources* (n 15) 113

60 NIEO Declaration, UN Doc A/RES/S-6/3201, para 4(e)

to nationalize or hand over ownership to its nations.[61] It is further provided in the NIEO Declaration that '[t]he right of all States, territories and peoples under foreign occupation, alien and colonial domination or apartheid to restitution and full compensation for the exploitation and depletion of, and damages to, the natural resources and all other resources of those States, territories and peoples'.[62] In addition, it also states that there should be a just and fair association between the costs of raw materials, primary goods, manufactured and semi-manufactured goods that emerging nations export and the costs of raw materials, primary goods, manufactures, capital goods and tools that emerging nations import, so as to create sustainable development of their terms of trade and the growth of the world economy.[63]

The new international economic order was set up by CERDS, which purportedly connects economic development with social development. CERDS presented a key principle regulating economic links amongst states, which pertained to the obligation of acting in good faith[64] by adhering to international standards, such as human rights.[65] According to CERDS, each state has the freedom to 'exercise full permanent sovereignty', which includes 'possession, use and disposal' of all of 'its wealth, natural resources and economic activities'.[66] It further asserts that every state has the freedom to control and exhibit control over foreign investment under its national jurisdiction, according to its laws and regulations and consistent with its national goals and priorities.[67] In addition, a state has the right to control and manage the activities of transnational companies that are under its national jurisdiction and to take steps to make certain that these activities are consistent with the laws, rules and regulations of the state and adhere to national 'economic and social policies'.[68] A state is also responsible for nationalizing, expropriating or transferring 'ownership of foreign property', and in this situation, appropriate compensation should be given by the state that is taking such steps, considering the relevant laws and regulations and all conditions deemed relevant by the state.[69] According to CERDS, when the call for compensation leads to a dispute, 'it shall be settled under the domestic law of the nationalizing State and by its tribunals, unless it is freely and mutually agreed' that other peaceful methods should be used, based on the 'sovereign equality of States' and as per the 'principle of free choice of means'.[70] Article

61 Ibid
62 Ibid para 4(f)
63 Ibid para 2(j)
64 CERDS, UN Doc A/Res/29/3281, ch I, principle j
65 Ibid ch I, principle k
66 Ibid ch II, Art 2(1)
67 Ibid ch II, Art 2(2)(a)
68 Ibid ch II, Art 2(2)(b)
69 Ibid ch II, Art 2(2)(c)
70 Ibid

2(2)(c) is indicative of the Calvo doctrine. However, this Article was not approved by the developed states.

Thus, following 1962, it was ensured that the right of each state to PSNR should be affirmed. Commitments may be accepted by a state not to exercise particular sovereign rights for some time so as to attract foreign investment; however, this does not suggest that the state is 'abandoning the doctrine of PSNR'.[71] This means that the recognition of the right of a state to propose investment incentives should not be considered as a decline in state sovereignty, as international law recognises that a state can commit itself on such terms, just as it recognises that a state has full authority over its natural resources.[72] Having a right is consistent with having the power or freedom not to exercise that right – but, of course, a state deciding not to exercise a right must make that decision for the people's benefit (not its own benefit).

Further phases in the evolution of resource sovereignty

A state has a sovereign right to use its natural resources. Nevertheless, environmental instruments are imposing certain restrictions on the sovereign rights of the state. The PSNR principle has both an environmental and developmental angle; therefore, it is closely related to the principle of sustainable development.

International cooperation in the management of natural resources: Rights of states

The 1972 Stockholm Declaration of the United Nations Conference on the Human Environment (Stockholm Declaration) and ensuing international legal instruments summarize the rights of states with respect to their natural resources. The focus of this stage of PSNR development was to achieve international cooperation in managing natural resources. It is asserted in the Stockholm Declaration that states, as per the UN Charter and the principles of international law, possess 'the sovereign right to exploit their own resources' according to the environmental policies enforced in their country, and the duty to make certain that the actions that are under their jurisdiction or control cause no harm 'to the environment of other States or of other areas' that are outside their jurisdiction.[73] Article 2 of the Rio Declaration on Environment and Development (Rio Declaration) of 1992 also asserts that all states have a sovereign right to make use of their natural resources according to the environmental and developmental policies within their country.

71 David Collins, *Performance Requirements and Investment Incentives under International Economic Law* (Edward Elgar Publishing, 2015) 4

72 Ibid

73 Principle 21

In addition, the topic of state sovereignty over natural resources is addressed in the 1982 United Nations Convention on the Law of the Sea (UNCLOS). The breadth of the territorial sea was increased by UNCLOS to 12 nautical miles.[74] In this area, the coastal state, excepting some exclusions linked to navigation, has full sovereignty over marine natural resources, including both living as well as non-living.[75] In the exclusive economic zone (EEZ), the coastal state has sovereign rights to explore and exploit living and non-living natural resources included in the water column, on the seabed and in the subsoil.[76] Nonetheless, it is also the duty of the coastal states to conserve and manage these resources. Sovereign rights are used by the coastal state to explore and exploit mineral and other non-living natural resources included within the continental shelf.[77] The deep seabed and its natural resources are declared by UNCLOS as the 'common heritage of mankind'.[78] At a depth of between 4,500 to 5,500 metres, deep sea mineral deposits are frequently found. It is quite challenging to carry out the mining of deep seabed resources. The commercial practicality of deep seabed mining is increasing, in the context of vast technological developments and increasing commodity prices. Yet notwithstanding its advantages, deep seabed mining has only attained limited investment,[79] suggesting international cooperation in the management of natural resources.

Sustainable use and conservation of natural resources: Rights and duties of states

With respect to natural resources and environmental issues, sustainable utilisation and conservation of natural resources necessitate regimes and systems which concentrate on avoiding and regulating environmental damage, instead of offering compensation for the damage that has already been caused.[80] It is stated in Article 1(2) of the ICCPR and ICESCR that the state's right to permanent sovereignty should be determined by the public benefit and should not, under any circumstances, have an effect on a people's livelihood. In Article 21(1) of the African Charter on Human and Peoples' Rights, 1981, it is mentioned that the people's interest should be the top priority in the right to permanent sovereignty, and that this right should not cause any obstacles to the people's freedom to exploit their resources.

74 Article 3
75 Article 2, Article 17
76 Article 56
77 Article 77
78 Preamble
79 Robert Makgill and Ana P. Linhares, 'Deep Seabed Mining: Key Obligations in the Emerging Regulation of Exploration and Development in the Pacific', in Robin Warner and Stuart Kaye (eds), *Routledge Handbook of Maritime Regulation and Enforcement* (Routledge, 2016) 231
80 Blanco and Razzaque (n 51) 251

The effects of unsustainable use of natural resources cannot be measured solely in economic terms, and cannot be resolved merely by implementing state responsibility or enforcing fines or other sanctions. Rather, it is vital for all the concerned parties to accept a regime that permits sustainable utilisation of resources without draining them. For this, resources should be accessible on a fair and equitable basis, and economic principles should be based on maintaining protection for the poor and the weak.[81] Thus economic management of PSNR is shifting in the direction of sustainable natural resources.

The concept of 'sustainable development' eventually highlighted the need to merge economic growth with environmental protection.[82] This term has become a key concept in environmental law from the early 1980s and various works have been published in this regard.[83] The Brundtland Report presents the highly popular explanation of sustainable development, which states that it is development that 'meets the needs of the present without compromising the ability of future generations to meet their own needs'.[84] It was suggested in the Brundtland Report that sustainable development indicates respect for restricting the capacity of the environment and natural resources to fulfil human requirements.[85] This is echoed in the legal principle that there should be sustainable exploitation of natural resources.[86] In 1992, the Earth Summit held at Rio de Janeiro approved of sustainable development as a key principle of international environmental law, despite the Rio Declaration not providing a specific definition of sustainable development. The Rio Declaration stressed that natural resources and ecosystem conservation shall be protected for sustainability.[87] Furthermore, poor communities' needs are to be assessed with a view to levelling inequalities and social, economic and environmental issues are to be managed.[88] In all, the 27 principles of the Rio Declaration and 40 chapters of Agenda 21 created the basis of the states' commitment to achieving sustainable development.

81 Ibid 251

82 Jane Holder and Maria Lee, *Environmental Protection, Law and Policy: Text and Materials* (2nd edn, Cambridge University Press, 2007) 217

83 Ibid

84 Chapter II, Article 1, World Commission on Environment and Development, *Our Common Future: Report of the World Commission on Environment and Development* [Brundtland Report 1987], <www.un-documents.net/wced-ocf.htm> accessed 27 February 2017

85 See Chapter II, Article 36, Article 38 and Article 39, ibid

86 S. Wood, 'Sustainability in International Law' in A.F. Munir Maniruzzaman and others (eds), *International Sustainable Development Law* (n 3) 137, 174

87 The Rio Declaration, Principles 3, 4, 8, 15 and 23

88 The Rio Declaration, Principles 5, 6 and 14. Federico Esu and Solenne Avet, 'The European Integration and the 2009 Renewable Energy Directive: A Sustainable Framework for the Implementation of the Sustainability Criteria for Biofuels Production in Third-States?' in Francesca Romanin Jacur, Angelica Bonfanti and Francesco Seatzu (eds), *Natural Resources Grabbing: An International Law Perspective* (Brill, 2016) 199, 204

The 1992 Convention on Biological Diversity (CBD) was developed by the Earth Summit. The CBD provides that sustainable use refers to using the elements of biological diversity in a manner and at a pace that does not bring about a reduction in biological diversity in the long run, thus ensuring the capacity to fulfil the needs and requirements of the existing and subsequent generations.[89] The United Nations Framework Convention on Climate Change (1992) (UNFCCC) and the United Nations Convention to Combat Desertification (1994) were also developed by the Earth Summit, and both also stressed the importance of sustainable development. Other significant findings of the Earth Summit were the establishment of the Global Environment Facility and the United Nations Commission on Sustainable Development. These two agencies performed critical roles in operationalizing sustainable development.[90] Environmental protection, in the exploration of natural resources for sustainable development, is emphasized by the CBD and the UNFCCC.

The United Nations Conference on Sustainable Development (Rio+20), which took place in Rio de Janerio in June 2012, emphasised *inter alia* the green economy and sustainable development, and international coordination for sustainable development. The Sustainable Development Goals (SDGs) of the 2030 Agenda for Sustainable Development were adopted on 1 January 2016, as a result of negotiations by world leaders in September 2015. The SDGs focus on three aspects of sustainable development: economic, social and environmental.

It is accepted on the international level that sustainable development is important and that FDI is an important element of any development scheme.[91] There are various soft instruments which have highlighted the significance of investment with respect to sustainable development. Agenda 21 puts forward this association, which is explicitly given in the final report of the International Conference on Financing for Development (Monetary Consensus).[92] FDI in the natural resources sector should be carried out in conformity with the idea of sustainable development.

89 Article 2

90 Tony George Puthucherril, *Towards Sustainable Coastal Development: Institutionalizing Integrated Coastal Zone Management and Coastal Climate Change Adaptation in South Asia* (Brill Nijhoff, 2015) 165–166

91 Markus Gehring and Andrew Newcombe, 'An Introduction to Sustainable Development in World Investment Law,' in Marie-Claire Cordonier Segger, Markus W. Gehring and Andrew Newcombe (eds), *Sustainable Development in World Investment Law* (Kluwer Law International, 2011) 3, 9

92 Paragraph 1, *Monetary Consensus of the International Conference on Financing for Development, Report of the International Conference on Financing for Development*, 22 March 2002, UN Doc A/CONF.1981/11, ch 1, resolution 1, annex (2002). Gehring and Newcombe, 'An Introduction to Sustainable Development in World Investment Law' in Segger, Gehring and Newcombe (eds), *Sustainable Development in World Investment Law*, ibid

Legal status of PSNR

It has been discussed earlier that the PSNR principle originates from UNGA resolutions. International law clearly states that the UNGA resolutions are not legally binding: Articles 10 and 14 of the Charter of the UN consider UNGA resolutions as simply 'recommendations'.

Given the non-binding nature of the UNGA resolutions, their legal position is still undecided. For instance, there was unanimous acceptance of the UNGA resolution on torture, whereas very few states ratified the 1984 Convention against Torture and Other Cruel, Inhuman or Degrading Treatment or Punishment. This meant that states saw a distinction between the two documents and were not ready to accept them. It is also asserted at times that certain UNGA resolutions have binding force, as a declaration involves serious issues and presents lasting obligations, as reflected in the 1948 Universal Declaration of Human Rights and the 1970 Declaration on Principles of International Law concerning Friendly Relations and Co-operation among States. These declarations involve issues that are of concern to the entire global community.[93]

In addition, UNGA members have official mandates from states, meaning that these people can officially function on the states' behalf while approving a resolution of the UNGA. Since they are working on the state's behalf, it is hard for the state to function against the approved resolution.[94] It was argued by Judge Lauterpacht in *South West Africa Voting Procedure* that, bearing in mind the circumstances of decolonization, the UN members have an indefinite but existing legal obligation to view UNGA resolutions in good faith, to prevent their consistent disregard by states resulting in the perception that they are against the purposes and principles of the Charter of the United Nations.[95]

The ICJ presented a judgment on the benefits of UN resolutions in the *Nicaragua* case, where the ICJ held that state consent to the various resolutions like Resolution 2625 (Declaration on Friendly Relations) may be interpreted 'as an acceptance of the validity of the rule or set of rules' presented by the resolutions.[96] This suggests that some UNGA resolutions can possess a legally binding force.[97] Under some standards, norms established by UNGA resolutions like Resolution 2625 may turn out to be part of customary international law. The PSNR principle has been developed in

93 Ulrike Barten, *Minorities, Minority Rights and Internal Self-Determination* (Springer, 2015) 66

94 Ibid

95 Hersch Lauterpacht (1995) South West Africa – Voting Procedure – Separate Opinion Advisory Opinion of 7 June 1995: ICJ Reports 1955, 90, 118–120

96 International Court of Justice (1986) *Case Concerning Military and Paramilitary Activities in and against Nicaragua* (*Nicaragua v United States of America*), Judgment on the Merits, 27 June 1986, ICJ Reports 1986, 14, para 188

97 Barten (n 93) 66–67

accordance with the notion of the 'permissive resolution', i.e., a resolution that does not impose obligations but that assigns rights not necessarily permitted by the international law at that time. For instance, Resolution 1803 diverges from the conventional global minimum standard of treatment of foreign citizens, as it creates novel principles regarding nationalization.[98] With respect to compensation, the triple standard ('prompt, adequate and effective') is not put forward; rather 'appropriate' compensation is, which calls for consideration of not just the destruction caused by investors, but also the social-economic circumstances of the nationalizing country, as well as its ability to make payments.[99]

Various states backed Resolution 1803, including countries that exported capital, as well as those that imported it. On this basis, the sole arbitrator Rene Jean Dupuy in the *Texaco Overseas Petroleum Co v Government of the Libyan Arab Republic* (Award of 19 January 1977) concluded that Resolution 1803 expresses the *opino juris communis* on nationalization of foreign property under international law.[100] In the *Armed Activities on the Territory of the Congo (Democratic Republic of the Congo v Uganda)*,[101] the ICJ asserted that Resolution 1803 is part of customary international law.[102]

Vaughan Lowe described the PSNR principle as being a potential example of a *jus cogens* norm of international law, on the same footing as the principle that prohibits an apartheid kind of racial discrimination.[103] He states that the sovereignty of states over their natural resources was never really questioned; rather, it was just the sovereignty of recently independent states that was, with a view to expanding their sovereignty over their natural resources. The actual query pertains to creating a balance between this principle and the principles of international law, so as to protect foreign investment.[104]

There is a progressive shift of this balance towards favouring the principles of international law, particularly in the span of the previous two decades.[105] Over the years, radical changes have been brought about by bilateral invest-

98 Paragraph 4, Resolution 1803; Schrijver, 'Permanent Sovereignty over Natural Resources versus the Common Heritage of Mankind', in Waart, Peters and Denters (eds), *International Law and Development* (n 1) 87, 91

99 Paragraph 4, Resolution 1803; Schrijver, ibid

100 Schrijver, ibid

101 Judgment of 19 December 2005

102 Para 244

103 See Vaughan Lowe, *International Law* (Oxford University Press, 2007) 59. Referred to by Melaku Geboye Desta, 'Sovereignty over Natural Resources and International Investment Law: The Elusive Search for Equilibrium' in Stephen W. Schill, Christian J. Tams and Rainer Hofmann (eds), *International Investment Law and Development: Bridging the Gap* (Edward Elgar Publishing Limited, 2015) 223, 253. However, this *jus cogens* assertion was not accepted by the International Arbitral Tribunal in the *Aminoil v Kuwait* (1982) case

104 Desta, 'Sovereignty over Natural Resources and International Investment Law: The Elusive Search for Equilibrium' in Schill, Tams and Hofmann (eds), *International Investment Law and Development: Bridging the Gap* (n 103)

105 Ibid

ment treaties (BITs) concluded between states, such that Judge Schwebel has commented on their capacity to signify what he, until recently, felt would be an 'ideal' law of international investment: 'BITs specify – in terms more explicit, detailed, and far-reaching than was ever advanced under what was customary international law in the time of Cordell Hull – what may be described as an ideal law of international investment.'[106]

Furthermore, several multilateral treaties, including the 1966 ICCPR and the 1966 ICESCR, the 1981 African Charter on Human and Peoples' Rights, and the 1982 United Nations Convention on the Law of the Sea, have referred to the PSNR principle. Therefore, there are very few international lawyers who presently refute the legal worth of the PSNR principle.[107]

Conclusion

This chapter argues that the PSNR principle emerged from the struggle of former colonies to attain political and economic self-determination following World War II. The peoples emerging from colonial rule sought to ensure their access to the economic benefits accruing from natural resources' extraction in their region.[108] Towards the end of the period of widespread decolonization, states were entitled to enjoy the right to permanent sovereignty, given that these states also adhered to the rights of their 'peoples' to use the natural wealth and resources in their areas.[109] The PSNR principle was also inspired by the apprehension amongst developing nations that conventional international law on foreign investment hindered the successful application of their sovereignty in the economic domain by giving preference to the concerns of capital-exporting nations.

The PSNR principle signified a victory for developing countries as it advanced the idea that sovereign states possessed the right to expropriate or nationalize foreign companies' assets in circumstances where there is 'public utility' and the owner has been appropriately compensated. It appeared to create a balance between developing states concerns over their control of

106 Quoted by Melaku, ibid, 253–254

107 Schrijver (n 1) 91

108 Maria Augusta Leon Moreta, *The Human Rights Fundamentals of Conservation in the Context of the Extraction of Energy Resources* (Vandenhoeck & Ruprecht GmbH & Co, 2015) 102

109 Ibid, 103–104. The inconsistency between the state sovereignty principle and the affirmation of peoples' rights creates various issues. One way through which this inconsistency can be eliminated is by considering the affirmation of peoples' rights as a means of comprehending the key idea that states should have control over their natural resources, however, the goal of this should be the benefit of their peoples. Jeremie Gilbert and Nadia Bernaz, 'Resources Grabbing and Human Rights: Building a Triangular Relationship between States, Indigenous Peoples and Corporation', in Francesca Romanin Jacur, Angelica Bonfanti and Francesco Seatzu (eds), *Natural Resources Grabbing: An International Law Perspective* (Brill/Nijhoff, 2016) 38, 43

their natural resources with the concerns of the developed states which wanted to guarantee investment protection to their corporate citizens.[110] In summary, earlier, peoples had a right to PSNR. However, the PSNR concept subsequently evolved more and more into an element of state sovereignty. The right to natural resources has been conferred on states on the understanding that states will use this right for the benefit of the peoples of those states. Therefore, states have duties as well as rights. Yet despite this evolution, in recent decades it can be noticed that PSNR is once again being framed as a right of peoples. This development may open the route towards more sustainable development.

The next phase of PSNR development involves international cooperation in the management of natural resources and the sustainable use and conservation of natural resources. This kind of cooperation is critical for fulfilling obligations to existing generations, without conceding the requirements of subsequent generations. Much attention needs to be given by states to the means of attaining this kind of cooperation and sustainability for the benefit of mankind. This is so, particularly as this kind of development would facilitate developing nations' capacity to encourage investors in natural resources to adopt more responsible behaviour.

110 Margot E. Salomon, 'Winners and Others: Accounting for International Law's Favourites', in Conor Gearty and Costas Douzinas (eds), *The Cambridge Companion to Human Rights Law* (Cambridge University Press, 2012) 271, 279

Part II

Balancing competing interests

Foreword

Kamal Hossain

The collection of papers published in this volume entitled *International Natural Resources Law, Investment and Sustainability* is timely as it comes soon after the adoption of the United Nations Declaration on Sustainable Development in September 2015 and the first report of the International Law Association's Committee on Sustainable Natural Resources Management for Development in 2016. The analyses of different legal aspects of the complex concept of sustainable development will be valuable, in particular, for those devising national strategies for implementation of the Sustainable Development Goals (SDGs).

The UN Declaration views SDGs as integrated and indivisible, and as aimed to balance three dimensions of sustainable development – economic, social and environmental. Juristic writings such as those published in this volume would promote a better understanding of the different dimensions of the complex concept.

These papers have dealt with a wide range of issues, which include: the role of law for resource protection and regulatory strategies devised for this purpose, protection provided by regional and bilateral investment agreements and an exploration of how these agreements have aimed to secure an equitable balance between the interests of host states and foreign investors. Another paper has analysed existing World Trade Organization (WTO) rules relevant for natural resources management and the relationship between those rules and the principle of sustainable development. Other papers have dealt with the impact of state-owned oil companies (North–South) and (South–South) on investments, and arbitration and natural resource protection.

The considerable body of juristic writings recognises the multifaceted character of the concept of sustainable development. The challenge of change which societies face in different stages of development has needed a framework which would identify and elucidate the different facets of sustainable development. Juristic writings such as those contained in this volume contribute to a better understanding of the different dimensions of the complex concept, which is necessary if appropriate policies and strategies are to be devised to realise sustainable development.

4 Natural resources management and sustainable development in the WTO legal system

Implications for the investment regime

Ilaria Espa

Introduction

Demand for natural resources has grown exponentially in recent years and, with it, international trade in commodities.[1] A number of structural and cyclical factors are responsible for the accrued attention on natural resources in the international markets. First, the major ongoing transformations occurring in China and other emerging economies, from urbanization to industrialization, have created unprecedented demand for energy and other extractive resources.[2] Second, the dynamics at the root of the 2000s commodity 'supercycle' have increased competition for scarce and heavily geographically concentrated natural resources,[3] challenging the traditional South–North patterns against the backdrop of skyrocketing commodities prices.[4] The sudden and profound reversal of this trend as of the mid-2010s,

1 Christophe Bellmann, 'Trade and Investment Frameworks in Extractive Industries: Challenges and Options' (E15 Expert Group on Trade and Investment in Extractive Industries Policy Options Paper, International Centre for Trade and Sustainable Development and World Economic Forum, January 2016) 4–5

2 The exceptional economic performances of China in the last decades were driven by the expansion of the construction sector: Masuma Farooki and Raphael Kaplinsky, *The Impact of China on Global Commodities Prices: The Global Reshaping of the Resource Sector* (Routledge, 2012) 117–139. More generally, emerging economies are at a stage of development which requires a much more intensive use of primary resources: Marian Radetzski, *A Handbook of Primary Commodities in the Global Economy* (Cambridge University Press, 2010) 7–12

3 Starting from the mid-2000s, the rising demand for natural resources met with a tight supply caused by the low investment that had followed decades of declining commodities prices: Gordon Peeling and others, 'Increasing Demand for and Restricted Supply of Raw Materials' in OECD, *The Economic Impact of Export Restrictions on Raw Materials* (OECD Publishing, 2010) 155, 156–157. Because of the lagged response of supply characterizing the extractive sector, actual capacity expansion could not timely materialize and the prices of commodities 'boomed': Radetzski (n 2) 70–72

4 These dynamics are thoroughly described in Ilaria Espa, *Export Restrictions on Critical Minerals and Metals: Testing the Adequacy of WTO Disciplines* (Cambridge University Press, 2015) 48–66

with energy and other natural resources prices plunging to their lowest levels in more than a decade, has moreover brought back the issue of commodity price volatility.[5]

Under such conditions, resource-abundant developing countries have focused on finding ways that would allow them to benefit from the wealth created by their endowments without getting locked into a pattern of commodity dependence.[6] At the same time, they have showed increased awareness of the social costs and the environmental impacts linked to extractive activities, from local communities' displacement to conflict, from health and environmental risks to exhaustible natural resources depletion.[7]

Economic, social and environmental concerns have led to the introduction of a wide range of policies and policy instruments revolving around the sustainability of natural resource extraction, use and disposal in these countries.[8] Some more directly respond to economic development rationales. Resource-rich countries have in particular balanced foreign direct investment (FDI) attraction policies and industrial policies such as local content requirements in the attempt to promote economic diversification, create local jobs and thus reduce poverty and boost prosperity.[9] Other measures clearly address non-economic objectives. Environmental protection in a broad sense, in particular, has inspired many natural resource management measures, including resource taxes, volume restrictions on mining and production and pollution taxes.[10]

5 Commodity price volatility translates into instability of export revenues, which in turn exposes countries to trade imbalances and, therefore, to balance of payments disequilibria and exchange rate fluctuations: Hannah Bargawi and others, 'Low-Income Countries and Commodity Price Volatility' in Thomas Cottier and Panagiotis Delimatsis (eds), *The Prospects of International Trade Regulation: From Fragmentation to Coherence* (Cambridge University Press, 2011) 452, 464–471

6 According to UNCTAD, two-thirds of all developing countries rely on primary resources (mineral, agricultural and energy commodities) for more than 50 per cent of their export earnings. This percentage grows to 80 per cent for half of the developing countries located in the African continent: UNCTAD, 'State of Commodity Dependence 2012' (UNCTAD, 2012) <www10.iadb.org/intal/intalcdi/PE/2012/12065.pdf> accessed 10 February 2016. Commodity-dependent developing countries are particularly vulnerable to strong price fluctuations over the business cycle

7 OECD, 'Minerals and Pro-Poor Growth: The Economics and Politics' (DAC Guidelines and Reference Series, OECD Publishing 2008) 138–139

8 Bellmann (n 1) 4–8

9 Isabelle Ramdoo, 'Unpacking Local Content Requirements in the Extractive Sector: What Implications for the Global Trade and Investment Frameworks?' (E15 Expert Group on Trade and Investment in Extractive Industries Think Piece, International Centre for Trade and Sustainable Development and World Economic Forum, September 2015)

10 E.g., Michele Ruta and Anthony J. Venables, 'International Trade in Natural Resources: Practice and Policy' (2012) 4 *Annual Review of Resource Economics* 331; Kristina Söderholm and others, 'Environmental Regulation and Mining Sector Competitiveness: Mining and Sustainable Development' (Luleå University of Technology, 2014) <www.ltu.se/cms_fs/1.124549!/file/rapport%20Environmental%20Regulation%20and%20Mining_low.pdf> accessed 11 February 2016

At times, however, the contours of a measure are more difficult to attribute neatly, and a single measure may practically fulfil a multiplicity of economic, social and/or environmental goals if it is implemented in the context of more comprehensive conservation policies encompassing a wider array of interacting measures.[11] In such cases, resource-abundant countries often insist on the need to respond to sustainable development concerns more generally, and frequently invoke the international law principle of permanent sovereignty over natural resources because of its strong developmental and environmental connotations.[12] Yet, in most cases, measures of this sort may have a de facto negative impact on investment on natural resource extraction inasmuch as their trade implications cause uncertainty in the international markets. The extractive sector is in fact particularly vulnerable to market fluctuations and trade disruptions due to the high geological concentration of natural resources, the time disconnect between investment decisions and extraction itself, and other sector-specific factors such as low supply elasticity induced by the high capital costs and the long-term payback perspectives characterizing the extractive industries.[13]

An illustrative example is the case of export restrictions (e.g., taxes, quotas, licensing schemes) imposed on extractive resources, namely minerals and metals and energy commodities.[14] Such measures have proliferated to alarming levels since the beginning of the financial and economic crisis at the end of the 2000s,[15] causing great turbulence in the international markets and de facto influencing investment choices on natural resources exploitation.[16]

11 European Commission Directorate-General for Trade, 'Ninth Report on Potentially Trade-Restrictive Measures Identified in the Context of the Financial and Economic Crisis September 2011 – 1 May 2012' (European Commission, 2012) <http://trade.ec.europa.eu/doclib/docs/2012/june/tradoc_149526.pdf> accessed 12 February 2016

12 Nico Schrijver, *Sovereignty over Natural Resources: Balancing Rights and Duties* (2nd edn, Cambridge University Press, 2008) 391–394; Bellmann (n 1) 5

13 Jane Korinek and Jeonghoi Kim, 'Export Restrictions on Strategic Raw Materials and their Impact on Trade and Global Supply' in OECD, *The Economic Impact of Export Restrictions on Raw Materials* (OECD Publishing, 2010) 103, 119; K.C. Fung and Jane Korinek, 'Economics of Export Restrictions as Applied to Industrial Raw Materials' (OECD Trade Policy Papers No. 155, OECD Publishing, 2013) 27–28

14 Ilaria Espa, 'Export Restrictions in Relation to Extractive Industries' (E15 Expert Group on Trade and Investment in Extractive Industries Think Piece, International Centre for Trade and Sustainable Development and World Economic Forum, November 2015)

15 *Report to the TPRB from the Director-General on Trade-Related Developments: Mid-November 2013 to Mid-May 2014*, WTO Doc WT/TPR/OV/W/8 (27 June 2014) 23; Espa, *Export Restrictions on Critical Minerals and Metals* (n 4) 8–11, 22–31

16 The use of export restrictions may have an impact on investment in natural resources owing to two main reasons: (1) companies may shift investment from the country imposing the export restriction to their mining operations elsewhere in order to benefit from higher world prices and avoid the restrictive measures; and (2) companies may engage in less investment than they would normally do due to the uncertainty caused by the introduction of such measures: Fung and Korinek (n 13) 27–29

The imposing governments contend that such measures form part of broader conservation policies aimed at achieving a more sustainable pace of extraction.[17] Standard economic theory indeed predicts that the use of export restrictions could mitigate the negative environmental externalities linked to extractive activities inasmuch as the reduction in the domestic price of restricted products may, under certain conditions, induce a decline in domestic production, thus preserving finite natural resources from depletion.[18] Net-importing countries, however, consider them as industrial policy measures, which subsidize domestic downstream producers to the detriment of foreign competitors.[19] Accordingly, they point to those cases where the empirical effects of export restrictions have contradicted or impaired alleged environmental rationales in the imposing countries, namely through inducing an increase in the exportation of higher value-added products on the part of domestic industries that avail themselves of restricted – and thus cheaper – raw materials.[20]

Because of their limiting effects on international trade, measures of this sort have gained centre stage in the World Trade Organization (WTO). At first, the tensions between resource-rich countries and net-importing countries crystallized around the question of whether WTO rules are well-equipped to ensure fair and predictable access to natural resources, given the heavily traded nature of extractive resources, on the one hand, and the increased competition for access to such resources, on the other hand.[21] It became soon clear, however, that the discourse on access could not capture alone the complex reality of natural resource management for development. Resource-abundant WTO members started evoking their inalienable right to manage national exhaustible resources in accordance with sustainable development needs.[22] In parallel, they have questioned the allegedly insufficient policy space left by WTO rules to ensure a fair distribution of the benefits arising from the exploitation of national resources in a way that still addresses social and environmental sustainability concerns.[23]

Against this backdrop, this chapter explores how key principles of the evolving international law of sustainable development have been reflected in the law and practice of the WTO, focusing on the principle of sustainable management of exhaustible natural resources for development. Assessing to

17 Espa, 'Export Restrictions in relation to Extractive Industries' (n 14)
18 Fung and Korinek (n 13) 27
19 For a thorough analysis of the effects of export restrictions in theory and in practice, Korinek and Kim (n 13); Fung and Korinek (n 13) 31–35. The complexity of the interface between declared policy goals of export restrictions, effects predicted by theoretical economic models, and empirical evidence is analysed in Espa, *Export Restrictions on Critical Minerals and Metals* (n 4) 101–123
20 Espa, *Export Restrictions on Critical Minerals and Metals* (n 4) 119–122
21 Bellmann (n 1) 4
22 Espa, *Export Restrictions on Critical Minerals and Metals* (n 4) 231–244
23 Bellmann (n 1) 8

what extent such principles have been integrated into the WTO legal system is instrumental to discussing what is the possible impact of WTO law on investment on natural resources exploitation due to the increased interaction between the international trade and investment regimes.[24] The chapter is organized as follows. The next section identifies the existing WTO rules and flexibilities relevant to sustainable natural resources management. After that the chapter examines how such rules and exceptions have been interpreted in recent WTO jurisprudence, paying due regard to the relationship between such rules and the principle of sustainable development enshrined in the Preamble of the WTO Agreement. The next section discusses what is the policy space left to WTO members to pursue natural resource management goals through trade-related policy instruments. In particular, it does so in light of how recent WTO case law has interpreted existing rules and flexibilities in light of other international law principles relevant to sustainable natural resources management. Accordingly, the next section discusses the potential impact of WTO law on sustainable investment in natural resources, namely by means of express usage of WTO-based flexibilities, including those relevant to sustainable natural resources management, in investment treaties. Finally, the chapter draws some conclusions on the adequacy of the global trading system to effectively respond to the major sustainable development challenges posed by natural resources exploitation and, in turn, on the appropriateness of the standards set by the WTO regime for the regulation of investment in the natural resources sector.

WTO rules relevant to sustainable natural resources management

The WTO legal system does not contain specific rules governing trade in natural resources. Issues of ownership are left outside the WTO mandate, and natural resources are subject to WTO rules once they are extracted and enter into trade.[25] Internationally traded natural resources are thus treated as any other goods in WTO law.[26] They fall within the scope of the generic WTO Agreement applicable to trade in goods, the General Agreement on Tariffs and Trade (GATT).[27]

24 Jürgen Kurtz, *The WTO and International Investment Law* (Cambridge University Press, 2016)

25 It is generally recognized that WTO rules do not apply to natural resources in their natural state: Alan Yanovich, 'WTO Rules and the Energy Sector' in Yulia Selivanova (ed.), *Regulation of Energy in International Trade Law* (Kluwer Law International, 2011) 1, 3

26 Concerns about the absence of sectoral rules have been expressed in particular with regard to energy resources: Thomas Cottier and others, 'Energy Law and Policy' in Cottier and Delimatsis (n 5) 211

27 *Marrakesh Agreement Establishing the World Trade Organization*, opened for signature 15 April 1994, 1867 UNTS 3 (entered into force 1 January 1995) annex 1A ('General Agreement on Tariffs and Trade 1994') [hereinafter GATT]

The GATT is based on the cornerstone principles of gradual elimination of tariffs and absolute prohibition of quantitative restrictions.[28] On a general level, WTO members may introduce and/or maintain tariffs and other domestic instruments in accordance with the most-favoured nation and the national-treatment clauses, namely two facets of the principle of non-discrimination that permeates the GATT.[29] Members may however deviate from GATT rules in accordance with the general exceptions recognized under Article XX GATT. Article XX lists a number of legitimate public policy goals under paragraphs (a) to (j), which may be invoked to justify otherwise GATT-inconsistent measures.[30] Among them are a number of non-economic public policy goals that may be of particular relevance for resource-abundant countries willing to address the array of sustainability concerns linked to natural resources exploitation. Under paragraph (b), in particular, WTO members may justify measures 'necessary to protect human, animal or plant life or health'; under paragraph (g), they can seek an exception from GATT rules for measures 'related to the conservation of exhaustible natural resources if such measures are made effective in conjunction with restrictions on domestic production or consumption'. Other Article XX exceptions protect economic interests more or less related to industrial policy concerns. Article XX(i) allows members to derogate from GATT rules when imposing 'restrictions on exports of domestic materials necessary to ensure essential quantities of such materials to a domestic processing industry during periods when the domestic price of such materials is held below the world price as part of a governmental stabilization plan', whereas Article XX(j) justifies measures 'essential to the acquisition or distribution of products in general or local short supply'. These latter grounds seem less directly relevant to sustainable natural resource management than the 'environmental' exceptions recognized under Article XX(b) and Article XX(g) GATT. If looked at from a natural resources perspective, Article XX(i) and (j) implicitly encourage members to maximize the exploitation of national resources domestically, irrespective of its impacts on sustainability.[31]

28 Petros C. Mavroidis, *Trade in Goods* (2nd edn, Cambridge University Press, 2012) 56–128

29 Ibid 129–152, 231–289

30 As per the chapeau of Article XX, moreover, a measure that falls within the range of policies enumerated under the letters (a) to (j) can seek justification only if it is not 'applied in a manner which would constitute a means of arbitrary or unjustifiable discrimination between countries where the same conditions prevail, or a disguised restriction on international trade'

31 In other words, they exclusively address the economic facet of resource exploitation (i.e. industrial development) from a national perspective. For an overview of the negotiating history of the 'industrial' exceptions under Article XX, see WTO, 'World Trade Report 2010' (WTO, 2010) 168 <www.wto.org/english/res_e/booksp_e/anrep_e/ world_trade_report10_e.pdf> accessed 18 February 2016

Importantly, the set of Article XX GATT exceptions are, together with all exceptions contained in the Agreement, incorporated by express reference in the Trade-Related Investment Measures (TRIMs) Agreement. As it is known, this WTO Agreement is based on existing GATT disciplines on trade in goods and, although not concerned with the regulation of foreign investment itself, it represents a first attempt to address the link between trade and investment.[32] In particular, it focuses on investment measures that infringe the cornerstone principles of national treatment and absolute prohibition of quantitative restrictions under GATT Articles III and XI. While the Agreement does not define the term 'trade-related investment measure', it contains in an annex an illustrative list of measures that are inconsistent with such principles, which includes local content requirements. Such measures are particularly widespread in the natural resources sector, with recent statistics showing that more than 90 per cent of resource-abundant countries maintain at least one form of local content requirement,[33] either in the form of quantitative requirements (e.g. legally binding targets such as the number of contracts to be granted to local suppliers or the number of local workers to be employed) or qualitative requirements (e.g. transfer of technology, staff training).[34] Accordingly, the deep integration model chosen to harmonize GATT general exceptions and TRIMs exceptions bears a relevance for the natural resource sector as trade-related investment measures employed in the extractives may be justified under the existing GATT exceptions relevant to natural resource management.[35]

The incorporation of non-economic public policy goals notwithstanding, neither the GATT nor the TRIMs Agreement mention the principle of sustainable development explicitly. Express reference to sustainable development can however be found in the preamble of the Agreement Establishing the WTO.[36] According to the first recital of the preamble, trade in and of itself is not the ultimate goal of the global trading system; rather, WTO members recognize that:

> their relations in the field of trade and economic endeavour should be conducted with a view to raising standards of living, ensuring full

32 WTO, 'Agreement on Trade Related Investment Measures' (WTO) <www.wto.org/english/tratop_e/invest_e/invest_info_e.htm> accessed 23 July 2016

33 Richard Dobbs and others, *Reversing the Curse: Maximising the Potential of Resource-Driven Economies* (McKinsey Global Institute, December 2013)

34 Ramdoo (n 9) 2

35 *Agreement on Trade-Related Investment Measures*, open for signature 15 April 1994, 1868 UNTS 186 (entered into force 1 January 1995) [hereinafter TRIMS Agreement], Art: 'All exceptions under GATT 1994 shall apply, as appropriate, to the provisions of this Agreement'

36 *Marrakesh Agreement Establishing the World Trade Organization*, opened for signature 15 April 1994, 1867 UNTS 3 (entered into force 1 January 1995) [hereinafter 'Marrakesh Agreement']

> employment and a large and steadily growing volume of real income and effective demand, and expanding the production of and trade in goods and services, ***while allowing for the optimal use of the world's resources in accordance with the objective of sustainable development, seeking both to protect and preserve the environment*** and to enhance the means for doing so in a manner consistent with their respective needs and concerns at different levels of economic development.
>
> (Emphasis added)

The preamble of the Marrakesh Agreement is particularly important when it comes to interpreting GATT rules relevant to natural resources management. Based on a consistent WTO jurisprudence, the preamble informs all the covered agreements including the GATT.[37] In *US–Shrimp*, in particular, the Appellate Body noted:

> this language demonstrates a recognition by WTO negotiators that optimal use of the world's resources should be made in accordance with the objective of sustainable development. As this preambular language reflects the intentions of negotiators of the WTO Agreement, we believe it must add colour, texture and shading to our interpretation of the agreements annexed to the WTO Agreement, in this case, the GATT 1994.[38]

This reasoning is all the more relevant as the measure at issue in the *US–Shrimp* dispute was an import ban implemented by the US for resource conservation purposes, namely the protection of sea turtles from certain harmful shrimp fishing techniques.[39] The Appellate Body affirmed in that occasion that the preamble of the Marrakesh Agreement imparts meaning to Article XX(g) GATT.[40] The objective of sustainable development can thus have a bearing in the interpretation of GATT rules that are relevant for natural resource management. This carries potential for the accommodation of greater levels of flexibility for states willing to pursue public policy objectives linked to sustainable management of natural resources in the investment. As we shall see below, investment treaties have in fact progressively envisaged express usage of GATT-based exceptions.[41]

37 E.g., Appellate Body Report, *European Communities – Conditions for the Granting of Tariff Preferences to Developing Countries*, WTO Doc WT/DS246/AB/R (20 April 2004) DSR 2004:III, 925, para 161

38 Appellate Body Report, *United States – Import Prohibition of Certain Shrimp and Shrimp Products* WTO Doc WT/DS58/AB/R (6 November 1998) DSR 1998:VII, 2755, para 153 [hereinafter '*US–Shrimp*']

39 For a complete yet synthetic overview of the dispute, Dukgeun Ahn, 'Environmental Disputes in the GATT/WTO: Before and After US-Shrimp Case' (1997) 20 *Michigan Journal of International Law* 819

40 Appellate Body Report, *US–Shrimp*, paras 129–131

41 See section 'Implications for the investment regime' below

Natural resource management and sustainable development in recent WTO jurisprudence

The existence of GATT general exceptions that are relevant for natural resource management and the language of the first recital of the preamble of the Marrakesh Agreement suggest that the multilateral trading system has the potential to accommodate sustainability concerns linked to natural resources extraction and exploitation. Yet, they do not say much about the scope of the policy space left to WTO members to legitimately pursue the goal of sustainable development in their natural resources laws and policies. The way Article XX(b) and (g) GATT have been interpreted in WTO case law can clarify these aspects and give a better understanding of the conditions that WTO members need to fulfil in order to successfully defend trade-relevant measures aimed at ensuring the sustainable management of natural resources.

So far, a number of disputes that relate to Article XX(b) and Article XX(g) GATT have been decided by WTO dispute settlement bodies.[42] In some cases, the challenged measures were allegedly aimed at promoting a more sustainable management of natural resources, broadly conceived as encompassing both living and non-living exhaustible resources.[43] In two recent disputes *China–Raw Materials* and *China–Rare Earths*, the measures at issue purportedly tackled the array of negative externalities linked to the extraction and the exploitation of minerals and metals.[44] These cases are of particular interest for this study irrespective of the fact that China could not justify its regime of export restrictions. By dissecting China's arguments and discussing the conditions upon which they would have passed the legal test construed under Article XX(b) and (g), the WTO dispute settlement bodies shed light on the scope left to WTO members to manage the extraction and use of their exhaustible resources in accordance with sustainable development needs.

42 For an overview of the WTO jurisprudence on Article XX, Aaditya Mattoo and Petros C. Mavroidis, 'Trade, Environment and the WTO: The Dispute Settlement Practice Relating to Article XX of GATT' in Ernst-Ulrich Petersmann (ed), *International Trade Law and the GATT/WTO Dispute Settlement System* (Kluwer Law International, 1997) 327

43 The possibility to consider biological resources such as sea turtles as exhaustible natural resources for the purposes of Article XX(g) GATT was confirmed by the Appellate Body in *US–Shrimp*. For the reasoning of the Appellate Body, see para 131

44 Appellate Body Reports, *China – Measures Related to the Exportation of Various Raw Materials* WTO Docs WT/DS394/AB/R, WT/DS395/AB/R and WT/DS398/AB/R (30 January 2012, adopted 22 February 2012) DSR 2012:VII, 3295 [hereinafter '*China–Raw Materials*']; Appellate Body Reports, *China – Measures Related to the Exportation of Rare Earths, Tungsten, and Molybdenum*, WTO Docs WT/DS431/AB/R, WT/DS432/AB/R and WT/DS433/AB/R (7 August 2014, adopted 29 August 2014) DSR 2014:III, 805 [hereinafter '*China–Rare Earths*']

Article XX(b)

Under Article XX(b) GATT, WTO members can lawfully adopt otherwise GATT-inconsistent measures that are 'necessary to protect human, animal or plant life or health'. WTO jurisprudence has interpreted all constituent elements of Article XX(b) GATT.[45] The meaning of such parameters for natural resource management measures was clarified in *China–Raw Materials* and *China–Rare Earths.*

In order to be justified under Article XX(b), a measure must be designed and structured to achieve the protection of human, animal or plant life or health.[46] The mere assertion that a measure forms part of a comprehensive environmental policy cannot be sufficient to meet the first test imposed under Article XX(b) GATT.[47] A defending party must, in other words, do more than 'simply produce a list of measures referring, inter alia, to environmental protection and polluting products'.[48] It must be able to explain how the measure in question operates to fulfil the objective it claims to address.[49] In the case of a measure adopted for the purpose of sustainable natural resources management, it must be designed to reduce pollution caused by extractive activities and thus the harmful impacts on environment and health linked to such activities.

The second test imposed under Article XX(b) GATT is the necessity test. Based on WTO case law, the necessity test imposes two sub-requirements: first, the measure must 'bring about' or be 'apt to make' a 'material contribution' to the achievement of its objective;[50] second, there must be a

45 In particular, Appellate Body Report, *United States – Standards for Reformulated and Conventional Gasoline* WTO Doc WT/DS2/AB/R (29 April 1996, adopted 20 May 1996) DSR 1996: I, 3 [hereinafter 'US–Gasoline']; Appellate Body Report, *European Communities – Measures Affecting Asbestos and Asbestos-Containing Products* WTO Doc WT/DS135/AB/R (12 March 2001, adopted 5 April 2001) DSR 2001:VII, 3243 [hereinafter '*EC–Asbestos*']; Appellate Body Report, *Brazil – Measures Affecting Imports of Retreaded Tyres* WTO Doc WT/DS332/AB/R (3 December 2007, adopted 17 December 2007) DSR 2007:IV, 1649 [hereinafter '*Brazil–Retreaded Tyres*']

46 E.g. Appellate Body Report, *US–Gasoline*, para 6.21; Appellate Body Report, *EC–Asbestos*, para 168; Appellate Body Report, *Brazil–Retreaded Tyres*, paras 140 and 210; Panel Reports, *China – Measures Related to the Exportation of Various Raw Materials* WTO Docs WT/DS394/R, WT/DS395/R and WT/DS398/R (5 July 2011, adopted 22 February 2012, as modified by Appellate Body Reports WTO Docs WT/DS394/AB/R, WT/DS395/AB/R and WT/DS398/AB/R) DSR 2012:VII, 3501 [hereinafter '*China–Raw Materials*'], para 7.479; Panel Reports, *China–Rare Earths*, *China – Measures Related to the Exportation of Rare Earths, Tungsten, and Molybdenum*, WTO Docs WT/DS431/R, WT/DS432/R and WT/DS433/R (26 March 2014, adopted 29 August 2014 as modified by Appellate Body Reports WTO Docs WT/DS394/AB/R, WT/DS395/AB/R and WT/DS398/AB/R) DSR 2014:IV, 1127 [hereinafter '*China–Rare Earths*'], para 7.145

47 Panel Reports, *China–Rare Earths*, paras 7.159–7.160

48 Ibid, paras 7.511 and 7.171

49 Ibid, paras 7.150–7.156

50 Appellate Body Report, *Brazil–Retreaded Tyres*, para 151

'genuine relationship of ends and means between the objective pursued and the measures at issue'.[51] If such analysis leads to the preliminary conclusion that the measure is necessary, the last step consists in assessing its trade restrictiveness compared to reasonably available alternatives that achieve the same level of protection.[52]

Importantly, a measure cannot be considered necessary based on these requirements if it solely targets foreign consumption while purportedly addressing environmental and health concerns that, by their very nature, are linked to domestic production. This was clarified in *China–Raw Materials* and *China–Rare Earths*. In such disputes, China contended that its export restrictions would bring environmental gains because, by reducing foreign demand of affected mineral resources, they would determine a decrease in the domestic production of such products. Yet, in the Panel's view, China had deliberately failed to take into account the 'pollution that may be generated by additional production in the downstream sectors' that is likely to occur after the imposition of export restrictions on mineral products, absent any corresponding measures targeting domestic consumption.[53] By the same token, the Panel rejected China's claim that the measures at issue were apt to make a material contribution to health and environmental protection by creating a 'virtuous circle of development and environmental protection' in accordance with the predictions of the environmental Kuznets curve.[54] According to the Panel, Article XX(b) could not be interpreted to allow such restrictions 'simply because they help increase growth, and, in turn, eventually reduce pollution'.[55] Here again, the Panel stressed that, when the environmental externalities that a measure claims to address derive from domestic production rather than from exports or imports, a measure that increases the price of a product when destined for foreign consumption only cannot qualify as necessary to pollution reduction within the meaning of Article XX(b) GATT.[56] What is more, measures of this sort could hardly be considered to be less trade restrictive than available alternative environmental measures.[57] This reasoning applies more generally to the case of natural resources inasmuch as the pollution generated by natural resources

51 Ibid, para 145
52 Ibid, para 156
53 Panel Reports, *China–Raw Materials*, para 7.533
54 As explained by the Panel, the empirical correlation between economic growth and pollution reduction depends upon a number of factors including: '(i) the composition of production and/or consumption that moves away from natural resources goods; (ii) the preference for environmental quality; (iii) the development of institutions introducing the proper regulatory measures to address environmental problems; and/or (iv) the arising economies of scale associated with pollution abatement technologies': Panel Report, *China–Raw Materials*, para 7.551. Also, Arik Levinson, 'Environmental Kuznets Curve' in *The New Palgrave Dictionary of Economics* (2nd edn, Palgrave Macmillan, 2008)
55 Panel Reports, *China–Raw Materials*, para 7.515
56 Panel Reports, *China–Rare Earths*, paras 7.173–7.176
57 Panel Reports, *China–Raw Materials*, paras 7.568–7.590

production (i.e. extraction and early processing) is not any different if such resources are consumed domestically or abroad.[58]

Article XX(g)

Article XX(g) GATT allows WTO members to deviate from GATT obligations when employing measures 'relating to the conservation of exhaustible natural resources if such measures are made effective in conjunction with restrictions on domestic production or consumption'. As for Article XX(b) GATT, the legal test to be applied for the consideration of Article XX(g) defences has been defined by WTO case law.[59] In the recent *China–Rare Earths* case, in particular, the Appellate Body clarified the contours of the conservation exception for those cases where the measures at issue target extractive resources.

Under the first prong of Article XX(g), an otherwise GATT-inconsistent measure can seek justification if it 'relates to' the 'conservation' of 'exhaustible natural resources'. The expression 'exhaustible natural resources' has been interpreted broadly by WTO dispute settlement bodies as encompassing both living and non-living exhaustible resources, from sea turtles to clear air,[60] to processed raw materials.[61] In *China–Rare Earths*, in particular, the Panel noted that the measures for which Article XX(g) is invoked do not need to be imposed on 'raw natural resources, so long as the[ir] object … is to conserve, directly or indirectly, such raw natural resources'.[62]

The term 'conservation' was also interpreted in a broad manner in recent WTO jurisprudence. In *China–Raw Materials* and *China–Rare Earths*, the panels posited that a proper reading of the term 'conservation' should take into account the objective of sustainable development as recognized in the preamble of the Marrakesh Agreement,[63] and the international law principle of sovereignty over natural resources[64] as a 'relevant rule of international law

58 Ibid, para 7.586

59 Appellate Body Report, *US–Gasoline*; Appellate Body Report, *US–Shrimp*; Panel and Appellate Body Reports, *China–Raw Materials*; Panel and Appellate Body Reports, *China–Rare Earths*

60 Appellate Body Report, *US–Gasoline*, 14

61 Panel Reports, *China–Rare Earths*, para 7.248

62 Ibid, para 7.250

63 Panel Reports, *China–Rare Earths*, para 7.261 and Panel Reports, *China–Raw Materials*, para 7.373. In both cases, the panels cited with approval the Appellate Body Report in *US–Shrimp*, according to which the preamble to the WTO Agreement forms part of the context of Article XX(g) GATT. See section 'WTO rules relevant to sustainable natural resources management' above

64 Panel Reports, *China–Raw Materials*, paras 7.377–7.381; Panel Reports, *China–Rare Earths*, para 7.262. The principle of sovereignty over natural resources allows states to 'freely use and exploit their natural wealth and resources wherever deemed desirable by them for their own development': UN General Assembly, 'Resolution 1803 (XVII) Permanent Sovereignty over Natural Resources' (14 December 1962); see also section 'Natural resource management between sustainability and availability concerns: How much policy space in the WTO?' below

applicable in the relations between the parties' in accordance with Article 31(3) of the Vienna Convention on the Law of Treaties.[65] Accordingly, the panels acknowledged that WTO members can determine their own conservation policies on the basis of a full range of policy considerations and goals, including their own economic and sustainable development needs,[66] also by means of comprehensive policies consisting of 'a series of interconnected measures and programmes ... which are designed to manage the extraction and supply of [the challenged] resources'.[67]

Building on this interpretation, the panels recognized that a measure adopted as part of comprehensive conservation policies may satisfy the 'relating to' criterion even if it reflects different policy objectives.[68] Critically, there must be a rational connection between the measure at issue and the conservation goal.[69] The existence of such a connection must be assessed in light of the 'design and structure' of the measure concerned[70] looked at 'in [its] policy and regulatory context'.[71] Evidence relating to 'the actual operation or the impact of a measure at issue' may also be considered on a subordinate basis.[72]

The implications of these requirements for measures that purport to ensure a sustainable management of extractive resources were explored in *China–Rare Earths*. Similar to the analysis pursued under Article XX(b) GATT, the WTO dispute settlement bodies clarified that the existence of a comprehensive conservation policy incorporating the challenged measures is not sufficient on its own to prove that they are 'related to' conservation within the meaning of Article XX(g) GATT.[73] More specifically, textual references to the goal of conservation, especially when combined with references to other policy objectives, can be considered towards establishing the required connection, but they 'cannot substitute for a full and proper explanation of how the [challenged measures] are designed to promote conservation'.[74]

65 *Vienna Convention on the Law of Treaties*, open for signature 23 May 1969, 1155 UNTS 33 (entered into force 27 January 1980) [hereinafter VCLT].

66 Panel Reports, *China–Raw Materials*, paras 7.375 and 7.381; Panel Reports, *China–Rare Earths*, paras 7.265–7.267

67 Panel Reports, *China–Rare Earths*, para 7.375

68 Ibid, paras 7.288–7.289, citing Panel Reports, *China–Raw Materials*, paras 7.375–7.376

69 Appellate Body Reports, *China–Raw Materials*, para 355; Appellate Body Reports, *China–Rare Earths*, para 5.90

70 Appellate Body Reports, *China–Rare Earths*, paras 5.96 and 5.111-5.114, citing Appellate Body Report, *US–Shrimp*, para 137; Appellate Body Report, *US–Gasoline*, 17, 20; Appellate Body Reports, *China–Raw Materials*, para 355

71 Appellate Body Reports, *China–Rare Earths*, para 5.108, citing Panel Reports, *China–Rare Earths*, para 7.289

72 Appellate Body Reports, *China–Rare Earths*, paras 5.113–5.114

73 Panel Reports, *China–Rare Earths*, para 7.390

74 Ibid, para 7.406; Panel Reports, *China–Raw Materials*, paras 7.422–7.426

As to the design and structure of conservation-related measures, the WTO dispute settlement bodies clarified that a measure cannot be 'disproportionately wide in its scope and reach in relation to the policy objective of protection and conservation'.[75] In this respect, the use of measures restricting exports, and thus burdening foreign consumers only, was not considered to have a rational connection to the goal of reducing consumption (and thus achieving conservation) domestically in *China–Rare Earths*.[76] This conclusion was reached after noticing the so-called perverse signalling function associated with export quotas, according to which '[w]hereas export quotas may reduce foreign demand for [the restricted goods], they will also *stimulate* domestic consumption by effectively reserving a supply of low-price raw materials for use by domestic downstream industries'.[77]

Through this reasoning, the Appellate Body elaborated on the extent to which sustainable economic development considerations may find protection under the conservation exception:

> Although … a Member's sustainable economic development needs are a legitimate consideration that may be taken into account when deciding whether and how to design and administer a conservation policy, they are not a standalone justification for the imposition of measures otherwise WTO-inconsistent … the panel in *China–Raw Materials* did not suggest that 'sustainable economic development' is itself a goal that can be pursued under Article XX(g), but simply indicated that resource-endowed Members may take their sustainable economic development needs into account in designing a conservation policy that 'manages the supply and use' of exhaustible resources in a way that 'take[s] into account the challenge of using and managing resources in a sustainable manner that ensures the protection and conservation of the environment while promoting economic development'.[78]

The essence of the panel's ruling is that WTO members cannot defend measures which have a 'sustainable economic development' objective, such as supply management, as conservation-related measures.[79]

Under the second prong of Article XX(g), a measure which relates to conservation must be 'made effective in conjunction' with 'restrictions on domestic production or consumption'. A domestic 'restriction' for the

75 Panel Reports, *China–Rare Earths*, paras 7.425–7.430, citing Appellate Body Report, *US–Shrimp*, para 141

76 Panel Reports, *China–Rare Earths*, paras 7.436–7.439

77 Appellate Body Reports, *China–Rare Earths*, para 5.186, citing Panel Reports, *China–Rare Earths*, para 7.444 (emphasis in original)

78 Panel Reports, *China–Rare Earths*, para 7.451, citing Panel Reports, *China–Raw Materials*, para 7.375

79 Panel Reports, *China–Rare Earths*, para 7.460

purposes of Article XX(g) is a measure 'which restricts someone or something, a limitation on action, a limiting condition or regulation'.[80] Examples of natural resource management measures that could be considered 'restrictions' within this meaning were given in *China–Rare Earths* and include: (1) resource taxes that increase the costs borne by mining companies operating domestically, provided that a defendant party is able to submit persuasive evidence that this tax was designed in such a way as to have a limiting effect on domestic consumption and/or production (e.g. by proving that the implementation and/or increase of a resource tax led to a reduction in the sales of a taxed product);[81] (2) extraction and production quotas, as long as they are set at a level which is below the level of expected demand;[82] and (3) volume restrictions on consumption.[83]

Any measure seeking justification under Article XX(g) GATT shall be 'made effective in conjunction' with such domestic restrictions. Based on a consistent jurisprudence, this legal benchmark embodies the notion of 'even-handedness' in the imposition of restrictions.[84] The even-handedness requirement prescribes that a member implement '"real" restrictions on domestic production or consumption that reinforce and complement the restrictions on international trade, and particularly so in circumstances where domestic consumption accounts for a major part of the exhaustible natural resource to be conserved'.[85] Factors considered as indicating that a measure fulfils the even-handedness requirement in *China–Rare Earths* include the existence of some coordination in the level and timing of the announcements of domestic and international trade restrictions, the correspondence in the product coverage of such measures and the absence of a temporal disconnect between domestic and international trade restrictions.[86]

The chapeau of Article XX GATT

The chapeau of Article XX GATT aims at preventing abuses of GATT general exceptions for protectionist purposes. Under the chapeau, a measure that falls within the range of policies that are provisionally justified under the letters (a) to (j) of Article XX shall not be 'applied in a manner which would constitute a means of arbitrary or unjustifiable discrimination between countries where the same conditions prevail, or a disguised restriction on international trade'.

80 Ibid, para 7.307
81 Ibid, para 7.554
82 Ibid, paras 7.521–7.544
83 Ibid, para 7.545–7.550
84 Ibid, paras 5.123–5.127, citing Appellate Body Report, *US–Gasoline*, 20
85 Appellate Body Reports, *China–Rare Earths*, paras 5.132–5.136
86 Panel Reports, *China–Rare Earths*, paras 7.572–7.599

Based on consistent WTO jurisprudence, the 'arbitrary or unjustifiable discrimination' clause is met when three conditions occur: (1) the application of a measure results in discrimination; (2) the discrimination is arbitrary or unjustifiable; and (3) it occurs in countries where the same conditions prevail.[87] In essence, countries can take into consideration different circumstances existing in different countries, but the reasons given for discriminating among them must bear a rational connection to the objective falling within the purview of a paragraph of Article XX and cannot go against that objective.[88] When alternative measures exist which could avoid or mitigate the discriminatory effects associated with a challenged measure,[89] without compromising the level of protection sought by the defending country,[90] the discrimination is 'arbitrary or unjustifiable' within the meaning of the chapeau of Article XX.[91]

In *China–Rare Earths*, the legal test imposed by the chapeau was applied for the first time to measures which were purportedly meant to manage the extraction and the supply of mineral resources in accordance with sustainable development needs, namely China's export quotas on minerals and metals. A number of factors were considered of particular relevance when determining whether the measures at issue had discriminatory impacts, which were not justified by the alleged conservation purposes: (1) differences in the denomination of export and production quotas leading to 'inflating the amount that appears to be exported';[92] (2) differences in the scope of the production and export quotas reflecting a 'structural imbalance' in favour of domestic users to the detriment of foreign consumers;[93] and (3) differences in the criteria used for the allocation of the quotas between domestic and foreign users.[94] The panel also considered that export quotas implemented for a prolonged period of time would still produce discriminatory effects within the meaning of the chapeau even when unused, due to the adjustment they would induce in the international markets over the long term.[95]

Finally, the Panel recalled that a '"disguised restriction" … may properly be read as embracing restrictions amounting to arbitrary or unjustifiable discrimination in international trade taken under the guise of a measure formally within the terms of an exception listed in Article XX'.[96] Accordingly,

87 Panel Reports, *China–Rare Earths*, para 7.350, citing Appellate Body Report, *US–Gasoline*, para 150. The first requirement refers to both most-favoured-nation and national-treatment types of discrimination

88 Ibid, para 7.352, citing Appellate Body Report, *Brazil–Retreaded Tyres*, paras 227–230

89 Ibid, para 7.354, citing Appellate Body Report, *US–Gasoline*, 26–27

90 Ibid, para 7.676

91 Panel Reports, *China–Rare Earths*, paras 7.675–7.677

92 Ibid, para 7.650

93 Ibid, para 7.651

94 Ibid, paras 7.652–7.657

95 Panel Reports, *China–Rare Earths*, paras 7.630–7.635

96 Ibid, para 7.349, citing Appellate Body Report, *US–Gasoline*, 16

it stated that a mere assertion that a measure forms part of a WTO member's environmental policy, without any explanation of the criteria used to design it, cannot be considered as 'tailored to' protect the environment.[97]

Natural resource management between sustainability and availability concerns: How much policy space in the WTO?

The analysis of how WTO rules that are relevant for natural resources management have been interpreted in recent case law has shown that there is still some policy space for WTO members to address the sustainability concerns linked to the extraction and use of natural resources. Article XX GATT explicitly lists environmental and health protection and natural resource conservation among the public policy goals that members can pursue, if need be, in derogation from GATT obligations.[98] The preamble of the Marrakesh Agreement, moreover, recognizes that free trade cannot be realized to the detriment of an optimal use of the world's resources, which should be managed in accordance with the objective of sustainable development.

While the preamble of the Marrakesh Agreement informs all the covered agreements, including the GATT, the principle of sustainable development was expressly considered by WTO dispute settlement bodies as relevant context to Article XX(g) GATT, and accordingly taken into account to 'stretch' the interpretation of the conservation exception. To the same end, importantly, the WTO adjudicators have also interpreted Article XX(g) GATT in the light of the principle of permanent sovereignty over natural resources.[99] They thus admitted that the term 'conservation' in Article XX(g) incorporates the notion of exercising rights over natural resources in the interests of a member's economic and sustainable development, and affirmed the right of WTO members to design their conservation programmes based on 'their own assessment of various, sometimes competing, policy considerations and in a way that responds to their own concerns and priorities'.[100]

97 Panel Reports, *China–Rare Earths*, paras 7.191–7.192

98 Yet, it should be noted that, according to economic literature, the employment of trade measures such as export taxes and other export restrictions is a second-best policy option compared to first-best policy options such as strengthening property rights. An adequate property right regime would in fact improve resource allocation by reducing the rate of extraction up to the point that would maximize rent, thus inducing a terms-of-trade gain for resource-abundant countries: WTO, *World Trade Report* 2010 (WTO, 2010) 132 <www.wto.org/english/res_e/booksp_e/anrep_e/world_trade_report10_e.pdf> (accessed 25 February 2016). Developing countries may, however, experience difficulties in implementing a strong property right regime due to institutional and socio-political limitations: ibid, 133

99 See section 'Article XX(g)' above

100 Panel Reports, *China–Rare Earths*, para 7.459

The explicit recognition that the principle of sovereignty over natural resources has a bearing in the interpretation of the GATT conservation exception suggests that resource-abundant members may have better chances to successfully defend national measures targeting the extraction and use of natural resources for sustainability purposes under Article XX(g) rather than Article XX(b) GATT, which imposes a stronger necessity text. Yet, WTO members cannot expect to legitimately transform the conservation exception into an exception protecting measures that pursue industrial policy goals.[101] This point was explicitly addressed by the panel in *China–Rare Earths*. In its view, the relationship between 'conservation', sustainable development and permanent sovereignty over natural resources cannot be intended as to allow a WTO member to allocate the available stock of a natural resource between foreign and domestic consumers under the purview of Article XX(g) GATT because, once extracted and in commerce, natural resources are subject to WTO law.[102] The Panels' conclusion lies in the premise that the permanent sovereignty over natural resources has to be exercised within the limits imposed by the requirements of Article XX(g) GATT:

> As noted by the panel in *China–Raw Materials*, a State's sovereignty is also expressed in its decision to ratify an international treaty and accept the benefits and obligations that such ratification entails. In becoming WTO Member[s], [States] ha[ve] of course not forfeited permanent sovereignty over [their] natural resources, which [they] enjoy as a natural corollary of [their] statehood. Nor [have they] 'given up' its right to adopt export quotas or any other measure in pursuit of conservation. [They have], however, agreed to exercise [their] rights in conformity with WTO rules, and to respect WTO provisions when developing and implementing policies to conserve exhaustible natural resources.[103]

Based on these considerations, the panels clarified that, while 'conservation' policies may take sustainable economic development into account, measures adopted for the purpose of economic development cannot be pursued under the rubric of 'conservation' within the meaning of Article XX(g) GATT.[104]

In light of the foregoing, Article XX(g) seems to leave WTO members with sufficient policy space to pursue natural resources policies aimed at managing extraction for sustainability purposes. Resource-abundant countries seem however very unlikely to successfully defend measures which have a 'sustainable economic development' objective, such as supply management, as conservation-related measures, especially when such measures discriminate

101 Ibid, paras 7.451–7.452 and 7.459–7.460
102 Ibid, para 7.462
103 Ibid, para 7.270
104 Ibid, para 7.451, citing Panel Reports, *China–Raw Materials*, para 7.375

between domestic and foreign consumers.[105] In this respect, economic sustainability concerns – which are still highly sensitive in commodity-dependent developing countries that are struggling to reap the benefits of natural resources exploitation – are not explicitly addressed in WTO rules relevant to natural resources management. Article XX GATT does include general exceptions addressing economic concerns, such as Article XX(i) and (j); yet, these industrial policy exceptions target very specific situations of emergency, which natural resources management measures inspired by sustainable economic development needs would hardly fit into.[106] The other GATT exceptions addressing economic development concerns, moreover, are only applicable to import quantitative restrictions, which are not of much relevance for resource-rich countries willing to manage national resources for economic sustainability purposes.[107]

Implications for the investment regime

Understanding how the WTO rules and exceptions relevant to natural resources management have been interpreted in recent WTO case law is instrumental to discussing the possible impact of WTO law on the regulation of investment on natural resources exploitation. As it is known, international investment law developed as a 'protective' framework for foreign investors but has progressively evolved into a much broader network whose goals are not limited to investment liberalization and protection. Rather, investment law includes investment 'regulation' through the achievement of an appropriate balance between the interests of investors and the interests of host states to maintain regulatory autonomy and pursue the public interest.[108] Emblematic of this complex and not always coherently pursued trend towards recalibration of investment treaty law[109] is the progressively more

105 In this respect, it is noteworthy that, during the London session of the Preparatory Committee, the proposal was made to drop the requirement under the second prong of Article XX(g) GATT to allow protection of newly industrialized countries with limited natural resources, which could be subject to depletion under a free trade regime. This proposal was rejected by saying that '[o]ne of the ways in which export prohibitions could be used ... is for protective purposes. ... It is possible for a raw material producing country, which wishes to industrialize, to do so behind a protective arrangement which is extremely effective, and that is preventing anybody else getting the raw material to use in his already existing industries': WTO, 'GATT Analytical Index' (WTO) <www.wto.org/english/res_e/booksp_e/gatt_ai_e/art20_e.pdf> (accessed 28 July 2016) 586

106 Espa, *Export Restrictions on Critical Minerals and Metals* (n 4) 221–223

107 For a thorough analysis of the gaps and inconsistencies of WTO disciplines on the export side, see ibid, 169–192

108 Jorge E. Vinuales, 'International Investment Law and Natural Resource Governance' (E15 Expert Group on Trade and Investment in Extractive Industries Think Piece, International Centre for Trade and Sustainable Development and World Economic Forum, September 2015)

109 For an analysis of the many contradictory outcomes in dispute settlement in the investment regime with respect to recalibration, see Kurtz (n 24)

substantial usage of WTO-based flexibilities in investment treaties. Among the exceptions frequently evoked are, in particular, those GATT general exceptions relevant to natural resources management, namely the public health exception under Article XX (b) and the natural resource conservation exception under Article XX (g).[110]

Importantly, recent years have not only seen a consolidation of this practice but a clear preference for more extensive uses of these exceptions in investment treaties, namely through techniques that are aimed at ensuring a closer interaction between the WTO and the investment regimes across various categories of investment treaty commitments, including guarantees of compensation for direct expropriation, fair and equitable treatment and non-discrimination.[111] In particular, newer investment treaties have opted for deeper forms of integration, where WTO law either provides 'the conceptual inspiration for the structure and operation of the investment treaty exception'[112] or is even incorporated by express reference into investment treaties, generally in the investment chapters of the new generation of free trade agreements (FTAs).[113]

The use of both the 'incorporation by reference' strategy and the 'modelling' strategy carries relevant implications for investment in natural resources exploitation due to the large environmental impact of this type of investment.[114] There seems in fact to be growing recognition that, in the case of incorporation by reference, this model entails a wider degree of transplant from the WTO to investment law, which includes the jurisprudence of WTO dispute settlement on the incorporated exceptions.[115] This would imply that investment tribunals would need to align to WTO panels and/or the WTO Appellate Body when they have ruled on any of the incorporated exceptions. When GATT environmental exceptions are expressly incorporated in investment treaties, considerations linked to the need to pursue natural resources management in accordance with sustainable development needs and the principle of sovereignty over natural resources may thus come into play when defining the contours of the regulatory autonomy of host states vis-à-vis foreign investors.[116] Yet, as seen above, such a direct jurisprudential transplant

110 Andrew D. Mitchell and Caterine Henckels, 'Variations on a Theme: Comparing the Concept of "Necessity" in International Investment Law and WTO Law' (2013) *Chicago Journal of International Law* 106

111 Kurtz (n 24) 168–228

112 Ibid, 202

113 Ibid, 194. According to Jürgen Kurtz, there is a third model of interaction based on 'thin commonality', which is common in older bilateral investment treaties (BITs): ibid, 209–227

114 Andrew Newcombe, 'General Exceptions in International Investment Agreements' in Marie-Claire Cordonnier Segger, Markus Gehring and Andrew Newcombe (eds), *Sustainable Development in World Investment Law* (Kluwer, 2011)

115 Kurtz (n 24) 198–199

116 See sections 'WTO rules relevant to sustainable natural resources management' and 'Natural resource management between sustainability and availability concerns: How much policy space in the WTO?' above

would itself pose limits as to permissibility of measures affecting investors in the name of environmental protection, requiring a direct means–end relationship between the exercise of the host state regulatory powers and its regulatory purpose.[117]

The same holds true when WTO rules and flexibilities relevant to natural resources management are used as a model to frame investment treaty exceptions. This 'modelling strategy' is used in a plurality of newer bilateral investment treaties (BITs).[118] In some cases, the wording of the exceptions contains some textual departures from Article XX GATT, which already reflect the state of WTO jurisprudence. This is the case, for instance, of Article 10(1) of the 2004 Canada Model BIT, which is clearly inspired by Article XX GATT and contains, inter alia, an Article XX(g)-like head on conservation that admits measures adopted 'for the conservation of *living and non-living* exhaustible natural resources'.[119] More generally, however, WTO law always has a bearing when interpreting an investment treaty exception modelled after Article XX GATT inasmuch as international law rules on treaty interpretation require that 'relevant international law rules applicable in the relations between the parties' to be taken into account in the interpretation of a provision.[120] As Jürgen Kurtz correctly noted, in particular, '[a]t an absolute minimum, an arbitral tribunal would need to actively consider the WTO jurisprudence on th[e] point and … explain why its ruling is more rigorous and justifiable than an alternative found in the WTO'.[121]

In light of the foregoing, the fact that WTO rules and exceptions relevant to natural resources management have been interpreted in the sense of placing sustainable development concerns over more economically focused development concerns may have a positive impact on the promotion of more sustainable investment on natural resource exploitation.

Conclusions

This chapter explored the interfaces between trade and sustainable natural resources management for development. It started from the premise that the interlinkages between these two areas of regulation crystallize around three main issues: (1) security of access on international markets, due to the

117 For an analysis of the possible shortcomings of a single doctrinal direction pursued by WTO adjudicators and investment tribunals when it comes to interpreting GATT-transplanted general exceptions, especially with respect to the fundamental institutional differences between the international trade and investment regimes, Kurtz (n 24) 199–202. For a thorough discussion on the concept of 'necessity' in international investment law and WTO law, Mitchell and Henckels (n 110) 95–164

118 Kurtz (n 24) 202–209

119 2004 Canada Model BIT, Art 10(1)(c) <www.italaw.com> accessed 29 July 2016 (emphasis added)

120 Vienna Convention on the Law of Treaties, Art 31(3)(c)

121 Kurtz (n 24) 204

increased competition for scarce and heavily geographically concentrated natural resources; (2) economic sustainability, given the risks entailed in commodity dependence and the need to ensure a fair distribution of benefits arising from the exploitation of national resources; and (3) social and environmental sustainability, in light of the negative externalities linked to extractive activities. This chapter focused on the question of policy space left to WTO members to manage national resources in a way that addresses such concerns, as a means to assess the adequacy of the global trading system to respond to the sustainable development challenges posed by natural resources exploitation. It analysed the WTO rules relevant to natural resource management and examined the relevance of key principles of international law of sustainable development for the interpretation of such rules. It discussed the implications of these interactions based on the analysis of the most recent WTO case law.

This chapter has concluded that, while environmental sustainability concerns figure prominently in GATT rules relevant to natural resources management, economic sustainability concerns linked to extractive activities are not explicitly addressed therein. Natural resources policies aimed at managing the pace of extraction for sustainable development purposes seem likely to be WTO-compatible, falling in particular within the scope of the conservation exception recognized under Article XX(g) GATT. Measures which have a sustainable *economic* development objective, such as supply management, are by contrast to run counter to WTO disciplines, falling within the range of policies to be 'sacrificed' in the interest of fair and predictable access to natural resources. Finally, the chapter stressed how the interpretation of WTO rules and exceptions relevant to natural resources management may have an impact on the regulation of investment on natural resources exploitation. It concluded that the closer interaction between the WTO and the investment regimes is likely to have a positive impact on the promotion of more sustainable investment in the natural resources sector.

5 Natural resource protection in regional and bilateral investment agreements

In search of an equitable balance for promoting sustainable development

Shawkat Alam

Introduction

International investment agreements (IIAs) have courted controversy in recent years, as demonstrated by the growing number of disputes between foreign investors and host states. Year-on-year there is a general increase in investor–state disputes reported by the United Nations Conference on Trade and Development (UNCTAD), with 42 new cases being initiated by foreign investors in 2014 alone.[1] Over the last decade, these cases have challenged a range of policy issues, including national measures relating to natural resource protection.[2]

Importantly, these cases have had a significant impact on a host state's ability to effectively regulate natural resources. In a claim brought by Lone Pine Resources, the company challenged Quebec's moratorium on hydraulic fracking that led to the revocation of the firm's gas exploration permits.[3] In another case, a foreign investor contended that a temporary ban on offshore wind farms, to allow for investigation of their health and environmental effects, breached its contract to supply electricity to Ontario, Canada.[4] These cases are indicative of the type of challenges being faced by host states and foreign firms wishing to invest in natural resources, in particular where host states express a policy preference for renewable energy.

Yet against this backdrop, IIAs play a critical role in achieving sustainable development and assisting developing countries to improve their capacity to

1 United Nations Conference on Trade and Development, *Recent Trends in IIAs and ISDS* (IIA Issues Note No. 1, UNCTAD, February 2015) 1 <http://unctad.org/en/PublicationsLibrary/webdiaepcb2015d1_en.pdf> accessed 30 September 2016

2 Ibid

3 *Lone Pine Resources Inc v Government of Canada* (UNCITRAL), Notice of Arbitration, 6 September 2013. Available at <www.italaw.com/cases/1606>

4 *Windstream Energy LLC v Government of Canada* (UNICTRAL), Notice of Arbitration (Amend), 5 November 2013. Available at <www.italaw.com/cases/1585> accessed 30 September 2016

undertake natural resource protection. The World Summit on Sustainable Development (WSSD) recognised the role that foreign direct investment (FDI) plays in achieving natural resource protection, agreeing that investment remains one of the highest priorities for improving economic, social and environmental outcomes into the future.[5] Indeed, in recent years, IIAs have been instrumental in encouraging and ensuring natural resources protection in developing countries. Of the 13 IIAs concluded in 2014, for instance, 11 contained clauses explicitly recognising that environmental measures by host state parties should not be relaxed in order to further investment opportunities.[6] Demonstrating this trend, Article 15 of the Canada–Tanzania BIT, concluded in 2013 and now in force, evinces recognition that departure from measures to protect the environment is inappropriate where this occurs to attract investment. The agreement therefore requires that each party should not waive or derogate from existing environmental measures in order to encourage establishment, expansion or retention of an investor's project within a host state's territory.[7]

So, given recent developments, why are IIAs under scrutiny to deliver on the promise of increased sustainable development? Why are IIAs often criticised for short-changing host states, including developing countries? One answer lies in the conflict between measures within IIAs which seek to uphold domestic measures and policies and provisions in the same instruments allowing for investor–state dispute settlement (ISDS) where national measures are seen to inhibit foreign investment. A recent analysis of ISDS case outcomes reveals that when states' measures are challenged under ISDS provisions in IIAs, it is usually the investor who wins the case.[8] The potential for inequity, based on the challenges posed to a developing state's financial capacity to withstand disputes with foreign investors, is problematic and could lead to a chilling effect with respect to environmental regulation. Of the 42 ISDS cases brought in 2014, 60 per cent of the respondents were host state developing countries, while the vast majority of claimants (35 of the 42) were investors from developed countries.[9]

5 Secretary-General of UNCTAD, *Making FDI Work for Sustainable Development*, UN Doc UNCTAD/DITC/TED/9 (2004) 4 <http://unctad.org/en/Docs/ditcted9_en.pdf> accessed 30 September 2016

6 United Nations Conference on Trade and Development (n 1)

7 *Agreement between the Government of Canada and the Government of the United Republic of Tanzania for the Promotion and Reciprocal Protection of Investments*, signed 16 May 2013 (entered into force 9 December 2013) Art 15

8 In 2015, investors won 72 per cent of jurisdictional determinations and 60 per cent of the decisions on the merits in ISDS disputes: Howard Mann, *ISDS: Who Wins More, Investors or States?* (Investment Treaty News, International Institute for Sustainable Development, June 2015) <www.iisd.org/itn/wp-content/uploads/2015/06/itn-breaking-news-june-2015-isds-who-wins-more-investors-or-state.pdf> accessed 30 November 2016

9 United Nations Conference on Trade and Development (n 1)

In light of the evident disparity between the movement toward sustainable development provisions in IIAs and the barriers potentially posed to the enforcement of environmental safeguards by the exercise of ISDS rights, this chapter will explore the complex relationship between regional investment treaties (RITs), bilateral investment treaties (BITs), IIAs and natural resource protection. After briefly considering some substantive provisions in select IIAs which directly address natural resource issues, this chapter will explore how IIAs – including their standard protection mechanisms and ISDS processes – can promote, and in some cases, hinder the ability for host states to achieve natural resource protection. This chapter will also consider options available to developing countries to improve natural resource protection through the incorporation of *amicus curiae* submissions into ISDS processes and the use of sustainability impact assessments (SIAs) in IIA negotiations.

The relationship between FDI and natural resource protection

FDI, as the Organisation for Economic Co-operation and Development (OECD) defines it, concerns the lasting interest established by an enterprise resident in one economy (that is, the interest of the 'direct investor') in an enterprise resident in an economy other than that of the direct investor.[10] FDI now forms a significant part of financial transfers and activity in the global economy. Each year, approximately US$1.7 trillion in FDI is transferred throughout the global economy, which continues to grow steadily following the Global Financial Crisis.[11] Most FDI can now be attributed to investment in developing or newly industrialised economies, with developing countries constituting 55 per cent of total FDI inflows in the last financial year.[12]

The significant volume and voracity of FDI in the global economy has augmented both the risks and opportunities for FDI to facilitate natural resource protection. To understand how it can create both risks and opportunities, arguments discussing the relationship between FDI and natural resource protection centre on how the scale, composition and technique of FDI can impact on natural resource protection.

First, where FDI generates positive economic growth, the associated rise in economic activity can place an extra strain on the protection of natural resources, as unsustainable practices and environmental externalities are not reflected in production processes or service delivery.[13] This 'scale' effect and

10 Secretary General of the OECD, *OECD Benchmark Definition of Foreign Direct Investment* (4th edn, OECD 2008) 48

11 United Nations, *Global Investment Monitor: January 2016* (No. 22, UNCTAD, 20 January 2016) 1

12 Ibid

13 Ibid

the failure to recognise the impact of externalities can drive domestic regulators to seek a false comparative advantage where the lack of environmental regulation (and therefore reduced cost to production) can be leveraged to obtain FDI inflows. In essence, this is the 'pollution haven' hypothesis that is often argued by critics of FDI when assessing its relationship with sustainable development. In this vein, Moran refers to the 'resource curse', whereby the commercial profits to be gained from FDI in natural resource industries in developing countries result in over-exploitation of natural resources without a corresponding gain in national growth.[14] Extra-market forces, such as the involvement of multilateral institutions in the harmonisation of environmental standards and capacity building for compliance with these, would greatly assist developing countries to ensure sustainable development is given priority. Indeed, leaving developing countries to provide for natural resource protection in the negotiation of BITs and RITs without this assistance may lead to vast sums of natural resources remaining vulnerable to unsustainable economic growth through depletion or potential destruction.

Notwithstanding these barriers, FDI in natural resources has the potential to also improve natural resource protection by changing the composition of economic activity within a host economy. The increased availability of capital in certain industries unlocks the opportunity for increased investment in potentially less pollution-intensive goods or services, and thus drives down the cost of these to the consumer through the facilitation of economies of scale. Moreover, the associated rise in economic activity and income[15] can change consumers' tastes and preferences for such goods towards more environmentally friendly products.

Additionally, FDI has a significant impact in changing the technique used to produce goods or services. This occurs through direct technology transfers between foreign and domestic firms, as well as technology spillovers resulting from domestic firms having to introduce new technology in response to increased competition.[16] This has occurred in Ghanaian gold

14 Theodore H. Moran, 'Is FDI in Natural Resources a "Curse"?' (*World Trade Organization*, 2010) <www.wto.org/english/res_e/publications_e/wtr10_forum_e/wtr10_moran_e.htm> accessed 30 November 2016

15 Cem Tintin, 'Does Foreign Direct Investment Spur Economic Growth and Development? A Comparative Study' (European Trade Study Group, 2012) 15–16. <www.etsg.org/ETSG2012/Programme/Papers/73.pdf> accessed 1 October 2016. See also S.L. Reita and H. Kevin Steensman, 'Human Development and Foreign Direct Investment in Developing Countries: The Influence of FDI Policy and Corruption' (2010) 32 *World Development* 1678, 1691

16 Emma Fan, *Technological Spillovers from Foreign Direct Investment: A Survey* (Asian Development Bank, 2002) 1; Carol Newman, John Rand, Theodore Talbot and Finn Tarp, 'Technology Transfers, Foreign Investment and Productivity Spill Overs' (2015) 76 *European Economic Review* 168, 170. See also World Trade Organization, *World Trade Report* (2010) 81

mining operations where the introduction of bacterial leaching operations has resulted in the elimination of cyanide treatments in gold extraction.[17]

The debate on the consequences of FDI on the measures to protect natural resources by governments is also coloured by several key trends emerging in global transfers. States are undertaking a stronger role in guiding and steering economic development, whilst recognising that unregulated economic growth has resulted in significant social and environmental costs. More than ever, states are becoming increasingly involved in promoting domestic participation in global value chains (GVCs) and using IIAs to encourage 'the right types of investment' to support comparative advantages.[18] This has a particular impact on the political will displayed by governments to protect certain natural resources, such as forestry and fishing, despite empirical evidence continually demonstrating that environmental regulations only marginally affect domestic productivity and international competitiveness.[19]

In addition, the type of investors participating in FDI is shifting. Institutional investors are now competing against sovereign wealth funds (SWFs) and state-owned enterprises (SOEs) for investment opportunities, particularly in the oil and gas industries.[20] Although SOEs constitute less than 1 per cent of the total number of multinational enterprises, SOE investments now constitute more than 10 per cent of global FDI, demonstrating that SOEs possess control of significant concentrations of wealth.[21] As the Natural Resources Governance Institute points out, in addition to increased domestic revenue, a primary benefit of SOEs' involvement in natural resource industries includes the opportunity for a host state to build domestic capacity within that industry,[22] with, ideally, the concomitant development of measures for sustainable exploitation. However, in countries where institutional controls are weaker, leading to corruption and over-exploitation, SOEs may actually inhibit rather than advance broader national development

17 Colin Noy Boocock, 'Environmental Impacts of Foreign Direct Investment in the Mining Sector in Sub-Saharan Africa' (Global Forum on International Investment, OECD, 7–8 February 2002) 20 <www.oecd.org/env/1819582.pdf>

18 United Nations, *Investment Policy Framework for Sustainable Development* (UNCTAD, 2015) 11

19 See Antoine Deschezlepretre and Misato Sato, 'The Impacts of Environmental Regulations on Competitiveness' (Grantham, Research Institute on Climate Change and the Environment, 2014)

20 Paul Blyschak, 'State-Owned Enterprises and International Investment Treaties' (2011) 6(2) *Journal of International Law and International Relations* 1, 5–6

21 United Nations (n 18)

22 Natural Resources Governance Institute, 'State Participation and State-Owned Enterprises: Roles, Benefits and Challenges' (NRGI Reader, Natural Resources Governance Institute, March 2015) 2. <www.resourcegovernance.org/sites/default/files/documents/nrgi_primer_state-participation-and-soes.pdf> accessed 30 November 2016

goals.[23] Therefore facilitation of the technological and institutional input available through FDI, and via RITs and BITs has, by contrast with SOE involvement, distinct advantages for developing countries as long as IIAs are drafted so as to provide effective protection for a developing host state's natural resources and to prevent erosion of this by ISDS action.

Linkages between IIAs and natural resource protection

Natural resource protection measures in RITs and BITs

Despite the importance that FDI plays in achieving natural resource protection, historically, RITs and BITs have not featured prominently as a vehicle for achieving natural resource protection. Generally, where RITs or BITs have reserved social or environmental policy space, the language reflects broad commitments contained in other multilateral trade instruments, including the 1948 General Agreement on Tariffs and Trade (GATT).[24] More specific concerns relating to natural resource protection, such as anthropogenic climate change, remain absent in the majority of RITs and BITs.[25] A study of the extensive range of BITs negotiated by developing South Asian states in recent years confirms that the space accorded to environmental provisions remains, problematically, very limited.[26]

Nevertheless, some RITs and BITs have introduced new measures to provide host states with sufficient policy space to regulate natural resources. Chapter 19 of the Australia–United States Free Trade Agreement (AUSFTA), concluded in 2005, contains several high-level commitments recognising the need for continued enforcement of existing environmental laws of the respective parties.[27] However, despite the commitment displayed by both states to capture foreign investment in extractive industries under the Agreement, Chapter 19 remains silent with respect to implementation of a governance mechanism to provide for adequate monitoring and enforcement.

Pre-dating AUSFTA by a decade, the 1994 Energy Charter Treaty (ECT) contains Article 19(3)(b) which adopts a broad approach to environmental

23 Ibid 5

24 Kathryn Gordon and Joachim Pohl, 'Environmental Concerns in International Investment Agreements: A Survey' (Working Papers on International Investment No. 2011/1, OECD 2011) 7–8

25 Ibid 7; OECD, 'International Investment Agreements: A Survey of Environmental, Labour and Anti-Corruption Issues' in *International Investment Law: Understanding Concepts and Tracking Innovations* (OECD, 2008) 135, 136

26 Pushkar Anand, 'South Asian Bilateral Investment Treaties and Regulatory Autonomy to Protect Environment: Is There a Threat?' (Working Paper No. 2016/119, presented at the Society of International Economic Law Conference, Johannesburg, 7–9 July 2016) 30

27 *Australia–United States Free Trade Agreement*, signed 18 May 2004, [2005] ATS 1 (entered into force 1 January 2005) Arts 1, 19.1, 19.2.2, 19.3.3

impacts.[28] Under the ECT, environmental impacts include human health and safety concerns, issues regarding flora, fauna, soil, air, water, climate and landscape as well as physical structures, cultural heritage and the interactions among these factors. The ECT significantly broadened the scope of what constitutes environmental factors in the RITs arena.

The text of the recently negotiated Trans-Pacific Partnership Agreement (TPP)[29] also contains a standalone environmental chapter that seeks to preserve a signatory state's right to regulate natural resources. Specifically, Article 20.3(2) of the TPP allows signatories to establish their own levels of environmental protection and to establish, adopt or modify their own environmental laws, in an approach that mirrors the North American Free Trade Agreement (NAFTA).[30] Article 20.3(3) also requires signatories to continue their existing levels of environmental protection, thus directly addressing the risk that the TPP may create pollution havens. Whilst it remains to be seen whether the TPP will be finalised in its current form,[31] again these provisions reflect developments which are occurring in multilateral trade instruments such as the GATT.

However, the environmental protections provided by the TPP must be read alongside existing obligations contained in all 30 of its chapters, including provisions relating to protection standards. As the following section discusses, in reality, the protection standards offered within IIAs play a critical role in determining the effectiveness of the environmental protections contained in RITs and BITs, where these are included. In practice, despite the high-level commitments displayed by host states to preserving natural resources, the translation of these commitments into tangible policies and regulations continues to be undermined by the competing obligations set by IIA protection standards and stabilisation clauses. This suggests that there is limited understanding as to the potential for RITs and BITs to impact on natural resource management and scant consideration of the possibility of strategic integration between the two policy communities.

28 *Energy Charter Treaty*, opened for signature 17 December 1994, 34 ILM 374 (entered into force 16 April 1998); see also Energy Charter Protocol on Energy Efficiency and Related Environmental Aspects, opened for signature 17 December 1994, 34 ILM 381 (entered into force 16 April 1998)

29 See 'TPP Text and Associated Documents' (Department of Foreign Affairs and Trade, 6 October 2015) <http://dfat.gov.au/trade/agreements/tpp/official-documents/Pages/official-documents.aspx> accessed 13 November 2016

30 *North American Agreement on Environmental Cooperation*, signed 14 September 1993, 32 ILM 1482 (entered into force 1 January 1994) Article 3.

31 David Smith, 'Trump withdraws from the Trans-Pacific Partnership amid flurry of orders' *The Guardian* (Washington, 24 January 2017) <www.theguardian.com/us-news/2017/jan/23/donald-trump-first-orders-trans-pacific-partnership-tpp> accessed 30 January 2017

Impact of IIA protection standards on natural resource protection

Traditionally, IIAs have primarily been concerned with creating a stable regulatory environment to enable or encourage FDI in a host state. IIAs have achieved this through two primary mechanisms supported by 'umbrella'[32] clauses: the development of 'standard' protection standards and the incorporation of stabilisation clauses. It is both protection standards and stabilisation clauses which present the most contested issues before ISDS arbitrations, and which play a critical role in determining the policy space afforded to host states to regulate natural resources.

Inbound FDI is supported by general investment protection standards provided by international investment law. Generally, these standards include:

1 national treatment, where the host state treats foreign investment no less favourably than it treats domestic investment;
2 most favoured nation treatment (MFN), where the host state treats a foreign investment at least as favourably as investment from other foreign sources;
3 fair and equitable treatment (FET), where the host state is required to avoid subjecting the foreign investor to arbitrary, discriminatory or fraudulent treatment, or treatment that would constitute a lack of due process or a denial of justice.[33]

In addition to these protections, 'standard' IIAs contain provisions which allow foreign investors to claim compensatory damages in the event of expropriation, full protection and security over their investments, guarantees of repatriation and recourse to ISDS mechanisms. Historically, ISDS arbitration decisions have not focused on specific language in IIAs addressing environmental matters or natural resource protection, but have instead examined how these IIA protection standards interplay with regulation seeking to achieve sustainable development objectives.[34]

FET remains the most frequently invoked standard in investment disputes,[35] especially where these disputes have involved natural resources, given FET's tendency to require parties to consider the context, objective, negotiating history and other intentions of parties in determining what constitutes fair and equitable treatment.[36] Gerstetter and Meyer-Ohlendorf

32 Umbrella clauses are provisions within IIAs which allow a breach in investor–host state obligations to be elevated into a breach of a governing treaty
33 Blyschak (n 20) 15
34 OECD, 'International Investment Agreements' (n 25) 135, 137
35 Moshe Hirsch, 'Between Fair and Equitable Treatment and Stabilization Clause: Stable Legal Environment and Regulatory Change in International Investment Law' (2011) 12 *Journal of World Investment & Trade* 789
36 Christine Gerstetter and Nils Meyer-Ohlendorf, 'Investor–State Dispute Settlement under TTIP: A Risk for Environmental Regulation?' (Ecologic Institute, 2013) 10

identify that ISDS disputes involving social or environmental issues, where violation of an FET clause has been raised, generally consider three types of conduct allegedly performed by the host state when implementing regulatory reform: a) arbitrariness and discrimination; b) lack of access to justice; and c) breach of an investor's legitimate expectations.[37]

In *Gold Reserve v Venezuela*, the Tribunal of the International Centre for Settlement of Investment Disputes (ICSID) was required to interpret an FET protection standard in Article II(2) of the Canada–Venezuela BIT which prescribes 'that each contracting party shall, in accordance with the principles of international law, accord investment or returns of investors of the other Contracting Party fair and equitable treatment'.[38] The Tribunal, in interpreting this provision, upheld the notion that investors can hold 'legitimate expectations' and, as this principle is replicated in domestic legal systems throughout the world, suggested that this principle remains a 'principle of international law'.[39] In *Achmea v Slovak Republic I*, the Tribunal also noted that whilst on one hand parties are 'free to adopt the policies that they choose', on the other:

> (investment treaties) focus on the manner in which policies may be changed and implemented, not the policies themselves. The decision in a case such as the present could be very different, if for example, reforms have been introduced in a phased manner together with the provision of compensations for (investors) who were caused loss by the reforms.[40]

This was later confirmed in *Perenco v Ecuador*, where 'the search is for a balanced approach between the investor's reasonable expectations and the exercise of the host state's regulatory and other powers'.[41]

These cases demonstrate that a complex relationship governs compliance with both international investment law and environmental law. In this

37 Ibid 10. The principle of 'legitimate expectations', invoked under the FET standard in investment treaty law, is intended to protect the individual from harm arising from the disappointment by a decision-maker of an expectation on which that individual relied, as a result of the decision-maker relying on a previous, publicly stated position: Michele Potestà, 'Legitimate Expectations in Investment Treaty Law: Understanding the Roots and Limits of a Controversial Concept' (2013) 28(1) *ICSID Review* 88, 93–94, 98

38 *Agreement between the Government of Canada and the Government of the Republic of Venezuela for the Promotion and Protection of Investments*, signed 1 July 1996, [1998] CTS No. 20 (entered into force 28 January 1998)

39 See *Gold Reserve Inc v Venezuela (Award)* (ICSID Arbitral Tribunal, Case No. ARB(AF)/09/1, 22 September 2014) para 567

40 *Achmea BV v Slovakia (Jurisdiction and Admissibility)* (UNICTRAL Arbitral Tribunal, PCA Case No. 2013-12, 20 May 2014) para 294. See also United Nations Conference on Trade and Development, *Investor–State Dispute Settlement: Review of Developments in 2014* (UNCTAD, May 2015) 15

41 *Perenco v Ecuador (Jurisdiction and Liability)* (ICSID Arbitral Tribunal, Case No. ARB/08/6, 12 September 2014)

regard, a central tenet of environmental law – that of due process and adequate participation by those affected by a decision – is also mirrored in IIA protection standards through the development of FET provisions. The challenge for developing countries wishing to improve their equitable natural resource management is in implementing an adequate process which allows foreign investors to exercise their right to due process, and where necessary, adequate compensation in instances of expropriation, but which also preserves the capacity of states to legislate domestically for the protection of natural resources where these are impacted by investment.

How developing countries respond to this challenge when developing IIAs remains a live issue. However, research suggests that the lack of trade expertise and awareness of the impact of arbitration processes and the requirements set forth by protection standards is a plausible cause of regulatory chill in this area.[42] This chill is further compounded by 'mailbox or shelf companies', who establish themselves under a protected home state in order to enjoy the benefits arising from an IIA. These issues, including the coverage of indirect FDI, have resulted in at least one BIT (Netherlands–Venezuela BIT) being terminated on this ground.[43]

Impact of stabilisation clauses on natural resource protection

Stabilisation clauses address the risk of 'capital flight' that may arise out of legislative change by the host state during the life of a project.[44] Stabilisation clauses vary between each IIA, however they are characterised by three different outcomes for domestic legislation: 'freezing' clauses that exempt an investment from the application of new laws introduced by the host state; financial 'equilibrium' clauses which cover the financial loss associated with the introduction of new laws; and 'hybrid' clauses which incorporate both elements as agreed upon by the parties.[45] Both freezing and hybrid clauses have particular implications for natural resources given the historical reliance by foreign investors on measures which protect their exposure to significant losses resulting from capital and start-up costs.[46]

42 See Christine Cote, *A Chilling Effect? The Impact of International Investment Agreements on National Regulatory Autonomy in the Areas of Health, Safety and the Environment* (London School of Economics and Political Science, 2014) 200

43 See Rosalin Diepevenn, Yulia Levashova and Tineke Lambooy, 'Bridging the Gap between International Investment Law and the Environment' (2014) 30(78) *Utrecht Journal of International and European Law and the Environment* 145, 154

44 Andrea Shemberg, *Stabilization Clauses and Human Rights* (IFC/SRSG Research Paper, 11 March 2008) <www.ifc.org/ifcext/sustainability.nsf/Content/Publications_LOE_Stabilization> 4 (accessed 13 November 2012)

45 Katja Gehne and Romulo Brillo, 'Stabilisation Clauses in International Investment Law: Beyond Balancing and Fair and Equitable Treatment' (NCCR Trade Regulation Working Paper No. 2013/46, 2014) 3

46 Ibid

Stabilisation clauses, in and of themselves, do not create a legal impediment for host states in their regulation of natural resource use. The ability to regulate natural resources remains a critical aspect of state affairs as recognised by the ICSID Tribunal in *Feldman v Mexico*: 'Governments must be free to act in the broader public interest through protection of the environment, new or modified tax regimes, the granting or withdrawal of government subsidies, reductions or increases in tariff levels, imposition of zoning restrictions and the like'.[47] However, where a host state decides to implement regulatory change which may affect the rights of foreign investors protected by an IIA stabilisation clause, it is generally accepted that such action is supported by compensation. In *Liberian Eastern Timber Corporation v Liberia*, the ICSID Tribunal concluded that the main purpose of stabilisation clauses was to protect against arbitrary actions of a contracting government through the supply of compensation, rather than to totally impair the sovereign power of states to manage their natural resources.[48] In a practical sense, from the dicta provided in *Feldman*, there is an overriding obligation on the part of host states to supply compensation to investors in circumstances where the state government's actions inhibit existing investment and the consideration of adequate compensation is not a *de jure* impediment to the exercise of state sovereignty.[49]

For developing countries, this obligation has significant consequences for effective natural resource management. Developing countries do not possess the financial capacity to supply adequate compensation, given the high start-up capital costs associated with natural resource extraction. As recent arbitrations reveal, compensation can be substantial. In 2014, ISDS arbitration awards to investors by both developed and developing countries ranged from \$8 million[50] to \$50 billion, the latter being the highest known award in the history of investment arbitration.[51] The expectation that compensation is to be provided to investors in situations of regulatory change can elicit a regulatory chill[52] with respect to natural resource management in developing

47 *Feldman Karpa v Mexico (Award)* (ICSID Arbitral Tribunal, Case No. ARB(AF)/99/1, 16 December 2002) para 103

48 *Liberian Eastern Timber Corporation v Republic of Liberia (Award)* (ICSID Arbitral Tribunal, Case No. ARB/83/2, 31 March 1986). See also Gehne and Brillo (n 45) 11

49 Gehne and Brillo (n 45) 11

50 *Angelia Auto Accessories, Ivan Peter Busta and Jan Peter Busta v Czech Republic*, 2014, SCC

51 See *Hulley Enterprises Limited (Cyprus) v Russian Federation (Final Award)* (UNCITRAL, Arbitral Tribunal, PCA Case No. AA 226, 18 July 2014); *Veteran Petroleum Limited (Cyprus) v Russian Federation (Final Award)* (UNCITRAL, Arbitral Tribunal, PCA Case No. AA 228, 18 July 2014); and *Yukos Universal Limited (Isle of Man) v Russian Federation (Final Award)* (UNCITRAL, Arbitral Tribunal, PCA Case No. AA 227, 18 July 2014)

52 See John Ruggie, *Stabilization Clauses and Human Rights* (International Finance Corporation 2009)

countries. This has a highly detrimental effect on the realisation of sustainable development in developing countries, where the need for legislative reform is most urgent.

Because of the risk borne by host states obligated to supply compensation, there has been a gradual shift towards limiting stabilisation clauses in contemporary IIA practice. This has been achieved through a variety of ways. However, the most common methods include restricting the application of compensatory measures to certain industries, providing compensation to enable compliance rather than for the withdrawal of investment, or applying compensation to a specific type of damage or only when a threshold amount is reached.[53]

Financial equilibrium clauses, which traditionally exist to give foreign investors operational and fiscal predictability,[54] have undergone significant reform to this extent. Contemporary IIA practice has shown the extensive use of these provisions, which allow host states to share in a financial windfall in the event of instituting legislative change, especially in natural resource sectors which contain high start-up costs.[55] Importantly, these measures demonstrate a movement away from 'stabilising' an entire regulatory environment to allowing some forms of regulatory change, as long as such change addresses foreign investors' needs for financial certainty and predictability.[56]

To date, the use of limited stabilisation clauses has been highly concentrated in favour of developed countries. In a study conducted by Ruggie, over 84 per cent of IIAs sampled by the OECD contained some form of limited stabilisation clause, compared to 27 per cent for sub-Saharan African IIAs, 15 per cent for Middle Eastern and Northern African IIAs and 10 per cent for Central Asian IIAs. Of the non-OECD countries which did possess a limited stabilisation clause, over 90 per cent of these clauses still provided an opportunity for the investor to claim compensation against social and environmental measures of general application, even if they are not discriminatory to a specific investor.[57] Importantly, studies such as these continue to highlight the general trend that the increased costs borne by foreign companies for regulatory compliance are passed onto consumers.[58] It remains to be seen as to what association, if any, exists between natural resource management regulation and commodity price fluctuations. However, the

53 Ibid 38

54 Howard Mann, 'Stabilization in Investment Contracts: Rethinking the Context, Reformulating the Result' IISD *Investment Treaty News* (7 October 2011) <www.iisd.org/itn/2011/10/07/stabilization-in-investment-contracts-rethinking-the-context-reformulating-the-result/>

55 Ruggie, above n 52, 38

56 See ICMM, 'Taxing Challenges II: A Studied Approach to Minerals Taxation Regimes' (ICMM Spotlight Series 13, September 2008)

57 Ruggie, above n 52, ix

58 Ruggie, above n 52, ix

introduction in domestic regulation of stronger natural resource protection measures may lead to a technological response resulting in the cost being passed onto the consumer,[59] rather than a total capital flight. This reflects an important reality, yet to be fully realised by host states negotiating IIAs, that social and environmental measures are generally a secondary concern for foreign firms, while other factors – such as the location of resources and associated labour and capital costs – are of primary importance in ensuring a competitive return on investment.

Impact of ISDS procedure on natural resource protection

Transparency in ISDS processes is vital for promoting effective natural resource management, especially in developing states. Not only does increased transparency enable adequate scrutiny of IIAs by civil society, transparency builds institutional knowledge of ISDS tribunals' interpretations of key IIA protection standards.

The current body of case law and arbitration decisions concerning IIA protections and stabilisation clauses remains largely inconsistent and underreported because of a lack of transparency measures in ISDS processes. As UNCTAD noted, there are 'divergent legal interpretations of identical or similar treaty provisions as well as different assessment of the merits of cases involving the same facts'.[60]

There are some measures to address this systemic concern relating to ISDS. The United Nations Commission on International Trade Law (UNCITRAL) Transparency Rules are a set of obligations which promote transparency and accessibility to the community for arbitrations initiated under UNCITRAL. Under Article 3 of the Transparency Rules, documents such as statements of claim, defences, written submissions, transcripts, orders and decisions shall be made publicly available through the Transparency Registry provided for under Article 8. The Transparency Rules provide for some exceptions to the need to make arbitration proceedings public, such as where there is commercial or protected information involved or where disclosure would impede law enforcement capabilities. At the time of writing, there were seven UNCITRAL arbitration cases which have been made publicly available through the UNCITRAL Transparency Register.

One of the strongest criticisms of the UNCITRAL Transparency Rules is that they only apply to IIAs that were concluded after 1 April 2014, unless parties agree otherwise. Under Article 2 of the UN Transparency Convention, the UNCITRAL Transparency Rules are applied to treaties

59 UNCTAD, 'Making FDI Work for Sustainable Development' (UNCTAD/DITC/TED/9, presented at the United Nations Conference on Trade and Development and Sustainable Business Institute at the European Business School, New York and Geneva, 2004) 14

60 UNCTAD 'Reform of the Investor–State Dispute Settlement: In Search of a Roadmap' (IIA Issues Note No. 2, UNCTAD, 2013) 3

concluded before 1 April 2014. Both the UNCITRAL Transparency Rules and the Transparency Convention provide important mechanisms to, at least, partially address transparency issues where parties choose to be bound by the UNCITRAL ISDS process.

In the absence of any requirement for a consistent application of a body of jurisprudence, ICSID decisions, which are usually immune from appeal, have the wide-ranging potential to override domestic law and policy concerning natural resource management.[61] A recent ICSID decision in a long-running case brought by the investor Niko Resources ('Niko') against Bangladesh and several of its SOEs confirms the extraordinarily broad jurisdictional scope enjoyed by the ICSID.[62] The case centred upon the liability of Niko for two blowouts which occurred at its gas wells in the Chattak field in 2005 and the ensuing claim by the Government of Bangladesh for consequent damages. In the context of environmental harm resulting from the blowouts, the High Court Division of the Supreme Court of Bangladesh issued injunctions in 2005 and in May 2016 restraining the provision of payment or benefit to Niko in return for the gas supplied by its operations.[63] In its decision of 19 July 2016, ICSID confirmed its sole and exclusive jurisdiction over any dispute brought under the relevant Joint Venture Agreement between the parties,[64] thus binding the Supreme Court, as an organ of the Bangladeshi state, to the ICSID ruling. In ordering that the parties take steps to ensure that any injunctions imposed by the Supreme Court would be terminated, the ICSID Tribunal upheld Bangladesh's international commitments to the ICSID Convention over and above any decision of the country's highest court.[65]

In disputes concerning the environmental harm accruing from natural resource investments, therefore, a host state's capacity to seek redress for the environmental consequences of FDI is ultimately contingent on ICSID recognition of the issues at stake and the willingness of the tribunal, in its exclusive jurisdiction over international trade agreement disputes, to prioritise environmental concerns over commercial considerations. However, for the time being, it appears that the immediate response by many states in

61 Thomas Faunce, 'Australia's Embrace of Investor State Dispute Settlement: A Challenge to the Social Contract Ideal?' (2015) 69(5) *Australian Journal of International Affairs* 595, 602. See <www.tandfonline.com/doi/full/10.1080/10357718.2015.1048781> accessed 30 November 2016

62 *Niko Resources (Bangladesh) Limited v Bangladesh Petroleum Exploration & Production Company Limited ('Bapex') and Bangladesh Oil Gas and Mineral Corporation ('Petrobangla') (Decision Pertaining to the Exclusivity of the Tribunal's Jurisdiction)* (ICSID Arbitral Tribunal, Case No. ARB/10/18, 19 July 2016)

63 Ibid 1

64 The *Joint Venture Agreement between Bapex and Niko* dated 16 October 2003.

65 *Niko Resources (Bangladesh) Limited v Bangladesh Petroleum Exploration & Production Company Limited ('Bapex') and Bangladesh Oil Gas and Mineral Corporation ('Petrobangla') (Decision Pertaining to the Exclusivity of the Tribunal's Jurisdiction)* (ICSID Arbitral Tribunal, Case No. ARB/10/18, 19 July 2016), 4–5

addressing the encroaching jurisdiction of the ICSID and other similar ISDS tribunals is to carve out environmental and sustainable development issues from being subject to ISDS.[66]

International soft law supporting natural resource protection in FDI

Significant reform is underway to improve IIA governance and align IIAs with best practices. This reform is primarily occurring at multilateral and regional levels, both of which provide a supportive framework for individual IIAs. This reform is further driven by several host states who remain critical of their respective FDI experiences, such as Brazil, and who are currently reviewing their participation in IIAs. For instance, Australia has declared its opposition to ISDS arbitration,[67] South Africa has cancelled its European BITs[68] and Venezuela, Ecuador and Bolivia have totally withdrawn from the ICSID Convention.[69]

International Finance Corporation Environmental and Social Performance Standards

The International Finance Corporation (IFC) Sustainability Framework and Environmental and Social Performance Standards[70] provide a mechanism for incorporating social and environmental issues into investment decision-making. The IFC Sustainability Framework, which only applies to investment and advisory clients who undergo the IFC's client review process after 1 January 2012, prescribes eight performance standards that are mandatory for projects directly financed by the IFC. Where a host country's

66 See *Korea–Australia Free Trade Agreement*, signed 8 April 2014, [2014] ATS 43 (entered into force 12 December 2014), Art 18.9, where 'Neither Party shall have recourse to dispute settlement under this Agreement for any matter arising under this Chapter (Environmental Matters), including such matters as referred to in Article 18.5'. Available at <http://dfat.gov.au/trade/agreements/kafta/official-documents/Pages/chapter-18-environment.aspx> accessed 3 February 2017

67 See Australian Government, Productivity Commission, Bilateral and Regional Trade Agreements (Productivity Commission, November 2010) section 14.2

68 Liang-Ying Tan and Amal Bouchenaki, 'Limiting Investor Access to Investment Arbitration: A Solution without a Problem?' in Jean E. Kalicki and Anna Joubin-Bret (eds), *Reshaping the Investor–State Dispute Settlement System: Journeys for the 21st Century* (Hotei Publishing 2015) 259–260

69 Sergey Ripinsky, 'Venezuela's Withdrawal from IISID: What It Does and Does Not Achieve' *Investment Treaty News* (13 April 2012): <www.iisd.org/itn/2012/04/13/venezuelas-withdrawal-from-icsid-what-it-does-and-does-not-achieve/>

70 See International Finance Corporation, 'Environmental and Social Performance Standards' (IFC, 2012) <www.ifc.org/wps/wcm/connect/115482804a0255db96fbffd1a5d13d27/PS_English_2012_Full-Document.pdf?MOD=AJPERES> accessed 2 October 2016

regulations differ from the Performance Standard, the more stringent standard applies unless justification is given by the investment or advisory client.[71]

IFC Performance Standard 6 requires consideration of biodiversity, ecosystem services and sustainable management of resources into projects subject to IFC funding agreements. Performance Standard 6, shaped by the language used in the Convention on Biological Diversity (CBD), requires IFC clients to manage the impacts on biodiversity throughout the life cycle of the project.[72] Indeed, the synergy between the IFC Performance Standards in promoting the obligations prescribed by the CBD is substantial, with the CBD 11th Conference of the Parties calling upon CBD signatories to incorporate the Principles into business practices.[73]

One of the most effective mechanisms under Performance Standard 6 is the requirement that IFC clients perform a supply chain review when purchasing primary commodities from regions with significant natural and critical habitats, so as to determine whether suppliers are contributing to effective natural resource management.[74] Although the review is limited to assessing the supply chain, instead of also examining how products may be used in environmentally damaging ways, the assessment encourages a greening of supply chains by IFC clients.

In addition, the IFC Performance Standard 1 establishes 'the importance of integrated assessment to identify environmental and social impacts, risks and opportunities' of IFC funded projects. Critically, Performance Standard 1 prescribes increased public participation and community engagement for these projects. Under Performance Standard 1 paragraphs 25–36, investment and advisory clients must engage in meaningful consultation with communities affected by an IFC project proposal, including implementing a grievance mechanism and ongoing reporting arrangements.

The IFC Environmental and Social Performance Standards are further supported by guidance material published by the IFC. The World Bank Group Environmental, Health and Safety Guidelines (the 'EHS Guidelines') are technical reference documents which illustrate these standards and best practices in industry-specific settings. Importantly, the guidance material provides an illustration as to application of the Performance Standards in

71 See International Finance Corporation, 'IFC Performance Standards on Environment and Social Sustainability' (IFC, 2012) 2 <www.ifc.org/wps/wcm/connect/c8f524004a73daeca09afdf998895a12/IFC_Performance_Standards.pdf?MOD=AJPERES> accessed 16 November 2016

72 Ibid 40

73 See *Convention on Biological Diversity*, 11th Conference of the Parties, Hyderabad, Decision XI/7 (2012) <www.cbd.int/decision/cop/default.shtml?id=13168> accessed 16 November 2016

74 See International Finance Corporation, 'IFC Performance Standards on Environment and Social Sustainability' (IFC, 2012) 40 <www.ifc.org/wps/wcm/connect/c8f524004a73daeca09afdf998895a12/IFC_Performance_Standards.pdf?MOD=AJPERES> accessed 16 November 2016

natural resource extraction industries, including in the agriculture, mining, oil and gas industries.

However, there are shortcomings with the use of these Standards. Regarding the IFC EHS Guidelines, there is no specific industry guidance as to public participation barriers that may be faced by certain natural resource extraction industries. For instance, although the EHS Guidelines on Mining recommend consultation with key stakeholders on certain stages in a mining proposal (such as water management and addressing competing land use and biodiversity concerns), there is limited guidance on how proponents can endeavour to create culturally appropriate dialogue with indigenous communities affected by the proposal.[75]

In addition, there is a further issue as to the application of these Standards to investment projects more generally. Notwithstanding that these Standards and the use of the supporting EHS Guidelines are only mandatory for projects directly funded by the IFC, the Standards and use of the EHS Guidelines are undermined by financial intermediaries who pass on IFC funding to firms which provide service delivery.[76] Due diligence in the observation of critical standards such as public participation or transparency arrangements does not rest with the IFC when third party financial intermediaries of IFC funding are involved, leaving such assessments of sub-clients to the intermediary itself. Unfortunately, and as the Office of the Compliance Ombudsman notes, this results in approximately 60 per cent of these sub-clients failing to improve on their environmental and social practices after IFC funding has been applied.[77]

Equator Principles[78]

The Equator Principles constitute a risk management framework, adopted by financial institutions, for determining, assessing and managing the environmental and social risk in projects.[79] Signatories to the Equator Principles are not to provide financial support to investors who cannot, or will not, comply with the principles.

75 See International Finance Corporation, 'Environmental, Health and Safety Guidelines: Mining' (IFC, 2007) <www.ifc.org/wps/wcm/connect/1f4dc28048855af4879cd76a6515bb18/Final%2B-%2BMining.pdf?MOD=AJPERES&id=1323153264157> accessed 1 October 2016

76 Office of the Compliance Advisor Ombudsman, 'CAO Audit of a Sample of IFC Investments in Third Party Financial Intermediaries' (CAO, 2012) <www.cao-ombudsman.org/newsroom/documents/Audit_Report_C-I-R9-Y10-135.pdf> accessed 1 October 2016

77 Ibid

78 For a further discussion relating to the Equator Principles and EITI, see Chapter 8 in this book

79 See Equator Principles Association, 'Environmental and Social Risk for Projects' (Equator Principles Association, 2011) <www.equator-principles.com/> accessed 16 November 2016

The third revision of the Equator Principles contains ten principles covering issues including how projects perform social and environmental impact assessments, facilitate stakeholder engagement, create effective grievance mechanisms with the community and implement reporting and transparency arrangements prescribed by the Principles. The Equator Principles also reiterate the importance of IFC Principle 6.

To date, there are 88 financial institutions, across the spectrum of developed and developing countries, currently participating in the Equator Principles scheme. Yet notwithstanding the growing participation in the scheme, the Equator Principles are not without their share of criticism. Despite a significant overhaul of the Principles in 2006 in order to extend their application to financial advisory services, the scope of the Principles has been criticised as being too narrow, with suggestions that it should extend to other forms of financial services.[80]

Furthermore, as the Equator Principles are implemented by financial institutions, they are also subject to the confidentiality arrangements between these institutions and investors. Significant information relating to project finance is thus withheld from key stakeholders on confidentiality grounds, while the lack of reporting by project owners further contributes to the denial of project transparency.[81]

Extractive Industry Transparency Initiative

The Extractive Industry Transparency Initiative (EITI) publishes a global standard for increasing transparency and civil society participation in the management of oil, gas and mineral reserves. The EITI Standard requires signatory countries to provide a description of the process used to award mining licences. The criteria used to award licences afford strategies for encouraging effective communication between investors and affected parties. The EITI also contains several standards concerning the transparency of production processes used by foreign firms and revenue collection transparency by government.

Initiatives such as the EITI are critical for obtaining increased alignment in IIAs with public participation obligations under international environmental law. This is vital not only to prevent conflict between environmental and IIA obligations, but as Diepevenn et al. observe, to also apply both environmental and investment obligations harmoniously.[82] This includes key

80 See Manual Worsdorfer, '10 Years of "Equator Principles": A Critical Economic-Ethical Analysis' (Osgoode CLPE Research Paper No. 54/2013) 16; see also Oliver Balch, 'Sustainable Finance: How Far Have the Equator Principles Gone?' *The Guardian* (15 November 2012) <www.theguardian.com/sustainable-business/sustainable-finance-equator-principles> accessed 12 November 2016

81 Worsdorfer, above n 80, 19–20

82 Rosalin Diepevenn, Yulia Levashova and Tineke Lambooy, 'Bridging the Gap between International Investment Law and the Environment' (2014) 30(78) *Utrecht Journal of International and European Law and the Environment* 145, 154

instruments such as Principle 10 of the UN Rio Declaration on Environment and Development which provides: 'At the national level, each individual shall have appropriate access to information concerning the environment that is held by public authorities, including information on hazardous materials and activities in their communities, and the opportunity to participate in the decision-making process'.[83]

The Rio Declaration is one among several international documents recognising public participation and which encourage host states to allow public participation in matters affecting the natural environment.[84] Critically, soft law mechanisms such as the EITI Standard allow increased policy cohesion between the obligations set under multilateral environmental agreements (MEAs) and international investment law.

Specific challenges for developing countries

The current trading environment for developing countries poses challenges for the achievement of effective natural resource protection through IIAs. Most significantly, although developing countries are often the sites for critically endangered fauna and flora species, they are also home to large quantities of extractive activities that are subject to FDI.

In Ghana, foreign firms own and control approximately 70 per cent of gold operations, many of which are located within forest reserves including the Tarkwa region.[85] Accordingly, the District Forestry Department of Tarkwa has reported extensive environmental damage due to the mismanagement of these operations, whereby 'flora and fauna species such as snails, mushrooms and medicinal plant[s] on which the local people depend for their livelihood have also become drastically reduced or extinct, leading to the impoverishment of the people'.[86]

The problem of determining investor liability for environmental damage is compounded where environmental laws and standards have failed to be sufficiently codified, or where information about local impacts or matters of environmental significance may be lacking due to inadequate institutional

83 United Nations Conference on Environment and Development, *Rio Declaration on Environment and Development*, UN Doc A/CONF.151/26 (Vol 1) (12 August 1992), annex 1, principle 10

84 See *Convention on Access to Information, Public Participation and Decision Making and Access to Justice in Environmental Matters*, signed 25 June 1998, 2161 UNTS 447 (entered into force 30 October 2001) (the 'Aarhus Convention'); *UN Framework Convention on Climate Change*, signed 9 May 1992, 1771 UNTS 107 (entered into force 21 March 1994), Art 6; *Cartagena Protocol on Biosafety to the Convention on Biological Diversity*, signed 29 January 2000, 2226 UNTS 208 (entered into force 11 September 2003), Art 23 for instance

85 See Aimann Sadik, 'Corporate Social Responsibility and the Gold Mining Industry: The Ghana Experience' (PhD Thesis, Montclair State University, 2013)

86 Ibid

investigation and monitoring by developing host states. Such issues have been raised in the *Niko v BAPEX* case, where the question of investor liability currently remains before the ICSID.[87]

As a significant proportion of natural resources are not directly controlled by host states through mechanisms such as SOEs, there is an urgent need to ensure that developing countries possess sufficient institutional capacity to effectively regulate natural resources to achieve sustainable outcomes. Yet unfortunately, many measures used to effectively regulate natural resources for long-term sustainability have been subject to ISDS, due to the short-term uncertainty that such measures may bring to FDI.

As the International Institute for Sustainable Development points out, the types of measures which have been subject to challenge under ISDS include:

- imposing or attempting to collect new taxes;
- changes in domestic fiscal policy;
- decisions regarding whether to grant developing permits;
- efforts to renegotiate investment contracts;
- government bans on the use of harmful chemicals;
- bans or restrictions placed on mining;
- requirements to undertake environmental impact assessments;
- regulations governing hazardous waste and delivery of water; and, amongst others,
- measures aiming to increase revenues gained from production and export of natural resources.[88]

The current foreign investment environment is becoming increasingly aware of the detrimental impact that previous, unrestricted IIA protections have had, as well as the proposed benefits that conventional IIA protections were meant to enable. In a study which examined the impact of conventional stabilisation clauses on perceived investment risk by foreign investors, OECD countries which adopted restricted stabilisation clauses demonstrated consistently low investment risk ratings, whereas sub-Saharan African economies which adopted similar protections possessed a high or speculative risk rating.[89] Institutional investors may perceive risk to lie in a host state's regulatory environment, even if the regulatory framework evinces similar, if

87 *Niko v Bapex and Petrobangla (Procedural Order No. 12)* (ICSID Arbitral Tribunal, Case No. ARB/10/18, 21 October 2015) 5

88 Nathalie Bernasconi-Osterwalder, Aaron Cosbey, Lise Johnson and Damon Vis-Dunbar, 'Investment Treaties and Why They Matter to Sustainable Development' (IISD, 2012) 6–7 <www.iisd.org/pdf/2011/investment_treaties_why_they_matter_sd.pdf> accessed 16 November 2016

89 Moody's Investment Services, Sovereign Risk Histories (September 2007) 1. Please note that care should be demonstrated with this Service, as a relative short ratings history was relied upon. This assessment was conducted before the Global Financial Crisis, which may affect investment risk perceptions of host economies

not the same, protections as found in the IIA. This tendency implies that wider considerations, such as the location of natural resources and the history that the host state possesses in facilitating FDI into certain sectors, are determinative factors in the decision of a foreign investor to invest in a host state.[90]

A future reform agenda for promoting natural resource protection in IIAs

Addressing transparency and participation in ISDS: A need for amicus curiae briefs?

ISDS remains a central issue for developing countries with current measures, including the lack of transparency, participation and the consistent application of jurisprudence. Yet importantly, and as previously discussed in this chapter, IIA protection standards, including FET, require adequate due process for affected stakeholders in order to achieve compliance. In this regard, the acceptance of *amicus curiae* submissions into ISDS arbitration may address concerns relating to transparency and participation, may also assist tribunals and arbitrators in applying investment law jurisprudence consistently, and may allow foreign companies to fairly contest decisions which impact on their investments.

In the *Suez* case, which considered the admissibility of *amicus curiae* submissions, the Tribunal noted: 'Given the public interest in the subject matter of this case, it is possible that appropriate non-parties may be able to afford the Tribunal perspectives, arguments and expertise that will help it arrive at a correct decision'.[91] The Tribunal went further to state that it will 'therefore only accept amicus curiae submissions from persons who establish to the Tribunal's satisfaction that they have the expertise, experience, and independence to be [of] assistance in this case'.[92]

There is a strong argument in favour of introducing *amicus curiae* submissions. As noted by Gomez, the introduction of *amicus curiae* submissions has increased transparency by requiring parties to a dispute to make available arbitration documents to non-parties for the purpose of preparing submissions.[93] This provides an important check and balance system by allowing

90 See UNCTAD, above n 59, 14 in which it is argued that other investment considerations, not the use of stabilisation clauses, determine if an investment into a host state will be made

91 *Suez, Sociedad General de Aguas de Barcelona, S.A. and Vivendi Universal, S.A. v Argentine Republic (Order in response to Petition for Participation as Amicus Curiae)* (ICSID Arbitral Tribunal, Case No. ARB/03/1919 May 2005), para 21

92 Ibid para 24

93 Katia Gomez, 'Rethinking the Role of Amicus Curiae in International Investment Arbitration: How to Draw the Line Favourably in the Public Interest' (2012) 35(2) *Fordham International Law Journal* 510, 547

non-governmental organisations (NGOs) to advance public interest advocacy, especially in arbitration involving developing country states who may otherwise lack the institutional and technical capacity to undertake lengthy and complex arbitration proceedings.

Nevertheless, the introduction of *amicus curiae* submissions into ISDS practice brings certain challenges for developing countries wishing to regulate their natural resources. Despite *amicus curiae* submissions offering technical expertise which often aligns with the arguments presented by states,[94] *amicus curiae* submissions by NGOs may not adequately reflect the nuanced social, political, economic and environmental concerns held by various communities affected by the dispute. This is a significant issue in natural resource disputes where, given the locality and scale of proposed economic activity, various communities, including indigenous people, may be directly impacted by an arbitration. Developing countries are cautioned to be aware of the principles and agenda driving *amicus curiae* submissions at the different stages of ISDS arbitration.

Maximising sustainability impact assessments

A significant way of improving transparency and participation levels in the negotiation of IIAs includes considering the use of risk assessment tools on IIAs themselves. Impact assessments and evaluation, such as SIAs, can be used to identify high-level social and environmental issues related to IIAs and can provide a mechanism for civil society and third-party stakeholders to offer submissions and participate in IIA creation.

Generally, SIAs begin with a brief, initial assessment or inception report which identifies the issues and objectives of an IIA or policy proposal. Inception reports should be completed before IIA negotiations, so as to frame IIA agenda items from the outset.[95] They should contain a preliminary scoping of the issues, identify which sectors require deeper analysis later in the consultation process, with a brief inception report produced for public consultation.[96] Following the inception report and preliminary stages, an interim report should be produced which implements the methodology stated in the inception report and provides a deeper analysis of social, economic and environmental issues relating to an IIA.[97] In the third and final stage of an SIA, a final report should be produced which considers the feedback obtained in

94 Ibid 551

95 See 'Draft Handbook for Sustainability Impact Assessments' (European Union, 2017) 39 <http://trade.ec.europa.eu/doclib/html/122363.htm> accessed 3 February 2017

96 European Commissioner for Trade, *Handbook for Trade Sustainability Impact Assessments* (Luxemburg Publications Office of the EU, 2nd edition, 2016) 12 <http://trade.ec.europa.eu/doclib/docs/2016/april/tradoc_154464.PDF> accessed 16 November 2016

97 Ibid

the interim report consultation process, with states producing a further position paper on the final reporting findings and recommendations, as well as outlining how they will implement their position in trade policy.[98]

To date, there has been limited use of risk assessment tools on IIAs. The EU Commissioner for Trade mandates that all major treaty negotiations entail SIA and consultation with stakeholders, which can in turn be fed back into treaty negotiations.[99] Over 20 EU IIAs have been subject to SIA, including the EU–Canada Comprehensive Economic and Trade Agreement (CETA). An additional three IIAs are currently undergoing assessment, including the EU–China IIA and EU–USA Transatlantic Trade and Investment Partnership (TTIP).[100]

Nevertheless, a push to incorporate SIAs as part of systemic trade practice comes with specific challenges for developing countries seeking to effectively incorporate sustainable development into natural resource management. Specifically, SIAs require extensive consultation with civil society and third party stakeholders, which comes with challenges for developing countries where their civil society remains relatively weak. Per the EU, institutional and governance measures, such as developing an independent advisory committee composed of trade academics and experts, can assist in the SIA consultation process and improve the quality of SIAs in this regard.[101] But over the long term, ensuring that SIAs remain publicly available and transparent remains an important measure. By increasing the transparency of SIAs and SIA reports, developing countries can share how similar social and environmental issues related to IIAs were addressed and thus improve the technical capacity of developing countries to effectively participate in trade negotiations and identify related social and environmental issues.

Conclusion

The current RITs and BITs framework governing IIAs lacks several important features essential for achieving equitable natural resource management for developing countries. Transparency and public participation are two such critical features missing in this regard. Soft law instruments, such as the IFC Performance Standards, will continue to play an important role in addressing the shortcomings of the current RITs and BITs framework.

However, the use of such instruments will not, in itself, suffice in achieving equitable and effective natural resource management. In this respect, two

98 Ibid 13

99 Ibid

100 European Commissioner for Trade, 'Assessments' (EU, 2016) <http://ec.europa.eu/trade/policy/policy-making/analysis/sustainability-impact-assessments/assessments/> accessed 16 November 2016

101 'Draft Handbook for Sustainability Impact Assessments' (European Union, 2017) 39 <http://trade.ec.europa.eu/doclib/html/122363.htm> accessed 3 February 2017

important reform measures are available to the international investment regime. First, significant reform of ISDS processes, which addresses several key weaknesses related to transparency, participation and a consistent application of international investment jurisprudence, is vital to help build stronger linkages between investment law, natural resource protection and sustainable development. This can be achieved through the introduction of *amicus curiae* submissions as part of mainstream ISDS practice, a practice which will assist developing countries who may otherwise lack the technical and institutional capacity to participate in complex arbitration.

Second, SIAs and other impact assessments are crucial for building the institutional capacity of host states and for encouraging better-informed decision-making. This is vital not only to ensure that a stable regulatory system exists which can address the need for investor certainty, but to also assist developing countries to address specific challenges associated with natural resource management including the lack of technical or institutional capacity to identify and address social and environmental issues relating to trade.

6 Arbitration and natural resource protection

Mariel Dimsey

Introduction

The influence of 'international arbitration' on natural resources is perhaps something of a misnomer. International arbitration, a process for resolving disputes whereby the parties agree to oust the jurisdiction of the courts, cannot in and of itself impact on natural resources. However, particularly in recent years the increase in and development of investment arbitration, has shown that international arbitration provides an appropriate and highly sought-after forum for the resolution of disputes involving natural resources.

Disputes about natural resources are invariably complex and often concern cases in which foreign investment, capital and know-how have been drawn upon in order to enable less-developed states to access and make effective use of their natural resources, often in the provision of essential services such as clean water. In developed countries and, increasingly, in developing and transition countries, natural resources are generally subject to complex regulatory frameworks. Infrastructure projects that aim to 'capture' and access natural resources, such as, for example, water concessions, are generally not short-term projects, but are entered into between governments and investors over long periods of time and involve considerable investment of capital, time and other resources.

The combination of complex regulatory frameworks and long-term investment bears a high risk of disputes arising. If, during the typically long term of a project, the regulatory framework concerning a particular resource changes, investors may be faced with changed circumstances that diverge from their initial expectations and pose challenges in the continued realisation of a project.

Moreover, in general, host states and foreign investors have different expectations from projects involving natural resources. Foreign investors are usually involved because of the promise of a certain financial return, while host states, themselves lacking the necessary technology and other resources, need the investment but cannot ignore the concerns, and in particular the purchasing power, of their population. This divergence of interests can lead to tension in which the potential for disputes is rife.

In certain circumstances, the interests of the public might suffer at the hands of both the host state and the foreign investor from the exploitation of a natural resource. A central aspect of the so-called 'resource curse', observed in many countries rich in non-renewable natural resources such as oil, minerals and gas, is the tendency of governments, upon discovery of such resources, to fail to respond effectively to public welfare needs. Instead, governments in such countries may look for a 'quick fix', which may often take the form of foreign investment, in order to harness large quantities of the resources as quickly as possible. As the cases in this chapter illustrate, this situation can lead to public outcry and unrest, and result in disputes. It more commonly falls to the host state to ameliorate the consequences.

If disputes arise in such a context, an obvious forum for dispute resolution is arbitration. Both commercial arbitration – between private entities, usually based on contract – and investment arbitration – between a foreign investor and a host state, usually based on a bilateral investment treaty (BIT) or other international investment agreement (IIA) – are equipped to resolve disputes about the protection of natural resources. From a merely practical point of view, however, investment arbitration is able to shed the most light on developments in this area, since investment arbitration is generally more transparent than commercial arbitration and the written submissions and awards are available for public review.[1]

This chapter seeks to examine a number of aspects of the relationship between arbitration and natural resources. After addressing the scope of relevant topics, this contribution will examine how natural resources were protected historically, and how their protection has changed since arbitration began being used as a means of dispute resolution in this field. This chapter will analyse both commercial and investment arbitration, both in principle and using case examples, to determine if and how protection is achieved today, and the notable developments in the area.

As this chapter will show, the core issue when examining any interaction between arbitration and natural resources is divergence of interests. In any (investment) arbitration dispute involving natural resources, differing interests are usually a primary cause. Up until now, arbitral tribunals have largely shied away from the task of setting out a clear 'pecking order' of priority of interests. Indeed, this reluctance is understandable because the task is a

1 See, for example, the changes brought about by the revisions to the ICSID Arbitration Rules in 2006, as explained in Antonio R. Parra, 'The Development of the Regulations and Rules of the International Centre for Settlement of Investment Disputes' (2007) 22 *ICSID Review – Foreign Investment Law Journal* 55, 65 et seq. See also in the field of investment such comprehensive transparency initiatives as the UNCITRAL Rules on Transparency in Treaty-Based Investor–State Arbitration (2014) and the commentary thereto by Dimitrij Euler, Markus Gehring, Maxi Scherer (eds), *Transparency in International Investment Arbitration: A Guide to the UNCITRAL Rules on Transparency in Treaty-Based Investor–State Arbitration* (Cambridge University Press, 2015)

difficult one. However, arbitral tribunals should summon more courage in addressing this difficult interaction of interests and tackle the issue head on, rather than sidelining a discussion of such issues or avoiding the need to address them at all.

Arbitration and natural resources: Points of contact

Definition of natural resources

The term 'natural resources' connotes the notion of resources available in the natural environment. Natural resources include basic human rights such as water,[2] but also include resources that are only able to be used when refined from their original state, such as oil, gas, sun and wind. For the purposes of the present analysis, the author has also included 'land' within this scope and focuses primarily on cases involving water, mining rights and land issues.

The Google definition of natural resources is 'materials or substances occurring in nature which can be exploited for economic gain'.[3] In the author's view, including 'economic gain' in a mere definition of 'natural resources' would appear to be going too far, but aptly enough, the 'economic gain' aspect of the definition is quite pertinent in the context of this contribution, since disputes involving economic gain from natural resources underlie many of the disputes discussed below.

Scope of international arbitration

International arbitration is a form of dispute resolution whereby the parties to a contract agree to have their dispute resolved by arbitration. The effect of such an agreement, when correctly drafted, is to oust the jurisdiction of the otherwise competent courts. International arbitration has a number of advantages which make it suitable for the resolution of international disputes. One of the main advantages is, of course, that agreeing to arbitration between parties from different countries means that no party to a contract is subjected to the jurisdiction of a foreign court. In the context of natural resources, this can potentially be a very important advantage because foreign investors will often not want to be subjected to the courts at the

2 On the classification of water as a basic human right see generally Mariel Dimsey, 'Foreign Direct Investment and the Alleviation of Poverty – Is Investment Arbitration Falling Short of Its Goals? in Krista Nadakavukaren Schefer (ed.), *Poverty and the International Economic Legal System: Duties to the World's Poor* (Cambridge University Press, 2013) 159–176

3 www.google.com.hk/?gfe_rd=cr&ei=wF2FWIaXDYSl8weQxojYDw&gws_rd=ssl#q=natural+resources accessed 23 January 2017. The definition could be made more precise by including both 'living' resources, such as agricultural species, and 'non-living' resources, such as oil, gas and minerals. In the context of arbitration, most disputes arise with respect to 'non-living' resources

location of the natural resources, not only due to unfamiliarity with laws and practices, but also often because of the perception that courts in the same country as the location of the natural resources concerned will oftentimes be biased against the foreign investor, corrupt or otherwise, predisposed to an outcome that may not necessarily represent a fair and neutral evaluation of the facts and issues.[4] Consequently, arbitration provides a sound means of addressing such concerns and offers an alternative means of dispute resolution.

Arbitration has other advantages over and above avoiding local courts with all the (perceived) pitfalls that litigation entails. Most of these advantages can be captured by the term 'party autonomy'.[5] Arbitration is generally a tailor-made process, subject to mandatory rules of law at the seat of arbitration. Parties can agree to have their dispute resolved in a particular way, often pursuant to the rules of an arbitral institution. Parties are also able to agree on methods of nominating and appointing their decision-makers, the arbitral tribunal, and can thus select a candidate (usually one of a three-member arbitral tribunal) who is, while still impartial and independent, suitable for resolving the dispute, whether due to the arbitrator's expertise in a particular field, the languages spoken by the arbitrator and/or the arbitrator's familiarity with particular legal systems.[6] Moreover, parties can agree, subject to certain limitations in some institutional rules,[7] that the arbitral proceedings, including written submissions and hearings, be kept confidential and out of the public eye.

Finally, one of the key advantages of international arbitration arises only at the end of the process. The Convention on the Recognition and Enforcement of Foreign Arbitral Awards (New York, 1958) (the 'New York Convention')[8] which has, as of June 2017, 157 member states worldwide, provides courts with internationally accepted standards for the enforcement of foreign arbitral awards. These include, in general terms, the potential for courts to refuse to enforce an arbitral award based on only extremely limited procedural and public policy-related grounds. Depending on the part of the world in which a party wishes to enforce an arbitral award, this international framework for enforcement can be considerably more reliable and certain than the international framework for the enforcement of foreign court judgments abroad.[9]

4 See, e.g., Gary B. Born, *International Commercial Arbitration* (2nd edn, Kluwer Law International, 2014) 72 et seq; Nigel Blackaby, Constantine Partasides et al., *Redfern and Hunter on International Arbitration* (6th edn, Oxford University Press, 2015) para 1.99 et seq

5 See, e.g, Born (n 4) 83 et seq

6 See, e.g., Born (n 4) 79 et seq

7 See section entitled 'International investment arbitration' below

8 330 UNTS 38; 21 UST 2517; 7 ILM 1046 (1968)

9 See, e.g., Born (n 4) 76 et seq, 98 et seq

Historical means of protection of natural resources

It is exceedingly difficult to make general statements about the ways in which natural resources have 'historically' been protected. The answer differs according to not only the resource concerned, but also the country or region in which it was protected. As a general matter, the United Nations General Assembly issued Resolution No. 626 (VII) on 21 December 1952,[10] providing for the right of peoples to exploit their natural resources as part of their sovereignty. This Resolution was the first text in which the United Nations General Assembly adopted the wording 'permanent sovereignty over natural resources'.[11]

The 1952 Resolution was followed – and modified – by Resolution No. 1803 (XVII) on 14 December 1962, which provided that nationalisation measures could only be implemented for public purposes, security or national interest, and subject to the investor receiving 'appropriate compensation' in accordance with domestic and international law.[12] Paragraph 8 of the Resolution clarified that investment agreements entered into by states were to be observed in 'good faith'.[13]

Resolution No. 1803 came at a time when earlier formulations of international investment law, often by way of state–state resolution, or 'gun boat diplomacy', were the norm.[14] This in turn evolved into the international investment law that is 'used' and continues to develop and evolve today. One commentator has described the evolution of natural resources protection through investment law as a:

> process through which a system that was initially a mere exception to the permanent sovereignty over natural resources grew out of proportion, particularly starting in the 1990s … came to be perceived as the rule at the expense not only of sovereignty but also of other considerations such as human rights and environmental protection.[15]

10 *Right to Exploit Freely Natural Wealth and Resources*, GA Res 626 (VII), UN GAOR, 7th sess, 411th plen mtg, UN Doc A/RES/626(VII) (21 December 1952)

11 See Chapter 2 of this book. See also Daniel E Vielleville, Baiju Simal Vasani, 'Sovereignty over Natural Resources versus Rights under Investment Contracts: Which One Prevails?' (2008) 2 *Transnational Dispute Management*, <www.transnational-dispute-management.com/article.asp?key=1211> accessed 23 January 2017, 3–4

12 *Permanent Sovereignty over Natural Resources*, GA Res 1803, UN GAOR, 17th sess, 1194th plen mtg, Supp No. 17, UN Doc A/RES/1803 (14 December 1962)

13 See Vielleville/Vasani (n 11) 4; R. Doak Bishop, James Crawford and W. Michael Reisman (eds), *Foreign Investment Disputes: Cases, Materials and Commentary* (2nd edn, Kluwer Law International, 2014) 4

14 See, e.g., M. Sornarajah, *Resistance and Change in the International Law on Foreign Investment* (Cambridge University Press, 2015) 81 et seq

15 Jorge E. Vinuales, 'International Investment Law and Natural Resources Governance' (International Centre for Trade and Sustainable Development (ICTSD) and World Economic Forum, 2015) 1 <http://e15initiative.org/wp-content/uploads/2015/07/Extractive-Vinuales-FINAL1.pdf> accessed 18 November 2016

The role of international arbitration in natural resources protection

Introduction

International arbitration tends to play a role in natural resources protection in cases of, to use a term coined by Sam Luttrell, 'resource nationalism'. Resource nationalism 'connotes policies or measures adopted by governments for the purpose of asserting control over natural resources for strategic, political or economic reasons'.[16] As stated above, international arbitration is increasingly becoming the means by which disputes involving natural resources, and primarily issues concerning 'resource nationalism', are resolved. Such disputes are often not limited to questions of 'protection', but extend to issues of accessibility, availability and, of course, to financial implications.

One aspect of the natural resources discussion common to most jurisdictions is the challenges arising from regulatory issues. As stated above, natural resources form part of a state's sovereign property. As such, they fall within the scope of a sovereign state's right to regulate. In addition, natural resources such as water, in particular, arguably constitute human rights and states are generally regarded as having an obligation to provide these services at affordable rates to their population.[17]

However, many states do not have the means of accessing their own natural resources. Those that do will employ specialist, often foreign, companies to access them in an efficient manner. International companies investing in a state in which the political environment is unstable, which is known to be corrupt, or which is still at an early stage of its economic development, generally require an incentive, one that is almost always financial and usually in the form of promises of returns on investment, to undertake the work of accessing and harnessing resources in what is perceived, for the above reasons, to be a 'risky' environment. Such incentives and promises of returns are often realised through concession contracts in many cases.[18] Should the

16 Sam Luttrell, 'Resource Nationalism: Old Problem, New Solutions' in Gabriël A. Moens and Philip Evans (eds), *Arbitration and Dispute Resolution in the Resources Sector* (Springer International Publishing, 2015) 197

17 See Dimsey (n 2) 168, quoting Pierre Thielbörger, 'The Human Right to Water versus Investor Rights; Double-Dilemma or Pseudo-Conflict?' in Pierre-Marie Dupuy, Francesco Francioni and Ernst-Ulrich Petersmann (eds), *Human Rights in International Investment Law and Arbitration* (Oxford University Press, 2009) 487, 498

18 See, for example, the seminal case of *Compania de Aguas del Aconquija, S.A. & Compagnie General des Eaux v Argentine Republic (Award)* (2001) 16 *ICSID Review – Foreign Investment Law Journal* 643, discussed at length in Christoph Schreuer, 'Investment Treaty Arbitration and Jurisdiction over Contract Claims – the *Vivendi I* Case Considered' in Todd Weiler (ed.) *International Investment Law and Arbitration: Leading Cases from ICSID, NAFTA, Bilateral Investment Treaties and Customary International Law* (Cameron May, 2005) 281, 281 et seq

returns offered pursuant to such concessions prove unrealistic or unworkable in practice, or should unanticipated circumstances associated with harnessing such resources arise, government intervention, whether indirectly in the form of changes to the regulatory framework or directly through measures against the company, has often been used as a response. The cases discussed below all concern disputes in which natural resources were accessed pursuant to an agreement between the foreign investor and the host state. In almost all cases, it was a change to the legal and regulatory framework that triggered the dispute on the basis that the investor could no longer reap the financial returns initially anticipated and contractually agreed due to the changes that had been imposed by the host state or a body attributable to it.

As the considerable number of cases in this area shows, disputes can take many forms and materialise in many situations. In the context of water, for example, disputes could – and have – involved issues of whether the tariff being charged for the water was actually affordable by the people to whom the water was being provided.[19] Of recent note, in the context of nuclear power, disputes often arise over changes in laws and/or taxes which arguably make the once profitable investment of a foreign company no longer so profitable.[20] In the context of oil and gas extraction and mining rights, issues regarding potential environmental damage, or encroachment on culturally sacred or otherwise protected lands, may also arise.[21]

As the above paragraphs show, regulation, an act of the state, is at the heart of most natural resources disputes. Issues arise when states enter into contracts with third parties that directly or indirectly influence the state's right to regulate. In a relatively recent development, many natural resources disputes arising out of regulation-related measures end up in investment arbitration, pursuant to a BIT signed between the investor's state and the

19 See *Aguas del Tunari SA v Republic of Bolivia* (ICSID Arbitral Tribunal, Case No. ARB/02/3) <www.italaw.com/cases/57> accessed 13 January 2017; *Suez, Sociedad General de Aguas de Barcelona, SA and Vivendi Universal, SA v Argentine Republic* (ICSID Arbitral Tribunal, Case No. ARB/03/19) <www.italaw.com/cases/1057> accessed 13 January 2017

20 See the oft-cited example of *Vattenfall AB, Vattenfall Europe AG, Vattenfall Europe Generation AG v Federal Republic of Germany* (ICSID Arbitral Tribunal, Case No. ARB/09/6) which concerned purported losses arising from Germany's decision to phase out its nuclear power plants by 2021

21 *Chevron Corporation (USA) and Texaco Petroleum Company (USA) v The Republic of Ecuador,* UNCITRAL ('Chevron I') (PCA Arbitral Tribunal, Case No. 34877) <www.italaw.com/cases/251> accessed 18 November 2016. For the second case see *Chevron Corporation and Texaco Petroleum Company v The Republic of Ecuador* (PCA Arbitral Tribunal, Case No. 2009-23) ('Chevron II') <www.italaw.com/cases/257> accessed 18 November 2016; *Glamis Gold, Ltd v United States* (NAFTA/UNCITRAL Arbitral Tribunal, *ad hoc*) <www.italaw.com/cases/487> accessed 10 November 2016; *Piero Foresti, Laura di Carli and Others v Republic of South Africa* (ICSID Arbitral Tribunal, Case No. ARB/(AF)/07/1) <http://italaw.com/cases/446> accessed 31 July 2016

host state, due to the suitability of arbitration as a forum for enforcing such rights.[22] It should be incumbent on investment arbitral tribunals to maintain the delicate balance between a state's right to regulate and the legitimate expectations that foreign investors derive from the BITs they have signed with host states.[23] The extent to which this balance has been achieved in practice will be examined in further detail below.

International commercial arbitration

Notwithstanding the fact that disputes in this area are often fought out in investment arbitration, it would be incorrect to say that there are no disputes in international commercial arbitration associated with natural resources protection. On the contrary, as most of these disputes are, by their very nature, contractual, it goes without saying that in addition to claims under a BIT, they would also have claims under contract. It is outside the scope of this contribution to discuss the procedural effect of whether claims brought under contract can also be brought under a BIT.[24] It is sufficient to say that when 'contractual' claims arise, commercial arbitration is often the (non-exclusive) forum for resolving such claims. In some countries, for example Brazil, arbitration is actually prescribed as the method of dispute resolution in the energy sector. Article 43, Item X of Law No. 9,478/1997, which created the National Agency of Petroleum, Natural Gas and Biofuels (ANP), provides that the concession contract shall contain provisions establishing 'the rules regarding dispute resolution, related to the contract and its execution, including conciliation and international arbitration'.[25]

In terms of case law, due to the confidential nature of most commercial arbitration proceedings, obtaining insight into case law on this subject is challenging. However, a recent International Chamber of Commerce (ICC) Award, rendered on 6 December 2015, in the matter of East Mediterranean Gas Company (EMG) against the Egyptian Natural Gas Holding Company (EGAS), the Egyptian General Petroleum Corporation (EGPC) and the

22 See generally Christina L. Beharry and Melinda E. Kuritzky, 'Going Green: Managing the Environment through International Investment Arbitration' (2015) 30 *American University International Law Review* 383, 384 et seq; Luttrell (n 16) 197

23 Beharry and Kuritzky (n 22) 422

24 See Schreuer (n 18); Jonathan B. Potts, 'Stabilizing the Role of Umbrella Clauses in Bilateral Investment Treaties: Intent, Reliance, and Internationalization' (2011) 51 *Virginia Journal of International Law* 1005

25 See the references quoted in Seema Bono and others, 'Sovereign Immunity and Enforcement of Arbitral Awards: Navigating International Boundaries' (Mayer Brown 2012) <https://m.mayerbrown.com/Files/Publication/2e0f7077-9b25-430e-8b70-6a8f8c1a9d76/Presentation/PublicationAttachment/1be4c54c-bfc2-4d78-9403-85e37c560f43/12270.PDF> accessed 27 August 2016

Israel Electric Corporation (IEC) has attracted some attention.[26] The facts of the case are complicated, but at its core was a contract between EMG and IEC, pursuant to which EMG had agreed to supply IEC with gas. Explosions and other attacks associated with the Arab Spring in 2011 damaged the gas pipelines and ultimately interrupted the gas supply to Egypt. The arbitral tribunal found in EMG's favour, but the payment thereunder was essentially 'waived' by IEC/Israel.

The enduring political agendas of both the Egyptian and the Israeli governments have since overshadowed the award itself. Both states are interested in pursuing a deal arising from the discovery of the Leviathan gas fields in the Eastern Mediterranean Sea, which fall within Israel's territory, and have decided to deal with the award in a kind of 'global settlement', which addresses all related issues at once.[27]

There has been considerable criticism of these proceedings and what happened in the aftermath of the award. First, it was argued that matters of such fundamental significance as the supply of gas for electricity – a core feature of infrastructure, many would argue – cannot be decided behind closed doors in confidential arbitration.[28] Second, and related to the first point, the proximity of the relevant Israeli and Egyptian companies to their own respective governments was so close that it was almost inevitable that the dispute would be motivated by politics. This in itself is neither new nor abhorrent; however, disputes concerning this subject matter, involving parties with patently close governmental ties, should arguably not fall to be resolved by private tribunals.[29] Finally, IEC's waiver of its determined right to compensation was clearly an act by the state of Israel. Again, *prima facie*, a party to an arbitration has the right to act in such a manner. However, the interruption of the gas supply to Israel had resulted in the state turning to alternate suppliers, which resulted in tariffs that were over 30 per cent higher than those previously charged for gas.[30] This increase was passed on to the Israeli people. One can therefore ponder whether or not Israel had the right to waive the compensation due to the IEC pursuant to the arbitral award without first putting the question to the Israeli people, since they ultimately bore the increased costs.

At first glance, this case appears to be about natural resources exploitation rather than protection, but it is useful to highlight typical issues that may arise in other cases concerning similar matters. In particular, the nature of

26 See, e.g., Ira Ryk-Lakhman, 'When Public Interests, State Strategy, and International Law Clash in One Confidential Commercial Arbitration' (*EFILA Blog*, 16 December 2015) <https://efilablog.org/2015/12/16/when-public-interests-state-strategy-and-international-law-clash-in-one-confidential-commercial-arbitration/> accessed 27 August 2016

27 Ibid

28 Ibid

29 Ibid

30 Ibid

natural resources means that disputes concerning them, even if resolved in 'private' commercial arbitration, will invariably contain a public interest element and be potentially influenced by political considerations.[31] Companies engaged to exploit natural resources are typically close to their governments and are likely to be subject to a similar degree of political influence. In the author's opinion, none of these factors is undesirable, but instead serves to highlight the issues that can arise when applying an essentially private form of dispute resolution to a matter involving the public interest and taxpayers' money.

Investor–state dispute settlement

Laws of foreign direct investment

Before turning to investment arbitration, it is appropriate to look briefly at the laws of foreign direct investment, since international investment arbitration as a dispute resolution mechanism is entrenched in legal instruments relating to the protection of foreign direct investment. As stated above, the usual manifestation of a legal framework for the protection of foreign direct investment is in treaties signed between two states, BITs, which guarantee certain protections to investors from one state in the territory of the other state.[32] Should the 'host' state allegedly fail to uphold its obligations of protection under the BIT in question, the BIT provides the purportedly injured foreign investor with a direct right of recourse against the host state.[33] In most BITs, this right of recourse takes the form of arbitration, often pursuant to the International Centre for Settlement for Investment Disputes (ICSID) Arbitration Rules, or as *ad hoc* arbitral proceedings under the United Nations Commission on International Trade Law (UNCITRAL) Arbitration Rules.[34]

Due to the nature of and contractual mechanisms for investments in the energy and natural resources sector, foreign direct investments generally fulfil the requirements for investment protection under the definitions of most BITs. Indeed, many BITs expressly include 'concessions' in the definition of 'investment'. As an example directly relevant in the present context, Article 1(e) of the 2003 Germany–China BIT provides that:

> the term 'investment' means every kind of asset invested directly or indirectly by investors of one Contracting Party in the territory of the other Contracting Party, and in particular, though not exclusively, includes: ... business concessions conferred by law or under contract

31 See, e.g., Luttrell (n 16) 197
32 See Bishop, Crawford and Reisman (n 13) 10 et seq
33 Ibid 11
34 Ibid 12 et seq

> permitted by law, ***including concessions to search for, cultivate, extract or exploit natural resources.***
>
> (emphasis added)

As the case law discussed below shows, concessions granted to foreign investors to access natural resources in a host state constitute perhaps the most typical example of an investment and have even been described as the '***paradigmatic example of a foreign investment transaction***',[35] satisfying both the requirements of the BIT concerned and the much-discussed requirements of Article 25 ICSID Convention.[36]

It is important to keep in mind that most BITs do not contain explicit language referring to environmental concerns, although almost 50 per cent of the BITs signed since 2005 contain some reference to the environment.[37] The 2012 US Model BIT, for example, makes express reference to environmental protection in its preamble[38] and the 2004 Jordan–Singapore BIT confirms that nothing in the BIT prevents the adoption and enforcement of measures '***relating to the conservation of exhaustible natural resources if such measures are made effective in conjunction with restrictions on domestic production or consumption***'.[39] Moreover, some BITs also explicitly preserve the state's right to regulate for legitimate public welfare objectives, which include the environment.[40]

35 Vinuales (n 15) 3

36 *Convention on the Settlement of Investment Disputes between States and Nationals of Other States*, opened for signature 18 March 1965, 757 UNTS 159 (entered into force 14 October 1966) (ICSID Convention). See, e.g., *Salini Costruttori S.p.A. and Italstrade S.p.A. v Morocco (Jurisdiction)* (ICSID Arbitral Tribunal, Case No. ARB/00/04, 31 July 2001) (2002) 129 *Journal du Droit International* 196 <www.italaw.com/cases/958> accessed 13 January 2017; *Malaysian Historical Salvors v Malaysia (Award)* (ICSID Arbitral Tribunal, Case No. ARB/05/10, 17 May 2007) <www.italaw.com/cases/646> accessed 13 January 2017, for cases discussing these requirements

37 See the discussion in Beharry and Kuritzky (n 22) 388 et seq. See also the comprehensive survey results in Kathryn Gordon and Joachim Pohl, 'Environmental Concerns in International Investment Agreements: A Survey' (2011) OECD Working Paper on International Investment 2011/01 <http://dx.doi.org/10.1787/5kg9mq7scrjh-en> accessed 18 November 2016

38 '2012 US Model Bilateral Treaty' (*Office of the United States Trade Representative*, 2012) <https://ustr.gov/sites/default/files/BIT%20text%20for%20ACIEP%20Meeting.pdf> accessed 18 November 2016 (US Model BIT)

39 'Bilateral Investment Treaty between the Government of the Hashemite Kingdom of Jordan and the Government of the Republic of Singapore' signed 16 May 2004 (entered into force 22 August 2005) (*Ministry of Trade and Industry Singapore*) Art 18(e) <www.mti.gov.sg/MTIInsights/Documents/app.mti.gov.sg/data/pages/2785/doc/Bilateral%20Investment%20Treaty%20Between%20Jordan%20and%20Spore.pdf> accessed 23 January 2017

40 US Model BIT (n 38) annex B(4)(b); 'Agreement between Canada and _________ for the Promotion and Protection of Investments' (*Global Affairs Canada*, 2003) annex B.13(1) <www.italaw.com/documents/Canadian2004-FIPA-model-en.pdf> accessed 18 November 2016 (2004 Canada Model BIT)

International investment arbitration

At the heart of any discussion on investment arbitration in the context of the protection of natural resources is the tension between public and private interests. An eminent expert on international law, Professor Philippe Sands,[41] opined on the role of arbitration in the protection of environmental interests as follows:

> [T]here remain certain areas of international law in which international environmental norms are yet to be recognized as having a material role to play. This is the case, for example, in the field of foreign investment laws, the rules of international law that seek to promote investment flows by establishing norms prohibiting expropriation or unfair or inequitable treatment ... [T]he key issue is the relationship between two different subject matter areas in international law. As issues become more interrelated it will be incumbent upon those involved in arbitrating disputes with an environmental element to strive for balance, balance between potentially competing objectives of environmental protection on one hand, and the protection of rights of foreign investors on the other hand. Neither of these important societal interests should trump the other, they should be treated in an integrated manner.[42]

Almost ten years have passed since Professor Sands made this insightful statement. The following sections will examine investment arbitration in the context of natural resources disputes and whether or not a '***balance between potentially competing objectives***' has been achieved. First, the author will examine the source of the tension and the reasons why a balance is needed. An examination of relevant institutions will follow, and investment arbitration case law involving natural resources will then be examined.

STATE'S RIGHT TO REGULATE VS. NEED FOR FOREIGN DIRECT INVESTMENT

As indicated by Professor Sands' quote above, there is an inherent tension between natural resources protection and international investment law.

Part of a state's sovereign prerogative is to protect its natural resources, and arguably part of the obligation to protect is an obligation to ensure that resources are properly managed and available to the population in adequate

41 Of course, many other scholars have also opined on this topic. See, e.g., Andreas Kulick, 'Sneaking through the Backdoor – Reflections on Public Interest in International Investment Arbitration' (2013) 29 Arbitration International 435, 425 et seq; Beharry and Kuritzky (n 22) 387

42 Philippe Sands, 'Litigating Environmental Disputes: Courts, Tribunals and the Progressive Development of International Environmental Law' (Global Forum on International Investment, OECD, 2007) 2 <www.oecd.org/investment/global forum/40311090.pdf> accessed 27 August 2016

measure.[43] In order to facilitate this, states often need external assistance, and will, in many cases, source competence and technical know-how from foreign investors. Indeed, many cases being fought out before international arbitral tribunals today are a result of a state's need to turn to foreign investment in order to enjoy its natural resources because it lacks the means to do so on its own.[44]

A need to access and utilise natural resources, but no experience in implementation, has in turn triggered the entry of multinational companies equipped with the know-how to make the resources available and accessible.[45] The problem with involving foreign investors in projects concerning natural resources is that many of the protections granted to foreign investors by BITs or other instruments will likely constitute limits to and place restrictions on a state's sovereignty over its natural resources.[46] Moreover, the pursuance of a foreign investment project may come at the expense of human rights or rights that fall thereunder, such as the right to water,[47] which states have an obligation to protect.[48]

There is another element to the tension between natural resources protection and foreign investment: oftentimes it may be a project commissioned by the state that incidentally jeopardises the protection of that state's natural resources.[49] Cutting down a forest in order to make way for a highway is as much a matter for natural resources protection as is the development of a system for clean water within a large city. In both scenarios, the state's interest in resource protection and the obligation to undertake appropriate measures for such protection may compete with the legitimate expectations of the foreign investor.

As stated above, a state's desire to harness its natural resources in circumstances where it lacks the means to do so, and a company's desire for a profitable return on its investment, have both been the subject of numerous disputes before arbitral tribunals.[50] By their very nature, disputes of this kind involve at the very least 'a tension and, at times, a direct conflict between competing obligations of the State to, on the one hand, promote foreign investment and, on the other hand, protect its population and territory from environmental harm while responsibly managing its natural resources'.[51]

43 See, e.g., the discussion in Beharry and Kuritzky (n 22) 387
44 See Dimsey (n 2) 161 et seq
45 Vielleville and Vasani (n 11) 1
46 See, e.g., the discussion in Vielleville and Vasani (n 11) 6
47 Dimsey (n 2)
48 See the discussion and the 'State-Investor-Population Triangle' in Vinuales (n 15) 4 et seq
49 See, e.g., the cases discussed below of *Glamis Gold* (n 21); *Piero Foresti* (n 21)
50 See, e.g., Luis Miguel Velarde Saffer and Amir Ardelan Farhadi, 'ISDS in the TPP: Is the Recent Uproar in the US Merited? – Part II' (*Kluwer Arbitration Blog*, 7 November 2016) <http://kluwerarbitrationblog.com/2016/11/07/isds-in-the-tpp-is-the-recent-uproar-in-the-us-merited-part-ii/?_ga=1.126074191.319367513.1483945641> accessed 9 January 2017. See also the cases examined below
51 Beharry and Kuritzky (n 22) 387, 396

Natural resources, an area of policy-making long left to governments and the public interest, has been increasingly affected by private interest in the form of foreign investors claiming an interest in natural resources based on a contract concluded with the state or an entity attributable thereto. The state, initially welcoming the investment due to the need for economic and social development, finds itself in a quandary when this aim competes with the public interest in a state's government maintaining a degree of control over natural resources.[52]

ICSID

ICSID, established in 1965 within the overall framework of the World Bank, overhauled its arbitration rules in 2006 in response to growing concerns about the legitimacy of investment arbitration. These concerns reflected the desire to have matters involving the public interest resolved in a more transparent and accountable manner. Since the 2006 revisions, most of the procedural documents in ICSID cases are made public on the ICSID website, and awards are generally made publicly available.[53]

Indeed, it is precisely the rules promulgated by ICSID that make it easy to find cases concerned with the protection of natural resources. Recent reports from ICSID indicate that over half of all investment disputes registered at ICSID involve the oil, gas, mining, electric power and other energy sectors.[54]

Consequently, many cases can be examined in this context, such as those addressing water concessions and mining rights, but also energy issues. The cases highlight the ongoing tension between a state's sovereign rights and the rights it promises to foreigners to entice them to provide – in most cases – much-needed investment.[55]

Specialist rules for the resolution of disputes involving natural resources

Of course, one of the better-known organisations for the resolution of energy disputes is the Energy Charter Secretariat, which performs the

52 See Vinuales (n 15) 3

53 See <https://icsid.worldbank.org/en/Pages/cases/AdvancedSearch.aspx> accessed 9 January 2017

54 See ICSID Annual Report 2016 <https://icsid.worldbank.org/apps/ICSIDWEB/resources/Documents/ICSID_AR16_ENG.pdf./> accessed 12 September 2016, 33: 35 per cent of registered cases in financial year 2016 involved the electric power and other energy sector; 20 per cent involved oil, gas and mining

55 Vinuales (n 15) 3; generally Julia Hueckel, 'Rebalancing Legitimacy and Sovereignty in International Investment Agreements' (2011) 61 *Emory Law Journal* 601 <http://law.emory.edu/elj/content/volume-61/issue-3/comments/rebalancing-legitimacy-sovereignty.html> accessed 9 January 2017. See in particular the cases discussed below

functions assigned to it pursuant to the Energy Charter Treaty (ECT). The ECT, which entered into force in 1998, was established to promote international cooperation in the energy sector. The ECT is less concerned with dispute resolution as such and focuses instead on legal and political issues relating to the creation of an open energy market.[56] It has gained attention in the context of investment arbitration because its dispute resolution mechanisms provide, in Article 26, for disputes between investors and states arising out of the ECT to be resolved by arbitration.[57]

The Permanent Court of Arbitration (PCA) has also undertaken measures to promote international arbitration as a dispute settlement mechanism for international environmental matters.[58] In 1991 the PCA approved the Permanent Court of Arbitration Optional Rules for Arbitration of Disputes Relating to Natural Resources and/or the Environment. While, unlike the Energy Charter Secretariat, the PCA does not currently have an active, natural resources-specific caseload, the PCA is active in the development of international environmental law and offers arbitration as a tool for compliance with the instruments of international environmental law.

The North American Free Trade Agreement (NAFTA), like the ECT, is not an investment arbitration instrument as such, but sets out rules for free trade between Canada, the United States and Mexico. Its Chapter 11 is concerned with 'Investment' and includes a section on the 'Settlement of Disputes between a Party and an Investor of Another Party'. Pursuant to Article 1120, a disputing investor may submit a claim to arbitration under either the ICSID Convention or the UNCITRAL Arbitration Rules.[59]

The UNCITRAL Arbitration Rules[60] should also be mentioned in this context, although they do not constitute 'specialist' rules. The UNCITRAL Arbitration Rules are a set of procedural rules for the conduct of arbitration promulgated by UNCITRAL. They are not institutional rules and there is no administering institution associated with the Rules. Rather, the UNCITRAL Arbitration Rules are a set of best practice procedural rules for parties to adopt. They are widely used in ***ad hoc*** arbitrations.[61]

56 *The Energy Charter Treaty*, 2080 UNTS 95 (signed and entered into force 16 April 1998) <www.energycharter.org/process/energy-charter-treaty-1994/energy-charter-treaty/> accessed 10 January 2017

57 See ECT website <www.energycharter.org/fileadmin/DocumentsMedia/Legal/ECTC-en.pdf> accessed 10 January 2017

58 See PCA website <https://pca-cpa.org/en/services/arbitration-services/environmental-dispute-resolution/> accessed 27 August 2016

59 See NAFTA website <www.nafta-sec-alena.org/Home/Legal-Texts/North-American-Free-Trade-Agreement?mvid=1&secid=539c50ef-51c1-489b-808b-9e20c9872d25> accessed 10 January 2017

60 See UNCITRAL website <www.uncitral.org/pdf/english/texts/arbitration/arb-rules-2013/UNCITRAL-Arbitration-Rules-2013-e.pdf> accessed 10 January 2017

61 Ibid

One should add in this context, however, that, as stated by Professor Philippe Sands, it is doubtful whether rules and committees[62] designated for the resolution of 'environmental' disputes will succeed in practice, since such disputes are rarely expressed to be solely 'environmental' in nature. Rather, environmental issues are often raised by host states as defences to claims of breaches of BITs brought by foreign investors, or may be raised by third-person participants in pursuit of the public interest. Thus, it would be difficult to classify a dispute as an 'environmental' dispute from the outset, since the investor, as claimant, would focus primarily on an alleged breach of the obligations under a BIT, which it is unlikely to classify as 'environmental' in the first instance.[63]

NATURAL RESOURCES CASE LAW

The investment arbitration cases concerning natural resources generally fall into two, sometimes overlapping categories. Many investment arbitral proceedings are related to mining and extraction rights in developing nations granted to foreign investors by the host state concerned, in which the implementation of the project causes public outcry based on environmental and public health concerns.[64] The second category of cases focuses on the resources themselves, including several cases involving water concessions.[65] At the heart of many of these cases has been a discussion of whether arbitral tribunals are mandated to take human rights concerns into account in evaluating claims brought by investors based on obligations arising from BITs.[66]

The discussion has been necessitated by the fact that many BITs do not explicitly refer to human rights as part of the spectrum of rights that the

62 Such as, for example, the Environmental Chamber at the International Court of Justice, which was established in 1993 and has since been dispensed with, see ICJ website <www.icj-cij.org/court/index.php?p1=1&p2=4> accessed 23 January 2017

63 Sands (n 42) 4, 6. See also the dispute resolution provision under the North American Agreement on Environmental Cooperation (NAAEC), negotiated and signed as a part of NAFTA, which was meant to be the 'teeth' of NAAEC, wherein 'one country [could] submit a claim against another for a persistent pattern of failure to effectively enforce its domestic environmental laws' in a way that affected trade between the two nations; however, the consultation and dispute resolution process has never been used. See NAAEC website <www.cec.org/about-us/NAAEC> accessed 23 January 2017

64 See Tamara L. Slater, 'Investor–State Arbitration and Domestic Environmental Protection' (2015) 14 *Wash. U. Global Stud. L. Rev.* 131 <http://openscholarship.wustl.edu/law_globalstudies/vol14/iss1/8> accessed 27 August 2016

65 See cases summarised below of *Aguas del Tunari* (n 19); *Suez / Vivendi* (n 19); *Biwater Gauff (Tanzania) Ltd v United Republic of Tanzania* (ICSID Arbitral Tribunal, Case No. ARB/05/22) <www.italaw.com/cases/157> accessed 10 November 2016

66 See, e.g., *Pac Rim Cayman LLC v The Republic of El Salvador (Submission of Amicus Curiae Brief by Centre for International Environmental Law)* (ICSID Arbitral Tribunal, Case No. ARB/09/12, 25 July 2014) <www.italaw.com/cases/783> accessed 13 January 2017

investor has to take into account when making its investment. The question has thus arisen in some cases as to whether human rights are even relevant in the context of realising a foreign investment. In the context of *amici curiae* submissions on the interdependence of investment treaty law and human rights law in the *von Pezold* case,[67] the arbitral tribunals found that neither party had put international human rights law questions in issue in the arbitration, and that the *amici curiae* were thus seeking to make submissions 'on legal and factual issues that are unrelated to the matters before the Arbitral Tribunals'.[68] The question that has to be asked as a response to such statements is whether arbitral tribunals have an *ex officio* right to consider human rights concerns regardless of whether any of the parties places them in issue in the proceedings.

One common feature of many cases involving natural resources is the attempted participation of non-disputing parties, often known as *amici curiae*, in the arbitral process. Perhaps par for the course for disputes with such a blatant public interest component, tribunals arbitrating natural resource cases are often faced with requests from non-disputing parties to make submissions or otherwise express views about the issues in dispute, and ideally offer a perspective on the issues not already provided by the parties themselves.[69]

The cases involving environmental issues, numbering 46 at recent count,[70] are too numerous for a detailed examination of each in this contribution. Instead, the following paragraphs seek to highlight specific types of cases and provide an overview of problems that are indicative of the tensions between natural resources protection and the rights of foreign investors pursuant to BITs.

Methanex v USA

In the case of *Methanex v USA* ('*Methanex*'),[71] Methanex, a Canadian manufacturer of the additive MTBE, a toxic gasoline additive, brought arbitration proceedings against the USA under Chapter 11 of NAFTA, claiming that a ban of MTBE by the State of California caused losses to Methanex's investment.[72] Since the case concerned the potential effect of MTBE on Californian drinking water, the case attracted significant public attention.

67 *Bernhard von Pezold and Others v Republic of Zimbabwe* (ICSID Arbitral Tribunal, Case No. ARB/10/15); *Border Timbers Limited, Border Timbers International (Private) Limited and Hangani Development Co (Private) Limited v Republic of Zimbabwe* (ICSID Arbitral Tribunal, Case No. ARB/10/25) <www.italaw.com/cases/1472> accessed 18 November 2016

68 *Von Pezold* (n 67) *(Procedural Order No. 2)* (26 June 2012), para 57

69 For a comprehensive overview of the issue of non-disputing parties in investment arbitration see Mariel Dimsey, 'Article 4. Submission by a Third Person' in Euler, Gehring and Scherer (n 1) 128 et seq

70 See Slater (n 64) 146

71 *Methanex Corporation v United States of America* (UNCITRAL/NAFTA Arbitral Tribunal, *ad hoc*) <www.italaw.com/cases/683> accessed 11 January 2017

72 NAFTA (n 59) Chapter 11, Article 1120(1)(c)

In rejecting Methanex's claims, the arbitral tribunal held that:

> as a matter of general international law, a non-discriminatory regulation for a public purpose, which is enacted in accordance with due process and, which affects, inter alios, a foreign investor or investment is not deemed expropriatory and compensable unless specific commitments had been given by the regulating government to the then putative foreign investor contemplating investment that the government would refrain from such regulation.[73]

The arbitral tribunal found further that Methanex had entered into the investment 'aware of and actively participating' in the 'notorious' regulatory environment of the US and could, consequently, not have held any expectation that restraint would be exercised regarding future regulatory actions.[74] The arbitral tribunal recognised that, unlike other cases, such as *Waste Management v Mexico*,[75] the claimant could not show 'representations made by the host State which were reasonably relied upon by the claimant'[76] and, on this basis, Methanex could not successfully argue a compensable expropriation of its investment.

This case constitutes early recognition of the principle, later included expressly in a number of BITs, that obligations entered into by a state pursuant to a BIT should not have the consequence that a state's right to regulate is impeded.[77] For example, the BIT negotiated between Canada and Benin in 2013 set out that the contracting parties 'may adopt or enforce a measure necessary to protect human, animal or plant life or health'.[78] Other BITs and model BITs have adopted the same approach.[79]

73 *Methanex* (n 71) (*Final Award of the Tribunal on Jurisdiction and Merits*) (3 August 2005) Part IV Chapter D [7]

74 *Methanex* (n 73) Part IV Chapter D [9]–[10]. See also the discussion in Mary E. Footer, 'Bits and Pieces: Social and Environmental Protection in the Regulation of Foreign Investment' (2009) 18(1) *Michigan State Journal of International Law* 33, 40

75 *Waste Management, Inc. v United Mexican States* ('Number 2') (ICSID Arbitral Tribunal, Case No. ARB(AF)/00/3) <www.italaw.com/cases/1158> accessed 11 January 2017

76 Ibid *(Award)* (30 April 2004) [98]

77 For a detailed discussion of the interaction between foreign investment and a state's right to regulate, see Catharine Titi, *The Right to Regulate in International Investment Law* (Nomos/Hart 2014)

78 See 'Agreement between the Government of Canada and the Government of the Republic of Benin for the Promotion and Reciprocal Protection of Investments' <http://investmentpolicyhub.unctad.org/Download/TreatyFile/438> accessed 23 January 2017, Article 20(1)(a)(i). See also the other instruments cited in Lone Wandahl Mouyal, 'International Investment Law and the Right to Regulate: A Human Rights Perspective' (Routledge 2016) 141; Beharry/Kuritzky (n 22) 391 et seq

79 Ibid. See also Gordon/Pohl (n 37) 14 et seq

Aguas del Tunari SA v Republic of Bolivia

The *Aguas del Tunari* case,[80] although not recent, represents perhaps the high-water mark of the implications of foreign investment in the natural resources sector of a nation's economy. In this case, the project at the centre of the dispute was a 40-year concession granted to the claimant to operate Cochabamba's sewage and water system.[81] In acting purportedly in compliance with the terms of its concession agreement, the claimant increased water tariffs for residents to such an extent that the population was unable to pay its water bills and its access to clean water was threatened. This situation led to increasing civil unrest and resulted in protests of such vigour that they ultimately led Bolivia's government to declare a state of emergency and terminate Aguas del Tunari's concession.[82]

The claimant claimed under the applicable BIT for loss of anticipated profits in the amount of several million US dollars. Notwithstanding the apparent voracity of the claim, the parties ultimately settled the dispute after the jurisdictional phase of proceedings amidst mounting international pressure and bad publicity. The claimant agreed to withdraw its claim in exchange for Bolivia absolving it of any liability.[83]

This case aptly illustrates the tensions that can, and often do arise between natural resource concerns and foreign investment. In the *Aguas del Tunari* case, the claimant was party to a concession agreement whereby it used its skills and know-how to develop the water and sewage system in a large Bolivian city. The claimant's 'service' arguably improved access to this critical resource for the population in general, in a country in which the government would have been unable to provide such a service on its own. Understandably, the claimant's services came at a price, namely in the form of the tariffs chargeable to the population of Cochabamba as agreed in the concession agreement.

It is likely that neither party anticipated that this doubtlessly well-meaning project would ultimately result in protests and a cancellation of the concession altogether. Therein lies the problem. Foreign investors will generally need an incentive to go to a foreign, less-developed country and invest time and capital in such a project. States need to provide such an incentive, which often takes the form of concessions. Unfortunately, as the *Aguas del Tunari* case demonstrated, the promise of concessions offering a particular rate of return by a host state is often at odds with the realities of the affected population, which may expect, or may only be able to afford, fundamental services to be supplied at a cost for which no foreign investor would normally be prepared to commit to an investment of its time, resources and expertise in

80 *Aguas del Tunari* (n 19)
81 See generally *Aguas del Tunari* (n 19) (*Decision on Respondent's Objections to Jurisdiction*) (21 October 2005) [52] et seq
82 Ibid [73] et seq
83 Summary generally taken from Dimsey (n 2) 169

a state in which it is exposed to political risk to an extent not present in its own jurisdiction.

Suez/Vivendi v Argentina

In *Suez/Vivendi v Argentina* ('*Suez/Vivendi*'),[84] a case bearing similarities to the *Aguas del Tunari* case, the project at the centre of the dispute was a concession for the provision of water and sewerage systems to the greater Buenos Aires area, which had been organised and managed by the claimants. Pursuant to the terms of the concession contract, the claimants were to make substantial investments in improving and developing the water distribution network, in return for which they would be compensated by the fees and tariffs paid by consumers. However, as a consequence of the Argentine financial crisis beginning in the year 2000, the Argentine government took a series of emergency measures, including depegging the Argentine peso from the US dollar, which devalued the peso to one third of its previous value. Argentina refused to revise upward the allowable tariffs and fees for the claimants' investment and sought to renegotiate the concession contract.[85]

Ultimately, Argentina terminated the claimants' concession and the claimants commenced ICSID arbitration under the relevant BITs, claiming expropriation of their investment.[86] In response, Argentina invoked the defence of necessity on the basis that it had adopted the measures in order to safeguard the human right to water of the inhabitants of Argentina.[87]

In the *Suez/Vivendi* case, like many investment arbitrations involving natural resources protection, the arbitral tribunal allowed *amicus curiae* to participate, reasoning that:

> The factor that gives this case particular public interest is that the investment dispute centers around the water distribution and sewage systems of a large metropolitan area ... Those systems provide basic public services to millions of people and as a result may raise a variety of complex public and international law questions, including human rights considerations. Any decision rendered in this case, whether in favor of the Claimants or the Respondent, has the potential to affect the operation of those systems and thereby the public they serve.
>
> These factors lead the Tribunal to conclude that this case does involve matters of public interest of such a nature that have traditionally led courts and other tribunals to receive amicus submissions from suitable non-parties. This case is not simply a contract dispute between private

84 *Suez / Vivendi* (n 19)
85 Ibid *(Award)* (2015) [3]
86 Ibid [5] et seq
87 *Suez/Vivendi* (n 19) *(Decision on Liability)* (30 July 2010) [202], [252]. For a general summary of the case see Dimsey (n 2) 170

> parties where non-parties attempting to intervene as friends of the court might be seen as officious intermeddlers.[88]

In its Decision on Liability,[89] in the context of examining whether Argentina had made its case on the defence of necessity, the tribunal held that Argentina was subject to both human rights and investment treaty obligations and must respect both obligations equally. It further held that these obligations were not inconsistent, contradictory or mutually exclusive.[90]

Unfortunately, the *Suez* tribunal failed to express a view on the potential consequences of a direct conflict between a state's obligation to respect human rights, and the obligations it enters into pursuant to a BIT. However, the case is significant in acknowledging the public nature of the issues in dispute and in allowing *amicus curiae* to present views going beyond those contained in the parties' submissions.[91]

Biwater Gauff v Tanzania

As the penultimate water concession case in this chapter, the *Biwater Gauff v Tanzania* case ('*Biwater*')[92] concerned a World Bank-funded project to repair, update and expand Dar es Salaam's water and sewerage infrastructure. Problems arose in the implementation of the project and disputes concerning water tariff increases occurred. These disputes led to the Tanzanian government taking back control over the water and sewerage system, seizing Biwater Gauff's assets and deporting some of its staff. Biwater Gauff commenced ICSID arbitration under the UK–Tanzania BIT. Here, as in the *Aguas* and *Suez* cases, non-party petitioners filed for *amici curiae* status in the proceedings, claiming that their interest in the case was that 'this arbitration process goes far beyond merely resolving commercial or private conflicts, but rather has a substantial influence on the population's ability to enjoy basic human rights'.[93]

In its final award, the tribunal referred to the *amici curiae* submissions.[94] In particular, the tribunal cited the concept raised by the *amici* of 'investor

88 *Suez/Vivendi* (n 19) *(Order in Response to a Petition for Transparency and Participation as Amicus Curiae)* (19 May 2005) [19], [20], partially quoted in *Order in Response to a Petition by Five Non-Governmental Organizations for Permissions to Make an Amicus Curiae Submission* (12 February 2007) [3]

89 *Suez/Vivendi* (n 87) [262]

90 Ibid

91 See also the discussion in J. Perez, M. Gistelink, D. Karbala, 'Sleeping Lions: International Investment Treaties, State–Investor Disputes and Access to Food, Land and Water' (2011) Oxfam Discussion Paper 19 <http://policy-practice.oxfam.org.uk/publications/sleeping-lions-international-investment-treaties-state-investor-disputes-and-ac-132350> accessed 10 November 2016

92 *Biwater Gauff* (n 65)

93 *Biwater* (n 65) *(Procedural Order No. 5)* (2 February 2007) [14]

94 *Biwater* (n 65) *(Award)* (24 July 2008) [355] [359] [392]

responsibility' in the context of sustainable development and human rights.[95] The *amici* had stated that the claimant had not fulfilled its obligations under the concession agreement and that the government:

> carrying [out] the duty to provide access to water to its citizens, had to take action under its obligations under human rights law to ensure access to water for its citizens. In this light, terminating the [concession] agreement cannot be found to be a breach of a contract whose very purpose was to promote and enhance the achievement of human rights.[96]

Interestingly, beyond referring to the *amici* submissions, the tribunal did not rely directly on them in making its findings. Notwithstanding this, it would appear that the tribunal had indirectly taken them into account, as it refused to award compensation to Biwater for Tanzania's alleged breaches of the BIT.[97]

The *amici* submissions referred to by the arbitral tribunal serve to highlight the tensions typical to water concession cases very appropriately here. On the one hand, the investment itself will be pursuant to a need to fulfil a basic human right, the access to water.[98] However, in order to provide the investor with a return on its investment and thereby create an incentive for the investment in the first place, tariffs will be set in the concession agreement. Should the tariffs prove unrealisable, or should the investor otherwise purportedly fail to fulfil its obligations, the very right which the investment was intended to preserve may be rendered unachievable through the actions of the same state that solicited the investment project.

Aguas Bilbao Bizkaia v Argentina

The most notable development in a line of 'water concession' cases is the recent award in the case of *Aguas Bilbao Bizkaia v Argentina*.[99] In this case, the claimants formed part of a consortium that, in early 2000, had been granted a concession for water and sewage services for the Province of Greater Buenos Aires. Similar to the *Suez/Vivendi* case discussed above, the

95 Ibid [379]
96 Ibid [387]
97 See also Kulick (n 41) 450
98 See generally Dimsey (n 2)
99 *Urbaser S.A. and Consorcio de Aguas Bilbao Bizkaie, Bilbao Biskaia Ur Partzuergoa v The Argentine Republic (Award)* (ICSID Arbitral Tribunal, Case No. ARB/07/26, 8 December 2016) <www.italaw.com/sites/default/files/case-documents/italaw8136_1.pdf> accessed 23 January 2017. See for a summary Jarrod Hepburn, 'In a First, BIT Tribunal Finds that It Has Jurisdiction to Hear a Host State's Counterclaim Related to Investor's Alleged Violation of International Human Rights Obligations' [2017] *IA Reporter* <www.iareporter.com/articles/in-a-first-bit-tribunal-finds-that-it-has-jurisdiction-to-hear-a-host-states-counterclaim-related-to-investors-alleged-violation-of-international-human-rights-obligations/> accessed 23 January 2017

concession encountered problems in connection with the Argentine economic crisis, which ultimately culminated in the province terminating the concession in July 2006.[100]

The claimants claimed breaches of the Spain–Argentina BIT relying on, *inter alia*, the obligation to protect foreign investment and the prohibition on adopting unjustified or discriminatory measures, the obligation of fair and equitable treatment and wrongful expropriation.

In the context of this contribution, one particularly interesting aspect of the case was that Argentina filed a counterclaim alleging that the claimants had violated their obligations in relation to the human right to water and claimed compensation. In a first for investment arbitration, the arbitral tribunal found that it had jurisdiction to hear Argentina's counterclaim on the basis of the broad wording of the BIT, and thus allowed Argentina to make an argument that the claimants had breached international human rights obligations. Of particular note, the arbitral tribunal did not follow the claimants' argument that any ruling on human rights obligations was outside its competence and found that as long as the dispute related to an investment, the tribunal was competent to hear it.[101]

Ultimately, the arbitral tribunal declined to find in favour of Argentina's counterclaim. Notwithstanding this, the tribunal made a number of positive statements about human rights and foreign investment that could be indicative of a changing trend with respect to the approach of tribunals to this issue.

The arbitral tribunal stated that it was 'reluctant'[102] to agree with the claimants' position that international law obligations could only be imposed on states, reasoning that nowadays, in light of the acceptance of corporate social responsibility (and thereby human rights) as a crucial standard for international companies and the now-accepted view that individuals and corporations enjoyed rights under international law, it would be logically flawed if they could not also be subjects of international law obligations.[103]

In refusing to find in favour of Argentina's counterclaim, the arbitral tribunal acknowledged that the claimants and Argentina did not hold equal obligations. Although individuals had an obligation to abstain from committing human rights violations, the human rights obligation to provide access to water was incumbent on the state, and could not give rise to a parallel obligation on the investor.[104]

Consequently, this case will likely be referred to by future arbitral tribunals faced with the question of the interplay between human rights obligations and natural resource protection, since it contains clear statements on the

100 Ibid [34]
101 Ibid [1153]
102 Ibid [1193]
103 Ibid [1193]–[1205]
104 Ibid [1210]–[1212]

hierarchy of human rights obligations in ensuring access to water. Equally, however, the potential exists for this case to be used as authority for the argument that investors do not have to actively enforce human rights, but rather need merely abstain from committing violations themselves. Such interpretations are likely to increase the burden on states to fulfil their human rights obligations while at the same time upholding their BIT obligations.

Glamis Gold v USA

In *Glamis Gold v USA* ('*Glamis Gold*'),[105] a dispute arose between Glamis, a Canadian mining company, and the USA concerning mining rights in California. The proposed mine in question was to be located close to sacred Native American lands. Glamis, the claimant, commenced proceedings under NAFTA Chapter 11 claiming breach of the 'fair and equitable treatment' standard and expropriation of its rights. Glamis' claims were based on a series of regulatory measures imposed by federal and state agencies in response to publicly expressed concerns about the environmental and cultural impact of the mining project, which resulted in additional costs being imposed on Glamis in order to meet the changed regulatory requirements.[106]

The tribunal ultimately dismissed Glamis' claim based on its failure to find that the state had breached its obligations under NAFTA. However, the factual background to the dispute provides a typical example of the tension between a state's right to regulate to protect environmental resources and an investor's right to realise its investment. Here, the state vested in Glamis a legitimate expectation that it had the right to mine the land concerned in the manner prescribed by the contract. Pressure from public interest groups – who also obtained consent to participate as *amici curiae* and make submissions in the arbitration concerning the protection of environmental and cultural resources – led to changes in the regulatory framework which allegedly had a direct impact on the value of Glamis' investment. Although the tribunal was not satisfied that this impact had devalued Glamis' investment to such an extent as to constitute expropriation, it had nevertheless impacted on Glamis' ability to fully realise its anticipated financial returns.

Piero Foresti v South Africa

The case of *Piero Foresti v South Africa* ('*Piero Foresti*')[107] concerned mining interests in South Africa. The claimants alleged breach of the relevant BITs

105 *Glamis Gold* (n 21)

106 For more detail on the dispute generally see Elizabeth Whitsitt, Damon Vis-Dunbar, 'Glamis Gold Ltd v United States of America: Tribunal sets a high bar for establishing breach of "Fair and Equitable Treatment" under NAFTA' [2009] *Investment Treaty News*, <www.iisd.org/itn/2009/07/14/glamis-gold-ltd-v-united-states-of-america-tribunal-sets-a-high-bar-for-establishing-breach-of-fair-and-equitable-treatment-under-nafta/> accessed 10 November 2016

107 *Piero Foresti* (n 21)

on the basis, among other things, that the introduction of the Mineral and Petroleum Resources Development Act (MPRDA) extinguished certain 'old order' mineral rights held by the claimants and thus amounted to an expropriation.[108] The respondents argued that even assuming the claimants' investment had been expropriated, such expropriation was lawful because it was undertaken for 'multiple and important public purposes'. Specifically, among the purposes contended by the respondents were 'reducing the economically harmful concentration of mineral rights and promoting the optimal exploitation of mineral resources; and ... protecting the environment and the communities living in the vicinity of mining operations'.[109]

The arbitral tribunal granted two South African and two international human rights groups[110] the right to participate in the arbitral proceedings. These *amici* referred to the public interest of the human rights and sustainable development dimensions of the dispute in their reasons for making the petition.[111]

Although this case was ultimately discontinued, the summary of the parties' positions contained in the award and the third-party petitioners' statements add the element of 'sustainable development' to the ambit of interests that an investment arbitral tribunal should aspire to balance.

Bernard von Pezold v Zimbabwe; Border Timbers Ltd v Zimbabwe

In 2010, Bernhard von Pezold as well as Border Timbers Limited, Border Timbers International (Private) Limited and Hangani Development Co (Private) Limited initiated two ICSID claims against the Republic of Zimbabwe ('*von Pezold*').[112] The disputes, which were ultimately conjoined by agreement of the parties and administered by the identically constituted tribunals, arose out of Zimbabwe's alleged breach of its obligations under its BITs with Switzerland and Germany by failing to provide fair and equitable treatment in conjunction with Zimbabwe's Land Reform Programme. At its heart, therefore, this dispute concerned the appropriation of land and the evolution of the land policies before and after Zimbabwe's independence.

Like other natural resources cases,[113] one of the issues fundamental to the dispute between the parties was the competing interests of, on the one hand, entitlement to land at a domestic, national level and, on the other, the promises allegedly made to a foreign investor to encourage investment.

Interestingly, a group of indigenous communities in Zimbabwe applied to present submissions on the interdependence of investment treaty law and

108 *Piero Foresti* (n 21) *(Award)* (4 August 2010) [69]

109 Ibid

110 And one additional petition by the International Commission of Jurists dated 19 August 2009, which was not made publicly available

111 *Piero Foresti* (n 21) [4.7] et seq

112 *von Pezold* (n 67)

113 See, e.g., *Glamis* (n 21)

human rights law, and to submit that human rights law was directly applicable to the dispute. With relevance to the issue of use of natural resources, in their submissions, the petitioners stated that they had a significant interest in the outcome of the proceedings since the case impacted on alleged rights over or in relation to the ancestral lands of the indigenous communities.[114]

Notwithstanding what appeared to be a valid ground for requesting *amicus curiae* participation, the tribunals refused to consent to the third-party petitioners participating in the arbitration. The tribunals stated that the petitioners were seeking to make submissions 'on legal and factual issues that are unrelated to the matters before the Arbitral Tribunals'[115] and that neither party had put the international human rights law issues concerned at issue in the proceedings.[116] They also found that a consideration of indigenous rights was not within the scope of their mandate under either the ICSID Convention or the applicable BITs.[117]

It remains to be seen how future investment arbitral tribunals will deal with the *von Pezold* approach when faced with the question of third-person participation, particularly in the context of human rights concerns.

Pacific Rim Cayman v El Salvador

On 30 April 2009, Pacific Rim Cayman commenced arbitral proceedings against El Salvador under the Dominican Republic–Central America–United States Free Trade Agreement (DR–CAFTA) for alleged breach of El Salvador's Investment Law on the basis that El Salvador had denied Pacific Rim Cayman a mining exploitation concession in the 'El Dorado' area.[118] El Salvador claimed that the moratorium, pursuant to which the claimant's concession was denied, was necessary in order to allow the government to study the environmental impact of mining on, *inter alia*, El Salvador's scarce water resources.[119]

On 2 February 2011, the tribunal issued a Procedural Order inviting any person or entity other than the disputing parties to make a written application to the tribunal for permission to file written submissions as an *amicus curiae*.[120] On 2 March 2011, member organisations of Mesa Nacional Frente a la Minería Metálica de El Salvador ('La Mesa'), on whose behalf the Center for International Environmental Law (CIEL) acted, made an application to the tribunal for permission to proceed as *amici curiae*.[121] In making its

114 *von Pezold* (n 67) *(Procedural Order No. 2)* (26 June 2012) [21]
115 *von Pezold* (n 114) [57]
116 *von Pezold* (n 114) [57]
117 *von Pezold* (n 114) [59]
118 *Pac Rim Cayman* (n 66)
119 See summary in Beharry/Kuritzky (n 22) 384
120 *Pac Rim Cayman* (n 66) (*ICSID News Release regarding Amicus Curiae*) (2 February 2011)
121 *Pac Rim Cayman* (n 66) *(Application for Permission to Proceed as Amici Curiae)* (2 March 2011)

application, CIEL stated that it could assist the arbitral tribunal in 'grappling with fundamental questions such as: whether metals mining is appropriate in a country with the highest population density in the Americas and a profound shortage of water'.

The application also referred to 'gains that *amici* and their allies have achieved in the last decade ... concern[ing] not just the mining debate but also much broader areas of civic participation, respect for human and environmental rights, and representative democracy'.[122] CIEL claimed that 'human rights obligations relating to the environment require that El Salvador design and apply a legal framework to ensure the full enjoyment of fundamental rights threatened by risky activities of third parties'.[123] The application went on to discuss the severe negative impact on access to and quality of water that the proposed mine would likely have.

On 23 March 2011, the tribunal issued an order granting CIEL permission to file a written submission as *amici curiae* under Article 10.20.3 of DR–CAFTA and ICSID Arbitration Rule 37(2) for the jurisdictional phase of the arbitration.[124] CIEL asserted that the tribunal's decision could impact on the communities that La Mesa represented.[125] CIEL filed similar submissions on environmental impact at the merits stage of the arbitration, stating that 'the measures adopted by El Salvador regarding the mining project proposed by Pac Rim Cayman LLC find support on the State's international obligations on human rights and environment' and discussed 'the environmental dimension of human rights'.[126]

Although the tribunal set out the submissions of the third person in the award on jurisdiction, it did not rely on them directly.[127] In the interim, extensive protests have occurred in connection with the case, with the claimant accused of using the arbitral process to 'subvert a democratic nationwide debate over mining and environmental health'.[128]

The award on the merits was rendered on 14 October 2016.[129] Unfortunately for the development of this area of the law, the tribunal found it 'unnecessary' to consider CIEL's case in full. It also stated that the

122 *Pac Rim Cayman* (n 121) 2

123 *Pac Rim Cayman* (n 66) *(Submission of Amicus Curiae Brief by Centre for International Environmental Law)* (25 July 2014) ii, 10

124 *Pac Rim Cayman* (n 66) *(Procedural Order No. 8)* (23 March 2011)

125 *Pac Rim Cayman* (n 124) 2

126 *Pac Rim Cayman* (n 123) 2

127 With respect to the abuse of process issue, the tribunal relied on the claimant's submissions and stated that it did 'not accept the arguments made to the contrary in the Amicus Curiae Submission' (n 66) *(Decision on the Respondent's Jurisdictional Objections)* (1 June 2012) [2.41] et seq. With respect to the denial of benefits argument, the tribunal did not expressly accept the amicus curiae argument, but stated in passing that a statement by the *amicus curiae* was in support of its findings, ibid, [4.85]

128 As quoted in Beharry/Kuritzky (n 22) 384 n 1

129 *Pac Rim Cayman* (n 66) *(Award)* (14 October 2016)

tribunal's decisions in the award 'do not require the Tribunal specifically to consider the legal case advanced by CIEL, and, in the circumstances, it would be inappropriate for the Tribunal to do so'.[130] In the context of an increasing number of cases being confronted with competing human rights and foreign investor commitments, the Tribunal's reluctance to provide a clear statement as to the interrelationship between the two is regrettable.

SUMMARY

As the cases discussed above show, natural resources concerns become relevant in investment disputes between foreign investors and host states in two main ways.

First, access to and affordability of the natural resource itself is at issue. This is demonstrated by the *Aguas del Tunari*, *Suez/Vivendi*, *Biwater* and *Aguas Bilbao Bizkaia* cases, in which the concessions granted by the host state to foreign investors resulted in tariffs for water that were, or became through acts of the host state, allegedly unaffordable for the local populations. In these cases, the foreign investor was setting tariffs pursuant to the concession agreements signed with the host state. However, public pressure ultimately forced the host state to renege on its obligations owing to the investor and a dispute ensued. These cases have been complicated by the circumstance often observed that the state itself has contributed considerably to the situation it then claims has resulted in infringement of its citizens' rights.[131]

Second, disputes have arisen with respect to the incidental protection of the environment in realising a foreign direct investment project. As shown by the cases of *Glamis Gold*, *von Pezold*, *Piero Foresti* and *Pacific Rim*, environmental concerns and actions by public interest groups advocating the protection of the environment have halted a number of investment projects. Here again, competing interests collide: the contractual right of the investor to realise its investment in the agreed manner, on the one hand, and a state's overarching obligation to protect the environment, on the other.

Finally, the case of *Methanex*, although also concerned with natural resources, does not fall into either of the above categories. Rather, this case is significant for providing an early clarification of the now well-established principle that obligations entered into by a state pursuant to a BIT should not have the consequence that a state's right to regulate is impeded.

Quo vadis?

As this contribution demonstrates, many challenges currently exist in the resolution of disputes involving natural resources through arbitration.

130 *Pac Rim Cayman* (n 129) [3.30]
131 See Kulick (n 41) 447

The cases discussed above make apparent that the interests of host states – at least when foreign investment is sought – cannot be equated with the interests of the local population and, particularly, the interest in natural resource protection. At the core of the challenges are competing interests: the interests of the foreign investor in having its investment realised in accordance with the contract and the underlying BIT, and the interests of the state in obtaining the necessary technology and at the same time appeasing the local population. Add to that the interests of third persons or *amici curiae*, who often claim to represent the 'public interest', and there are many cooks to potentially spoil the broth.

Generally, arbitral tribunals seem to be intent on avoiding an explicit discussion of the often directly competing obligations incumbent upon states: on the one hand, to protect natural resources for the benefit of their citizens, as enshrined in a number of international instruments and also pursuant to basic human rights, and, on the other, to uphold alleged promises made to foreign investors that often promote the economic needs of the state. However, users of arbitration desperately need to engage in this discussion, particularly since the difference in interests between the parties involved often appears to be irreconcilable.

The investor is primarily interested in upholding the promises made both in the contractual document underlying the project and in the applicable BIT. This often collides with the role of states as that role evolves over the course of a project. States may face public outcry and even make changes to the regulatory framework in order to appease the population, which may result in mismanaged expectations for the investor. Finally, an increase in the use of third person, or *amicus curiae*, participation can be observed. When used sparingly and properly, third-person participation may contribute to the tribunal's understanding of the relevant issues, and should ideally lead to better reasoning in the award. However, tribunals have hitherto appeared reluctant to rely directly on third-person submissions when rendering a finding in their ultimate award, and have only addressed public interest concerns 'through the back door'.[132]

In terms of the future approach in investment arbitration, the increasing recognition of a state's right to regulate, both in academic discourse and in the wording of recent BITs, may go a long way towards empowering arbitral tribunals to confront this question.

Indeed, it will be incumbent on arbitral tribunals to bring about a change in approach to environmental and natural resource concerns in arbitration. Positive steps in this direction can be inferred from the recent *Aguas Bilbao Bizkaia* case, in which the arbitral tribunal made clear statements about the nature of human rights obligations on both states and investors. The resolution of the competing interests of a foreign investor, which has contractually

132 See in particular Kulick (n 41) 449 et seq

promised returns, the host state and the general public (or particular sections of the general public, often represented by *amici curiae*), which all claim often competing rights, is unlikely to be achievable in general terms and will require new and innovative approaches that reconcile competing rights in a manner appropriate to the specific circumstances of a given case. In practice, this will likely consist not of preferring one set of interests over the other, but instead of undertaking a balancing exercise which seeks to respect the differing objectives and 'public interest' concerns inherent to projects that typically attract foreign investment.

7 Expropriation, nationalisation and resource protection – 'resource nationalism' and international law

Jürgen Bröhmer

Introduction

The notion of 'resource nationalism', though not new at all, has gained some currency in recent times, not least because of the activities of some leftist regimes in South America, most prominently, but by no means exclusively, Venezuela and Bolivia. The term 'resource nationalism' is not closely defined. One broad definition explains this notion as 'policy regimes, where resource policies are designed to direct economic activity in the mining and energy sectors towards politically defined national goals'.[1] The definition does reflect the reality that such policies can and do come in many guises. Having said that, it is hard to see any national policy, including the most liberal laissez-faire policy approach conceivable, that could be described as not pursuing defined national goals. A rather broad understanding of 'resource nationalism' appears to be prevalent among those who operate in the field and presumably mainly on behalf of foreign investors. Consulting giant EY published a 'Resource Nationalism Update' in June 2015 which gives an overview of 'resource nationalism' activities by nations across the globe.[2] In it, the overview commences by pointing to Australian government plans 'to introduce new measures and penalties to prevent multinationals from avoiding tax via loopholes and profit shifting'.[3] Clearly those initiatives by the Australian government are not specifically directed at the resource industries. Here the notion of 'resource nationalism' is apparently understood as any policy measure that is seen to diminish the position of a market participant for whatever reason.

This chapter rests on a much narrower understanding of 'resource nationalism': expropriations and measures of equivalent effect. Such measures attempt to shift a greater portion of the economic benefits of resource exploitation to

1 Jeffrey D. Wilson, 'Understanding Resource Nationalism: Economic Dynamics and Political Institutions' (2015) 21 *Contemporary Politics* 399.

2 EY, Mining & Metals, 'Resource Nationalism Update' June 2015, <www.ey.com/Publication/vwLUAssets/resource-nationalism-june-2015/$FILE/EY-resource-nationalism-june-2015.pdf> accessed 20 February 2017.

3 Ibid 2.

the state (nation) and away from private interests.[4] This chapter will attempt to analyse the legal framework for expropriations and measures of equivalent effect in the resources sector under international law, notwithstanding the fact that in developed constitutional systems constitutional law would also play a decisive role in determining the legality of expropriations or measures of equivalent effect. As will be shown, the framework is rather broad ranging from general public international law concepts, such as customary international law rules protecting foreigners from expropriations, to secondary rules or quasi rules of international organisations and specialised provisions prevalent in many bilateral investment treaties (BITs) protecting foreign investors against expropriations and measures of equivalent effect. Finally, a brief excursion into European Union (EU) law will show that there are other ways to protect local interests in core economic sectors such as the resource sector. In the EU, specific arrangements around powers attributed to certain shares have been used to secure national control in the private sector.

The legal framework

Customary international law on expropriation and compensation

The protection of property held by aliens is by no means a new issue in public international law. In fact, one could refer to it as one of the first developments arising out of what today is often referred to as globalisation. The increasing trade between nations caused the increasing presence of foreigners within the various countries for trading and production purposes, thus increasing the number of assets held by these foreigners and the necessity for their protection.[5] The procedural avenue for that protection is the rules of diplomatic protection. Under this body of customary international law, the

4 There are mainly two approaches to explain why this is happening. The market cycle model sees a link to the boom–bust cycle in the resource sector and argues that high prices and the ensuing competition between companies puts governments in a stronger position to raise demands on the industry, whereas low prices have the opposite effect. The second approach, the so-called obsolescing bargaining model, posits, in somewhat similar fashion, that states will first be more conducive to policies that attract investment but subsequently, when those policies were successful and once investments have been undertaken and investors are to some degree 'stuck' with their assets, states feel empowered to increase regulatory pressures to derive more benefit for the state. For an overview over these theories see Wilson (fn. 1) 402 with further references to the origin of these approaches. Wilson adds to these two theories interesting thoughts on political and institutional factors to enhance and complement the economic approach of the two main models, 402 ff.

5 From a Eurocentric perspective, these developments reach back to the northern Italian city states of, for example, Genoa and Venice from about the twelfth century or the Hanseatic League, a confederation of merchant cities from about 1400 onwards situated along what is now the German and Dutch North Sea coast, and cities along the coastlines of the present-day Baltic Sea nations. For more information see Richard B. Lillich, *The Human Rights of Aliens in Contemporary International Law* (Manchester University Press, 1984) 7.

home state of a national is deemed to have suffered a violation of its rights if a host state violates international law in the treatment of the foreign national, for example by expropriating the foreigner without compensation. Exercise of diplomatic protection is contingent on the injured individual being and having been a citizen of the state exercising diplomatic protection and on the allegedly injured individual having exhausted all available local remedies to seek redress in the host state.[6] If these requirements are fulfilled, the injured state (the state of which the injured individual was and is a citizen) is entitled to pursue the violation and seek redress from the host state according to the rules of state responsibility. The rules of diplomatic protection demonstrate that under general international law the individual (as a natural person or as a corporation)[7] plays no role and is mediated by the state of nationality. Individuals enter the legal arena only insofar as they are empowered to do so in specific treaties elevating them to this plane, such as human rights treaties or the investment treaties to be examined below.

One major issue in the context of the protection of the property of foreigners from expropriation[8] lies in the determination of the amount of compensation and whether the determination of the level of compensation is in the hands of the expropriating state. The dividing line ran – and to some degree still runs – between capital-exporting countries, which tend to insist on a higher level of compensation, and the host countries of the investment. This position favouring the investor has found its most famous expression in the so-called Hull rule (or formula), according to which the legality of an expropriation of property held by a foreigner rests on the payment of 'prompt, adequate and effective' compensation.[9] The much more restrictive

6 See, for example, Annemarieke Vermeer-Künzli, 'Diplomatic Protection as a Source of Human Rights Law' in Dinah Shelton (ed.), *The Oxford Handbook of International Human Rights Law* (Oxford University Press, 2013) 250.

7 For corporations see *Ahmadou Sadio Diallo (Guinea v Democratic Republic of the Congo) (Merits)* [2010] ICJ Rep 639 para 156 which refers to the leading case concerning the allocation of corporations to states for purposes of diplomatic protection, ICJ, Judgment of 5/2/1970, *Barcelona Traction, Light and Power Company, Limited (Belgium v Spain) (Second Phase)* [1970] ICJ Rep 3 paras 70 ff.

8 *Factory at Chorzów (Germany v Poland) (Indemnity)* [1928] PCIJ (ser A) No. 17, paras 121 ff.

9 This language came out of an exchange between US Secretary of State Cordell Hull and his Mexican counterpart in 1938 around the issue of the expropriation of agrarian lands owned by American citizens in Mexico. The exchange has been published in (1938) 32 AJIL Supplement: Official Documents 181. In his first note, the secretary laid out the basic principles around expropriation, including the undisputed right of a state to expropriate in the first place: Letter from Cordell Hull to Don Francisco Castillo Najera (21 July 1938) 184. The Mexican foreign minister challenged the view and maintained that there is no such rule of international law requiring 'payment of immediate nor even of deferred compensation': Letter from Eduardo Hay to American Ambassador to Mexico (5 August 1938) 186. It is not clear whether the payment of any compensation at all was challenged, because the language subsequently suggests that Mexico reserves to determine the 'time and manner' of such compensation payments, id. at 187 and this view is largely based on the notion of equality, i.e. that foreigners must not be treated differently to nationals, at 188.

view has its origins in the equally famous 'Calvo doctrine'.[10] This doctrine emphasised the territorial sovereignty of the host state and its right to treat everybody within its territory equally and hence not to privilege foreigners by way of allowing recourse to diplomatic protection by their home country. The doctrine gained a particular foothold in South America, not least because of the policies of the US and European powers, who did not hesitate to use military force to protect their nationals' pecuniary interests.[11] From the doctrine ensued the respective clause which came to be inserted in many contracts, often concession contracts, between South American states and foreigners in which the latter waived their right to seek diplomatic protection from their home state,[12] and limited themselves, in essence, exclusively to whatever redress is available locally.[13] Implied in this approach is the notion that compensation is a matter of domestic law only. In principle, this notion applies not only to the calculation of the compensation actually to be paid but even to the question whether any compensation will be paid at all. Having said that, state practice, not least countless investment treaties and many cases of expropriations and nationalisations since World War II, persuasively suggests that compensation is a prerequisite for a lawful expropriation from foreigners.[14]

In summary, general public international law does set a framework but little else. Expropriation is legally possible, however there is a requirement for the payment of compensation to foreigners. What this compensation must look like, whether it is the 'just compensation' standard of the US Constitution (5th Amendment), which is generally interpreted as referring to the market value of the property understood in the sense of 'what a willing

10 Named after the Argentinian publicist and international law scholar of the nineteenth century, Carlos Calvo.

11 See Lillich (n 5) 15; see also Jürgen Bröhmer, 'State Immunity and Sovereign Bonds' in Anne Peters and others (eds), *Immunity in the Age of Global Constitutionalism* (Brill/Nijhoff 2015) 182, 184–185.

12 Patrick Juillard, 'Calvo Doctrine/Calvo Clause', *Max Planck Encyclopedia of Public International Law* (Oxford University Press, January 2007) para 5, <http://opil.ouplaw.com/home/EPIL> accessed 20 March 2017.

13 From the perspective of international law a futile attempt because diplomatic protection assumes – at least also – a violation of the home state of the foreigner affected and not only of the foreigner herself and an individual cannot sign away any rights her home state has under international law.

14 Compensation was often paid through lump sum, negotiated agreements. See Alice Ruzza, 'Expropriation and Nationalization', *Max Planck Encyclopedia of Public International Law* (Oxford University Press, March 2013) para 3, <http://opil.ouplaw.com/home/EPIL> accessed 20 March 2017. For more authority on the requirement to pay compensation see M.H. Mendelson, 'What Price Expropriation – Compensation for Expropriation: The Case Law' (1985) 79 *American Journal of International Law* 414, 415 ff; C.F. Amerasinghe, 'Issues of Compensation for the Taking of Alien Property in the Light of Recent Cases and Practice' (1992) 41 *The International and Comparative Law Quarterly* 22.

buyer would pay a willing seller'[15] or whether there is only a very minimum standard for compensation, i.e. some appropriate compensation to be determined by the law of the expropriating state with wide discretion to take into account the concrete circumstances, remains unclear under general public international law. One major consequence of this insecurity has been the proliferation of more concrete protective clauses in BITs.[16]

General Assembly Resolution on Permanent Sovereignty over Natural Resources

One of the reasons for the vagueness of general public international law regarding expropriation and compensation was the emergence of newly independent nations from the yoke of colonialism. This happened first in South America and hence the restrictive Calvo doctrine. The other major independence wave took place after World War II in Africa and Asia. It is not surprising that these newly independent states were more interested in establishing their sovereignty, fostering their economic development and recalibrating the web of relationships with their former colonial power, which all too often had exercised their colonial rule mainly to their own advantage without being overly concerned with the development of the colony as such. This struggle for independence and subsequent development came to the fore in the development and ultimate passage by the General Assembly (GA) of the United Nations (UN) of the Resolution on Permanent

15 *United States v Miller*, 317 U.S. 369, 374 (1943).

16 It is interesting to note in this context that the European Convention on Human Rights does not contain a property protection clause because in the period around 1950 the notion of property as a human right, the relationship of property on the one hand and expropriation and nationalisation on the other and the concept of compensation were generally highly controversial. Especially Sweden and the UK were concerned that such a right could restrict the nationalisation of industries for political or social reasons. See Monica Carss-Frisk, *The Right to Property – A Guide to the Implementation of Article 1 of Protocol No. 1 to the European Convention on Human Rights* (Human Rights Handbooks No. 4, Directorate General of Human Rights, Council of Europe, 2001) 5–6, para 3. The right was subsequently and as a compromise included in the first additional protocol to the Convention, however, without mentioning compensation at all. Despite this the European Court of Human Rights has consistently held in its jurisprudence that the requirement to pay compensation is a consequence of the application of the principle of proportionality, see *James v UK* App. No. 8793/79 (ECtHR, 21 February 1986), para 54, or, more recently, *Žilinskien v Lithuania* App. No. 57675/09 (ECtHR, 1 December 2015), para 53. The German Constitution, also drafted just before 1950, resolved a similar drafting conflict by emphasising that property must also serve the public good (Article 14.2) and by including directly after the property protection clause of Article 14 Basic Law a socialisation provision in Article 15 which permits the transfer into public ownership of 'land, natural resources and means of production'. However, both expropriation possibilities, i.e. Article 14.3 and socialisation under Article 15 Basic Law, are contingent on the payment of compensation which in effect has rendered Article 15 totally obscure as the nationalisation of entire industries is financially out of reach.

Sovereignty over Natural Resources (PSNR).[17] It is important to note that resolutions of the GA of the UN cannot create hard legal obligations, i.e. such resolutions have by themselves no binding effect on the member states.[18]

The UN-PSNR resolution was the culmination of a number of efforts, especially since the end of World War II, addressing on the one hand the growing realisation that the adequate supply of various natural resources was of ever growing importance for the achievement of economic growth in the industrialised world.[19] At the same time, newly independent states brought to the fore the need for development and for establishing their sovereignty and self-determination and natural resources were to play a major role in that as well. This led to the establishment by the GA of the UN of a Commission to conduct a full survey of the status of the concept of permanent sovereignty over natural resources, which the GA regarded as a 'basic constituent of the right to self-determination'.[20] The work of this Commission led to the passage of the UN-PSNR in December 1962. From a legal perspective, the core passages of the eight enumerated paragraphs that make up the core Part 1 of the Resolution are contained in paragraphs 3, 4 and 8 which, perhaps surprisingly, given the existing political environment during the lead-up to the Resolution, confirm the legal situation under general public international law. The Resolution repeatedly emphasises that the sovereignty of natural resources exists within the confines of general public international law and one of the main tenets of general public international law is the principle of *pacta sunt servanda*. In the Resolution, this is expressed most clearly in paragraph 8 which states that '[f]oreign investment agreements freely entered into by or between sovereign States shall be observed in good faith'.

As far as expropriation and nationalisation are concerned the Resolution also remains well within the bounds of established customary international

17 *Permanent Sovereignty over Natural Resources*, GA Res 1803, UN GAOR, 17th sess, 1194th plen mtg, Supp No. 17, UN Doc A/RES/1803 (14 December 1962) (UN-PSNR).

18 E.g., Jan Klabbers, *An Introduction to International Institutional Law* (2nd edn, Cambridge University Press, 2009) 188–189. It is an entirely different question whether the content of such resolutions could, where applicable, evolve into customary international law with the voting by the states in the General Assembly being one expression of necessary state practice and/or *opinio juris*: at 190–191 (both with further references).

19 For a comprehensive analysis of these developments see Nico Schrijver, *Sovereignty over Natural Resources – Balancing Duties and Rights* (Cambridge University Press, 1997) 33 ff. A shorter genesis by the same author can be found at Nico Schrijver, 'Natural Resources, Permanent Sovereignty over', *Max Planck Encyclopedia of Public International Law* (Oxford University Press, June 2008), <http://opil.ouplaw.com/home/EPIL> accessed 20 March 2017.

20 GA Resolution 1314 (XIII) of 12 December 1958 – Recommendations Concerning International Respect for the Right of Peoples and Nations to Self-Determination, text accessible via <www.un.org/documents/ga/res/13/ares13.htm> accessed 20 March 2017.

law as explained above. Paragraph 4, the core part of the Resolution for the purposes of this chapter, determines that:

> Nationalization, expropriation or requisitioning shall be based on grounds or reasons of public utility, security or the national interest which are recognized as overriding purely individual or private interests, both domestic and foreign. In such cases the owner shall be paid appropriate compensation, in accordance with the rules in force in the State taking such measures in the exercise of its sovereignty and in accordance with international law. In any case where the question of compensation gives rise to a controversy, the national jurisdiction of the State taking such measures shall be exhausted. However, upon agreement by sovereign States and other parties concerned, settlement of the dispute should be made through arbitration or international adjudication.

Expropriations are possible if they are in the public interest[21] but they require 'appropriate compensation'. The adjective appropriate reflects the fact, as evidenced by the previously mentioned conflict between the Hull formula and more restrictive notions espoused especially in South America, that general public international law never quite reached an understanding on what exactly the correct level of compensation should be. The referral to both domestic and international law can only mean that international law defines the minimum standard of what an 'appropriate' compensation could be whereas everything else is a matter of domestic law. The reference to the procedure around the payment of compensation also reflects standard international law practice. Either the parties have both agreed to refer any arising conflicts to arbitration (as is often the case under investment treaties, see below) or possibly to international jurisdiction (e.g., to the International Court of Justice) or the matter remains in the hands of the domestic courts. If such a matter remains in the hands of the domestic courts, it is inherent

21 The public interest restriction is, of course, one that is hardly contestable as a matter of international law. Whereas one could easily construe scenarios where an expropriation would theoretically fail the test, for example transfer of natural resources property to the private estate of a leasing politician in the country, in practice states enjoy the widest conceivable discretion in the determination of what such a public purpose could be. It should be noted that even in countries with a very strong property ethos the taking of property can fulfil the public purpose test even if the taken property is transferred to another private party. For the US see *Kelo v New London* 545 U.S. 469 (2005), available through <www.supremecourt.gov/opinions/boundvolumes/545bv.pdf> accessed 20 March 2017. See also the Boxberg decision of the German Constitutional Court, BVerfGE 74, 264, available in German at <www.servat.unibe.ch/dfr/bv074264.html> accessed 20 March 2017. For a South African perspective and with references to cases in other jurisdictions see B.V. Slade, 'Public Purpose or Public Interest and Third Party Transfers' (2014) 17 *Potchefstroom Electronic Law Journal/Potchefstroomse Elektroniese Regsblad (PER)* 6, available at <www.saflii.org/za/journals/PER/2014/6.pdf> accessed 20 March 2017.

that the avenue to diplomatic protection remains open, a process which itself is contingent on local remedies having previously been exhausted. The UN-PSNR Resolution thus fits perfectly in the existing framework of international law.[22]

The 'new international economic order' and the Charter of Economic Rights and Duties of States

The discussion did not stop there. In the 1970s, further attempts were made to shift the balance towards more unfettered state rights. The GA adopted a 'Declaration on the Establishment of a New International Economic Order'.[23] This equally legally unbinding document explicitly lists 'the right to nationalization or transfer of ownership to its nationals' as a core element for states to safeguard their national resources and goes on to say that this right is 'an expression of the full permanent sovereignty of the State'.[24]

At the end of 1974, the GA added another resolution to the fold, the Charter of Economic Rights and Duties of States.[25] Article 2 of this Charter stipulates that states have the right: 'To nationalize, expropriate or transfer ownership of foreign property, in which case appropriate compensation should be paid by the State adopting such measures, taking into account its relevant laws and regulations and all circumstances that the State considers pertinent'. The contentious word is the word 'should' when it comes to payment of compensation. The UN-PSNR resolution described above used stronger language and required that compensation 'shall be' paid. This does not change the law as it stands. Although the Charter does not constitute binding law, it also states in Chapter 1(j) that the '[f]ulfillment in good faith of international obligations' is a fundamental principle in international economic relations.

22 Cf., Award on the Merits in the Dispute between Texaco Overseas Petroleum Company/ California Asiatic Oil Company and the Government of the Libyan Arab Republic (Compensation for Nationalized Property), 17 ILM 1 (1977), paras 81 et seq., 90. The political fight over this Resolution, however, makes it very clear that serious attempts were made to achieve a result which would have been plainly outside the scope of existing international law. For example, an amendment proposal by the then Soviet Union to confirm the 'inalienable right of peoples and nations to the unobstructed execution of nationalization, expropriation and other essential measures', see Schrijver, Sovereignty over Natural Resources (n 19) 73. At the same time, the fact that not only developing states but also Western states, including the USA, voted in favour of the resolution, likewise points in the direction of the Resolution sitting well within the general public international law framework.

23 *Establishment of a New International Economic Order*, GA Res 3201 (S-VI), 6th special sess, 2229th plen mtg, Agenda Item 7 UN Doc A/RES/S-6/3201 (1 May 1974).

24 Ibid para 4(e).

25 *Charter of Economic Rights and Duties of States*, GA Res 3281, 29th sess, 2315th plen mtg, UN Doc A/RES/29/3281 (12 December 1974).

These resolutions have little effect on the underlying principles. Of course, if one were to be of the view that international customary law required full 'market value' compensation, these resolutions would be part of the empirical case against this notion and for a softer standard of appropriate compensation. In any case, the uncertainty about what compensation must look like in practice remains. So does the right of a state to expropriate if compensation is paid.

International Covenant on Civil and Political Rights (ICCPR)

The ICCPR and natural resources

The ICCPR[26] contains references to the issue at hand in several places, most notably in Articles 1(2) and 47.[27] There is very little evidence of any impact these provisions have had on the problem of outward resource sovereignty. The Human Rights Committee, which oversees the application of the ICCPR and adjudicates individual complaints brought under the Optional Protocol to the ICCPR,[28] has referred to Article 1(2) in the context of domestic conflicts between the government and indigenous peoples and their participation and rights concerning land and resource allocation[29] but those references bear little relevance to the problem at issue here. This is not surprising. The language of Article 1(2) makes it quite clear that whatever this provision may yield for the 'peoples' referred to is yielded only within the confines of general public international law and specifically does not

26 *International Covenant on Civil and Political Rights*, opened for signature 16 December 1966, 999 UNTS 171 (entered into force 23 March 1976) (ICCPR).

27 Ibid Art 1(2): 'All peoples may, for their own ends, freely dispose of their natural wealth and resources without prejudice to any obligations arising out of international economic co-operation, based upon the principle of mutual benefit, and international law. In no case may a people be deprived of its own means of subsistence'. Art 47: 'Nothing in the present Covenant shall be interpreted as impairing the inherent right of all peoples to enjoy and utilize fully and freely their natural wealth and resources'.

28 Text at <www.ohchr.org/EN/ProfessionalInterest/Pages/OPCCPR1.aspx> accessed 20 March 2017.

29 See *Concluding Observations of the Human Rights Committee*, (1999) UN Doc CCPR/C/79/Add.105, para 8. See also *Concluding Observations of the Human Rights Committee*, (2002) UN Doc CCPR/CO/74/SWE, para 15 (both texts accessible through the database provided at <http://tbinternet.ohchr.org/_layouts/ TreatyBody External/TBSearch.aspx> accessed 20 March 2017). See also S. Joseph and M. Castan, *The International Covenant on Civil and Political Rights* (3rd edn 2013), paras 7.20, 7.21 (pp. 162–163). In 2004 French citizens brought a claim against Algeria arising from the independence struggle of Algeria which might have given cause for the HRC to address questions around the expropriation of property but the complaint was decided to be inadmissible, see Communication No. 1922/2009, Gilbert Martinez and others, 28/10/2013, CCPR/C/109/D/1922/2009, text available through database at <http://juris.ohchr.org/search/Documents> accessed 20 March 2017.

create exemptions from these principles. Article 47 ICCPR[30] likewise does not give licence to suspend basic rules such as *pacta sunt servanda*. In fact, much of what happens in the space of resource exploration, exploitation and management happens in the context of resource possessing states entering various arrangements with other states or private corporations aimed at the exploitation of these resources precisely to achieve the outcome envisaged by Article 47 ICCPR, namely to 'to enjoy and utilize fully and freely their natural wealth and resources'.

The ICCPR and the protection of property

The ICCPR does not contain an explicit provision protecting property against expropriation and nationalisation.[31] However, the jurisprudence of the Human Rights Committee (HRC) has consistently employed the anti-discrimination clause of Article 26 ICCPR to afford at least some degree of protection against expropriations or lack of compensation, if such measures or subsequent remedies to restitution or compensation could be found to be discriminatory.[32] The HRC has held that such unjustifiable discrimination existed and hence Article 26 was violated when restitution or compensation for property expropriated by a previous regime in the country was limited to nationals and residents of the state thus excluding persons who had left the country because of their opposing political opinions and who had in the meantime taken on a new citizenship.[33] However, it is important to keep in mind that Article 26 ICCPR can only be invoked if a case for discrimination can be made either in circumstances of the expropriation itself or in the context of subsequent restitution or compensation matters.[34]

30 Text cited supra fn. 27.

31 See most recently *T.W. and G.M. v Slovak Republic*, Communication No. 1963/2010, UN Doc CCPR/C/110/D/1963/2010 (2014), para 8.2, <www1.umn.edu/humanrts/undocs/1963-2010.html> accessed 20 March 2017.

32 Unlike the anti-discrimination clause of the European Convention on Human Rights (Article 14 ECHR), Article 26 ICCPR is not tied to a violation of an existing substantive right and is therefore applicable to any and all discriminatory measures. See Hans-Joachim Cremer, 'Eigentumsschutz' in O. Dörr et al. (eds), *EMRK/GG Konkordanz-Kommentar* (Mohr Siebeck, 2nd edn 2013), 1466, 1607–1608, para 145, also with references to the case-law under the ICCPR in fn. 994.

33 *Josef Frank Adam v The Czech Republic*, Communication No. 586/1994, UN Doc CCPR/C/57/D/586/1994 (1996), <www1.umn.edu/humanrts/undocs/html/VIEW586.htm> accessed 20 March 2017. See also similar case and findings *Simunek, Hastings, Tuzilova and Prochazka v The Czech Republic*, Communication No. 516/1992, UN Doc CCPR/C/54/D/516/1992 (1995), <www1.umn.edu/humanrts/undocs/html/dec516.htm> accessed 20 March 2017.

34 Not every differentiation amounts to a discrimination. See *Nikolaus Fürst Blücher von Wahlstatt v Czech Republic*, Communication No. 1491/2006, UN Doc CCPR/C/99/D/1491/2006 (2010), para 10.3 and cases cited there in fn. 15, <www1.umn.edu/humanrts/undocs/1491-2006.html> accessed 20 March 2017.

For the purposes of this study, the ICCPR can thus only yield relief if the expropriation of resource-related property is conducted on the basis of differentiating criteria which amount to discrimination in the sense of Article 26 ICCPR. This could be the case, for example, if only certain foreign nationals or corporations suffered expropriation or if any compensation regimes instituted were to similarly differentiate in a discriminatory manner, i.e. if the differentiation at issue is not 'based on objective and reasonable grounds'.[35]

Lex specialis: International investment treaties

The question of expropriation has been shaped foremost by international investment agreements (IIAs), often BITs. These BITs are a relatively young phenomenon and their rise began in the late 1950s in parallel to the resource nationalism debate. There are now more than 3000 BITs around the globe.[36] The reason for their relevance in the context of expropriation is simple. As shown above, the framework presented by customary international law, valuable as it is, is somewhat vague especially about the calculation of compensation to be paid. The debate over resource sovereignty, while unable to change the legal tenets in this regard, has added to the need for more legal certainty around the matter. It is precisely the role of international treaties to afford more clarity by creating a special regime tailor-made to the needs of the parties.

Expropriation and compensation: Examples from BITs/IIAs with Australian participation

Australia has concluded bilateral BITs with 21 countries and is party to a further 18 free trade and similar IIAs with significant investment chapters.[37] These treaties contain similar clauses pertaining to expropriation and compensation and are a good reflection of (very similar) treaty practice around the world. The standard template places restrictions on the power of the host country to engage in measures of expropriation. Expropriation encompasses both the direct taking of the asset but also indirect forms of expropriation, i.e. administrative measures tantamount to or with equivalent effect to expropriation.[38] For a foreign investor it makes little difference

35 *Nikolaus Fürst Blücher von Wahlstatt v Czech Republic*, supra fn. 32, para 10.2.

36 According to the Investment Policy Hub of the UNCTAD a total of 3282 BITs and other IIAs have been concluded and 2562 BITs/IIAs are currently in force, <http://investmentpolicyhub.unctad.org/IIA> accessed 20 March 2017.

37 See <http://dfat.gov.au/trade/topics/investment/Pages/australias-bilateral-investment-treaties.aspx>. For IIAs see <http://investmentpolicyhub.unctad.org/IIA> both links last accessed on 20 March 2017.

38 See, for example, Article 7(1) of the Australia–Mexico BIT which states that 'Neither Contracting Party expropriate or nationalise an investment either directly or indirectly through measures tantamount to expropriation or nationalisation', <www.austlii.edu.au/

whether the mining operation is expropriated and continues to operate under the ownership of the host country or a corporate entity controlled by the host country,[39] or whether the operation is brought to a halt because of administrative law or other legal changes brought about by parliament or the executive branch of government. In both cases the foreign investor is unable to continue to reap the economic benefits of the investment. Direct or indirect expropriations are not prohibited by international law per se but their legality is contingent on such measures being undertaken for a public purpose, on a non-discriminatory basis, under due process of law and, importantly from the perspective of the investor, on being 'accompanied by the payment of prompt, adequate and effective compensation'.[40]

The standard for compensation in BITs generally pivots around payment without undue delay of the 'fair market value of the expropriated investment immediately before the expropriation occurred' to be calculated using certain standard indicators.[41] This standard is favourable to the foreign investor especially given that the fair market value just before the expropriation will also include at least to some degree the future profit potential for the investment. It must be emphasised in this context that admitting foreign investment is entirely in the hands of the host country and hence the host country can fully control the potential future risk arising from expropriation measures and that BITs, which address both the admitting of foreign investment and compensation for direct or indirect expropriations, can be negotiated with any content the parties will agree on. BITs and IIAs usually

au/other/dfat/treaties/2007/20.html> accessed 20 March 2017. Article 7 of the Australia–Poland BIT expresses the same principle using slightly different language and describing indirect expropriations as 'measures having effect equivalent to nationalisation or expropriation', see <www.austlii.edu.au/au/other/dfat/treaties/1992/10.html> accessed 20 March 2017. Most recently see Chapter 9 'Investment' of the Trans-Pacific Partnership Agreement, signed on 4/2/2016 (not yet in force). Article 9.8 of the chapter refers to direct measures of expropriation and to indirect measures 'equivalent to expropriation or nationalisation', <http://dfat.gov.au/trade/agreements/tpp/official-documents/Documents/9-investment.pdf> accessed 20 March 2017. Annex 9-B and 9-C contain further clarifications of what constitutes indirect expropriation.

39 Cf. L. Nottage and S. Butt, 'Recent International Commercial Arbitration and Investor–State Arbitration Developments Impacting on Australia's Investment in the Resources Sector' in G.A. Moens and P. Evans (eds), *Arbitration and Dispute Resolution in the Resources Sector* (Springer 2015), 153 at 160 et seq. with the illustrating example of newly introduced divestment requirements to shift majority control of companies holding Indonesian mining licences to Indonesian owners.

40 See for example Article 7(1)(c) of the Australia–Argentina BIT, <www.austlii.edu.au/au/other/dfat/treaties/1997/4.html> accessed 20 March 2017.

41 See for example Article 7(2)(b) of the Australia–Mexico BIT: 'Valuation criteria shall include generally recognised principles of valuation and equitable principles such as the going concern value, asset value (including declared tax value of tangible property), capital invested (minus capital already repatriated), depreciated value, replacement value and other relevant factors', <www.austlii.edu.au/au/other/dfat/treaties/2007/20.html> accessed 20 March 2017.

have a lifespan of 10 or 15 years and are subject to termination by the treaty partners after giving notice. However, there is usually an ongoing effect of these treaties into the future after their termination because the treaties usually provide for ongoing protection of previously undertaken investments in the host country for a further 10 or 15 years.[42]

The problem of indirect expropriation

Today the focus has shifted somewhat from direct expropriation to indirect expropriation through regulatory interference in the broadest sense. The reason for this lies in the fact that international treaties create international obligations of a longer-term nature. Getting out of these obligations takes much more time than the duration of the usual election cycles of the parliaments around the globe.[43] Thus indirect expropriation clauses have come under increased scrutiny in developed countries. In the past, as the debate on the permanent sovereignty resolution of the GA has amply illustrated, these treaty clauses tended to protect developed countries from political changes often in developing countries, including newly independent states. As such, the value of these indirect expropriation clauses was much more evident. Globalisation has, however, changed this rather simplistic view of the world. Now the industrialised and highly developed countries themselves must balance the interests of foreign investors whose money they seek with conflicting political interests at home which could threaten the investments undertaken by these foreign investors. Especially relevant in this context are public policy interests in environmental protection (including climate change) and health and social policy. In these policy areas, it is easily conceivable that domestic legislative and regulatory action, for example around environmental standards, could have a measurable impact on the value and profitability of a foreign investment and hence could give rise to the question whether such regulatory action by the host state constitutes a compensable measure of indirect expropriation. If that were the case and the adversely affected investors were entitled to perhaps substantial amounts of compensation, this could have a chilling effect on otherwise legitimate domestic legislative undertakings in these policy fields.

Example: Carmichael coal mine project in Queensland

That brings to the fore the issue of democratic legitimacy versus transnational governance in the form of international obligations arising in this context from investment treaties. The controversy over the Carmichael coal

42 See, for example, the final Articles of the above cited BITs.

43 Ranging from two years for the US House of Representatives to six years for the US and Australian Senate and everything in between with four years perhaps being most popular.

mine project in Northern Queensland provides an illustrative example.[44] The project is driven by Indian mining corporation Adani with a prospective investment value of AUD$16 billion. It is not yet clear whether the project will overcome all legal obstacles and to what degree the lower prices for coal at the time of writing have made this project less attractive for the foreign investor. But it can be safely assumed that if the project went ahead it would remain highly controversial politically. The economic benefits must be weighed against the environmental risks of the whole mining operation from extracting the coal to transporting it to the coast to shipping it through the Barrier Reef. The project could only go ahead if that balancing act was resolved in favour of the economic benefits. However, if, as a result of subsequent political changes after future elections, the project came under renewed scrutiny with a different outcome of the balancing act in favour of environmental and climate change concerns, and the project were stopped or confronted with additional and significant regulatory burdens, the Indian investor could take recourse under the Australian–Indian BIT.[45]

Article 7 of the Australian–Indian BIT protects foreign investors against measures of expropriation or measures having equivalent effect in very similar ways to the BITs and IIAs cited above. If the Carmichael project were to go ahead with considerable investment by Adani, subsequent significant changes in policy that impact this mining project could only be implemented by compensating Adani for the loss if those policy changes amounted to an expropriation or measures of equivalent effect. Given the projected investment volume of $16 billion, the price tag for such a policy change could be politically prohibitive. Terminating the treaty could be an option under Article 17, but previous investments would be protected for a total of 16 years, i.e. for a 1 year notice period (Article 17.2) plus a further 15 years' protection period for investments preceding termination of the agreement (Article 17.3).

The matter is further complicated by the fact that disputes arising under investment agreements are often subject to external arbitration under so-called 'investor–state dispute settlement' (ISDS) clauses. Under these clauses, such disputes can be brought to international commercial arbitration institutions by foreign investors against the host state thereby circumventing the host state's domestic court system. This is regarded by some as an undue privilege for foreign investors and the perception of a problem is often aggravated by the lack of transparency and publicity that often govern commercial arbitration.[46]

44 For more detail see <www.statedevelopment.qld.gov.au/assessments-and-approvals/carmichael-coal-mine-and-rail-project.html> accessed 20 March 2017.

45 <www.austlii.edu.au/au/other/dfat/treaties/2000/14.html> accessed 20 March 2017.

46 R. Dolzer and C. Schreuer, *Principles of International Investment Law* (Oxford University Press, 2nd edn 2012) 286–288.

The concept of indirect expropriation

The extent of the problem will greatly depend on what is construed to be an indirect expropriation, i.e. what kind of measures qualify as being of 'equivalent effect' to an expropriation. The standard rules of treaty interpretation as codified in Article 31 of the Vienna Convention on the Law of Treaties already strongly imply that not every measure having a potential or actual negative effect on the investment can be regarded as having equivalent effect to a full-scale expropriation. However, beyond that statement the definitional waters have remained rather murky. It is beyond the scope of looking at the relevant jurisprudence and literature in depth,[47] but there are some common threads which can be identified to distinguish non-compensable state action from action amounting to compensable indirect expropriation.

The core parameter for that distinction is the severity of the measure in terms of its impact on the value of the investment. It is not entirely clear to what extent economic effect alone can be a decisive criterion,[48] or to what extent other criteria such as proportionality, striking a fair balance between the public and private interests involved,[49] legitimate expectations by the affected party[50] and the principle of non-discrimination[51] are additional

47 For more detail see OECD (2004), 'Indirect Expropriation' and the 'Right to Regulate' in International Investment Law, OECD Working Papers on International Investment, 2004/04 (OECD Publishing), <http://dx.doi.org/10.1787/780155872321> accessed 20 March 2017; S. Olynyk, 'A Balanced Approach to Distinguishing between Legitimate Regulation and Indirect Expropriation in Investor-State Arbitration' (2012) 15 *Int'l Trade & Bus. L. Rev.* 254; UNCTAD (2012), *Expropriation – A Sequel*, UNCTAD Series on Issues in International Investment Agreements II, <http://unctad.org/en/Docs/unctaddiaeia2011d7_en.pdf> accessed 20 March 2017.

48 The Iran–US Claims Tribunal stated with regard to regulatory measures that 'it is an accepted principle of international law that a State is not liable for economic injury which is a consequence of bona fide "regulation" within the accepted police powers of States' but added in a footnote (fn. 25) that this would have to be different if such regulation damages the property to a 'substantial or excessive degree', Iran–US Claims Tribunal, *Sedco Inc. v National Iranian Oil Company*, Interlocutory Award, 24/10/1984, Award No. ITL 55-129-3, 84 ILR 483, 513.

49 See the jurisprudence of the European Court of Human Rights on Article 1 of the First Additional Protocol, most recently ECtHR, *Grigaliūnien v Lithuania*, Appl. No. 42322/09, 23/2/2016, paras 27 et seq, 31, with reference to *Pyrantien v Lithuania*, Appl. No. 45092/07, 12/11/2013, paras 37–40.

50 *Metalclad Corporation v United Mexican States*, ICSID Case No. ARB(AF)/97/1, text available at <https://icsid.worldbank.org> (go to 'cases') or at <www.italaw.com/sites/default/files/case-documents/ita0510.pdf> both accessed on 20 March 2017, para 103 where the Tribunal stated that expropriation under NAFTA also includes 'covert or incidental interference with the use of property which has the effect of depriving the owner, in whole or in significant part, of the use or reasonably-to-be-expected economic benefit of property even if not necessarily to the obvious benefit of the host State'.

51 *Methanex v United States* (2005) 44 ILM 1345, Part IV Ch. D para 7, text at <www.italaw.com/sites/default/files/case-documents/ita0529.pdf> accessed 20 March 2017: 'In the Tribunal's view, Methanex is correct that an intentionally discriminatory regulation against a foreign investor fulfils a key requirement for establishing expropriation. But

constitutive elements of this determination rather than just additional criteria to assist in the determination and evaluation of the economic effect. The European Court of Human Rights uses a test comprising of several criteria pivoting around the principle of proportionality.[52] The Iran–US Claims Tribunal has stated that for an expropriation to occur, the measures in question must deprive the owner 'of fundamental rights of ownership' without being merely 'ephemeral'.[53]

The bottom line is that the action in question by the allegedly expropriating state needs to be of sufficient gravity to qualify as equivalent or tantamount to expropriation. Some forums achieve that qualification by looking at a corresponding economic effect, others draw on assisting criteria to allow for the conclusion that a regulatory matter is serious enough to constitute an equivalent effect or be tantamount to an expropriation. All have in common that grammatical treaty interpretation of the relevant treaty clauses dictates a restrictive understanding of what constitutes an indirect expropriation. This is because all property rights exist exclusively within the framework of the respective governing legal order and not outside of that legal order. The states that define the property rights also bear the ultimate political responsibility for the welfare of the population. It follows that the scope for exercising their regulatory police power to pursue these welfare objectives can only be restricted in very limited circumstances when strong reasons can be cited in favour of the competing private property interest to either prevail entirely or at least fiscally by way of compensation.

In other words, the threshold for qualifying state regulatory measures as equivalent to expropriation remains high. Disputes involving Ecuador illustrate this finding.[54] These disputes arose in the context of legislative measures passed in Ecuador regarding participation of the state in any profits derived from hydrocarbon exploration and subsequent exploitation, i.e. sale of crude oil. One of the measures passed was Law 42 which initially provided for a 50 per cent tax (levy) payable to Ecuador on the price difference between a low statutory price set in the legislation and the higher market price. This 50 per cent tax was later raised to 99 per cent.[55] Despite what appears to be a

as a matter of general international law, a non-discriminatory regulation for a public purpose, which is enacted in accordance with due process and, which affects, inter alios, a foreign investor or investment is not deemed expropriatory and compensable unless specific commitments had been given by the regulating government to the then putative foreign investor contemplating investment that the government would refrain from such regulation'.

52 See cases cited in fn. 47.

53 *ITT Industries Inc. v Islamic Republic of Iran*, Award No. 47-156-2, Concurring Opinion of Judge Aldrich, para 352, 72 ILR 223, 229 (para 352).

54 *Perenco Ecuador Ltd v Ecuador*, ICSID Case No. ARB/08/6, Decision on Remaining Issues of Jurisdiction and on Liability, 12/9/2014 ('Perenco'); *Burlington Resources Inc. v Ecuador*, ICSID Case No. ARB/08/5, Decision on Liability, 14/12/2012 ('Burlington').

55 Burlington, paras 30 et seq.; Perenco, paras 88 et seq. with detailed legislative and implementation history.

devastating tax rate, the Tribunals in both cases did not regard even the 99 per cent rate as a measure tantamount to an expropriation. The main reason was that this tax only pertained to that amount of money that was achieved on the markets over and above the statutory reference price. The evidence had shown that even at that lower statutory price operations continued. The 99 per cent tax rate, whereas 'disadvantageous to Perenco, did not bring its operation to a halt or, to revert to the tests previously cited, effectively neutralise the investment or render it as if it had ceased to exist'.[56]

The 'tests' referred to by the Tribunal concerned decisions by other Tribunals which had characterised an (indirect) expropriation measure as having to amount to a 'complete or near complete deprivation of value' or such a radical deprivation of the economical use and enjoyment of its investments, 'as if the rights related thereto ... had ceased to exist', i.e. 'the assets involved have lost their value or economic use for their holder' or that the measures had to 'effectively neutralize the benefit of the property of the foreign owner'.[57]

'Golden shares'

Pursuing the national interest in matters of economic strategic importance can also be achieved in other ways and this is of particular relevance in the resources sector. So-called 'golden shares' are a phenomenon of the post-privatisation era of the 1980s and 1990s when formerly state-owned enterprises and monopolies were opened up for private ownership. These 'golden shares' created special rights, often vested in just one share held by the government, to afford special powers to the holder regarding changes to the company's charter, foreign ownership or other strategic issues. In other words, 'golden shares' are an instrument to retain governmental control and limit the effect of privatisation in certain sectors of the economy. The resources sector is one of the sectors considered to be of strategic importance in many countries. One practical example in the resource sector are the 'golden shares' in Brazilian resource

56 Perenco, para 685; Burlington, para 456 ('the investment preserved its capacity to generate a commercial return'). The disputes also highlight that, from an accounting perspective, it can be very difficult to determine whether an undertaking is making a loss or a profit, see paras 434 et seq.

57 Perenco, para 672 with reference to *Compañía de Aguas del Aconquija S.A. and Vivendi Universal S.A. v Argentine Republic*, ICSID Case No. ARB/97/3, Award, 20/8/2007, para 7.5.11; *Técnicas Medioambientales Tecmed S.A. v United Mexican States*, ICSID Case No. ARB(AF)/00/2, Award, 29/5/2003, para 115; *CME Czech Republic, B.V. (the Netherlands) v the Czech Republic*, UNCITRAL Partial Award, 13/9/2001, para 604. See also *Grand River Enterprises Six Nations, Ltd, et al. v United States of America*, UNCITRAL, Award, 12/1/2011, <www.state.gov/documents/organization/ 156820.pdf> accessed 20 March 2017, which summarises the equally strict NAFTA approach: 'Other NAFTA Tribunals have regularly construed Article 1110 to require a complete or very substantial deprivation of owners' rights in the totality of the investment, and have rejected expropriation claims where (as here) a claimant remained in possession of an ongoing business'.

giant Vale.[58] The relevance of these 'golden shares' lies in the fact that they are an instrument which can be used preventively to avoid scenarios which might lead interested parties in a country to the conclusion that resorting to expropriation might provide a persuasive benefit. 'Golden shares' can be an instrument to 'pre-balance' the interests of foreign investors with the host state's interest in having access to the world capital markets and being attractive to foreign investors by providing ownership security yet having a transparent system for core strategic control retention.

This instrument has in the recent past played a significant role in the legal order of the EU where the free movement of capital is one of the fundamental market freedoms of the EU's internal market.[59] Critically, this market freedom applies not only to market participants within the EU, but also to market participants in non-member states.[60] In principle, the free movement of capital can therefore be claimed by anybody engaging in capital transactions within the EU and between the EU and non-member states. Foreign direct investment, e.g. buying shares in an EU corporation, is such a capital transaction and any restrictions placed on buying certain shares or exercising standard rights flowing from the ownership of these shares, such as limiting the percentage that can be held by foreign owners or other ownership restrictions, are an infringement on the right to freely move capital. That would also apply in the resources sector.

However, no right is absolute and neither is the free movement of capital. The European Court of Justice (ECJ) has decided several cases in this regard. They are commonly referred to as the 'golden share' cases because they usually involve iconic national corporations in the areas of finance, transport, energy and natural resources that previously were often state owned and then privatised during the worldwide privatisation drive in the 1980s and 1990s.[61]

58 See <www.vale.com/australia/EN/investors/company/corporate-governance/golden-share/Pages/default.aspx> accessed on 20 March 2017, for a description of the rights associated with these shares which are held by the Brazilian government.

59 Article 26 TFEU: 'The internal market shall comprise an area without internal frontiers in which the free movement of goods, persons, services and capital is ensured in accordance with the provisions of the Treaties'.

60 Article 63 TFEU: 'Within the framework of the provisions set out in this Chapter, all restrictions on the movement of capital between Member States and between Member States and third countries shall be prohibited'.

61 ECJ, Case C-367/98, ECR 2002, I-4731 (Commission/Portugal); Case C-483/99, ECR 2002, I-4781 (Commission/France); Case C-503/99, ECR 2002, I-4809 (Commission/Belgium); Case C-463/00, ECR 2003, I-4581 (Commission/Spain); Case C-98/01, ECR 2003, I-4641 (Commission/UK); Case C-174/04, ECR 2005, I-4933 (Commission/Italy); Joined Cases C-282 u. C-283/04, ECR 2006, I-9141 (Commission/Netherlands); Joined Cases C-463 und C-464/04, ECR 2007, I-10419 (Federconsumatori); Case C-326/07, ECR 2009, I-2291 (Commission/Italy); Case C-171/08, ECR 2010, I-6817 (Commission/Portugal); Case C-543/08, ECR 2010, I-11241 (Commission/Portugal); Case C-212/09, ECLI:EU:C:2011:717 (Commission/Portugal).

In dealing with these cases the ECJ strictly stuck to its consistent jurisprudence in the construction of the market freedoms. The fact that 'national champions' may be subject to takeovers by foreign investors cannot as such serve as a valid justification for restricting such investment under the Treaty on the Functioning of the European Union (TFEU). However, national public interests such as public security and, for example, reliability of the energy supply can be invoked as justifications for infringements by the EU member states if the measures taken to that effect are proportional, i.e. if these measures can reach the proclaimed objective and do not go beyond what is absolutely necessary to reach that goal. To this end, criteria must be spelled out and it must be assured that these criteria can be subjected to judicial scrutiny in a court of law by an investor whose intentions to invest or whose position in the protected corporation are stymied by the restrictions imposed, e.g. the 'golden share'.[62]

In other words, EU member states retain the possibility to limit access to ownership or the ability to determine corporate strategic decision-making of important energy or resource corporations if and insofar as tangible overriding and justiciable public policy interests are formulated and invoked. These public policy interests are the same interests which tend to drive domestic legislation in the exercise of the domestic police powers and which, as demonstrated above, could lead to claims of indirect expropriation. Regarding third countries, the ECJ has in effect shut out third country investors from the benefits of the free movement of capital clauses in the TFEU if and insofar as the foreign (third country, non-EU member state) investment is not merely a financial investment but one with the intention to actively influence corporate decision-making. Such investments are regarded as primarily falling under the freedom of establishment (Articles 49 et seq. TFEU) which grants rights only to EU citizens and not to third country nationals or corporations.[63]

Outside the EU the matters related to ownership of corporations, types and classes of stock and in fact all matters concerning corporation law are part of the sovereign law-making function of the state in question. There are no general limitations in international law to structuring domestic corporation law in a certain way. Free movement of capital is not part of general international law and even investment treaties, which could provide rights similar to the free movement of capital right in the EU, often do not grant a substantive right for foreign investors to have their

62 See cases cited in fn. 57 and J. Bröhmer, 'The Free Movement of Capital in the European Union and the Problem of "Golden Shares" and Similar Instruments' (2007) 25 (2) *Law in Context* 144, 156; see also J. Bröhmer, 'Articles 63–66' in C. Calliess and M. Ruffert, *EUV/AEUV-Kommentar* (Verlag C.H. Beck, 5th edn 2016).

63 See J. van Bekkum, 'Golden Shares: A New Approach' (2010) 7 *European Company Law* 14.

investment admitted by the host state or, insofar as they do, contain sweeping exceptions.[64]

Conclusion

The notion of 'resource nationalism' is strictly political and devoid of any legal meaning. The legal framework for dealing with natural resources is entirely unaffected by this term and primarily governed by domestic law. The policies pursued by states regarding their natural resources are for the states themselves to determine. The scope for shaping the legal framework in that regard is broad and subject mainly to limitations by domestic, often constitutional, law. Additional limitations arising from public international law can either flow from customary public international law or from treaty law. Whereas it is a trademark of customary international law that it can exist without the proactive contribution of a state in its conception through state practice, the impact of such international law norms on resources management and policy are very limited indeed and are mainly restricted to the protection of foreigners against expropriation (public purpose, no intentional discrimination, proportionality, compensation).[65]

Of much more relevance in a practical sense is treaty based international law, i.e. IIAs. These treaties confirm what customary international law already suggests, namely that expropriation or nationalisation is by no means illegal but requires certain safeguards, most importantly the duty to pay compensation, and these safeguards are in essence the same as prescribed by customary international law. In fact, these safeguards and their description in many treaties has in the meantime yielded an impressive body of state practice to strengthen the customary law regime in this regard vis-à-vis even those states not party to such treaties. One of the major questions in this regard has been the delineation of takings in the narrow sense, i.e. where the property right as such changes hands, and indirect expropriations, i.e. where the property right as such remains untouched but the usefulness of the property is diminished. This question goes to the balancing of the private interest reflected in the property right and the public interest in exercising the state's regulatory (police) powers. Relevant treaty law requires such regulatory measures to be of 'equivalent effect' to an expropriation which explains that

64 E.g. *White Industries Australia Ltd v The Republic of India*, Final Award of 30/11/2011, <http://opil.ouplaw.com/view/10.1093/law:iic/529-2011.case.1/IIC529%282011%29D.pdf> last accessed on 28 February 2016, para 9 at 9.2.5 et seq. C. Schreuer, 'Investments, International Protection' in *Max Planck Encyclopedia of Public International Law [MPEPIL]* (Oxford University Press reference ID: MPEPIL 1533), para 43 et seq.

65 And some core basic concepts of environmental protection, e.g. the no harm principle established in the *Trail Smelter Arbitration USA–Canada*, Arbitral Trib., 3 UN Rep. Int'l Arb. Awards 1905 (1941), available at <http://legal.un.org/riaa/cases/vol_III/1905-1982.pdf> last accessed on 7 May 2016.

not every diminishing of the value of a property right because of regulation qualifies.

States maintain a very broad margin of appreciation in determining what regulatory action they take; such regulatory action can only lead to a claim for compensation if the measures render the property right effectively economically useless. A public policy interest to nationalise can as such and by itself not serve to legitimise expropriations even if the nationalisation equally affected all foreign held property rights as that would render the minimum standard rules under customary international law for the protection of aliens useless. Finally, the same discussions prevalent in the context of 'resource nationalism', the thoughts underpinning the Calvo doctrine and the balancing of public and private interest are currently a major force in the discussion around the advantages and disadvantages of major free trade agreements, such as the Trans-Pacific Partnership (TPP) or the Transatlantic Trade and Investment Partnership (TTIP). The major concern of those opposed to these efforts is the perceived impact of these treaties on the regulatory power of the states and especially in the context of the investment chapters of these treaties where the measures of equivalent effect to expropriation are situated.

8 Regulatory strategies, CSR and resource protection

Paolo Galizzi and Emily Smith Ewing

Introduction

While states have the sovereign right to exploit the natural resources within their jurisdictions,[1] it is very often multinational corporations (MNCs)[2] who use, extract and profit from those resources the most.[3] Further, corporate activities in this regard often cause significant damage to the environment and development process.[4] Destruction of ecosystems, environmental pollution, reduction of available resources for local communities, conflict and corruption are just some of the issues that result from natural resource use

1 Declaration of the United Nations Conference on the Human Environment 1972 Principle 21 (Stockholm Declaration); Principle 2, Rio Declaration on Environment and Development 1992 (Rio Declaration). See also Nico Shrijver, *Sovereignty over Natural Resources* (Cambridge University Press, 1997)

2 In this chapter, 'multinational corporation' will have the same meaning as that used in the OECD Guidelines for Multinational Enterprises: 'companies or other entities established in more than one country and so linked that they may co-ordinate their operations in various ways. While one or more of these entities may be able to exercise a significant influence over the activities of others, their degree of autonomy within the enterprise may vary widely from one multinational enterprise to another. Ownership may be private, state or mixed'. In OECD, *OECD Guidelines for Multinational Enterprises* (OECD Publishing, 2011) <http://dx.doi.org/10.1787/9789264115415-en> accessed 21 April 2016, 17 para 4. For a discussion on the various definitions of MNCs, see Elena Blanco and Jona Razzaque, *Globalization and Natural Resources Law, Challenges, Key Issues and Perspectives* (Edward Elgar Publishing, 2011)

3 For a sampling of literature see: United Nations Economic and Social Council, 'The Impact of Multinational Corporations on Development and on International Relations, Report of the Group of Eminent Persons to Study the Role of Multinational Corporations on Development and on International Relations', UN Doc E/5500/Add.1 (Part 1); Macartan Humphreys, Jeffrey D. Sachs and Joseph E. Stiglitz (eds), *Escaping the Resource Curse* (Columbia University Press, 2007); Andreas Georg Scherer and Guido Palazzo, 'Globalization and Corporate Social Responsibility' in Andrew Crane and others (eds), *The Oxford Handbook of Corporate Social Responsibility* (Oxford University Press 2008); Blanco and Razzaque, *Globalization and Natural Resources Law* (n 2) 212–250

4 Ibid. See also United Nations Environment Programme, *Industry as a Partner for Sustainable Development. 10 Years after Rio: The UNEP Assessment* (United Nations Environment Programme, 2002) for failings of industry in natural resource protection

and exploitation by MNCs.[5] At the same time, the global reliance on natural resources provides a powerful incentive for exploration and sustained rates of extraction.

However, MNCs have much to contribute to the protection of natural resources. They have far-reaching influence over policy, legislation and enforcement at the global and domestic levels.[6] They can provide technological and research capabilities to evaluate environmental policies and procedures, and bring innovative solutions to natural resource degradation such as the development of and investment in renewable energy such as solar and wind power.[7]

In order to protect natural resources, MNCs are primarily regulated by domestic law both in the host state in which the natural resources are located and, in some circumstances, in the home state in which the corporation is headquartered.[8] However, due to weak legal frameworks, inadequate enforcement mechanisms, lack of coordination between government agencies, legal complexity surrounding the nature of MNCs, limitations in extraterritorial prescription of home state law, widespread corruption and an imbalance of negotiating power that favours MNC interests over states, MNCs can appear to proceed in their exploitation of natural resources with limited regulation and accountability.[9] Partly in response to these perceived inadequacies, the idea of corporate self-regulation through voluntary

5 See Chapter 10 in this volume

6 Evidenced recently by the strong corporate lobbying that took place at the Paris Climate Change meeting in December 2015 where business groups, such as the International Chamber of Commerce and the B Team, spoke out in favour of stronger targets: International Chamber of Commerce <http://cop21.iccwbo.org/>; B Team group of CEOs led by Richard Branson <http://bteam.org/planb/>; the Caring for Climate private sector initiative of the United Nations Global Compact, United Nations Environment Programme and United Nations Framework Convention on Climate Change <http://caringforclimate.org/>

7 Which now reportedly sees twice the investment as fossil fuels globally: Tom Randall, 'Wind and Solar Are Crushing Fossil Fuels' *Bloomberg* (6 April 2016)

8 For an interesting discussion on the challenges of regulating MNCs see Blanco and Razzaque, *Globalization and Natural Resources Law* (n 2) 217–220; for an argument for greater home state regulation of MNCs see generally Edwin Mujih, *Regulating Multinationals in Developing Countries: A Conceptual and Legal Framework for Corporate Social Responsibility* (Gower, 2012)

9 Patricia Birnie, Alan Boyle and Catherine Redgwell, *International Law and the Environment* (3rd edn, Oxford University Press 2009) 326–329; Shanta Martin, 'Corporate Social Responsibility and the Defence of Human Rights' in Elena Blanco and Jona Razzaque (eds), *Natural Resources and the Green Economy: Redefining the Challenges for Peoples, States and Corporations* (Nijhoff 2012) 186–189; Jona Razzaque, 'Corporate Responsibility in Tackling Environmental Harm: Lost in the Regulatory Maze?' (2013) 16 *The Australian Journal of Natural Resources Law and Policy* 197; Gare A. Smith, 'An Introduction to Corporate Social Responsibility in the Extractive Industries' (2008) 11 *Yale Human Rights and Development LJ* 1

principles and standards, often referred to as corporate social responsibility (CSR), has emerged.[10]

Initially a philanthropic activity to 'give back' (in addition to being an effective marketing tool to attract customers, clients and talented employees), CSR has evolved into a broader agenda that sets voluntary standards for business enterprises in regard to the environmental and social impacts of their products, services and operations.[11] In practical terms, CSR is generally understood to require companies to respect and conserve the environment, contribute to sustainable development, ensure respect for workers' rights, address human rights harms, avoid corrupt practices and be transparent in their CSR efforts.[12] These CSR principles may be codified in intergovernmental agreements such as the Organisation for Economic Co-operation and Development (OECD) Guidelines for Multinational Enterprises, voluntary initiatives such as the United Nations Global Compact, and industry codes of conduct such as the International Council on Mining and Metals Sustainable Development Principles, as discussed further below.[13] While technically non-binding, these CSR principles derive from an international agreement on the minimum standards that companies are expected to adhere to in their activities, regardless of domestic regulation. Often, compliance with domestic law will form the minimum basis for the various CSR guidelines and codes of conduct, but where domestic law or enforcement are inadequate, companies are expected to meet these higher voluntary standards.[14] At the same time, there are examples of states starting to enact legislation that seeks to strengthen CSR principles, such as recent non-financial reporting requirements at the European Union that encourage greater transparency, which suggest future opportunities to reinforce both regulatory and self-regulatory approaches.[15]

10 For an in-depth discussion on the development and rise of CSR see Jennifer A. Zerk, *Multinationals and Corporate Social Responsibility: Limitations and Opportunities in International Law* (Cambridge University Press, 2006) 15–29

11 For a detailed overview of the history and development of CSR see Archie B. Carroll, 'A History of Corporate Social Responsibility: Concepts and Practice' in Andrew Crane and others, *The Oxford Handbook of Corporate Social Responsibility* (Oxford University Press, 2008) 19

12 For an in-depth examination of the different definitions and interpretations of CSR see Matthew Genasci and Sarah Pray, 'Extracting Accountability: The Implications of the Resource Curse for CSR Theory and Practice' (2008) 11 *Yale Human Rights and Development LJ* 37

13 See sections 'Development of international expectations of MNCs: International environmental law and policy' and 'Soft law, MNCs and natural resource protection' below

14 Blanco and Razzaque, *Globalisation and Natural Resources Law* (n 2) 212–250; Razzaque (n 9)

15 Directive 2014/95/EU of the European Parliament and of the Council of 22 October 2014 amending Directive 2013/34/EU as regards disclosure of non-financial and diversity information by certain large undertakings and groups [2014] OJ L330/1

Focusing on a CSR approach to natural resource protection,[16] this chapter will examine three aspects of MNC regulation: international soft law instruments, voluntary industry initiatives, and the role of other non-state actors such as international organizations and non-governmental organizations (NGOs). Following a brief examination of the impact of MNCs on natural resource conservation, the chapter will outline the development of international expectations for MNC behaviour that have emerged from a series of landmark intergovernmental conferences. It will then examine some of the most prominent international soft law instruments that directly address corporations and natural resource protection. The chapter will then move on to explore the impact of voluntary initiatives and industry standards using the extractive industry as a case study.[17] Finally it will briefly discuss the role of non-state actors, such as international organizations and NGOs, in regulating MNCs.

The impact of MNCs on natural resources

Under international law, states have a sovereign right to use, manage and dispose of the natural resources that lie within their boundaries pursuant to their own environmental and development policies (albeit with certain limitations).[18] However, it is very often MNCs that exploit and profit from these resources the most.[19] Private sector investment can of course benefit states that cannot otherwise manage and extract the resources themselves.[20] MNCs may provide necessary infrastructure, technical capabilities and employment, and can stimulate economic growth. However, very often there is little or no

16 While there are examples of domestic legislation incorporating CSR principles, such as the EU non-financial reporting requirements mentioned above, new legislation in the area of human trafficking (such as the California Transparency in Supply Chains Act 2012 and the UK Modern Day Slavery Act 2015), and the widely adopted requirement for states to use Environmental Impact Assessments to guide decision-making for certain proposed corporate activities (as highlighted in the section 'Development of international expectations of MNCs: International environmental law and policy' below), a full review of domestic regulation of corporations in regard to natural resource protection is beyond the scope of this chapter

17 On the one hand the extractive industry is perceived to cause significant damage to natural resources and the environment often as a result of inadequate regulation, however the industry has also started to attempt to address concerns through a series of industry initiatives, thus making it an interesting case study for the purposes of this chapter

18 n 1. On the relationship between states and individuals as owners of natural resources as well as the other limitations that apply to state ownership of resources see Lorenzo Cotula, *Human Rights, Natural Resources and Investment Law in a Globalised World* (Routledge, 2012); Jorge E. Vinuales, 'The Resource Curse: A Legal Perspective' (2011) 17 *Global Governance* 197; Blanco and Razzaque, *Globalization and Natural Resources Law* (n 2)

19 n 3

20 Bede Nwete, 'Corporate Social Responsibility and Transparency in the Development of Energy and Mining Projects in Emerging Markets; Is Soft Law the Answer?' (2007) *8 German Law Journal* 311

long-term economic benefit or improvement in the standard of living for people of that host state.[21] Further, in the use and extraction process, corporate activities can cause or contribute to serious environmental damage. This has been demonstrated by the vast quantities of water that are used for factory processes and the pollution caused to water systems due to factory outlets;[22] catastrophic mining events such as the Deepwater Horizon oil spill in 2010;[23] rapid deforestation in Borneo and Sumatra for palm oil plantations;[24] the extraction of fish stocks beyond their maximum sustainability levels due to over fishing;[25] or soil degradation due to the development of oil pipelines such as reported in Colombia in 2014.[26] Additionally, as has been evidenced by cases and reports against Shell in Nigeria, many of the corporate activities that cause environmental damage also have negative social implications including human rights abuses, increased conflict, increased corruption, poor working conditions and denying economic benefit to the host state through beneficial tax treatment of MNCs.[27]

Of course, as noted above, companies do not only negatively impact the environment. The private sector can and does contribute to the protection of natural resources on many levels, for example through corporate influence over policy and legislation at the international and domestic levels, the provision of technological and research capabilities to evaluate environmental policies and processes, the development of innovative solutions to natural resource degradation and the exploration of alternative sources of resources, such as renewable energy.[28]

21 Martin (n 9); Smith (n 9)

22 One example frequently reported is that of the textile industry: Leon Kaye, 'Clothing to Dye for: The Textile Sector Must Confront Water Risks' *The Guardian* (London, 12 August 2013)

23 National Commission on the BP Deepwater Horizon Oil Spill and Offshore Drilling, *Report to the President, Deep Water: The Gulf Oil Disaster and the Future of Offshore Drilling* (Government Publishing Office, 2011)

24 WWF Market Transformation Initiative, 'Making Better Production Everybody's Business, Results of 5 Years of WWF Market Transformation Work' (World Wide Fund for Nature, 2014)

25 According to United Nations Food and Agriculture Organization (FAO), 90 per cent of fish stocks have now been depleted beyond maximum sustainability levels: Food and Agriculture Organization of the United Nations, 'The State of World Fisheries and Aquaculture: Opportunities and Challenges' (FAO, 2014). See also Malgosia Fitzmaurice, 'Natural Resources Management: Protecting Fisheries in the 21st Century' in Blanco and Razzaque (eds), *Natural Resources and the Green Economy Redefining the Challenges for People, States and Corporations* (Nijhoff, 2012)

26 Jane Croft, 'Colombian Farmers Sue BP over Oil Pipeline's Alleged Impact' *Financial Times* (12 October 2014)

27 For example Shell's activities in the Niger Delta against the Ogoni people in the 1990s, see *Ken Wiwa, et al. v Royal Dutch Petroleum*, US District Court of the Southern District of New York (complaint), and more recently Mark Leftly, 'Shell Attacked for its Part in "Extraordinary" £2.3bn Nigerian Tax Break' *Independent* (19 January 2016)

28 n 6; n 7

Development of international expectations of MNCs: International environmental law and policy

International law, including international environmental law, traditionally regulates relations between states and does not impose rights and obligations on non-state actors, such as corporations, individuals and other entities.[29] However, a series of landmark conferences over the last 50 years has helped to establish a global consensus on basic international environmental norms and policies, some of which are of particular relevance for business activity, as highlighted below.[30] In addition to forming the basis of domestic environmental law of host and home states,[31] over the years these principles and processes have been translated into a number of soft law documents, international guidelines and voluntary industry initiatives directed specifically towards MNCs.

The equal responsibility that enterprises share alongside states to protect the environment and natural resources was initially highlighted at the first intergovernmental conference on the environment, the 1972 United Nations Conference on Human Development, and the resulting Stockholm Declaration on the Human Environment (Stockholm Declaration).[32] The provisions of the Stockholm Declaration focus on protecting the environment and natural resources for future generations while taking into account the need for economic and social development.[33] The Stockholm Declaration codified one of the first principles of international environmental law: the prohibition on causing transboundary environmental harm.[34] Principle 21 affirms that while states have the sovereign right to exploit their own natural resources, they have an equally important responsibility to ensure that 'activities within their jurisdiction or control do not cause damage to the environment of other States or of areas beyond the limits of national jurisdiction'.[35] Furthermore, the Stockholm Declaration endorses the principle of prevention of environmental

29 Zerk (n 10)

30 For a comprehensive overview of the general principles and rules of international environmental law see Philippe Sands and others, *Principles of International Environmental Law* (Cambridge University Press, 2012) Ch 6. For a detailed analysis of how these principles apply to MNCs see Paolo Galizzi, 'From Ignorance, to Indifference, to Limited Familiarity: An Analysis of the Relationship between International Environmental Law and Multinational Corporations' in Mariarosa Cutillo, Fabian Novak Talavera and Tullio Scovazzi (eds) *La responsabilità sociale d'impresa in tema di diritti umani e protezione dell'ambiente. Il caso del Perù* (Giuffrè, 2014)

31 As an example, the use of environmental impact assessments has been widely endorsed around the world, and in particular in the EU (Environmental Impact Assessment (EIA) Directive 2014/52/EU newly amended). See Peter G.G. Davies, *European Union Environmental Law, An Introduction to Key Selected Issues* (Ashgate, 2004) Ch 5

32 Para 7, Stockholm Declaration

33 Ibid para 6

34 Ibid Principle 21

35 A principle that originated from a dispute involving a lead and smelting complex in Canada that caused damage to crops and forest land in the United States, *Trail Smelter Arbitration, United States v Canada*, 3 RIAA 1905 (1941), p. 1965

damage,[36] which according to the International Court of Justice puts an obligation on states to exercise due diligence 'in respect of all activities' within their jurisdictions including in regard to private operators.[37]

During the subsequent decades, following environmental disasters such as the industrial gas disaster at Bhopal, India, the impact of corporate activities on the environment became an increasing concern for the international community.[38] Following a series of failed attempts to launch a voluntary code of conduct for MNCs, the General Assembly, in the convening resolution of the UN Conference on Environment and Development in Rio de Janeiro in 1992 (the Earth Summit), referred specifically to the role and responsibilities of large industrial enterprises, including transnational corporations, to protect and enhance the environment in all countries.[39] While the resulting Rio Declaration on Environment and Development (Rio Declaration) encompasses only voluntary, self-regulatory initiatives (argued by some as the result of the notable corporate presence and participation in the negotiations),[40] it does set out a number of important environmental norms that impact corporate activities. In addition to reiterating the prohibition on causing transboundary environmental harm as codified in the Stockholm Declaration outlined above,[41] the Rio Declaration affirms the precautionary principle/approach which, while widely debated, in essence suggests that action should be taken to counter any threat of environmental damage even in the case of scientific uncertainty as to the activities causing, or existence of, a given problem.[42] The importance of precaution as a principle for MNCs is highlighted by its inclusion as a stand-alone provision of the UN Global Compact's 10 Principles for private sector members.[43] The Rio Declaration also affirms the principle of polluter pays, which arguably contemplates the private sector as being expected to compensate damage caused by polluting activities.[44]

36 Stockholm Declaration principles 6, 7, 15, 18 and 24

37 See International Court of Justice *Pulp Mills on the River Uruguay (Argentina v Uruguay)*, Judgment of 20 April 2010, paragraph 197

38 For a detailed overview of the efforts of the United Nations to engage with MNCs and urge socially and environmentally responsible behaviour, see Tagi Sagafi-Nejad, *The UN and Transnational Corporations: From Code of Conduct to Global Compact* (Indiana University Press, 2008)

39 United Nations Conference on Environment and Development, General Assembly Resolution 44/228 (1989) para 10

40 Jennifer Clapp, 'Global Environmental Governance for Corporate Responsibility and Accountability' (2005) 5 *Global Environmental Politics* 23; Birnie, Boyle and Redgwell (n 9)

41 Rio Declaration Principle 2

42 Rio Declaration Principle 15. For a discussion of the meaning of the precautionary principle, see David Freestone, 'The Road from Rio: International Environmental Law after the Earth Summit' (1994) 6 *Journal of Environmental Law* 193

43 See section 'United Nations Global Compact' below

44 Rio Declaration Principle 16. For a comprehensive analysis of the polluter pays principle see Sanford E. Gaines, 'The Polluter-Pays Principle: From Economic Equity to Environmental Ethos' (1991) 26 *Texas International Law Journal* 463

Further, Chapter 30 of Agenda 21, a comprehensive programme of action accompanying the Rio Declaration, specifically recognizes the crucial role that business and industry play in social and economic development.[45] Chapter 30 calls upon all businesses to acknowledge environmental management as 'among the highest corporate priorities'[46] and emphasizes the role that policies and efficient production systems can play in reducing the impact on resource use and waste.[47] Companies are asked to consider two programmes: promoting cleaner production that is less polluting and increases the efficiency of resource use, reuse and recycling,[48] and promoting responsible entrepreneurship which includes increasing self-regulation, such as through codes, charters and initiatives.[49]

The World Summit on Sustainable Development in Johannesburg in 2002 (WSSD) reaffirmed the importance of CSR in sustainable development efforts. WSSD called upon the duty of the private sector 'to contribute to the evolution of equitable and sustainable communities and societies'[50] and highlighted the need to enhance corporate responsibility and accountability to address poverty eradication, change patterns of consumption, promote sustainable development and protect and manage national resources as a base for economic and social development.[51]

At the United Nations Conference on Sustainable Development (Rio+20 Summit),[52] the business sector formally participated in negotiations through the Business Action for Sustainable Development (BASD).[53] Confirming commitments made to implement the Rio Declaration, Agenda 21, and the Johannesburg Declaration, the outcome document of the Summit, *The Future We Want*, re-acknowledges the importance of engaging the private sector in advancing sustainable development goals through promoting responsible business practices.[54]

Soft law, MNCs and natural resource protection

While the international conferences discussed above have played an

45 Earth Summit, Agenda 21, Ch 30, para 30.1
46 Ibid para 30.3
47 Ibid paras 30.2 and 30.4
48 Ibid paras 30.5 to 30.16
49 Ibid paras 30.16 to 30.30
50 Plan of Implementation of the World Summit on Sustainable Development chs II–V and XI
51 Ibid Chs II–V and XI
52 The conference was established to mark the twentieth anniversary of the 1992 Rio Conference and the tenth anniversary of the World Summit on Sustainable Development
53 BASD is a joint initiative of the International Chamber of Commerce, World Business Council for Sustainable Development and the United Nations Global Compact. See: <http://basd2012.org> accessed 21 April 2016
54 United Nations Conference on Sustainable Development, outcome document *The Future We Want* paras 46 and 47

important role in establishing the international expectations on corporations in natural resource protection, a combination of domestic regulation, soft law and CSR initiatives guide corporate activity in practice.[55] This chapter will focus on soft law instruments. Although criticized for the fact that it is not binding,[56] soft law remains an important mechanism for influencing corporate decision-making outside domestic law.

First, soft law codifies international expectations as to corporate activities, providing an avenue for the public and civil society organizations to pressure companies to improve their behaviour and governments to set laws and hold companies accountable for environmental damage. For example, the OECD Guidelines for Multinational Enterprises reflect society's expectation of good corporate conduct by drawing on the principles contained in international agreements such as the Rio Declaration and further provide a system through which companies can be held accountable for their actions against the prescribed standards (as discussed further below).[57]

Second, in the absence of a strong legal framework that meets international standards, soft law instruments set the benchmark by which companies can assess their own environmental and social performance and set goals for improvement. For example, under the Communication on Progress process, United Nations Global Compact members are expected to report annually on their efforts to meet a set of ten principles (as discussed further below).[58]

Third, where international soft law is developed in partnership between governments, civil society and MNCs, it secures legitimacy and garners support across stakeholders and business sectors, thus strengthening the framework and encouraging greater engagement. For example, the Forest Stewardship Council is a notable and credible certification standard based on principles for the responsible management of forests that engages environmentalists, local communities and companies.[59]

Soft law instruments fall into a number of categories including international guidelines, business initiatives and sector specific guidance. The following section will examine a selection of four of the most prominent international instruments that can be used to guide corporate activity in regard to natural resource protection.

OECD Guidelines for Multinational Enterprises

The OECD Guidelines for Multinational Enterprises (OECD Guidelines)

55 Razzaque (n 9)

56 Anthony D'Amato, *International Soft Law, Hard Law, and Coherence*, Northwestern University School of Law Public Law and Legal Theory Series No. 08-01, available at <http://ssrn.com/abstract=1103915>

57 OECD (2011), *OECD Guidelines for Multinational Enterprises*, OECD Publishing, para 60

58 United Nations Global Compact <www.unglobalcompact.org> accessed 31 August 2016

59 See Forest Stewardship Council website: <https://us.fsc. org/en-us>

are a set of voluntary principles and standards that seek to promote corporate responsibility and governance consistent with domestic law and international obligations.[60] Focusing on a wide spectrum of CSR issues, the provisions of the OECD Guidelines are divided into eight chapters: human rights; employment and industrial relations; environment; bribery; consumer interests; science and technology; competition; and taxation. As '[r]ecommendations addressed by governments to multinational enterprises',[61] the Guidelines form part of the Declaration on International Investment and Multinational Enterprises, which has been adopted by all 34 OECD countries and 12 non-OECD countries. The OECD Guidelines were first adopted in 1976 and have been revised and updated five times, with the most recent revision in 2011.

The Environment Chapter of the OECD Guidelines reflects the principles and objectives of Agenda 21 and requires companies to recognise the 'need to protect the environment, public health and safety, and generally to conduct their activities in a manner contributing to the wider goal of sustainable development'.[62] While the Guidelines expect MNCs to comply with domestic and international laws and standards generally,[63] they specifically encourage companies to: adequately evaluate environmental impacts of activities; strive to improve and monitor environmental performance; engage with communities directly affected by the company's activities; conduct appropriate environmental impact assessments; and adopt a precautionary approach[64] to potential environmental harms.[65] They also encourage companies to continually seek improvements in environmental performance at every level of the supply chain and develop products and services that are sensitive to consumption of energy and natural resources.[66]

While the OECD Guidelines are not binding on the companies to which they are addressed, adhering governments are obliged to encourage MNCs operating in or from their territories to comply.[67] Further, adhering governments are required to establish National Contact Points (NCP) whose role is, *inter alia*, to promote the OECD Guidelines and handle complaints against companies that have allegedly failed to adhere to Guidelines' standards.[68] The NCP system has been criticized for a number of reasons

60 OECD (n 57)

61 Ibid

62 OECD Guidelines, Text and Commentary, Part VI Environment

63 Ibid 42–44

64 n 43

65 OECD (n 62)

66 Ibid

67 OECD Guidelines; see also Decision of the Council on the OECD Guidelines for Multinational Enterprises (June 2000) <www.oecd.org/investment/mne/theoecdguidelinesformultinationalenterprisesdecisionofthecouncil.htm> accessed 23 April 2016

68 OECD Guidelines, Part II, Implementation Procedures of the OECD Guidelines for Multinational Enterprises, Amendment of the Decision of the Council on the OECD Guidelines for Multinational Enterprises, I 1-4 (n 2). For an in-depth discussion of the

including a lack of formal process causing a variance in procedure in each country, inconsistency of the treatment of cases submitted to the same NCP, the lack of independent human rights experts hearing the NCP cases, and the inability to enforce decisions against companies, as evidenced by the refusal by Vedanta Resources to comply with the recommendations of the UK NCP in its failure to consult with indigenous groups concerning its mines in Orissa, India.[69] However, supporters have argued that the procedure as a whole can bring about change in corporate behaviour by raising public awareness of particular issues or concerns.[70]

United Nations Global Compact

Launched in 2000, the United Nations Global Compact (UNGC) is the world's largest voluntary corporate citizenship and sustainability initiative. Comprising over 12,000 participants from over 145 countries from across the business sector and civil society, the UNGC provides a platform for the development, implementation and disclosure of responsible and sustainable corporate policies and practices, as well as providing a forum for learning and exchange of experiences.[71]

Companies joining the UNGC commit to aligning their operations, strategy and organizational culture to ten universally accepted principles in the areas of human rights, labour rights, the environment and anti-corruption. In the area of the environment, there are three relevant provisions: Principles 7, 8 and 9.[72] Principle 7 calls upon businesses to adopt a 'precautionary approach' to environmental matters as introduced by the Rio Declaration as

legal obligations of the NCP system on states see Scott Robinson, 'International Obligations, State Responsibility and Judicial Review under the OECD Guidelines for Multinational Enterprises' (2014) 30(78) *Utrecht Journal of International and European Law* 68

69 OECD, *Final Statement by the UK National Contact Point for the OECD Guidelines for Multinational Enterprises, Complaint from Survival International against Vedanta Resources plc* (September 2009): <www.oecd.org/investment/mne/43884129.pdf> accessed on 11 May 2016. See also Amnesty International Obstacle Course, *How the UK's National Contact Point Handles Human Rights Complaints under the OECD Guidelines for Multinational Enterprises* (Amnesty International UK, February 2016)

70 For discussions as to the effectiveness of the NCP systems see: Robinson (n 53); Jernej Letnar Cernic, 'Corporate Responsibility for Human Rights: A Critical Analysis of the OECD Guidelines for Multinational Enterprises' (2008) 4(1) *Hanse Law Review* 71; OECD Watch, *Guide to OECD Guidelines for Multinational Enterprises' Complaint Procedure: Lessons from Past NGO Complaints* (2006); Evaristus Oshionebo, 'The OECD Guidelines for Multinational Enterprises as Mechanisms for Sustainable Development of Natural Resources: Real Solutions or Window Dressing' (2013) 17 *Lewis and Clark Law Review* 545

71 United Nations Global Compact (n 58)

72 UN Global Compact, *The Ten Principles of the UN Global Compact*, available at <www.unglobalcompact.org/what-is-gc/mission/principles>

discussed above.[73] The UNGC asks companies to apply risk assessments and management to environmental challenges and to consider scientific-technology evaluations, economic cost–benefit analyses and political considerations to determine an appropriate response to a perceived risk of environmental harm resulting from activities. Reflecting the provisions of Chapter 30 of Agenda 21, UNGC Principle 8 encourages businesses to undertake initiatives to promote greater environmental responsibility, through greater self-regulation (codes of conduct, charters and other initiatives) and open dialogue with the public. Principle 9 recommends that companies encourage the 'development and diffusion of environmentally friendly technologies' that protect the environment, cause less pollution and use natural resources in a sustainable manner, as defined in Agenda 21.

The initiative requires a certain degree of transparency and accountability through the annual public disclosure of progress made by member companies in implementing the ten principles (known as a Communication on Progress). Despite this, there is some criticism towards the level of accountability that the UNGC establishes and therefore inability to bring about any real change in corporate behaviour, leading to potential 'blue washing'.[74]

Equator Principles

The Equator Principles (EPs) are a voluntary risk management framework for financial institutions to measure and manage social and environmental risks associated with projects that they finance.[75] The EPs are intended to provide a minimum standard for due diligence to support responsible financing. They apply globally, to all industry sectors. As of September 2016, 84 financial institutions in 35 countries have officially adopted the Equator Principles, covering over 70 per cent of international project finance debt in emerging markets.[76]

Equator Principles Financial Institutions (EPFIs) commit to implementing the EPs in their internal environmental and social policies and procedures for financing projects and are expected to refuse financing or other loans to projects where clients will not, or are unable to, comply with the EPs. EPFIs are required to conduct an initial review of a proposed project to determine its potential social and environmental risks.[77] According to the identified risk level, clients are requested to conduct a formal environmental and social assessment and propose ways to mitigate any negative environmental or

73 See n 43
74 Clapp (n 41)
75 Equator Principles (EPs), <www.equator-principles.com> accessed 23 April 2016
76 EPs association members and reporting <www.equator-principles.com/index.php/members-reporting> accessed 23 April 2016.
77 EPs III (2013), Principle 1 <www.equator-principles.com/resources/equator_principles_iii.pdf> accessed 23 April 2016

social impacts that have been identified.[78] The assessment must also address compliance with relevant domestic laws and legislation, or, in some instances, International Finance Corporation (IFC) Performance Standards on Environmental and Social Sustainability and World Bank Group Environmental, Health and Safety Guidelines.[79] EPFIs must also compel their clients to establish an action plan to address issues identified, engage in dialogue with stakeholders and establish a grievance mechanism such as a locally based complaints procedure or system of mediation for the community to raise concerns with the company.[80]

While some applaud the EPs for increasing uniformity across the lending sector and bringing many projects to a higher environmental and social standard,[81] there has been criticism for the perceived lack of transparency, vague and discretionary nature of the EPs, absence of any formal grievance mechanism and their limited scope.[82]

International Chamber of Commerce Business Charter for Sustainable Development

Originally adopted in 1991, the International Chamber of Commerce Business Charter for Sustainable Development (ICC Charter) is a voluntary framework to support companies in the development of their own business sustainability strategy.[83] Originally focusing on environmental management, the ICC Charter was updated in 2015 and broadened to cover the subject of sustainable development more holistically. The provisions of the ICC Charter now focus on the themes of governance and collaboration, environmental innovation, societal innovation and economic innovation.[84]

Specifically the eight principles refer to (1) recognising sustainable development as a key priority, (2) the importance of inclusive economic growth and development, (3) environmental responsibility and management, (4)

78 EPs, Principle 2
79 EPs, Principle 3
80 EPs, Principles 4–6
81 John Hodges, 'Equator Principles III: Helping Banks "Get It Right"' (*BSR*, December 4, 2012) <www.bsr.org/en/our-insights/blog-view/equator-principles-iii-helping-banks-get-it-right> accessed 24 April 2016
82 Robert F. Lawrence and William L. Thomas, 'The Equator Principles and Project Finance: Sustainability in Practice?' (2014) *NR&E* 20; Andrew Hardenbrook, 'The Equator Principles: The Private Financial Sector's Attempt at Environmental Responsibility' (2007) 40 *Vanderbilt Journal of Transnational Law* 197; Watch Dog, Bank Track: <www.banktrack.org/show/pages/equator_principles> accessed 24 April 2016; Freshfields Bruckhaus Deringer, 'Banking on Responsibility: Equator Principles Survey 2005: The Banks' (2015) <www.banktrack.org/manage/ems_files/download/banking_on_responsibility/050701_banking_on_responsibility.pdf> accessed 24 April 2016
83 ICC, *Inspire and Grow Your Business in the 21st Century: Business Charter for Sustainable Development* (2015)
84 Ibid

social responsibility, (5) developing safe products and services that provide value while minimizing adverse environmental and social impacts, (6) promoting sustainable development values through the supply chain, (7) encouraging transparency, communications and reporting, and (8) fostering innovative collaboration and partnerships with other businesses, governments and stakeholders.[85]

The Charter applies to businesses of all sectors, geographies and sizes, including small- and medium-sized enterprises. While the Charter is voluntary, companies that sign commit to respect the eight principles. Although it is difficult to determine how many companies follow the Charter, the ICC intended to reach over 6 million companies, chambers of commerce and business associations worldwide through its own networks and those of its partner organizations when it was launched in 2015.[86]

United Nations Guiding Principles on Business and Human Rights

There is a growing understanding of the important role that human rights instruments can play in the protection of the environment and natural resources. This perspective was first introduced in the Stockholm Convention and has been an important theme of environmental protection and sustainable development since then.[87] While a full discussion of the human rights approach to natural resource protection is outside the scope of this chapter, the United Nations Guiding Principles on Business and Human Rights (UNGPs) can be understood as another non-binding instrument to protect natural resources through CSR mechanisms.

Endorsed by the United Nations Human Rights Council in 2011, the UNGPs clarify existing standards and practices for businesses in regard to human rights using a 'Protect, Respect and Remedy' Framework relating to the different and combined responsibilities of states and companies.[88] Although the UNGPs have received widespread uptake and support from both private sector and civil society, a number of criticisms have been raised including against their lack of specificity of the obligations, and lack of clarity in regard to action to be taken by companies towards those with whom

85 Ibid

86 The partner organizations include OECD, WTO, WCO, World Bank, UN, regional organizations, national organizations and NGOs. See ICC, 'Sponsorship Opportunities, ICC Business Charter for Sustainable Development' <www.iccwbo.org/uploadedFiles/Data/Policies/2015/ICC_BusinessCharter_SponsorshipOpp_2015.pdf> accessed 5 May 2016

87 For an in-depth discussion on the role that human rights can play in environmental protection see Birnie, Boyle and Redgwell (n 9); Martin (n 9)

88 UN General Assembly, Human Rights Council Resolution, *Human Rights and Transnational Corporations and Other Business Enterprises*, A/HRC/RES/17/4 (July 2011)

they interact, such as their supply chain.[89] Further, while a notable number of companies have adopted and published human rights policies, and have conducted human rights due diligence for proposed projects,[90] concerns have been raised that this allows companies to identify human rights issues without adequately addressing them.[91]

Industry initiatives in the extractive sector

Industries and companies themselves have responded to criticism of their environmental impact with their own codes and initiatives. Although voluntary in nature, these instruments are powerful tools for governments and civil society to regulate corporate activity. First, they can be used to identify the standards to which companies and industries believe themselves to be held thus offering an avenue for corporate accountability. Further, they can create pressure for non-signatory companies to subscribe to the principles, thereby improving industry behaviour as a whole. Finally, they can provide stakeholders (including consumers, clients and investors) with a benchmark by which to value the company.[92]

In terms of negative impact on natural resources, the extractives industry is one of the most frequently criticized offenders.[93] This is compounded by the fact that 90 per cent of these resources are now found in developing countries where weak legal frameworks, poor enforcement mechanisms and efforts, and corrupt practices reduce corporate regulation and accountability for damage to the environment.[94] A notable example is the Niger Delta area in Nigeria where the United Nations Development Programme has claimed that environmental degradation from the oil and gas industry activities is pushing the area towards 'ecological disaster'.[95] Further, while the enormous revenue generated by these activities might be expected to reduce poverty and improve national development in the states in which the natural

89 For an in-depth academic review of opportunities and criticisms of the UNGPs see Radu Mares (ed), *The UN Guiding Principles on Business and Human Rights: Foundations and Implementation* (Nijhoff, 2012)

90 The Business and Human Rights Resource Center (BHRRC) is an excellent source of examples of companies that have taken steps to implement the UNGPs. These examples can be accessed through the BHRRC website <http://business-humanrights.org/en> accessed 24 April 2016

91 Christine Parker and John Howe, *Ruggie's Diplomatic Project and Its Missing Regulatory Infrastructure*; Mares (ed), *The UN Guiding Principles on Business and Human Rights: Foundations and Implementation* (n 89)

92 For a full discussion on the benefits of voluntary codes, see Paul Collier, 'Laws and Codes for the Resource Curse' (2008) 11(1) *Yale Human Rights and Development LJ* 9

93 Jim Walker and Steve Howard, *Finding the Way Forward, How Could Voluntary Action Move Mining towards Sustainable Development* (IIED, 2002)

94 Hossein Razavi, 'Financing Oil and Gas Projects in Developing Countries' (IMF, 1996); Birnie, Boyle and Redgwell (n 9), Ch 5; Genasci and Pray (n 11)

95 UNDP Nigeria, 'Niger Delta Human Development Report' (2006)

resources are located, in reality there is little improvement to living standards or meaningful advantage to society in the long run, in some instances even creating a disadvantage to other non-extractive sectors of the economy.[96]

Extractive Industries Transparency Initiative

The Extractive Industries Transparency Initiative (EITI) is an international standard to encourage accountability in the management of natural resources. Announced at the WSSD in 2002, EITI aims to increase transparency by requiring states and extractive companies operating within their territories to publicly report on any payments made by the company to the government.[97] In turn, civil society and the public are able to compare payments reported by both the company and government and are therefore empowered to hold the government accountable for resource revenue it has received.[98]

While the EITI is voluntary for governments, reporting obligations become mandatory for any extractive company operating within the territory of an implementing or member state.[99] However, as a multi-stakeholder initiative, extractive companies do play an important role in encouraging states to both implement and comply with EITI. EITI also relies on the active participation of civil society to oversee national implementation processes, and demand greater transparency of government spending of resource revenues.[100]

EITI currently has 41 implementing countries,[101] 31 member countries[102] and 90 of the world's largest oil and gas companies are EITI supporting companies.[103] While some argue that it is too soon to tell how effective EITI has been in improving social and environmental performance, it is without doubt that increased transparency improves market stability, strengthens governance institutions, reduces the risk of corruption and encourages a fair and competitive business environment.[104]

96 For a detailed explanation of what is described as the 'Resource Curse' see Genasci and Pray (n 11); Collier (n 93)

97 Extractive Industries Transparency Initiative (EITI), Principles 4 and 5: <https://eiti.org/eiti/principles>

98 EITI, Principles 5, 8, 9, 12: <https://eiti.org/eiti/principles>

99 EITI, Frequently Asked Questions <https://eiti.org/faqs#Standard> accessed 25 April 2016. Indeed in some countries, EITI principles may be enforced through domestic law, for example through specific EITI legislation (Nigeria and Liberia), provisions in mining, petroleum or mining laws (Ghana and Sierra Leone) or other decrees, see EITI FAQ <https://eiti.org/faqs#Standard>

100 Ibid

101 Implementing countries are countries who are currently candidates for EITI membership but are not yet in compliance <https://eiti.org/countries> accessed 25 April 2016

102 States that are compliant with all the requirements of EITI <https://eiti.org/countries> accessed 25 April 2016

103 For a list of stakeholders see <https://eiti.org/supporters/companies> accessed 25 April 2016

104 Genasci and Pray (n 12)

International Council on Mining and Metals Sustainable Development Principles

The International Council on Mining and Metals (ICMM) is a consortium of metals and mining companies and business associations established to address sustainable development concerns across the industry. Member companies make public commitments to improve their sustainability performance and report annually on their progress.[105] The work of ICMM is built around five core values in the areas of health and safety of workers and communities, respect for the environment and the values of host societies, integrity in stakeholder engagement, accountability and collaboration.[106]

In 2003, ICMM committed member companies to meet ten principles that seek to address priority issues within the sector. Benchmarked against leading international standards,[107] the ICMM Sustainable Development Principles include, among other provisions, the improvement of environmental performance, conservation of biodiversity and responsible product use, recycling and disposal.[108] Specifically, these principles require member companies to consider the environmental impact of projects and set up environmental management systems to review, prevent, mitigate and ameliorate adverse environmental impacts.[109] Companies are also required to respect legally designated protected areas and develop and support inclusive and transparent procedures for integrated approaches to planning, biodiversity, conservation and mining.[110] Finally, companies are asked to participate in research and innovation that promotes the safe and efficient use of energy and natural resources, and provide regulators and stakeholders with scientifically sound data and analysis for regulatory decisions.[111]

Member companies are required to report on their sustainable development performance in accordance with the Global Reporting Initiative (GRI), a leading global standard in sustainability reporting.[112] In particular, ICMM companies report against both the GRI G4 Guidelines and also the sector-specific Mining and Minerals Sector Disclosures.[113]

105 The International Council on Mining and Metals (ICMM), *Public Reporting*: <www.icmm.com/our-work/sustainable-development-framework/public-reporting>

106 ICMM <www.icmm.com/about-us/about-us> accessed 25 April 2016

107 Rio Declaration, Global Compact, OECD Guidelines, Global Reporting Initiative, World Bank Operational Guidelines, OECD Convention on Combating Bribery, ILO Conventions, and the Voluntary Principles on Security and Human Rights, see <www.icmm.com/our-work/sustainable-development-framework/10-principles> accessed 25 April 2016

108 ICMM Sustainable Development Principles 6, 7 and 8

109 Ibid, Principle 6

110 Ibid, Principle 7

111 Ibid, Principle 8

112 Global Reporting Initiative <www.globalreporting.org/Pages/default.aspx> accessed 25 April 2016

113 ICMM Public Reporting <www.icmm.com/our-work/sustainable-development-framework/public-reporting> accessed 25 April 2016

Initiative for Responsible Mining Assurance

Founded in 2006, the Initiative for Responsible Mining Assurance (IRMA) is a coalition of NGOs, mining companies, mineral and metal purchasing companies, community groups and trade unions that are working towards developing a responsible mining assurance system to improve environmental and social performance in the mining sector.[114] Targeted towards industrial-scale metals and minerals mines, the standard is expected to cover all stages of the mine life cycle from exploration to closure.[115]

While the IRMA Standard for Responsible Mining is still under development,[116] the fundamental provisions focus around four key principles: (1) business integrity, meaning conducting business transparently and in compliance with local and international laws, regulations and best practices; (2) social responsibility, meaning engaging with stakeholders to ensure that mining operations respect human rights and cultural heritage and maintain health, safety and quality of life of workers and communities; (3) environmental responsibility, meaning that mining companies engage with stakeholders to ensure that operations maintain or enhance environmental values and avoid or minimize impact to the environment and communities; and (4) planning and managing for positive legacies, meaning engaging with stakeholders to ensure that mining projects leave positive social and environmental legacies.[117] The first draft met with a mixed response from different business and civil society organizations and IRMA is currently receiving comments on the second draft.[118]

Non-state actors, MNCs and natural resource protection

Other non-state actors play an important role in the regulation of MNCs and protection of natural resources.

While civil society organizations might lack the size and, arguably, power of many of the largest MNCs today, these actors are essential for the effective enforcement of many of the regulatory strategies discussed above. To

114 The Initiative for Responsible Mining Assurance (IRMA) <www.responsiblemining.net> accessed 25 April 2016

115 IRMA, 'IRMA Standard for Responsible Mining IRMA-STD-001 Draft v 2.0' (April 2016)

116 The most recent draft inviting comments was published in April 2016: <www.responsible mining.net/images/uploads/IRMA_Standard_Draft_v2.0_with_MOV.pdf> accessed 11 May 2016

117 n 116

118 Comments on version 1 and IRMA's responses can be accessed from IRMA's website <www.responsiblemining.net> accessed 2 September 2016. The public consultation period for version 2 was extended until 30 July 2016 although no comments have been made public at this time <www.responsiblemining.net/irma-standard/stakeholder-feedback/stakeholder-consultation-timeline/> accessed 2 September 2016

start, civil society is comprised of sophisticated NGOs, lawyers and other individuals with technical skills and understanding of environmental and sector specific issues. These groups are able to work with MNCs and governments to promote environmental responsibility, or alternatively have been known to effectively use tactics such as adverse publicity campaigns, boycotts, legal suits or shareholder action as more forceful means to demand response or remedy from companies.[119]

Additionally, while the presence of the private sector at international conferences has increased over the years, so too has the presence of civil society groups who now actively engage in policy-making and negotiation of international instruments fighting for the highest possible standards to be imposed on MNCs.[120] Further, these on-the-ground actors are also often best placed to ensure that international agreements are properly implemented into domestic law and effectively complied with in practice by governments and MNCs, as demonstrated by the participation of civil society in the implementation process of the UNGPs referred to above.[121] Finally, when issues arise, civil society groups can play an active role in dispute resolution processes, such as in the OECD NCP complaint process against Vedanta Resource noted above, where Survival International, a UK NGO, brought the complaint against Vedanta on behalf of the affected indigenous community.[122]

International organizations like the World Bank Group also play a role in the regulation of MNCs through the provision of loans, knowledge, advice and other resources to developing countries.[123] The World Bank can engage with MNCs on a number of levels: the Bank provides companies with advice on social and environmental sustainability practices and standards;[124] the Bank can demand greater environmental responsibility from private sector parties in Bank-funded projects; and the Bank can halt projects until standards are met.[125]

119 For a detailed discussion of the role that NGOs play in both the regulation of MNCs and cooperation with the business community, see Mujih (n 8)

120 Jem Bendell and David F. Murphy, *Partners in Time? Business, NGOs and Sustainable Development* (UNRISD Discussion Paper No. 1091999)

121 See, for example, UK Government, Press Release, 'UK first to launch action plan on business and human rights' (2013)

122 n 70

123 World Bank Group, 'The World Bank Group A to Z' (2015) <https://openknowledge.worldbank.org/bitstream/handle/10986/20192/9781464803826.pdf?sequence=9&isAllowed=y> accessed 25 April 2016

124 Ibid

125 An example of this can be seen in the Chad–Cameroon Oil and Pipeline Project. See Audrey C. Cash, 'Corporate Social Responsibility and Petroleum Development in Sub-Saharan Africa: The Case of Chad' (2012) 37(2) *Resources Policy* 144; Mujih (n 8)

Conclusion

The private sector plays a prominent role in the exploitation and extraction of natural resources with often negative social and environmental consequences. While domestic law in both home and host states might be the primary means of regulating MNCs, these legal frameworks are often inadequate to effectively regulate MNCs for the reasons outlined above. As a result, CSR has developed as an important tool for natural resource protection in its own right.

CSR instruments can include intergovernmental agreements, soft law principles or industry initiatives that refer to standards established at the international level. Compliance with domestic legislation often forms the basis for these instruments, however where such law is weak or inadequate, higher standards are proposed in line with international expectations that seek to reduce the negative impact of natural resource degradation, often through various practical means. This includes *inter alia,* environmental impact assessments, stakeholder engagement, use and development of environmentally friendly technology, corrective action where damage occurs and encouraging transparent business transactions. However, as highlighted above, due to their voluntary nature, these initiatives often lack adequate monitoring and enforcement mechanisms, thus limiting their potential strength and impact, in some cases effectively granting companies a licence to 'greenwash'.

While new legislation is arising in the area of CSR offering the opportunity to strengthen these CSR principles,[126] for the time being, the private sector must be encouraged to comply with the voluntary guidelines and initiatives discussed above. This includes multi-party engagement between governments, international organizations, civil society, business associations and companies themselves to understand the necessary action that companies need to take as well as enabling robust accountability where such standards are not met. Given current patterns of global use and consumption of natural resources, the international community must act now to reinforce and strengthen CSR and regulate MNCs where traditional legal channels fall short.

126 Such as new EU non-financial reporting requirements and environmental impact assessments as required by a large number of pieces of legislation globally; see n 16

9 State owned oil companies, North–South and South–South perspectives on investment

Elena Merino Blanco

Introduction

The involvement with and interest of multinational corporations (MNCs) on natural resource trade and investment is often traced back to the sixteenth century[1] when colonial outposts such as the British East India Company (EIC)[2] and the Dutch Vereenigde Oost-Indische Compagnie (VOC)[3] traded with distant lands and overseas territories. Both companies started out as speculative vehicles to import precious spices and exotic materials but as their activities expanded from the spice trade to other resources and commodities, so did their powers and reach. These powers included quasi-governmental prerogatives such as the ability to wage war, imprison and execute convicts, negotiate treaties, strike their own coins and establish colonies.[4] While the VOC is widely considered to be the first MNC, the EIC, in turn, ruled over one-fifth of the world's population at the time and its revenues were greater than those of many European countries.[5] Both companies were central actors in forging the structural history of foreign direct investment (FDI) through what has been described as 'coerced imperialism and monopolistic mercantilism'.[6] The territorial control enjoyed by the EIC enabled the manipulation of terms of trade, the extraction of taxes and, in general, the financing of

1 Kate Miles, *The Origins of International Investment Law: Empire, Environment and the Safeguarding of Capital* (Cambridge University Press 2013) 18–19

2 Anthony Wild, *The East India Company: Trade and Conquest from 1600* (Harper Collins 1999); 'The East India Company: The Company That Ruled the Waves' *The Economist* (17 December 2011) <www.economist.com/node/21541753> accessed 30 November 2015

3 That literally means the United East Indian Company and is referred to by the British commonly as the Dutch East India Company. See <http://entoen.nu/voc/en> for a brief introduction to the origins an early expansion of the VOC

4 Wild (n 2) with reference to the EIC

5 Nick Robins, 'Loot: In Search of the East India Company, The World's First Transnational Corporation' (2002) 14 *Environment & Urbanization* 79

6 Glenn J Ames, *The Globe Encompassed: The Age of European Discovery, 1500–1700* (Pearson, 2007) 102–103

Britain's own industrial revolution through the plunder and de-industrialisation of the colonies.[7]

The early companies engaged in commercial transactions under the so-called 'colonial encounter'[8] that was to lay the foundations of future interactions between the 'Old World' and the 'New'; between what became known as 'the West' and, later, 'the North' (the capital exporting, developed countries) and the resource rich, raw material exporting (ex)colonies, the developing South. For many, this 'encounter' is accountable for today's uneven and much criticised system of international law in general and FDI in particular.[9] Watched through this prism current British affluence is not just a consequence of the nation's superior ingenuity and industrial past; it has also, on the contrary, much to do with a planned, ruthless drive to conquer and plunder through a 'remorseless logic of its eternal search for profit, whether through trade, through taxation or through war'.[10]

This chapter examines MNCs' relationship with home and host states in the course of resource extraction. It begins by looking at the early extractive imperial companies from a North–South perspective and tries to contextualise the lasting legacy of colonial plunder as resource extraction politics evolved through the decolonisation period first and the advent of globalisation later, until the emergence and growth of South–South investment in the postcolonial world. The chapter focuses on a particular type of resource – oil, and on a particular type of company – state owned. Oil is the world's wealthiest industry[11] and the companies involved in its extraction and commercialisation have particular ties with their home and host states.[12] Oil

7 Robbins (n 5) 80

8 Anthony Anghie, *Imperialism, Sovereignty and the Making of International Law* (Cambridge University Press, 2004) 6–7; Nico Schrijver, *Sovereignty over Natural Resources: Balancing Rights and Duties* (Cambridge University Press 2008) 173

9 The literature in this area draws mostly from two historical secondary sources, Anghie (n 8) and Charles Lipson, *Standing Guard: Protecting Capital in the Nineteen and Twentieth Centuries* (University of California Press 1985); Miles (n 1) expands upon this idea and so did, previously, Elena Blanco and Jona Razzaque in *Globalisation and Natural Resources Law* (Edward Elgar 2011) advancing the theory that the quest for resources was the driving engine of the globalisation process

10 Robbins (n 5) 80–81

11 Approximately US$2 billion a day of petroleum is traded worldwide, which makes petroleum the largest single item in the balance of payments and exchanges between nations. Silvana Tordo, Brandon S. Tracy and Noora Arfaa, 'National Oil Companies and Value Creation' (2011) World Bank Working Paper No. 218 at xi. For the most up-to-date and comprehensive 'guide' to the politics, trends and issues surrounding oil and its governance see Gavin Bridge and Philippe Le Billon, *Oil* (Polity 2013)

12 Michael Watts, *Empire of Oil: Capitalist Dispossession and the Scramble for Africa* (2006) Monthly Review <http://monthlyreview.org/2006/09/01/empire-of-oil-capitalist-dispossession-and-the-scramble-for-africa/> accessed 10 July 2016 for a critical account of the relationship between the US and the governments of Saudi Arabia, the Gulf Oil States, Venezuela and Nigeria and the absurdly high profits of 'Big Oil'. Visit also the think tank 'Price of Oil Campaign'<http://priceofoil.org/campaigns/separate-oil-and-state/> accessed 10 July 2016

companies, whether state owned or privately owned, have a substantial impact on a country's economy that often translates itself into political influence and economies of corruption and clientism.[13] The importance of state owned oil companies cannot be overstated. The IEA expects over 80 per cent of growth in oil production between 2010 and 2035 to come from just six countries of the Organization of the Petroleum Exporting Countries (OPEC), Saudi Arabia, Iraq, Kuwait, Iran, Qatar and Abu Dhabi; in all of them state oil companies play the leading role.[14]

The second part of the chapter traces the growth and expansion of national or state owned natural resource extraction companies alongside the emergence of the Global South as an economic force, and the subsequent growth of South–South investment. The focus in this part remains on national oil companies (NOCs), and the historical and political factors that determined their development, highlighting the tenuous yet dynamic divide between the 'public' and the 'private' in the global economy.

The third section considers the goals and aims of state owned enterprises (SOEs) in the Global South and links these to the international investment strategy of many national oil companies. Advancement of the public interest and economic expansion are considered against the backdrop of existing investment rules. The fourth part examines both the external and internal corporate governance structures of NOCs and considers the special risks associated with the close relationship between state and enterprise activity in the context of resource extraction and management. Two related aspects are highlighted: the first one is the danger of and opportunities for corruption and clientism and how these are addressed and managed within the increased demands for transparency and good governance. The second relates to the drive to ensure a so-called 'level playing field' and the proper separation between the state and the enterprise in the context of a variety of corporate governance codes including the Organisation for Economic Co-operation and Development (OECD) Guidelines on Corporate Governance of State Owned Enterprises (OECD SOEs Guidelines).[15] The role played by the state as a public power in the control and management of the enterprise and the definition of SOEs are considered in the context of investment dispute resolution, with emphasis on the standing of SOEs as both claimants and

13 Daniel Yergin, *The Prize: The Epic Quest for Oil, Money and Power* (Free Press 1999) 3

14 Bernice Lee and others, 'Resources Futures' (Chatham House Report 2012) <www.chathamhouse.org/sites/files/chathamhouse/public/Research/Energy,%20Environment%20and%20Development/1212r_resourcesfutures.pdf> 40, accessed 10 July 2016

15 OECD, *OECD Guidelines on Corporate Governance of State-Owned Enterprises, 2015 Edition* (OECD, 2015) <http://dx.doi.org/10.1787/9789264244160-en> accessed 10 July 2016. Please note that throughout the chapter national or state owned oil companies will be referred to as NOCs while the term SOE will be reserved to identify state owned companies in general to follow the OECD Guidelines terminology and the nomenclature chosen by most of the literature. NOCs are, of course, SOEs

respondents in investment arbitration disputes. The interpretation given to the doctrine of attribution and the applicability of the structural and functional tests developed by investment arbitration tribunals is examined in turn to establish the potential liability of the state alongside that of state owned companies.

Some of the points raised in the third and fourth sections are developed in the fifth section, which considers state liability within the context of the International Law Commission's (ILC) Draft Articles on State Responsibility (ILC Articles)[16] and the United Nations Guiding Principles on Business and Human Rights (UNGPs).[17] The potential shortcomings in using the ILC Articles and on the UNGPs are considered in the conclusion within the context of the work and findings of the UN Intergovernmental Working Group on Business and Human Rights for drafting an 'international legally binding instrument' on business and human rights.[18] Human rights claims against SOEs face potential obstacles of immunity from jurisdiction and lack of neutrality of state based courts, leading to suggestions for independent, transnational tribunals that may provide a more impartial forum.[19] Investment arbitration was indeed developed to address problems of state immunity and local court bias in favour of states, however, and despite some arguments in favour of extending investment arbitration tribunals' scope to cover human rights claims against corporations, the lack of expertise in human rights issues of the tribunal and the need to include public interest considerations in the evaluation of state policy may pose an insurmountable obstacle to siting human rights related claims in those tribunals.[20]

The chapter concludes by highlighting that state ownership of national oil companies is not a monolithic concept; on the contrary it takes multiple shapes and contours to serve varied, combined political, social and economic goals. In the context of South–South expanding trade and investment and, more specifically, in the context of increased natural resource demands and consumption by emerging economies, state ownership enables a policy

16 *Report of the International Law Commission*, UN GAOR 56th sess, Supp No 10., UN Doc A/56/10 (2001) (ILC Articles)

17 John Ruggie, Report of the Special Representative of the Secretary-General on the Issue of Human Rights and Transnational Corporations and Other Business Enterprises: Guiding Principles on Business and Human Rights: Implementing the United Nations 'Protect, Respect and Remedy' Framework, 17th sess, Agenda Item 3, UN Doc A/HRC/17/31 (21 March 2011) annex

18 *Elaboration of an International Legally Binding Instrument on Transnational Corporations and Other Business Enterprises with Respect to Human Rights*, HRC Res 26/9, 26th sess, Agenda Item 3, UN Doc A/HRC/RES/26/9 (July 14, 2014)

19 Claes Cronstedt and Robert C Thompson, 'A Proposal for an International Tribunal on Business and Human Rights' (*IHRB*, 21 July 2015) <www.ihrb.org/other/remedy/a-proposal-for-an-international-arbitration-tribunal-on-business-and-human/?> accessed 10 November 2016

20 Ioannis Glinavos, 'Public Interests, Private Disputes: Investment Arbitration and the Public Good' (2016) 13 *Manchester Journal of International Economic Law* 50

informed economic option that can greatly facilitate positive social and economic outcomes. For this, a system that implements, transparency, accountability and sustainability in respect of both states and business actors is crucial.

The rise of state owned companies and the Global South

In colonial times, land use regulations were often deployed as a control mechanism against the indigenous and local communities.[21] Access to natural resources was a priority for the *metropolis* and regulation facilitating resource extraction often laid down the foundations of ecological degradation.[22] At the same time international investment law, an offshoot of public international law, developed within European nations and under the auspices of liberal capitalism, exercised a legal quasi-colonialism that ensured, alongside the supply of raw materials, the subjection to European rule.[23] The cycle of resource extraction that followed resulted in the commodification of nature,[24] while the displacement of local resource management practice[25] created poverty, environmental damage and fractured economies. In this fertile ground the early incarnation of the MNC[26] thrived with closely aligned interests to those of the 'home' state.[27]

The well known English or the Dutch East (and West, another company) India Company (the VOC) were private companies pursuing private gain but, at the same time, acted as instruments of the home state, establishing a system of diplomacy and trade that was to shape and poison international markets and the global economy for centuries.[28] The common interests of early companies and states explain partly the high degree of 'home' state involvement in their expansion and activities, and the vesting of powers and prerogatives in the companies that would be considered

21 Susan Marks, 'Empire's Law' (2003) 10 *Indiana Journal of Legal Studies* 449; Joseph Murphy, 'Environment and Imperialism: Why Colonialism Still Matters' (SRI Papers No. 20, 2009) at 6 SRI available at <www.sse.leeds.ac.uk./sri> accessed 10 July 2016

22 Patricia Kameri-Mbote and Philippe Cullet, 'Law, Colonialism and Environmental Management in Africa' (1997) 6 *Review of European Community and International Environmental Law* 23

23 Schrivjer (n 8) 173; Miles (n 1); Anghie (n 8) 224, 238–239

24 Ellen Meiksins Woods, *Empire of Capital* (Verso 2005) 139; Anthony Allot, 'Modern Changes in African Land Tenure' in Neville Rubin and Eugene Cotran (eds), *Readings in African Law* (vol 1, Franck Cass 1970), 236

25 Shalini Randeira, 'Global Designs and Local Lifeworlds: Colonial Legacies of Conservation, Disenfranchisement and Environmental Governance in Postcolonial India' 9 *Interventions* (2007) 12

26 Janet McLean, 'The Transnational Corporation in History: Lessons for Today?' (2004) 79 *Indiana Law Journal* 363

27 Peter Muchlinski, *Multinational Enterprises and the Law* (2nd edn, Oxford University Press 2009) 8–10

28 Ibid 9

'public' today.[29] In respect of the host state, these early overseas companies had an 'extractive' and colonial relationship not dissimilar to that of contemporary multinationals investing in developing countries.[30]

Notwithstanding their activities and public involvement, these companies remained private enterprises. It was necessary to wait until the early twentieth century for the creation of the first national oil company. It was the government of Austria–Hungary which was the first to build and operate a plant to supply oil products in 1908, in the years of instability preceding World War I.[31] As war loomed on the horizon and oil entered the war machinery, it did not take long for other European powers to follow suit, either creating companies to supply the domestic market or in upstream operations from their colonial territories. Security of supply was a key motivation on the eve of World War I and alongside the creation of national oil companies European private oil companies (POCs) took advantage of the protection and diplomatic weight of their home countries to prospect and extract oil in the colonies.[32] Strategic control battles of the new oil fields[33] in the Middle East, in territories which had been for centuries under either Ottoman or European control, saw the UK investing in the Anglo–Persian Oil Company (later to become British Petroleum – BP),[34] while new private oil giants rapidly expanded into oil rich countries such as Venezuela (1910), Egypt (1911), Trinidad and Mexico (1913).[35]

In Latin America, where oil was found at the beginning of the twentieth century, NOCs didn't take long to emerge. The first of them was Argentina's Yacimientos Petrolíferos Fiscales (YPF) in 1922 followed by Bolivia's Yacimientos Petrolíferos Fiscales Bolivianos (YPFB) in 1936, and Chile's Empresa Nacional del Petroleo (ENAP) in 1950.[36] However it was Mexico's Petróleos Mexicanos (Pemex) that in 1938 rocked the industry by taking over the operations of foreign private firms in the first large scale expropriation/nationalisation within the oil sector.[37]

29 Miles (n 1) 30; Ann Carlos and Stephen Nicholas, 'Giants of an Earlier Capitalism: The Chartered Trading Companies as Modern Multinationals' (1988) 62 *Business History Review* 398

30 Carmen Gonzalez, 'China's Engagement with Latin America, Partnership or Plunder?' in Elena Blanco and Jona Razzaque (eds) *Natural Resources and the Green Economy* (Brill 2012) 37

31 Tordo (n 11) 15

32 Ibid

33 Wilfred Nunn, *Tigris Gunboats, The Forgotten War in Iraq 1914–1917* (Chatham 2007) 21

34 Yergin, *The Prize* (n 13) 142

35 Tordo (n 11) 16–17

36 Osmel Manzano and Francisco Monaldi, 'The Political Economy of Oil Production in Latin America' (2008) *Economía* 59

37 Noel Maurer, 'The Empire Struck Back: Sanctions and Compensation in the Mexican Oil Expropriation of 1938' (2011) 71 *Journal of Economic History* 590

Following the instability of the interwar period at the wake of the post-colonial era, a very different type of foreign domination emerged, that of international oil companies (IOCs) or POCs. These private companies had been expanding silently while cashing in on the profits of war.[38] In the Middle East, for example, petroleum production remained controlled by a variety of private oil companies until the wave of nationalisations in the 1950s, 1960s and 1970s, which eventually led to the declaration on permanent sovereignty over natural resources,[39] the new international economic order (NIEO)[40] and the establishment of national oil companies for the first time in the region.[41]

From the postcolonial NOCs' creation to today's post global order, national oil companies have increased both their power and their market share.[42] It is estimated that 75 per cent of global oil production and 90 per cent of proven oil reserves today are controlled by state owned companies.[43] Saudi Arabia's Aramco, for example, is the world's largest oil company,[44] while Petrobas, Petrochina, Sinopec and Snooc have eclipsed traditional oil giants like Exxon Mobil, BP and Royal Dutch Shell.[45] The weight of the public sector in oil extraction and distribution in emerging economies can partly be explained by their recent political history.[46] Countries like Saudi Arabia, Iraq and Libya were subject to colonial rule and one of the first post independence priorities consisted in the nationalisation of the oil industry.[47] Private oil companies were perceived to be backed up by foreign, imperialistic governments and therefore opposed to national interests.[48] Government

38 Yergin, *The Prize* (n 13) 150

39 *Permanent Sovereignty over Natural Resources*, GA Res 1803, UN GAOR, 17th sess, 1194th plen mtg, Supp No. 17, UN Doc A/RES/1803 (14 December 1962)

40 *Establishment of a New International Economic Order*, GA Res 3201 (S-VI), 6th special sess, 2229th plen mtg Agenda Item 7 UN Doc A/RES/S-6/3201 (1 May 1974)

41 In Saudi Arabia, five US companies set up the Aramco Oil Company, today nationalised and under control of the Saudi Royal family. Schrjiver (n 8) 167

42 Christopher Helman, 'The World's Biggest Oil and Gas Companies – 2015' *Forbes* (19 March 2015) <www.forbes.com/sites/christopherhelman/2015/03/19/the-worlds-biggest-oil-and-gas-companies/>

43 Tordo (n 11) xi

44 'Saudi Aramco Sale of the Century?' *The Economist* (9 January 2016)

45 'Really Big Oil' *The Economist* (10 August 2006)

46 An analysis of ownership of oil companies shows that with the exception of Norway, most NOCs are in emerging economies. Przemyslaw Kowalski, and others, 'State-Owned Enterprises: Trade Effects and Policy Implications' (Trade Policy Papers No. 147, OECD, 2013) 5 <www.oecd.org/officialdocuments/publicdisplaydocumentpdf/?cote=TAD/TC/WP(2012)10/ANN/FINAL&docLanguage=En> accessed 12 June 2016

47 Schrijver (n 8) 82–100

48 Daniel Yergin, *The Quest: Energy, Security, and the Remaking of the Modern World* (Penguin 2011) 285. Political and economic interest lurked heavily in the Middle East where governments were topped or financed depending on their friendliness or openness to the big oil companies. Dictators were kept in place as long as they allowed a steady supply of the drug to which the economy had become addicted. See Tordo (n 11) for the rise and fall of the Shah in Iran's post independence

control of the oil industry became the logical corollary of the much fought for principle of sovereignty over natural resources,[49] while ideological and practical reasons contributed to the growth of the state sector in oil extraction. The combination of a weak domestic private sector and the practical benefits of natural monopolies' management for interlocking sectors made public ownership of oil companies a clear favourite. State ownership of oil production was used as a policy tool that enabled the collection of revenue and the redistribution of wealth and privileges.[50]

NOCs are an example of strategic state owned companies whereby the state pursues socioeconomic goals alongside economic priorities. They provide cheap oil to the local population, local jobs and serve as the motor for other industries.[51] These NOCs can be structured in different ways. In some cases, the state has full ownership like Aramco in Saudi Arabia or Pemex in Mexico.[52] The state may also operate through a majority share that enables control of their operations. This is the case with ENI in Italy, Statoil in Norway, Sinopec in China, Petrobras in Brazil or Gazprom in Russia. This second type of NOC is generally publicly traded.[53] The choice depends on the type of objectives that policy makers wish to achieve by the NOC and the country specific context, including exogenous factors such as oil and gas prices, economic cycles or even the existence of international sanctions.[54]

The above discussion should not encourage the assumption that the close link between oil companies and states is limited to those oil companies that are state owned fully or in part. Private oil companies also have close ties with their 'home governments' either because they were initially under public ownership – BP – or due to their strategic role in securing access to one of the world's most precious natural resources. The history of BP illustrates this special relationship well. BP's origins date back to 1908 when the Anglo-Persian Oil Company was originally established as a subsidiary of the Burma Oil Company to exploit oil discoveries in what was then Persia (today, Iran).[55] Following World War II, and the subsequent process of decolonisation, the new government of Iran nationalised the oil industry in 1951 creating the Iranian National Oil Company. The British government, which failed to retain control by legal means,[56] staged a *coup d'état* in 1953 with the

49 Schrijver (n 8) 41–100

50 Robert Pirog, 'The Role of National Oil Companies in the International Oil Market' (CRS Report for Congress, 21 August 2007) 4 <http://fas.org/sgp/crs/misc/RL34137.pdf> accessed 20 October 2016

51 Ibid 4

52 Tordo (n 11) 67 provides examples of the various ownership models of NOCs

53 Ibid. This will be of particular relevance to qualifying as claimants and defendants in investment arbitration and it is discussed in section 4 of this chapter

54 Tordo (n 11) xii

55 Yergin, *The Quest* (n 48) 285

56 *Anglo-Iranian Oil Co (United Kingdom v Iran) (Preliminary Objection)* [1952] ICJ 2. The case can be found at <www.icj-cij.org/docket/index.php?p1=3&p2=3&k=1ba&case=16&code=uki&p3=4> accessed 10 July 2016

help of the CIA.[57] A new pro-Western government allowed the Anglo-Iranian Oil Company to return to Iran and operate there until the triumph of the theocratic Islamic Revolution of 1978–1979.[58] The Anglo-Iranian Company changed its name to British Petroleum and expanded its operations beyond the Middle East as far as Alaska and, in 1965, it became the first company to strike oil in the North Sea.[59] BP became a public limited company and one of the world's 'supermajors' oil and gas companies.[60] Registered in England and with headquarters in London, BP is a vertically integrated company operating in all areas of the oil and gas industry.[61] Of the various environmental disasters it has been involved with,[62] the recent Deepwater Horizon oil spill off the coast of the US illustrates especially well the very close relationship between oil companies (private as well as publically owned) and their 'home' governments. Indeed the British government involvement at the diplomatic level in the resolution of the case didn't escape the scrutiny of those who have long denounced the indifference with which the suffering by victims of MNCs abroad has been met in similar scenarios.[63]

Strategies, goals and investment by state owned companies in the Global South

Servicing of national markets, operations of natural monopolies and the pursuit of public interest may have all been behind the creation of state or national companies in the oil sector in what is known as the Global South but there is, today, a discernible trend towards expansion into international markets by state owned oil companies. This is particularly the case in respect of large national oil companies from emerging Asian economies, and, in particular, China. China was one of the first emerging economies that encouraged its state owned companies to invest and acquire a market share

57 Yergin, *The Quest* (n 48) 300

58 Stephen Kinzer, *All the Shah's Men: An American Coup and the Roots of Middle East Terror* (Wiley 2003) 272

59 'Our History' (BP) <www.bp.com/en/global/corporate/about-bp/our-history.html> accessed 10 July 2016

60 It was privatised by the British Government in stages between 1979 and 1987

61 Bridge and Le Billon (n 11) at 35–40

62 For an overview of these see Corporate Watch <https://corporatewatch.org/company-profiles/bp-plc> accessed 12 July 2016; Ishaan Tharoor, 'A Brief History of BP' *Time Magazine* 2 June 2010

63 The Deepwater Horizon oil spill is considered the largest accidental oil spill in the history of the oil industry. It has cost the group around $54 billion in penalties, damages and clean-up costs. <www.theguardian.com/environment/bp-oil-spill> accessed 12 July 2016. In contrast, one can cite the outcome of the tragedy in Bhopal <www.bhopal.com/> accessed 12 July 2016. For an overview of the current state of corporate accountability see Anna Grear and Burns H. Weston, 'The Betrayal of Human Rights and the Urgency of Universal Corporate Accountability: Reflections on the Post-Kiobel Lawscape' *Human Rights Law Review* (2015) 21–44

abroad, pursuing a 'Going Out' strategy and progressing from market seeking to resource seeking.[64] Natural resources were always at the heart of this 'Going Out' policy[65] with oil, on which China had become increasingly dependent, occupying a prominent role.[66] This has become a type of South–South investment that many praise while others loathe.[67]

Chinese investments in the oil industry in two countries – Angola and Ecuador – exemplify the advantages and perils of this type of South–South resource seeking relationship. Chinese presence in Angola[68] began during the cold war with China supporting the three major liberation movements in the country: the Movimento Popular de Libertação de Angola (MPLA), União Nacional para a Indêpendencia Total de Angola (UNITA), and the Frente Nacional para Libertação de Angola (FNLA).[69] This relationship got caught up with China's own struggles against Soviet dominance during the cold war. After almost 30 years of civil war following independence from Portuguese rule, Angola, with large oil, mineral and diamond reserves, exemplifies the so-called resource curse or paradox of plenty[70] as it scores in the lowest ranks of the Human Development Index and suffers from endemic poverty, malnutrition and underdevelopment.[71] It is with this already challenging governance climate that Chinese involvement began. Spurred by Mao Zedong's ideology, the initial involvement of China in Africa was driven by what China claimed as a 'shared history of grievances as victims of Western imperialism and colonization and a strong will to cultivate and protect national sovereignty'.[72] Initial relations, thus, were driven by political as well as economic interests.

64 In this period Chinese investment rose from $3 billion to $60 billion in the five years from 2005 to 2010. Susan Harris *China's Foreign Policy* (Polity 2014)

65 Bo Kong (ABC, Clio 2010) *China's International Petroleum Policy* at 46 and 'China's Quest for Oil in Africa Revisited' SAIS Working Papers in African Studies 01-2011

66 Jeremy Glenn and Hinrich Voss (2012) 'Chinese Overseas Investment in the European Union', Europe China Exchange and Research Network (ECRAN) 15–16 <wwweeas.europa.eu/china/docs/division_ecran/ecran_chinese_investment_in_the_european_union_jeremy_clegg_and_hinrich_voss_en.pdf> accessed 3 October 2015

67 Andrew Bracken and others, 'China's Quest for Energy Security: Redefining and Driving Foreign Aid. An Analysis of China's Involvement in Central Asia and Africa' (2013) 10 *The Michigan Journal of Public Affairs* 4

68 See, Indira Campos and Alex Vines, 'Angola and China: A Pragmatic Partnership', Center for Strategic and International Studies (Chatham House 2008) available at <www.china-briefing.com/news/2011/05/25/the-china-angola-partnership-a-case-study-of-chinas-oil-relationships-with-african-nations.html> accessed 3 October 2015

69 Iain Taylor, *China and Africa: Engagement and Compromise* (Routledge 2006)

70 Jeffrey D. Sachs and Andrew M. Warner 'Natural Resources and Economic Development The Curse of Natural Resources' (2001) 45 *European Economic Review* 827–838

71 The 2015 Human Development Report for Angola can be found at <http://hdr.undp.org/sites/all/themes/hdr_theme/country-notes/AGO.pdf> accessed 10 October 2016

72 Bracken et al. (n 67) 12.

After joining the OPEC in 2007, Angola became the biggest oil exporter in Africa, with China as its main client.[73] China, as is common in its international resource seeking relations, provided Angola with loans for infrastructure, without imposing any stipulations to improve transparency, corruption, human rights or democratisation in exchange.[74] Instead a 'no-strings attached' policy based on China's 'Eight Principles'[75] respected the sovereignty and political choices of the aid recipient. This respect offered a stark contrast with the conditions often attached to International Monetary Fund (IMF) loans.[76] It also took place when no other concessionary loans were available to Angola due to the different priorities of Western powers at the time.[77] Chinese national oil companies invested $7.989 billion in Africa between 1995 and 2006, including crude and refined oil ventures.[78] However, and for the much trumpeted Sino influence in Africa in general and in Angola in particular, a detailed look at the figures shows that international oil companies like Texaco, Exxon Mobil or Total still dominate the oil market in the country[79] and that trading relations with the US and Europe are still important.[80] The Angolans have also expressed their dissatisfaction at the exaggerated emphasis on their ties with China and the implications commonly drawn from these ties. Although China, moved by economic considerations such as resource access and the opening of new markets for Chinese products, would not insist on the staff monitoring programmes that were initially suggested by the IMF in respect of transparency and anti-corruption initiatives, these are important for both Angola and China.[81] Angola is currently working with the IMF to improve transparency standards in the country and has recently published reports on payments to and from

73 China imports 41 per cent of Angola's oil, followed by the US which imports 23 per cent. The Economist Intelligence Unit (EIU). <www.eiu.com/industry/energy/sub-saharan-africa/angola> accessed 10 October 2016

74 Ethan Cramer-Flood, 'Chinese Oil Investment in Angola and the Quest to Evade the Resource Curse' *Perspectives on Global Issues* 2007 <www.perspectivesonglobalissues.com/archives/fall-2009-energy/chinaangola/> accessed 10 October 2016

75 Premier Zhou Enlai proposed what is called the 'Eight Principles Governing China's Aid to Other Countries'. In Bracken et al. (n 67) at 5

76 Dambisa Moyo, *Dead Aid*, 'The Chinese are our friends' (Penguin 2009) 98–114

77 Tony Hodges, *Angola: From Afro-Stalinism to Petro-Diamond Capitalism* (James Currey 2001)

78 Campos and Vines (n 68) 16

79 According to data from the EIU among the largest players are ChevronTexaco (US), ExxonMobil (US), TotalFinaElf (France), BP (UK) and Agip/Eni (Italy). Mike Hodel, 'The Scramble for Energy: China's Oil Investment in Africa' *The Journal on International Policy Solutions* University of California, San Diego 51 <www.irps.ucsd.edu/assets/017/7168.pdf 3> accessed 30 April 2016

80 Alec Russel, 'The New Colonialists' *Financial Times Magazine* November 17, 2007

81 Sara Lengauer, 'China's Foreign Aid Policy: Motive and Method' (2011) 9 2 *Culture Mandala: Bulletin of the Centre for East–West Cultural & Economic Studies* 35 <www.internationalrelations.com/CM2011/PRC-Foreign-Aid-2011.pdf> accessed 30 April 2016

its extractive sector that surpass the information supplied by many members of the Extractive Industry Transparency Initiative (EITI).[82] China is keen on reducing corruption in its national owned companies and has developed a variety of initiatives to this end, including ratifying the United Nations Convention against Corruption (UNAC)[83] and agreeing to accept that other State Parties to the Convention assess its compliance with the treaty during the 2010–2015 review cycle.[84] China, the biggest economy of the Global South, shows in its aid and investment policy very similar motives to those of traditional OECD donors in economic terms[85] but a radically different political positioning. What emerges from these recent investment encounters is that whether South–South investment replicates conventional Western prescriptions for good governance or chooses to develop its own rules within a different paradigm will be decided by those participating in the process.

In the case of Ecuador a crippling foreign debt and several decades of legal battle with American private owned oil companies for damages related to environmental destruction in the Amazon[86] pushed the populist government of Eduardo Correa towards China's offer of loans for oil.[87] China approached the transaction within the same parameters that it used for its investments in Angola and other Global South countries: it prioritised its own economic needs and strictly pursued a policy of non-intervention in the political affairs of the recipient country.[88] China's oil interests in Ecuador, however, have been blamed for the failure to maintain the oil drilling moratorium in the Yasuni National Park.[89] This park offers an exciting and novel example of payments for ecosystem services[90] global scheme devised by Correa's government with

82 Campos and Vines (n 68) 27

83 New York 31 October 2003, United Nations, Treaty Series, vol 2349, p. 41; Doc A/58/422

84 Pursuant to Article 63 of UNCAC by a body created by and dependent on the conference of the parties. Giovanni Nicotera, 'China's commitment to the United Nations Convention against Corruption' (2013) <www.f3magazine.unicri.it/?p=617> accessed 16 November 2016

85 'White Paper on China's Foreign Aid' State Council Information Office of the PRC (2011) in Sara Lengauer, 'China's Foreign Aid Policy: Motive and Method' (2011) 9 2 *Culture Mandala: Bulletin of the Centre for East–West Cultural & Economic Studies* 41 <www.internationalrelations.com/CM2011/PRC-Foreign-Aid-2011.pdf> accessed 30 April 2016

86 For an overview of the ongoing legal battle visit <www/business-humanrights.org/en/texacochevron-lawsuits-re-ecuador> accessed 12 July 2016

87 Joshua Cheynder and Nicolas Medina Mora, 'Special Report: How China Took Control of an OPEC Country's Oil' <www.reuters.com/article/2013/11/26/us-china-ecuador-oil-special-report-idUSBRE9AP0HX20131126> accessed 12 July 2016

88 Bracken et al. (n 68) 4

89 <www.sosyasuni.org/en/index.php?option=com_content&view=article&id=99:oil-extraction-moratorium-in-the-yasuni-national-park-&catid=1:news&Itemid=3> accessed 12 July 2016

90 For a discussion on payments for ecosystem services see Elena Blanco and Jona Razzaque, 'Ecosystem Services and Human Well-Being in a Globalized World' (2009) 31 *HRQ* 692–720

the help of civil society and international donors.[91] Failure to raise enough contributions from the international community, together with Chinese pressure to extract oil in payment for the loans advanced, meant that the scheme was suspended in August 2013.[92] This suspension reinforced the perhaps partisan but extended view that China's appetite for resources is so insatiable that it will contribute to the ecological destruction of the planet, conveniently forgetting the decades of Western led resource depletion and its environmental cost.[93]

In other emerging economies it is difficult to discern a single trend. While some countries concentrate on the promotion of the national oil sector, others have clearly moved towards foreign expansion and are engaging in what is has been described as 'South–South Neo-extractivisim'.[94] In India, for example, special schemes have been developed in the last few years with a clear emphasis on natural resource acquisition, particularly oil.[95] In Brazil, the 1988 Constitution made private participation in protected sectors, of which oil is one, more difficult, therefore restricting private sector investment.[96] In Russia, an oil exporting country, the Strategic Investment Law of 2008 specified strict rules of engagement for foreign investors interested in the sector.[97]

While these transactions could be and are, in some cases, an excellent example of South–South cooperation, they often simply reproduce neocolonial and imperialist extractive systems.[98]

Corporate governance of state owned enterprises and investment law

One of the worries surrounding the expansion of SOEs abroad is the potential anti-competitive effects and distortions in respect of local or foreign

91 Gonzalo Escribano, 'Ecuador's Energy Policy Mix: Development versus Conservation and Nationalism with Chinese Loans' (2013) 57 *Energy Policy* 152–159

92 Jeremy Watts, 'Ecuador Approves Oil Drilling in the Yasuni National Park' (*The Guardian* 16 August 2016) <www.theguardian.com/world/2013/aug/16/ecuador-approves-yasuni-amazon-oil-drilling> accessed 10 July 2016

93 U. Thara Srinivasan, et al., 'The Debt of Nations and the Distribution of Ecological Impacts from Human Activities' (2008) 105 *PNSA* 1768–1773. Dries Lesage, Thijs van de Graaf, Kirsten Westphal, 'Prospects for Energy Cooperation in a Multipolar World' in Lesange et al. (eds) *Global Energy Governance in a Multipolar World* (Ashgate 2010) 177–195

94 Tordo (n 11) 67–72

95 The foreign exchange expenditure of five of the largest Indian SOCs in 2010–2011 exceeded foreign exchange earnings by almost $60 billion. Fernanda Ribeiro Cahen, 'Internationalization of State-Owned Enterprises through Foreign Direct Investment' (2015) 55 *Rev. Adm. Empresa* 645–659

96 Tordo (n 11) 67–72

97 William Pomeranz, 'Russian Protectionism and the Strategic Sectors Law' (2010) 25 2 *American University International Law Review* 213–214

98 Gonzalez (n 30) 39

competitors for the host's state resources.[99] In today's global markets and despite the growing participation of SOEs there is still very little reliable information on their scope and the type of benefits these companies may be enjoying vis-à-vis their private counterparts.[100]

Concerns about both the internal and external corporate governance of SOEs are warranted when the state sector comprises a large number of national oil companies. The strategic importance of the oil industry in many countries' economies has already been discussed. Income from oil exploitation directly contributes to the national budget and pays for various policy tools and interventions.[101] The OECD has addressed some of these concerns in a variety of working documents and guidelines: *Accountability and Transparency: A Guide for State Ownership* (2011);[102] *Competitive Neutrality: Maintaining a Level Playing Field between Public and Private Business* (2012);[103] *Boards of Directors of State-Owned Enterprises* (2013);[104] *Financing State-Owned Enterprises: An Overview of National Practices* (2014);[105] and *State-Owned Enterprise Governance: A Stocktaking of Rationales for State Ownership* (2015).[106] The OECD Guidelines on Corporate Governance of SOEs ('OECD SOE Guidelines')[107] are the first international benchmark on good practice for governments on corporate governance of SOEs. Other relevant OECD instruments include the OECD Guidelines for Multinational Enterprises;[108] auxiliary guidance in the articulation on the so-called 'level playing field' and corporate governance of state owned companies may also be sought from other sources, such as the

99 Pradaig Carmody, *The New Plunder of Africa* (Polity 2013) 95–112

100 Przemyslaw Kowalski, Max Büge, Monika Sztajerowska and Matias Egeland, 'OECD Trade Policy Paper' No. 147 TAD/TC/WP(2012)10/ANN/FINAL at 5 <www.oecd.org/officialdocuments/publicdisplaydocumentpdf/?cote=TAD/TC/WP(2012)10/ANN/FINAL&docLanguage=En> accessed 1 October 2015

101 Cf discussion in previous section

102 <www.oecd-ilibrary.org/governance/accountability-and-transparency-a-guide-for-state-ownership_9789264056640-en> accessed October 2015

103 <www.oecd.org/daf/ca/corporategovernanceofstate-ownedenterprises/50302961.pdf> accessed October 2015

104 <www.oecd-ilibrary.org/docserver/download/5kg9xfg6n4wj.pdf?expires=1444598012&id=id&accname=guest&checksum=46AB83F44003209BEA56AFAFE2E738E3> accessed October 2016

105 <www.oecd-ilibrary.org/finance-and-investment/financing-state-owned-enterprises_9789264209091-en> accessed 10 October 2016

106 <www.oecd.org/publications/state-owned-enterprise-governance-9789264239944-en.htm> accessed October 2016

107 The Guidelines were first published in 2005 and later updated in 2015. The updated version can be found at <www.oecd.org/daf/ca/guidelines-corporate-governance-soes.htm> accessed 10 October 2016

108 2011 Update of the OECD Guidelines for Multinational Enterprises, available at <www.oecd.org/document/33/0,3746,en_2649_34889_44086753_1_1_1_1,00.html> (hereinafter OECD Guidelines). A much criticised instrument, see Blanco and Razzaque (n 9) 226–227

OECD Policy Framework for Investment[109] and the OECD Competition Assessment Toolkit.[110]

The Guidelines are intended as a complement to the OECD Principles of Corporate Governance,[111] with which they are fully compatible. The Guidelines state that 'the ultimate purpose of state ownership of enterprises should be to maximise value for society, through an efficient allocation of resources',[112] while recommending the maintenance of a level playing field between state owned and privately owned companies through the implementation of a number of guiding principles. Concerns and priorities reflected in the principles revolve around three areas: 'transparency and accountability', 'the State acting as an owner' and 'the functioning of SOE Boards'. We will consider these concerns in turn in the following subsections.

The majority of SOEs in OECD countries are incorporated according to ordinary company law and need to comply with regular corporate governance requirements. In addition, SOEs are often subject to more stringent financial disclosure and transparency standards than their private counterparts due to the danger posed by their proximity to policy makers and regulators.[113] For example Statoil (Norway) publishes financial statements and annual reports with disaggregated data on both their payments and the cost of their operations.[114]

Political interference in the affairs of the company and the complexity of the accountability chain are often manifested in oil based economies as a version of the 'resource curse' in the form of the so-called 'rentier state theory'.[115] The 'rentier state' typically experience governance failures that range from cronyism and clientism, the picking up of certain firms that receive privileges in exchange for funds and political backing,[116] to poor

109 Updated in 2015, available at <www.oecd.org/investment/investment-policy/pfi-update.htm> accessed 10 October 2016

110 First published in 2007 and updated in 2010 <www.oecd.org/daf/competition/assessment-toolkit.htm> accessed 10 October 2016

111 OECD Principles of Corporate Governance 2015. Originally developed in 2004, modified in 2009 and 2015 <www.oecd.org/corporate/principles-corporate-governance.htm> accessed 10 October 2016

112 Ibid

113 Sofia Wickberg 'Transparency of State-Owned Enterprises' (Transparency International 2013) <www.transparency.org/files/content/corruptionqas/Transparency_of_state_owned_enterprises.pdf> accessed 10 October 2016

114 Ibid at 2

115 The term was crafted by Hussein Mahdavy, 'Patterns and Problems of Economic Development in Rentier States: The Case of Iran' in M.A. Cook (ed) *Studies in Economic History of the Middle East* (Oxford University Press 1970) 428–467; and developed by Hazem Beblawi, 'The Rentier State in the Arab World,' in Hazem Beblawi and Giacomo Luciani (eds) *The Rentier State* (Routledge 1987) 49–62

116 Oliver Falck, Christian Gollier and Ludger Woessmann, 'Arguments for and against Policies to Promote National Champions' in Falck, Gollier and Woessmann (eds) *Industrial Policy for National Champions* (MIT Press 2011) 3

economic diversification and lack of an independent press or opposition.[117]

Countries with large NOCs are at a greater risk of cronyism or clientism than other economies. In many of the oil rich Middle Eastern states like Saudi Arabia, Bahrain, Kuwait, Qatar, Oman and the United Arab Emirates (UAE) politics are heavily conditioned by oil. Redistribution of wealth takes precedence and forsakes democratic bargaining.[118] Populations are bought off by oil wealth and those who dissent are repressed.[119] A very small but important group within society is involved in the generation of the rents and in sustaining the ruling elite.[120] In fact, many oil producing states and their national oil companies fall in a slightly more sophisticated version of the rentier state theory called neopatrimonialism, whereby rulers develop new economic opportunities for themselves and their clients.[121] The Guidelines address these perils by stating that a clear rationale for state ownership needs to be published and always guided by the ultimate purpose of providing the highest service to society, considering whether an alternative ownership structure or taxation could achieve the same or better results.[122] This approach enshrines societal service into the government's policy choice and ensures that the debate about ownership policy is subject to appropriate procedures of political accountability and disclosed to the general public.[123] However private oil companies also influence policy and politics in countries without a large SOE sector.[124]

Chapters III,[125] IV,[126] V,[127] VI[128] and VII[129] of the OECD SOE Guidelines

117 See Matthew Gray, 'A Theory of "Late Rentierism"', in *Arab States of the Gulf* (Center for International and Regional Studies, Georgetown University School of Foreign Service in Qatar 2011), for an up-to-date account of rentier state theory <www/repository.library.georgetown.edu/bitstream/handle/10822/558291/CIRSOccasionalPaper7MatthewGray2011.pdf?sequence=5> accessed 10 November 2016

118 Falck et al. (n 116) 58

119 Gray (n 117) 4

120 Belawi (n 115) at 78

121 Gray (n 117) 7 discussing Gero Erdmann and Ulf Engel, 'Neopatrimonialism Revisited – Beyond a Catch-All Concept' GIGA Working Paper 16-2006 (Hamburg, GIGA German Institute of Global and Area Studies, 2006) 17–20 <http://repec.giga-hamburg.de/pdf/giga_06_wp16_erdmann-engel.pdf.> accessed 10 July 2016

122 <www.oecd.org/daf/ca/OECD-Guidelines-Corporate-Governance-SOEs-2015.pdf> at 30 accessed 10 July 2016

123 Ibid at 31–32

124 Indeed the financing of political parties in the US by, among others, oil companies was recently exposed in respect of the 2016 presidential election by Nicholas Confessore, Sarah Cohen and Karen Yourish (*New York Times* 10 October 2015) <www.nytimes.com/interactive/2015/10/11/us/politics/2016-presidential-election-super-pac-donors.html?_r=0> accessed 10 October 2016

125 Chapter III: '[t]he legal and regulatory framework for SOEs should ensure a level playing field and fair competition in the marketplace ...'

126 Chapter IV: Equitable treatment of shareholders and other investors

127 Chapter V: Stakeholder relations and responsible businesses

128 Chapter VI: Disclosure and transparency

129 Chapter VII: The responsibilities of the boards of state owned enterprises

further expand upon the idea of a 'level playing field' that will allow free competition without unjustified privileges be granted to SOEs.

Transparency, accountability and the 'level playing field'

National oil companies account for over two-thirds of the total revenue in countries such as Azerbaijan, Congo-Brazzaville, Iraq and Yemen.[130] They not only sell and distribute the country's oil but often collect payments and revenue from private oil companies,[131] yet, despite the volume and value of the transactions involved, their accounts are often opaque and the transfer of funds between the government and the state owned national oil company is not transparent.

Lack of transparency on resource revenue reporting is linked to poor development outputs. Revenue Watch estimated that in Angola poor reporting from the national oil company produced a $32 billion gap in public funds sorely needed for public support projects.[132] In other African countries the figures are not dissimilar. Nigeria, for example, had a gap of several million in its gross domestic product (GDP).[133] The EITI has published some guidelines on the type of information it suggests NOCs provide.[134] Membership and implementation of EITI is however no guarantee of compliance. For example Azerbaijan and Kazakhstan, both EITI members, publish barely any information about their national oil companies.[135] Cameroon, by contrast, reports on royalties, bonus bonds, payments and transfers to the treasury from national oil companies and so do national oil companies like Statoil (Norway), Pemex (Mexico), Petrobas (Brazil) and Petroecuador (Ecuador) who without EITI membership publish audited financial statements and annual reports with disaggregated data on both their payments and the cost of their operations.[136]

A different attempt to address lack of transparency is that of introducing 'integrity pacts'. India, with a large SOE sector, began to implement in 2005 the so-called integrity pacts with the aim of reducing the endemic culture of

130 Revenue Watch (2012) 'Advancing State-Owned Transparency through the EITI' <www//eiti.org/files/SWG/RWI_SWG_Paper_State_owned_enterprises_April_2012.pdf> accessed 30 April 2016

131 Ibid

132 J.R. Mailey, 'The Anatomy of the Resource Curse: Predatory Investment in Africa's Extractive Industries' 24 <htts://www.africacenter.org/wp-content/uploads/2015/12/Africa-Center-Special-Report-No.-3-EN.pdf> accessed 10 July 2016

133 OECD, 'Corporate Governance of State-Owned Enterprises: Change and Reform in OECD Countries since 2005' (OECD Publishing 2011) <www.oecd.org/daf/ca/corporategovernanceofstate-ownedenterprises/48455108.pdf> accessed 30 April 2016

134 'EITI as a Tool for Improving the Trading Climate with National Oil Companies (NOCs)' (2015) <https://eiti.org/sites/default/files/documents/EITI_Brief_NOC_FirstTrade_March2015.pdf> at 5 accessed 9 October 2016

135 Ibid at 5

136 OECD (n 134) 2

bribery around state owned enterprises providing public services and exploiting natural resources.[137] The pacts consist of an undertaking by the government office – or the SOE – that public officials will not demand or accept any bribes or gifts and that disciplinary or criminal sanctions will be imposed in case of violation of this rule while the private sector, in turn, undertakes to disclose all payments made and makes a 'non-bribery' commitment. Many state owned companies have signed up to the pacts[138] and despite criticism indicating that more stringent measures are needed to address the endemic bribery that also plagues the private sector,[139] the Central Vigilance Commission, an autonomous governmental body that addresses public sector corruption, published a report stating that 95 per cent of the participating state owned companies believed that integrity pacts have 'helped [in] making procurement processes transparent'.[140]

The state as owner

Definition of what constitutes an SOE and what type of criteria – control, management, majority share or subordination to state activity or goals – are to be used for defining SOEs are of paramount importance as they will have a direct impact on the type of transparency requirements, access to foreign markets and dispute resolution procedures.

It is not always easy to establish, a priori, what constitutes an SOE due to the different ways in which these can be structured. For national oil companies the state may have full ownership of the company, like in the case of Aramco, the national oil company in Saudi Arabia or Pemex, the national oil company in Mexico.[141] The state may also operate through a majority share that enables control of their operations, as happens with ENI in Italy, Statoil in Norway, Sinopec in China, Petrobras in Brazil or Gazprom in Russia. This second type of NOC is generally publicly traded.[142] These variations in structure make it necessary to define SOEs in investment treaties in order to avoid situations of preferential treatment by the state. For example the US model bilateral investment treaty (BIT) defines SOEs in its Article 1 as 'an enterprise owned, or controlled through ownership interests, by a state [Party] … Excluding governmental, administrative or regulatory acts and public functions'.[143]

137 'Integrity Pact in the Public Sector Undertaking (PSU) in India' <www.integritypact.in/page.php?pid=136> accessed 30 April 2016

138 Among them the Oil and Natural Gas Corporation, Hindustan Petroleum Corporation and Gas Authority of India. Ibid

139 Integrity Pact in the Indian Private Sector, Ibid. ACSS Special Report No. 3 May 2015 Africa Center for Strategic Studies <http://africacenter.org/wp-content/uploads/2015/12/Africa-Center-Special-Report-No.-3-EN.pdf> accessed 30 April 2016

140 <www.transparencyindia.org/page.php?pid=23> accessed 30 April 2016

141 Tordo (n 11) 67 provides examples of the various ownership models of NOCs

142 Ibid

143 The text of the BIT can be found at <www.state.gov/documents/organization/188371.pdf>

The Trans-Pacific Partnership Agreement (TPPA)[144] reflects the preoccupation of those countries with a market economy and a privately owned oil sector with the presence of state owned companies in the natural resource extraction sector in particular.[145] The TPPA negotiations were seen as an opportunity to improve treatment of (mostly American) private investors vis-à-vis SOEs.[146] The US tried to eliminate any potential or actual unfair competition effects of state subsidies to foreign state enterprises that could potentially make American products uncompetitive. It did so by establishing a clear definition of what constituted an SOE and then creating some specific transparency requirements. Article 17.1 of the TTPA defined state owned enterprise/s as:

> an enterprise that is principally engaged in commercial activities in which a Party: (a) directly owns more than 50 per cent of the share capital; (b) controls, through ownership interests, the exercise of more than 50 per cent of the voting rights; or (c) holds the power to appoint a majority of members of the board of directors or any other equivalent management body.[147]

These requirements should, in principle, be considered disjunctive and the presence of any one of them would suffice to consider an enterprise as state owned.[148]

The Agreement states that it will seek to enhance transparency in respect of SOEs (Article 17.10), eliminate unrecorded subsidies that may harm other countries' (to the TPPA) businesses and workers and seek to ensure that there is no discrimination against goods or services of other treaty parties while enabling them to provide public goods and domestic public services. There are, however special provisions for those countries with a large SOE

144 The TPPA is a free trade agreement currently being negotiated by nine countries: US, Australia, Brunei Darussalam, Chile, Malaysia, New Zealand, Peru, Singapore and Vietnam. The US text can be found at <https://ustr.gov/trade-agreements/free-trade-agreements/trans-pacific-partnership/tpp-full-text> accessed 12 October 2016. Note that following the US presidential election of November 2016 it is doubtful that US will ratify the TPPA

145 In this context some countries like Vietnam, Malaysia, Peru and Chile have a larger presence of SOEs in natural resource exploitation

146 According the Office of the United States Trade Representative, the TPPA is offering much better protection in terms of levelling the playing field in respect of regulatory preferential treatment and competition law. See, <https://ustr.gov/trade-agreements/free-trade-agreements/trans-pacific-partnership/tpp-chapter-chapter-negotiating-7> accessed 1 October 2015

147 <https://ustr.gov/sites/default/files/TPP-Final-Text-State-Owned-Enterprises-and-Designated-Monopolies.pdf> accessed 10 October 2016

148 It will be necessary to await the interpretation of a tribunal in this point. See discussion below in n 163 and accompanying text in respect of Broches' test for SOEs in the context of investment arbitration

sector like Vietnam, Malaysia[149] and Brunei Darussalam.[150] The negotiations of these exceptions take into account the role played by the state in the economy and especially in the oil sector, often through national oil companies.[151]

The OECD Guidelines, similarly to bilateral and multilateral investment treaties, aim at standardising corporate governance duties and erasing the differences between private and state owned companies.[152] The Guidelines are generally not intended to apply to entities or activities whose primary purpose is to carry out a public policy function, even if the entities concerned have the legal form of an enterprise.[153] In practice this distinction is not always straightforward.[154] They establish that for the purpose of the Guidelines 'any corporate entity recognised by national law as an enterprise, and in which the state exercises ownership, should be considered as an SOE'.[155] This includes joint stock companies, limited liability companies and partnerships limited by shares. Statutory corporations are also considered SOEs if their purpose is mostly economic.[156] In parallel with the investment

149 Article 17.10.1 provides that 'Viet Nam and Malaysia, respectively, separately, within six months after the date of entry into force of this Agreement for Viet Nam and Malaysia, respectively, each Party shall provide to the other Parties or otherwise make publicly available on an official website a list of its state owned enterprises that have an annual revenue derived from their commercial activities of more than SDR [Special Drawing Rights] 500 million in one of the three preceding years, and shall thereafter update the list annually, until the obligation in this paragraph applies and replaces this obligation'

150 'For Brunei Darussalam, Article 17.10.1 requiring of each party publication of the full list of SOEs shall not apply until five years from the date of entry into force of this Agreement for Brunei Darussalam. Separately, within three years after the date of entry into force of this Agreement, Brunei Darussalam shall provide to the other Parties or otherwise make publicly available on an official website a list of its state-owned enterprises that have an annual revenue derived from their commercial activities of more than SDR 500 million in one of the three preceding years, and shall thereafter update the list annually, until the obligation in this paragraph applies and replaces this obligation'

151 Annex IV lists excluded sectors and enterprises for each country party to the agreement. Exceptions for national oil companies are provided for Vietnam, Brunei, Chile and Peru <https://ustr.gov/trade-agreements/free-trade-agreements/trans-pacific-partnership/tpp-full-text> accessed 10 October 2016

152 Chapter II (OECD SOE's Guidelines) 'State's role as an owner'. See, Hans Christensen, 'Balancing Commercial and Non-Commercial Priorities of State-Owned Enterprises' (OECD Corporate Governance Working Papers No. 6 2013) 6–8, explains the Swedish 'Guidelines for External Reporting by State-owned Companies'

153 Chapter I (OECD SOEs Guidelines 2015) 'Applicability: "The Guidelines are applicable to all SOEs pursuing economic activities, either exclusively or together with the pursuit of public policy objectives or the exercise of governmental authority or a governmental function"'

154 Investment tribunals have clarified this point famously in *Maffezini v Kingdom of Spain*, Award on Jurisdiction ICSID Case ARB/97/7 (Jan, 25, 2000) discussed later in this section. It is also one of the contentious points in the negotiation of the TPPA and other investment agreements

155 Definitions (OECD SOEs Guidelines) <www.oecd.org/daf/ca/OECD-Guidelines-Corporate-Governance-SOEs-2015.pdf> 17

156 Ibid

treaty provisions discussed above, once an enterprise is considered an SOE, requirements are applied such as the reporting of objectives, composition, activities carried out in the public interest, remuneration of state members, governance ownership and voting structure, financial assistance by the state and transactions with state agencies or state related entities as specified in Chapter VI (Disclosure and Transparency).[157]

SOEs as claimants in investment arbitration

Investment arbitration coexists with both state–state arbitration[158] and commercial arbitration for private international commercial disputes. It was developed to bridge the gap between those two forms of arbitration (inter-state and private) and sought to address the problem posed by sovereign immunity to jurisdiction and enforcement therefore encouraging foreign ventures by private commercial actors.[159]

Investment arbitration has developed, mostly, around the World Bank's International Centre for the Settlement of Investment Disputes (ICSID) Washington Convention (ICSID Convention),[160] the ICSID Additional Facility[161] and the United Nations Commission on International Trade Law (UNCITRAL) Arbitration Rules.[162] In order to fall within the remit of the ICSID, the dispute must be one between an 'investor' of a state party to the convention and another state party (Article 25 (1) ICSID Convention).[163] In

157 Ibid at 26

158 Which can be submitted to the International Court of Justice (ICJ). See Nathalie Bernasconi-Osterwalder, 'The State–State Dispute Settlement Clause in Investment Treaties' (IIED 2014) <www.iisd.org/sites/default/files/publications/best-practices-state-state-dispute-settlement-investment-treaties.pdf> accessed 28 October 2016

159 Christoph H. Schreuer, *The ICSID Convention: A Commentary* (Cambridge University Press 2009) 2. Due, mostly, to the privileged enforcement mechanisms facilitated by Articles 53(1) and 54(1) of the ICSID Convention. See Michael Feit, 'Responsibility of the State under International Law for the Breach of Contract Committed by a State Owned Entity' (2010) 28 *Berkeley Journal of Int'l Law* 142 1–36

160 Convention on the Settlement of Investment Disputes between States and Nationals of Other States (opened for signature 18 March 1965, entered into force on October 14, 1966). Available at <https://icsid.worldbank.org/apps/ICSIDWEB/icsiddocs/ Pages/ICSID-Convention.aspx> accessed 28 October 2016

161 The ICSID Additional Facility was created on 27 September 1978. It offers arbitration, conciliation and fact finding services for certain disputes that fall outside the scope of the ICSID Convention. <https://icsid.worldbank.org/apps/ICSIDWEB/process/Pages/Overview-ICSID-Additional-Facility-Arbitration.aspx> accessed 10 July 2016. Aurélia Antonietti, 'The 2006 Amendments to the ICSID Rules and Regulations and the Additional Facility Rules' (2006) 21 2 *ICSID Review – Foreign Investment Law Journal* 427–448

162 <www.uncitral.org/uncitral/en/uncitral_texts/arbitration/2010Arbitration_rules.html> accessed 10 July 2016

163 Article 25(1) ICSID Convention. Aron Broches, *Selected Essays, World Bank, ICSID, and Other Subjects of Public and Private International Law* (Martinus Nijhoff Publishers 1995) 202

respect of SOEs, in principle, and unless the BIT indicates otherwise, those that fall within the definition of 'investor' can trigger the process[164] but potentially SOEs may be precluded from acting as claimants in investment arbitration if applying the doctrine of attribution they are considered to be a state or state organ which would render the dispute state-to-state and thus excluded from investment arbitration.[165]

The duality of SOEs as commercial and public interest enterprises poses other important challenges on a system that already has difficulties accommodating the equitable treatments of foreign investors and the public interests of host states.[166] The attitudes of states and investors in respect of public interest protection are unsurprisingly radically different. Investors will not hesitate to initiate investment arbitration claims to protect their investment and profit in cases where another state would perhaps appreciate the legitimate policy reasons behind certain measures.[167] States should be aware when negotiating trade and investment deals, especially multilateral ones that agree to investor/state arbitration will certainly reduce the regulatory autonomy of a host country. In some cases, the investment treaty will expressly provide that 'government-owned' or 'state' enterprises can bring claims by including them within the definition of 'investor'.[168] In fact, only two BITs were found to expressly exclude state owned entities from access as claimants in investment arbitration.[169] While BITs and investment chapters of free trade agreements (FTAs) adopt a range of approaches to potential claims against states by states or state enterprises, the ICSID Convention simply excludes state-to-state disputes from its coverage: a state cannot qualify as a 'national' of a Contracting Party under ICSID Convention Article 25, even in a

164 Jo En Low, 'State-Controlled Entities as "Investors" under International Investment Agreements' *Columbia FDI Perspectives* 80 (8 October 2012)

165 Mark Feldman, 'The Standing of State-Owned Entities under Investment Treaties' in Karl Sauvant (ed.) *Yearbook on International Investment Law & Policy 2010–2011* (Oxford University Press 2012) 615

166 Jan Paulsson, 'The Public Interest in International Arbitration', *Proceedings of the Annual Meeting (American Society of International Law)* (2012) 106 *Confronting Complexity* 300–303

167 Bernasconi-Osterwalder (n 158) at 20

168 Mark Feldman, 'State Owned Enterprises as Claimants in Investment Arbitration' (2016) 31 *ICSID Review* 26; n 7 'USA–Korea Free Trade Agreement (signed 30 June 2007, entered into force March 15, 2012) Art 11.28 (KORUS) (including 'state enterprise' within the definition of 'investor of a Party'); Agreement between the Government of the United Mexican States and the Government of the People's Republic of China on the Promotion and Reciprocal Protection of Investments (signed 11 July 2008, entered into force 6 June 2009) Art 1 (China–Mexico BIT) (including within the definition of 'investor of a Contracting Party' an 'enterprise,' which is defined to include 'governmentally owned entities').

169 Jo En Low, 'State-Controlled Entities as "Investors" under International Investment Agreements', *Columbia FDI Perspectives* No. 80 (8 October 2012) (citing Panama's BITs with Switzerland and Germany)

subrogation context.[170] 'The broad purpose of the Convention is the promotion of private foreign investment and the balancing of the investors and host state interest.'[171] Based on Broches' analysis, SOEs 'acting as an agent for the government' or 'discharging an essentially governmental function' should be precluded from accessing ICSID (and other forms of) investment arbitration.[172] The test put forward by Broches was originally formulated as a disjunctive. However the only case to date where an ICSID tribunal has examined whether an SOE can be considered an 'investor' and qualify as a claimant in ICSID investment arbitration proceedings applied the two propositions cumulatively,[173] arguably extending the scope for SOE to bring cases as claimants. To ascertain whether an SOE is acting as an agent of the state, Articles 5 and 8 of the ILC's Draft Articles on State Responsibility[174] provide guidance to the factors considered by the customary international law attribution rules: the 'conduct of a person' is attributable to a state if the person: (1) 'is in fact acting on the instructions of, or under the direction or control of, that State in carrying out the conduct' (ILC Article 8), or (2) 'is empowered by the law of that State to exercise elements of the governmental authority ... provided the person ... is acting in that capacity in the particular instance' (ILC Article 5).[175] Applying this criteria in *Československa Obchodní Banka, as v Slovak Republic* (COB v Slovak Republic),[176] and *Hrvatska Elekroprivreda DD v Republic of Slovenia* (HEP),[177] the tribunal found that CBO and HEP (the SOEs' claimants in each case respectively) were acting under state control and/or exercising delegated state authority. However as the activities of a state owned entity were commercial in nature, a claim submitted by such an entity to ICSID arbitration could be brought as an investor–state, rather than a state–state, dispute.[178] This was so even if the entity is engaged in activities that are 'driven by' state governmental policies and is controlled by the state such that it is 'required' to do the state's 'bidding'.[179] The test under international law is set extremely high and 'would not extend to cases where a State does not actively exercise its right

170 Broches (n 163) at 202
171 Ibid
172 Ibid
173 Feldman (n 168) 27
174 Cf (n 16); Feldman (n 168) 27. We discuss attribution in the next sections
175 Ibid
176 ICSID Case No. ARB/97/4, Decision on Objections to Jurisdiction (24 May 1999) (CSOB)
177 Case No. ARB/05/ 24, Decision on the Treaty Interpretation Issue (12 June 2009) (HEP)
178 Ji Li, 'State-Owned Enterprises in the Current Regime of Investor–State Arbitration' in Shaheeza Lalani and Rodrigo Polanco (eds) *The Role of the State in Investor–State Arbitration* (Brill 2014) 404 (asserting that 'all multitasking SOEs except those discharging clear and narrowly-defined governmental functions' should be able to bring claims against states under the ICSID Convention)
179 Discussed by Feldman (n 168) 29

to control'.[180] Annacker, however, disagrees with this analysis and opines that '[t]he attribution criteria of the rules of State responsibility ... have no general applicability, and should not be used to override definitions and standards laid down in specific investment treaty provisions or the ICSID'.[181]

The growth of overseas investment activities of SOEs will, no doubt, provide an opportunity for the re-examination of the applicable criteria in the determination of what constitutes state activity and what doesn't and on the availability or not of investment arbitration for the settlement of disputes involving SOEs.

SOEs as defendants in investment arbitration

In order to sue an SOE as a defendant in investment arbitration proceedings the conduct of the SOE must be attributable to the state. Investment disputes susceptible of resolution by an ICSID tribunal need to be disputes between an investor, national of a state party, and a state party. If in the previous section we discussed in which cases the SOE activities are non-governmental and enable the SOE to qualify as an 'investor' to trigger the investment arbitration mechanism, in this section we turn our attention to the opposite scenario, that of SOEs displaying or performing governmental activities or functions, acting under the direction or control of the state and therefore treated as 'the state' for the purposes of being defendants to investment arbitration cases.

Investment tribunals have applied several tests to establish a connection (attribution) between the acts of the SOE and the state.[182] In *Maffezini v Spain*[183] the arbitral tribunal found that the defendant, SODIGA, was not only a *state owned* company (the so called 'structural test') but that it was also *state controlled* ('control test') and operated within government objectives ('functional test'). The tribunal in *Maffezini* went further by establishing that a 'finding that the entity is owned by the State, directly or indirectly, gives rise to a rebuttable presumption that it is a State entity' even though 'company ownership or control alone is, however, not sufficient to define a company as a State entity'.[184] A further 'functional test' was necessary to determine whether the company's operations were commercial or governmental in nature.[185] The tribunal concluded that SODIGA represented an

180 Feldman id, discussing *White Industries Australia Limited v Republic of India*, UNCITRAL, Award (30 November 2011) para 5.1.25

181 Claudia Annacker, 'Protection and Admission of Sovereign Investment under Investment Treaties' (2011) 10 *Chinese J Intl L* 531 564

182 See Michael Feit, 'Responsibility of the State under International Law for the Breach of Contract Committed by a State Owned Entity' (2010) 28 *Berkeley Journal of Int'l Law* 142 1–36, at 6

183 Maffezini (n 154) para 77

184 Ibid

185 Feldman (n 168) 27

entity of the Spanish state because the latter owned more than 88 per cent of the company's capital (control and structural test) and because it carried out governmental functions of regional development (functional test).[186]

These tests of attribution of conduct to the state, it has been suggested, can be used in another context to attribute responsibility for violation of human rights under international law to states.[187] This idea is developed in the next section.

State owned companies and human rights

While there is a consensus today that MNCs have a duty to respect human rights,[188] there is still a vigorous debate about the exact nature of that obligation and about the way it can and should be enforced.[189] SOEs not only share the duty to respect human rights with their private counterparts but their public nature could potentially generate (1) a higher expectation on standards of conduct and (2) facilitate accountability for violations of human rights through the use of the doctrine of attribution either under the principles of state responsibility in international law (ILC Articles)[190] or the first pillar of the state duty to protect under the UNGPs.[191]

Under customary international law on state responsibility, conduct by any organ of the state can trigger state responsibility for an internationally wrongful act (Article 2 ILC Articles).[192] SOEs, however, have distinct legal

186 Maffezini (n 154) para 75. The case is amply discussed in the investment law literature; see Feldman (n 169), Feit (n 159) or 'Investor–State Dispute Settlement and Impact on Investment Rulemaking' (UNCTAD 2007) <http://unctad.org/en/Docs/iteiia20073_en.pdf> accessed 28 October 2016

187 Camilla Wee, 'Regulating the Human Rights Impact of State-Owned Enterprises: Tendencies of Corporate Accountability and State Responsibility' (2008) <www.reports-and-materials.org/sites/default/files/reports-and-materials/State-owned-enterprises-Oct-08.pdf> accessed 12 July 2016

188 John Ruggie, 'Protect, Respect and Remedy: A Framework for Business and Human Rights', Report of the Special Representative of the Secretary-General on the issue of human rights and transnational corporations and other business enterprises, 7 April 2008, A/HRC/8/5, at 3

189 Olivier De Schutter, Gwynne Skinner and Robert McCorquodale, *The Third Pillar: Access to Judicial Remedies for Human Rights Violations by Transnational Business* (British Institute of International and Comparative Law 2013)

190 Cf n 146. James Crawford, *International Law Commission's Articles on State Responsibility, Introduction, Text and Commentaries* (Cambridge University Press 2002) 249

191 'Business and Human Rights: The Evolving International Agenda' John Ruggie, John F. Kennedy School of Government – Harvard University June 2007 RWP07-02. Olivier De Schutter, et al., *Human Rights Due Diligence: the role of states* (ICAR 2012). Michael Hakimi, 'State Bystander Responsibility' (2010) 21 2 *European Journal of International Law* 341

192 For a comprehensive study on attribution see Kaj Hober, 'State Responsibility and Attribution' in Peter Muchlinski, Federico Ortino and Christopher Scheuer (eds) *Oxford Handbook of International Investment Law* (Oxford University Press 2008) 549–583

personality from the state – even if the state is the majority (or even the only) shareholder.[193] Indeed in respect of the legal effects of conduct of SOEs, the United Nations Convention on Jurisdictional Immunities of States and their Property 2004[194] Article 10(3) provides that the immunity of a state is not affected by acts of SOEs if the enterprise has separate legal personality.[195] It will become necessary thus to establish the actual relationship between the state and the SOE in each case, arguably according to the same criteria discussed in the previous section.[196]

In principle, conduct of SOEs is not, *per se*, attributed to a state, for this to happen the SOE will need to exercise governmental authority or elements of it.[197] Indeed the combined reading of ILC Articles 4, 5 and 8 sets out a 'functional' test of attribution by stating that persons or entities that are not in principle state organs (as defined in Article 4) but which are *de facto* empowered to exercise state authority can be considered organs of the state for the purposes of attribution. Article 5 read in conjunction with Article 8 deal with actions which do not necessarily involve state activity[198] but which nevertheless can be attributed to the state because they have been authorised by the state.

These provisions bear some commonalities with the doctrine of 'lifting the corporate veil' in cases of litigation involving private companies.[199] In the case of private companies in some instances it is necessary to pierce the so-called corporate veil in order to avert the use of the doctrine of separate personality to commit fraudulent acts or human rights violations by the company.[200] If the corporate veil is lifted, or pierced, then the parent company, and not only the subsidiary, can be found to be liable on the basis that the subsidiary's conduct is its own conduct.[201] This device is used for several reasons. One of them is

193 'Commentary to International Law Commission Articles on State Responsibility', ILC Annual Report 2001, Ch. IV 107–108 <www.lcil.cam.ac.uk/Media/ILCSR/ ILC2001 chptIV.pdf>

194 Adopted by the General Assembly of the United Nations on 2 December 2004. Not yet in force. See General Assembly resolution 59/38, annex, Official Records of the General Assembly, Fifty-ninth Session, Supplement No. 49 (A/59/49)

195 Wee (n 187) 18

196 The SOE is 'acting as an agent for the government' or 'discharging an essentially governmental function' cf n 177–181 and accompanying text

197 Attribution was discussed by the ICSID tribunal in *Maffezini*, discussed above. ICSID Case No. Arb/97/7. It has also been discussed in *Salini v Jordan* ICSID Case No. Arb/02/13 Decision on Jurisdiction, 29 November 2004, 44 ILM 573 (2005) and *Trendex v Albania* ICSID Case No. Arb/94/2 Decision on Jurisdiction 24 December 1996

198 Hober (n 192) 557

199 Robert B. Thompson, 'Piercing the corporate Veil: An Empirical Study' (1990) 76 *Cornell L. Rev.* 1036

200 According to the *Barcelona Traction Case* ICJ Reports (1970), 3. In Hober (n 192) 557

201 The principle set by *Salomon v Salomon & Co Ltd* (1897) AC 22 (HL) is not set in stone. A court in certain circumstances has justifiably lifted the corporate veil and disregarded the separate existence of a corporation and held shareholders liable for ccorporation's actions as if they were their own

that of securing jurisdiction in a more favourable forum (that of the parent company). The other is to access greater resources to satisfy any potential liability. In the case of SOEs, if the state is found to be liable for the SOE's conduct as a principal for the acts of its agent, a new array of rules and resources become available to the victim to satisfy potential liability for human rights violations. This was done, as discussed in the previous section, in the case of *Maffezini* where the tribunal considered the relationship between SODIGA and the Spanish state in order to establish the jurisdiction of the tribunal.[202] A note of caution must be made, however, as the conduct attributable to the state under Article 5 will be limited to those acts and omissions which are deemed to be particularly governmental or public in their nature; therefore, if the violation of human rights by an SOE took place in 'commercial' acts or omissions, these may not be attributable to the state.[203] Although in principle the three terms 'instructions', 'direction' and 'control' of Article 8 of the ILC Draft Articles 'are disjunctive and it should be sufficient to establish any one of them'[204] to establish state responsibility, in practice claimants face an extremely difficult to discharge test, particularly when valuable resources are involved in areas with poor governance.[205]

The issue of state responsibility for the acts of a state owned national oil company was brought to the African Commission of Peoples' and Human Rights in respect of the destruction of the Ogoni's lands and resources.[206] The Commission, unfortunately, didn't make a clear statement as to whether acts of the state owned oil company, the Nigerian National Petroleum Company (NNPC), were directly attributable to the state. Only in respect of the destruction of food sources by NNPC, Shell Petroleum Development Corporation (SPDC) and security forces did the Commission establish a link between the acts of the NNPC to the state in connection with the violation of the right to food.[207] In this case the African Commission on Human and Peoples' Rights found that Nigeria had failed in its 'duty to protect' on

202 Cf n 154

203 Hober (n 192) 557–558

204 Crawford (n 159) and 'Commentary to International Law Commission Articles on State Responsibility' (ILC Annual Report 2001) Ch. IV, 107–108 <www.lcil.cam.ac.uk/Media/ILCSR/ILC2001chptIV.pdf> accessed 12 June 2016

205 'The Role of States in Effectively Regulating and Adjudicating the Activities of Corporations with Respect to Human Rights' Summary Report 2 <www.business-humanrights.org/Documents/Ruggie-Copenhagen-8-9-Nov-2007.pdf> accessed 12 June 2016. For an overview of the duty to protect and due diligence see Dangood Mzikenge Chirwa, 'The Doctrine of State Responsibility as a Potential Means of Holding Private Actors Accountable for Human Rights' (2004) 5 *Melbourne Journal of International Law* 11–18

206 African Commission on Human and Peoples' Rights, Case No. ACHPR/COMM/A044.1, 27 May 2002

207 Decision Regarding Communication 155/96 (Social and Economic Rights Action. *Centre for Economic and Social Rights v Nigeria*), African Commission on Human and Peoples' Rights, Case No. ACHPR/COMM/A044.1, 27 May 2002

several counts, including 'failure to investigate human rights violations, to conduct environmental and social impact assessments, and to provide information to the affected people' for human rights violations caused by a consortium consisting of a Nigerian SOC and Shell.[208]

In many cases it is arguable that the state duty to protect, which constitutes one of the three pillars of the Ruggie Framework on Business and Human Rights,[209] may be more easily enforceable in respect of acts of state owned companies than of privately owned companies since the level of information, relative control and influence are all relevant factors to the duty of the state[210] and it is likely that these will be more easily established in the case of state owned companies. As one commentator has noted 'because ownership places the State in a better position to protect against violations of human rights by SOEs, the corresponding duty will be equally higher'.[211]

The European community case of *Foster v British Gas*[212] interestingly took a different angle in the relationship between the state and a state owned company when it held that obligations of the state could be claimed directly against privatised entities[213] under the so-called 'horizontal' application of fundamental rights. Whereas under Article 5 ILC Draft Articles attribution is directed against the state, in *Foster* it was held that the claimants could rely on an equal treatment directive directly against the privatised entity rather than the state, when the state had failed to implement the directive within the prescribed period.[214] The European Court of Justice held that when the transition of the entity from the public to the private sphere adversely affected individual rights, the privatised entity 'inherited' some of the state's obligations.[215] It is doubtful that such an extension of state obligations could be expected of SOEs (or even POCs) deploying state activities in countries with weak governance. While states indisputably have a duty to protect those within their jurisdiction against rights abuses by third parties, including business actors, they are not required, at the moment, to exercise extraterritorial jurisdiction over human rights violations by business.[216]

208 Discussed in Dinah Shelton, 'International Decisions: Decision Regarding Communication 155/96' (2002) 96 *American Journal of International Law* 937–942. Wee (n 187) at 33

209 Wee (n 187) at 33

210 Ibid

211 Ibid at 36

212 *Foster v British Gas Plc.* [1991] ICR 84, ECJ Case C 188/89, see especially § 16–20

213 In this case an equal treatment directive was brought against British Gas, recently privatised by the British government. Council Directive 76/207/EEC of 9 February 1976 on the implementation of the principle of equal treatment for men and women as regards access to employment, vocational training and promotion, and working conditions. This is the so-called 'horizontal' effect of constitutional and fundamental rights

214 *Foster* (n 212) para 20

215 See discussion in Wee (n 187) 26

216 Stephanie Lagoutte, 'The State Duty to Protect against Business-Related Human Rights Abuses. Unpacking Pillar 1 and 3 of the UN Guiding Principles on Human Rights and Business' (September 15, 2014). Matters of concern Human rights' research papers Series No. 2014/1 <http://ssrn.com/abstract=2496355>

To summarise, state ownership has at least three immediate effects on the likelihood of victims of human rights violations by SOEs obtaining protection. The first one is the strengthening of the standard of human rights observance expected and demanded of SOEs; the second is the possibility of engaging the direct responsibility of states when an SOE acts in violation of international law and the conduct can be attributed to such states; and the third is an increased likelihood of state responsibility for the failure to protect against human rights violations.[217]

Conclusion

While sustainable use of resources is vital for both economic growth and human development, the experience of decades of market liberalisation suggests that certain public goods and human values may be better served by public bodies. Yet, the policy space of countries in their developmental path is increasingly constrained by the neoliberal agenda, the proliferation of free trade and investment agreements and multinational company friendly laws and policies. Investment arbitration is a timely and highly contested exponent of the subrogation of public interests to commercial pursuits, but it is not the only one. In the case of state owned companies, the overview of existing regulation shows that SOEs face, perhaps, more stringent conditions than private companies and that aside from the ideological misconceptions and certain economic bias against state commercial activity, real danger exists within the potentially incestuous role of the state as both regulator and owner. Corruption, renterism and clientism are some of the ills surrounding this, at times, dysfunctional relationship. A survey of the historical context of national oil companies however illustrates that state ownership is not a monolithic concept; on the contrary it takes a variety of shapes and forms and can serve multiple political and social goals. In the context of South–South expanding trade and investment and, more specifically, in the context of increased natural resource consumption by emerging economies, state ownership enables the development of a policy informed economic option that can facilitate growth and provide a variety of public services. What is crucial, thus, is not the fact that state ownership is used as a policy tool in the context of resource extraction and of meeting natural resource consumption needs, but that transparency requirements and clear boundaries between the fundamentally different roles of the state as regulator and the state as owner are established.[218]

217 Joylon Ford 'Business and Human Rights. Bridging the Governance Gap' (Chatham House, September 2015) <www.chathamhouse.org/sites/files/chathamhouse/field/field_document/20150226BusinessHumanRightsFord.pdf> for an excellent up-to-date overview of the agreed parameters and future challenges of the business and human rights debate, including accepted standards of duties for companies and states

218 Mushtaq H. Khan ' Governance and Anticorruption Reforms in Developing Countries: Policies, Evidence and Ways Forward' (UNCTAD G-24 Discussion Paper 2006) <http://unctad.org/en/Docs/gdsmdpbg2420064_en.pdf> accessed 10 November 2016

Companies involved in resource extraction often impose a high toll in the form of environmental damage and human rights abuses in the countries where they operate. A commitment to responsible growth from state and private companies can only crystallise with clearer, faster and more effective mechanisms of accountability, irrespective of whether the companies are private or state owned. Those mechanisms, arguably, are not value neutral and require a wider understanding of the political and historical responsibilities acquired by the Global North, and facilitated by international law, in resource extraction from the Global South.[219] The legacy that the ruthless and destructive machinery of capital accumulation introduced in colonial times, is still, sadly, stealing the future of millions of innocent people in resource rich but governance poor countries.

Accountability of companies (state or private owned) appears to depend largely on political factors that invariably reproduce colonial patterns.[220] Victims in developed countries are more likely to receive compensation from violations by corporate actors.[221] Victims of human rights violations by private or state owned companies in host countries in the Global South are mostly not so lucky. A combination of poor governance in host countries, insufficient funding to enable access to justice and reduced political leverage by the host state make both private litigation[222] and interstate actions[223] difficult and unpredictable.

Despite the many criticisms against the proposal put forward by Ecuador and South Africa for a binding regime regulating business and human rights,[224] it is indeed imperative that a global binding system that partially levels the extraterritorial reach of transnational corporations with extraterritorial liability is agreed. How this should be achieved is however the subject of debate. Those against adopting a binding instrument argue that the

219 Akinpelu O. Olutayo and Ayokunle O. Omobowale, 'Capitalism, Globalisation and the Underdevelopment Process in Africa: History in Perpetuity' (2007) XXXII *Africa Development* 97

220 Sabelo J. Ndlovu-Gatsheni, 'Genealogies of Coloniality and Implications for Africa's Development' (2016) *Africa Development* 16

221 As was the case on the Deepwater Horizon Oil Spill discussed above (n 63) and accompanying text

222 Claims are highly dependable on civil society organisations' willingness to take the case. For example claims pursued under the US ACTA, much more restricted arguably since the Supreme Court decision in *Kiobel v Shell*. See Liesbeth Enneking, 'The Future of Foreign Direct Liability? Exploring the International Relevance of the Dutch Shell Nigeria Case' (2014) 1 *Utrecht Law Review* 1 <www.utrechtlawreview.org> accessed 12 July 2016

223 Penelope Simons and Audrey Macklin, *The Governance Gap: Extractive Industries, Human Rights and the Host Country Advantage* (Routledge 2014) 9–13

224 Human Rights Council Res. 26/9, Elaboration of an international legally binding instrument on transnational corporations and other business enterprises with respect to human rights, UN Doc A/HRC/RES/26/9 (July 14, 2014) <http://ap.ohchr.org/documents/al> accessed 10 July 2016. Norway proposed a parallel resolution A/HRC/26/20 adopted by UN Human Rights Council on 27 June 2014 and signed by 21 countries

UNGPs, approved not long ago and widely adopted, provide enough of an accountability framework.[225] Proponents of the binding instrument argue that despite its success the UNGPs as a voluntary instrument of accountability present serious deficits, especially in respect on the third pillar – provision of a remedy. The new instrument will focus on this deficit either through the inclusion of suitable procedural rules in existing instruments like BITs or multiparty international investment agreements.[226] Technical issues of jurisdiction are often the main impediment in the exercise of the victims' right of access to justice.[227] Clear and non-discretionary jurisdictional grounds, whereby the victims can rely on a choice between the host and the home country of MNCs or SOEs to hear and determine disputes involving violations of human rights or environmental damage, could both advance the right to a suitable remedy[228] and reduce expenses, delay and uncertainties in litigation involving MNCs.[229] Another option could consist of allowing victims of human rights abuses to bring cases in a redefined ICSID or in another investment tribunal where arbitrators with human rights backgrounds would have the power to grant damages in cases of violation of human rights.

The landscape of transnational companies operating in the natural resource sector shouldn't be reduced to simplistic 'North–South' narratives. The debate on the binding treaty suggests that much. China, for example, voted in favour of such treaty,[230] despite being a global economic player with a large state sector. Brazil, by contrast, abstained, perhaps reflecting the

225 See on the debate surrounding the proposed treaty commentary by John Ruggie <www.ihrb.org/other/treaty-on-business-human-rights/a-business-and-human-rights-treaty-international-legalisation-as-precision> accessed 10 November 2016

226 Nadia Bernaz, 'Multilateral Agreement on Investment: Time to Awaken the Beast? – A Contribution to the "Business and Human Rights Treaty" Debate' (2014) <http://rightsasusual.com/2014/02/mai-beast-treaty/> accessed 10 November 2016

227 <www.ihrb.org/other/treaty-on-business-human-rights/beyond-the-guiding-principles-examining-new-calls-for-a-legally-binding-ins> accessed 28 October 2016

228 Richard Meeran, 'Tort Litigation against Multinational Companies for Violations of Human Rights: A Position outside the United States' (2011) 3 *City University of Hong Kong Law Review* 1–41

229 The regime could be imaged from that of the Regulation (EU) 1215/2012 of the European Parliament and of the Council of 12 December 2012 on jurisdiction and the recognition and enforcement of judgments in civil and commercial matters (recast) (Brussels Regulation (recast)). In the case of torts the case can be brought under the general rule of domicile in the place where the defendant is domiciled or according to Art 7(3) in the place where the tort has occurred or may occur at the plaintiff's discretion and without power of the courts to decline jurisdiction

230 UN Human Rights Council Resolution 26/9 was adopted by a recorded vote of 20 to 14, with 13 abstentions.
In favour: Algeria, Benin, Burkina Faso, China, Congo, Côte d'Ivoire, Cuba, Ethiopia, India, Indonesia, Kazakhstan, Kenya, Morocco, Namibia, Pakistan, Philippines, Russian Federation, South Africa, Venezuela (Bolivarian Republic of) and Viet Nam.
Against: Austria, Czech Republic, Estonia, France, Germany, Ireland, Italy, Japan, Montenegro, Republic of Korea, Romania, the former Yugoslav Republic of Macedonia, UK and USA

increased global exposure of its state owned and private mining, energy and agribusiness companies.[231] The dominance of SOEs in energy and natural resources exploitation in emerging economies is an opportunity to reconsider the objectives of BITs and to move on from what could be described as the dogmatic fixation with the narrow protection of investors' interests[232] onto a new stage in investment law that addresses and includes the public interest issues[233] that often arise in the context of investment claims. A shift in focus – from investor protection to sustainable investment that is inclusive of social and environmental criteria[234] – would facilitate combining efforts to address two of the most controversial and current issues in the field of business and human rights: the correct regulation of state owned companies and the accountability of MNCs for human rights violations through the fast evolving matrix of international investment law.

Abstaining: Argentina, Botswana, Brazil, Chile, Costa Rica, Gabon, Kuwait, Maldives, Mexico, Peru, Saudi Arabia, Sierra Leone, United Arab Emirates.
Joe Zhang, 'Negotiations Kick Off on a Binding Treaty on Business and Human Rights' (November 26, 2015) <www.iisd.org/itn/2015/11/26/negotiations-kick-off-on-a-binding-treaty-on-business-and-human-rights/#_edn1>
For the latest news and developments in respect of the calls for a Binding Treaty on Business and Human Rights see <https://business-humanrights.org/en/binding-treaty/latest-news-on-proposed-binding-treaty> accessed 12 June 2016

231 Ford (n 217) at 9 and J. Ruggie, 'Closing Remarks' (3rd UN Forum on Human Rights and Businesses, Geneva, 3 December 2014) 2

232 Glinavos (n 20) 50

233 Bernasconi-Osterwalder (n 158) 24

234 A term that encompasses the respect of human rights alongside environmental sustainability concerns

Part III
Changing dynamics

Foreword

Philippe Cullet

The use of natural resources plays a central role in most countries of the Global South. Most people use natural resources for meeting basic needs and realising human rights, such as the rights to life, food, water or health. Further, they often derive their livelihood and sustenance from biological resources, land, water and other natural resources. The individual, small-scale use of natural resources is thus indispensable to poverty eradication strategies. Even at that level, it needs to be conceived in a context that reflects the finite nature of many natural resources.

The use of natural resources is also central to economic activities of the private sector and economic development strategies of countries. Large-scale use of natural resources is meant to contribute to economic development but it can also have significant negative consequences for individuals and communities/indigenous peoples. This includes, for instance, situations where natural resource use leads to displacement through acquisition of land or indirect displacement where people do not lose their land but where their access to resources is affected or stopped, such as fisher people downstream of a large dam.

Large-scale use of natural resources must be undertaken in a context giving equity a central place since impacts of natural resource use tend to fall disproportionately on the weaker and more marginalised people, as confirmed by the fact that many large dam projects are found in territories occupied by indigenous peoples.[1] Further, since large-scale use of natural resources is often environmentally unfriendly, it must be planned in the context of the need to protect the environment, including with a view to ensuring availability of resources to future generations. Issues that arise in this context include pollution that may be caused in the context of the extraction of resources (e.g. water pollution caused by coal mining), pollution caused using the resource extracted (coal/oil-related greenhouse gas emissions) and exhaustion of resources in the case of finite resources.

1 E.g. World Commission on Dams, *Dams and Development – A New Framework for Decision-Making* 110 (London: Earthscan, 2000)

Natural resources use is so important that it sits at the crossroads of the most crucial law and policy debates of our time. This is nowhere better reflected than in the notion of sustainable development that originally sought to provide a new framework for environmental protection that would integrate the need to use resources for poverty eradication in the South.[2] The malleability of sustainable development has allowed multiple understandings to emerge. Sustainable development was originally understood as an environmental concept, as confirmed by the fact that it became the umbrella concept for environmental law. Yet, the adoption of the Sustainable Development Goals (SDGs) in 2015 capped a transformation whose roots can be traced at least to the 2002 World Summit on Sustainable Development (WSSD). From a notion meant to give environmental policy a stronger footing that could bring together the North and the South to pursue similar environmental policy goals, sustainable development is now the centrepiece of international development policy. This transformation has come with a heavy price for the environment. Sustainable development remains *the* central environmental policy umbrella notion but SDGs are essentially developmental goals within which the environment plays second fiddle.

The transformation of sustainable development towards a concept encompassing all dimensions of development contributed for a time to mainstreaming the environment. Yet, the triangular relationship between the environment, society and economy formalised at WSSD that was never really a relationship of equals became progressively more biased towards its economic dimension. This is well illustrated by the Rio+20 summit that introduced the concept of the green economy in an apparent bid to recast the debate on environmental protection.[3]

The changing understanding of sustainable development over time can be seen in parallel to the changes affecting natural resource use policy and practice in the past few decades. On the one hand, the progressive mainstreaming of the environment has ensured that it is considered where it may have been ignored a few decades ago. This does not mean that environmental considerations are comprehensively addressed but are at least usually considered, for instance, through a form of impact assessment.[4] On the other hand, natural resource use has been affected by overall changes brought about by the neoliberal economic reforms starting from the 1980s onwards. This has included state disengagement from natural use through privatisation and

2 World Commission on Environment and Development, *Our Common Future* (Oxford: Oxford University Press, 1987)

3 Cf Sam Adelman, 'Rio+20: Sustainable Injustice in a Time of Crises', (2013) 4/1 *Journal of Human Rights and the Environment* 6–31

4 E.g. Olufemi Elias, 'Environmental Impact Assessment', in Malgosia Fitzmaurice, David M. Ong and Panos Merkouris (eds), *Research Handbook on International Environmental Law* 227–242 (Cheltenham: Edward Elgar, 2010)

making individuals and communities increasingly responsible for their own access to natural resources based on the demand-led paradigm.[5]

This part of the book highlights several key natural resource sectors where significant changes have taken place in the past couple of decades. These chapters are framed around concerns that affect particularly the Global South and reflect the structural inequalities that traverse the current law and policy framework. Changing dynamics are visible both in terms of evolving patterns of use and appropriation of resources and the commodification of new substances that may not have been recognised as a good having economic value, such as in the case of drinking water.[6]

The expansion of natural resources use is linked to the search for new economic opportunities that lead to the creation of new markets, as in the case of carbon trading.[7] A general trend that can be identified is that the more the use of natural resources is emphasised, the more the environmental or conservation dimension of use is sidelined. The balance between use and protection that was at the centre of sustainable development in its early years is thus particularly affected. This is not surprising in a context where the strengthening of environmental regulation tapered off by the beginning of the century and where various countries now attempt to claw back some of the existing environmental standards or institutions.[8] This means that use increasingly trumps conservation, in what is looking increasingly suspiciously like a return to an era where 'development' is largely equated with economic growth. At the same time, this is not a movement backward in time. New challenges are thrown up by new natural resource uses. Biofuels may, for instance, be contributing to climate change mitigation but those produced from feed stocks have direct negative impacts on food sovereignty and the realisation of the right to food.[9] Others replicate a number of challenges already identified with large-scale commercial agriculture, in particular regarding land use and land acquisition.

One of the significant challenges in large-scale natural resource use is investment. Diminishing public investments have had the impact of conversely increasing the role and visibility of the private sector. In this context, one of the main causes for concern is the extent to which private sector investments contribute to a development that is sustainable. The development of the concept of green economy that reflects the stronger

5 E.g. concerning water, David Hemson, 'Water for All: From Firm Promises to "New Realism"?' in David Hemson et al. (eds), *Poverty and Water – Explorations of the Reciprocal Relationship* 13, 26 (London: Zed Books, 2008)

6 On commodification of water, e.g. Karen Bakker, 'Neoliberalizing Nature? Market Environmentalism in Water Supply in England and Wales', (2005) 95(3) *Annals of the Association of American Geographers* 542–565. See Chapter 10 (Bates) in this volume

7 Chapter 15 (Garcia) in this volume

8 E.g. United States, 115th Congress, 1st Session, H.R. 861 To terminate the Environmental Protection Agency, 3 February 2017

9 Chapter 16 (Lesniewska) in this volume

position of the private sector in natural resource use highlights the challenges that arise. This is, for instance, the case with mining where the limited legal instruments and principles developed at the international level, such as prior informed consent,[10] struggle to be implemented effectively in practice. Where environmental or democratic concerns prevail, it is often where the domestic legal framework has inbuilt safeguards that provide for the same.[11] Domestic law can be used to an extent to mediate between natural resource use and environmental and social concerns but this is not possible in all countries to the same extent.

Private investment is in principle bound by relevant principles of international law as expounded in the Rio Declaration.[12] Investments in natural resource use must follow these principles, from integration of environmental protection in development to the precautionary principle and common but differentiated responsibilities. This implies that investment is, for instance, to be reconciled with the imperatives of protection, precaution and equity. This is a challenge since the legal principles that define sustainable development were developed by states in a context where states were still either the major users of natural resources or able to effectively impose their will on private actors. That this is not necessarily the case anymore is confirmed by the proliferation of bilateral treaties that include clauses whereby the host state consents to International Centre for Settlement of Investment Disputes arbitration that may be triggered by a national of the other state.[13]

New thinking is urgently needed in a context where the law and policy framework governing natural resources use has failed to ensure equitable access to resources and environmentally benign exploitation of resources, and failed to prevent significant human rights violations linked to such use as well as effectively tackle armed conflicts related, for instance, to mining. This calls for rethinking the bases upon which the current framework is built. Indeed, while sustainable development was first conceptualised in the Brundtland Report with a focus on the poor, three decades later there has only been limited structural change and the poorest countries remain comparatively as poor as they were then.

The first step must be to move away from the discourse of development, including that of 'sustainable' development in favour of a discourse that puts poverty and impoverishment as the driving forces behind policies and laws governing use and conservation of natural resources. This would in turn lead

10 Chapter 13 (Erueti, Down and Ruru) in this volume

11 E.g. Niyamgiri case involving Vedanta. See *Orissa Mining Corporation v Ministry of Environment and Forest*, Writ Petition (Civil) No. 180 of 2011, Supreme Court of India, 18 April 2013

12 Declaration of the United Nations Conference on the Human Environment, Stockholm, 16 June 1972

13 E.g. Organisation for Economic Co-operation and Development, Dispute Settlement Provisions in International Investment Agreements: A Large Sample Survey (Paris: OECD, 2012)

to putting the social and environmental dimensions of natural resource use at the centre of the regulatory framework. Achieving this can be done in part by effectively implementing existing legal principles that are already virtually universally recognised at least in their most generic form. These include solidarity and equity, two founding principles of international law related to natural resource use that need to be implemented more effectively.[14]

It is also imperative to think beyond existing categories. This includes, for instance, rethinking the place of sovereignty as a marker of state control over natural resources. Indeed, the concept of permanent sovereignty over natural resources that was meant to provide safeguards to developing countries against predatory moves by foreign private sector investors has failed to play its role effectively. It has neither protected the weak in international perspective, as confirmed for instance by the imposed introduction of plant variety protection in all World Trade Organization member states that mostly favours foreign private actors,[15] nor stopped venal elites from depriving most people from the benefits of natural resource use. Ideally, solidarity among peoples should call for recognising natural resources as a common heritage of humankind, as is already the case, for instance, with deep seabed resources. Yet, in a context where solidarity is in retreat and where international institutions have failed to effectively represent and uphold the interests of smaller and weaker states, it is probably more appropriate to trust the principle of subsidiarity and local control, if some form of effective local democratic control can be established. Local or international solidarity is much needed at this juncture. It goes against the interests of large-scale investors in natural resource use but is imperative to maintain the legitimacy of the existing law and institutional framework in place.

14 E.g. R.St.J. McDonald, 'The Principle of Solidarity in Public International Law', in Christian Dominicé et al. (eds), *Etudes de droit international en l'honneur de Pierre Lalive* (Helbing, 1993), 275

15 E.g. Philippe Cullet, *Intellectual Property Protection and Sustainable Development* 246–248 (New Delhi: Butterworths/Lexis-Nexis, 2005)

10 Water, investment and sustainability

Rebecca Bates

Introduction

This chapter will examine the issues surrounding water, investment and the sustainable use of water resources. In particular it will focus on the area of water privatisation and its relationship with the General Agreement on Trade in Services (GATS).[1] Whilst there are a number of instruments that influence this area, most notably, bilateral investment treaties, the most global and wide ranging of these is the GATS. Due to the scope of this chapter and the intention to consider water services from a universal perspective, this chapter will focus on the GATS. The GATS has a substantial capacity to influence the water and sanitation services sector, perhaps more than any other instrument, as it enables member states of the World Trade Organization (WTO) to nominate their water markets to be subject to global trade rules and market access. There is however also substantial uncertainty as to how the GATS provisions apply to water services and how this 'openness' will impact markets, consumers and the environment. The global nature of this Agreement means that this uncertainty is a significant issue for both water markets and water managers.

Water privatisation is not a new phenomenon, however the potential scope of investment treaties, such as the GATS, means that existing water markets may be subject to new forces such as foreign investment and competition. As the private sector continues to play an increasing role in water supply it is important to understand how these interactions may impact supply from both a consumer and environmental perspective. Sustainability in this context will be examined through the perspective of sustainable water management as this form of sustainability applies directly to water services and water managers. Generally, the issue of sustainability is not one that is regularly considered in this context, however this is an area where international agreements and non-government agents have a direct impact on

1 *Marrakesh Agreement Establishing the World Trade Organization*, opened for signature 15 April 1994, 1867 UNTS 3 (entered into force 1 January 1995) annex 1B (*General Agreement on Trade in Services*) ('GATS')

sustainability outcomes. This chapter will conclude by considering how measures, including regulation, may be taken to ensure non-economic outcomes receive adequate priority in the process.

Background: Water, neoliberalism and free trade

Water privatisation has been one of the most important trends in the water sector over the past 50 years.[2] Water privatisation is both separate and linked to international investment. At the basic level water privatisation involves the operation of a non-government entity owning and managing supply infrastructure. This function may either be performed by a local or foreign entity. Global investment treaties, such as the GATS, however, provide a framework through which foreign corporations may enter local markets and the respective obligations of the state to provide access. The role of the private sector in the provision of water and sanitation services in and of itself is not a new phenomenon, however investment treaties are changing how these firms can operate in local markets.

The management and control of water and sanitation services has generally been viewed as a public good and therefore a public sector responsibility. However, the great need to improve the level of water and sanitation connection to communities across the world has led some to reconsider the status quo.[3] The shift towards privatisation, however, is more than a search for additional infrastructure funding. It is also frequently a decision driven by the ideological motivations of governments and a belief in the efficiency of the private sector over government.[4] Privatisation, 'private sector participation' or 'public–private partnerships' in the water and sanitation sector involve 'transferring some or all of the assets or operations of public water systems into private hands'.[5] Johnstone and Wood[6] assert that the case for private sector participation in the water and sanitation services sector results in part from a belief that private sector firms are 'better placed' to undertake the forms of investment needed to 'expand and rehabilitate the infrastructure', and that the desire to 'relieve' the burden on public finances only forms part of the motivation for the shift towards privatisation.[7] The authors note that there are four broad reasons which are generally cited for the

2 Jason Morrison and Peter Gleick, 'Freshwater Resources: Managing the Risks Facing the Private Sector' (Research paper, Pacific Institute, 2004); Maude Barlow and Barry Clarke, *Blue Gold: The Battle against the Corporate Theft of the World's Water* (Earthscan, 2002)

3 Peter Gleick and others, *The New Economy of Water: The Risks and Benefits of Globalization and the Privatization of Fresh Water* (Pacific Institute, 2002), 22; Nick Johnstone and Libby Wood (eds), *Private Firms and Public Water: Realising Social and Environmental Objectives in Developing Countries* (Edward Elgar, 2001) 1–19

4 Gleick and others (n 3) 22

5 Ibid i

6 Johnstone and Wood (n 3)

7 Ibid 7–10

involvement of the private sector within water and sanitation services.[8] First, they cite the inefficiencies that result from the nature of public sector management as being a central motivation of private sector participation. Second, the authors identify the problem of 'flexibility and autonomy' where the operations of water utilities are significantly constrained by the nature and scope of their bureaucratic obligations, and third, the 'absence of competitive discipline' where public utilities lack market discipline and incentives to minimise costs. Fourth, Johnstone and Wood cite the argument of the limitations of the public sector in accessing sufficient capital and the greater perceived capacity of the private sector in accessing financial and human capital as being a key reason for the shift from public to private.[9] However, these reasons alone fail to sufficiently explain how private firms are 'better placed' to provide water and sanitation services as they do not actively define the positive contribution private firms are capable of making to the sector. Rather these define the private sector's strengths through the perceived failures of the public sector. Perhaps this is a result of there being greater elements at play in this process than public sector inefficiency.

Commentators such as Petrella view privatisation as a broader phenomenon resulting from an 'ideological, political, economic, social and cultural transformation of regulatory systems'; the privatisation of telecommunications, mail services, electricity, gas, electricity and airlines may be seen as part of the broader movement towards smaller government.[10] This trend towards 'smaller government' stems from the broader movement towards and political acceptance of neoliberal economic theory in Western democracies since the late 1970s which draws upon classical theories of the free market to achieve the maximum benefit for the population.[11] These will be discussed in greater detail later in the chapter. Ultimately, the search for additional funds must be viewed as only part of the broader movement towards the privatisation of water and sanitation services[12] because, while increased investment has the potential to deliver improved outcomes, government attitudes regarding the status and role of water utilities within the community should be viewed as one of the key drivers of the privatisation process.

The private sector was responsible for the first formal provision of water and sanitation services in Western Europe and North America in the

8 Ibid
9 Ibid 8
10 Riccardo Petrella, *The Water Manifesto: Arguments for a World Water Contract* (Zed Books, 2001) 59–60
11 Jessica Budds and Gordon McGranahan, 'Are the Debates on Water Privatisation Missing the Point? Experience from Africa, Asia and Latin America' (2003) 7 *Environment & Urbanisation* 87; Christopher Sheil, *Water's Fall: Running the Risks with Economic Rationalism* (Pluto Press, 2000)
12 The World Bank and Public Private Infrastructure Advisory Facility, *Approaches to Private Participation in Water Services: A Toolkit* (World Bank, 2006) 2

nineteenth century[13] and, at the present time, is again a dominant force within the water services sector. The capacity of the private sector to provide additional funds to improve and expand water supply systems and infrastructure is a significant driver behind this shift in ownership. However, investment is not the only factor that has influenced the decision to privatise. The pattern of water and sanitation privatisation is also linked to the dominance of classical and later neoclassical economic thought within social and political thought as these policy approaches influence attitudes towards investment and the role of government.

The rise to dominance of neoliberal economic policies in Western democracies in the later 1970s brought privatisation back to the fore and supported the creation of the water market as we know it today. Briefly, neoliberal doctrine holds that social functions, such as the provision of public goods and economic development, are best undertaken by the private sector operating within 'free markets'.[14] In this model, the functions of the state are restricted to regulating and facilitating private enterprise. The adoption of this doctrine marked a significant ideological shift from the previously prevailing 'statist' ideology which believes that society's 'problems and needs are best addressed by the state through the political process'.[15] The Chicago School of Economics, led by Milton Friedman and Fredrick von Hayek, rejected Keynesian theory and championed the rise of neoclassical economics which dismissed Keynes' interventionist approach and promoted the return of free market principles to enable the market to find its own natural equilibrium.[16] The new neoclassical movement advocated the introduction of a denationalised and privatised monetary system, the removal of all international trade barriers and the 'wholesale privatisation of public services', supported by a voucher system for those unable to meet the price demanded by private market forces.[17] Consequently, the Chicago School was fundamental to the rise of economic rationalism around the world and engineered the shrinkage of the public sector and the reliance on free market mechanisms to deliver the maximum good to the maximum number of people.[18]

Linked to the increased role of the private sector in the supply of services, the free market approach of the Chicago School also supported the expansion of free trade and globalisation policies such as those supported by the WTO.[19] Globalisation challenges the concept of state boundaries, as national governments no longer possess total sovereignty in managing their economic affairs. The process also demonstrates the dominance of neoliberal economic

13 Budds and McGranahan (n 11) 90–92
14 Ibid
15 Ibid 90–92
16 Sheil (n 11) 27
17 Ibid 27–28
18 Ibid 33–34
19 Budds and McGranahan (n 11)

theory as it aims to remove global barriers to the free flow of commerce and trade.[20] Since the 1970s, it has not been a static process. Jurgen Habermas argues that, since the formation of the WTO, the rate of globalisation has rapidly augmented, as a result of the increased imposition of free trade imperatives on economic activity.[21] Consequently, national boundaries diminish in significance as the instruments of liberalisation take effect.

Globalisation and the tools of trade liberalisation have the potential to radically change the operation of water markets, in particular those that have traditionally operated under monopoly government control. The primary instrument of the WTO focused on the area of water services, is the GATS.[22] The GATS is the sector-specific agreement negotiated by WTO member states during the Uruguay Round of negotiations. It formed part of the 'new' WTO replacing the previously stand alone General Agreement on Tariffs and Trade (GATT). The GATS is responsible for establishing 'binding rules' on the international trade of services.[23] However, despite the high level of private sector participation in the water services sector, the industry operates generally outside the direct influence of trade liberalisation and the WTO. At present, there are no specific commitments with respect to water services under the GATS. There is also a significant degree of uncertainty as to how the agreement would classify a water service if a related commitment were to be made by a member state.[24] It is therefore important to understand how GATS applies to the water services sector and whether there is any scope to provide greater clarity to their relationship and to ensure the sustainable management of water resources.

Overview of the General Agreement on Trade in Services

The GATS is the sector-specific agreement negotiated by WTO member states during the Uruguay Round of negotiations. It formed part of the 'new' WTO replacing the previously stand alone GATT. The GATS is responsible for establishing 'binding rules' on the international trade of services.[25] Leroux argues that this Agreement is 'somewhat complex' as a result of the substantial challenges faced by the negotiators in achieving their

20 Jurgen Habermas, 'The European Nation-State and the Pressures of Globalisation' (1999) 235 *New Left Review* 46

21 Ibid 52

22 GATS (n 1)

23 World Trade Organization, 'The General Agreement on Trade in Services (GATS): Objectives, Coverage and Disciplines' (World Trade Organization) <www.wto.org/english/tratop_e/serv_e/gatsqa_e.htm> accessed 4 August 2016; David Hunter, James Salzman and Durwood Zaelke, *International Environmental Law and Policy* (4th edn, Foundation Press, 2011) 1216

24 Rebecca Bates, 'The Trade in Water Services: How Does GATS Apply to the Water and Sanitation Services Sector?' (2009) 31 *Sydney Law Review* 121–142

25 World Trade Organization (n 23); Hunter, Salzman and Zaelke (n 23) 1216

goal of drafting a 'comprehensive set of disciplines governing the multilateral trade in services'.[26] As a result, the GATS is a mixture of mandatory and voluntary obligations, which at times create substantial interpretative difficulties.[27] Interestingly, the Agreement does not define the meaning of 'services'[28] within its text. However, it is clear that GATS applies to all forms of trade in services and ensures that the liberalisation commitments made by member states apply to all services nominated by a member for liberalisation.[29] The Agreement does, however, define the meaning of 'trade in services' as being the supply of a service:

> (a) from the territory of one Member into the territory of any other Member;
> (b) in the territory of one Member to the service consumer of any other Member;
> (c) by a service supplier of one Member, through commercial presence in the territory of any other Member;
> (d) by a service supplier of one Member, through presence of natural persons of a Member in the territory of any other Member.[30]

Article 1(3)(b) excludes the application of the Agreement from government services.[31] The list of services sectors and their classification for liberalisation are broadly contained within two documents, the W/120 Scheduling Guidelines[32] and Central Product Classification (CPC).[33] The nature of the classification process and its application to water services will be discussed in depth in the following section.

The GATS document is divided into two key sections – the framework Agreement containing the general rules and the accompanying schedules which list national commitments on specific domestic access for foreign suppliers.[34] The GATS, like the GATT, contains a number of key provisions designed to promote equality between member states, market access and

26 Eric Leroux, 'Eleven Years of GATS Case Law: What Have We Learned?' (2007) 10 *Journal of International Economic Law* 749, 749–750
27 Ibid
28 The exclusion of a definition was the intention of the drafters: see Aly K. Abu-Akeel, 'Definition of Trade in Services under the GATS: Legal Implications' (1999–2000) 32 *George Washington Journal of International Law and Economics* 189, 190–191
29 Ibid
30 GATS Art I
31 GATS Art I:3(b). Art I:3(c) defines a service supplied in the exercise of government authority to be 'any service which is supplied neither on a commercial basis, nor in competition with one or more service suppliers'
32 *Services Sectoral Classification List*, WTO Doc MTN.GNS/W/120 (10 July 1991) (Note by the Secretariat)
33 Central Product Classification (CPC) Version 1.0, Statistical Papers Series, M, No. 77 Ver 1.0, United Nations 1998
34 World Trade Organization (n 23)

non-differential treatment of like products. These are Articles II, III and XVI. Article II:1 'Most Favoured Nation' (MFN) provides that 'each Member shall accord immediately and unconditionally to service and service suppliers of any other Member treatment no less favourable than it accords to like services and service suppliers of any other country'; Article III 'Transparency' requires each member state to 'publish promptly … all relevant measures of general application which pertain to or affect the operation of this Agreement'. Finally, Article XVI 'Market Access' requires member states to 'accord services, and service suppliers of any other Member, treatment no less favourable than that provided for under the terms, limitations and conditions agreed and specified in its Schedule'.

Despite the existence of similar principles in the two Agreements,[35] the GATT and GATS differ as a result of the mixed approach adopted by the GATS. This approach allows for the core provisions of Article XVII (National Treatment) and Article XVI (Market Access) only to apply to individual service sub-sectors nominated by the member state for liberalisation whereas Articles II (Most Favoured Nation) and III (Transparency) apply 'horizontally' across all sectors in a similar manner to the GATT.[36] Consequently, Articles XVI and XVII will only apply in circumstances where a member state has specifically nominated it for inclusion thus making GATS an 'opt in' Agreement. Therefore, member states are required to nominate their service sectors for liberalisation before Articles XVII and XVI have national application.

Specifically, the MFN principle requires member states to 'automatically and unconditionally' provide other member states with treatment no less favourable than they would afford any other country. The concept of like services has not yet been fully explored by the WTO adjudication bodies. However, it did find in *Canada – Autos*[37] that 'manufacture beneficiaries' and 'non-manufacture beneficiaries' were like service suppliers 'regardless of whether they have production facilities in Canada'.[38] Members are required to afford this access without delay and to all WTO members.[39] The GATS, however, allows a member to 'maintain a measure inconsistent with [the MFN principle] provided that such a measure is listed in, and meets the conditions of, the Annex on Article II Exemptions',[40] thus enabling members to exclude themselves from the operation of the provision for both legal and

35 Leroux (n 26) 752

36 Hunter, Salzman and Zaelke (n 23) 1216; World Trade Organization (n 23)

37 Panel Report, *Canada – Certain Measures Affecting the Automotive Industry*, WTO Docs WT/DS139/R, WT/DS142/R (11 February 2000); Appellate Body Report, *Canada – Certain Measures Affecting the Automotive Industry*, WTO Docs WT/DS139/AB/R, WT/DS142/AB/R, AB-2000-2 (31 May 2000)

38 Mitsuo Matsushita, Thomas J. Schoenbaum and Petros C. Mavroidis, *The World Trade Organization: Law, Practice and Policy* (2nd edn, 2006) 619–620

39 Ibid 620–621

40 GATS Art II.2

political reasons.[41] Similarly, Article II, the Market Access provision, requires members wishing to liberalise a service sector to specifically nominate the sector for liberalisation and then enter into commitments under Articles XVI, XVII and XVIII.[42] Once nominated, the provision operates to restrict a member from limiting the number of suppliers in the country, value of services imported, quantity of service output, number of service operations, number of persons employed, participation of foreign capital and certain forms of legal entities.[43] However, Article XVI.2 creates an exception to the rule, allowing members to meet its requirements 'according to services and service suppliers of any other Member, either formally identical treatment or formally different treatment to that it accords to its own like services and service suppliers'.[44] Mitsuo Matsushita, Thomas Schoenbaum and Petros Mavroidis argue that this allows members to make exceptions through a number of means, including the use of population density tests to determine the number of service suppliers permitted to operate or limiting the operation of foreign subsidiaries to a percentage of total domestic assets in an industry sector.[45] Consequently this provision, like the MFN principle, does not apply to all members in all circumstances. Finally, Article XVII, the National Treatment provision, requires that members treat the 'like services' of members in a manner no less favourable than their domestically produced 'like services'. This provision has a potentially large scope of operation, having the capacity to cover all the GATS measures. However, in reality, its operation is limited to the areas affecting the trade in services excluding those already covered by Articles XVI and VI.[46] In *EC – Bananas III*,[47] the dispute resolution panel developed a four-pronged test to determine the inconsistency of a measure with the GATT National Treatment provision.[48] First, the test requires that the complainant establish that the member had taken a 'specific commitment in the relevant sector and mode of supply'. Second, the member must have adopted a measure that 'affected the supply of services in the sector and the mode of supply concerned'. Third, the disputed measure must have been 'applied to foreign and domestic like services and/or services suppliers' and finally, the measure must have accorded the foreign suppliers 'treatment less

41 Matsushita, Schoenbaum and Mavroidis (n 38) 623–626
42 Ibid 648
43 Ibid
44 GATS Art XVI.2
45 Matsushita, Schoenbaum and Mavroidis (n 38) 468–469
46 Ibid 659–660; GATS Art VI (the Domestic Regulation provision) provides that in circumstances where a member has made a GATS commitment, the member must apply regulations that may affect the trade in services 'in a reasonable, objective and impartial manner'
47 Panel Report, *European Communities – Regime for the Importation, Sale and Distribution of Bananas*, WTO Doc WT/DS27/R/USA (22 May 1997); Appellate Body Report, *European Communities – Regime for the Importation, Sale and Distribution of Bananas*, WTO Doc WT/DS27/AB/R, AB-1997-3 (9 September 1997) ('*EC – Bananas III*')
48 Matsushita, Schoenbaum and Mavroidis (n 38) 662

favourable than that accorded their domestic counterparts'.[49] However, it remains to be seen whether this approach will by applied by a dispute resolution panel with respect to the GATS National Treatment provision.

The GATS, however, creates a number of general exceptions under Article XIV which provide for circumstances in which members are allowed to take certain otherwise-prohibited actions on a number of limited grounds in the same manner as Article XX of the GATT. These actions must not be applied in a discriminatory manner or act as a distinguished restriction on the trade in services.[50] Specifically of interest with respect to the water services sector, Article XIV(b) provides that: 'nothing in this Agreement shall be construed to prevent the adoption or enforcement by any Member of measures … necessary to protect human, animal or plant life or health'.[51]

Similarly, Article XIV also provides an exception for measures designed to protect 'public morals and public order',[52] however, not as in the case of GATT Article XX(g) 'exhaustible' natural resources. The failure to replicate GATT Article XX(g) reflects the focus of the Agreement on services rather than physical resources. Water is one of the few physical resources that is subject to both the GATT and GATS as a result of being both a physical resource and a service. As will be discussed below, the absence of such a provision does not limit the possibly of higher water and sanitary standards being imposed by member states given the possibility of an expansive interpretation of XIV(a). Generally the Article XX/Article XIV case law has demonstrated a willingness of the WTO Panel and Appellate Body to accept the merits of trade restrictive measures in genuine circumstances, however, a general failing of the member state to construct the measures in a non-discriminatory manner.[53] An exception to this trend can be found in the recent Appellate Body decision, *EC – Seals Products*[54] where measures adopted by the European Union (EU) to prohibit the importation and marketing of seal products were the subject of a complaint by Canada and Norway. In this dispute the EU justified the application of its measures under GATT XX(a), and the 'protection of public morals and public', on the basis

49 Ibid; *EC – Bananas III* (n 47)

50 GATS Art XIV

51 GATS Art XIV(b)

52 GATS Art XIV(a)

53 See for example Panel Report, *United States – Measures Affecting the Cross-Boundary Supply of Gambling and Betting Services*, WTO Doc WT/DS285/R (10 November 2004); Appellate Body Report, *United States – Measures Affecting the Cross-Boundary Supply of Gambling and Betting Services*, WTO Doc WT/DS285/AB/R, AB-2005-1 (7 April 2005) ('*US – Gambling*'); Appellate Body Report, *United States – Import Prohibition of Certain Shrimp and Shrimp Products*, WTO Doc WT/DS58/AB/R, AB-1998-4 (12 October 1998); Appellate Body Report, *Brazil – Measures Affecting Imports of Retreaded Tyres*, WTO Doc WT/DS332/AB/R, AB-2007-4 (3 December 2007)

54 Appellate Body Reports, *European Communities – Measures Prohibiting the Importation and Marketing of Seal Products*, WTO Docs WT/DS400/AB/R, AB-2014-1 and WT/DS401/AB/R, AB-2014-2 (22 May 2014)

that animal welfare concerns were of high importance to public morals in Europe.[55] These arguments were upheld by both the Panel and Appellate Body, despite the measure being discriminatory under Articles I(i) and III(iv).[56] The finding in *EC – Seal Products* therefore has the potential to inform the interpretation of Article XVI(a) as the 'protection of public morals' has been a key issue in the very limited case law to date.[57] There is also scope for such an approach to be adopted within Article XIV(a) regarding human rights concerns. This is particularly important with respect to water services in light of the recent recognition of the right to water by the United Nations General Assembly and Human Rights Council.[58] If such an approach were to be endorsed by the Panel or Appellate Body this would allow human rights considerations, such as access and affordability, to be a valid justification for discriminatory practice. The application of this provision in such a way would also arguably compensate for the absence of an 'exhaustible natural resources exception'.

GATS and service classification

The classification of water services is an area of relative uncertainty under the GATS. As previously mentioned, service classification within the Agreement is governed by the W/120 and CPC documents which categorise and define service areas and subcategories. The CPC agreement was created by the United Nations Statistical Office in 1991 with the goal of classifying goods and services in a 'comprehensive and mutually exclusive manner'.[59] Mirelle

55 Appellate Body Reports, *European Communities – Measures Prohibiting the Importation and Marketing of Seal Products*, WTO Docs WT/DS400/AB/R, AB-2014-1 and WT/DS401/AB/R, AB-2014-2 (22 May 2014); World Trade Organization, 'European Communities – Measures Prohibiting the Importation and Marketing of Seal Products' <www.wto.org/english/tratop_e/dispu_e/cases_e/ds401_e.htm> accessed 4 August 2016

56 Appellate Body Reports, *European Communities – Measures Prohibiting the Importation and Marketing of Seal Products*, WTO Docs WT/DS400/AB/R, AB-2014-1 and WT/DS401/AB/R, AB-2014-2 (22 May 2014); Rob Howse, Joanna Langille and Katie Sykes, 'Sealing the Deal: The WTO's Appellate Body Report in EC – Seal Products' (2014) 18(2) *ASIL Insights* <www.asil.org/insights/volume/18/issue/12/sealing-deal-wto's-appellate-body-report-ec-—-seal-products> accessed 4 August 2016

57 See for example Panel Report, *US – Gambling*, WTO Doc WT/DS285/R (10 November 2004); Appellate Body Report, *US – Gambling*, WTO Doc WT/DS285/AB/R, AB-2005-1 (7 April 2005); Appellate Body Report, *China – Measures Affecting Trading Rights and Distribution Services for Certain Publications and Audiovisual Entertainment Products*, WTO Doc WT/DS363/AB/R, AB-2009-3 (21 December 2009)

58 *The Human Right to Water and Sanitation*, GA Res 64/292, UN GAOR, 64th sess, 108th plen mtg, Agenda Item 48, UN Doc A/RES/64/292 (28 July 2010); *Human Rights and Access to Safe Drinking Water and Sanitation*, HRC Res 15/9, 15th sess, 31st mtg, Agenda Item 3, UN Doc A/HRC/RES/15/9 (6 October 2010)

59 Mireille Cossy, 'Water Services at the WTO' in Edith Brown Weiss, Laurence Boisson de Chazournes and Nathalie Bernasconi-Osterwalder (eds) *Fresh Water and International Law* (Oxford University Press, 2005) 117–125

Cossy notes that originally the document was created for statistical purposes but was later adopted by member states as the guiding classification document following the Uruguay Round. Since 1991, the document has been revised twice but now, however, shares the responsibility for service classification with the W/120.[60] The W/120 was drafted by the GATT Secretariat in 1991 and creates 12 broad service sectors which are divided in 160 subsectors and, as Cossy notes, is generally viewed as a 'simplification' of the CPC. Member states are free to use either classification system or to adopt another of their choosing.[61] This 'freedom' has been a significant cause of the general uncertainty surrounding service classification as there are no definitive boundaries or groupings.[62] This, as will be discussed subsequently in relation to *US – Gambling*, presents challenges in terms of defining both the nature and boundaries of GATS commitments. Specifically, with respect to water services the issue of classification is particularly fraught. Neither the CPC or the W/120 contains a specific reference to water services, however, the related areas of sanitation and sewage services are included within the environmental services category.[63]

The area of environmental services has seen a growth in the number of commitments made by member states over recent years. The W/120 creates four subcategories within this sector namely 'sewage services', 'refuse disposal services', 'sanitation and similar' and 'other', which may include cleaning, noise abatement and landscaping.[64] At present there are over 60 commitments in the area, 54 of which are with respect to sanitation.[65] This number is however minimal compared to the number of commitments made in other areas such as tourism and financial services.[66] The low level of commitments in this area can be partly explained by the operation of the public services exception in Article 1(3)(b) as many environmental services are state operated, and particularly in the case of sanitation, have monopolistic tendencies. There are, however, generally higher levels of community concern regarding the liberalisation of essential services, such as water and sanitation, which has made liberalisation in these areas more politically sensitive than other areas such as financial services.[67]

60 Ibid 122–125
61 Ibid
62 Ibid 121–122
63 Ibid
64 *Services Sectoral Classification List*, WTO Doc MTN.GNS/W/120 (10 July 1991) (Note by the Secretariat)
65 WTO/World Bank, Services Database <http://i-tip.wto.org/services/(S(5s22pd0bjgendtvmrsulcamk))/SearchResultGats.aspx>
66 WTO (n 17)
67 See for example World Trade Organization (WTO), *GATS – Fact and Fiction* at <www.wto.org/english/tratop_e/serv_e/gatsfacts1004_e.pdf> accessed 4 August 2015; see also Shiva (n 14)

The European Community submitted a proposal in 2000 to the WTO for greater clarity regarding the classification of environmental services. The proposal argued for the creation of seven new categories of 'purely environmental services' which it asserted would support the enhanced take up of commitments by member states.[68] Importantly, it allocated a specific category for water services, 'water for human use and water management'.[69] This proposal, while gathering a great degree of interest, was not formally adopted by the WTO due to a difficulty in achieving consensus.[70] As a result, water services are not specifically mentioned within the classification system and to date there has been no member state commitment in this area.[71] However, the increasing rate of commitments in the environmental services sector and in particular with respect to sewage and sanitation, raises the question of how long water services may remain outside the Agreement. Sewage and sanitation services both rely heavily upon water for their processes and clearly their water needs feed into water use and resource allocation. Water services therefore in their broadest meaning may be subject to GATS commitments while the specific area of drinking water may remain outside. This fragmentation of water supply in terms of the Agreement may raise domestic challenges for water managers given the tendency of the sector towards a natural monopoly and require co-existence of public and private actors.[72] The complexity and uncertainty surrounding the classification of water services is a significant challenge for the WTO and the GATS agreement.

Challenges of uncertainty

Water supply: Natural monopoly and long-term investment

The possibility of liberalisation and the uncertainty surrounding service classification under the GATS raises significant issues for water managers and challenges regarding sustainability and sustainable water management. The nature of water supply and water infrastructure tends towards natural monopoly and encourages longer-term investment and ownership structures. Traditionally, water and sanitation services have been viewed as a classic example of a natural monopoly as their total operational cost will always be at its lowest point when there is a 'single enterprise' producing 'the entire output for a given market' rather than multiple operators dividing 'the

68 WTO, 'Communication from the European Communities and their Member States' GATS 2000: Environmental Services S/CSS/W/38 (22 December 2000)

69 Ibid II, 8, 6A

70 Cossy (n 59) 123–124

71 World Bank and WTO, I-TIP Services <http://i-tip.wto.org/services/(S(r2sl0omoomrwnqs4bwb02o4i))/default.aspx> accessed 4 August 2015

72 Budds and McGranahan (n 11) 93; Peter Gleick, Garry Wolff, Elizabeth Chalecki and Rachel Reyes (n 3) 5–6

production amongst them'.[73] Moreover, in such a market, a 'natural' outcome of competition would be for one owner to buy out its competitors and receive the maximum return by achieving economy of scale.[74] It is believed that under this model the lowest cost to consumers will be achieved through one, rather than multiple, suppliers in the market as it is generally viewed as inefficient to lay competing systems of water and sewerage pipes.[75] This tendency towards natural monopoly has meant that decisions regarding planning and investment have tended to be focused on the longer term and a limited number of participants.

Investment in water and sanitation services involves providing funds to support the 'financing of long-term physical assets'. The long-term nature of the investment has generally led governments to be the main investor in this area.[76] High entry costs into the water market restrict the opportunity for competition and reinforce the monopolistic nature of the market. While long-term contracts have the potential to provide investment security, Nicola Tynan argues that recent and past experiences demonstrate that high entry costs 'do act as fairly robust barriers to inefficient entry by suppliers seeking purely to capture an incumbent's existing customers'.[77] Clearly, the long-term nature and payback period of investment in this area have tended to favour the involvement of governments and established private water firms in the supply of water services leading to a high level of consistency over the longer term. However, as the water-related classification sectors of the GATS demonstrate, the supply of water is also being fragmented into sectors such as storage, treatment, supply and waste and traditional participants can be forced to compete with other operators to perform these services. Moreover, new technologies such as recycling, dual piping and desalination are also being performed by different operators. This therefore means that the supply of water services is increasingly becoming subject to competition and fragmentation. The issue here, however, is not to distinguish between upstream and downstream users but rather the potential for the increased fragmentation of supply and for the possibility of bracket creep from areas subject to a commitment. Whilst this change is likely to be a positive experience for consumers, this change reflects a significant shift for water management and sustainability planning as multiple suppliers and users must be considered within the policy mix. Moreover, the possibility that a service area may be subject to a GATS commitment means firstly that the member state will be

73 Ibid at 93–94

74 Ibid

75 Michael Klein, *Economic Regulation of Water Companies*, World Bank Policy Research Working Paper No. 1649 (1996) 2

76 James Winpenny, *Report of the World Panel on Financing Water Infrastructure: Financing Water for All* (World Panel on Financing Water Infrastructure, 2003) 6–7

77 Nicola Tynan, 'Private Participation in Infrastructure and the Poor: Water and Sanitation', Paper presented at Infrastructure for Development: Private Solutions for the Poor (London, 2000) 7

required to ensure that foreign and domestic suppliers are treated in the same manner[78] and secondly the possibility of opening the market to additional suppliers.

The right to water

There is a strong and interconnected relationship between the adequacy of a nation's water and sanitation system and its level of economic development. Investment is the key for developing countries to improve their water and sanitation infrastructure and service, however, foreign investors generally avoid nations with 'unpredictable food production, health problems related to poor water quality and unreliable electrical supplies' and therefore do not assist in the 'breaking' of the poverty cycle.[79] International law has increasingly recognised the right to water over recent years, most notably in 2010 with the United Nations General Assembly[80] and Human Rights Council Resolutions[81] acknowledging the existence of the right within international law. This international recognition has lead to the increased application of the right at the regional and domestic level.[82]

The right to water has developed within international law over a number of years. The right to access adequate drinking water was first directly acknowledged by the international community in 1977 at the United Nations Water Conference.[83] Since this time the right has been recognised in a number of international instruments, including the Stockholm Declaration,[84] the Convention on the Rights of the Child[85] and the International Convention on the Elimination of All Forms of Discrimination against Women,[86] which have supported the development of different elements of the right.

78 As per Article XXIV

79 The World Bank, *Water and Poverty Linked* at <http://web.worldbank.org/WBSITE/EXTERNAL/NEWS0,print:Y> accessed 5 March 2006 (document on file with author)

80 The Human Right to Water and Sanitation, UNGA Res 64/292 (28 July 2010); Human Rights and Access to Safe Drinking Water and Sanitation (6 October 2010) A/HRC/RES/15/9

81 Ibid

82 Rebecca Bates, 'The Road to the Well: An Evaluation of the Customary Right to Water' (2010) 9(3) *Review of European Community and International Environmental Law* 282, 289–292

83 Report of the United Nations Water Conference, Mar del Plata (March 25, 1977) UN Publication, E77 II A 12 (Mar Del Plata Action Plan)

84 Declaration of the United Nations Conference on the Human Environment (1972) UN Doc A/CONF.48/14/Rev.1, reprinted 11 ILM 1416 (Stockholm Declaration)

85 Convention on the Rights of the Child, UNGA Res 44/25 of 20 November 1989 (2 September 1990) (CRC)

86 Convention on the Elimination of All Forms of Discrimination against Women (entered into force 3 September 1981) UNTS No. 20378 vol 1249 (CEDAW)

In July 2010, the UN General Assembly endorsed Resolution 64/292, 'The Human Right to Water and Sanitation'[87] which recognised the right to water in light of previous UN commitments and the significant numbers of individuals still lacking basic water services.[88] The resolution acknowledged 'the importance of equitable access to safe and clean drinking water as an integral component of the realization of all human rights'.[89] The resolution also called upon states to 'scale up [their] efforts' to provide 'safe, clean, accessible and affordable drinking water and sanitation for all' through the provision of additional technology transfer, capacity building and financial resources.[90] This should be viewed as a highly significant development in the right, both in terms of the acknowledgement of previous developments and moving the right forward in terms of status and acceptance.[91]

In September 2010, the United Nations Human Rights Council added to the General Assembly Resolution, with its own Resolution entitled 'Human Rights and Access to Safe Drinking Water and Sanitation'.[92] This Resolution added to the recognition of the General Assembly affirming that the right to water and sanitation formed part of the existing body of international law and the binding nature of the right.[93] Importantly, the Resolution recalls the General Assembly Resolution, and in Principle 3 affirms:

> that the human right to safe drinking water and sanitation is derived from the right to an adequate standard of living and inextricably related to the right to the highest attainable standard of physical and mental health, as well as the right to life and human dignity.[94]

The Resolution again recalled the vast body of international instruments which have supported and recognised the right including the Universal Declaration of Human Rights,[95] International Covenant on Economic Social and Cultural Rights (ICESCR), Convention on the Elimination of All Forms of Discrimination against Women[96] and Convention on the Rights of the Child[97] and the relevant provisions of declarations and programmes of action adopted at major United Nations conferences such as Mar del Plata. It also

87 The Human Right to Water and Sanitation (n 80)
88 Ibid; Bates (n 82) 289–292
89 The Human Right to Water and Sanitation (n 80), Principle 2
90 Ibid
91 Inga Winkler, *The Right to Water: Significance, Legal Status and Implications for Water Allocation* (Hart, 2014) 79–80
92 Human Rights and Access to Safe Drinking Water and Sanitation (n 80)
93 The Right to Water and Sanitation, 'International Timeline' <www.righttowater.info/international-timeline/#sep2010>, accessed 4 April 2011
94 Principle 3, Human Rights and Access to Safe Drinking Water and Sanitation (n 80)
95 *Universal Declaration of Human Rights*, GA Res 217, UN Doc A/64 (1948) (UNDR)
96 CEDAW (n 86)
97 CRC (n 83)

makes reference to regional commitments and initiatives recognising the right to water and international commitments.[98] Winkler argues that the Resolution places the rights to water within 'the context of legally binding human rights instruments and reinforces its understanding as a component of the right to an adequate standard of living'.[99]

The presence of the right to water within international law has both the capacity to inform principles of water management and how the Panel and Appellate Body could treat water services in the case of a dispute. As previously mentioned, the existence of the right could support the application of an exception under Article XXIV(a) as the acceptance of the right within international law may inform arguments supporting public morals in light of *EC – Seals*. Moreover, the central components of the right, namely accessibility and affordability, are key elements to achieving sustainability.

Sustainable water management

Sustainability is a fundamental principle to the management of water resources and the supply of water based services. The origins of the principle may be found in Principle 2 of the Stockholm Declaration: 'the natural resources of the earth including the air, water, land, flora and fauna and especially representative samples of natural ecosystems must be safeguarded for the benefit of present and future generations through careful planning or management, as appropriate'.[100] More broadly the concept is inherently connected to the overall objective of sustainable development and concepts of sustainable use.[101] In 2016 the World Water Development report defined the concept as:

> Sustainable water management in its broadest sense encompasses ecosystems protection and restoration, integrated water resources management (IWRM), as well as infrastructure development, operation and maintenance. Combined with access to a safe, reliable and affordable supply of water and adequate sanitation services, it creates an enabling environment for long-term employment opportunities, as well as development and growth across different economic sectors.[102]

The idea of sustainability is particularly suited to the area of water services given its capacity to link environmental, economic and social considerations.

98 Resolution on Human Rights and Access to Safe Drinking Water and Sanitation (n 80)

99 Winkler (n 91) 81

100 Declaration of the United Nations Conference on the Human Environment (1972) UN Doc A/CONF.48/14/Rev.1, reprinted 11 ILM 1416 (Stockholm Declaration) Principle 2

101 See Rio Declaration on Environment and Development (1992) UN Doc A/CONF.151/26 (vol I) 31 ILM 874 Principles 3–8

102 The United Nations World Water Development Report 2016 available at <http://unesdoc.unesco.org/images/0024/002439/243938e.pdf> accessed 15 February 2017

More widely it also links supply with the wider body of law governing water resources. The idea of sustainability is supported by customary international law, which has for a number of years recognised the sustainable use of water resources.[103] In 2010 the International Court of Justice (ICJ) in *Argentina v Uruguay* (*Pulp Mills*),[104] acknowledged the link between the principle of equitable and reasonable utilisation of water resources and the goal of sustainable development.[105] This in effect, as Alan Boyle notes, located the right of equitable utilisation within 'the larger framework of sustainable development'.[106] In particular the Court emphasised that Article 27 of the 1975 Statute of the River Uruguay demonstrated an 'interconnectedness between equitable and reasonable utilisation of a shared resource and the balance between economic development and environmental protection that is the essence of sustainable development'.[107] This, as Boyle asserts, is in keeping with the UN Watercourses Convention and other modern river treaties.[108] As the judgment of *Pulp Mills* demonstrates, the purpose of sustainability is to reconcile the competing imperatives of development and environmental protection. Practically, it also has the capacity to include both economic and environmental considerations within the planning process.[109]

In terms of its scope, the Global Water Partnership (GWP) defines sustainable water management as including water allocation, river basin planning, stakeholder participation, pollution control, monitoring, economic and financial management and information management.[110] In practice, it focuses on all aspects of water use and the interdependencies between each stage. It also balances environmental factors such as precipitation, pollution, run-off and recharge rates and climate change to balance the supply and demand for water resources. Emphasis is also placed upon balancing the requirements of different water users. A recent report undertaken by the Australian Academy

103 *Gabcikovo-Nagymaros (Hungary v Slovakia)* (1997) ICJ Reports 7; See also Law of Non-Navigational Use of International Watercourses (n 9)

104 *Pulp Mills on the River Uruguay (Argentina v Uruguay)* (Judgment) General List 135, 20 April 2010; *Pulp Mills on the River Uruguay (Argentina v Uruguay)* (Provisional Measures) Order of 13 July 2006 (2006) ICJ Reports 113

105 *Pulp Mills on the River Uruguay (Argentina v Uruguay)* (Provisional Measures) (n 148) [80]; Patricia Birnie, Alan Boyle and Catherine Redgwell, *International Law and the Environment* (3rd edn, Oxford University Press, 2009) 149

106 Alan Boyle, 'Pulp Mills: A Case Commentary' <www.biicl.org/files/5167_pulp_mills_case.pdf> accessed 25 October 2012, 4

107 *Pulp Mills on the River Uruguay (Argentina v Uruguay)* (n 104) at [177]; Boyle (n 106)

108 Boyle (n 106) 4

109 See for example the concept of ecologically sustainable development in Australia: Australian Government, Department of Environment and Energy, *National Strategy for Ecologically Sustainable Development* available at <www.environment.gov.au/about-us/esd/publications/national-esd-strategy-part1> accessed 5 October 2016

110 The Global Water Partnership, Water Resource Management available at <www.gwp.org/en/The-Challenge/Water-resources-management/) accessed 15 February 2017

of Technological Sciences and Engineering highlighted this point in their consideration of sustainable water management:

> Water cannot be considered in isolation. A systems dynamic approach can be applied to encapsulate the complex feedback mechanisms associated with the interactions between water, energy, climate change, population and agriculture. There are strong interdependencies between water and energy, food and the carbon cycle. Water is required for a broad range of energy systems – recent droughts severely impacted electricity production across much of eastern Australia.[111]

One of the key elements in achieving this balancing between users, uses and resources is the capacity to plan. The challenge for water managers is how to achieve this goal in the face of a changing water market, in particular with respect to the vulnerability of water supplies and the increased numbers of participants in the water market. For instance with regard to climate change, Dan Tarlock argues that the changing hydrological system and the presence of climate change mean that water managers cannot continue to rely upon the assumption of 'regional water balances' and that current hydrological models are unreliable and may contribute to an 'underestimation of available supplies'.[112] The same must be said with respect to the presence of multiple suppliers and the diversification of water uses within the market. Consequently, there are multiple challenges for water managers planning for and attempting to realise the goal of sustainable water management. These have the potential to be exacerbated by the forces of liberalisation and the uncertainty surrounding the application of the GATS with respect to water services.

Impact of liberalisation (GATS)

The application of the GATS to water services has always been a controversial issue in light of the associated 'threats' of enhanced privatisation and foreign control over water services. Whilst there are currently no member states with a specific commitment with respect to drinking water, there are, as previously mentioned, increasing number of commitments in related areas of water supply such as sewage and sanitation. The challenge in this area relates to how these commitments would be interpreted by the WTO Panel or Appellate Body in the case of a dispute. It is this uncertainty that presents

111 The Australian Academy of Technological Sciences and Engineering, 'Sustainable Water Management: Securing Australia's Future in a Green Economy', ii available at <www.atse.org.au/Documents/reports/sustainable-water-management-report.pdf> accessed 15 January 2017

112 Dan Tarlock, 'How Well Can Water Law Adapt to the Potential Stresses of Climate Change' (2010) 14(1) *University of Denver Water Law Review* 1, 2

the greatest challenge for water managers and the attainment of sustainable water management as the outcome of a dispute could grant access to additional market participants or place requirements on how foreign and domestic suppliers are regulated.

The Appellate Body decision, *US – Gambling*,[113] demonstrated that the Dispute Settlement Understanding (DSU) is willing to adopt a broad interpretation of a service commitment. The dispute brought by Antigua and Barbuda concerned the United States' GATS commitment to 'other recreational services (except sporting)' and considered whether the commitment included 'gambling and betting services' within its scope'.[114] The Panel and Appellate Body found that the US had made a specific commitment with respect to gambling and betting services by applying the W/120[115] and 1993 Scheduling Guidelines[116] as a 'supplementary means of interpretation' under Article 32 of the Vienna Convention.[117] The US had continually asserted during this dispute that this was a service commitment that it had not intended to make.[118] As a result the US was found to have made a commitment with respect to online gambling and betting services and was required to provide equal treatment to foreign and domestic suppliers.

The prospect of an expansive interpretation of service commitments by the DSU raises significant challenges with respect to water services given the fluid nature of supply and service 'sectors'. Water resources and networks are interconnected meaning that it can be difficult to fully separate water supplied for the purposes of household and commercial consumption, sanitation and sewage. In light of the existing commitments with respect to sanitation and sewage and the likely expansive interpretation of commitments by the DSU in the case of a dispute, it is clear that there is a risk of 'bracket creep' between water sectors and for the line between different water services to become blurred. This complication and uncertainty presents a significant challenge for water management and ultimately the operation of sustainable water management as it creates a state of flux in what has generally been a more certain area of water services. This uncertainty will interplay existing hydrological and physical challenges to make the planning for sustainable outcomes additionally burdensome and at times uncertain. Arguably, greater certainty regarding the scope of the Agreement would

113 Appellate Body Report, *United States – Measures Affecting the Cross-Boundary Supply of Gambling and Betting Services* WT/DS285/AB/R, adopted 20 April 2005; Panel Report WT/DS285/R, adopted 20 April 2005 (*US – Gambling*)

114 Leroux (n 26) 762–765, 761; WTO, *US – Gambling* (n 113)

115 *Uruguay Round, Group of Negotiations on Services, Service Sectors Classification List*, MTN.GNS/W/120, 10 July 1991

116 *Scheduling of Initial Commitments in Trade in Services: Explanatory Notes*, MTN.GNS/W/164, 3 September 1993

117 *Vienna Convention on the Law of Treaties*, 23 May 1969, 1155 UNTS 331; 8 ILM 679

118 *US – Gambling* (n 113)

assist water managers in the context of planning and the overall attainment of sustainable water management outcomes.

Conclusion

The application of the GATS to water services has been one of the more controversial topics within globalisation discourses since the adoption of the Agreement in 1995. The liberalisation of water services under the GATS is inherently linked to the processes of globalisation and privatisation, areas which have both been a topic of significant public debate. These concerns have stemmed in part from the sector's traditional mode of public sector supply and also water's fundamental role in human health and survival. However, another contribution to these sentiments has been the challenge of reconciling the economisation of what has traditionally been viewed as a public good. Service liberalisation is not, however, a new process having been widely adopted within more traditionally commercial spheres such as banking and telecommunications. It has, however, struggled to make similar inroads within the environmental services sector and with respect to water services themselves.

Environmental services are a relatively new area of liberalisation activity under the GATS. The recent increase in commitments by member states under the Agreement indicates a likely expansion of this area in coming years. However, the challenges regarding service classification present a number of difficulties in this area with respect to water services. The absence of a specific reference to the service area within the W/120 or the CPC means that a member state is not able to specifically nominate their water services for liberalisation or in the alternate, not able to specifically exclude their water services from a liberalisation commitment. The interconnected nature of water supply and the growing number of commitments in the areas of sanitation and sewage raises the risk that part of a member state's water services may be included within a commitment. This uncertainty has been supported by the lack of GATS-specific case law and the prospect of the broad interpretation service commitments raised by the Appellate Body decision, *US – Gambling*. This raises particular challenges with respect to water services due to the interconnected nature of supply and the lack of clarity regarding their classification.

Sustainability is the ultimate goal of water management. As a concept it has the capacity to integrate environmental, economic and practical elements such as infrastructure and capacity within one operational model. In practice, however, it represents a constant challenge to balance these factors while delivering adequate services and maintaining the capacity of the ecosystem to continue doing so. The monopolistic nature of the water market and the tendency towards long-term investment means that planning is a fundamental element in achieving this objective. Investment treaties, such as the GATS, and their capacity to open markets to new providers, create an additional layer of uncertainty within an already challenging task. In this sense the uncertainty surrounding the application of the GATS does pose a threat to the operation of sustainable water management. This is clearly an area that should be re-examined by the WTO in order to support the long-term and sustainable provision of water services.

11 Sustainable agricultural investment and the Global South

Jona Razzaque and Phuong Le

Introduction

Agricultural investment contracts have extensive implications for the livelihoods and wellbeing of people affected by many of these investment projects. From the large-scale coffee plantation in Uganda[1] in Africa to oil palm plantations in Colombia or Indonesia[2] – there are increased concerns regarding the sustainability of these projects. These concerns underscore that social and environmental considerations need to be effectively integrated not only during the implementation of the project but also throughout the contracting process. Investment contracts for agricultural investments, especially in some African and Asian countries in recent years, have a lack of transparency regarding practices and the commitments in contractual provisions which have resulted in major social and environmental risks.[3]

The focus of this chapter is the foreign investment contracts signed between host states and foreign investors[4] and they are usually considered as a state contract.[5] State contracts are generally of a hybrid nature where elements of private law (e.g., consent of the parties, breach, damages) and public law (e.g., subject matter and legislative approval of the contract,

1 FIAN International, 'Uganda – Coffee Plantations in Mubende' <www.fian.org/what-we-do/case-work/uganda-mubende/> accessed 17 January 2017

2 Emily Polack and others, *Agricultural Investments in Southeast Asia: Legal Tools for Public Accountability* (International Institute for Environment and Development, 2013) <http://focusweb.org/sites/www.focusweb.org/files/Agric%20Invest%20in%20SEA%20Legal%20Tools.pdf> accessed 17 January 2017

3 Lorenzo Cotula, *Investment Contracts and Sustainable Development: How to Make Contracts for Fairer and More Sustainable Natural Resource Investments*, Natural Resource Issues No. 2 (International Institute for Environment and Development, 2010) <http://pubs.iied.org/pdfs/17507IIED.pdf> accessed 17 January 2017

4 Bilateral investment treaties may or may not guide an investment contract

5 State contract is defined as 'a contract made between a state or a state entity vested with monopolistic control of a sector of state's economy and a foreign entity entering that state with the intent of establishing a long term business relationship with the state or the state entity in that economic sector'. M Sornarajah, *International Commercial Arbitration: The Problem of State Contracts* (Longman, 1990) 3

protection of public interest) coexist.[6] In addition, the involvement of the state, 'the long duration of mutual commitments' and the continuous need for the balance between 'commercial interest' and 'public interest' create an extra layer of risk for the investment contract.[7] This is exemplified due to the dual role that host states play as a contracting partner as well as a sovereign legislator; therefore, the state contract may not be simply to attain commercial profit.[8] Almost all large-scale foreign agricultural projects involve commitments to improve infrastructure for a local area, the use of local human resources and the reduction of poverty.[9]

In an agricultural investment contract, safeguards for land rights, compensation for affected communities, environmental protection, water resource use and strict impact assessments may be required because of the critical nature of the agricultural sector and its impact on communities and the environment.[10] In addition, to protect public interests, national law may impose specific terms that state contracts must apply on a wide range of matters (e.g. protection of human rights and security). Thus, negotiations for agricultural investment contracts can be complex because they typically involve many sophisticated technical, financial, legal, economic, social and environmental issues.

With the increasing acknowledgment of the sustainable development (SD) agenda in the international investment law,[11] a state contract needs to offer safeguards not only to prospective investors to attract their investments, but also to people in the host state to improve their living standards while respecting the environment.[12] In practice, many past investments have resulted in an unsatisfactory contribution to SD.[13] The extent to which

6 Jan Ole Voss, *The Impact of Investment Treaties on Contracts between Host States and Foreign Investors* (Martinus Nijhoff Publishers, 2011) 17

7 Ibid 16

8 Jeswald W. Salacuse, *The Three Laws of International Investment: National, Contractual, and International Frameworks for Foreign Capital* (Oxford University Press, 2013) 164

9 Columbia Centre on Sustainable Investment (CCSI) and International Senior Lawyers Project (ISLP), 'Guide to Land Contract: Agricultural Projects' (CCSI and ISLP, March 2016) <http://ccsi.columbia.edu/files/2016/03/Ag-Guide-2016.pdf> accessed 17 January 2017

10 Ibid

11 John Anthony Vanduzer, Penelope Simons and Graham Mayeda, *Integrating Sustainable Development into International Investment Agreements: A Guide for Developing Country Negotiators* (Commonwealth Secretariat, 2013); Marie-Claire Cordonier Segger, Markus W. Gehring and Andew Newcombe (eds), *Sustainable Development in World Investment Law* (Wolters Kluwer, 2011)

12 Lorenzo Cotula, 'Rethinking Investment Contracts through a Sustainable Development Lens' in Elena Blanco and Jona Razzaque (eds), *Natural Resources and the Green Economy: Redefining the Challenges for Peoples, States and Corporations* (Martinus Nijhoff Publishers, 2012) 13

13 Lorenzo Cotula and Kyla Tienhaara, 'Reconfiguring Investment Contracts to Promote Sustainable Development' in Karl P Sauvant (ed.), *Yearbook on International Investment Law and Policy 2011–2012* (Oxford University Publishing, 2013) 308

investment contracts contribute to SD can be assessed in light of the linkage between the key aspects of SD (e.g., transparency, public participation and scrutiny) and the process and content of contracts. Given the importance of foreign investment contracts and their implications, key SD concerns during the contracting process include local participation and public accountability in decision-making.[14]

The goal of SD in agricultural investment contracts is to maximise economic benefits for people in the host country, minimise negative impacts on people's lives and minimise environmental damage from project implementation. Structuring contracts to gain the most of the economic deal may include public revenues and non-revenue benefits, such as capital contributions, positive linkages with the local economy through job creation and business opportunities, capacity building, technology transfer as well as infrastructure development.[15] At the same time, the contract must minimise negative impacts on people's lives. If land taking occurs, fundamental human rights may be at risk, including the right to food,[16] the rights of indigenous people over their ancestral territories[17] and the right to property.[18] Tackling social impact also includes ensuring that economic benefits are equitably distributed and used for poverty eradication. Shaping a contract to achieve SD should also include commitments to minimise environmental damage such as water pollution or natural resource degradation, to consider liability for such damage and to promote investment projects by using, for example, low-carbon technology or renewable energy.[19] Indeed, each contract represents trade-offs and compromises between conflicting interests of the parties and their multiple objectives. As the examples from an International Institute for Sustainable Development report[20] highlight, parties may decide to compromise on one aspect in exchange for concessions on another, and prioritise certain issues or diminish certain benefits to achieve a fairer contract for all stakeholders.

14 For instance, Principles 1 and 10 of the Rio Declaration 1992

15 Cotula and Tienhaara (n 13) 284; Cotula, *Investment Contracts* (n 3)

16 *Universal Declaration of Human Rights*, GA Res 217A, 3rd sess, 183rd plen mtg, UN Doc A/810 (10 December 1948) Art 25; *International Covenant on Economic, Social and Cultural Rights*, opened for signature 16 December 1966, 993 UNTS 3 (entered into force 3 January 1976) Art 11

17 Articles 13–19, *Convention Concerning Indigenous and Tribal Peoples in Independent Countries*, opened for signature 27 June 1989, 72 ILO Official Bull 59 (entered into force 5 September 1991)

18 *Universal Declaration of Human Rights*, GA Res 217A, 3rd sess, 183rd plen mtg, UN Doc A/810 (10 December 1948) Art 17

19 Cotula, *Investment Contracts* (n 3)

20 Carin Smaller and others, *Investment Contracts for Agriculture: Maximizing Gains and Minimizing Risks* (Agricultural Global Practice Discussion Paper 03, World Bank Group and International Institute for Sustainable Development 2015) <www.iisd.org/sites/default/files/publications/world-bank-agri-investment-contracts-web.pdf> accessed 17 January 2017

With this background, this chapter first examines the legal nature of the foreign investment contract with its hybrid public–private nature and the involvement of sovereign states in an agricultural investment. The chapter will then focus on how investment contracts strike a balance between state responsibility and liability of the investors when public interests are at stake. The final section explores challenges for the Global South to 'green' the agricultural investment contract. The chapter concludes that the 'green' agenda requires the state to provide effective legal safeguards to be included in relevant national laws. In addition, state responsibility lies in providing adequate procedural tools (e.g. environmental impact assessment and effective local consultation), along with national remedies for liability and compensation as part of national legal mechanisms as well as being integrated into the contract. The chapter argues for better incentive mechanisms and collaborative business practices to reduce governance gaps.

Interaction between agricultural investment contract and national law

National legal frameworks are diverse, although they may have many common characteristics as they encourage foreign investment by providing investors and investments increased freedom of action and various incentives, as well as regulating foreign investment by imposing rules and restrictions. National laws and the investment contracts interact in several ways. According to Salacuse, '[n]ational law creates, gives meaning to, and enforces the contractual framework for the investment transaction' and '[i]nvestment contracts often refer to specific items of national legislation either to integrate them into or exclude them from the investment transaction'.[21] He adds that '[n]ational law usually controls and regulates the negotiation process, defines the scope of parties' negotiating authority, and specifies the contents of relevant investment contracts'.[22]

The difference between national law and investment contracts is clear. While investment contracts reflect the interest of the parties to the investment, the national law is a 'manifestation of the will of the governing authorities of the state'.[23] In addition, 'investment contracts are the product of bargaining and negotiation' between the host state and the foreign investors and the national law 'results from the legislative and regulatory processes of a specific country'.[24] Moreover, investment contracts are 'designed to govern a particular transaction' while the national law contains 'rules of a certain level of generality in order to cover a class of transaction'.[25]

21 Salacuse (n 8) 405
22 Ibid
23 Ibid 159
24 Ibid
25 Ibid

The power play between the national law and the investment contracts shows that they both try to influence each other.[26] For example, the investment agreement may include a 'stabilisation clause' to exempt the investments from negative future changes in laws and regulations; or include 'international arbitration clauses which enable them to avoid the jurisdiction of national courts with respect to settling disputes relating to the investments'.[27] In addition, investment contracts may include a choice-of-law clause to avoid entirely the application of national law.[28] Moreover, as Salacuse highlights, host states where national laws are not 'highly developed or which lack relevant legislation' may create a 'special legal regime' for investment projects.[29]

Generally, national law in the host state is the primary source of law that is used to govern foreign direct investment (FDI) in agriculture.[30] In the Global South, the national legal system on social, economic and environmental issues is generally weak or ineffective while the investment treaties and contracts provide greater rights and protections to foreign investors.[31] This is more so in the case of foreign agricultural investments where 'domestic land tenure rights, water rights, environmental management regimes relating to chemicals, labour law on farms and so on can be weak or absent'.[32] Thus, the asymmetric nature of investment contracts imposes obligations on host states but does not impose similar responsibilities on investors. The interests of the Global South are at stake due to the lack of clear, comprehensive and effective national legal systems to efficiently regulate this kind of investment.[33]

In many areas of foreign agricultural investment, national law plays a less important role while investment contracts play a significant role over national law in their interplay.[34] National laws governing agricultural investment and land tenure are critical but they are often inadequate and lack enforcement

26 Ibid 406
27 Ibid
28 Ibid
29 Ibid. The author brings an example from the Kenana Sugar Company of Sudan
30 Carin Smaller and Howard Mann, 'Foreign Purchases for Agriculture: What Impact on Sustainable Development' (Sustainable Development Innovation Briefs Issue 8, United Nations Department of Economic and Social Affairs, January 2010) <https://sustainabledevelopment.un.org/content/documents/no8.pdf> accessed 17 January 2017
31 Nadia Cuffaro and David Hallam, '"Land Grabbing" in Developing Countries: Foreign Investors, Regulation and Codes of Conduct' (Paper presented at the International Conference on Global Land Grabbing, April 2011) <www.iss.nl/fileadmin/ASSETS/iss/Documents/Conference_papers/LDPI/8_Nadia_Cuffaro_and_David_Hallam.pdf> accessed 17 January 2017
32 Smaller and Mann (n 30) 3
33 Mahnaz Malik, 'Foreign Investment into Agriculture: Investment Treaties and the Ability of Governments to Balance Rights and Obligations between Foreign Investors and Local Communities' (Paper presented at the International Conference on Global Land Grabbing, April 2011) <www.ids.ac.uk/files/dmfile/MahnazMalik2.pdf> accessed 17 January 2017
34 David Hallam, 'Foreign Direct Investment in Developing Country Agriculture: Issues, Policy Implications and International Response' (Global Forum on International Investment VIII, OECD, 7–8 December 2009) <www.oecd.org/dataoecd/30/39/44231828.pdf> accessed 17 January 2017; Smaller and Mann (n 30) 3–8

in many southern countries.[35] Mann brings examples from Africa where many countries may have no or limited law relating to the use of pesticides, or workers' health and safety standards in farms, or land protection for small-holder farmers.[36] Hence, when an investment contract comes into play upon that weak and narrow national legal framework, it can cause disadvantages to host states.

Agriculture investment contracts: Balancing state responsibility and liability of investors

Agricultural investment contracts raise concerns because they are closely related to the public interest and have major implications for SD. Provisions in the investment contract seek to reduce the perceived risk to the investor of nationalisation and expropriation, but also create many social and environmental consequences for local communities. Many investment contract provisions give priority to the interests of the investor and ensure stability for their investment, but may not address social and environmental aspects of SD.[37] In the agricultural sector, while there are challenges at the global level such as promoting environmental sustainability of agricultural production, mitigating and adapting to climate change, and eradicating food insecurity in least developed countries, it is critically important for the Global South to attract foreign investment.[38] Two substantive areas in investment contracts can be highlighted where the balance between state responsibility to promote SD and the liability of investors is apparent: stabilisation clauses and dispute settlement clauses.

First, 'stabilisation clauses'[39] either preclude the application of, or require

35 Food and Agriculture Organization of the United Nations (FAO), *Trends and Impacts of Foreign Investment in Developing Country Agriculture: Evidence from Case Studies* (FAO, 2013) 337

36 Howard Mann, 'Foreign Investment in Agriculture: Some Critical Contract Issues' (2012) 17 *Uniform Law Review* 129, 134 <www.iisd.org/pdf/2012/uniform_law_review_foreign_inv_ag_2012.pdf> accessed 17 January 2017

37 Dominic Ayine and others, 'Lifting the Lid on Foreign Investment Contracts: The Real Deal for Sustainable Development' (Sustainable Markets Briefing Paper No. 1, International Institute for Environment and Development, September 2005) <http://pubs.iied.org/pdfs/16007IIED.pdf> accessed 17 January 2017

38 Wanki Moon, 'Is Agriculture Compatible with Free Trade?' (2011) 71 *Ecological Economics* 13

39 Stabilisation is grouped into three broad categories, such as the *freezing clause* that 'freezes' the law of the host state with respect to the investment project over the life of the project. The *economic equilibrium clause* requires that the investor comply with new laws but also requires that the investor be compensated for the cost of complying with them. The *hybrid clause* requires the state to restore the investor to the same position it had prior to changes in law, including, as stated in the contract, by exemptions from new laws. See: Andrea Shemberg, 'Stabilisation Clauses and Human Rights' (Research Paper conducted for the International Finance Corporation, 27 May 2009) <www.ifc.org/wps/wcm/connect/9feb5b00488555eab8c4fa6a6515bb18/Stabilization%2BPaper.pdf?MOD=AJPERES> accessed 17 January 2017

compensation for, new or modified national regulatory measures that affect the investment.[40] These clauses are likely to protect investors from having to implement new national laws (e.g. environmental law, land law) or to provide investors with an opportunity to be compensated for compliance with such laws.[41] They provide 'formal tools for investor protection pursuant to a claim of breach of contract', and seek to ensure the terms and conditions of an investment project are stable during the lifetime of the project, thereby contributing to manage non-commercial risk.[42] Thus, concerns about stabilisation clauses in agricultural investment stem from fears that they may limit the ability of government to make new laws applicable to the investment, even to protect human rights or environment or legitimate public policy objectives.[43] Stablisation clauses can be controversial and problematic, especially when they are deemed unconstitutional.[44] In the Global South, stabilisation clauses trigger concerns about the constitutionality of these provisions, and the legitimacy of state action in agreeing to them.[45] Especially, in many Southern countries, there is a need to have constant change and reform in social and environmental matters to achieve the Sustainable Development Goals.[46] But signing up to excessive and broadly defined stabilisation commitments may limit the policy space of developing countries and constrain their ability to undertake regulatory changes during the long term of the investment projects.

As a way forward, many suggest the parties should renegotiate the contract or parts of it when changes are needed.[47] This suggestion includes explicit renegotiation clauses (e.g., a sunset clause, periodic review clause) in the contract that may reduce uncertainty. The aim of the renegotiation would be to restore the economic equilibrium of the contract after the regulatory change. These clauses combine features of stabilisation and renegotiation, as they stabilise the economic equilibrium rather than the regulatory framework

40 Cotula, 'Rethinking investment' (n 12) 33

41 Shemberg (n 39)

42 Ibid ix–x

43 Lorenzo Cotula, 'Regulatory Takings, Stabilization Clauses and Sustainable Development' (Global Forum on International Investment VII, OECD, 27–28 March 2008) <www.oecd.org/investment/globalforum/40311122.pdf> accessed 17 January 2017; also see: CCSI and ISLP (n 9)

44 Cotula, ibid 25

45 Ayine and others (n 37); Katja Gehne and Romulo Brillo, 'Stabilization Clauses in International Investment Law: Beyond Balancing and Fair and Equitable Treatment' (January 2014) NCCR Trade Working Paper No. 2013/46, 11 <www.nccr-trade.org/fileadmin/user_upload/nccr-trade.ch/wp2/Stab_clauses_final_final.pdf> accessed 17 January 2017

46 Ana Novik, 'Investment for Sustainable Development' (OECD Post-2015 Reflections Element 11, Paper 3) <www.oecd.org/dac/Post%202015%20Investment%20for%20sustainable%20development.pdf> accessed 17 January 2017

47 Cotula, *Investment Contracts* (n 3)

48 Ibid 73

itself.[48] In addition, carve-out provisions can help to limit the scope of protected investments and safeguard the right to regulate in the public interest.[49] In agricultural investments, it is crucial to reduce the risk of chilling effects on environmental laws and to increase the variety of measures a host state may undertake to pursue SD objectives without giving rise to mandatory compensation.

Second, the method and legal framework for dispute settlement is considered as an essential element in a contract. Foreign investors generally have rights to compensation from host states if their contractual rights are breached. Investment disputes may be settled through negotiation, mediation or conciliation. In case of a dispute, cases can be brought in the national courts of the host state as a default option.[50] However, investment contracts normally contain provisions to deal with dispute settlement and may enable parties to settle disputes through international arbitration rather than in national courts.[51] International treaties and national laws may also give investors direct access to international arbitration. In the past few years, a number of arbitrations have been brought by foreign investors against host states and many of these cases raise concerns about their implications for SD.[52] From a SD perspective, it is crucial that dispute settlement mechanisms adequately address all the interests involved in investment disputes, including both commercial and public interests.[53] Because of the public policy consequences, investor–state arbitration has been characterised as a method of 'transnational governance'.[54]

The 'public interest' element in investment disputes suggests that there is a need for greater legitimacy and public participation. One of ways to increase the transparency is the participation of third-party submissions (e.g., *amicus curiae* briefs). The involvement of these non-disputing parties (e.g., non-governmental organisations, civil society groups) in the arbitral proceedings can be seen as a representation of public interest including health and SD.[55] Nevertheless, the issues of confidentiality, the increase of costs to the disputing party or delays, and potential politicisation are some of the

49 United Nations Conference on Trade and Development (UNCTAD), *World Investment Report 2015: Reforming International Investment Governance* (United Nations, New York and Geneva, 2015) 133
50 Cotula, *Investment Contracts* (n 3) 75
51 Ibid
52 See Chapter 5 (Alam) and Chapter 6 (Dimsey) in this volume
53 Cotula, *Investment Contracts* (n 3) 75–84
54 Gus van Harten, 'Private Authority and Transnational Governance: The Contours of the International System of Investor–State Protection' (2005) 12 *Review of International Political Economy* 600
55 Examples of such cases can be found in Eugenia Levine, 'Amicus Curiae in International Investment Arbitration: The Implications of an Increase in Third-Party Participation' (2012) 29 *Berkeley Journal of International Law* 200

negative effects of this mechanism and may lead to the chilling of FDI flows to less stable nations, which are often the Southern countries.[56]

A green foreign agricultural investment regime? Challenges for the Global South

While FDI in agriculture is a complex issue relating to investment, trade and SD, the hierarchy of rights and obligations of the legal regime regulating these remains uncertain.[57] The international obligations on the investor to undertake the investment in accordance with the host state's food security, human right to food and property and indigenous people's rights are likely to be contained in the national laws, including the constitution, and the obligations on the host state to protect the investor are contained in the investment agreements. There is an additional concern in relation to agricultural investments where there is food or water shortage. The host state's right to expropriate the investor right may be limited as it may constitute a breach of the 'fair and equitable treatment' standard and frustrate the legitimate expectation of the investor.[58] In some cases, government intervention to protect the local population may cause a violation of broad protection guarantees in investment agreements, resulting in the government having to pay compensation to the investor.[59]

Moreover, as discussed below, a common problem of the Global South is the lack of clear property rights, water rights, land rights and impact assessment laws. If these rights are vague or based on local traditions, not only do these rights create a problem for the traditional natural resource users, investors may impose rights acquired under investment contracts over these forms of ambiguous or non-formalised rights.[60] In addition, national laws of many countries of the Global South do not provide an adequate framework for negotiation between investors and local people who are affected by the agricultural investment.[61] The bargaining power in negotiation of the investments often favours foreign investors, especially when the host country supports their objectives. This inequality is aggravated and becomes a critical issue when small landholders run the risk of being displaced without adequate consultation or effective and proper compensation.[62] Acquisition of

56 Ibid

57 Howard Mann, *International Investment Agreements, Business and Human Rights: Key Issues and Opportunities* (International Institute for Sustainable Development, February 2008) 20

58 Ibid

59 Shemberg (n 39) 9

60 Smaller and Mann (n 30) 5

61 Polack and others (n 2)

62 Evadne Grant and Onita Das, 'Land Grabbing, Sustainable Development and Human Rights' (2015) 4 *Transnational Environmental Law* 289

agricultural land is essentially a political issue with land reform and land rights issues often leading to conflicts and at times to violence.[63]

Environmental impact assessment

During the negotiation as well as during the implementation of the agricultural investment agreements, the projects have to be monitored against, *inter alia*, depletion of soils, loss of critical biodiversity, increased greenhouse gas emissions or significant diversion of water from other human or environmental uses.[64] National laws often do require an impact assessment to be carried out prior to the land transfer and many low and middle-income countries have adopted national legislation that prioritises environmental impact assessment (EIA).[65] Where government authorities approve an impact assessment, they issue the environmental permits or licences needed to implement the agricultural project. In practice, the implementation of EIA often faces difficulties.[66] There are many reported shortcomings in impact assessments, including violations of information and consultation requirements, for example in relation to large-scale land acquisitions for agricultural investments.[67]

Though environmental laws require an EIA to be conducted before the approval of the investment projects, evidence indicates that there are many weaknesses in administrative and institutional systems in the Global South to make EIAs work effectively from the process of licensing to monitoring and enforcement. The negative environmental effects resulting from agricultural investments are often due to the lack of a proper EIA prior to the investment

63 Cuffaro and Hallam (n 31)

64 Matthias Görgen and others, 'Foreign Direct Investment in Land in Developing Countries' (Deutsche Gesellschaft für Technische Zusammenarbeit Division 45, December 2009) <www.giz.de/fachexpertise/downloads/Fachexpertise/giz2010-en-foreign-direct-investment-dc.pdf> accessed 17 January 2017

65 Examples are available from Jennifer C. Li, 'Environmental Impact Assessments in Developing Countries: An Opportunity for Greater Environmental Security?' (2008) USAID Working Paper No. 4 <www.fess-global.org/workingpapers/eia.pdf> accessed 17 January 2017; John Kakonge, 'Improving Environmental Impact Assessment (EIA) Effectiveness: Some Reflections' (Global Policy, 5 March 2013) <www.globalpolicyjournal.com/blog/05/03/2013/improving-environmental-impact-assessment-eia-effectiveness-some-reflections> accessed 17 January 2017

66 Lorenzo Cotula, *Foreign Investment, Law and Sustainable Development: A Handbook on Agriculture and Extractive Industries* (1st edn, International Institute for Environment and Development, 2013)

67 Ibid. Also examples from developing countries can be found in George C. Schineveld, Laura A. German and Eric Nutakor, 'Towards Sustainable Biofuel of Development: Assessing the Local Impacts of Large-Scale Foreign Land Acquisitions in Ghana' (Paper presented at the World Bank Land Governance Conference, 26–27 April 2010); Isilda Nhantumbo and Alda Salomão, *Biofuels, Land Access and Rural Livelihoods in Mozambique* (International Institute for Environment and Development, 2010)

and the absence of an effective environmental management system.[68] Many EIAs are one-off assessments, not supported by implementation, ongoing monitoring, modification and adherence to recommendations for changes to operations.[69] For example, in Lower Mekong countries, the implementation of the EIA process usually commences too late, when other major project decisions have already been made, and their current EIA regimes do not adequately address the 'follow up' process.[70] Therefore, robust accountability and meaningful public participation are crucial for the EIA process. Citizens and civil society can also play an important role in scrutinising impact and in monitoring subsequent compliance with social and environmental management plans.[71] In addition, strong legal review mechanisms, as discussed below, will be required allowing affected communities to bring their grievances.

Investments in agriculture are typically implemented over a long time frame. It is important that any permits or licences issued reflect the recommendations included in impact assessment studies or in separate management plans based on those studies. These permits can include detailed conditions (e.g., to safeguard groundwater resources or regulate waste management), either directly or through reference to the management plans.[72] It is important that government authorities have the power to monitor compliance and withdraw or suspend permits in case of non-compliance.[73] It is also essential that the government institutions mandated with approving EIA and monitoring compliance during project implementation are properly resourced, equipped with the full range of skills needed (including skills to deal with social and environmental impacts) and backed up by strong political support.[74]

68 FAO, *Trends and Impacts of Foreign Investment in Developing Country Agriculture: Evidence from Case* Studies (Food and Agriculture Organization of the United Nations, Rome, 2013)

69 UNCTAD, *The Practice of Responsible Investment Principles in Larger-Scale Agricultural Investments: Implications for Corporate Performance and Impact on Local Communities* (World Bank Report Number 86175-GLB, Agriculture and Environmental Services Discussion Paper 08, 2014)

70 Matthew Baird and Richard Frankel, 'Mekong EIA Briefing: Environmental Impact Assessment – Comparative Analysis in Lower Mekong Countries' (Mekong Partnership for the Environment, 2015) <www.pactworld.org/eia%20comparative%20analysis> accessed 25 February 2017; William J. Schulte and Ashlee Stetser, 'On the Path to Sustainable Development: An Assessment of Cambodia's Draft Environmental Impact Assessment Law' (2014) 3 *Cambodia Law and Policy Journal* 98

71 Lorenzo Cotula and others, 'Agricultural Investment and International Land Deals: Evidence from a Multi-Country Study in Africa' (2011) 3 *Food Security* 99

72 FAO, *Environmental Impact Assessment: Guidelines for FAO Field Projects* (FAO, 2012) <www.fao.org/3/a-i2802e.pdf> accessed 17 January 2017

73 Cotula, *Foreign Investment* (n 66)

74 Ibid

Regulating local land rights

Land tenure is one of the most contentious issues in agricultural investments. The right of local communities who were prior users of purchased or leased land is a critical issue in the debate over land acquisition.[75] The processes of land acquisition to enable project implementation can have far-reaching implications for people who depend on that land and natural resources for their livelihoods.[76] Land also has important cultural and spiritual value and provides the basis for social identity and social networks. In the investment regime where public consultation and transparency are often lacking, problems concerning land acquisition are likely to arise in the initial stages of project implementation at the land clearance and construction stages.[77] Moreover, where consultation does take place, it may not adequately reflect the view of many marginalised community and sub-community groups, including women within indigenous communities who are often under-represented in decision-making activities.[78]

Where agricultural investment projects involve the acquisition of local land rights, such action may trigger the application of legal safeguards protecting the human right to property.[79] Where people depend on land for their food security, there may be a breach of the right to adequate food.[80] Another human right that may be at stake is the right to housing, which is also part of the broader right to an adequate standard of living. Well-developed land tenure systems with clearly structured rights for local owners or users make it easier to determine how the land will be allocated to the investor.[81] In cases of local opposition to an investment agreement, the government may decide to expropriate the land subject to the relevant laws and compensation requirements.[82]

75 Smaller and Mann (n 30)

76 World Bank, 'Principles for Responsible Agricultural Investment that Respects Rights, Livelihoods and Resources' (A Discussion Note prepared by FAO, IFAD, UNCTAD and the World Bank Group to contribute to an ongoing global dialogue, January 2010) <http://siteresources.worldbank.org/INTARD/214574-1111138388661/22453321/Principles_Extended.pdf> accessed 17 January 2017

77 Cotula, *Foreign Investment* (n 66)

78 United Nations Office of the Special Adviser on Gender Issues and Advancement of Women and the Secretariat of the United Nations Permanent Forum on Indigenous Issues, *Gender and Indigenous Peoples* <www.un.org/esa/socdev/unpfii/documents/Briefing%20Notes%20Gender%20and%20Indigenous%20Women.pdf> accessed 17 January 2017

79 This right is internationally recognised by the Universal Declaration of Human Rights (Article 17)

80 The right to food is recognised as part of the broader right to an adequate standard of living under the Universal Declaration of Human Rights (Article 25) and the International Covenant on Economic, Social and Cultural Rights (Article 11)

81 Smaller and Mann (n 30)

82 Carin Smaller, 'Investment Contracts for Farmland and Water: Ten Steps' (International Institute for Sustainable Development, April 2013) <www.iisd.org/pdf/2013/investment_contracts_farmland_en.pdf> accessed 17 January 2017

In many Southern countries, land rights are 'often not formally recognised, vague, based on local customs or simply non-existent'.[83] Smaller adds that:

> Instead, title is often vested in the government, in local chiefs or other community structures. This can lead to a situation in which the investor is allocated secure tenure to land and water, while local communities are left with weak or non-existent tenure rights. Access to land and water for the local community would be undermined as a consequence, a reality that has now been documented by the World Bank, several United Nations agencies and civil society organizations. The issue of land and water tenure for local owners and users must be clearly identified before the contract is negotiated.[84]

In agricultural investment, large-scale land acquisitions for plantation farming have generated much controversy about land grabbing. There are increasing concerns that such investment disproportionately affects rural communities as such projects often deprive them of their land and, at the same time, cause environmental problems through overexploitation.[85] The countries where large numbers of contracts have been reported are poor and often in conflict or post-conflict situations.[86] These countries tend to have weak governance – 'in terms of regulatory frameworks, government effectiveness, the rule of law, corruption control, investor protection and land governance'.[87] According to the FAO, '[w]eak governance marginalises the poor who lose out because they lack the political force to influence decisions, and because they lack the financial resources to bribe corrupt officials'.[88]

83 Ibid
84 Ibid
85 S. Haralambous, H. Liversage and M. Romano, 'The Growing Demand for Land: Risks and Opportunities for Smallholder Farmers' (Discussion Paper prepared for the Round Table organised during the Thirty-second session of IFAD's Governing Council, 18 February 2009) <www.ifad.org/documents/10180/72144de7-3ef9-4c96-8e6b-f54 5964fe6e4> accessed 17 January 2017
86 Ibid; Rabah Arezk, Klaus Deininger and Harris Selod, 'What Drives the Global Land Rush?' (International Monetary Fund (IMF) Working Paper WP/11/251, November 2011) <www.imf.org/external/pubs/ft/wp/2011/wp11251.pdf> accessed 17 January 2017; and Klaus Deininger and Derek Byerlee, 'The Rise of Large-Scale Farms in Land Abundant Developing Countries: Do They Have a Future?' (Policy Research Working Paper 5588, World Bank, March 2011) <http://elibrary.worldbank.org/doi/pdf/10.1596/1813-9450-5588> accessed 17 January 2017
87 Claire Schaffnit-Chetterjee, 'Foreign Investment in Farmland: No Low-Hanging Fruit' (Deutsche Bank Research, Current Issues – Natural Resources, 13 November 2012) <www.dbresearch.com/PROD/DBR_INTERNET_EN-PROD/PROD0000000000 296807/Foreign+investment+in+farmland%3A+No+low-hanging+fruit.pdf> accessed 17 January 2017
88 Food and Agriculture Organization of the United Nations (FAO), *Voluntary Guidelines on the Responsible Governance of Tenure of Land, Fisheries and Forests in the Context of National Food Security* (FAO, 2012)

Thus, the risks associated with large-scale land acquisitions, according to Deininger, include weak land governance and a failure to recognise, protect or properly compensate local communities' land rights; lack of legal capacity to offer inclusive and participatory consultations that result in clear and enforceable agreements; and resource conflict with negative distributional and gender effects.[89] Large-scale investments have also led to increased land concentration and even to forced evictions.[90]

In many Southern countries, particularly in sub-Saharan Africa,[91] the land tenure regime includes customary land rights as well as formal property rights. Smallholders may use land based on customary or communal practices which may not be formally recognised. Such weak legal recognition of customary rights is one of the reasons for limited protection of local resource rights.[92] In some jurisdictions, customary rights afford no legal protection.[93] As Cotula suggests, '[n]ational law may formally protect these local land rights but they are often construed as conditional use rights, rather than ownership'.[94] Weak land rights lead to the eviction of the local population and create significant risks of further conflict for investors.[95] There is an additional risk for local people of losing access to land without adequate compensation.[96] One suggestion is to strengthen customary and common property rights and effective enforcement of existing laws.[97] The enforcement of land rights can be improved through clarification and documentation of land use rights of smallholders. But even where legal protection is afforded on paper, weak implementation mechanisms may prevent local land rights from becoming more secure.[98]

89 Klaus Deininger, 'Challenges Posed by the New Wave of Farmland Investment' (2011) 38 (2) *The Journal of Peasant Studies* 225

90 Oxfam, 'Land and Power: The Growing Scandal Surrounding the New Wave of Investments in Land' (151 Oxfam Briefing Paper, 22 September 2011) <www.oxfam.org/sites/www.oxfam.org/files/bp151-land-power-rights-acquisitions-220911-en.pdf> accessed 17 January 2017

91 Vara Songewe and Klaus Deininger, 'Foreign Investment in Agricultural Production: Opportunities and Challenges' (Agriculture and Rural Development Notes, Land Policy and Administration, World Bank, Issue 45, January 2009)

92 Olivier De Schutter, 'How Not to Think of Land-Grabbing: Three Critiques of Large-Scale Investments in Farmland' (2011) 38 (2) *Journal of Peasant Studies* 249

93 Lorenzo Cotula, 'Land Tenure Issues in Agricultural Investment' (SOLAW Background Thematic Report – TR05B, November 2011) <www.fao.org/fileadmin/templates/solaw/files/thematic_reports/TR_05B_web.pdf> accessed 17 January 2017

94 Ibid

95 Ibid

96 Görgen and others (n 64)

97 Cotula, *Foreign Investment* (n 66)

98 Schutter (n 92)

Local consultation and transparency

For both government and investors, recognising local claims is critical to prevent conflict and promote local support for the project. Where investment projects affect indigenous peoples, international law requires governments to seek the free, prior and informed consent of these groups.[99] The UN Declaration on Indigenous Peoples' Rights (UNDRIP) incorporates the right to participation in decision-making in matters which would affect their rights,[100] and the duty of the state to consult before the adoption and implementation of legislative or administrative measures that may affect them.[101] However, national laws in many countries of the South often do not ensure meaningful consultation. Even if consultations are mandatory, their usefulness may be limited due to a lack of clarity about who must participate, what information needs to be made available to the key stakeholder and whether the outcome of such meetings is formally recognised or enforceable.[102] This lack of transparency undermines the ability of affected people to participate and inform decision-making. It is also crucial to note that consultation is not necessarily consent and the duty to consult is significantly deeper than mere consultation. In the *Endorois* case,[103] the African Commission on Human and Peoples' Rights noted that for 'any development or investment projects that would have a major impact within the Endorois territory, the State has a duty not only to consult with the community, but also to obtain their free, prior, and informed consent, according to their customs and traditions'. Even with better information provisions provided to stakeholders prior to consultation, additional challenges in the Global South remain, for example, making investment contracts available on the internet or for open viewing in capital cities may not be appropriate for projects which affect poor rural communities with limited technological infrastructure.

Although the content of investment contracts has direct implications for the people and the environment, the contracting process remains important. Many investment contracts are out of reach for the public from negotiation and implementation stages to dispute settlement.[104] This lack of public engagement contrasts with the access rights (e.g., right to information and

99 1989 Convention Concerning Indigenous and Tribal Peoples in Independent Countries, adopted by the International Labour Organization (Convention No. 169). United Nations Declaration on the Rights of Indigenous Peoples, Resolution adopted by the General Assembly, 2 October 2007, A/RES/61/295 (hereafter, UNDRIP) <www.refworld.org/docid/471355a82.html> accessed 2 February 2017

100 UNDRIP, Article 18

101 UNDRIP, Article 19

102 Deininger (n 89) 238

103 African Commission on Human and Peoples' Rights, 276/03 Centre for Minority Rights Development (Kenya) and Minority Rights Group International on behalf of Endorois Welfare Council v Kenya, para 162 and 291 (May 2009) <www.achpr.org/files/sessions/46th/comunications/276.03/achpr46_276_03_eng.pdf> accessed 17 January 2017

104 Ibid

public participation in decision-making) integrated in the concept of SD and in the national law of many countries.[105] However, host governments and foreign investors are still reluctant to be transparent about their investment activities, particularly in disclosing investment contracts.[106] Most foreign investment contracts are hidden from public view and negotiated behind closed doors between only the lawyers, government officials and corporate executives directly involved in the negotiation.[107] These closed-door negotiations undermine public accountability and raise a question mark over the state's role to protect the public interest.[108]

Indeed, public disclosure of agricultural investment contracts may promote fairer contractual terms as it may increase pressure for more balanced contracts and strengthen the negotiating capacity of host governments.[109] Requirements for transparency in the contracting process may also attract 'quality' investors.[110] Under national law, some countries have included local consultation and/or consent requirement as part of the approval processes of the investment agreement in order to open space for local negotiation.[111] However, there is a gap in the good intention and the poor implementation of these consultation or consent requirements

> ... due to the major asymmetries in information, capacity and negotiation power that affect relations between foreign investors, host governments and affected people. The outcome of a consultation is often not a legally binding agreement between the community and the company. This limits the ability of communities to hold investors to account in case of non-compliance.[112]

There is an argument that investment contracts usually deal with highly sensitive commercial issues that need high levels of confidentiality of the negotiation in order for parties to effectively negotiate, such as key project information and the contract itself.[113] Thus, the decision-makers need to

105 Principle 10 of Rio Declaration 1992; and Convention on Access to Information, Public Participation in Decision Making and Access to Justice in Environmental Matters 1998. For national examples, see <www.accessinitiative.org/resources> accessed 17 January 2017
106 Carin Smaller, 'Going Public to Improve Investment in Agriculture' (International Institute for Sustainable Development, October 2011) <www.iisd.org/pdf/2012/going_public_improve_investment_ag.pdf> accessed 17 January 2017
107 Ayine and others (n 37)
108 Smaller (n 106)
109 Peter Rosenblum and Susan Maples, 'Contracts Confidential: Ending Secret Deals in the Extractive Industries' (Revenue Watch Institute, Washington DC, 2009) <www.resourcegovernance.org/sites/default/files/RWI-Contracts-Confidential.pdf> accessed 17 January 2017
110 Cotula, *Foreign Investment* (n 66) 101
111 Ibid 99
112 Ibid
113 Rosenblum and Maples (n 109)

strive for a balance between commercial confidentiality and public scrutiny.[114] In agricultural FDI, information about large-scale agricultural projects, such as the extent of the projects and the substantial use of land and water resources, needs to be made open to the public.[115] It is necessary to clarify which information and aspects of the contract are confidential and protected, and which information needs to be made public when the public interest is greater than commercial considerations.[116]

Land acquisition and compensation

The terms for compulsory land acquisition are usually set by national laws. Most countries have legislation that allows the government to issue compulsory orders rescinding land rights if it is in the public interest to do so.[117] In such cases, the law also requires the government to comply with certain procedures and pay compensation. Such compulsory orders allow the government to acquire land in the public interest for social projects and for commercial investment projects in the natural resource sectors.[118] The national law may allow certain types of private investment to serve a public purpose and trigger compulsory acquisition of local resource rights.[119] Guidance issued by the FAO states: '[a] compulsory acquisition is inherently destructive. Even when compensation is generous and procedures are generally fair and efficient, this displacement of people from established homes, business and communities will still entail significant human costs'.[120] Although compulsory acquisitions are widely used to transfer land to investors, this practice narrows the range of options for negotiation and lacks local consultation or mechanisms for appeal. It may also 'encourage rent-seeking and political meddling'.[121]

In some instances, monetary compensation can play a role to ensure the continued enjoyment of human rights, such as the right to food and the right to housing. However, such compensation may not be adequate when it does not enable affected communities to gain access to alternative land or in the case 'where the land has special cultural and spiritual values'.[122] Apart from

114 Cotula, *Investment Contracts* (n 3) 86
115 Smaller (n 106)
116 Cotula, 'Rethinking investment' (n 12) 22
117 Cotula, *Investment Contracts* (n 3) 56
118 Ibid 57
119 Lorenzo Cotula and Emily Polack, 'Land Tenure and Agricultural Investment – Investing in Local Tenure Security for Inclusive and Sustainable Development' (The European Report on Development 2011/2012)
120 Simon Keith and others, 'Compulsory Acquisition of Land and Compensation' (FAO Land Tenure Studies 10, 2008) <www.fao.org/3/a-i0506e.pdf> accessed 17 January 2017
121 Deininger (n 89) 238
122 Cotula, *Investment Contracts* (n 3) 58

cash compensation or in-kind compensation (for example, alternative land), Cotula adds that 'affected communities may be able to contribute land rights into a joint venture with the investor, in which they obtain an equity stake'.[123] Such arrangements may lead to a balance of power between the communities, the investor and the government. However, conflicts surrounding the compensation regime in many countries of the South highlight the weak protection such a regime provides to local interests.[124]

When national law does not provide adequate safeguards, international standards can play a role in improving the investment agreements. For example, Performance Standard 5 of the International Finance Corporation concerning land acquisitions calls for the minimisation of involuntary resettlement with preference to be given to negotiated settlements over compulsory acquisition.[125] When displacement is inevitable, displaced communities and persons should receive 'compensation for loss of assets at full replacement cost and other assistance to help them improve or restore their standards of living or livelihoods'.[126] It also calls for 'the appropriate disclosure of information, consultation, and the informed participation of those affected'[127] along with suitable systems to deal with grievances.[128]

In cases of compulsory acquisition, low valuations of land are common.[129] According to Deininger:[130]

> Undervaluation of land has not only negative distributional consequences but also encourages projects that would otherwise not be viable, in addition to possibly fostering rent-seeking. As a result, land users may receive less than the benefits they derived from the land earlier, making them objectively worse off.

Thus, 'cash compensation levels should be sufficient to replace the lost land and other assets at full replacement cost in local markets'.[131] According to Deininger, compensation 'requires either a comprehensive valuation of affected people's current livelihoods/income streams or a voluntary decision (and market transaction) based on adequate information and their agreement

123 Ibid 59
124 Cotula and Polack (n 119)
125 International Finance Corporation (IFC), 'Performance Standard 5: Land Acquisition and Involuntary Resettlement', paragraph 3 (1 January 2012) <www.ifc.org/wps/wcm/connect/3d82c70049a79073b82cfaa8c6a8312a/PS5_English_2012.pdf?MOD=AJPERES> accessed 17 January 2017
126 Ibid, paragraph 9
127 Ibid, paragraph 3
128 Ibid, paragraph 11
129 Deininger (n 89) 239
130 Klaus Deininger and others, *Rising Global Interest in Farmland: Can It Yield Sustainable and Equitable Benefits* (World Bank, 2011) 108
131 IFC (n 125), paragraph 21

to exchange their land in ways that protect their livelihoods and food security'.[132]

In addition, the compensation schemes targeting economically displaced persons should provide 'opportunities to improve, or at least restore, their means of income-earning capacity, production levels, and standards of living'.[133]

Local content requirement

Agricultural investments maximise several positive economic outcomes including public revenues, income generation through employment and business links, export promotion, growth in foreign reserves, technology transfer and infrastructure development. However, a persistent challenge in agricultural investments is that they may not be effectively linked to the local economy and examples from long-term land lease and concessions in Africa and Asia support this view.[134] Concerns are raised about the possible impacts, including loss of local rights to land, water and other natural resources; threats to local food security; and more generally, the risk that large-scale investments may marginalise smallholders.[135] Employment opportunities are also limited 'because of the capital-intensive nature of extractive industries and mechanised farming'.[136] Therefore, agricultural investment projects may not effectively contribute to SD or poverty alleviation.

In the agricultural sector, investment contracts can seek to maximise local employment, processing and business opportunities through local content requirements. The local content requirements may be 'a way to promote investment in strengthening local business capacity, for instance through on-the-job learning, formal training opportunities and transfer of know-how'.[137] Such provision in the investment contract or in the national law may create greater support for the investment in the host country and also enable 'longer-term savings by using local labour or reducing transportation costs for supplies'.[138] While these clauses may require the investor to source a specified share of labour, goods and services from local workers and suppliers, the preferential treatment of such requirements for local suppliers vis-à-vis foreign goods and services providers can be viewed as protectionist measures.[139] In

132 Deininger (n 89) 239

133 IFC (n 125), paragraph 28

134 Lorenzo Cotula, 'The International Political Economy of the Global Land Rush: A Critical Appraisal of Trends, Scale, Geography and Drivers' (2012) *Journal of Peasant Studies* 1

135 Ibid

136 Cotula and Tienhaara (n 13) 291–292

137 Cotula, *Investment Contracts* (n 3) 45

138 Ibid

139 Theodore H. Moran, 'Enhancing the Contribution of FDI to Development: A New Agenda for the Corporate Social Responsibility Community, International Labour and Civil Society, Aid Donors and Multilateral Financial Institutions' (2011) 20 (1) *Transnational Corporations* 69

addition, the host government may not be able to use local content requirements if there are international obligations restricting such measures. For example, the World Trade Organization Agreement on Trade Related Investment Measures (TRIMs) prohibits any measure that discriminates against foreign products or that leads to quantitative restrictions.[140]

Thus, before signing the investment agreement, a host government needs to understand the potential ramifications on their ability to use local content requirements. At the same time, the government must be clear about the objective of the local content requirement, understand the qualitative and quantitative requirements that can be included in the investment contract, and the incentives that can be offered to the investors to stimulate effective implementation of the local content requirements.[141]

Agricultural investment and small-scale farmers

Regarding the farming systems, around half of the global population is found in rural areas of the Global South.[142] Around 50 per cent of developing country rural populations are smallholders and smallholder farms constitute about 85 per cent of all farms.[143] These small-scale farmers, more than 1 billion in total, play a central role in management of agricultural landscapes in the Global South.[144] They suffer in varying degrees from similar problems associated with complex, diverse and risk prone farming systems and a low level of technology.[145] Thus, there is a need to change agricultural practices dealing with small-scale farmers to reduce the negative impacts of agriculture on

140 The TRIMs Agreement includes a list of prohibited local content requirements. Agreement on Trade-Related Investment Measures, April 15, 1994, Marrakesh Agreement Establishing the World Trade Organization, Annex 1A, The Legal Texts: The Results of the Uruguay Round of Multilateral Trade Negotiations 143 (1999), 1868 UNTS 186

141 Isabelle Ramdoo, 'Unpacking Local Content Requirements in the Extractive Sector: What Implications for the Global Trade and Investment Frameworks?' (2015) <http://ecdpm.org/wp-content/uploads/Unpacking-Local-Content-Requirements-Isabelle-Ramdoo-September-2015-ECDPM.pdf> accessed 17 January 2017

142 Gustavo Anríquez and Libor Stloukal, 'Rural Population Change in Developing Counties: Lessons for Policymaking' (ESA Working Paper No. 08-09, Agricultural Development Economics Division, FAO, November 2008) <ftp://ftp.fao.org/docrep/fao/011/aj981e/aj981e00.pdf> accessed 17 January 2017

143 UNCTAD, *Technology and Innovation Report 2010: Enhancing Food Security in Africa through Science, Technology and Innovation* (United Nations Conference on Trade and Development, Geneva, Switzerland, 2010); and International Food Policy Research Institute IFPRI, *The Future of Small Farms: Proceedings of a Research Workshop* (Wye, UK, June 26–29 2005. Washington, DC)

144 FAO and PAR, *Biodiversity for Food and Agriculture – Contributing to Food Security and Sustainability in a Changing World* (FAO, 2011)

145 Jonn F. Morton, 'The Impact of Climate Change on Smallholder and Subsistence Agriculture' (2007) 104 (50) PNAS 19680:19785 <www.pnas.org/content/104/50/19680.full.pdf+html> accessed 17 January 2017

environment while continue to increase productivity and improve sustainability.[146] For this to happen, collaboration with local farmers or communities needs to be prioritised rather than large-scale land acquisitions.[147] In order to boost the agricultural sector, the government needs to design mechanisms that link outside investors and local communities in a sustainable and mutually beneficial way.[148]

Collaborative farming schemes (e.g. contract farming, out-grower schemes) may involve a series of separate contracts between an investor and local farmers.[149] According to Cotula:

> These arrangements vary widely, depending on the countries, crops and companies involved. Usually, local farmers grow and deliver a specified quantity and quality of agricultural produce at an agreed date. In exchange, the investor (usually an agribusiness company) makes certain contributions upfront, such as credit, seeds, fertilisers, pesticides and technical advice, all of which may be subtracted from the final purchase price. The company also agrees to buy the produce supplied, which is usually at a specified price.[150]

These collaborative business models, on the one hand, may minimise the risk undertaken by the investor as they have available land and a guaranteed supply of produce. On the other hand, the small farmers may keep control over their land and at the same time, gain access to improved technologies and a reliable market.[151] However, to be effective, there are a number of issues that should be taken into account during the negotiation of these schemes (e.g., the investor needs to commit to purchase the produce at the agreed price, specification of quality standards of the produce).[152] The danger remains where the trade-offs between productivity increase, land expansion and environmental risks lead to unsustainable farming practices. Concurrently, there has been a push by developed countries to examine local

146 FAO and PAR (n 144)

147 Lorenzo Cotula and Rebecca Leonard, 'Alternatives to Land Acquisitions: Agricultural Investments and Collaborative Business Models' (International Institute for Environment and Development, 2010) <http://pubs.iied.org/pdfs/12567IIED.pdf> accessed 17 January 2017

148 Haralambous, Liversage and Romano (n 85)

149 Cotula, *Investment Contracts* (n 3) 32

150 Ibid

151 Schaffnit-Chetterjee (n 87); and Joachim von Braun and Ruth Meinzen-Dick, '"Land Grabbing" by Foreign Investors in Developing Countries: Risks and Opportunities' (International Food Policy Research Institute IFPRI Policy Brief, 13 April 2009) <www.ifpri.org/pubs/bp/bp013.asp> accessed 17 January 2017

152 Charles Eaton and Andrew W. Shepherd, 'Contract Farming: Partnership for Growth' (Agricultural Services Bulletin 145, FAO, 2001) <www.fao.org/docrep/014/y0937e/y0937e00.pdf> accessed 17 January 2017

sustainable farming practices and knowledge, and to commodify these practices through the intellectual property system.[153] These challenges emphasise yet again the need for well-defined land rights, clear criteria for land transfer including provision for compensation, accessible information and meaningful consultation that may benefit the small farmers without compromising their food security or land rights. In addition, the time is ripe for the developing countries to allocate adequate research funds to utilise the intellectual property system to their advantage.

Conclusion

To say that the Global South requires enabling policy and legal environment and good land governance is one thing, but to implement these enabling regulatory mechanisms that safeguard social and environmental standards and attract external investments is extremely difficult. Most of the host countries based in the Global South lack the capacity to manage the investment sustainably and often fail to protect the interest of the local communities.[154] Support by the government and non-governmental agencies (e.g. capacity building initiatives) and collective action by the farming communities will be critical to promote leverage to legal rights.

First, capacity building in negotiating investment agreements should be a priority for most host countries of the Global South. In many Southern countries, governments may not have adequate capacity to negotiate an investment agreement and there are 'imbalances in negotiating capacity between investors and governments'.[155] Cotula adds that '[b]esides differential access to skills and expertise, other factors may put the host government in an unfavourable position during the negotiation: high staff turnover in key government agencies, inadequate preparation, poor use of the expertise available in the country and corruption'.[156]

Another area for further improvement is the national regulations targeting investment in farmland and the impacts from such agricultural investments.[157] These improvements may include mapping of agricultural land and rules regulating the land tenure system, evictions and compensation, corruption as well as traditional and customary land rights. In addition, investment law may introduce the 'screening of the investors and the analysis of the economic and technical viability of the project'.[158] Post monitoring

153 Philippe Cullet, 'Food Security and Intellectual Property Rights in Developing Countries' (Les Cahiers du RIBios – n° 6, March 2004) <www.ruig-gian.org/ressources/ Brochure6FoodsecDPI.pdf?ID=195&FILE=/ressources/Brochure6FoodsecDPI.pdf> accessed 17 January 2017

154 Schutter (n 92)

155 Cotula, *Investment Contracts* (n 3) 5

156 Ibid

157 Schutter (n 92) 265

158 Ibid

of the investment contract as well as adequate penalties for non-compliance should be integrated either in the investment agreement or in the national law.[159]

Third, incentive is one of the most important policy tools countries can seek to attract FDI. The rationale for providing investment incentives is to captures spillovers such as 'technological upgrading, improvement of managerial know-how and employee skills, transfer of firm-specific assets to the host country, and improved market access for exports'.[160] Another rationale for incentives is to compensate for an unfavourable policy environment.[161] There are a number of incentives that can be found to promote investment in the agriculture sector, for instance, no restriction on capital repatriation, no foreign-exchange control, no price control and quantitative trade restrictions.[162] At the same time, it is also crucial to encourage incentives that promote sustainable investment, for example, government incentives to producers to use sustainable harvesting methods, or incentives for certification to agricultural products.[163]

Fourth, leaving the challenges aside, collaboration between investors and small rural producers that takes into account 'the needs, capabilities and constraints of smallholder farmers' can contribute to poverty reduction, agriculture-led development and economic growth.[164] Schaffnit-Chetterjee adds that: 'collaborative business models between small farmers and investors (for instance contract farming) can be mutually beneficial, boosting agricultural productivity while reducing poverty and hunger, without necessitating transfer of land'.[165]

This chapter has argued that a 'green' investment contract needs to offer safeguards not only to prospective investors to attract their investments, but also to people in the host state to improve their living standards while respecting the environment. It also needs to be well negotiated and enforced to receive the desired economic outcomes that balance social and environmental considerations. The extent to which investment contracts positively or negatively contribute to sustainable investments can be assessed in the way the contract balances the key principles of sustainable development and the process and content of contracts. With the different types of agricultural investment contracts across jurisdictions, this balancing act is not an easy

159 Ibid
160 B.V.R. Subrahmanyam, 'Investment Incentives and Multilateral Disciplines' in Simon J. Evenett and Bernard M. Hoekman (eds), *Economic Development and Multilateral Trade Cooperation* (World Bank, 2006) 302
161 Ibid
162 FAO, 'Investment Policy Support: Foreign Agricultural Investment Profile (Cambodia)' (2011) <www.fao.org/fileadmin/user_upload/tcsp/docs/Cambodia_Profile_Final.pdf> accessed 17 January 2017
163 Görgen and others (n 64)
164 Haralambous, Liversage and Romano (n 85) 8
165 Schaffnit-Chetterjee (n 87) 1

task. Indeed, a well-designed and well-implemented contract may protect livelihoods of local people and ecosystems affected by the investment project. The concern remains when the investment regime fails to take into consideration the broader concerns of human rights or environmental sustainability. The pursuit of liberalisation of agricultural FDI must not come at the expense of overarching public interest matters.

12 Sustainable mining, human rights and foreign investment

Nexus and challenges

Abdullah Al Faruque

Introduction

The development of mineral resources has been one of the important factors in plans and programmes of any country's economic development. In particular, mineral resources constitute valuable assets for countries in a situation of considerable and increasing global scarcity. Many developing countries attract foreign investment in exploration of their mineral resources in order to accelerate their economic growth. Foreign investment in mining can have both positive and negative social, environmental and economic outcomes in recipient countries. By contributing capital, know-how and market links, foreign investment can help promote economic development, generate public revenues, develop infrastructure and create employment in host countries.[1] However, it is also now widely acknowledged that such exploration and development can potentially be an environmentally damaging and socially disruptive process if not carried out in sustainable manner. Human rights and environmental issues have emerged as one of the most important factors in mineral extraction in recent times.[2] The adverse social impacts of mineral extraction and the associated human rights violations of local and indigenous communities by mineral companies is a significant risk factor for individuals, as well as for local and indigenous communities.

There has been a change in perception among developing countries about the urgency of the need for human rights and environmental protection in mineral extraction since the late 1980s. This has been driven by three factors: increased global awareness of environmental issues; public concern about the environmental and human rights consequences of mineral exploration; and the emergence of sustainable development as a paradigm, including the idea of intergenerational equity. This change of attitude has been reflected in the mineral industry through increased integration of human rights and

1 See Lorenzo Cotula, *Foreign Investment, Law and Sustainable Development: A Handbook on Agriculture and Extractive Industries* (International Institute for Environment and Development, 2014) 3.

2 See generally Lorenzo Cotula, *Human Rights, Natural Resources and Investment Law in a Globalised World: Shades of Grey in the Shadow of the Law* (Routledge, 2012).

environmental concerns into laws and policies on mineral extraction in developing countries. In addition, the demand for greater corporate accountability, the activism of non-governmental organisations (NGOs) and civil society, and an enhanced understanding of the social dimension of mineral projects, driven by the notion of corporate social responsibility, have furthered the integration of human rights in laws regulating mineral extraction.

However, despite the geographic remoteness of most mineral operations, they tend to have a substantial and profound impact on local communities and can generate significant social tensions among community stakeholders. The negative social impact of mineral operations can in part be attributed to the inevitable consequence of the extractive process and in part to the unsustainable practices and negligence of the operating company towards the local community. Adverse social impacts may arise in all phases of mineral extraction, albeit in varying degrees.[3] However, the exploration and development stage can cause the greatest disruptions, including displacement of indigenous peoples and their livelihood, environmental pollution, loss of biological diversity, deforestation, destruction of cultural properties, severe health problems and other social problems. At the abandonment and closure phase of the project, local communities may also lose their main source of employment. At this stage, inequitable distribution of economic rents from the project can also generate social tension in the producing areas.

The objective of this chapter is to examine the emerging social and human rights dimensions and trends in mineral extraction in developing countries. It notes that these new paradigms increasingly constitute an important factor in contract negotiation and contract planning in the mineral sector. The chapter focuses on how the adverse social impacts of mining operations and the human rights violations by mining companies that have occurred in recent times can be translated into a risk factor for the company as a result of individual or collective action by local or indigenous communities. It examines preventive measures that can be taken by the host state and mineral companies in order to address these issues. It is argued that socially responsible behaviour on the part of the company can reduce much of the tension between the company and host community and can contribute to the long-term sustainability of a given mineral project.

3 The social and human rights impacts pertaining to the process of exploration, development, extraction and transportation of petroleum resources have been well discussed in recent times. See George S. Akpan, 'Host Community Hostility to Mining Projects: A New Generation of Risk?' in Elizabeth Bastida, Thomas Waelde and Janeth Warden-Fernandez (eds), *International and Comparative Mineral Law and Policy: Trends and Prospects* (Kluwer Law International, 2005) 311–330.

Human rights and social issues associated with mineral extraction

Mining extraction can become entangled with human rights abuses by unaccountable security forces, may undermine the livelihoods of families forced to relocate to make way for it, and may fuel government corruption, thereby increasing poverty and conflict in resource-rich countries. A mining company can indirectly or directly violate human rights by its complicity in the abuse of human rights by the host government through the support of, or acquiescence in, the activities of such governments. Mineral companies operating in countries with an autocratic regime may easily fall prey to complicity with human rights violations by maintaining silence and inactivity in the face of oppression by such governments.[4] The government's overriding need for foreign investment may exacerbate the situation. A host country may attract foreign investment at the expense of human rights considerations, or violations of human rights by petroleum companies may simply be overlooked. Mining companies may also be implicated in human rights violations for their investment in countries with poor human rights records and rampant corruption.[5]

The operation of mineral projects may produce negative socio-economic and cultural impacts, including changes in land-use patterns, human rights abuses and destruction of cultural heritage and biodiversity. In particular, if mining extraction takes place in remote areas where mineral deposits are located, the indigenous or local people living in those areas can be negatively affected by the mining extraction. Such negative impacts can be attributed to unsustainable practices adopted by mineral companies. Examples of unsustainable mining practices can include lack of involvement of relevant stakeholders or communities in mining exploration, use of technology that can damage the environment, lack of environmental and social impact assessment of a particular mining project and lack of a proper rehabilitation and mine closure plan.

Although mining companies can wield significant social, economic and political power in developing countries, these companies are also capable of

4 See Sir Geoffrey Chandler, 'The Responsibilities of Oil Companies' in Asbjorn Eide, Helge Ole Bergesen and Pia Rudolfson Goyer (eds), *Human Rights and the Oil Industry* (Intersentia, 2000) 5, 14.

5 For instance, the Chad–Cameron oil pipeline project, a joint venture of Exxon, Elf Aquitaine and Royal Dutch/Shell, had been criticised by civil society and NGOs because of allegations of corruption, the poor human rights record in Chad and incidence of human rights violations in the area surrounding the pipeline, and lack of adequate environmental safeguards in the project. See criticisms of the World Bank's involvement in the project as discussed in Genoveva Hernandez Uriz, 'To Lend or Not to Lend: Oil, Human Rights, and the World Bank's Internal Contradictions' (2001) 14 *Harvard Human Rights Journal* 197. See also Korinna Horta, 'The Chad/Cameroon Oil and Pipeline Project – Reaching a Critical Milestone' (World Rainforest Movement, January 2003) <http://wrm.org.uy/oldsite/countries/Cameroon/Horta.html> accessed 12 July 2015.

producing a significant impact on the enjoyment of human rights within developing countries. Activities of both state-owned and private mining companies can lead to human rights abuses in several ways. Both the unintended and intended social impacts of mineral extraction can significantly impair enjoyment of the social, economic and cultural rights of the local community, including the right to self-determination, the right to an adequate standard of living, the right to life, the right to employment and the right to social security of the host community. Moreover, the current trend of viewing environmental degradation as a violation of human rights can add to the complexity of the problem.

The linkage between the environment and human rights is now well established under international soft law.[6] The relationship between human rights and environmental protection has been conceived in two ways. First, environmental protection provides a mechanism for the fulfilment of human rights standards.[7] Since degraded physical environments contribute directly to infringements of the human rights to life, health, and livelihood, acts leading to environmental degradation may constitute an immediate violation of internationally recognised human rights.[8] Second, the legal protection of human rights is an effective means for achieving the ends of conservation and environmental protection since the broader notion of human rights also includes the right to a safe and healthy environment. Thus, the full realisation of human rights can be possible only in a society and political order in which claims for environmental protection are more likely to be respected.[9]

Finally, an important source of human rights violation, which leads to violation of social and economic rights in a broader context, relates to the inequitable allocation of project revenues. It is now widely believed that the contractual and legal arrangement of mineral development, which denies equitable distribution of resource rent from a given mineral project, can generate a conflict between the local community and the host government.[10] Depriving the local communities and indigenous people of the economic

6 For instance, the 1972 Stockholm Declaration on the Human Environment recognises the environment as an aspect of human rights. Principle 1 of that Declaration states that: '[m]an has the fundamental right to freedom, equality and adequate conditions of life in an environment of a quality that permits a life of dignity and wellbeing, and he bears a solemn responsibility to protect and improve the environment for present and future generations'. Report of the United Nations Conference on the Human Environment, UN Doc A/CONF.48/14/Rev.1 (5–16 June 1972) pt 1, ch I ('Declaration of the UN Conference on the Human Environment').

7 Michael R. Anderson, 'Human Rights Approaches to Environmental Protection: An Overview' in Alan E. Boyle and Michael R. Anderson (eds), *Human Rights Approaches to Environmental Protection* (Clarendon Press, 1996) 3.

8 Ibid.

9 Ibid.

10 Abdullah Al Faruque, 'Transparency in Extractive Revenues in Developing Countries and Economies in Transition: A Review of Emerging Best Practices' (2006) 24 *Journal of Energy and Natural Resources Law* 68.

outcome of mineral projects can ultimately generate frustration, conflict and hostility toward the companies involved and the government.

Transparency in mineral contract negotiation and revenue management is now considered an integral part of the human rights dimension of mineral extraction.[11] Transparency and accountability are fundamentally important for ensuring that wealth derived from natural resources is best managed for the benefit of the community. However, lack of transparency and accountability in contract negotiation and non-disclosure of contracts can facilitate embezzlement, corruption and misappropriation, and thereby further fuel social inequality.[12] The transparency requirement should be incorporated in contractual arrangements, in the bidding process, in equity participation and in the fiscal regimes of the contract.[13] It is also acknowledged that a legislative and contractual requirement mandating disclosure of the contract terms used in any exploration and development of natural resources can facilitate openness.[14] Disclosure should not only entail public accessibility to these contractual arrangements but also complete disclosure of incoming revenues, comprising of taxes, profit share, royalties, bonus payments and mining companies' payments to the governments of host countries.[15]

Thus, the human rights issues arising from mineral investment necessitate public participation, addressing human rights abuses, developing an adequate compensation regime and meeting stakeholders' demands for consultation in mineral extraction. Critically, these are issues that cannot be addressed by traditional legal and contractual mechanisms which mostly deal with the economic aspects of mineral exploration and rights and duties of transnational mining corporations. Rather, they need to be addressed through the regulation of corporate behaviour which recognises the social aspects of mineral extraction and which consequently seeks to enhance human rights and the proactive engagement of mining companies with the community.

The concept of stakeholders' interest in natural resource exploitation and management has emerged as a new paradigm in the mineral industry and the demands of stakeholders for increased openness, public participation and consultation with mining companies appear to be the dominant theme in the current context of natural resource development.[16] It is now acknowledged

11 See, Lorenzo Cotula, *Investment Contracts and Sustainable Development: How to Make Contracts for Fairer and More Sustainable Natural Resource Investments* (International Institute for Environment and Development, 2010) 85–90.

12 Al Faruque, 'Transparency in Extractive Revenues in Developing Countries and Economies in Transition' (n 10) 69.

13 Ibid 71.

14 Ibid.

15 Ibid 86.

16 A 'stakeholder' has been defined as 'somebody' or a group of 'somebodies' who have an interest, be it economic, legal, political or ethical, in the outcome of a project or a process and who therefore 'holds a stake' in it: Olle Ostensson, 'The Stakeholders: Interests and

that the interest and concern of local and indigenous people, who are also referred to as a 'host community', is widely regarded as key, given their specific vulnerability to disruptive mining practices and the impact these practices may have on the expression of a local, indigenous community's cultural values.[17] Improved communication and information technology, and recognition of their rights at the legal and normative level, have made it possible for local and indigenous communities to articulate their voices more clearly and to acquire greater leverage in the negotiation of mineral development than ever before.[18] Since the Brent Spar incident in the North Sea, NGOs and civil society have also emerged as important stakeholders in mineral and petroleum projects.[19]

The human rights violations and environmental pollution caused by mineral operations can give rise to conflict between companies and local or indigenous communities.[20] Similarly, human rights violations by companies can give rise to resentment amongst the local community and indigenous people, which can erupt into resistance to continuation of the mineral project. Such resistance often leads to substantive changes to or total abandonment of a project. For our purpose, the expression 'conflict' can be used to describe both violent conflict and conflict short of violence which nevertheless entails hostility and disruptive actions towards companies as a

Objectives' in James M. Otto and John Cordes (eds), *Sustainable Development and Future of Mineral Investment* (United Nations Environmental Programme, 2000) 1–3. The author categorises stakeholders into 'core' and 'secondary' groups. The 'core' stakeholders include those who are materially affected by individual mining projects, such as petroleum and mining companies, local communities and government authorities at different levels. A second group of stakeholders consists of those whose objectives are generally of a broader political, ideological or cultural nature, for instance, NGOs: 2–3.

17 The expression 'host community' generally refers to the communities that host the development of a petroleum project and usually comprises local people or indigenous groups of people of a particular locality in which the project is to be carried out. The expressions 'local or indigenous community' and 'host community' have been used interchangeably in this chapter.

18 See Sergei Vinogradov and Ibibia Lucky Worika, 'Global Stakeholders: The Impact of International Law on the Resources Industry' in *International Resources Law and Projects*, Mineral Law Series (1999), Number 2, pp. 11A(1–22). See also Philippe Le Billon, 'Getting It Done: Instruments of Enforcement' in Ian Bannon and Paul Collier (eds), *Natural Resources and Violent Conflict: Options and Actions* (World Bank, 2003) 215.

19 Ibid.

20 See for useful discussion on contexts of extractive company–community conflict: Gary MacDonald and Timothy McLaughlin, 'Extracting Conflict' in Rory Sullivan (ed), *Business and Human Rights: Dilemmas and Solutions* (Greenleaf Publishing, 2003) 232; Manuel Eduardo Echeverra, 'Conflicts between Resource Development and Indigenous People' in *Mining and Oil and Gas Development in Latin America* (Mineral Law Series, Rocky Mountain Mineral Law Foundation, 2001) (discussing many incidents of community/petroleum company conflict in Ecuador); George S. Akpan, 'Host Community Hostility to Mining Projects: A New Generation of Risk?' in Elizabeth Bastida, Thomas Walde and Janeth Warden-Fernandez (eds), *International and Comparative Mineral Law and Policy: Trends and Prospects* (Kluwer Law International, 2005) 311.

consequence of social pressures and campaigns. The conflict can be fuelled by pressure groups including local NGOs, whose coalition with other local and international activist groups can build vehement resistance to the development of a project. This can be reflected through actions such as the dissemination of information, awareness-raising activities undertaken in the host community concerning the negative impact of the mineral exploration, exposing companies' environmental and human rights abuses to the media, and mobilising public support against companies' activities. As a result, companies can sometimes be compelled to withdraw operations from the host nation.[21]

The negative social impacts of operations and human rights abuses by a mining company can result in significant NGO campaigns, media coverage and public outrage. This concerted effort of accusation and publicity may bring serious negative consequences with financial implications. One of the most important consequences is the loss of an accused company's reputation, which can prompt boycotting of the company's products and can lead to decreasing market value of the company's shares. The disrepute brought to the company by the negative publicity may also lead to denial of access to new deposits in a particular country.[22]

The mining companies accused of violations of human rights can be sued in both the host countries and their home countries as a measure of accountability for human rights abuses.[23] The threat of litigation as a consequence of negative social and environmental impacts and human rights abuses is now considered to be one of the significant risk factors for mining companies. In host states, the possibility of litigation against a company by non-state actors has been facilitated by the opportunity for public interest groups to bring class actions against companies in their host countries.[24] Public interest litigation may be initiated by public interest groups drawing inspiration from the growing body of international environmental law which provides for the

21 For example, Shell chose to discontinue its operations in Colombia when the indigenous U'wa people threatened to commit mass suicide if Shell continued its drilling operations on their traditional lands.

22 For instance, oil exploration by the Consortium of Talisman (a Canadian company), Petrochina (the Chinese state-owned company) and Petronas (the Malaysian company) in Sudan, where civil conflict and human rights violations are regular phenomena, and where the oil profits have fuelled governmental repression in the southern region, gave rise to huge public pressures on the operating companies. In particular, the Canadian company Talisman, which faced severe criticism both in Canada and in the US, was compelled to sell its share to another company and pulled out of operations in Sudan due to the fact that a divestment campaign caused the plummeting of its shares: Jane Lampman, 'Battle against Oppression Abroad Turns to Wall Street Religious and Human Rights Activities Target Stocks and Capital Markets to Stop a War of "Genocide" in Sudan', *Christian Science Monitor* (3 March 2000) 1.

23 Abdullah Al Faruque, *Petroleum Contracts: Stability and Risk Management in Developing Countries* (Bangladesh Institute of Law and International Affairs, 2011) 238.

24 Ibid.

prevention of harmful activities. Alternatively, public interest litigation may seek redress for the damage caused by mining companies. Publicity generated by court action can also be a very useful tool for NGOs or other pressure groups seeking to launch campaigns for change to the ways in which environmental and human rights issues are dealt with by mining companies.

The possibility that companies can be sued in the domestic courts of their home states under extra-territorial application of domestic laws of some states has also developed into a significant risk factor for mineral companies. For instance, on 6 October 2016 the British Columbia Supreme Court of Canada ruled that a lawsuit by Eritrean miners, who allege they were forced to work in a mine owned by Nevsun Resources Ltd, a Canadian mining company, can proceed to trial.[25] Similarly, US companies may be sued in the US courts under the Alien Tort Act, 1769 for violation of the law or a treaty of the US. The value and implications of the suits lies not only in the legal result of financial relief but also their importance should be viewed from the context of the public pressure, reputation loss and the negative publicity that can be generated from these legal actions.[26] Generally, such litigation entails significant costs for the companies forced to defend these claims.

Preventive strategies: The way forward

It should be acknowledged that the social and human rights dimensions of mineral operation go beyond economic imperatives such as the profit motives of mining companies and revenue generation of the host states. Rather, they embrace the questions of the equitable distribution of revenues, the mitigation of any adverse social and environmental impact of operations, and the rectification of human rights abuses.[27] Most of the potential social impacts and consequent risks can be avoided through preventive strategies. Preventive strategies can include the use of social planning and social impact assessments (SIAs), stakeholder consultation, negotiating agreements with the host community, proactive internal change to address human rights issues and payment of compensation to affected communities. Adoption of preventive strategies has proved to be the most viable approach to resolving the social and human rights risks. However, mitigation measures are a retroactive solution for social impacts and require their implementation by way of the provision of compensation and rehabilitation programmes to the

25 Kevin Coon and Christopher Burkett, 'BC Case against Canadian Mining Company for Overseas Human Rights Violations to Proceed to Trial' (Baker McKenzie, 10 November 2016) <www.labourandemploymentlaw.com/2016/11/bc-case-against-canadian-mining-company-for-overseas-human-rights-violations-to-proceed-to-trial/> accessed 13 January 2017.

26 See George S. Akpan, 'Litigating Problems that Arise from Natural Resources Exploitation in Foreign Courts: Impediments to Justice' (2002) 20 *Journal of Energy and Natural Resources Law* 55, 76–77.

27 Al Faruque, *Petroleum Contracts* (n 23) 244.

affected local and indigenous communities.[28] Compared to preventive measures, the mitigation measures can be a costly and complicated process.

Social planning and social impact assessment

Considering the fact that failure to understand community needs and aspirations at the initial stage of the project can sow the seeds of social tensions and potential conflict in the future, social planning and its integration are often seen as a legal requirement of project design and implementation.[29] Carrying out social planning to address any social and human rights issues arising from a mineral project is important for increasing the public acceptability and success of the project, obtaining a licence to operate and reducing the risk of potential conflict and consequent uncertainties.[30] However, SIA is more than a company's preventive strategy and it requires an appropriate legal mechanism in contracts or mining legislation.

Be that as it may, integration of social concerns is not an easy task. Successful integration depends on factors which can be divided into two broad categories. First, human resource issues within companies determine the successful integration of human rights concerns into mining operations. This includes developing an appreciation of the importance of integration, recognition of the value of building social and human capital, appointment of social scientists at the project level and fostering an understanding among technical, environmental and social specialists of the legitimacy and importance of each other's contributions.[31] Second, the process of implementing SIA into company practice and procedure promotes the successful integration of social issues into mining operations.[32] As communities' expectations may change and evolve over the lifespan of the project, companies' social policies may need to be revised and updated to match a changing scenario.

Apart from social planning, SIA is crucial for understanding the social and human rights risks the company may face in carrying out a project. An SIA is the main instrument for balancing social concerns, on the one hand, and the economic gains from petroleum, on the other. An SIA generally includes the study of the social, economic, cultural and health impacts of a given operation in a particular area, such as the local history, populations and demographic change, political institutions, social and power structures in the local community, and likely changes in the values and norms of the society

28 Ibid 245.

29 Elizabeth Bastida, 'Integrating Sustainability into Legal Frameworks for Mining in Some Selected Latin American Countries' (No. 120, International Institute for Environment and Development, January 2002).

30 Al Faruque, *Petroleum Contracts* (n 23) 245.

31 Ibid.

32 Kathryn McPhail and Aidan Davy, 'Integrating Social Concerns into Private Sector Decision Making: A Review of Corporate Practices in the Mining, Oil and Gas Sectors' (Discussion Paper No. 384, World Bank, 1998) 55–56.

by the operation of the project.[33] The SIA denotes a process of evaluation, prediction and reflection on both intended and unintended consequences of the proposed project on a given society. The main objectives of an SIA are to identify and assess the potential social impact of a proposed project, to suggest alternative solutions, to integrate community concerns in the project design and to develop management and measures to mitigate any negative social impact and to make the project more compatible with human rights norms.[34]

While companies are familiar with environmental impact assessments (EIAs) and carry these out comprehensively, the area of SIAs is less developed and is usually carried out as part of an EIA. This can be attributed to several factors such as a lack of understanding of the significance of social aspects of a project, and priority being accorded to environmental considerations over social ones. However, in view of the fact that the social impacts of an operation can be a significant risk factor for a mining company, a separate and self-contained SIA increasingly becomes essential. The necessity of a separate SIA can be justified on the basis that there are inherent underlying differences between the environmental and the social impacts of mining operations. While environmental impact is largely limited to the physical environment and can be mostly mitigated through technological solutions, the social impact can have far-reaching effects on society and its management requires different approaches and strategies. However, consideration of both environmental and social issues associated with mineral development should be viewed as an integrated way toward achieving sustainable development.

Carrying out an independent and comprehensive environmental and social impact assessment in all phases of a contract – from the project evaluation stage to the abandonment stage – and the continuing monitoring of social and human rights developments which may arise as a result of exploration, constitute valuable tools for eliminating early misunderstandings and conflicts and for achieving sustainable development.[35] While it should be carried out on a mandatory basis in all mineral projects, the level of assessment can depend on the sensitivity of the project location. For instance, extensive impact assessment is especially needed for any project undertaken in the sensitive physical and human environments where indigenous peoples typically live.

The public perception of fairness in the process of SIAs is crucial for ensuring their credibility and effectiveness. Transparency and impartiality in the SIA process, its exposure to external independent verification and the

33 See, *Mining & Environment Research Network, Research Bulletin* (1997) (Special Edition No. 11/12) 130.

34 Margaret Jungk, 'A Practical Guide to Addressing Human Rights Concerns for Companies Operating Abroad' in Michael K. Addo (ed), *Human Rights Standards and the Responsibility of Transnational Corporations* (Kluwer Law International, 1999) 184.

35 Al Faruque, *Petroleum Contracts* (n 23) 246.

opportunity to appeal against a decision to approve a project can enhance public confidence in SIAs. Participation of the community by way of involving the interested and affected parties and accommodating their input and concerns in the whole process is seen as a prerequisite for ensuring credibility and public acceptability of the SIA.[36] An SIA should not be carried out for the mere purpose of obtaining approval of the project, but it should truly reflect a consultative process.

Stakeholder consultation

Currently, the negotiation process of most of the mineral agreements is carried out between a government and company participant to the exclusion of the local community or indigenous people. In view of the fact that total exclusion of host communities in natural resource development is one of the underlying causes of conflict, public participation in natural resource development and consultation with stakeholders has emerged as an essential component of the sustainable development process and is considered to be the most significant new trend in natural resource development and management in the twenty-first century.[37] Consultation appears to be the principal modality of public participation in resource development projects for the purposes of facilitating engagement of a company with various stakeholders and for identifying appropriate measures for reducing the scope of disagreements.[38] Consultation should be a continuing process of participation of all

36 Institute of Environmental Assessment UK and International Association for Impact Assessment, 'Principles of Environmental Impact Assessment Best Practice' (1999).

37 Participation 'explosion' has occurred due to the following reasons:

(1) the democratisation trends and pressures of the 1990s in the former Soviet Union countries, Africa, and Asia and Latin America;
(2) adoption of the new international legal paradigm of sustainable development, of which public participation is a central tenet;
(3) the international environmental movement;
(4) incorporation of public participation in lending requirements;
(5) human rights law regimes designating public participation as a political right;
(6) increasing recognition of the rights of indigenous and tribal and local communities; and
(7) the Internet, which has so greatly increased the public's ability to obtain, analyse, and disseminate information and views.

See George (Rock) Pring and Susan Y. Noé, 'The Emerging International Law of Public Participation Affecting Global Mining, Energy and Resource Development' in Donald N. Zillman, Alastair Lucas and George (Rock) Pring (eds), *Human Rights in Natural Resource Development: Public Participation in the Sustainable Development of Mining and Energy Resources* (Oxford University Press, 2002) 13.

38 Public consultation has been defined by the International Finance Corporation as follows: 'Public consultation … is a tool for managing two way communications between the project sponsor and the public. Its goal is to improve decision-making and build understanding by activity involving individuals, groups and organisations with a stake in the project. This involvement will increase a project's long-term viability and enhance its

stakeholders in decision-making throughout the formulation and execution of a project.

The importance of stakeholder consultation as a means of public participation has assumed wider significance in mineral and petroleum development since the Ok Tedi case, which for the first time dealt with social conflict between the company and the community in participatory ways.[39] However, stakeholder consultation often constitutes more than a company's preventive strategy. In some countries, the right to be consulted is part of the constitution as well as the national law.[40] Stakeholder consultation can be prescribed in the legal and contractual framework of host countries. The value of stakeholder consultation lies in the fact that it is one of the ways of involving civil society and indigenous peoples in the decision-making processes of mineral development, allows for ventilation and consideration of their concerns, and also serves to ensure provision of the free and informed consent of local communities prior to commencement of the project. In these ways, stakeholder consultation prevents the tragic consequences of destructive resource development and includes host communities in resource management decisions that can help improve the social environment of business.[41]

Public participation and stakeholder consultation in natural resource management have been institutionalised to some extent by the efforts of the United Nations (UN). One of the fundamental principles of the inaugural UN-initiated 'Berlin Guidelines' of 1991[42] is that states and mining

benefit to locally affected people and other stakeholders'. See, IFC, *Doing Better Business through Effective Public Consultation and Disclosure: A Good Practice Manual* (1998), <www.ifc.org/wps/wcm/connect/54c46b8048855702bb44fb6a6515bb18/PublicConsultation.pdf?MOD=AJPERES> accessed 26 March 2017.

39 In the Ok Tedi case, local communities brought legal action against BHP, an Australian company, for compensation for environmental pollution. However, the parties settled the dispute out of court and entered into a negotiated agreement while the case was pending. The agreement spells out a new trend of environmental participation by local communities in developing countries. Second, the local communities not only received compensation for past pollution of their environment but also secured a commitment to payment for future pollution. The case exposed BHP/Ok Tedi Mill Limited (OTML) and the government of Papua New Guinea to adverse local and international publicity. See, Zhiguo Gao, George Akpan and Jim Vanjik, 'Public Participation in Mining and Petroleum in Asia and the Pacific: The Ok Tedi case and its Implications' in Zillman, Lucas and Pring (n 37) 679.

40 See for example the 1998 Constitution of Ecuador and the 2011 Law on the Right of Consultation of Indigenous Peoples of Peru.

41 See Gerald P. Neugebauer, 'Indigenous Peoples as Stakeholders: Influencing Resource-Management Decisions Affecting Indigenous Community Interests in Latin America' (2003) 78 *New York University Law Review* 1227.

42 Environment Guidelines for Mining Operations were adopted at the International Round Table on Mining and the Environment Berlin 25–28 June 1991. See the guidelines at <https://commdev.org/userfiles/files/814_file_UNEP_UNDESA_EnvGuidelines.pdf> accessed 26 March 2017.

companies should ensure participation and dialogue with affected communities and other directly interested parties to a mining proposal. The Berlin Guidelines II for Mining and Sustainable Development particularly emphasise the reduction of conflict that is associated with public participation.[43] The Guidelines provide that:

> The participation of the affected communities in the decision-making process is an essential pre-condition for a responsible environmental policy and for avoiding subsequent conflict. Notwithstanding the possibility of granting more extensive rights, participation is primarily ensured by giving affected communities access to relevant information at all stages of mining activities.[44]

The 1998 Aarhus Convention on Access to Information, Public Participation in Decision-Making and Access to Justice in Environmental Matters[45] contains the broadest and most detailed requirements to date for public participation in decision-making. Among other things, it requires states to implement public involvement in decisions on specific development activities, including metals production and processing facilities, other mineral industry developments, mining projects, energy sector facilities (such as refineries, large power plants and nuclear plants), chemical plants, waste disposal and incineration facilities, dams and large water projects, pipelines and roads.

A host community's participation in a project that is perceived to be open-ended, transparent and fair can develop trust in the host community and company relationship. Furthermore, this can contribute to the building of a sustainable contractual relationship for the long-term project. Effective participation of the community in the mineral project can empower the affected communities and strengthen their role, reduce conflict among competing indigenous and local interests, ensure accountability of the decision-makers and increase public acceptance of a given project. Public participation can play an instrumental role in making the project sustainable by ascribing a greater degree of legitimacy and acceptability to the project.[46] The evolving norms of international human rights law clearly recognise the rights of

43 United Nations, 'Berlin II: Guidelines for Mining and Sustainable Development' (United Nations, 2002) <www.commdev.org/userfiles/files/903_file_Berlin_II_Guidelines.pdf> accessed 23 August 2015.

44 Environmental Guideline for Mining Operations, UN Doc ST/TCD/20 (November 1999), ch 5 <https://commdev.org/userfiles/files/814_file_UNEP_UNDESA_ Env Guidelines.pdf> accessed 26 March 2017

45 *Convention on Access to Information, Public Participation in Decision-Making and Access to Justice in Environmental Matters*, opened for signature 25 June 1998, 2161 UNTS 447 (entered into force 30 October 2001).

46 Faruque, *Petroleum Contracts* (n 12) 251.

indigenous peoples to participation in natural resource development in their lands.[47]

However, it should be acknowledged that to yield desired goals, consultation should not be carried out in order to achieve mere regulatory compliance. It should be spontaneous, demonstrate equitable representation of the communities and be channelled through a transparent process. Consultation between the company and local communities may encounter various problems, such as relevant information being inaccessible or vulnerable communities not receiving adequate consultation.[48]

It should, however, be acknowledged that the community consultation process can be extremely difficult when local communities raise unrealistically high expectations from the project. Under these circumstances, reaching consensus on all the demands voiced by heterogeneous communities with opposing interests could be a particularly frustrating task. This underscores the necessity for a genuine and realistic consultation process, which seeks a balance between the needs, interests and constraints of all stakeholders and acknowledges the project's limitations in meeting those needs.

Negotiating agreements with the host community

A company's negotiation of a separate agreement with the local community can also be an important means of channelling concerns and community interests. The negotiation of such community agreements is already a well-established practice in the mining industry,[49] and it can address a number of community rights issues, such as project-related employment and business opportunities for community members, access to information relating to environmental data, planned operational policies, safety and health concerns, revenue for local municipalities and community relations. Negotiation of a separate agreement is increasingly becoming a viable alternative for

47 For instance, Article 15(2) of the *Convention (No. 169) Concerning Indigenous and Tribal Peoples in Independent Countries*, opened for signature 27 June 1989, 1650 UNTS 383 (entered into force 5 September 1991), requires the state to consult with indigenous peoples in case of exploration or exploitation of natural resources in their land with a view to ascertaining whether and to what degree their interests would be prejudiced by such activities. Article 17(2) states that the peoples concerned shall be consulted whenever consideration is being given to their capacity to alienate their lands or otherwise transmit their rights outside their own community. See also the 2007 UN Declaration on the Rights of Indigenous People, <www.un.org/esa/socdev/unpfii/documents/DRIPS_en.pdf> accessed 26 March 2017. Article 30 of the Declaration emphasises the informed consent of and participation of the indigenous people in the exploitation of natural resources on their land.

48 Al Faruque, *Petroleum Contracts* (n 23) 252.

49 Boubacar Boccoum and others, 'Mining Community Development Agreements: Source Book' (World Bank, 2012) <http://siteresources.worldbank.org/INTOGMC/Resources/mining_community.pdf> accessed 18 November 2016.

articulating and accommodating public participation, social provision and the question of compensation.[50]

Negotiating with local communities who may be unrepresented or particularly vulnerable can be problematic, if the objective is to develop an agreement which is contractually or legislatively enforceable. Inequality of bargaining power between the company and the local or indigenous community may be of concern. These communities are often economically disadvantaged and lack the appropriate legal skills to negotiate with companies in possession of sophisticated negotiating skills. Local and indigenous groups may often not be effectively represented in the negotiation process, particularly when language or cultural mores pose a barrier. For this reason, establishing a consensus among the key stakeholders on core interests and demands is needed in order to facilitate such negotiation. This problem can be resolved by the formation of a small, appropriately resourced and skilled group from the community to negotiate, and by providing external legal and financial support and community development programmes for meaningfully engaging the communities with the company.[51]

Addressing human rights

It is increasingly realised that mining companies should address human rights concerns in their operating areas in order to meet community expectations from the mining industry. Companies' proactive efforts to protect human rights within their own operations and to promote human rights, in circumstances where the corporation has the possibility of influencing the host government's human rights record, can be seen as key elements of their compliance with human rights obligations.[52] In their internal operation, companies' human rights responsibilities should ensure that the basic rights of company workers are well protected and that their subcontractors conform to the same levels of human rights standards. In the sphere of its external influence, a company should make efforts to persuade the host government not to resort to an illegitimate use of force with regard to demonstrators and striking workers in the local field of operations of the company.[53] Companies' recognition that human rights protection and

50 Sunrita Sarkar and others, 'Mining Community Development Agreements – Practical Experiences and Field Studies' (Final Report for the World Bank, Environmental Resources Management, June 2010) <www.sdsg.org/wp-content/uploads/2011/06/CDA-Report-FINAL.pdf>.

51 Geoff Gishubl, 'Negotiating Community Agreements: Some Issues Arising from the Yandicoogina Experience' (Paper presented at International Bar Association Seminar on Minerals, Energy and Resources Law, Edinburgh, April 2002).

52 See Jens Scierbeck, 'Operational Measures for Identifying and Implementing Human Rights Issues in Corporate Operations' in Eide, Bergesen and Goyer (eds) (n 4) 168.

53 Asbjorn Eide, 'Globalisation and the Human Rights Agenda: The Petroleum Industry at Crossroads' in Eide, Bergesen and Goyer (eds) (n 4) 43.

promotion can matter as much as their profit motive can have a profound impact on any sustained relationship with the host community. For this purpose, it is essential that companies operate in accordance with international human rights norms and respect the basic civil and political rights of local or indigenous community members in the operating area.

Payment of compensation to the affected communities

Payment of compensation is one of the most contentious issues in any conflict between the community, the state and mining companies. In most jurisdictions, compensation is payable to individual landowners for acquisition of surface rights or land.[54] Sometimes this compensation remains the only direct fiscal benefit to the local communities or indigenous peoples in the mining operation areas. Generally, compensation is payable by the host state under the relevant legislation and the rate and amount of compensation are determined by the host state's land acquisition laws.

Payment of compensation by companies can encounter various problems. The local and indigenous communities' demand for compensation can be hindered by the non-recognition of traditional rights by the formal laws of a country.[55] Moreover, communities can claim that the compensation paid is not fair or inadequate, or they may face inordinate delay and complex procedures before any compensation is paid. These problems can be resolved by the legal and contractual framework for mining activity, which should lay down a transparent procedure for the early determination of the compensation issue prior to a project commencing operations. Attention to fairness in determination of the amount of compensation is crucial for satisfaction of the key stakeholders.

Apart from being available in cases of land acquisition, compensation should be payable to the affected communities for negative social impacts, as a mitigatory measure. However, an inadequate amount of compensation, lack of transparency or delay may be a source of friction between the company and community. To ensure fairness in compensation, quantum should be measured according to established principles and in concert with the consultation of affected communities, where appropriate.

Another fundamental problem relating to payment of financial compensation can arise in circumstances where the local or indigenous community may not have sufficient institutional and management capacity to deal with an influx of cash flow. Financial compensation may produce only short-term benefits, ignoring the interests of future generations who will bear the legacy

54 For example, section 10 of the *Acquisition and Requisition of Immovable Property Ordinance 1982* (Ordinance II of 1982) (Bangladesh), available at <http://bdlaws.minlaw.gov.bd/pdf_part.php?id=619> accessed 26 March 2017.

55 For example, in Bangladesh, collective ownership of land of indigenous people is not recognised by formal law.

of the negative social and environmental impact of the operation. Thus, financial compensation for the acquisition of land may merely be a short-term solution. In terms of addressing social impact, it is suggested that social investment in the establishment of schools, hospitals, enhanced employment opportunities and training aimed at overall improvement of social and economic conditions in those affected areas should be among the most desirable alternatives to lump sum compensation.

The role of host governments

Legal and regulatory measures

At the national level, the appropriate legal framework, monitoring mechanisms and capacity building of relevant government agencies are imperative for managing social risks and the equitable distribution of a share of rent to affected local communities. It is imperative that a state's legal and policy measures should posit SIAs as a precondition for approval and development of any project so as to properly address fundamental human rights and social issues. A clear legal framework, either in the domestic mineral law, in the code of a host state or in impact assessment legislation, can remove much of the uncertainty regarding the extent of a company's commitment to mitigating the social and human rights impacts of an operation. The host government's development of the legal or contractual framework can also furnish the legal basis for the social and human rights obligations of mining companies, obligations which may otherwise be seen by those companies as merely voluntary in nature. However, for such legislation to be credible and effective, it is essential that the relevant government seek consultation with and input from industry and stakeholders, such as communities and NGOs, in its formulation.

Only a few states require companies to carry out SIA prior to undertaking a mineral project. For instance, Papua New Guinea's Oil and Gas Act of 1998 makes social mapping and landowner identification studies a condition for granting a petroleum licence to the licensee. The Act provides that, prior to the entry into the licence area for the purpose of exploration, the licensee shall undertake a preliminary social mapping study and landowner identification study of the customary owners and the occupants of the land comprised in the licence area. Following discovery of petroleum, the licensee is required to conduct a full-scale study of both aspects.[56]

Many developing countries might be more interested in gaining large economic benefits from the mineral project and may ignore the social and

56 Article 47 of the Oil and Gas Act 1998 (No. 49 of 1998) (Certified on: 5 February 1999) (Papua New Guinea), Barrows supplement Asia and Australasia (Basic Oil Laws and Concession Contracts), No. 146, 40, Barrows Company (2000) New York.

environmental aspect of the operation. The governments' efforts to deal with human rights abuses and social impacts can be severely compromised by their desire to attract foreign investment over and above the social and human rights aspects of mining projects.

Equitable revenue sharing

A source of discontent on the part of host communities lies in their deprivation of the revenue extracted from the mineral project. A mineral agreement fiscal regime that is insensitive to the needs of the local communities and indigenous people will likely be considered by them to be inequitable and unjust. Host communities can be dissatisfied with existing compensation arrangements and social provisioning, given the high rate of economic benefits associated with mineral extraction. This dissatisfaction can lead to tension between the local and indigenous communities and the host government. To counter this, it is imperative that government allocates an appropriate share of revenue from mineral extraction to affected communities. In several countries, local 'rights' to a share of resource revenues have been codified in constitutions or legislation. The Constitution of Peru of 1979 mandated for the first time that a percentage of the revenue from exploitation of mineral resources should be allocated to mineral producing regions.[57] In 2001, Canon Minero of 27506 stipulated that local governments of the producing province would be allocated 20 per cent of revenue and the urban and rural population of the producing region would be allocated 60 per cent, based on their population.[58] The mining law of 2002 of the Democratic Republic of Congo sets the sharing rates for natural resources revenue at 60 per cent to the national government and 40 per cent to the provinces, from which 10 per cent is allocated to their local communities.[59] The Mineral Development Fund of Ghana established in 1993 receives 20 per cent of the mining royalty payments. Half of the fund is distributed in the mining areas for projects to mitigate the effects of mining, in the proportion of 25 per cent via the district assemblies and the rest to local communities.[60] The according of rights to resource revenues should be premised on the promotion of social justice, which can be achieved through affirmative action towards affected communities who are marginalised compared to other communities. Equity and social justice

57 María Lasa Aresti, 'Mineral Revenue Sharing in Peru' (Natural Resource Governance Institute, 2016) <www.resourcegovernance.org/sites/default/files/documents/mineral-revenue-sharing-in-peru_0.pdf> accessed 10 March 2017.

58 Ibid.

59 Giorgio Brosio and Raju Jan Singh, 'Revenue Sharing of Natural Resources in Africa: Reflections from a Review of International Practices'(Background Paper, World Bank, April 2014) <http://documents.worldbank.org/curated/en/890931468209041225/pdf/902520WP0P1437000Final00April020140.pdf> accessed 12 March 2017.

60 Ibid.

perspectives underscore the philosophy of revenue sharing with the community or local government.

However, revenue sharing encounters the following problems. First, the community's demand for a share of revenue can be constrained by legal and constitutional arrangements which vest management or control over natural resources in a state. Second, determination of fair and equitable revenue sharing can be inherently problematic due to the competing claims of many groups. Third, it may be difficult to make an equitable balance between the interests of the affected area where minerals are exploited and other areas of a country. Distribution of a project's revenue among federal, state and local governments and also local and indigenous communities may, moreover, be highly complex and may be fraught with a lack of consensus among the political units concerned with that distribution.

These issues can be addressed by delineating the rights of the communities to a share of the revenue in a clear legal framework, supported by appropriate contractual rights, and on the basis that many of the external costs of exploring mineral resources are localised. In addition, an appropriate formula should be devised for sharing revenue between the central government, affected communities and local governments and other parts of the areas of a country. In determining a fair and equitable division of revenue among these actors, there are two accepted principles which should be taken into consideration. First, the 'derivation' principle denotes the proportion of contribution to production in the particular area and should be utilised in determining appropriate compensation to local communities and government. For example, in Nigeria, the principle of derivation has evolved as part of the efforts by the federal government of Nigeria to address the inequities and injustice inherent in the revenue allocation system, whereby oil revenue collected by the federal government is redistributed to the constituent units.[61] The principle of derivation is based on the notion of distributive justice, which posits fair allocation of benefits and burdens by the state.[62] Second, the principle of 'need' is fundamental, which entails sharing of revenue on the basis of the number of affected populations, the level of economic and social development among them, the degree of impact on them and, in the case of allocation to local governments, the level of their

61 Adangor, Z., 'The Principle of Derivation and the Search for Distributive Justice in the Niger Delta Region of Nigeria: The Journey So Far,' (2015) 41 *Journal of Law, Policy and Globalization*.

62 See Gene R. Laczniak and Patrick E. Murphy, 'Distributive Justice: Pressing Questions and Emerging Directions and the Promise of Rawlsian Analysis' (2008) 28 *Journal of Macro Marketing* 1; Karen S. Cook and Karen A. Hegtvedt, 'Distributive Justice, Equity, and Equality' (1983) 9 *Ann. Rev. Sociol.* 217, 218; Ronald L. Cohen, 'Distributive Justice: Theory and Research' (1987) 1 *Social Justice Research* 19, 20–21, 24; Wulf Gaertner, 'Distributive justice: Theoretical foundations and empirical findings' (1994) 38 Euro*pean Economic Review* 711, 712.

financial expenditures and obligations and the number of populations affected within the particular local area.[63]

The right of affected local governments and communities to negotiate a participating interest in the mineral project warrants further consideration in determining adequate compensation for mining proposals. Such a participation right has been recognised in Papua New Guinea, where affected provincial governments, local governments and project area landowners of a mineral project can negotiate with a licensee to acquire from the licensee, on freely negotiated commercial terms, a participating interest in a mineral project, in addition to the state's participating interest.[64] However, the efficacy of such community equity participation is yet to be tested.

Transparency in revenue management

The importance of improving transparency and accountability of mineral revenues in many developing countries and economies in transition lies in the fact that misappropriation or mismanagement of revenue and the resultant exclusion of the vast majority of people from the economic benefits accruing from projects, can fuel conflict and increase social instability which, in turn, may negatively affect the investment climate. Lack of transparency in mineral revenue management can breed corruption, strengthen authoritarian regimes, increase the poverty level and social inequality, and consequently can create an unstable business environment within a state.[65]

Ensuring revenue transparency requires that the host state adopt measures which allow for the disclosure of basic information on revenue earned from resource extraction and which encourage the maintenance of proper accounts, establish linkages to the overall state budget and measures for public expenditure management, identify priority areas for expenditure and ensure oversight in terms of monitoring and control of that expenditure.[66] Legal and policy reform of the public disclosure requirements relating to payments made to governments by mining companies and to government expenditure can contribute to transparency and accountability in revenue management and augment the positive public outcomes from projects.

Mining companies' responses: An appraisal

Many mining companies have realised the need to integrate social concerns into the decision-making process and have acknowledged the urgency of

63 See Ike Oguine, 'Nigeria's Oil Revenues and the Oil Producing Areas' (1999) 17 *Journal of Energy and Natural Resources Law*, 114.

64 Article 175 of the Oil and Gas Act 1998.

65 Abdullah Al Faruque, 'Transparency in Extractive Revenues in Developing Countries and Economies in Transition' (n 10).

66 Ibid.

addressing human rights issues as one of their core responsibilities.[67] This corporate response to social and human rights issues has mainly been driven by growing criticism against companies in the context of the negative environmental and social impacts of mining. The risk of litigation resulting from any failure to comply with domestic regulations also drives this response. Since the mid-1990s, mining companies have placed increasing emphasis on the integration of stakeholder concerns into the overall project management cycle. Mining companies now consider socially responsible behaviour as an essential element of good business practice and a means of fulfilling social expectations arising from mining company activities, which may eventually enhance the prospects of gaining access to new exploration licences.[68] The recent movement toward corporate social responsibility (CSR) is also considered an important contributory factor behind recent corporate initiatives.[69] CSR encompasses a company's responsibility toward a broad range of stakeholders. It denotes the idea that companies should not be seen as merely legal entities operating for the benefit of shareholders, but that they are also expected to be agents assuming greater responsibility for the economic and social impacts of their corporate activities and for the well-being of society.[70]

The current social responses of mining companies can be divided into two broad categories, the first being adoption of voluntary codes and principles on social responsibilities.[71] Many mining companies have responded to demands for improved social and human rights performance by adopting voluntary codes for internal management of social and environmental concerns, accepting the industry-specific voluntary codes and guidelines,

67 Heledd Jenkins and Louise Obara, 'Corporate Social Responsibility (CSR) in the Mining Industry – The Risk of Community Dependency', available at <www.dlist.org/sites/default/files/doclib/CSR_mining%20industry_risk%20of%20community%20dependency.pdf> accessed 12 March 2017.

68 For example, Rio Tinto, one of the world's largest mining companies, has adopted CSR as its strategy to address social, human rights and environmental concerns. See the Rio Tinto *2016 Sustainable Development Report*, available at <www.riotinto.com/documents/RT_SD2016.pdf> accessed 12 March 2017.

69 Abdullah Al Faruque, *Petroleum Contracts: Stability and Risk Management in Developing Countries* (n 23) 258.

70 David Crowther and Guler Aras, *Corporate Social Responsibility* (Ventus Publishing, 2008); Cynthia A. William, 'Corporate Social Responsibility in an Era of Economic Globalisation' (2002) 35 *UC Davis Law Review*, 705.

71 In this regard, three types of self-regulating code can be identified. Some codes relate to minimum standards regulating the conditions of work by the company and its associates. Some codes support increased involvement by the company in human rights in the larger community in which it operates. Some establish ethical criteria by which a company's investment should be guided: Christopher McCrudden, 'Human Rights Codes for Transnational Corporations: What Can the Sullivan and MacBride Principles Tell Us?' (1999) 19 *Oxford Journal of Legal Studies* 169.

making policy statements, incorporating CSR principles into their business principles or accepting voluntary international standards.[72]

While these codes and guidelines acknowledge the trend toward the acceptance of ethical, social and human rights responsibilities by mining companies, the effectiveness of this self-regulation is questionable. Moreover, the credibility of such codes can be eroded by the lack of their binding force and implementation. Even when they are implemented, such codes are not subject to monitoring and external verification. According to Ratner, the overall impact of such codes on corporate behaviour is unclear, with different companies and industries adopting stronger or weaker codes, each of which is observed with varying degrees of commitment.[73] However, these codes can provide an ideal mechanism for creating awareness and respect for human rights within the structure of a company.

The second category of company response constitutes efforts such as stakeholder consultation, community programmes, partnership building, social benefits and the provision of training and education to the local and indigenous community.[74] Many mining companies have undertaken to provide community consultation, healthcare and education for the local people in the area of operation, in order to build trust.

The above discussion clearly demonstrates that a change is currently taking place in mining companies' attitudes towards community participation and the accommodation of community interests. This emerging practice of making policy commitments to address social and community concerns reflects an increased understanding of the social and ethical dimensions of the mining industry.

However, a note of caution should be sounded regarding the limits on the ability of mining companies to discharge social responsibilities. A company's ability to shoulder social responsibility is constrained by its financial capacity. The concerns expressed by local communities may also reflect issues which do not have a rational basis and that cannot be calculated with the degree of certainty preferred by private sector mining operations.

72 See, J. Walker and S. Howard, 'Voluntary Codes of Conduct in the Mining Industry. Mining, Minerals and Sustainable Development Project (MMSD)' (IIED, 2002); MMSD, 'Breaking New Ground: Mining, Minerals, and Sustainable Development, World Business Council for Sustainable Development' (2002).

73 Steven R. Ratner, 'Corporation and Human Rights: A Theory of Legal Responsibility' (2001) 111 *Yale Law Journal* 443, 532.

74 In the Camisea project in the Inca region of Peru, Shell Prospecting and Development Peru (SPDP) has undertaken an extensive consultation process, has provided social benefits to the local communities in the key areas of health, training and education, and has reached agreement with Red Ambiental Peruana, a network of 35 social and environmental NGOs in Peru, to undertake independent third party monitoring of the company's social and environmental performance.

Conclusion

An understanding of the human rights and social issues in mineral operations by mining companies is a prerequisite for mineral extraction and for a sustained community and company relationship. In the planning and implementation of mineral projects, social, human rights and environmental issues should be taken into consideration to ensure sustainability of the project as well as to protect the legitimate interests of the wider community. A better integration of social and environmental concerns into the decision-making process of companies can enhance the stability of the relationship between the host communities and companies, particularly those which are operating in environmentally sensitive and socially fragile areas. Developing a strong community relations programme early in the project, enhancing employment opportunities for local communities, strengthening community participation, improving social provision and integrating social policy into companies' decision-making are all measures widely considered as essential to the success of a project.[75] However, in implementing these measures, a balance has to be struck between the necessity of mineral extraction, which can accelerate economic and social development, and the need to address societal concerns in the development of such a project. Successful implementation also requires that a host government's legislative and policy measures for addressing human rights issues and social impacts include a clear legal framework for impact assessment, consultation and the equitable distribution of revenue among the affected communities.

75 See, Elizabeth Bastida, Thomas W. Waelde and Janeth Warden-Fernández, *International and Comparative Mineral Law and Policy: Trends and Prospects* (Kluwer Law International, 2005); Heledd Jenkins and Natalia Yakovleva, 'Corporate Social Responsibility in the Mining Industry: Exploring Trends in Social and Environmental Disclosure' (2006) 14(3–4) *Journal of Cleaner Production* 271–284.

13 International indigenous rights, investment and sustainability in the mining sector

Andrew Erueti, Sarah Down and Jacinta Ruru

Introduction

Indigenous peoples throughout the world have deep connections and relationships with their lands, waters, forests and coastlines.[1] Indigenous peoples have long developed governance systems and economies for owning, managing and valuing natural resources that make entire sense within Indigenous societies. Contemporary world globalisation, including prospects for foreign investment, offers both serious challenges and opportunities for Indigenous peoples to support and realise their own goals and aspirations for their communities. Foreign investment must be guided by best principles in law and policy and not repeat the catastrophes of European colonisation. International law is now at the forefront in presenting these expectations to recognise and respect Indigenous peoples' rights, interests, responsibilities and relationships with natural resources. With many natural resource extraction activities now conducted in Indigenous peoples' traditional areas,[2]

1 There is no universally accepted definition of the term 'Indigenous peoples' but a statement made by the former Special Rapporteur José Martínez Cobo is instructive: '[Indigenous peoples] are those which, having a historical continuity with pre-invasion and pre-colonial societies that developed on their territories, consider themselves distinct from other sectors of the societies now prevailing in those territories, or parts of them. They form at present non-dominant sectors of society and are determined to preserve, develop and transmit to future generations their ancestral territories, and their ethnic identity, as the basis of their continued existence as peoples, in accordance with their own cultural patterns, social institutions and legal system'. José Martínez Cobo, Special Rapporteur of the Sub-Comm'n on Prevention of Discrimination & Prot. of Minorities, *Study of the Problem of Discrimination against Indigenous Populations*, UN Docs E/CN.4/Sub.2/1986/7 & Addendum 1–4.

2 For example, in Australia it is estimated that more than 60 per cent of mineral operations neighbour Indigenous communities. Minerals Council of Australia website: 'Indigenous Economic Development' (Minerals Council of Australia) <www.minerals.org.au/policy_focus/Indigenous_economic_development> accessed 4 May 2016.

significant issues exist and are continuing to arise.[3] This chapter explores this international law and considers its application in Aotearoa, New Zealand within the context of the business of natural resource extraction.

International law

Free, prior, informed consent

Central to the increased recognition of Indigenous peoples' rights over natural resource extraction is the development of the right of 'free, prior, informed consent' (FPIC). In 2005, the United Nations' Permanent Forum on Indigenous Issues described FPIC in the following terms.[4] 'Free' intimates the absence of coercion, intimidation or manipulation.[5] 'Prior' implies that consent should be sought in advance of any authorisation or commencement of activities and further that sufficient time be given for consultation to take place in a way that coheres with traditional decision-making processes.[6] 'Informed' expects that Indigenous peoples should receive satisfactory information in an accessible form which should include the nature, size, pace, reversibility and scope of the proposed project, the reasons for launching it, its duration and a preliminary assessment of its economic, social, cultural and environmental impact.[7] 'Consent' requires a process of consultation and participation undertaken in good faith with the full and equitable participation of Indigenous peoples leading to agreement.[8] The Forum expects that Indigenous peoples should also have equal access to financial, human and material resources in order to engage constructively in discussions.[9] Elements of this definition have been disputed by state governments and others, in

3 There is a vast amount of literature on mining and Indigenous peoples in different countries. See for example, Chris Ballard and Glenn Banks, 'Resource Wars: The Anthropology of Mining' (2003) 32 *Annual Review of Anthropology* 287; Saleem Ali, *Mining, the Environment and Indigenous Development Conflicts* (University of Arizona Press 2003); Ciaran O'Faircheallaigh and Saleem Ali (eds), *Earth Matters: Indigenous Peoples, the Extractive Industries and Corporate Social Responsibility* (Greenleaf Publishing 2008); Jon Altman and David Martin (eds), *Power, Culture Economy: Indigenous Australians and Mining* (ANU E-Press 2009). See also: James Anaya, 'Indigenous Peoples Participatory Rights in Relation to Decisions about Natural Resource Extraction: The More Fundamental Issue of What Rights Indigenous Peoples Have in Land and Resources' (2005) 22 *Arizona Journal of International and Comparative Law* 7.

4 Permanent Forum on Indigenous Issues, *Report of the International Workshop on Methodologies Regarding Free, Prior and Informed Consent and Indigenous Peoples*, 4th Session, Provisional Agenda Item 4, UN Doc E/C.19/2005/3 (17 February 2005).

5 Ibid para 46.

6 Ibid.

7 Ibid.

8 Ibid paras 47–48.

9 Ibid para 48.

particular, whether 'consent' provides Indigenous peoples with a right to veto projects or whether it is a right to be consulted.[10]

Development of Indigenous rights at international law

One of the earliest international legal instruments to give substance and recognition to the FPIC obligations was the International Labour Organization's Convention concerning Indigenous and Tribal Peoples in Independent Countries 1989 ('ILO 169').[11] Article 6(2) requires that consultations must be in good faith, through culturally appropriate procedures, and with the objective of reaching an agreement. Article 15 requires states to safeguard Indigenous peoples' rights to the natural resources throughout their territories, including the right 'to participate in the use, management and conservation' of resources and to participate in benefits and receive fair compensation for any damage. The Convention does not provide for Indigenous peoples' ownership of minerals, if the state has claimed ownership of these resources. In applying the Convention, the ILO monitoring body has repeatedly called on states to respect their obligations to consult with Indigenous peoples prior to exploration and exploitation of natural resources within their traditional territories, and has insisted on the adoption and implementation of domestic legislation in order to facilitate such consultations.[12] However, while the Convention is binding on states

10 For example, the UN Workshop on Indigenous Peoples in a 2001 conference on the issue of natural resources, mining and human rights made clear that FPIC gives Indigenous peoples the right, as land and resource owners, to say 'no' to proposed development projects at any point during negotiations with governments and or/ extractive industries. UN Workshop on Indigenous Peoples, *Private Sector Natural Resource, Energy and Mining Companies and Human Rights Workshop*, UN Doc E/CN.4/Sub.2/AC.4/ 2002/3 (Geneva, 5–7 December 2001) para 52. The World Bank in its Operational Policy 4.10 made changes to its influential social and environmental governance procedures to require its clients to ensure 'free, prior and informed *consultation*' of affected communities leading to their '*broad community support*' (emphasis added). World Bank, 'Operational Manual', *Indigenous Peoples*, Operational Policy 4.10, July 2005, Washington (USA) at 1.

11 *Convention (No. 169) Concerning Indigenous and Tribal Peoples in Independent Countries*, opened for signature 27 June 1989, 1650 UNTS 383 (entered into force 5 September 1991) ('ILO 169'). See also, *Convention (No. 107) Concerning the Protection and Integration of Indigenous and Other Tribal and Semi-Tribal Populations of Independent Countries*, opened for signature 26 June 1957, ILO No. 10, (entered into force 2 June 1959). For comment on the Conventions see Luis Rodríguez-Piñero, *Indigenous Peoples, Post Colonialism and International Law: The ILO Regime* (Oxford University Press 2005). See also Athanasios Yupsanis, 'ILO Convention No. 169 Concerning Indigenous and Tribal Peoples in Independent Countries 1989–2009: An Overview' (2010) 79 *Nordic Journal of International Law* 433.

12 Tara Ward, 'The Right to Free, Prior, Informed Consent: Indigenous Peoples' Participation Rights within International Law' (2011) 10(2) *Northwestern Journal of International Human Rights* 54, 60.

that ratify it, to date it has only been ratified by 22 states, predominantly in Latin America.[13]

Earlier legal instruments such as the International Covenant on Civil and Political Rights, while not formulated in the language of FPIC, also provide protections.[14] Article 27 states that 'persons belonging to such minorities shall not be denied the right, in community with the other members of their group, to enjoy their own culture, to profess and practise their own religion, or to use their own language'.[15] In interpreting Article 27, the UN Human Rights Committee (HRC) has held it includes the protection of Indigenous peoples' ways of life which are connected to the control over, and use of, lands and resources.[16] This protection was found to include a positive duty of the state to 'ensure the effective participation of members of minority communities in decisions which affect them'.[17]

Article 1(1) of the International Covenant on Civil and Political Rights and the International Covenant on Economic, Social and Cultural Rights states that, 'All peoples have the right of self-determination. By virtue of that right they freely determine their political status and freely pursue their economic, social and cultural development'.[18] In interpreting this provision,

13 International Labour Organization, *Convention (No. 169) Concerning Indigenous and Tribal Peoples in Independent Countries*, opened for signature 27 June 1989, 1650 UNTS 383 (entered into force 5 September 1991) ('ILO 169'). See also, *Convention (No. 107) Concerning the Protection and Integration of Indigenous and Other Tribal and Semi-Tribal Populations of Independent Countries*, opened for signature 26 June 1957, ILO No. 10 (entered into force 2 June 1959). For comment on the Conventions see Luis Rodríguez-Piñero, *Indigenous Peoples, Post Colonialism and International Law: The ILO Regime* (Oxford University Press 2005). See also Athanasios Yupsanis, 'ILO Convention No. 169 Concerning Indigenous and Tribal Peoples on Independent Countries 1989–2009: An Overview' (2010) 79 *Nordic Journal of International Law* 433.

Ratifications of C169 – Indigenous and Tribal Peoples Convention, 1989 (ILO No. 169)' <www.ilo.org/dyn/normlex/en/f?p=1000:11300:0::NO:11300:P11300_INSTRUMENT_ID:312314> accessed 17 March 2016. For an analysis of the implementation of ILO 169 in Bolivia see Laurie Sargent, 'The Indigenous Peoples of Bolivia's Amazon Basin Region and ILO Convention No. 169: Real Rights or Rhetoric?' (1997–1998) 29 *University of Miami Inter-American Law Review* 451.

14 International Covenant on Civil and Political Rights, opened for signature 16 December 1966, 999 UNTS 171 (entered into force 23 March 1976).

15 Ibid Art 27.

16 Human Rights Committee, *Addendum: General Comment No. 23(50) (Art. 27)*, UN Doc CCPR/C/21/Rev.1/Add.5 (26 April 1994) para 3.2.

17 Ibid. For concluding statements by the HRC on countries' obligations to consult see: Human Rights Committee, *Concluding Observations of the Human Rights Committee: Chile*, 89th Session, UN Doc CCPR/C/CHL/CO/5 (18 May 2007) para 19; Human Rights Committee, *Concluding Observations of the Human Rights Committee: Panama*, 92nd Session UN Doc CCPR/C/PAN/CO/3 (17 April 2008) para 21; Human Rights Committee, *Concluding Observations of the Human Rights Committee: Nicaragua*, 94th Session, UN Doc CCPR/C/NIC/CO/3 (December 2008) para 21.

18 International Covenant on Economic, Social and Cultural Rights, opened for signature 16 December 1966, 993 UNTS 3 (entered into force 3 January 1976).

both the UN HRC and the Committee on Economic, Social and Cultural Rights have urged states to obtain the FPIC of Indigenous peoples before engaging in extractive activities in their territory.[19] Furthermore, the International Convention on the Elimination of All Forms of Racial Discrimination, under General recommendation 23, provides that all peoples are entitled to enjoy and exercise human rights and fundamental freedoms in all spheres of public life and that no decisions directly relating to their rights and interests should be taken without their informed consent.[20]

The United Nations Declaration on the Rights of Indigenous Peoples

The United Nations Declaration on the Rights of Indigenous Peoples ('the Declaration') is a significant achievement in the setting of standards for the protection of Indigenous peoples' rights including their interests in natural resources and protection against displacement and despoliation caused by natural resource extraction. The most powerful suite of norms in the Declaration are the rights to self-determination[21] and self-government;[22] FPIC;[23] and the obligation of states to recognise traditional land rights.[24]

The Declaration is not a legally binding international instrument. Technically, it is a resolution of the UN General Assembly. However, it is vested with significant legitimacy given the active role Indigenous advocates and state delegates played in negotiating the text over the course of 24 years.[25] The Declaration also elaborates fundamental human rights contained in treaties that have been ratified by many states.[26] In addition, the Declaration

19 Human Rights Committee, *Views: Communication No. 1457/2006*, 95th Session UN Doc CCPR/C/95/D/1457/2006 (24 April 2009) (*Angela Poma Poma v Peru*); UN Committee on Economic, Social and Cultural Rights, *Concluding Observations by the Committee on Economic, Social and Cultural Rights: Colombia*, 27th Session, UN Doc E/C.12/1/Add.74 (6 December 2001) para 33.

20 *International Convention on the Elimination of All Forms of Racial Discrimination*, opened for signature 21 December 1965, 660 UNTS 195 (entered into force 4 January 1969). For more on how General Recommendation 23 has been interpreted by the UN Committee on the Elimination of Racial Discrimination see Committee on the Elimination of Racial Discrimination, *Concluding Observations of the Committee on the Elimination of Racial Discrimination: Russian Federation*, 73rd Session, UN Doc CERD/C/RUS/CO/19 (22 September 2008).

21 *United Nations Declaration on the Rights of Indigenous Peoples*, GA Res 61/295, UN GAOR, 61st Session, 107th plenary meeting, Supp No. 49, UN Doc A/RES/61/295 (13 September 2007) Art 3 (Indigenous Peoples Declaration).

22 Ibid Art 4.

23 See ibid Arts 10, 11(2), 19, 28–29, 32.

24 See ibid Arts 26–27.

25 See generally Claire Charters and Rodolfo Stavenhagen (eds), *Making the Declaration Work: The United Nations Declaration on the Rights of Indigenous Peoples* (International Work Group for Indigenous Affairs 2009).

26 James Anaya, *Indigenous Peoples in International Law* (2nd edn, Oxford University Press 2004).

has been formally endorsed by an overwhelming majority of UN member states. While Australia, Canada, New Zealand and the USA voted against the Declaration in the UN General Assembly, they later reversed their position and endorsed it.[27] Of all the rights in the Declaration, so far FPIC has generated the most attention and discussion.[28] The Declaration cites the right to FPIC several times but Article 32 specifically addresses the requirement to obtain Indigenous peoples' FPIC with respect to mining activities within their traditional lands. It provides:

> States shall consult and cooperate in good faith with the Indigenous peoples concerned through their own representative institutions in order to obtain their free and informed consent prior to the approval of any project affecting their lands or territories and other resources, particularly in connection with the development, utilization or exploitation of mineral, water or other resources.

States were generally opposed to the inclusion of FPIC in the Declaration, arguing that it provided Indigenous peoples with a right of veto.[29] However, a body of policy, scholarship and jurisprudence has provided greater clarity about the content of the right to FPIC. In particular, the Inter-American Court of Human Rights has given perhaps the most comprehensive authoritative guidance on the content of FPIC. In 2007, the Court held that Indigenous peoples have the right to say 'no' to activities that have potential to significantly impact them and their territories.[30] The former UN Special Rapporteur on the Rights of Indigenous Peoples, James Anaya, has stressed the need to focus not only on consent, but on establishing a process that will result in Indigenous peoples' full engagement with a proposed development. The key is ensuring that Indigenous peoples are involved early in the process,

27 'Chair of UN forum welcomes Canada's endorsement of indigenous rights treaty' *UN News Centre* (12 November 2010) <www.un.org/apps/news/story.asp?NewsID=37102&Kw1=canada&Kw2=declaration&Kw3=#.WMsSJfJaDIU> accessed 17 March 2016; 'United States' backing for indigenous rights treaty hailed at the UN' *UN News Centre* (17 December 2010) <www.un.org/apps/news/story.asp?NewsID= 37102&Kw1=canada&Kw2=declaration&Kw3=#.WMsVV_JaDIU> accessed 17 March 2016.

28 Cathal Doyle, *Indigenous Peoples, Title to Territory, Rights and Resources: The Transformative Role of Free Prior and Informed Consent* (Routledge Research in Human Rights Law 2015).

29 Explanation of Vote by H.E. Rosemary Banks, New Zealand Permanent Representative to the United Nations, 13 September 2007.

30 *Saramaka People v Suriname (Preliminary Objections, Merits, Reparations and Costs)* (Inter-American Court of Human Rights, Series C No. 172, 28 November 2007) paras 129–134. The Court ruled that, regarding large-scale development or investment projects that would have a *major impact* within Saramaka territory, the state has a duty, not only to consult with the Saramakas, but also to obtain their free, prior, and informed consent, according to their customs and traditions.

including in the preparation of regulatory frameworks on relevant areas such as the environment, and natural resource allocation and strategic planning for resource extraction.[31]

Indigenous peoples' rights to lands and natural resources and self-determination

In addition to FPIC, there is the issue of Indigenous peoples' rights to lands and natural resources. Often states do not recognise Indigenous peoples' ownership of their traditional lands – assuming them to be 'state-owned' – despite many Indigenous peoples' having occupied and used the lands for many generations.[32] The Declaration requires states to demarcate and recognise those rights.[33] The Declaration does not however have a strong position on ownership of minerals, noting only that Indigenous peoples have rights to their 'lands, territories and resources'.[34] However, the right to natural resources like minerals and petroleum can be inferred from the right to self-determination in that Indigenous peoples have rights of control over the natural resources in their traditional area.

The Declaration states: 'Indigenous peoples have the right to self-determination'[35] and, 'as a specific form of exercising their right to self-determination, have the right to autonomy or self-government in matters relating to their internal and local affairs'.[36] The right to self-determination is contentious in international law given its close association with the UN-sponsored decolonisation movement.[37] This was the reason why Indigenous advocates sought its inclusion in the Declaration – it indicated that Indigenous peoples might possess the right of independence should there be no agreement between the state and Indigenous peoples about their terms of co-existence in the state.[38] There remains disagreement about the meaning of self-determination in the UN Declaration especially given the express reference to the need to maintain territorial integrity in Article 46. However,

31 James Anaya, *Report of the Special Rapporteur on the Rights of Indigenous Peoples: Extractive Industries and Indigenous Peoples*, 24th Session, UN Doc A/HRC/24/41 (1 July 2013) paras 49–51.

32 See *Mayagna (Sumo) Awas Tingni Community v Nicaragua (Merits, Reparations and Costs)* (Inter-American Court of Human Rights, Series C No. 79, 31 August 2001) (*Awas Tingni*).

33 *Indigenous Peoples Declaration*, UN Doc A/RES/61/295, Art 26. See also, *Awas Tingni* (n 32).

34 *Indigenous Peoples Declaration*, UN Doc A/RES/61/295, Art 26. See also ILO 169 (n 13) Art 15.

35 *Indigenous Peoples Declaration*, UN Doc A/RES/61/295, Art 3.

36 Ibid Art 4.

37 Karen Engle, *The Elusive Promise of Indigenous Development: Rights, Culture, Strategy* (Duke University Press 2010).

38 Andrew Erueti, 'UN Declaration on the Rights of Indigenous Peoples: A Mixed-Model Interpretative Approach' (SJD thesis, University of Toronto 2016).

at the very least the right to self-determination indicates that Indigenous peoples should have control over matters of concern to them, including the use of natural resources in their traditional lands.

Indigenous peoples and business and human rights

During the early 1990s, the international community began to focus its attention on whether human rights might extend to businesses. This was a marked departure from the orthodox approach of regarding human rights as obligations owed by the state to its citizens. However, it was clear that many businesses were now encroaching into areas formerly administered by governments and that specific business practices, including mining activities, were violating human rights.

In the last two decades a number of codes and standards have been developed about how to conduct business in a manner consistent with human rights and ethics. One of the earliest and most important was the UN Global Compact which was established in 2000 by the UN Secretary-General in order to encourage businesses worldwide to voluntarily adopt a framework for business enterprises and which outlines ten key principles in the areas of human rights, labour, the environment and anti-corruption.[39] The Global Compact remains the world's largest sustainability initiative with over 12,000 signatories in 170 countries.[40] Of particular relevance to Indigenous peoples are principles 1 and 2 which provide that businesses should support and respect the protection of internationally proclaimed human rights and should not be complicit in human rights abuses. A number of guidance documents have been released by the UN Global Compact about how businesses should implement these principles with regard to Indigenous peoples, including with respect to the Declaration and the right of FPIC.[41]

In 2011 the UN HRC unanimously endorsed the United Nations' Guiding Principles on Business and Human Rights.[42] These Guiding

39 'Overview of UN Global Compact' (United Nations Global Compact) <www.unglobalcompact.org/> accessed 17 March 2016.

40 'The World's Largest Corporate Sustainability Initiative' (United Nations Global Compact) <www.unglobalcompact.org/what-is-gc> accessed 17 March 2016. For discussion of the motivations of why businesses join and remain part of the UN Global Compact see: Dilek Cetindamar, 'Corporate Social Responsibility Practices and Environmentally Responsible Behavior: The Case of the United Nations Global Compact' (2007) 76(2) *Journal of Business Ethics* 163.

41 UN Global Compact, 'A Business Reference Guide: United Nations Declaration on the Rights of Indigenous Peoples' (UN Global Compact 2013); Amy K. Lehr, 'Indigenous Peoples' Rights and the Role of Free, Prior and Informed Consent' (Practice note, UN Global Compact, 20 February 2014).

42 See John Ruggie, *Report of the Special Representative of the Secretary- General on the Issue of Human Rights and Transnational Corporations and Other Business Enterprises: Guiding Principles on Business and Human Rights: Implementing the United Nations 'Protect, Respect and Remedy' Framework*, 17th Session, Agenda Item 3, UN Doc A/HRC/17/31 (21 March 2011).

Principles provide governments, companies and international organisations with a normative framework to guide company practice and policy. Several states have already established plans of action outlining how they intend to give effect to the Guiding Principles and many companies including mining and petroleum companies have established policies on corporate accountability to communities affected by their activities.[43] The Guiding Principles have also been highly influential in the development and revision of other important policies and guidelines including the revised Organisation for Economic Co-operation and Development (OECD) Guidelines for Multinational Enterprises, adopted in May 2011[44] and the International Organization for Standardization (ISO) 26000, adopted in late 2010.[45]

Multilateral development finance institutions, in particular the World Bank and its private sector lending arm, the International Finance Corporation (IFC), have come under fire for their financing of projects that have detrimentally impacted Indigenous peoples. The negative impacts of World Bank-funded projects have been identified in a number of internal World Bank performance evaluations and documented by non-governmental organisations (NGOs) and intergovernmental human rights bodies.[46] As recognised by one World Bank study, Indigenous peoples 'have often been on the losing end of the development process'.[47]

Since the 1980s the World Bank has developed a series of policies regarding Indigenous peoples and project finance.[48] Yet the efficacy of these policies has been questionable. For example, an internal implementation review conducted in 1986–1987 found that only 2 out of 33 World Bank Group projects substantially complied with their policies.[49] Further, an evaluation of the later Operational Policy (OP) 4.20 found that:

43 See Ministry for Foreign Affairs, *Action Plan for Business and Human Rights* (Government Offices of Sweden, 24 August 2015).

44 See Kathryn Gordon, 'The OECD Guidelines and Other Corporate Responsibility Instruments: A Comparison' (Working Papers on International Investment 2001/05, OECD December 2001).

45 ISO 26000 clarifies what social responsibility is and provides guidance on translating principles into best practice. It is not certification like other ISO standards. For more information see: 'ISO 26000' (International Organization for Standardization) <www.iso.org/iso/home/standards/iso26000.htm> accessed 17 March 2016.

46 Fergus MacKay, 'Indigenous Peoples' Rights to Free, Prior and Informed Consent and the World Bank's Extractive Industries Review' (Summer 2004) *Sustainable Development Law and Policy* 43.

47 World Bank, *The World Bank Participation Source Book* (World Bank 1996) 251.

48 See World Bank Group, 'Tribal People in Bank-Financed Projects' (Operational Manual Statement 2.34, World Bank February 1982).

49 Fergus McKay, 'The Draft World Bank Operational Policy 4.10 on Indigenous Peoples: Progress or More of the Same?' (2005) 22 *Arizona Journal of International and Comparative Law* 65, 66. See also McKay, 'Indigenous People's Right to Free, Prior and Informed Consent' (n 44).

> Project results for [Indigenous peoples] were not as satisfactory in the energy and mining, transportation, and environment sectors, which comprised 65 percent of Bank commitments evaluated for this second phase, and include projects with significant potential to harm IP [Indigenous peoples]. The majority of these projects neither mitigated adverse effects on IPs nor ensured that they received an equitable share of benefits.[50]

The latest policy OP4.10 provides under paragraph 1 that for all projects proposed for Bank financing that affect Indigenous peoples, the borrower must engage in 'free, prior and informed *consultation*' with Indigenous peoples.[51] The World Bank's formulation has been termed 'FPICon' to distinguish it from FPIC which requires consent. It continues that the Bank 'will provide project financing only where [FPICon] results in broad community support to the project by the affected Indigenous Peoples'. Paragraph 1 further states that Bank-financed projects will include measures to avoid potential adverse effects or where avoidance is 'not feasible' to 'minimize, mitigate, or compensate for such effects'. Paragraph 1 provides that Bank projects will be designed to 'ensure that Indigenous Peoples receive social and economic benefits that are culturally appropriate and gender and inter-generationally inclusive'.

However, Indigenous rights groups have levelled the criticism that the policy fails to uphold international standards of human rights.[52] Issues arise on a number of fronts. First, the phrasing of 'broad community support' has been criticised as setting a confusing and potentially damaging threshold for the amount of community support required by the community.[53] Second, the wording and construction of FPICon requires consultation opposed to consent which can be seen as a watering down of the right. Third, reviews of the World Bank's operations show that:

> Meaningful Indigenous participation remains absent or superficial in the Bank's adjustment and programmatic loans that now form a growing part of its portfolio. At the project and programme level, the assessment confirms that participation is often low grade and so many projects are still experienced as top-down interventions.[54]

50 Cited in McKay, 'The Draft World Bank Operational Policy 4.10' (n 47) 68.

51 World Bank, 'Operational Manual', Indigenous Peoples, Operational Policy 4.10, July 2005, Washington (USA) at 1.

52 See Tom Griffiths, 'Indigenous Peoples and the World Bank: Experiences with Participation' (Forest Peoples Programme 2005).

53 Office of the Compliance Advisor/Ombudsman (CAO) IFC and MIGA, World Bank Group Advisory Note 'IFC's Policy and Performance Standards on Social and Environmental Sustainability and Disclosure Policy, Commentary on IFC's Progress Report on the First 18 Months of Application', 17 December 2007.

54 Griffiths (n 50) at 1.

The Equator Principles have become the most adopted framework for financial institutions and currently 89 financial institutions in 37 countries have adopted the Equator Principles, covering over 70 per cent of international project finance debt in emerging markets.[55] Banks which are signatories are expected to follow procedures for undertaking environmental and social impact studies before disbursing money, and to consult with potentially affected communities.[56] These Principles adopt the Performance Standards of the IFC which include Performance Standard 7 directed at protecting Indigenous rights, including rights to traditional lands and FPIC.

The focus of the Equator Principles and the IFC Performance Standards, which underpin them, is on consultation with affected Indigenous peoples, ensuring proper process and mitigation of effects. Some commentators have argued that the International Performance Standards and the Equator Principles lack substantive standards, procedures and effective grievance mechanisms.[57] Others have argued that not withstanding uncertainty regarding their real impact, the Equator Principles have improved the situation by placing the private sector in a proactive environmental role and strengthening the public's ability to hold the financial sector accountable for its actions.[58]

Case study: Aotearoa, New Zealand

Māori were the first peoples to make their homes in the South Pacific islands of Aotearoa, New Zealand. Europeans began arriving in numbers in the early 1800s. In 1840, the British Crown assumed sovereignty of the country partly in accordance with the Treaty of Waitangi. The 1840 Treaty between many Māori chiefs and the British Crown was signed in two language versions: English and Māori. The Māori version guaranteed ongoing Māori sovereignty of the country while welcoming the British to reside in these lands and govern themselves. In comparison, the English version recorded a transfer of sovereignty from Māori to the British Crown but still recognised the continuing Māori ownership of property including of lands, forests and fisheries until they wished to sell or gift this property to the Crown. Despite the Treaty, the New Zealand government proceeded to pursue policies which

55 To view these Principles see: <www.equator-principles.com/> accessed 17 March 2016.

56 The Equator Principles apply to projects of a total capital cost exceeding US$10 million. Benjamin J. Richardson, 'Protecting Indigenous Peoples through Socially Responsible Investment' (Fall 2007) 6(1) *Indigenous Law Journal* 1, at 21.

57 See Steven Herz and others, 'The International Finance Corporation's Performance Standards and the Equator Principles: Respecting Human Rights and Remedying Violations? A Submission to the U.N. Special Representative to the Secretary General on Human Rights and Transnational Corporations and other Business Enterprises' (August 2008).

58 Andrew Hardenbrook, 'The Equator Principles: The Private Financial Sector's Attempt at Environmental Responsibility' (2007) 40 *Vanderbilt Journal of Transnational Law* 197.

oversaw the transfer of the vast majority of Māori land to the New Zealand government and the new European arrivals. By the end of the 1800s, Māori remained in ownership of very little land. In the 1970s and 1980s, the government began to accept that its actions, or inactions, both historically and currently, could be considered in breach of the Treaty of Waitangi.[59] The government has since been negotiating settlements with Māori tribes with the help of the Waitangi Tribunal, a special commission of inquiry with a mandate to consider Crown breaches of the Treaty. Settlements include financial, commercial and cultural redress.[60]

This part of this chapter provides a brief glimpse into New Zealand law and a contemporary case study of a company seeking to extract iron sand off the west coast of the North Island: the 2016 Trans-Tasman Resources Limited (Trans-Tasman) marine consent application. This case study serves to highlight some of the issues that confront Indigenous peoples and the difficulties they face in ensuring international law and principles are implemented in practice.

Overview of relevant legislation

New Zealand is regarded as a mineral rich country, most prominently in petroleum, iron sands, coal, gold and silver. Three key statutes regulate mining activities in New Zealand. The Crown Minerals Act 1991 provides that all petroleum, gold, silver and uranium are owned by the Crown.[61] Other minerals may be owned by the Crown if a specific reservation has been made.[62] The Crown Minerals Act supports the minerals programmes that establish the policies, procedures and provisions for mining Crown-owned minerals including information on how to seek mining permits.

The Resource Management Act 1991 provides the basis for local authorities to design rules for the sustainable management of natural and physical resources including minerals. In particular, no persons or companies can do anything with land, including mining it, unless the activity is permitted in a local authority plan. If persons and companies wish to extract minerals from land, including seabed land out to the 12 nautical mile boundary, that is not already permitted by a local authority, then resource consents must be sought from the appropriate local authority.

The Exclusive Economic Zone and Continental Shelf (Environmental Effects) Act 2012 (EEZ Act) is relevant in the context of mineral exploration and exploitation in the seabed. This Act promotes the sustainable manage-

59 See Treaty of Waitangi Act 1975 (NZ).

60 For example, see one of the first settlements, the Ngai Tahu Claims Settlement Act. See Janine Hayward and Nicola Wheen (eds), *The Waitangi Tribunal: Te Roopu Whakamana i Te Tiriti o Waitangi* (Bridget William Books 2004).

61 Crown Minerals Act 1991 (NZ) s 10.

62 Crown Minerals Act 1991 (NZ) s 11.

ment of natural and physical resources in the exclusive economic zone and the continental shelf. The general rule is that no person can do any activity in the exclusive economic zone or in or on the continental shelf unless the activity is a permitted activity authorised by a marine consent. The Environmental Protection Authority issues marine consents.

All three of these statutes require those making decisions to have a certain level of regard to the principles of the Treaty of Waitangi and to Māori interests in natural resources. For example, section 124 of the EEZ Act sets out steps that decision makers under the Act must take 'in order to recognise and respect the Crown's responsibility to give effect to the principles of the Treaty of Waitangi'. Meanwhile, section 8 of the Resource Management Act provides 'All persons exercising functions and powers under this Act shall have regard to the principles of the Treaty of Waitangi (Te Tiriti o Waitangi)'.

In New Zealand, those seeking to extract minerals need to obtain a series of government consents and permits. Depending on the mineral sought, mineral permits under the Crown Minerals Act, marine consents under the EEZ Act for activities in the EEZ, and resource consents under the Resource Management Act will typically be required. Local governments regulate resource consents. The Environmental Protection Authority regulates marine consents. Decisions can be taken on appeal to the Environment Court and then onto the subsequent appeal courts.

While New Zealand's legislation has a number of distinct provisions which provide a degree of recognition that Māori should be consulted and considered in decision-making regarding minerals, it has not fully embraced relevant international law standards. The Waitangi Tribunal, in its Petroleum Report, found that these Acts were deficient in ensuring Māori interests, finding that there is a lack of protections for sacred sites, unsuitable time frames for consultation, no requirements to fund Māori participation and insufficient consideration given to Māori interests in decision-making.[63] With respect to companies, the Report discussed how Māori tribes were disappointed that they had been unable to secure benefits from petroleum developments, how they felt their interests were not fully considered by companies, and that companies had not been unwilling to pay for Māori participation in petroleum developments (including the provision of cultural impact assessments).[64] Furthermore, the government asserted ownership of petroleum and gold is a particularly contentious issue. Māori have sought to negotiate their continuing customary ownership of petroleum and gold, but the government has so far refused to recognise any continuing Māori property interests in these minerals.[65] The exception is the

63 Waitangi Tribunal, *The Petroleum Management Report* (Legislation Direct, 2011) at 173.

64 Ibid, at 83, 96–97.

65 Waitangi Tribunal, *The Petroleum Report* (Legislation Direct 2003); Waitangi Tribunal, *The Hauraki Inquiry* (Legislation Direct, 2006); Craig Coxhead, 'Māori Title to Petroleum: The Waitangi Tribunal Petroleum Report' (2004) 7 *Yearbook of New Zealand Jurisprudence* 66.

culturally significant jade (pounamu) that is now recognised as the property of one tribe.[66]

Investment in New Zealand's mining sector

The New Zealand government is actively seeking to grow the economic potential of mineral extraction. New Zealand Petroleum & Minerals is the government agency established to lead and actively manage New Zealand's petroleum and minerals portfolio. One of its flagship initiatives is to promote 'doing business in New Zealand'. It prominently highlights that companies should invest in New Zealand on its website for these reasons:[67]

- stable and predictable regime delivering certainty for investors with a simple tax system noting 28 per cent corporate income tax and no capital gains tax;
- sophisticated infrastructure and skilled workforce with established and reliable transport and electricity markets and high quality technical support sector services;
- active jurisdiction for investment in petroleum, ranked 14th in investment attractiveness among 126 countries and ranked 8th in the geological database;
- ranked 1st for ease of doing business among 190 nations;
- low country risk, corruption free and transport governance providing certainty to investors;
- a government focused on business growth reputation.

Many companies with significant foreign connections already operate (or seek to operate) in New Zealand including Shell New Zealand (as a subsidiary of Royal Dutch Shell), Newmont Mining Corporation, Oceana Gold, OMV, Orcia and up until recently Anadarko and Petrobras. This chapter now turns to briefly discuss the Trans-Tasman Resources Limited marine consent application.

Trans-Tasman Resources Limited's marine consent application

Trans-Tasman Resources Limited is recorded as a privately owned New Zealand company established in 2007, although it likely has international links through shareholding. In November 2013, Trans-Tasman applied to

66 See Ngai Tahu (Pounamu Vesting) Act 1997 (NZ). Nicola Wheen, 'Legislating for Indigenous Peoples' Ownership and Management of Minerals; A New Zealand Case Study on Pounamu' (2009) 20(5) *Management of Environmental Quality: An International Journal* 551.

67 New Zealand Petroleum and Minerals, 'Why Invest in New Zealand' <www.nzpam.govt.nz/doing-business/why-invest> accessed 9 March 2017.

the Environmental Protection Authority ('Authority') to undertake iron ore extraction in an area of 65.76 square kilometres off the coast of South Taranaki in the west of the North Island.[68] This was the first application in New Zealand to be decided under the EEZ Act. In 2014, the Authority refused the marine consent because the application was premature.

The decision cited numerable concerns with the overall uncertainty and inadequacy of information presented by Trans-Tasman, including lack of clarity about the extent of economic benefits for New Zealand as opposed to impacts, and the potential adverse effects it could have on existing interests such as Māori and fishing interests.

The decision set a strong precedent as to how the EEZ Act should be interpreted to provide for meaningful Māori input. The Authority interpreted the EEZ Act's Treaty provision to be 'more fulsome'[69] than its counterpart in section 8 of the Resource Management Act. The decision listed that under the EEZ Act the Authority has to notify relevant Māori groups of marine consent applications, receive advice from the Authority's statutorily required Māori Advisory Committee and take into account existing interests of Māori among others.[70] The Authority understood the EEZ Act to anticipate the special relationship of Māori with the sea and their role as cultural guardians as 'an integral part of the factual matrix within which decisions on natural resource use, development and protection should be made'.[71] Furthermore, it acknowledged the necessity of understanding how Māori existing interests are defined and how a proposal might affect Māori including Māori knowledge.

The Authority held that Trans-Tasman's marine consent application could adversely affect the local tribes 'in more than a minor way',[72] especially potentially impacting on Māori customary and commercial fishing, sacred sites, social and economic implications and responsibilities of guardianship. The Authority noted problems with Trans-Tasman's consultation with tribes as weakening its proposal, at least in terms of Trans-Tasman's ability to assess and provide for the tribe's existing interests.[73] Similarly, the Authority expressed concerns that Trans-Tasman had proposed conditions for its project that would provide a significant role for the tribe if the marine consent was granted, but had not involved the tribe in designing these conditions; nor had Trans-Tasman demonstrated that the tribe were willing and able to be involved in the manner proposed or that they felt the conditions were

68 Environmental Protection Authority, *Trans-Tasman Resources Limited Marine Consent Decision* (17 June 2014). See Benjamin Ralston and Jacinta Ruru, 'Landmark EPA Decision' [2014] NZLJ 284.

69 *Trans-Tasman Resources Limited Marine Consent Decision* (n 64) [95].

70 Ibid [96].

71 Ibid [97].

72 Ibid [624] and [642].

73 Ibid [128] and [624].

appropriate.[74] While this initial 2014 decision illustrated that the provisions in New Zealand's legislation can be effective in protecting Māori interests, the essential message in that decision was that the application was 'premature' rather than fatal.

Unsurprisingly perhaps, in August 2016, Trans-Tasman reapplied to undertake iron ore extraction and processing in the South Taranaki Bight. At the time of writing, the Environmental Protection Authority is considering the marine consent application. The local Māori tribes remain opposed to the application.[75]

The initial Trans-Tasman application, and now the subsequent application, illustrate how Indigenous peoples often need to fight hard to have their basic rights based in domestic and international law heard and recognised. Key components of FPIC, such as the right to sufficient information and consultation periods that are in line with traditional decision-making, often prove difficult in the domestic consenting process. For example, when filing its application in August 2016 for a marine consent, Trans-Tasman Resources sought to restrict publication of what it considered sensitive information. The Environmental Protection Authority agreed with Trans-Tasman Resources resulting in the information becoming confidential. Several environmental groups and a Māori tribe appealed this decision to the Environment Court seeking to make the entire redacted documents available to the public. The Environment Court accepted their argument finding that the 'public's right to participate effectively in the consent process, outweigh[s] any trade secret or business prejudice interest of Trans-Tasman by a considerable margin'.[76]

The fast moving and short time frames of domestic consenting application processes often frustrate Indigenous peoples' abilities to participate in the process. This has certainly been a feature of both the first and second Trans-Tasman marine consent applications. Both applications were submitted in spring, therefore requiring those opposing the applications to prepare expert evidence over the traditional Southern Hemisphere summer holidays. The 2016 application in particular, required expert evidence to be submitted at the height of the holidays in January. These tight deadlines can make it near impossible for many Indigenous groups to prepare a well-evidenced defence.

In the view of the tribes, the need to consult has been triggered because the excavating of iron sands will impact on their self-determination and cultural guardianship responsibilities over the area by damaging the fragile ecosystem. They are also concerned that the activity could negatively impact

74 Ibid [632], [636] and [641].

75 Jeremy Wilkinson, 'All eight Taranaki iwi united against 'misleading' mining company' *Stuff news online* (29 September 2016) <www.stuff.co.nz/business/84664185/All-eight-Taranaki-iwi-united-against-misleading-mining-company> accessed 9 March 2017.

76 *Kiwis against Seabed Mining Incorporated v Environmental Protection Authority* [2016] NZEnvC 217 at [68].

their commercial fisheries interests. While Trans-Tasman are seeking to engage with the tribes, the nature of consultation including when and to what purpose are pressing questions for the tribes.

Even though Trans-Tasman might consider that their proposed activity will not have a significant impact on the tribes, any activity carried out in tribal territory should be treated with caution given the close association they have with their lands and waters and their interests in fisheries and other offshore resources. The fact that the tribes do not formally own the seabed where the iron sands lie should not undermine the right to FPIC. While land rights may not have received formal recognition domestically, international law recognises continuing customary ownership, use and occupation.

New Zealand's legislation does not make provision for Māori, as distinct from the general population, to share in the benefits of mining. The domestic legislation is also weak on requirements for company engagement with tribes and has not been particularly responsive to business and human rights. The New Zealand government, for example, has no national strategic plan on business and human rights and has been slow to prompt a shift in the culture of mining companies in New Zealand. The Ministry of Business, Innovation and Employment has a link on its website to the Treaty of Waitangi which lists principles for companies to consider when engaging with Māori, including the recommendation to engage with tribes 'before a permit application is lodged but most certainly once an application has been accepted and granted'.[77] Detailed advice in a 'Best Practice Guidelines for Engagement with Māori' commissioned partly by the Ministry and prepared by a tribe provides excellent advice, but there are no legal requirements for companies to follow these guidelines.[78]

Research has identified that the surrounding legal framework has a strong role to play in the extent to which companies build successful relationships with Indigenous peoples.[79] Domestic law should keep up with international law developments to ensure investments in resource extraction are respectful of Indigenous peoples. And, businesses must be both cognisant and active in implementing international law principles in all their activities.

In New Zealand, the Crown Minerals Act requires businesses with mineral permits to produce annual Māori engagement reports.[80] This is a positive requirement, however, legislation does not provide for any repercussions if companies fail to engage with Māori and reports are not made public.

77 'Permit holder engagement with Māori' <www.nzpam.govt.nz/doing-business/maori-waitangi/permit-holder-engagement> accessed 9 March 2017.

78 See 'Best Practice Guidelines for Engagement with Māori' (August 2014) <www.nzpam.govt.nz/assets/Uploads/doing-business/engagement-with-maori-guidelines.pdf> accessed 9 March 2017.

79 Ciaran O'Faircheallaigh and Tony Corbett, 'Indigenous Participation in Environmental Management of Mining Projects: The Role of Negotiated Agreements' (2005) 14(5) *Environmental Politics* 629, 644.

80 Crown Minerals Act 1991 (NZ) s 33.

Confidentiality is a core issue that affects transparency of foreign and domestic investments in natural resources.[81] It would also be useful for domestic legislation to require that the past relationship that companies have had with Māori and/or other Indigenous peoples be taken into account when consent authorities are considering permits. This would give companies a consequential interest in proper engagement with Indigenous peoples.

Conclusion

This chapter has discussed some of the advancements made in international human rights law regarding mineral rights for Indigenous peoples, particularly the right of FPIC which has found recognition in numerous UN reports and in the UN Declaration. Furthermore, business and human rights, as expressed in the United Nations' Guiding Principles on Business and Human Rights and the UN Global Compact, have made clear that companies and financial institutions must respect human rights. Such developments have prompted some states to revise their practices, while a number of companies including mining and petroleum companies have established policies on corporate accountability to communities affected by their activities.[82] International financial institutions such as the World Bank have also adopted policies.

In many respects, New Zealand has a robust regulatory process for environmental regulation and extractive industry, including important distinctive protections for Maori interests. However, in some regards it falls short of international standards, demonstrating that significantly more attention is required about how to translate rights, such as the right to FPIC, into domestic regimes. The analysis presented demonstrates that in practice Māori experience significant obstacles in having their right to FPIC respected. Key issues include short time frames for consultation and processes which are not cognisant of the limited resources and time that tribes have. Furthermore, in the case of Trans-Tasman, affected tribes experienced significant issues in obtaining the information they needed to make an informed decision about the proposal, in the end resorting to judicial proceedings to obtain the information they wanted. International literature demonstrates that these are issues are not unique to Māori and that reform is needed to ensure Indigenous rights are effectively implemented in practice.[83]

81 Ciaran O'Faircheallaigh and Tony Corbett, 'Indigenous Participation in Environmental Management of Mining Projects: The Role of Negotiated Agreements' (2005) 14(5) *Environmental Politics* 629.

82 See Ministry for Foreign Affairs, *Action Plan for Business and Human Rights* (Government Offices of Sweden 24 August 2015).

83 Jon Altman, 'Indigenous Rights, Mining Corporations and the Australian State' in Suzana Sawyer and Edmund T. Gomez (eds), *The Politics of Resource Extraction: Indigenous Peoples, Multinational Corporations, Multilateral Institutions and the State* (Palgrave Macmillan Ltd 2012) 46–74.

Research has also shown that the surrounding legal framework has a strong role to play in whether or not companies build successful relationships with Indigenous peoples.[84] We argue that while businesses must be active in implementing international law in their activities irrespective of the domestic setting, states also need to ensure that the surrounding legislation encourages companies to respect human rights.

Furthermore, for Indigenous peoples there are outstanding questions about the ownership of natural resources including minerals. As discussed, international laws such as ILO 169 and the Declaration do not expressly confer Indigenous peoples with minerals rights (in the case of ILO 169 the right of states to continue to manage nationalised minerals is explicitly recognised).[85] However, Indigenous rights over natural resources can be inferred from the right of self-determination. It is our view that states such as New Zealand need to engage seriously with Indigenous claims to ownership of minerals, including minerals that have been nationalised in the public interest, such as petroleum.

84 Ciaran O'Faircheallaigh and Tony Corbett, 'Indigenous Participation in Environmental Management of Mining Projects: The Role of Negotiated Agreements' (2005) 14(5) *Environmental Politics* 629, 644.

85 ILO 169 (n 13) Art 15.

14 Financing energy resources and sustainable development

Priscilla Schwartz

Energy and sustainable development policy

Developing countries particularly in sub-Saharan Africa need access to basic infrastructure services, improved service quality and efficient service delivery. Energy is a creative force of life from which human beings and the environment are sustained for development.[1] It is required to fuel hospitals, schools, transportation and other productive activities that support development. Demand for primary energy will reportedly increase by 80 per cent in lower-income countries (LICs) by 2035, requiring an additional annual average investment of US$36 billion.[2]

Energy resources refer to the means by which we obtain energy to generate power for electricity and energy services for household, industrial or commercial use. They include renewable energy resources like wind power, hydropower, solar power, tidal power, geothermal power, bio-power (agro residues or cogeneration-bagasse), waste to energy (e.g. municipal solid waste to energy or industrial waste energy) and fossil fuel resources.[3]

Generally, most energy resources policies do not focus on the social dimension beyond the environmental impact of burning fossil fuel, pollution issues, public unrest for energy security and the domestic 'energy rich' and 'energy poor' gap problems.[4] However, over the past decades the role that energy plays in sustainable development policy has become more defined through several international instruments integrating energy in the three dimensions of sustainability: economic, environmental and social.[5]

1 'In the beginning God created the heaven and the earth ... And the Spirit of God moved upon the face of the waters. And God said, Let there be light: and there was light'. Genesis 1:1–3 (KJV)

2 Richard K. Lattanzio, 'The World Bank Group Energy Sector Strategy Analyst in Environmental Policy' (Congressional Research Services Report, April 16, 2013) 4

3 Nuclear energy is in a unique category outside identified sustainable energy resources

4 A.F. Alhaji, 'What Is Energy Security? Economic, Environmental, Social, Foreign Policy, Technical and Security Dimensions' (2008) 3 *Oil, Gas & Energy Law Journal* 3; Lattanzio (n 2) 4

5 See *Report of the United Nations Conference on Environment and Development*, UN Doc A/CONF.151/26 (Vol 1) (12 August 1992) annex 1 Rio de Janeiro, 3–14 June 1992

In designating the 'International Year of Sustainable Energy for All', the United Nations stressed the need for an integrated approach to energy issues for the promotion of synergies across the global energy agenda for sustainable development.[6] Sustainability in energy policy has evolved from nuanced contemplation in Agenda 21, to an explicit poverty reduction tool, an environmental protection mechanism and an energy efficiency and climate enhancing agenda.[7] The international community has stressed the importance of energy in a call for joint action to improve access to reliable and affordable energy towards mitigating poverty and for investments in clean energy technology, renewable energy and an appropriate regulatory framework.[8]

More recently, Agenda 2030 Sustainable Development Goal 7 (SDG7) calls on states to take practical actions to 'ensure access to affordable, reliable, sustainable, and modern energy for all'.[9] It identifies specific strategies for financing the implementation of the SDGs, including the mobilisation of financial resources to developing states, especially the role of public and private sector finance.[10] Agenda 2030 adopts the Addis Ababa Action Agenda (AAAA) on financing for development as integral to attaining full

and Vol I, Resolutions Adopted by the Conference (United Nations Publication, Sales No. E.93.I.8) Resolution 1, annex I: and Agenda 21 annex II (UNCED Report); *Report of the World Summit on Sustainable Development*, UN Doc A/CONF.199/20 (4 September 2002) Chapter I, Resolution 2, annex 4 (WSSD Report); *The Future We Want*, GA Res 288, UN GAOR, 66th sess, 123rd plen mtg, Agenda Item 19, UN Doc A/RES/66/288 (11 September 2012, adopted 27 July 2012) annex Energy Section D paras 125–129 (Rio+20, 2012); *Transforming our World: The 2030 Agenda for Sustainable Development*, GA Res 1, 70th sess, 4th plen mtg, Agenda Items 15 and 116, UN Doc A/RES/70/1 (21 October 2015) (Agenda 2030); see generally Priscilla Schwartz, 'Sustainable Energy Infrastructure: Law, Policy and Practice' (2009) 2 *International Journal of Private Law* 135

6 *International Year of Sustainable Energy for All*, GA Res 151, 65th sess, 69th plen mtg, Agenda Item 20, UN Doc A/RES/65/151 (16 February 2011); see also *Promotion of New and Renewable Sources of Energy: Report of the Secretary-General*, UN GAOR, 69th sess, provisional Agenda Item 19(i), UN Doc A/69/323 (18 August 2014)

7 Agenda 21, Chapters 7, 9 and 14. Energy and mining are key sectors not included as individual chapters; see UNCED Report. See also *Review of Implementation of Agenda 21 and the Rio Principles* (Stakeholder Forum for a Sustainable Future, United Nations, 2012) <https://sustainabledevelopment.un.org/content/documents/641Synthesis_report_Web.pdf> accessed 3 April 2016; also *Report of the World Summit on Sustainable Development*, UN Doc A/CONF.199/20 (4 September 2002) annex ('World Summit on Sustainable Development: Plan of Implementation') (WSSD/POI) <www.un.org/esa/sustdev/documents/WSSD_POI_PD/English/WSSD_PlanImpl.pdf> accessed 23 May 2016; and *Transforming our World: 2030 Agenda for Sustainable Development*, UNGA Resolution A/RES/70/1 (Agenda 2030)

8 WSSD/POI ibid s.II (9); WSSD Report Ch. I, Resolution 2, para. 20 (e)

9 Sustainable Energy for All (SE4All) (a global UN initiative); see www.se4all.org/. See also Agenda 2030 para 27

10 Agenda 2030 SDG 17(1)–(5)

implementation and realisation of the SDGs.[11] The AAAA sets out core financing principles (AAAA/CFPs) for achieving the Agenda 2030 SDGs and identifies the role of multilateral development banks (MDBs) as particularly essential to this purpose.

The following section of this chapter presents the global financing framework through analyses of the AAAA/CFPs in the context of energy sustainability and the role of MDBs as the essential catalyst in addressing the objectives of Sustainable Energy for All (SE4All). The chapter then examines financing and investment arrangements of MDBs especially the World Bank, the Global Environmental Facility (GEF) and the Africa50 initiatives, in an attempt to illustrate the practice of applying the AAAA/CFPs in addressing varying forms of energy resources to ensure SE4All. The following section then engages in a critical assessment of energy resources financing practice in the sector in relation to the AAAA to reveal the pertinent issues of sustainability. The issue areas serve to provide guidance for energy policy planning and investment decision-making on the choice of financing instruments, sources and methods, relative to the energy resources, that are viable to promote sustainable energy development, particularly for developing countries.

The global financing framework in energy context

One of the main objectives of the AAAA is to strengthen the financial framework and the means of implementation of sustainable development post-2015.[12] It envisages a holistic implementation approach to the SDGs that integrates the economic, environmental and social dimensions of sustainable development.[13] The AAAA calls for the mobilisation of international and domestic public finance to provide essential energy resources (e.g. fossil fuel and renewable energy sources) for electricity and energy services. States and MDBs are to mobilise official development assistance (ODA) and catalyse private sector energy investment.[14]

States should endeavour to provide support (financial and technical) for initiatives that facilitate the development of sustainable, accessible and

11 See Agenda 2030 *supra* note 5 ss.40 and 62; *Addis Ababa Action Agenda of the Third International Conference on Financing for Development* UNIGA /RES/69/313, s.2 ('the AAAA'). Previous financing strategy can be found in the Rio+20 *supra* note 5 section VI para 252; *Doha Declaration on Financing for Development: Outcome Document of the Follow-up International Conference on Financing for Development to Review the Implementation of the Monterrey Consensus* Doha, Qatar, 29 November–2 December 2008 UN (2009). A/CONF.212/L.1/Rev.; and *Report of the International Conference on Financing for Development*, Monterrey, Mexico, 18–22 March 2002 (United Nations publication, Sales No. E.02.II.A.7), chap. I, resolution 1, annex (Monterrey Consensus)

12 AAAA s.2

13 AAAA ss.2 and 11

14 AAAA s.14; e.g. micro-enterprises; cooperatives; MNCs; civil society organisations; and philanthropic organisations

resilient quality energy infrastructure in developing countries and emerging economies in order to bridge the global infrastructure gap.[15] The Global Infrastructure Facility (GIF) of the World Bank and the Africa50 Infrastructure Fund are notable among the new financing initiatives.[16] Also, the GEF must play a role in energy resources financing, especially in mainstreaming environmental concerns into energy development efforts.[17]

Aiming to channel public and private investments in energy infrastructure, renewable energy, clean energy technologies, energy efficiency and conservation, the AAAA recognises the need for international cooperation on energy research and technology, the need to expand infrastructure and upgrade technology, and the need for the supply of modern sustainable energy services to all developing countries.[18] States are called on to take action (e.g. develop action agendas and investment prospectuses) to raise 'over $100 billion in annual investments by 2020, through market-based initiatives, partnerships and leveraging development banks'.[19] The AAAA thus lends support to several cooperative initiatives on energy, including SE4All.[20]

On the institutional front, the AAAA endorses the launch of the new infrastructure gap-bridging forum initiative that will encourage 'greater range of voices to be heard, particularly from developing countries', on how to identify and address the energy infrastructure and capacity gaps in poor countries.[21] This global infrastructure forum is structured on existing multilateral collaboration that is led by the MDBs.[22] The forum functions to identify investment opportunities for the infrastructure gap economies and to ensure that such investments are environmentally, socially and economically sustainable.[23] It also provides a platform to advocate the transfer of environmentally sound energy technologies to developing countries, on favourable concessional or preferential terms.[24]

15 AAAA s.14
16 AAAA s.14; others are Asian Infrastructure Investment Bank; the Global Infrastructure Hub; the New Development Bank; the Asia Pacific Project Preparation Facility; as well as the increase in the capital of the Inter-American Investment Corporation
17 AAAA s.76
18 AAAA s.49
19 AAAA s.49
20 <www.se4all.org/about-us> (accessed 24/05/2016). Other energy initiatives include: Power Africa, NEPAD's Africa Power Vision and IRENA's Global Renewable Energy Islands Network
21 AAAA s.14
22 The forum is to hold periodic meetings that will enhance 'alignment and coordination' among infrastructure initiatives (old and new), MDBs, national development banks, UN agencies, domestic institutions, development partners and the private sector
23 AAAA s.14
24 AAAA s.2

Energy resources financing methods

The main financing methods proposed in the AAAA to ensure SE4All goals derive from the following broad categories: effective use of domestic resources, domestic and international private business finance, international development cooperation, international trade, debt sustainability, technology innovation and capacity building.

Domestic resources mobilisation policies and strategies focus on how to maintain effective taxing systems, including efficient tax collection, combating tax evasion and avoidance, transparency and to broaden the base to include the informal sector and to improve tax policy generally.[25] In addition to an effective tax system, states agree to take steps to rationalise inefficient fossil fuel subsidies, remove market distortions and phase out harmful subsidies.[26] They further commit to also establish or strengthen bond markets to help subnational authorities finance necessary energy resources investments. National and regional development banks have a role to ensure sound private sector lending for sustainable energy infrastructure and to finance medium and small–medium enterprises (MSMEs) in the credit market segment in complicity with environmental and social safeguards.[27] MDBs (and other financial institutions) are encouraged to assist in financing the necessary domestic investments and especially cater for risk mitigation mechanisms.[28]

In terms of domestic and international private business, the AAAA calls for support (public and private) of business activity through finance, investment and innovation. Private international capital flows, particularly foreign direct investment (FDI), are vital for this purpose. It also seeks to encourage 'impact investing', i.e. the combination of return on investment with non-financial impacts. Incentives such as insurance and guarantee schemes and new and innovative financial instruments are important tools for attracting FDI into energy resources in developing countries, but these must be aligned with public goals, including incentivising the adoption of sustainable practices.[29]

Moreover, the AAAA advocates increased lending to MSMEs (including women-owned enterprises) in project arrangements that are aligned with national and regional sustainable energy projects. Direct investment is invaluable in this regard, especially to aid the development of know-how and energy technology through establishing linkages with domestic suppliers and integrating local MSMEs from developing countries into regional and global value chains.[30]

25 AAAA ss.20–27
26 AAAA s.31
27 AAAA ss.31–33
28 AAAA s.34
29 AAAA ss.35–37 and 45
30 AAAA ss.43 and 45

The AAAA envisages that a high up-take of renewable energy projects is desired in order to complement the use of fossil fuels and mitigate the threat of climate change and ensure energy efficiency to achieve SE4All by 2030. This outcome can only be realised through financing the development of renewable energy technologies, transfers of such technologies, knowledge and skills and skills trading programmes within a market-based framework, which fosters *inter alia*, linkages between MNCs and MSMEs through mutually agreed terms.[31] Also, 'philanthropic donors' can leverage additional funds through multi-stakeholder partnerships to develop innovative energy technology projects.[32] Public finance and policies should play an important role in research and technological development and setting up innovation funds on a competitive basis.[33]

One of the main sources recommended for financing infrastructure projects at all levels are development banks and development finance agencies. Development partners are called on to support energy projects through concessional and non-concessional financing and to ensure that ODA assistance for LICs is generally secure.[34] Development banks are to begin lending for energy infrastructure projects and also leverage contributions and capital, and play a catalytic role in mobilising resources from capital markets.[35] The range of 'tools and mechanisms' that they could utilise includes public–private partnerships (PPP),[36] blended finance,[37] nonrecourse project financing,[38] special purpose vehicles, risk mitigation instruments and pooled funding structures.[39] Parties in blended energy resources financing

31 AAAA ss.116–118

32 AAAA s.42; for examples of such partnerships, see L.M. MacLean and J.N. Brass, 'Foreign Aid, NGOs and the Private Sector: New Forms of Hybridity in Renewable Energy Provision in Kenya and Uganda in Africa Today' 62(1) Special Issue: *The Politics of Non-State Provision of Public Goods in Africa* (Indiana University Press 2015) 57–82

33 AAAA ss.116–118

34 AAAA ss.50–54; the ODA target is 0.7 per cent of ODA/GNI and 0.15 to 0.20 per cent of ODA/GNI

35 AAAA s.70

36 For insight into PPPs, see P. Schwartz, 'Public Private Partnerships and Government Services in LDCs: Regulatory Paradoxes' in Szyszczak et al. (eds) *Developments in Services of General Interest* (TMC Asser Press, 2011) 197–228

37 Blended finance (including PPPs) combines concessional public finance with non-concessional private finance and expertise from the public and private sector. It tends to lower investment specific risks and incentivise additional private sector finance in the sector

38 This is a financing structure in which debt, equity and credit enhancement combine for use in the construction and operation or the refinancing of a capital-intensive power facility. It is 'nonrecourse' because the debt terms are predicated completely on the merits of the particular project (i.e. on the assets, revenue-producing project contracts and other cash flow generated by the facility). For insight on energy project finance, see Donggen Xu, 'Legal Aspects of International Project Finance for Sustainable Energy Development' in Bradbrook et al. (eds) *The Law of Energy for Sustainable Development* (IUCN Academy of Environmental Law Research Studies, 2012) 487–506; K.C. Baragona, 'Project Finance' (2004–2005) *Transnational Law* 18 139

39 AAAA s.48

arrangements should share the risks and rewards fairly and should include clear accountability mechanisms for meeting social and environmental standards.[40] Countries must build capacity to be involved in PPP arrangements, especially in the areas of 'planning, contract negotiation, and management, accounting and budgeting for contingent liabilities'.[41] The GEF must play a role in energy resources financing especially in mainstreaming environmental concerns into energy development efforts.[42]

Within the framework of these strategic sources and action points, the role of both public and private finance and investment is crucial to facilitating the achievement of SE4All. The next section examines the World Bank's GIF, the GEF and Africa50 in financing and investment practices applying the AAAA/CFPs in energy infrastructure projects, renewable energy and low-carbon technology development and commercialisation.

Application of AAAA in energy financing practice

To achieve SDG7, the AAAA recommends public and private financing and investments in energy infrastructure (grid and off grid), renewable energy, clean energy technology that promotes energy efficiency in demand and supply and innovative projects and programmes that aim at substantially increasing the share of renewable energy, efficiency and conservation.

The AAAA core principles for financing energy resources are:

- effective taxing regimes that include the informal sector and combat tax avoidance;
- MDBs and national and regional development banks (NRDBs) to facilitate energy infrastructure lending and risk mitigation mechanisms to local MSMEs with environmental and social safeguards;
- NRDBs to finance energy technology development and know-how, establish linkages with domestic suppliers and MSMEs and integrate them into regional and global value chains;
- MDBs to catalyse the mobilisation of resources from capital markets using project finance, blended finance, special purpose vehicles (SPVs) and risk management instruments;
- encourage FDI with consideration for 'impact investing';
- public and private financing of renewable energy technology and transfer, research and development of innovative technology, setting up innovation funds and skills trading programmes within a market -based framework;
- development partners to support energy projects on concessional and non-concessional financing including through the target ODA for LICs.

40 AAAA s.48
41 AAAA s.48
42 AAAA s.76

The World Bank

The World Bank[43] adopts a strategy that pursues its core mission of poverty alleviation and environmental sustainability.[44] The AAAA/CFPs advocating infrastructure lending, risk mitigation mechanisms and environmental compliance procedures are basic to World Bank energy resources financing. Its policy on energy infrastructure finance aims to provide access to energy services to foster economic development, support household energy programmes, and ensure long-term environmental sustainability of the sector while addressing climate change.[45] In 2010, lending for energy infrastructure projects by the Bank accounted for upstream exploration, new and upgraded power generation facilities, 'transmission and distribution systems, demand side management and energy efficiency programs, and policy and technical advice, totalling investment of $13 billion'.[46]

The World Bank is ahead in mainstreaming risk mitigation tools like guarantees and risk insurance (e.g. partial risk guarantee, partial credit guarantees and Multilateral Investment Guarantee Agency (MIGA) guarantees) to cushion developing countries' borrowing vulnerability and calm investor risk perception to enhance capital flows into energy infrastructure. For example, the Kenya Private Sector Power Generation Support Project used ODA as credit enhancements to leverage International Development Association (IDA) resources through a partial risk guarantee (PRG) of $166 million equivalent 'to back-stop liquidity support for certain ongoing payment obligations from Kenya's national power utility to private project developers'.[47] It has also developed 'catastrophic risk insurance', which works to transfer disaster risk from the government to the financial market, thereby increasing the financial resilience of developing countries.[48] Under the India Solar Power Guarantee Facility ($150 million) for instance, the World Bank covered up to 50 per cent of the payment default risk on commercial bank loans of up to 15 years to developers of small solar power projects in the private sector.[49]

43 'World Bank' is used loosely to refer also to the affiliates including the International Bank for Reconstruction and Development (IBRD), International Finance Corporation (IFC), the International Development Association (IDA) and the Multilateral Investment Guarantee Agency (MIGA), but more specific references will be made to the activities and practice of the respective entity as appropriate

44 World Bank *Energizing Sustainable Development: Energy Sector Strategy of the World Bank Group* (World Bank ESS, 2011)

45 World Bank/ESS, ibid.

46 R.K. Lattanzio, *supra* note 2, 5; see generally G.E. Metcalf, 'Investment in Energy Infrastructure and the Tax Code' (2010) 24 *Tax Policy and the Economy* 1 1–34

47 World Bank *Financing for Development Post-2015* (World Bank, 2013) 21–22 (World Bank/FfD Post-2015). The IDA allocation involved was $41.5 million. Note that in Kenya only 25 per cent of the population has access to electricity and rural grid access is only 5 per cent

48 Ibid 25

49 Ibid. See critique on the Bank's risk guarantee system: A. Oni, 'The World Bank/Nigerian Government Partial Risk Guarantee and the Nigerian Gas to Power Challenge: An Introduction' (2011) *Oil, Gas & Energy Law* 5

A more modern risk mitigating instrument used by the World Bank (and MDBs) is the first loss guarantee in equity or debt funds.[50] Under the scheme, governments participate in the 'equity tranche' of a product (e.g. energy technology) in return for taking the first loss risk. So that while the government gets to provide a first loss guarantee to private investors, the taxpayers get to share the profit on the investment.[51]

The conventional fossil fuels industry and service industry remain capital intensive and the most revenue oriented and economically attractive enterprises for the host country and international oil companies. Oil rich states commonly rely on tax instruments, regulation or direct state equity participation as a vehicle to achieve their petroleum development goals.[52] Key financing techniques to access capital for oil and gas exploitation include equity kicker transactions and net profit interest deals, volumetric production payments net, royalty trusts and mezzanine finance[53] and modern asset pricing methods.[54] But in a depressed economic environment triggered by financial crises, suppressed commodity prices and lower asset values, term loans and revolvers, which have been the financing modus over decades, face tightened underwriting criteria and increased regulatory constraints.[55]

The World Bank aims to move away from financing climate-harmful coal fired power generation by eliminating loans for new coal based projects and providing finance to improve the efficiency of existing plants.[56] All new energy investment projects, commencing after 2012, undergo a greenhouse gas emissions analysis programme.[57] But the Bank has been criticised for funding the Medupi Power Station project, a coal fired power plant in Lephalale, South Africa.[58] The project obtained Bank approval for Clean Development Mechanism (CDM) funding, despite the prospect of the plant emitting an estimated 25 million tons of carbon a year.[59]

50 World Bank/FfD Post-2015, *supra* note 47 25

51 Ibid; other de-risking instruments include currency loans, swaps and derivatives

52 See generally Adebola Ogunlade, 'How Can Government Best Achieve its Objectives for Petroleum Development: Taxation and Regulation or State Participation?' (2010) 8 *Oil, Gas & Energy Law Journal*, available at <www.ogel.org/article.asp?key=3052>

53 Craig W. Murray, 'Energy Finance in the New Industry Economics' (2009) *Annual Institute on Mineral Law* 56 394–420 at 411. Mezzanine finance is a level of financing which exceeds the risk profile of traditional bank finance and commands higher interest rates. For investment legal frameworks, see N. Mustafayev, 'The Legal Frameworks for Foreign Investments in Upstream Petroleum Industry of Azerbaijan' (2013) *Oil, Gas & Energy Law Journal* 11

54 David G. Laughton, 'The Potential for Use of Modern Asset Pricing Methods for Upstream Petroleum Project Evaluation' (1998) 19 *The Energy Journal* 1

55 Murray (n 53) 394–395

56 World Bank/ESS *supra* (n 44) 11–13 (i.e. an enhanced focus on 'Greenfield' and 'Brownfield' projects

57 Ibid

58 The Medupi project is owned by the state-owned utility company Eskom Holdings, Ltd. See <www.power-technology.com/projects/medupi-power/> (accessed 02/05/2016)

59 Ibid

Another AAAA core principle visible in the World Bank practice relates to public and private financing of infrastructure, renewable energy technology development and transfer and skills trading programmes within a market-based framework. The Bank aims to expand access to modern energy services to about 30 million people between 2012 and 2020 and to ensure additional energy access to 65 million to 80 million people in sub-Saharan Africa through financing the construction of generation capacity of about 8–12GW.[60] For example the World Bank has entered into a 'joint engagement' with the IDA, IFC and MIGA for the recently approved $138 million 'comprehensive and complementary financial package' to finance the Western Area Power Generation Project for the development of a 57MW heavy fuel oil greenfield thermal power plant in Sierra Leone.[61] The IFC will also lead in organising a credit line of $70 million for the project.[62] Two further World Bank projects for network upgrades (the Energy Access Project and the Energy Sector Utility Reform Project) are planned. These aim to enhance the overall availability of energy and commercialisation within the sector as well as to facilitate the 'integration of renewables, in line with the World Bank Group Climate Change Action Plan (2016)'.[63]

In the area of renewable energy and clean energy, the World Bank is clearly active in financing especially large-scale hydropower projects that meet environmental and social sustainability criteria. It has increased its share of lending for clean energy projects, thereby paving the way for over 100 countries, including low-income ones, to set policy targets and incentives to attract these.[64] The World Bank pursues its clean energy strategy by linking climate finance and development finance. It supports energy efficiency and low emissions projects and programmes that aim to address both climate change and poverty reduction within the market-based framework, thereby promoting the AAAA/CFPs. Its energy efficiency initiatives work towards removing technical barriers that will ensure energy efficiency in all economic sectors.[65]

Bank energy financing has also been dominant in 'household fuel and distributed energy programmes' that encourage 'local community engagement and empowerment' and in supporting initiatives that provide solar-based energy services, efficient cookstoves and biomass-based energy.[66]

60 World Bank/ESS *supra* note 44 11–13

61 The package includes an IDA Guarantee (up to $40 million), an IFC A-Loan (up to $30 million), an IFC interest rate swap representing a loan-equivalent exposure (up to $3 million) and a MIGA Guarantee (up to $60 million). See <www.worldbank.org/en/news/press-release/2016/07/14/world-bank-group-supports-western-area-power-generation> (WBG/WAPGP 2016) (accessed 25/07/2016)

62 Ibid

63 Ibid

64 Note that only projects classified as 'energy efficiency', 'renewable energy', 'energy policy' and 'electricity transmission and distribution' will attract World Bank financing

65 World Bank/ESS *supra* note 44 11–13

66 Ibid

For example, the IFC provided a $30 million loan to the ResponsAbility Energy Access Fund[67] to facilitate the production and distribution of affordable solar powered devices for lighting and power. These devices are frequently used for charging mobile phones and other appliances that support economic activity and enhance livelihoods.[68] Similarly, several funding sources[69] are available from public and private financing to support regional efficient lighting strategies and activities in order to promote increased demand for efficient lighting products, both on-grid and off-grid.[70] The World Bank also promotes carbon market mechanisms which generate new revenue streams or encourage investments in low emissions projects. This is touted as a promising option to mobilise higher investment returns.[71]

The AAAA calls for the public sector to act as a catalyst to attract private sector financing of innovation, energy technologies, research and development and the setting up innovation funds, as represented in the World Bank practice. The Bank creates new financial models, instruments and innovative policy tools to promote private sector participation to address energy investment barriers.[72] In its catalytic role to attract private sector financing, it brings together financing partners into specific deals through syndications or co-financing arrangements.[73] The GIF exemplifies this private financing catalytic function. It coordinates PPPs and pools the private sector and institutional investor capital to enable the estimated $1 trillion a year of financing and investments in energy infrastructure that is needed in emerging markets and developing economies.[74] Applicable instruments under such schemes include ownership of direct equity in an energy project or indirect investing

67 <www.responsability.com/investing/en/975/Investing-in-the-energy-sector.htm> (accessed 08/02/2016)

68 World Bank, *Shock Waves: Managing the Impacts of Climate Change on Poverty, Climate Change and Development Series* (Washington DC 2016) 195 (World Bank 'Shockwaves')

69 These sources include: the World Bank Carbon Partnership Facility; the Sustainable Energy for All initiative; the Energising Development Programme; Fonds Africain de Garantie et de Coopération Économique; and Green Climate Fund

70 E.g., ECOWAS energy efficient lighting strategy ensures support for distribution of 'free' or subsidised lighting products, efficient lighting equipped social housing projects and financing schemes to cover the upfront cost to selected communities; see ECOWAS *Regional Strategy on Energy Efficient Lighting* Draft (Praia, Cape Verde May 2014) 5 (ECREE)

71 World Bank/FfD Post-2015 *supra* note 47 35. Note that the total value of the carbon market reached $176 billion in 2011; see also World Bank *Clean Energy for Development Investment Framework Report* (World Bank CEDIF-Report, 2007)

72 World Bank/ESS *supra* note 44 11 –13; see also; Lattanzio, *supra* note 2

73 World Bank/FfDPost-2015 *supra* note 47 26

74 The GIF became operational in April 2015, with an initial capitalisation of $100 million. See <www.worldbank.org/en/programs/global-Infrastructure-facility> (accessed 20/03/2016)

in private equity funds, 'funds of funds' financing[75] and mezzanine financing[76] instruments.

Further new innovative mechanisms have been developed to generate financing for development that could be applicable in financing energy resources to achieve the SDG7 by 2030.[77] The 'pull mechanisms for development' (PMfD) and the 'advanced market commitment' (AMC) schemes are notable. A form of economic incentive for innovation, the PMfD links payments to the actual impact of the innovation, ensuring for the relevant product, a self-sustaining, competitive market.[78] In the AMC, public finance may be used to subsidise the cost of the energy product (e.g. solar lighting products) actually demanded and produced for the target market.[79] Then there is the 'resources-for-infrastructure' model, in which the standard tax and royalty regimes are complemented by exchanging oil rights for turnkey infrastructure,[80] such as hydropower dams and plants and other electrical power projects. Africa alone has signed resources for infrastructure swaps amounting in value to an estimated $28 billion, in spite of the huge risks that the mechanism entails for both the private sector and government.[81]

The World Bank (and other international financial institutions) utilise a variety of innovative financing techniques to develop the supply of energy service industries as a tool to encourage investment, particularly in energy efficiency and renewable energy projects.[82] 'Energy performance contracting' (EPC)[83] is one such technique, entailing two broad financing options: energy service company (ESC) financing (i.e. either the ESC's own financing or

75 Where a public entity invests a relatively small amount of long-term capital in a range of private, professionally managed funds

76 Leveraging a hybrid of debt and equity capital from a mix of sources; WBG/FfDPost-2015 *supra* note 47 26–27

77 WBG/FfDPost-2015; ibid 33

78 Ibid 33–34. Note however that the PMD entails two major shortcomings: (1) the failure of markets to reflect the social value of such innovations; and (2) imperfect information

79 Ibid

80 Ibid 35. Note that in such cases, the financing frequently takes the form of export credit because the infrastructure project financing is premised on future oil (or mineral) revenues

81 Ibid 36

82 Energy Charter Secretariat, 'Third Party Financing Achieving its Potential' (2004) 2(5) *Oil, Gas & Energy Law Journal* (ECS-TPF) <www.ogel.org/>. Also see generally Ali Liaqat, 'Financing New and Renewable Sources of Energy' (1981) 16 *Economic and Political Weekly* 91; Hillard Huntington and Christine Jojarth, 'Financing the Future: Investments in Alternative Sources of Energy' in Andreas Goldthau and Jan Martin Witte (eds) *Global Energy Governance: The New Rules of the Game* (Brookings Institution Press, 2010) 161; Lars Holstenkamp, 'An Overview of European Programs to Support Energy Projects in Africa and Strategies to Involve the Private Sector' in Paul Hoebink (ed), *European Development Cooperation: In Between the Local and the Global* (Amsterdam University Press, 2010) 95

83 Note that 'Third Party Financing' (TPF) and 'Contract Energy Management' (CEM) are similar terms usually employed in such schemes. See ECS-TPF 108

debt finance) and 'energy user financing/guaranteed energy savings'.[84] In the former, the ESC takes over the technical risk of the project in terms of the performance of equipment as designed, the budgetary risk in implementation and the operational and maintenance risks.[85] In the latter, the financing is based on the ESC performance to achieve the energy savings, the performance contract and the transfer of the management risks from the end-user to the ESC.[86] The energy user takes on a commitment for fixed payments for a specific time.[87] The World Bank and the GEF have been involved in these ESC financing approaches in the Krakow Energy Efficiency Project in Poland and the Romanian Fund for Energy Efficiency.

Two further financing mechanisms applied to enhance energy service supply to attract investment are the 'finance leasing' programme and 'mortgage financing'. The leasing programmes allow end-users to opt for leasing rather than outright purchase of the energy equipment, while mortgage financing allows the homeowner to incorporate the cost of installing renewable energy systems into the cost of their homes.[88] The choice of a particular financing approach considers the size of the renewable energy project, the operational technicality and the characteristics of the system, which could be non-grid,[89] isolated grid[90] and grid-connected systems.[91]

The World Bank seems to have ticked all the boxes for applying the AAAA/CFPs in practice in various areas of traditional, innovative and more modern techniques for financing energy resources to ensure the supply of sustainable energy and energy services for all. The question to ponder however is to what extent these instruments and techniques are 'new' financing practices that are directly connected with the outcome of Agenda 2030 and the AAAA. It could be that the AAAA global financing principles and framework present as a 'new wine', but really reiterate 'old skins' practices but in a more comprehensive and cohesive way with varying permutations that make them attractive for domestic energy policy consumption.

84 ECS-TPF 22; see also Jayarao Gururaja, 'Financing Energy for Sustainable Development' in Adrian J. Bradbrook and others (eds), *The Law of Energy for Sustainable Development* (Cambridge University Press, 2004) 222, 228–229

85 ECS-TPF 18

86 Ibid 6, 15

87 Ibid 77

88 Gururaja *supra* note 84 228–229

89 Ibid. Non-grid systems (small-scale) are energy equipment, which is sold or leased directly to the end-user, e.g., solar PV home systems or wind battery chargers

90 Ibid. Isolated grid systems (medium-scale) are energy systems within the range of 100kW to 10MW including small hydropower plants, biomass gasifiers and cogeneration systems and hybrids (wind/diesel/solar)

91 Ibid. Grid-connected systems (large-scale) would be those renewable energy projects requiring mobilisation of investment capital, from private sector IFIs, commercial banks and host government institutions in long-term power-purchase agreements, usually entailing incentives for tax and risk management and other conditions

The Global Environmental Facility in energy finance

GEF[92] energy financing generally supports projects for emissions reduction, energy efficiency, renewable energy development and commercialisation of renewable energy technology. The GEF investment portfolio for energy efficiency is to the tune of $850 million in direct funding and $5.9 billion in co-financing and has been used in an estimated 131 projects.[93] The renewable energy portion (between 1991 and 2012) was worth about $1.22 billion, with an average of $4.9 million per project, with $9.59 billion in co-financing.[94] The largest source of funds for clean energy projects on concessional terms is the GEF.[95] It adopts measures that reduce the cost of renewable energy technology and encourage commercial competitiveness by bringing onto the market renewable energy technologies and underutilised efficient energy technologies that are commercially competitive.[96]

The GEF leverages investment to promote renewable energy and energy efficiency objectives through key strategic mechanisms to achieve lasting policy reforms. It uses indirect engagement financing mechanisms to create markets and conditions (e.g. equitable energy pricing and agreed industrial inputs standards) that allow pro-environment firms in the renewable energy business and their equipment to boom.[97] GEF direct engagement financing strategy seeks to induce companies' consciousness and conduct of environmentally friendly business. Its funding/co-finance scheme promotes a transition to a green economy by supporting the development of clean technologies and energy efficiency.[98]

GEF renewable energy financing initiatives are designed to facilitate access at the local level, including through the enhanced integration of renewable energy options into the energy supply system, the adaptation of technology locally or the building of technical and financial capacities to stimulate

92 The GEF is a financial organisation of partnerships providing grants for projects that address global environmental issues and supporting national sustainable development initiatives. The World Bank is host to the facility

93 GEF Investing in Energy Efficiency: The GEF Experience (2014) <www.thegef.org/sites/default/files/publications/GEF_EnergyEff-Oct17-2013_3.pdf> (accessed 20/03/2016)

94 GEF Renewable Energy <www.thegef.org/sites/default/files/publications/GEF_EnergyEff-Oct17-2013_3.pdf> (accessed 20/03/2016)

95 In 21 years, GEF has 'invested directly $11.5 billion and co-financed $57 billion and supported 3,215 projects' in over 165 countries

96 See Alan S. Miller, 'Financing Clean Energy for Development' in Adrian J. Bradbrook et al. (eds), *The Law of Energy for Sustainable Development* (Cambridge University Press, 2004) 473, 480

97 Priscilla Schwartz, 'The Polluter-Pays Principle' in Jorge E. Viñuales (ed), *The Rio Declaration on Environment and Development: A Commentary* (Oxford University Press, 2015) 429, 445

98 Ibid

renewable energy project development.[99] These are implemented in line with the GEF Private Sector Strategy, which aims to collectively contribute to the goals of SE4All.[100]

For example, the GEF helps countries identify innovative business models involving low-carbon options that the private sector can adopt. It also supports private or public energy service companies, MSMEs and women to ensure their participation in the renewable energy market opportunities in rural areas.[101] The Facility has funded projects that pertinently demonstrate the commercialisation of power production from bagasse and other agricultural resources using established local technologies.[102] Other similar projects in rural areas show that renewable energy technology and capacity building efforts can be integrated with financing grants to buy-down capital costs that increase affordability of solar home systems and increase awareness among consumers and providers.[103]

It is clear from the foregoing that the focus of the GEF energy financing strategy and initiatives and the range of renewable, efficiency and clean technology projects it supports are within a predominantly commercialised and market-based framework. Certainly, domestic energy policy design that aims to facilitate commercial activity and innovation within the economy could benefit much from the GEF strategy, initiatives and financing. It is doubtful however whether the opportunities that may be created for sustainable energy businesses or entrepreneurs will be amenable to all or that the energy products and services will provide reliable and affordable sustainable energy for all, pursuant to the AAAA and Agenda 2030 energy objectives.

Africa Investment Bank for Infrastructure

Africa50 covers the energy financing need for the African region, especially high-impact national and regional projects in energy.[104] It aims to mobilise African savings alongside non-African institutions and the private sector to increase and accelerate the number of bankable infrastructure projects in Africa. The Africa50 financing strategy uses the mechanisms known as

99 GEF/Renewable Energy <www.thegef.org/sites/default/files/publications/GEF_EnergyEff-Oct17-2013_3.pdf> (accessed 20/03/2016)

100 Ibid

101 GEF/RE <www.thegef.org/sites/default/files/publications/GEF_EnergyEff-Oct17-2013_3.pdf>

102 Miller *supra* note 96 480–481. See, e.g., the GEF/UNDP funded biomass power generation in Brazil and the cogeneration of electricity and steam using sugarcane bagasse and trash in Cuba

103 Ibid; see World Bank Rural Electrification and Renewable Energy Development project in Bangladesh, implemented by rural electricity cooperatives, community based organisations, NGOs, microfinance institutions and the private sector

104 'Developers' (*Africa50*) <www.africa50.com/focus-areas/developers/> (accessed 20/03/2016)

project finance companies (PFCs) and project development companies (PDCs), which are public–private institutions that are commercially managed and profit oriented.[105]

The PDC energy projects will come from governments, public institutions and state-owned enterprises. The project finance will cover *inter alia* environment and social impacts assessments (ESIAs), environment and social management plans (ESMPs) and the development and social impacts and negotiations of power-purchase agreements, concessions and licences.[106] The interests of the poor and vulnerable are usually envisaged in the general ESIA and ESMP requirements and in specific industry standards that provide for the protection of the public from social and environmental impacts of energy projects. The financing model places emphasis on strong asset management during the construction and commercial operations, the best rules for risk management and the preservation of the value of the liquid assets and returns.[107]

It is important to note that the Africa50 focus is on financing large-scale, regional energy infrastructure projects and on sustainability considerations for project impact on people and the environment rather than on clean energy, efficiency, technology and domestic innovation and capacity, which is the target of the AAAA and Agenda 2030.[108] Its concern with the economic viability of infrastructure projects (i.e. investment protection, risk mitigation, assets security and profits) is however in line with the AAAA/CFPs. But the model considers the interest of the poor and vulnerable only in the ESIA and ESMP, as opposed to during negotiations of power purchase agreements, concessions and licences which have a greater potential to secure accessible and affordable energy. With an approach to infrastructure finance that is centralised and top-down, it may be difficult to include the voices of the poor or no-income groups, who usually utilise energy resources outside the formal, competitive, market-led and commercialised framework. They are likely to be marginalised in decision-making on the choice of energy access that may be feasible in their local context and for their capacity and needs.

The AAAA, energy finance and sustainability issues

Policy and institutional level sustainability

One mechanism advocated by the AAAA is the security of targeted ODA. While ODA and aid contributions may ameliorate the difficulty for LICs to access international capital markets, it is worth noting that the aid landscape

105 *Africa50*
106 Ibid
107 Ibid
108 See core financing principles of the AAAA in section 'Application of AAAA in energy financing practice' above

has evolved in fundamental shifts that hold implications for its effectiveness. New or 'emerging donors'[109] on the ODA scene tend to promote their own economic strategic interests with a focus on physical infrastructure development, a trend that could be particularly problematic where LICs do not share similar strategic economic interests. Also, private new actors including non-governmental organisations (NGOs) are participating in various donor-funded energy efficiency and technology innovation projects and yielding approximately $60–70 billion per year.[110] While the involvement of these new private actors in the energy sector is laudable, LICs should ensure that there is proper energy policy and planning to direct such activities and to have in place tighter transparency and accountability mechanisms over and above the donor-country reporting mechanisms.

Also, the World Bank applies considerable pressure through conditions attached to the release of its energy sector loans and provides technical assistance as the basis for the privatisation of the management of the electricity utilities.[111] Adopting this energy service financing 'needs' approach, without also considering policy changes, institutional improvements and linkages with other parts of the development strategy is unsustainable practice.[112] It is imperative that financing is viewed as 'one component of a strategy that includes private sector efficiency and public sector productivity improvements'.[113] Achieving the objectives of SDG7 depends as much on the efficiency of implementing quality policies and practice as making more efficient use of existing infrastructure and improving the quality of projects and management.

Another policy sustainability concern is that the World Bank assists LICs to adapt to its G8 members' renewable energy investment strategies that are designed to overcome the recent financial crisis, with a $100 billion economic stimulus to support a 'green' economic recovery.[114] There is a danger in promoting and using 'special support schemes' in the transition of energy supply from thermal to renewable energy. Such financing schemes engender increased power prices for energy consumers, leading some states to roll back support for new and existing installations and causing losses to

109 These include non-DAC members of the OECD and EU; upper middle-income countries (in Latin America, the Middle East and East Asia); and other developing countries and Arabia, South Korea and Turkey; see World Bank/FfDPost-2015 *supra* note 47 18–19

110 Ibid

111 See generally World Bank, 'Toward a Sustainable Energy Future for All: Directions for the World Bank Groups Energy Sector' (Report No. 7597, World Bank, 9 July 2013)

112 Background Paper for the Post-2015 HLP meeting in Bali, *Summary of Financing for Development*, March 2013

113 Ibid

114 See Priscilla Schwartz, 'Powering the Right to Development: Sustainable Energy in a Changing Climate' (Speech, OHCHR, 2016) <www.ohchr.org/Documents/Issues/Development/Dignity/PriscillaSchwartz.pdf> (accessed 20/06/2016)

investors' non-recourse project finance.[115] Financing policies on renewable energy and low-carbon technology should build indigenous capabilities and be based on service needs, convenience, productivity and sustainability within specific contexts.

Moreover, the World Bank's linking of energy resources finance with climate and development finance promotes climate-informed energy strategies. Such strategies focus mainly on policies and projects with implications for consumers and consumption in terms of low energy tariffs, awareness and attitudinal changes in demand management for energy efficiency and up-take of clean energy technology and energy efficient products. However, its financing agreements, as with the GEF and Africa50, could do more to address the effective management of energy product life-cycle impacts and disposal.[116] Embedding EIA laws and international standards for public participation[117] in financing commitments to address public interest issues does not impose strict legal obligations on firms or businesses that the poor in particular could directly claim.

Sustainability challenges at project initiation level

Renewable energy and energy efficiency projects generate incremental cost savings that can be turned into growing cash flows to the lender or the energy service entity to repay the costs of the project,[118] but financing problems have been identified with such projects. Compared to conventional energy systems, renewable energy projects have a high capital to operations and maintenance cost ratio and do not benefit from the economies of scale.[119] The growing demand for electricity may not sufficiently be met by solar power, wind and biofuels in an affordable and reliable manner.[120] Also, large investors are not usually attracted to such projects because they have disproportionately small total investment requirements compared to the cost of undertaking 'due diligence' and the perceived risks.[121]

115 See generally Alexander Reuter, 'Retroactive Reduction of Support for Renewable Energy and Investment Treaty Protection from the Perspective of Shareholders and Lenders' (2015) 3 *Oil, Gas & Energy Law Journal*

116 Appropriate measures could include testing new materials and processes, expanding recycling technologies and designing products for easy recycling. See Kari Larsen, 'End-of-Life PV: Then What? Recycling Solar PV Panels' (Renewable Energy Focus, 2009) <www.renewableenergyfocus.com/view/3005/end-of-life-pv-then-what-recycling-solar-pv-panels/>; see also Alhaji *supra* note 4 3

117 See World Bank (IBRD/IDA) Safeguard policies (OP 4.01) on Environmental Assessment (2012) <http://go.worldbank.org/3GLI3EECP0>; and IFC Performance Standards for Private Sector Activities (2012) <http://go.worldbank.org/GCH411QCR0>

118 ECS/TPF *supra* note 82 6, 15

119 Gururaja *supra* note 84 227

120 Lattanzio *supra* note 2

121 Gururaja *supra* note 84 227

Further, preparing energy services performance contracting projects is complex and entails conditions that could be difficult to achieve without causing hardship for the poor and other vulnerable groups. For example conditions requiring the setting of energy prices at market level, elimination of cross subsidisation between classes of consumers (e.g. commercial and residential) and insisting on metered consumption billing and cash payments[122] could impact on the poor.

Implementation and post-project monitoring sustainability issues

The AAAA recommendation for supporting domestic revenue mobilisation via the tax regime, if effectively implemented, could garner savings that could be used to finance renewables, clean energy, efficiency technologies and research and development projects. But domestic revenue mobilisation is a huge challenge in LICs. Even if tax collection capacity and revenue could be enhanced, it will be insufficient to address the huge infrastructure deficit costs.[123] Modern energy infrastructure – power plants, oil refineries, transmission systems and renewable energy and clean energy systems – are capital-intensive projects and for developing countries particularly, having limited credit and varying needs, lowest costs societal options can be difficult.[124] And LICs continue to be largely sidelined by FDI, which is a major energy financing tool. More challenging is the state of play in the petroleum industry where the ongoing tightening of credit, suppressed commodity prices and the consequential drop in asset values make access to capital even harder in the oil and gas sector and service support industry.[125]

In light of the heavy fiscal pressures on major donors, constrained MDBs and a weak global recovery, developing countries are urged to make themselves attractive destinations for resources from the private sector and donors.[126] Countries could embed in their sustainable development programmes resilient energy infrastructure investment plans. But the collapsing of energy investment policy with global financial recovery could undercut the environmental and social dimensions of sustainability. The challenge for energy policy planners will be how to balance the competing interests without losing sight of energy policy needs. Albeit, while energy access and availability may be attainable with successful infrastructure project finance, affordability for low-income earners and the no-income poor will be difficult unless costs and pricing issues are resolved.

The financing instruments and strategies covering energy efficient technology and renewable energy (e.g. marketing efficient lighting products and

122 ECS/TPF *supra* note 82 108–109
123 World Bank/FfDPost-2015 *supra* note 47 12
124 Miller *supra* note 96 474–475
125 Murray *supra* note 53 394
126 World Bank/FfDPost-2015 *supra* note 47

low cost solar powered devices) have potential to support economic activity. Financing grants apply to buy-down capital costs and increase the affordability of solar home systems. Biofuels, biomass and bagasse and other agriculture resources are used in power generation or cogeneration projects that focus on the adaptation of technology locally.[127] The bigger picture in all energy resources financing initiatives is a concern for enhancing market effectiveness and the competitive sustainability of climate friendly energy products. They are less about accessibility or affordability issues for the no-income poor as opposed to low-income groups. These technologies tend to attract higher prices that squeeze poor people's consumption and remain a challenge.[128] MDBs' public-financed energy agreements and project agreements (or contracts) should specify accessibility and affordability conditions for the poor as a risk instrument (power supply risk) that must be insured before the commencement of the project.

Conclusion

This chapter has identified the AAAA core financing principles and broad categories of sources of financing, including domestic resources mobilisation, public resources such as MDBs and global donor facilities, private businesses, FDI and ODA. The finding is that the financing principles and sources accord with promoting the objectives of SDG7 and the implementation design under SDG7 of Agenda 2030. The AAAA principles and implementation framework are already largely operational within the practice of energy resources financing of the World Bank (including the new GIF), the GEF and Africa50. It was also argued that the financing mechanisms are not essentially 'new' to their respective institutions. Their application in individual developing countries and LICs however could be novel as the allure of public and private finance could incentivise these countries to embrace a market-based competitive structure rather than traditional government control over energy policy and market structure.

Practice reveals financing and catalysing private sector resources for investment in oil and gas exploitation, energy infrastructure, renewable energy, energy efficient technology and clean energy technology and several innovative financing instruments and mechanisms to promote financing for electricity and energy services. Financing for renewable energy resources does not cancel out funding for fossil fuel powered plants and generation and the latter seem to attract the major investments, in spite of the vast 'clean energy' rhetoric.

127 Miller *supra* note 96 481; for pertinent examples, see *supra* notes 102 and 103

128 S.K Kar and P.K. Sinha, 'Ensuring Sustainable Energy Security: Challenges and Opportunities for India' (2014) *Oil, Gas & Energy Law* 7–12; J. Arevalo, P. Halder, J. Kortelainen and B. Mola-Yudego, 'Bioenergy: From Local Conflicts to Global Governance' (2014) 12 *Oil, Gas & Energy Law* 4 4; see World Bank 'Shockwaves' *supra* note 68 195

Energy finance is invariably linked with broader objectives like climate change and development. Financing strategies and instruments therefore focus on mitigating climate change threats, reducing poverty while increasing energy access and availability, and inclusive energy commercialisation and economic activity for MSMEs. Energy policy planners will need to overcome the challenge of balancing these competing interests without losing sight of energy policy needs. Also, the market imperative, commercialisation and innovation competitiveness in both the design of financing instruments and energy products and services will require domestic energy experts to acquire a range of technical and project management skills.

The chapter further argued that the emphasis placed on bringing low-cost energy devices and high-cost energy technology into the market creates a challenge for energy regulators: how to ensure affordability for poorer households without government support and in the face of depressed donor assistance. LICs could consider an arrangement whereby MDBs' public-financed energy agreements and project agreements (or contracts) specify *accessibility* and *affordability* conditions for the poor as a risk instrument (e.g. power supply risk or guarantee) that can be insured before the commencement of all energy projects and programmes in LICs.

15 Carbon trading as a climate change mitigation tool

Beatriz Garcia

Introduction

Market-based mechanisms, including carbon trading, have been used as a climate change mitigation tool for several years now in the framework of the United Nations Framework Convention on Climate Change (UNFCCC). Carbon trading occurs under compliance carbon markets, established by the 1997 Kyoto Protocol, under national and regional trading schemes such as the European Union Emissions Trading System (EU ETS) and under the voluntary carbon market[1] where millions of carbon offsets are transacted each year.[2]

The 2015 Paris Agreement foresees the use of carbon market mechanisms to assist the parties to meet their emission reduction goals. The Agreement avoids reference to the words *carbon trading* or *markets*, but Article 6 refers to *voluntary cooperation* between countries that involves trading emission reductions, or the so-called *internationally transferred mitigation outcomes.* In addition, Article 6(4) proposes a mechanism to contribute to the mitigation of carbon emissions while also fostering sustainable development, which has been named as the Sustainable Development Mechanism. Parties are also encouraged to implement actions aimed at reducing emissions from deforestation and forest degradation (REDD+) to conserve and enhance carbon sinks, including forests and other ecosystems.[3] REDD+ has also been used as a market tool in the voluntary market to capture the economic value of

* The author would like to acknowledge Emma Shea Thornton for her assistance in proofreading this chapter.

1 See classification in David Freestone and Charlotte Streck (eds), *Legal Aspects of Carbon Trading: Kyoto, Copenhagen and Beyond* (Oxford University Press, 2009).

2 The volume and types of carbon offsets transacted in the voluntary market can be found in the reports published by Ecosystem Market Place, 'State of the Voluntary Carbon Markets' and 'State of Forest Carbon Finance' (Ecosystem Marketplace, 2017) <www.ecosystemmarketplace.com/publications> accessed 27 March 2017. Examples and details about existing carbon projects in the voluntary market are available at Verified Carbon Standard, 'Standards for a Sustianable World' <www.v-c-s.org> accessed 27 March 2017.

3 Paris Agreement 2015, Art 5.

forests and remunerate landowners and communities for safekeeping forest areas.[4]

It is well known that *new and additional* resources are needed to help developing countries mitigate and adapt to climate change.[5] In 2009 at the Conference of the Parties 15 (COP15) in Copenhagen, developed countries pledged to jointly mobilise US$100 billion per year by 2020.[6] Funding will come from a wide variety of sources including public and private, bilateral and multilateral partnerships and alternative sources of finance. The mitigation costs associated with keeping the global temperature below 2°C could bear a significant burden on developing countries. Indeed, it is estimated that these costs could reach $139–175 billion per year by 2030.[7] In view of the scale of financing required, there is no doubt that private capital flows (and alternative sources) will be part of the global climate finance architecture.[8] In 2014, at the United Nations Climate Summit in New York, governments, businesses and the financial sector committed significant sums, adding up to $200 billion, to help address climate change.[9] The World Bank also announced an increase of its climate change financing to potentially reach $29 billion per year by 2020.[10] Private capital investment in conservation is growing rapidly. In just two years, the total private capital committed to conservation investments increased by 62 per cent to a total committed private capital of $8.2 billion tracked from 2004 to 2015.[11] The carbon market plays a role in scaling up funding and investment needed to keep the global temperature well below 2°C. According to the UNFCCC, it is an optimal combination of mechanisms and tools that will ensure the investment and financial flows necessary to address climate change. These include

4 Stephanie O'Donnell and others, *Forest Carbon and the Protection of Native Forests: A Real Life Australian Example* (2011) <www.redd-net.org> accessed 27 March 2017.

5 Decision 2/CP.15, Copenhagen Accord, para 8.

6 Ibid.

7 World Bank, 'State and Trends of the Carbon Market 2011' (World Bank, 2011) 47 <http://documents.worldbank.org/curated/en/270781468157764739/State-and-trends-of-the-carbon-market-2011> accessed 31 March 2017.

8 According to the UNFCCC, private sector investment already is an important means of enhancing financial flows towards climate change mitigation as it constitutes the largest share of investment and financial flows (86 per cent), UNFCCC, 'Dialogue on Long Term Cooperative Action to Address Climate Change by Enhancing Implementation of the Convention', Dialogue Working Paper 8 (2007) 2.

9 Climate Funds Update, '10 Things to Know about Climate Finance in 2014' (Climate Funds Update, 2014) <www.climatefundsupdate.org> accessed 27 March 2017.

10 To date, about 21 per cent of the Bank Group's funding is climate related. Under the plans, that could rise to 28 per cent in 2020, representing a one-third increase in climate financing, information available at: World Bank, 'Funding Boost for Climate Action' (2015) <www.worldbank.org/en/news/feature/2015/10/10/funding-boost-for-climate-action> accessed 27 March 2017.

11 Kelley Hamrick, *State of Private Investment in Conservation 2016: A Landscape Assessment of an Emerging Market* (Ecosystem Marketplace, 2016) 9.

the carbon markets, the financial mechanism of the Convention, overseas development assistance and national policies.[12]

The use of market mechanisms as a tool to mitigate climate change has become a common practice. However, questions remain. Is carbon trading indeed an effective mitigation tool? Can it help countries achieve mitigation targets established under their nationally determined contributions? What are the investment opportunities and challenges associated with these mechanisms?[13] More fundamentally, is carbon trading only delaying real changes, which involve phasing out carbon emissions and transitioning away from fossil fuels? This chapter examines how carbon market mechanisms operate, both in the compliance and voluntary markets and may evolve after the 21st COP (COP21) in Paris. It enquires whether carbon offset projects and trading of emission reductions, particularly in the land use and forestry sector, have been an effective market tool to reduce emissions, conserve and enhance carbon sinks and protect natural resources.

Market-based mechanisms and carbon trading under the UNFCC

The Kyoto Protocol's flexibility mechanisms

The Kyoto Protocol[14] was a milestone in international climate change policy. For the first time, a group of countries committed, under the Protocol, to reducing greenhouse gas (GHG) emissions as part of a global effort to tackle climate change. The Protocol also introduced three market mechanisms as one of its main features, thereby creating what is now known as the *carbon market.*[15] It established specific and mandatory limits on industrialised countries' emissions (Annex I parties), known as *Qualified Emission Limitation or Reduction Commitments.* Annex I parties were expected to reduce emissions of six major GHGs[16] by at least 5 per cent below 1990 levels in the first commitment period, from 2008 to 2012. The sectors targeted include energy, industrial processes, agriculture and waste. Each Annex I party had different reduction commitments listed in Annex B of the Kyoto Protocol. Based on the

12 UNFCCC, (n 8) 2.

13 According to Art 4(2), parties are required to prepare, communicate and maintain nationally determined contributions, which involves the efforts and emissions reduction goals that each country intends to achieve.

14 The Kyoto Protocol was adopted in 1997 at the third COP to the UNFCCC and entered into force in 2005.

15 See UNFCCC, 'The Mechanisms under the Kyoto Protocol: Clean Development Mechanism, Joint Implementation and Emissions Trading' (UN, 2014) <http://unfccc.int/kyoto_protocol/mechanisms/items/1673.php> accessed 27 March 2017.

16 The GHG emissions and sectors covered by the Kyoto Protocol are listed in Annex A.

principle of *common but differentiated responsibility*,[17] the Kyoto Protocol imposed legal obligations to reduce emissions only on Annex I countries, leaving developing country parties exempted during the first commitment period.

In addition to setting emission reduction targets, the Kyoto Protocol introduced a framework for trading emission rights through the well-known 'flexibility mechanisms'. Therefore, Annex I parties wishing to emit more than their limit had the option to purchase additional rights from other countries that have managed to reduce emissions. The three mechanisms established under the Kyoto Protocol are: Joint Implementation (JI) (Article 6), the Clean Development Mechanism (CDM) (Article 12) and Emissions Trading (Article 17). These mechanisms are intended to assist Annex I parties in reducing the costs involved in meeting their Kyoto targets. They are in line with the principles of the UNFCCC, including that of cost effectiveness. Per Article 3 of the Convention, policies and measures set to deal with climate change should be cost effective so as to ensure global benefits at the lowest possible cost. It also recognises the need for developed countries to take immediate action in a *flexible manner* (Preamble).

JI consists of collaborations between Annex I parties. It allows one Annex I country to invest in another's emission reduction projects. These projects generally aim to reduce carbon emissions or enhance removals by sinks compared to a baseline scenario. They generate emission reduction units (ERUs) that can be used by an Annex I party to meet its Kyoto targets, as an alternative to reducing emissions domestically.[18]

The CDM involves projects developed by an Annex I party, in the territory of a non-Annex I party, which reduce carbon emissions. These projects generate Certified Emission Reductions (CERs) that can be used by Annex I parties to meet their obligations under the Protocol. The CDM is also intended to help developing countries foster sustainable development and contribute to the objectives of the UNFCCC.

Finally, Annex I countries can engage in emissions trading. The emission reduction targets established under the Kyoto Protocol for each Annex I party can be expressed as levels of allowed emissions, or *assigned amounts* over the first commitment period. These allowed emissions are divided into *Assigned Amount Units* (AAUs).[19] Emissions trading allows Annex I countries that have emission units to spare to sell this excess capacity to countries that exceeded their targets.[20] In any case, per Article 17, emissions trading should be supplemental to domestic actions.

17 1992 Rio Declaration on Environment and Development, A/CONF.151/26 (Vol. I) 1992, principle 7.

18 See UNFCCC, 'Kyoto Mechanisms – Background' (UN, 2014) <http://unfccc.int/kyoto_protocol/mechanisms/items/2998.php> accessed 27 March 2017.

19 Kyoto Protocol, Art 3(7). See also UNFCCC, 'International Emissions Trading' (UN, 2014) <http://unfccc.int/kyoto_protocol/mechanisms/emissions_trading/items/2731.php> accessed 27 March 2017.

20 Ibid.

The three flexibility mechanisms created trading relationships only among parties.[21] In other words, a party to the Kyoto Protocol would not be allowed to trade emission permits with a non-party. In 2001, at COP7, most of the Kyoto Protocol's operational rules for the three flexibility mechanisms were finalised under the agreement known as Marrakesh Accords.[22]

The reduction commitments under the Kyoto Protocol were rather modest, but achieving them still involved significant costs to Annex I parties.[23] Therefore, by reducing compliance costs for Annex I countries, the flexibility mechanisms were crucial in engaging countries that would not be part of the Protocol otherwise.[24]

Each of the three Kyoto Protocol mechanisms anticipates a role for the private sector in transnational climate mitigation activities, thus implicating the international investment law regime.[25] Climate change concerns are now part of many international investment agreements and confer some flexibility as to how such treaties must be interpreted in order to protect a host country's social and environmental values.[26] The CDM is explicitly designed to stimulate low-carbon foreign direct investment in developing countries, which indicates its interplay with the international investment law regime.[27] The flexibility mechanisms allow market participants to invest in emissions reductions through various channels, such as JI and the CDM. However, private sector investment is traditionally guided by the risk–return ratio for a given project.[28] This has been demonstrated by the preference to invest in countries with higher levels of development. For example, CDM projects have not been implemented evenly across developing countries; 70 per cent of CDM projects have been located in only three countries: China (41.2 per cent), India (22.3 per cent) and Brazil (7.1 per cent). Only 1.9 per cent of registered projects are in Africa, with South Africa leading the continent.[29] This inequity of investment is also likely to occur with the market mechanisms under the Paris Agreement.

21 Aaron Cosbey and James Cameron, *Trade Implications of the Kyoto Protocol* (International Institute for Sustainable Development, 2008) 23, 24.

22 The Marrakesh Accords, FCCC/CP/2001/13/Add.1, 2002.

23 Michael Grubb and Duncan Brack, *The Kyoto Protocol, a Guide and Assessment* (Earthscan, 1991) 191.

24 Ibid.

25 Daniel M. Firger and Michael Gerrard, 'Harmonizing Climate Change Policy and International Investment Law: Threats, Challenges and Opportunities', in Karl Sauvant (ed) *Yearbook on International Investment Law & Policy 2010–2011* (Oxford University Press, 2012) 8.

26 Ibid. According to this paper, climate-friendly provisions in international investment law agreements take two forms. First, they preserve host-country flexibility in promulgating climate regulations, by including exceptions that specify measures necessary to protect human, animal or plant life or health, or the environment. Second, countries can make use of new and existing provisions in international investment agreements to incentivise low-carbon foreign direct investment flows.

27 Ibid 8.

28 Ibid 41.

29 Ibid 35.

The Kyoto Protocol and forests

Under the Kyoto Protocol, emission reductions can be achieved in two ways: by reducing emissions and by increasing carbon sequestration and storage.[30] In this context, the role of forests particularly has been the object of much debate. Forests can be a source of carbon emissions (i.e. coming from burning forests, land clearance, degradation and soil erosion), or a *sink*, considering they remove carbon dioxide (CO_2) from the atmosphere through photosynthesis and store terrestrial carbon.[31]

The role of forests as sinks was controversial under the Kyoto Protocol negotiations. Some countries proposed that CO_2 absorption should be directly offset against emissions (the *net approach*), because absorption is equivalent to reduced emissions from an atmospheric standpoint.[32] Other countries feared that this would detract from the goal to limit emissions and allow countries to claim credit for purely natural sink processes. This was known as the *Amazonian picket fence* problem, i.e. allowing parties simply to erect a fence around natural forests to be able to take credit for what nature was already doing. The issue of sinks could also potentially divert the focus on the core problem of reducing emissions and carry overtones concerning sovereignty over land use for developing countries.[33]

The Kyoto Protocol finally established a regime of sinks that allowed accounting only for absorption due to *direct, human-induced* changes limited initially to forestry related activities, including afforestation and reforestation and deforestation after 1990.[34] Afforestation and reforestation later became one modality of CDM projects.[35]

Forests gradually gained importance under the Kyoto Protocol regime for their role in climate change mitigation. Advances in technology and practical experience showed a growing body of research and evidence that demonstrated forest conservation as a credible part of the fight against

30 Convention on Biological Diversity Secretariat, 'Markets for Carbon Offsets' (CBD, 2002) <www.cbd.int/financial/offsets/g-offsetclimatecarbon.pdf> accessed 27 March 2017.

31 Sinks are defined as 'any process, activity or mechanism which removes a greenhouse gas, an aerosol or a precursor of a greenhouse gas from the atmosphere'. Forests and other vegetation are considered sinks because they remove carbon dioxide through photosynthesis, see UNFCC, 'Glossary of climate change acronyms and terms' (UNFCC, 2014) <http://unfccc.int/essential_background/glossary/items/3666.php> accessed 31 March 2017.

32 This discussion can be found in Grubb, Vrolijk and Brack (n 23) 76.

33 Ibid.

34 Kyoto Protocol, Art 3(3).

35 UNFCCC, *Afforestation and Reforestation Projects under the Clean Development Mechanism: A Reference Manual* (2013) 12. A total of 51 afforestation/reforestation CDM projects were registered (as of 10 October 2013). Of the registered project activities, eighteen project activities had successfully secured their first issuances amounting to 10.327 million credits.

climate change.[36] Scientific evidence also indicated that land-use changes including deforestation accounted for 15 per cent to 20 per cent of CO_2 emissions, a significant portion of global GHG emissions.[37]

The idea of reducing carbon emissions through avoided deforestation (initial acronym: RED) was first proposed by Papua New Guinea and Costa Rica in 2005 at COP11 in Montreal.[38] Not long after, the Bali Action Plan, adopted at COP13 in 2007, firmly incorporated the issue of reducing emissions from deforestation and forest degradation in the climate change international legal framework.[39] In Bali, countries agreed to conserve forests, manage them sustainably and enhance forest carbon stocks in developing countries (acronym became: REDD+).[40] The focus shifted from exclusively achieving carbon emission reductions to having multiple objectives.[41] A core idea underlying REDD+ is that of performance or results-based payments, which means paying forest owners and users for reducing emissions and increasing removals.[42]

In 2010, at COP16 in Cancun, countries agreed to implement REDD+ in three phases, which involved: (1) developing national REDD+ strategies, action plans, policies, measures and capacity building, (2) implementing such policies and measures, and carrying out results-based demonstration activities, evolving into (3) results-based actions that should be measured, reported and verified.[43] Since then, there have been many REDD+ pilot and demonstration activities, notably to help developing countries prepare and implement REDD+ policies and strategies.[44] Sources of funding for REDD+ activities include the World Bank's Forest Carbon Partnership Facility (FCPF) and Forest Investment Programme (FIP), the United Nations REDD Programme (UN-REDD) and the REDD-plus Partnership, among others.

REDD projects currently rely mostly on public funding rather than private investment, but private sector investment is growing and may generate

36 Nicole R. Virgilio and others, *Reducing Emissions from Deforestation and Degradation (REDD): A Casebook of On-the-Ground Experience* (Nature Conservancy, Conservation International and Wildlife Conservation Society, 2010) 13.

37 Intergovernmental Panel on Climate Change, *Climate Change 2007, Mitigation of Climate Change* (Cambridge University Press, 2007) 28.

38 Maria Brockhaus and Monica Di Gregorio, 'National REDD+ Policy Networks: From Cooperation to Conflict' (2014) 19(4) *Ecology and Society* 1.

39 Rosemary Lyster, Catherine MacKenzie, Constance McDermott, *Law, Tropical Forests and Carbon: The Case of REDD+* (Cambridge University Press, 2013) 3.

40 Decision 1/CP.13 Bali Action Plan, 1 (iii).

41 Brockhaus and Di Gregorio (note 38) 1.

42 Arild Angelsen and others, *Realising REDD+: National Strategy and Policy Options* (Center for International Forestry Research, 2009).

43 Decision 1/CP.16 para 73.

44 See UN-REDD Programme, 'Homepage' (UN-REDD Programme Collaborative Online Workspace, 2017) <www.unredd.net> accessed 31 March 2017.

future investment disputes under applicable international investment agreements.[45] As in other sectors, additional investment and financial flows are needed in forestry and in the reduction of deforestation and forest degradation.[46] Therefore, private sector investment tends to become more significant. REDD is also an area where climate policy and the investment law regime might interact.[47]

The Kyoto Protocol regime has been criticised for many reasons, including its flexibility mechanisms. A common criticism is that the strong focus on cost effectiveness through the use of such mechanisms and the enormous effort to develop them has diverted attention from the core goal of the Protocol.[48] In reality, the flexibility mechanisms, in particular the CDM, have been actively used and have generated a carbon price and market valuing ecosystem services.

The Kyoto Protocol, and especially the CDM, has given rise to the first international market in an environmental commodity, the CERs.[49] The CDM exceeded expectations in terms of the number of projects registered.[50] The estimated amount of emission reductions from the CDM and JI was 1 billion tons of CO_2 during the Kyoto Protocol's first commitment period.[51] In practice, about 2.2 billion CERs have been transacted for approximately US$26 billion (between 2002 and 2009).[52] These mechanisms did help industrialised countries meet their Kyoto targets more cost effectively. There are also many examples of how the Kyoto Protocol mechanisms have contributed to sustainable development in host countries, for example by improving energy access and services, providing solutions for solid waste management, reducing air and water pollution, generating employment, etc. In addition, CDM and JI have involved technology transfer that was beneficial to developing countries.[53] JI suffered from a late start compared to the CDM and has not materialised as expected. Over time, high supply in the market coming from both Kyoto Protocol units and regional trading schemes, together with low

45 Firger and Gerrard (n 25) 38.

46 For forestry, additional investment and financial flows are estimated at about $21 billion and an indicative estimate of the cost of reducing deforestation and forest degradation to zero in 2030 is $12 billion, see UNFCCC (n 8) 3.

47 Firger and Gerrard (n 25) 38

48 Javier de Cendra de Larragan, 'The Kyoto Protocol with a Special Focus on the Flexibility Mechanisms', in Daniel Farber and Marjan Peeters (eds) *Climate Change Law, Elgar Encyclopedia of Environmental Law* (Edward Elgar Publishing, 2016) vol 1, 230.

49 Charlotte Streck and Jolene Lin, 'Making Markets Work: A Review of CDM Performance and the Need for Reform' (2008) 10 (2) *The European Journal of International Law* 420.

50 This review of the Kyoto Protocol can be found in World Bank, *10 Years of Experience in Carbon Finance, Insights from Working with the Kyoto Mechanisms* (World Bank, 2010).

51 Ibid.

52 Ibid.

53 Ibid.

demand,[54] have depressed the carbon price and brought the markets to a standstill.[55]

The Paris Agreement: Movement away from the Kyoto Protocol

The 2015 Paris Agreement moves away from the Kyoto Protocol's approach to differentiation, putting an end to the divide between Annex I and non-Annex I countries.[56] Thus, both developed and developing countries must now work together towards a *global response to the threat of climate change.* All parties must undertake *ambitious efforts* defined under their *Nationally Determined Contributions* (NDCs), which describe a country's mitigation status and goals.[57]

While a small group of countries opposed the inclusion of a market-based provision in the Paris Agreement, the majority contemplated the use of carbon markets in their *Intended NDCs* (INDCs).[58] The Agreement finally foresees the use of carbon market mechanisms, but avoids references to the words *markets* or *carbon trading.* Instead, Article 6 refers to *voluntary co-operation* between countries that involve trading emission reductions, or *internationally transferred mitigation outcomes* (ITMOs). In other words, it allows for emissions trading. To ensure integrity of a market mechanism, parties must apply robust accounting rules in order to avoid double counting.[59] Article 6.4 also establishes a new mechanism to promote the mitigation of GHG emissions while fostering sustainable development, which has been named the *Sustainable Development Mechanism* (SDM). The SDM will be able to generate offsets for emission reductions deriving from projects located both in developed and developing countries. Therefore, it merges the roles of the Kyoto Protocol's CDM and JI.[60] Unlike the CDM, the SDM will not be limited to project-based reductions, but may also include policies or activities that may lead to emission reductions. Similarly to the CDM, the SDM is likely to attract private capital investment in developing countries, as

54 One of the main reasons that explains the low demand for Kyoto Protocol units relates to the uncertainties surrounding a post-2012 international agreement. This has led to a decline of the CDM and JI market volume and value of carbon units. The slow economic recovery in Europe and other parts of the world from the global financial crisis is another factor, see World Bank (n 7) 48.

55 de Cendra de Larragan (n 48) 236.

56 Daniel Bodansky, 'The Paris Climate Change Agreement: A New Hope?' (2016) 110 *American Journal of International Law* 18.

57 Ibid 8.

58 Ibid 8.

59 About double counting see, Lambert Schneider, Anja Kollmuss and Michael Lazarus, 'Addressing the Risk of Double Counting Emission Reductions under the UNFCCC' (2015) 131 (4) *Climatic Change* 473: 'Double counting of emission reductions can occur when a single greenhouse gas emission reduction or removal, achieved through a mechanism issuing units, is accounted more than once towards attaining mitigation pledges'.

60 Bodansky (n 56) 8.

it involves project activities to incentivise the use of clean technology, waste reduction and adaptation, among others, all of which require funding.

In sum, the Paris Agreement provides for two market-based approaches: ITMO between two or more parties and the SDM.[61] They are both voluntary and must have a transparent reporting system and robust accounting procedures to ensure that carbon emission reductions are accurately calculated and not counted twice. The outcomes of both mechanisms shall be *real, measurable and* contain *long-term* mitigation benefits.

In relation to forests, the Paris Agreement encourages parties to implement REDD+ to conserve and enhance carbon sinks, including forests and other ecosystems. Under Article 5, parties are required to reduce emissions from deforestation and forest degradation through both results-based payments and policy approaches, such as joint mitigation and adaption.

Carbon markets beyond the United Nations

Carbon trading outside Kyoto: Compliance national and regional schemes

Beyond the UN, countries have used two types of market instruments to reduce carbon emissions: carbon taxes and emissions trading. Both put a price on carbon emissions. The key distinction between the two is that with a carbon tax, the government sets the price and allows the market to determine the quantity of emissions, whereas with emissions trading, the government sets the quantity of emissions and allows the market to determine the price.[62] Hybrid systems combining the two approaches also exist. Currently, about 40 national jurisdictions and over 20 cities, states and regions opted for putting a price on carbon as a key mitigation tool, notably through emissions trading schemes (ETSs).[63]

There are two kinds of carbon markets: regulatory (or compliance) and voluntary. Compliance markets refer to the creation and trade of emission reductions pursuant to treaties and laws that place a legally binding cap or limit on certain sources of GHG emissions.[64] Examples of compliance markets include the Kyoto Protocol and the EU ETS. Under the voluntary carbon market, there are no legal obligations to reduce emissions. Therefore, companies, organisations and individuals, without government-mandated obligations, can engage in activities to offset their emissions, for example

61 Anju Sharma and others, *Pocket Guide to the Paris Agreement* (European Capacity Building Initiative, 2016) 11.

62 Partnership for Market Readiness, *Emissions Trading in Practice, A Handbook on Design and Implementation* (World Bank, 2016) 7.

63 Ibid 3.

64 Michelle Passero, 'The Voluntary Carbon Market: Its Contributions and Potential Legal and Policy Issues' in Freestone and Streck (n 1) 517.

through projects that meet the Voluntary Carbon Standard (VCS) and/or the Climate, Community and Biodiversity (CCB) Standards.[65] The voluntary carbon market is also called an *over-the-counter* (OTC) marketplace.[66]

Compliance markets outside Kyoto take place at the regional, national and sub-national levels. The EU ETS is an example of a regional scheme. National trading schemes include for example the New Zealand Emissions Trading Scheme (NZ ETS), Swiss Emissions Trading System and the Korean Emissions Trading Scheme. At the sub-national level, trading schemes can involve cities, states or groups of states. Examples include the Tokyo Cap-and-Trade, the California Cap-and-Trade Program, Québec Cap-and-Trade System and the United States' Regional Greenhouse Gas Initiative (covering Connecticut, Delaware, Maine, Maryland, Massachusetts, New Hampshire, New York, Rhode Island and Vermont).[67] A range of regional pilot ETS schemes is also in place in China and may be incorporated into an overall Chinese cap-and-trade system by 2017. According to the World Bank, ETSs currently operate across four continents in 35 countries, 13 states or provinces and 7 cities, covering 40 per cent of global GDP.[68]

Carbon trading in the voluntary market: The land-use and forestry sector

In the voluntary market, there are no legal obligations to reduce emissions. Therefore, carbon offset buyers, including private sector companies and other entities, are driven for example by ethical or branding reasons. In 2015, a total of 84.1 million tonnes of carbon dioxide equivalent ($MtCO_2e$) were transacted in the voluntary market.[69]

Consumer demand for 'green' goods and services is a factor that pushes firms into voluntary carbon markets. Corporate social responsibility (CSR) is also driving a subsequent response towards eco-friendly actions. The first common reason for purchases in the voluntary market is branding and CSR, followed by a 'pre-compliance buy' (i.e. those buying in anticipation of regulation).[70] Offset buyers have different motivations, but the two most cited reasons for offsetting are: '*demonstrating climate leadership within industry*', and '*pursuit of a GHG emissions target*' driven by a CSR policy or public relations team.[71] Companies are looking to market themselves as 'green' or

65 Forest Trends and others, *Investing in Forest Carbon: Lessons from the First 20 Years* (BioLogical Capital, 2011) 2.

66 Ibid.

67 These examples and figures can be found in Forest Trends (n 65) 3.

68 Ibid.

69 Ecosystem Marketplace, *Raising Ambition, State of Voluntary Carbon Markets* (Forest Trends, 2015) 1 (Hereinafter: State of Voluntary Carbon Markets 2016).

70 Markit Environmental Registry, *Beginner's Guide to the Voluntary Carbon Market* (Katoomba Group, 2009).

71 Ibid.

environmentally friendly[72] as a way to capture growing conscious-consumer trends.

There are different types of projects in the voluntary market in different sectors, such as energy, industrial processing, agriculture and forestry, among others.[73] The most sought-after project type in 2015 was offsets from wind, due to its attractive price for buyers.[74] REDD+ projects usually have higher average prices, when compared to other types of projects. Most offsets in 2015 have been bought by private sector buyers in the energy, transportation, finance/insurance sectors, as well as in the events/entertainment and service sectors.

Forest carbon projects are implemented in both the compliance and voluntary markets. Examples of such projects in the regulatory market include CDM afforestation and reforestation projects. In the voluntary market, there are various types of forest carbon projects, for example, improved forest management, REDD+, afforestation and reforestation projects.[75] Historically, most forest carbon deals (73 per cent or 15 $MtCO_2$) have occurred in the voluntary carbon market.[76] Much of the demand for forest credits has been from buyers who purchase credits to offset their own emissions. They opt for forest carbon offsets for many reasons, for example because they are easier to communicate than other types of carbon offsets, through compelling images of standing forests with clear branding benefits. Also, these projects usually lead to positive land-use change that can be bundled with other social and environmental co-benefits, from environmental conservation, to poverty alleviation and social justice.[77]

However, the social and environmental impacts of carbon projects are better assessed on a case-by-case basis. For example, some CDM afforestation/reforestation projects have been criticised for leading to non-permanent monoculture plantations of non-native species, which lead to negative environmental impacts on natural habitats and biodiversity, such as

72 Overseas Development Institute, 'What Are Carbon Markets?' (ODI, 2017) <www.odi.org/sites/odi.org.uk/files/odi-assets/publications-opinion-files/6088.pdf> accessed 27 March 2017.

73 See Verified Carbon Standard (VCS), 'Find a Methodology' (VCS, 2017) <http://database.v-c-s.org/methodologies/find> accessed 27 March 2017.

74 This information can be found in Ecosystem Marketplace (n 69) 3.

75 Forest Trends and others (n 65) 3. Definitions are as follows: (1) afforestation involves growing forests on land that has not been forested in recent history, while reforestation, re-growing forests in areas where forests have been previously. Afforestation and reforestation (A/R) projects are commonly considered simultaneously, as both refer to projects where trees are grown; (2) improved forest management includes activities that enhance carbon stocks on currently forested lands; (3) REDD avoids carbon emissions by preserving existing forests threatened by activities that reduce the carbon storage of the forest.

76 Ibid 5.

77 Ibid 6.

excessive water consumption.[78] Some CDM projects have also failed to include local communities through measures like credible benefit sharing and participatory mechanisms.[79]

Over the past 20 years, forest carbon markets have evolved and their methodologies have become more sophisticated. Carbon standards are increasingly being used for establishing consistency and quality benchmarks, particularly those that account for co-benefits of forest carbon projects and third-party verification.[80] The VCS is the most used of all standards, holding 49 per cent of market share.[81] Besides the VCS, several other carbon standards also propose regulations, methodologies, or guidelines for forest carbon projects. Examples include: the American Carbon Registry (ACR) Forest Project Standard, Climate Action Reserve, Plan Vivo Standards, ISO 14064 and SocialCarbon, among others.

Apart from the direct results-based payments for emission reductions, in the voluntary and compliance markets, support for forest conservation and improved management also occurs in the form of 'non-market' funding. This may include for example finance for *REDD+ readiness* or activities involving tree planting, carbon-conscious agriculture and forest management, among others.[82] Over time, the majority of forest carbon finance ($2.8 billion, tracked in 13 key tropical forest countries) has gone towards 'readiness' efforts as countries prepare for implementing REDD+ mechanisms.[83]

Forest carbon projects in practice

Forest carbon projects have been developed and credits have been transacted primarily in the voluntary market.[84] A forest carbon project is an activity that prevents the deforestation and/or degradation of forest habitats and provides an economic benefit, through the selling of carbon credits, to those who cease detrimental activities in favour of conservation and sustainable management. The project proponent can be an individual landowner, a community, an organisation or a private entity (e.g. mining, agriculture or a

78 See discussion about CDM afforestation/reforestation projects at Carbon Market Watch, 'Forestry Land Use Projects' (CMW, 2017) <http://carbonmarketwatch.org/category/sustainable-development/forestry-land-use-projects/ CDM> accessed 27 March 2017.

79 Ibid.

80 Almost all (98 per cent) offsets that found a buyer in 2015 were verified by an independent third-party standard, see Ecosystem Marketplace (n 69) 3.

81 Ibid 12.

82 Ecosystem Marketplace, 'Converging at the Crossroads, State of Forest Carbon Finance 2015' (Forest Trends, 2015) 3: 'REDD+ "readiness" finance refers to money committed to tropical forest countries earmarked for activities that will prepare them for payments for avoided deforestation. "Readiness" encompasses Phases 1 and 2 of REDD+ under the UNFCCC (developing and implementing a REDD+ strategy) but *not* Phase 3 (payments for emissions reductions)'.

83 Ibid 4.

84 Forest Trends and others (n 65) 1.

livestock company).[85] The main objectives of forest carbon projects are to protect or restore forest areas, reduce GHG emissions, remunerate project proponents with revenues from carbon sales and protect other environmental assets, such as biodiversity, water, cultural values or other ecosystem services.

The first step in any forest carbon project is to identify a suitable standard and methodology. Currently, the VCS is the most used and comprehensive carbon standard.[86] It is often combined with the CCB Standards, which accounts for other environmental and socioeconomic co-benefits, such as water and biodiversity conservation, recreational values and community participation, among others.

The VCS has various approved methodologies to address specific situations, or *baseline scenarios*, in different sectors: energy, transport, waste, agriculture, forestry, etc.[87] In the land-use sector, those methodologies address different baseline scenarios, for example illegal degradation and deforestation (VCS-REDD); deforestation of areas where logging has been sanctioned (VCS-IFM Improved Forest Management); or restoration and re-establishment of forest areas (afforestation and reforestation) (UNFCCC-CDM Afforestation/Reforestation).

Despite the differences in existing methodologies, forest carbon projects involve five basic steps from the initial design to the completion of the project. These include:

1 Feasibility study of the potential carbon credits and associated costs and benefits. A feasibility study entails:
   a. An evaluation of landownership or concession holdings and any required engagement/awareness activities with relevant stakeholders. There must be an *eligible project area*. In other words, the project proponent must demonstrate a right of use over the area, by providing legally recognised evidence (e.g. land titles, concession contracts, etc.).
   b. Stratification using Geographic Information System (GIS) and fieldwork to prepare a comprehensive forest inventory.
   c. Calculation of avoided carbon emissions and corresponding carbon credits generated.
   d. Assessment of risks, such as leakage and non-permanence.

85 The information regarding how forest carbon projects are implemented in practice can be found in *Seeking Synergies and Project Opportunites Combining Biotrade and Forest Carbon Projects*, Concept Note, Prepared by Forests Alive for discussion at the Rio+20 Conference, 2012.

86 Johannes Ebeling and Jacob Olander (eds), *REDD Guidance: Technical Project Design in Building Forest Carbon Projects* (Forest Trends, 2011) 2.

87 See VCS (n 73).

2 Field survey of standing carbon, which is an on-ground survey to confirm the projected carbon within the forest.
3 Preparation and submission of all required project documents to the selected standard (e.g. project design document, monitoring plan, etc.).
4 Verification and validation of the project by independent auditors. To generate carbon credits project developers must demonstrate real and measurable reductions in emissions. For this reason, projects are validated and verified by external third parties to ensure that they meet the criteria of the selected standard (VCS, CCB or other). Carbon credits are generated after each verification event, once demonstrated that emission reductions have been achieved.
5 Monitoring report and risk assessment, usually submitted every year during the project life cycle, unless stated otherwise in the methodology. Calculations are also revisited periodically.

Forest carbon projects must meet some basic requirements. The forest must be under threat by the conversion to other land uses or degradation. There must be evidence of ***additionality***, which is proof that the baseline scenario (e.g. planned deforestation and/or degradation, or illegal deforestation and/or degradation, etc.) will take place in the absence of the project. In other words, all projects must demonstrate that they are additional to what would have happened under a business-as-usual-scenario.[88] Also, there must be evidence that the project avoids *leakage*, which is evidence that the baseline activity will not be carried out elsewhere as a result of the project.

Forest carbon projects generate carbon credits, which can be used in different ways. They can be sold in compliance or voluntary carbon markets and act as a source of revenue for the project proponent. They can also be used to offset the project proponent's own emissions, for example, from stock raising, agriculture, mining or other activities. These projects often involve other *co-benefits*, apart from delivering emission reductions. Co-benefits may include biodiversity conservation, watershed protection and recreational and scenic values (environmental benefits), as well as community engagement, training, research and knowledge and employment (social benefits).

Forest carbon projects can be initiated in both developed and developing countries, while REDD+ projects are only implemented in developing countries.[89] Latin America hosts the greatest number of REDD+ projects, followed by Asia and then Africa.[90] The countries that host the majority of

88 These definitions can be found in David Shoch, James Eaton and Scott Settelmyer, *Project Developer's Guidebook to VCS REDD Methodologies* (Conservation International, 2013).

89 For an overview of existing projects see VCS 'Project Database' (VCS, 2017) <http://vcsprojectdatabase.org/#/vcus/vac> accessed 27 March 2017.

90 Isilda Nhantumbo and Marisa Camargo, *REDD+ for Profit or for Good? Review of Private Sector and NGO experience in REDD+ Projects* (International Institute for Environment and Development, 2015).

REDD+ demonstration projects are: Brazil, Indonesia, Mexico and Peru. Examples of forest carbon projects, including REDD+ projects, are: the Suruí Forest Carbon Project (Brazil), the Ankeniheny-Zahamena Corridor (Madagascar) and the April Salumei REDD project (Papua New Guinea).[91]

Forest carbon projects are not for the faint-hearted.[92] These projects are costly, complex and risky. Each of the five steps listed above involves significant costs. There are yet other expenses to factor in for REDD+ (or other project types) when carried out in developing countries. They often take place in community areas inhabited by local or indigenous populations. Therefore, various actions are needed, such as stakeholder consultations, community engagement and the design of effective benefit-sharing mechanisms, all of which involve costs. Adding up all these costs, forest carbon projects turn out to be very expensive. Overall, a forest carbon project, from initial development and preparation of the project design document (PDD), can easily cost $100,000 or more, depending on project characteristics.[93]

These considerations are also valid for private investors who must also face the complexities and risks associated with forest carbon projects. Given the high costs of REDD+ (and other project types), some projects have triggered public–private partnerships. For example, the Kasigau Corridor REDD project in Kenya, developed by Wildlife Works, issued its first VCS credits in 2011. Pursuant to a financing agreement between BNP Paribas and Wildlife Works, BNP Paribas had the option to purchase 1.25 million tons of these carbon offsets over five years.[94]

However, risks in forest carbon projects are still a factor limiting private sector investment. For example, a survey of private investors indicated that they intend to deploy $5.6 billion in conservation impact investments before 2018 (almost triple the $1.9 billion they spent between 2009 and 2013).[95] Yet only 1 per cent of past investment ($58 million) went to land-based funding mechanisms such as REDD+. According to investors, the limiting factor to growth is not available capital, but rather a shortage of deals with the appropriate risk/return profiles.[96] Investment tends to concentrate on countries with higher levels of development and political stability. For example, a select few countries host the majority of REDD+ demonstration projects: Brazil, Indonesia, Mexico and Peru.[97] Public–private partnerships have helped to address risk-related concerns. For example, the Althelia

91 See VCS (n 89).
92 Forest Trends and others (n 65) 23.
93 Ibid 9.
94 World Bank (n 7) 58.
95 Ecosystem Marketplace (n 82) 35.
96 Ibid.
97 See VCS (n 89).

Climate Fund found a way to reduce risks to its REDD+ investors by securing a $133.8 million loan guarantee from the United States Agency for International Development.[98]

The challenge for project developers is that many project costs are borne early in the development process, usually before carbon sales. These include costs associated with project design and start-up, such as on-ground assessments, fieldwork, carbon calculations, legal services, etc. Thus, most projects experience a financing gap and need to secure start-up funding. This financing gap is currently bridged by philanthropic sources, often funneled through NGOs,[99] organisations, private sector companies or investors.[100] Due to the complexities and costs associated with forest carbon projects, they normally have higher average prices when compared to other project types.[101]

Forest carbon projects are also complex from both a policy and technical perspective. Governments set the legal and policy context for forest carbon projects from land ownership, carbon rights rules and contract laws to tax rules for the trading of carbon offsets.[102] The existing policy and legal frameworks need to be well understood by project developers, investors, project proponents and other participants. For example, sometimes it is unclear for project developers to understand which government agencies and officials have the authority to discuss and determine carbon rights and negotiating with government officials can be lengthy and intricate.[103] Also, forest carbon projects can be impacted by fluid policy both at the domestic and international levels.

In general, forest carbon projects are more likely to succeed in countries with clear land ownership and carbon rights policies, a certain level of economic and political stability to attract investment, credible institutions to build partnerships with and anti-corruption and other measures to improve governance. But this is easier said than done. There are many well-known barriers to overcome in implementing such projects in developing countries, such as uncertainty over land ownership, potential land disputes, corruption and weak governance, threat of exclusion of forest-dependent communities or insufficient or unclear policies and rules.[104] Fortunately, there exists a conscious effort to address those issues. For example, most countries in Latin America and the Caribbean have anti-corruption laws and specialised control institutions in place to promote accountability and transparency in areas such

98 Ecosystem Marketplace (n 82) 35.

99 Ibid.

100 See discussion about financing gap in REDD+ project implementation in UN-REDD Programme, 'Economics of Forests and Forest Carbon Projects' (UN REDD, 2013) 72.

101 Ecosystem Marketplace (n 82) 3.

102 Forest Trends and others (n 65) 14.

103 Ibid.

104 Arild Angelsen and others, *Analysing REDD+: Challenges and Choices* (Centre for International Forestry Research, 2012).

as procurement, public administration and election campaigns, some of which are directly related to the land-use sector.[105]

Forest carbon projects are also challenging from a technical point of view. They require several technical requirements, for example tools to map forest areas through GIS, measuring and calculating carbon stocks and preparing lengthy project documents (e.g. PDDs, monitoring and risk reports). In addition, it may be difficult to understand rates and drivers of deforestation, conduct modelling and monitor land-use changes in landscapes undergoing rapid changes from urbanisation or shifting agricultural frontiers. The lack of accurate on-ground data can also be a hindrance to measuring carbon stocks, understanding land-use changes and estimating precisely future carbon revenues. The risks associated with forest carbon projects vary from natural risks (e.g. forest fires, floods, landslides, etc.) or human-induced deforestation and/or degradation to changes in policy or market uncertainties. These may involve, for example, a decline in a credit's average price if supply of carbon offsets exceeds demand.[106]

The question is whether forest carbon projects, with their potential and shortcomings, can be an effective mitigation tool and help countries meet their NDCs. Are these projects a good market tool to reduce emissions, conserve and enhance carbon sinks and protect natural resources? Overall, is carbon trading only delaying real changes that involve phasing out carbon emissions and transitioning away from fossil fuels? Will carbon markets help mobilise new and additional resources and investments? What are investment opportunities and challenges related to those mechanisms?

Ideally, countries should reduce carbon emissions without relying on carbon offsets or other forms of market instruments that make compliance with emission reduction targets more attractive to polluters and legal obligations more palatable. One main criticism to carbon trading and a genuine concern, is that CO_2 emissions in industrialised countries are not declining at the necessary rate to avert catastrophic climate change.[107] The efforts to build credible carbon market mechanisms probably divert attention from the real issue: that global carbon emissions must be cut as soon as possible, before it is too late. Instead of driving aggressive structural and behavioural changes, countries seem focused on reducing emissions more cost effectively.

Yet despite these challenges, there are many forest carbon projects that have delivered positive outcomes, in terms of protecting forests and

105 About anti-corruption measures in the forestry sector, see B. Garcia, *Local Governance, Anti-Corruption and REDD+ in Latin America and the Caribbean: Exploring Synergies to Strengthen Transparency and Accountability* (United Nations Development Programme, 2011).

106 About a supply-and-demand analysis of forest carbon offsets, see Ecosystem Marketplace (n 82) 3.

107 Jutta Kill, Saskia Ozinga, Steven Pavett and Richard Wainwright, *Trading Carbon, How It Works and Why It Is Controversial* (FERN, 2010).

introducing best management practices. Third-party verification of carbon offsets to stringent carbon standards developed for REDD+ (and other project types) also helps to ensure that emission reductions can be real, measurable and verifiable.[108] As noted, REDD+ offers the potential for a triple benefit: climate change mitigation, community development and biodiversity conservation. The most robust projects capture all three.[109] However, there are still various challenges associated with these projects that need to be addressed. For example, a review of 115 demonstration projects in different countries in Africa, Asia and Latin America indicates that benefit-sharing arrangements with local communities are usually unclear and that community participation is not optimal.[110] In any case, a thorough review and evaluation of existing REDD+ (and other project types) across different regions of the world, using clear and robust indicators, is still needed in order to clarify the real benefits and problems of existing forest carbon projects.

Carbon markets can attract both public funding and private sector investment at a great scale and pace. The public sector alone will not be able to finance current climate mitigation and adaptation needs. Therefore, although those mechanisms play a role in scaling up climate finance, challenges remain. As noted earlier, investments in carbon projects tend to be unevenly distributed among countries. Current and future carbon projects must also achieve positive social and environmental outcomes. This requires adequate monitoring and oversight from independent bodies. In addition, achieving the right balance between the interests of investors and host countries (and communities) may prove challenging.

The future of carbon markets after Paris

In an ideal world, countries would reduce net carbon emissions as quickly and widely as possible in all different economic sectors, through efforts by industries, households and individuals, without offsetting or trading carbon emissions. However, this is unlikely to happen, as carbon markets are currently the largest environmental market in the world and worth almost $144 billion.[111] As noted, more than half of the UNFCCC parties indicated in their national submissions that they plan or hope to use market-based mechanisms to meet reduction targets.[112] Beyond the UN, voluntary carbon markets are well established and generate millions of dollars per year.[113]

108 See Nicole R. Vigillio (n 36) 5.
109 Ibid.
110 Nhantumbo and Camargo (n 90) 68.
111 Carbon markets, measured by volume, are the largest type of environmental market in the world. In 2009, the value of global carbon markets reached almost $144 billion, 'Investing in Forest Carbon: Lessons from the First 20 Years' (n 73) 2.
112 Ecosystem Marketplace (n 2), 'State of the Voluntary Carbon Market 2016' 4.
113 Voluntary value reached $128 Million, 'State of Forest Carbon Finance 2015' 4.

A significant benefit from carbon markets and the voluntary carbon market in particular, is that at minimum they raise awareness regarding how entities or individuals contribute to global climate change, how to measure GHG emissions and how these emissions may be avoided or mitigated.[114] The voluntary market has also fostered the development of GHG accounting standards and registries.

Carbon trading is a reality and is likely to grow. Therefore, one of the main challenges after Paris is to ensure environmental integrity of the market mechanisms under the UN system. This requires robust accounting rules to ensure that emission reductions are real and counted only once. The carbon market mechanisms proposed under the Paris Agreement must ensure transparency, rigorous verification and compliance with UNFCCC rules. Given that parties are highly heterogeneous, developing this common accounting system may prove challenging.[115] This might be a key topic of discussion for the years ahead.

Carbon market mechanisms also play an important role in mobilising public funding and private investment in developing countries. Therefore, together with other types of initiatives, policies and measures, these mechanisms will help scale up climate finance. One of the main challenges associated with carbon projects is ensuring that they bring tangible social and environmental benefits to host countries and communities. This requires effective monitoring and oversight of project activities. Moreover, those mechanisms shall benefit developing countries more broadly, including least-developed countries.

The carbon market space tends to grow in volume and complexity. In practice, carbon trading will take place at different levels, under and beyond the UNFCCC. One important consideration for the future is how existing trading schemes will co-exist and interact. Several questions may arise, for example: how will market mechanisms under the Paris Agreement interact with other trading schemes? Will carbon units generated under one scheme be used under another scheme? Will existing methodologies, rules and verification procedures under different standards be harmonised in any way? Will different trading schemes be guided by a common set of principles and how can this be achieved? Will different trading schemes be linked in any way?

Moreover, it is yet to be seen what role the voluntary carbon market will play in a world in which nearly every country is under a compliance agreement to reduce emissions.[116] In practice, will projects validated under the VCS, CCB or other standards meet the technical requirements and safeguards of a future UNFCCC compliance regime? How will the hundreds of pilot forest carbon projects around the world co-exist with domestic and

114 Passero (n 64) 520.

115 Bodansky (n 56) 29.

116 Ecosystem Marketplace (n 2), 'State of the Voluntary Carbon Market 2016' 4.

international carbon trading schemes? Will the offsets generated by those projects be incorporated into other markets? Experience shows that compliance markets often serve to catalyse voluntary markets, rather than suppress them and that there will always be companies willing to demonstrate 'above-and-beyond' action as part of a CSR strategy or for other reasons.[117] The rules for the market mechanisms under the Paris Agreement, and their potential interaction with other carbon trading schemes, will be shaped in the years to come. Hopefully, the negotiations started in Marrakesh will eventually deliver market mechanisms that are as simple as possible, transparent and credible, as well as being technically robust.

117 Ibid.

16 Modern biofuels

The road to integrated sustainability

Feja Lesniewska

Introduction

Today biofuels are the single largest renewable energy source globally. They provide over 10 per cent of the world's primary energy supply.[1] Two thirds of biofuels are 'traditional' and locally sourced, primarily in developing countries.[2] Yet biofuels production, processing and trade are undergoing a transformation at the start of the twenty-first century. World biofuel production capacity nearly trebled from 2000 to 2014, with over 30 per cent being so-called 'modern biofuels'.[3]

According to the World Energy Council, there is significant potential to expand modern biofuels supply to be a sustainable energy source, especially in the Global South, in the fight against climate change as well as energy poverty.[4] Globally, the International Renewable Energy Agency predicts that the demand for non-traditional uses of bioenergy energy will increase over the next 20 years, more than tripling over the period 2013–2035.[5] Yet these outcomes are only feasible if modern biofuel production, processing and trade are truly sustainable.

With over 40 countries currently possessing policy frameworks to promote the use of modern biofuels, ensuring sustainability is vital if negative

1 World Energy Resources, *Bioenergy* (World Energy Council, 2013)

2 Traditional bioenergy refers to the use of biomass such as wood, charcoal, agricultural residues and animal dung for cooking and heating, at a small scale, by poor, marginal and frequently vulnerable communities. They can have negative social, environmental and economic impacts: see Fiona Lambe and others, 'Bringing Clean, Safe, Affordable Cooking Energy to Households Across Africa: An Agenda for Action' (Stockholm Environment Institute, 2015) working paper 21 available <www.sei-international.org/mediamanager/doucments/Publications/NCE-SEI-2015-Transforming-household-energy-sub-Saharan-Africa-LR.pdf> accessed 5 February 2017

3 Modern bioenergy is the use of bioliquids and biomass at large scale for transport, electricity generation and urban heating: Olivier Lavagne d'Ortigue, Adrian Whiteman and Samah Elsayed, 'Renewable Energy Capacity Statistics 2015' (International Renewable Energy Agency, 2015) 36

4 World Energy Resources (n 1)

5 d'Ortigue, Whiteman and Elsayed (n 3) 36

environmental, economic and social impacts are to be avoided.[6] Negative impacts are experienced inequitably due to transnational modern biofuels investment occurring primarily in least-developed countries, with poor, vulnerable and marginalised rural communities being the most impacted.[7] Without rigorous and effective regulations in place biofuels' environmental and social impacts will undermine efforts to improve law and governance, especially in least-developed countries. This needs to be achieved however without perpetuating existing injustices and inequities in access to resources between the elite and other citizens. To achieve sustainable biofuel production, processing and trade, multiple law and policy interconnections across a multilevel global governance landscape need to be identified, understood and reconciled.

An integrated approach to biofuel standards is a prerequisite to achieving real sustainability. It must support the realisation of human and indigenous peoples' rights as well as international environmental law objectives, including climate change mitigation. Several international, public and private, voluntary, non-legally binding initiatives are coalescing towards a more integrated approach towards biofuels sustainability.[8] Obstacles continue to remain, not least embedded governance structures, states' political agendas as well as an unsustainable international trade system.[9] A final threat to biofuels sustainability could be the large-scale uptake of bioenergy carbon capture and storage projects undertaken as part of the United Nations Framework Agreement on Climate Change's Paris Agreement parties' efforts to mitigate climate change, which some argue will result in net positive rather than net negative emissions, as well as serious environmental and social impacts.[10]

This chapter argues that an integrated framework approach towards biofuels sustainability regulation is emerging internationally. International guidelines, both specifically in relation to biofuels as well as natural resources, are coalescing into a normative foundation that can be the basis for designing effective biofuels sustainability regulation. However, as this chapter illustrates, there are serious political, economic and legal limitations

6 As well as EU member states, these include Armenia, Brazil, Canada, China, Dominican Republic, Ecuador, Ghana, India, Indonesia, Israel, Japan, Malawi, Malaysia, Pakistan, Palestine, Philippines, Serbia, South Africa, Switzerland, Syria, Thailand, Turkey, Uganda, United States and Uruguay: ibid

7 Countries include Cambodia, Congo, Ethiopia, Ghana, Kenya, Laos, Madagascar, Malawi, Mali, Mozambique, Nigeria, Sierra Leone, Somalia, South Sudan, Tanzania, Uganda, Vietnam, Zambia and Zimbabwe: Kate Geary, *'Our Land, Our Lives': Time Out on the Global Land Rush* (Oxfam Briefing Note, October 2012)

8 Rebecca Efroymson and others, 'Environmental Indicators of Biofuel Sustainability: What about Context? (2013) 51 *Environmental Management* 291

9 Ibid 302

10 Naomi Vaughan and Clair Gough, 'Expert Assessment Concludes Negative Emissions Scenarios May Not Deliver' (2016) 11 *Environmental Research Letters* 9 available <iopscience.iop.org/article/10.1088/1748-9326/11/9/095003/pdf> accessed 5 February 2017

hindering more rapid progress that make it questionable whether modern biofuels can be sustainable soon, and that many initiatives are a dangerous distraction from this reality.

The chapter begins by introducing modern biofuels classifications to clarify the different feedstocks and their associated impact factors. The impacts of biofuels are then discussed to illustrate how modern production can conflict with existing international environmental law and human rights law. The tensions between the UN Framework Convention on Climate Change objectives and other international law are also highlighted. The following section outlines how an integrated approach to determining biofuels sustainability is emerging internationally. This is followed by the European Union case study that demonstrates the biofuels sustainability criteria shortcomings, despite being heralded as the 'most stringent in the world'. The final section concludes that despite developments on international biofuels sustainability, a fully integrated approach would need to reverse current trends to increase demand driven by climate change policy.

Modern biofuels classifications

Modern biofuel feed stocks have different economic, environmental and social impacts.[11] 'Conventional' first-generation modern biofuels are usually produced from feedstocks that are also used in food and feed markets. Examples include corn and sugarcane for ethanol (in the US and Brazil, respectively), soy, palm oil and rapeseed for biodiesel (with major production in the Americas, Southeast Asia and Europe, respectively).[12] The increasing demand for conventional modern biofuels has resulted in concerns over the direct and indirect impacts on food security due to land use competition, as well as land rights, ecosystem resilience and climate change mitigation.

'Advanced' second-generation modern biofuels are being promoted and developed to be commercially viable in an effort to reduce threats to food security, especially in producer countries in the Global South.[13] Second-generation biofuels are made from lignocellulose biomass or woody crops, agricultural residues or waste.[14] Feedstock for second-generation biofuels can be established either on currently existing cropland, converted land or marginal land thereby avoiding the need to convert land. However, economically competitive second-generation biofuel feedstocks do not necessarily

11 FAO Forestry Department, *Unified Bioenergy Terminology* (Food and Agriculture Organization of the United Nations, 2004)

12 Julie Witcover, Sonia Yeh and Daniel Sperling, 'Policy Options to Address Global Land Use Change from Biofuels' (2013) 56 *Energy Policy* 63

13 Stefan Bringezu and others, *Towards Sustainable Production and Use of Resources: Assessing Biofuels* (United Nations Environment Programme, 2009) 18

14 Ibid

reduce biofuel production land use impacts, they can merely lead to indirect impacts nationally and/or transnationally.[15]

Concern over land use change, direct or indirect, from both first and second-generation biofuels impacts has led to an interest in identifying 'marginal' land for production.[16] There is substantial uncertainty, as well as lack of reliable data, over the global land reserve that could be deployed for the production of biofuels.[17] Growing energy crops on 'marginal' land is seen as a way of ensuring that biofuel production involves an acceptable and sustainable use of land.[18] The meaning of the term 'marginal land' is significantly open to interpretation. The term 'marginal land' is one of a number of labels used to characterise the type of land promoted for second-generation biofuels production; others being 'idle', 'unused', 'free', 'spare', 'abandoned', 'set aside', 'degraded', 'fallow', 'additional', 'appropriate' and 'under-utilised' land.[19] Shortall notes that 'the definitions of these terms are ambiguous and fluid' and, as such, 'many interesting conceptual issues [are] raised, particularly in relation to the linguistic negotiation of "free" and "unused" land'.[20] Consequently national law and policy on defining, categorising and zoning 'marginal lands' has significant implications for land users. The Food and Agriculture Organization of the United Nations (FAO) has cautioned that liquid biofuels production, using feedstock such as *jatropha curcas* might contribute to the socio-economic marginalisation of women and female-headed households.[21] The conflicts between users is multiplied with feedstock from forests used for biomass where access and user rights are not clearly defined for local communities. This is particularly the case in developing countries where land tenure rights are unclear

15 Rebecca Efroymson and others, 'A Causal Analysis Framework for Land-Use Change and the Potential Role of Bioenergy Policy' (2016) 59 *Land Use Policy* 516

16 Carmen G. Gonzalez, 'Energy Poverty and the Environment' in Carmen G. Gonzalez (ed), *International Energy and Poverty: The Emerging Contours* (Seattle University, 2015)

17 Chidi Oguamanam, 'Sustainable Development in the Era of Bioenergy' in Shawkat Alam and others (eds), *International Environmental Law and the Global South* (Cambridge University Press, 2015) 237, 242; Petr Havlik and others, 'Global Land-Use Implications of First and Second Generation Biofuel Targets' (2011) 39 *Energy Policy* 5690

18 Göran Berndes, Neil Bird and Annette Cowie, 'Bioenergy, Land Use Change and Climate Change Mitigation' (International Energy Agency Bioenergy 2010) 4 <http://task39.org/files/2013/05/Bioenergy-Land-Use-Change-and-Climate-Change-Mitigation.pdf> accessed 5 February 2017

19 Witcover, Yeh and Sperling (n 12)

20 Orla Shorthall, '"Marginal land" for Energy Crops: Exploring Definitions and Embedded Assumptions' (2013) 62 *Energy Policy* 19

21 Andrea Rossi and Yianna Lambrou, 'Gender and Equity Issues in Liquid Biofuels Production: Minimizing the Risks to Maximize the Opportunities' (FAO, 2008), cited in Nicola Colbran and Eide Asbjorn, 'Biofuel, the Environment, and Food Security: A Global Problem Explored through a Case Study of Indonesia' (2008) 9 *Sustainable Development Law and Policy* 4

and/or insecure, and where communities lack political power to claim their rights.[22]

The following section will expand on the issues regarding land use as the impacts of biofuel production are presented through a legal lens.

Biofuels: Environmental and human rights law dimensions

At the international level, law is an important driver pushing the increase in demand for biofuels but it also provides the normative framework to safeguard the environment and peoples' rights from their negative impacts.

UNFCCC, biofuels and conflicts

Behind the increase in modern biofuels demand since the late 1990s are policies and measures adopted to transition from fossil fuels to renewable energy in an effort to mitigate climate change. The 1997 Kyoto Protocol to the UN Framework Convention on Climate Change (UNFCCC) was a turning point internationally as it contained legally binding commitments by developed country parties to limit greenhouse gas (GHG) emissions.[23] Kyoto Protocol Annex I parties could develop policies and measures in the land use, land use change and forestry (LULUCF) sector to meet their emission reduction targets.[24] This prompted both developed and developing countries to adopt national renewable energy legislation including biofuel targets.[25] Nearly a decade later 37 UNFCCC parties in their Intended Nationally Determined Contribution (INDC) submissions for the Paris Agreement negotiations at the Conference of the Parties (COP) 21 in December 2015 included biofuels proposals to reduce GHGs by replacing fossil fuels with renewable energy sources.[26] The environmental, social and economic impact of this is yet to be seen on the ground but there are reasons to be concerned as ongoing issues remain as to the effectiveness in reducing GHG emissions from biofuels.

For GHG emissions reductions to contribute to climate change mitigation strategies, the reductions need to be real. There is an assumption, which

22 Saturnino Borras Jr and Jennifer Franco, 'From Threat to Opportunity – Problems with the Idea of a Code of Conduct for Land-Grabbing' (2010) 13 *Yale Human Rights and Development Law Journal* 507

23 *Kyoto Protocol to the United Nations Framework Convention on Climate Change*, opened for signature 16 March 1998, 2203 UNTS 162 (entered into force 16 February 2005) Art 3(1)

24 Ibid Arts 3(3), 3(4) and 3(7)

25 Jolene Lin, 'Governing Biofuels: A Principal – Agent Analysis of the European Union Biofuels Certification Regime and the Clean Development Mechanism' (2012) 24 *Journal of Environmental Law* 45

26 Vanessa Meadu and others, 'The Paris Climate Agreement: What It Means for Food and Farming' (CGIAR, December 2015)

originates from the GHG inventory and reporting guidance developed by the Intergovernmental Panel on Climate Change (IPCC) for the national GHG inventories submitted under the UNFCCC, that biofuels are carbon neutral.[27] It is claimed that by substituting biofuels for fossil fuels, a 'carbon debt' is created. A 'carbon payback period' is then determined in order to repay the debt. During the payback period, landscape restoration activities need to be undertaken. These activities, in time, are meant to result in carbon neutrality. This carbon payback period is critical to the contribution of biofuels to climate policy goals. As Brack notes, a range of factors affect this figure, including the type of forest and feedstock used, the amount of energy consumed in cultivation, collecting and transporting the biofuels and the combustion efficiency.[28] As a result, calculations suggest that the carbon payback period can vary enormously, from less than 20 years to many decades, and in some cases even centuries. By failing to adequately address loopholes and inconsistencies, the IPCC reporting guidelines for LULUCF GHG emissions reductions continue to be contentious and, as Dooley argues, continue to deliver 'misleading numbers' that inform future law and policy.[29] One perverse outcome illustrates this: proposals for bioenergy carbon capture and storage, permissible under the Paris Agreement, to achieve negative GHG emissions may ultimately result in an increase in GHGs.[30]

The increase in modern biofuel production has resulted in conflicts with other multilateral environmental agreements' objectives including the UN Convention on Biological Diversity (CBD)[31] and the UN Convention on Combating Desertification (UNCCD).[32] The CBD, because it is a framework convention that applies to all ecosystems, offers a useful case study to highlight the interconnections between biofuel expansion and the impacts on the environment.

Biofuel expansion is a threat to the 1992 CBD objectives: conservation, sustainable use and fair and equitable benefit sharing.[33] Threats to ecosystems from biofuels production include the potential spread of alien invasive

27 Simon Eggleston and others (eds), *2006 IPCC Guidelines for National Greenhouse Gas Inventories* (Institute for Global Environmental Strategies, 2006)

28 Duncan Brack, *Burning Matter: Making Bioenergy Policy Work for People and Forests* (FERN, 2015)

29 See Kate Dooley, *Misleading Numbers: The Case for Separating Land and Fossil Based Carbon Emissions* (FERN, 2014)

30 Oliver Geden, 'The Paris Agreement and the Inherent Inconsistency of Climate Policymaking' (2016) 7 *Wiley Interdisciplinary Reviews: Climate Change* 790

31 *Convention on Biological Diversity*, opened for signature 5 June 1992, 1760 UNTS 79 (entered into force 29 December 1993)

32 *Convention to Combat Desertification in those Countries Experiencing Serious Drought and/or Desertification, particularly in Africa*, opened for signature 14 October 1994, 1954 UNTS 3 (entered into force 26 December 1996)

33 *Convention on Biological Diversity* (n 31) Art 1

species, loss of wildlife habitat, land degradation, deforestation and degradation, water pollution from chemicals (fertilisers and pesticides) and synthetic impacts from the introduction of genetically modified feedstocks.[34] The risks are often interconnected.[35] For example under the CBD, parties are obliged to adopt a precautionary approach to prevent the spread of alien invasive species.[36] However, many countries have expanded biofuel production using exotic non-food crops, such as the *jatropha curcas*. To increase *jatropha* yields, producers regularly use fertilisers and pesticides; this is especially the case where alien invasive species feedstocks are intensively used.[37]

Due to the potential threats identified, CBD parties have actively sought to integrate the issue of biofuel production and incorporate it into several work programmes, including those on agricultural biodiversity and forests.[38] The CBD's 2020 Aichi biodiversity targets require not only the protection of some biodiversity hotspots such as old-growth forests, but also sustainable management of larger areas providing bioenergy feedstocks.[39] Due to the extensive nature of these threats, CBD parties have called for strict guidelines to prevent the negative impacts of biofuel production on biodiversity and ecosystem functions.[40] The CBD Secretariat also collaborates with other initiatives on developing biofuel sustainability criteria, including the Global Bioenergy Partnership (see below).[41]

International environmental law includes instruments that embrace the human dimensions of environmental issues. Adopting a human rights perspective to the critique of biofuels could lend additional value to the environmental perspective. International human rights law goes beyond other

34 Annie Webb and David Coates, *CBD Technical Series No. 65: Biofuels and Biodiversity* 65 (2012): 69 <www.cbd.int/doc/publications/cbd-ts-65-en.pdf> accessed 5 February 2017

35 Deborah Scott, Sarah Hitchner and Edward M. Maclin, 'Fuel for the Fire: Biofuels and the Problem of Translation at the Tenth Conference of the Parties to the Convention on Biological Diversity' (2014) 14(3) *Global Environmental Politics* 84

36 *Convention on Biological Diversity* (CBD) (n 31) Art 8(h) states that, 'Each contracting Party shall, as far as possible and as appropriate, prevent the introduction of, control or eradicate those alien species which threaten ecosystems, habitats or species'

37 Alexandros Gasparatos and Neil Christopher, 'Uncovering Hidden Trade-Offs in the Green Economy' in Alexandros Gasparatos and Katherine J. Willis (eds), *Biodiversity in the Green Economy* (Routledge, 2015) 61

38 *CBD* Conference of the Parties (COP) Decision IX/1 IX/1. In-depth review of the programme of work on agricultural biodiversity, UNEP/CBD/COP/DEC/IX/1 9 October 2008 para 31 Bonn (19–30 May 2008)

39 CBD COP Decision IX/2 Agricultural biodiversity: biofuels and biodiversity UNEP/CBD/COP/DEC/IX/2 9 October 2008 Bonn (19–30 May 2008)

40 CBD COP Decision X1/27 Biofuels and biodiversity, UNEP/CBD/COP/DEC/XI/27 5 December 2012 Hyderabad, India (8–19 October 2012)

41 CBD COP decision X/37 Biofuels and biodiversity, UNEP/CBD/COP/DEC/X/37 29 October 2010, Nagoya, Japan (18–29 October 2010)

areas of international law by providing a framework wherein individuals are the subject of its obligations.[42] This is important given that modern biofuel production, processing and trade impact people's human rights as well as indigenous peoples' rights. The remainder of this section will discuss three rights: water, land and food, which are commonly identified as being threatened by expanded biofuels production.[43]

The right to water

The right of an individual to access safe drinking water is recognised either implicitly or explicitly in several international instruments.[44] The UN General Comment 15 set out that 'a human right to water entitles everyone to sufficient, safe, acceptable, physically accessible and affordable water for personal and domestic uses'.[45] Ten years later the UN General Assembly adopted the Declaration on the Human Right to Water and Sanitation.[46] On this basis, states should guarantee the access of the population to water by avoiding, or

42 Philippe Cullet, 'Human Rights and Climate Change: Broadening the Right to Environment' in Cinnamon P. Carlene, Kevin R. Gray and Richard G. Tarasofsky (eds), *The Oxford Handbook of International Climate Change Law* (Oxford University Press, 2016) 495

43 This chapter will not be focusing on other rights such as labour, anti-discrimination, children and women's rights, all of which equally warrant attention when considering modern biofuel production, processing and trade impacts

44 Explicit reference to the right to access to water in human right instruments: *Convention on the Rights of the Child*, opened for signature 20 November 1989, 1577 UNTS 3 (entered into force 2 September 1990) (CRC) Art 24(2)(c); *Convention on the Elimination of All Forms of Discrimination against Women*, opened for signature 18 December 1979, 1249 UNTS 13 (entered into force 3 September 1981) (CEDAW) Art 14(2)(h); *Convention on the Rights of Persons with Disabilities*, opened for signature 30 March 2007, 2515 UNTS 3 (entered into force 3 May 2008) Art 28(2)(a); International Labour Organization Convention (ILO) No. 161 on Occupational Health Services, Art 5(b); *African Charter on the Rights and Welfare of the Child*, opened for signature 1 July 1990 (1990) OAU Doc CAB/LEG/24.9/49 (entered into force 29 November 1999) Art 14(1)(2)(c); *Protocol to the African Charter on Human and Peoples' Rights on the Rights of Women in Africa*, opened for signature 11 July 2003 (entered into force 25 November 2005) Art 15(a). Implicit references in human rights treaties: *UN Charter* Art 55; *Universal Declaration of Human Rights*, GA Res 217A, UNGAOR, 3rd sess, 183rd plen mtg, UN Doc A/810 (10 December 1948) Art 25(1); *International Covenant on Civil and Political Rights*, opened for signature 16 December 1966, 999 UNTS 171 (entered into force 23 March 1976) (ICCPR) Art 6; *International Covenant on Economic, Social and Cultural Rights*, opened for signature 16 December 1966, 993 UNTS 3 (entered into force 3 January 1976) (ICESCR) Arts 11 and 12

45 Committee on Economic, Social and Cultural Rights, *General Comment No. 15 The Right to Water (Arts 11 and 12 of the International Covenant on Economic, Social and Cultural Rights*, 29th sess, Agenda Item 3, UN Doc E/C.12/2002/11 (20 January 2003) para 2

46 *The Human Right to Water and Sanitation*, GA Res 64/292, 64th sess, 108th plen mtg, Agenda Item 48, UN Doc A/RES/64/292 (3 August 2010, adopted 28 July 2010)

reducing, the negative impacts, both depletion and contamination, during biofuels production and processing.[47]

Both first and second-generation biofuels require water resources for production and processing.[48] On average for the production of 1 litre of agrofuels, 2,500 litres of crop evapotranspiration and 850 litres of irrigation water are required.[49] The impacts, both on the quantity and quality of water, will differ depending on the type of feedstock, methods of irrigation and cultivation and processing technologies, as well as according to the location, e.g. semi-arid or water-abundant regions. Water resources are not only appropriated by large-scale investors in biofuel plantations but are frequently polluted with chemicals, including pesticides. This can infringe the quality of water, as well as the human right to health and human dignity.[50] The use of fertilisers or pesticides in the production of agrofuels has significant environmental impacts, not only on the surface water and groundwater but also on soil productivity as well as ecological systems and services depending on water.[51] Given the predicted biofuel demand in the coming decades, production and processing will pose significant competition to the rights of other users for available water resources.[52] This is a situation that will be exacerbated by the impacts of climate change, especially in least-developed countries, where water stress is predicted to become more extreme.

Rights and land

Existing international human rights law does not recognise a human right to land as such: no treaty affirms such a right in general terms.[53] However, it is

47 Maria León-Moreta, 'Biofuels: A Threat to the Environment and Human Rights – An Analysis of the Impact of the Production of Feedstock for Agrofuels on the Rights to Water, Land and Food' (2011) 4 *European Journal of Legal Studies* 122

48 Deepak Rajagopal, 'On Mitigating Emissions Leakage under Biofuel Policies (2016) 8 *GCB Bioenergy* 471

49 Richard G. Allen and others, *Crop Evapotranspiration: Guidelines for Computing Crop Water Requirements* (FAO Irrigation and Drainage Paper No. 56, 1998) cited in León-Moreta (n 47)

50 Shiney Varghese, *Biofuels and Global Water Challenges* (IATP, 2007) 2

51 León-Moreta (n 47)

52 Ibid

53 Jerome Gilbert, 'Land Rights as Human Rights: The Case for a Specific Right to Land' (2014) 10(18) *Sur: Journal on Human Rights* 114. For an example of international jurisprudence favouring the emergence of a human right to land, see Miloon Kothari, *Report of the Special Rapporteur on Adequate Housing as a Component of the Right to an Adequate Standard of Living*, UN Doc A/HRC/4/18 (5 February 2007) <http://daccess-dds-ny.un.org/doc/UNDOC/GEN/G07/106/28/PDF/G0710628.pdf?OpenElement>, accessed 5 February 2017. The report states that the Special Rapporteur 'strongly believes that the Human Rights Council should consider devoting attention to the question of the human right to land and should conduct studies in this regard which build on the work of organized peasant and indigenous peoples' movements' (para 31)

widely recognised that land rights are closely linked to the realisation of several human rights, including the rights to property, to food and to housing, and people's right to freely dispose of their natural resources.[54]

Investments, both domestic and transnational, can threaten communities' access to land.[55] National governments, especially in the Global South, prefer, for short-term economic reasons, to offer preferential access rights to large-scale biofuel business, either national or foreign investors.[56] The term 'land grabbing' characterises this system of land acquisition and concentration.[57] Domestic or transnational enterprises in the agro-business sector may buy or lease large extensions of arable land to the host state or even force farmers off their land to produce food or feedstock for biofuels.[58] Land appropriation and consolidation impact vulnerable groups. Indigenous people, and communities, minorities, women and farmers are evicted because they do not possess formal property titles and their ownership over land is generally based on customary law which is not recognised under statutory law.[59] Vulnerable groups' right to land constitutes the protection against forced evictions and displacement, included forced sales, founded on the right to housing.[60] In its General Comment No. 4, the Committee of Economic, Social and Cultural Rights determined that an important aspect of the right to housing is the legal security of tenure. The Commission on Human Settlements catalogued forced evictions as 'gross violations of human rights'.[61] The impacts of the concentration of land for modern biofuels production are experienced most by women in the Global South who play a special role in agriculture.[62]

A key point in the protection of the human right to property is the recognition of not only the individual but also the collective right to land of vulnerable groups when energy or development projects are planned to take

54 Gilbert (n 53)

55 Lorenzo Cotula, *Land Rights and Investment Treaties: Exploring the Interface* (International Institute for Environment and Development, 2015)

56 Asbjørn Eide, *The Right to Food and the Impact of Liquid Fuels* (FAO, 2008) 17–18

57 The Land Matrix – a useful resource documenting investments in land made globally – see <www.landmatrix.org/en/>

58 *Report of the Special Rapporteur on the Right to Food*, UN Doc A/62/289 (22 August 2007) para 38

59 Lorenzo Cotula, 'Property in a Shrinking Planet: Fault Lines in International Human Rights and Investment Law' (2015) 11(2) *International Journal of Law in Context* 113, 1241 *African Human Rights Law Journal* 40 127

60 ICESCR (n 44) Art 11(1)

61 Committee on Economic, Social and Cultural Rights, *General Comment No. 4 The Right to Adequate Housing (Art 11(1) of the Covenant)*, UN Doc para 8(a)

62 Asbjørn Eide (n 56): see Committee on Economic, Social and Cultural Rights, *General Comment No. 7 The Right to Adequate Housing (Article 11(1)): Forced Evictions* para 10. Women in all groups are especially vulnerable given the extent of statutory and other forms of discrimination which often apply in relation to property rights (including home ownership) or rights of access to property or accommodation, and their particular vulnerability to acts of violence and sexual abuse when they are rendered homeless

place in their land or territories.[63] Indigenous peoples and minority communities frequently experience displacement from lands as governments conclude foreign direct investment deals and/or trade deals that include extraction rights for overseas investors.[64] For indigenous peoples, control over land is associated with the right to self-determination. Convention No. 169 of 1989, of the International Labour Organization, Concerning Indigenous and Tribal Peoples in Independent Countries, requires states to recognise the rights of ownership and possession of indigenous peoples over the lands they traditionally occupy, and to safeguard these peoples' rights to the land they have access to, even if they do not occupy the land exclusively.[65]

The 2007 UN General Assembly Declaration on the Rights of Indigenous Peoples (UNDRIP) Article 26 states that 'indigenous peoples have the right to the lands, territories and resources which they have traditionally owned, occupied or otherwise used or acquired'. The expropriation of lands that provide the basis of traditional ways of life also violates the right of minorities to enjoy their own culture, affirmed in Article 27 of the International Covenant on Civil and Political Rights.[66] UNDRIP, although non-legally binding, provides a normative framework for indigenous people to challenge incursions of their recognised rights.

In September 2016 the International Criminal Court added to its priority list the investigation of crimes that result in the illegal dispossession of land, the illegal exploitation of natural resources and the destruction of the environment.[67] The move comes ahead of a decision by the prosecutor whether to investigate a case filed in 2014 that catalogues mass human rights abuses linked to systematic land seizures in Cambodia.[68] This development could set an international case law precedent that may lead to the strengthening of the right to land, as well as interconnected rights outlined above, for vulnerable individuals, including women and communities.

63 James Anaya, 'Indigenous Peoples' Participatory Rights in Relation to Decisions about Natural Resource Extraction: The More Fundamental Issue of What Rights Indigenous Peoples Have in Lands and Resources' (2005) 22(7) *Arizona Journal of International and Comparative Law* 7

64 Cotula (n 55)

65 Article 14; ILO Convention No. 169 has been ratified by 22 states. See also Articles 10 and 19 of the 2007 UN Declaration on Indigenous Peoples' Rights

66 General Comment No. 23, 'Article 27 (Rights of Minorities)', Human Rights Committee, 8 April 1994, UN Doc HRI/GEN/1/Rev.1, <www.refworld.org/docid/453883fc0.html> para 7 accessed 5 February 2017

67 John Vidal and Owen Bowcott, 'ICC Widens Remit to Include Environmental Destruction Cases (15 September 2016) *The Guardian*, London, UK <www.theguardian.com/global/2016/sep/15/hague-court-widens-remit-to-include-environmental-destruction-cases> accessed 5 February 2017

68 Global Witness, 'Company Executives Could Now Be Tried for Land Grabs and Environmental Destruction', Press Release (September 15 2016) <www.globalwitness.org/en/press-releases/company-executives-could-now-be-tried-land-grabbing-and-environmental-destruction-historic-move-international-criminal-court- prosecutor/> accessed 5 February 2017

The right to food

The right to land is closely connected to the right to food. The right to adequate food is considered a fundamental human right in international law. Like any other human right, it imposes duties on states: the obligations to respect, to protect, promote and to fulfill. The right to adequate food and the obligations on the state should be understood in two ways. The right to food ensures, on the one hand, that people have access to sufficient, safe and nutritious food to satisfy their dietary needs. On the other hand, this right guarantees also the access, especially of vulnerable groups, to resources for food production.[69]

International and regional cooperation play a fundamental role in the fulfillment of the right to adequate food. According to the Special Rapporteur on the Right to Food, the obligations of states regarding the right to food are not only to be fulfilled, protected and respected at the national level.[70] Also on the basis of Article 56 of the UN Charter and Article 23 of International Covenant on Civil and Political Rights, states are also called upon to contribute to the realisation of the right to food in other countries and to shape an international environment that enables national governments to realise the right to food under their own jurisdiction.[71]

The first significant international community response to global biofuel expansion came in the form of the Declaration resulting from the High-Level Conference on World Food Security in 2008.[72] The Special Rapporteur on the Right to Food, drawing on Article 11 of the International Covenant on Economic, Social and Cultural Rights, had already claimed that states must provide citizens with opportunities to obtain sufficient, nutritionally adequate, and safe food.[73] To realise the right to food, the state must refrain from infringing on the ability of individuals and groups to feed themselves, and must also protect this ability from infringements by third parties, including foreign direct investment.[74] Land dispossessions resulting from

69 Maria León-Moreta (n 47)

70 *UN Conference on Trade and Development, Sao Paulo Consensus* (2004) para 5

71 Human Rights Council, *Building Resilience: A Human Rights Framework for World Food and Nutrition Security*, 8 September 2008 A/HRC/9/23 para 24, available <www2.ohchr.org/english/bodies/hrcouncil/docs/.../A.HRC.9.23.doc> accessed 5 February 2017

72 Declaration of the High-Level Conference on World Food Security: *The Challenges of Climate Change and Bioenergy – Declaration of the High-Level Conference on World Food Security: The Challenges of Climate Change and Bioenergy* (FAO, IFAD, CGIAR, 5 June 2008) available <www.fao.org/fileadmin/user_upload/foodclimate/HLCdocs/declaration-E.pdf> accessed 5 February 2017

73 Oliver De Schutter, 'The Emerging Human Right to Land', *International Community Law Review* 12 (2010) 303–334

74 General Comment No. 12, *The Right to Adequate Food* (Article 11), Committee on Economic, Social and Cultural Rights, UN Doc E/C.12/1999/5 (12 May 1999), available <www.unhchr.ch/tbs/doc.nsf/0/3d02758c707031d58025677f003b73b9.> accessed 5 February 2017

biofuels-related investments would violate the right to food if people were deprived of the land on which they depend for their livelihoods without a suitable alternative.[75] Despite such clarity, a public appeal by the UN Special Rapporteur on the Right to Food in 2009, calling for evidence on the interface between land rights and the right to food, resulted in 117 case submissions.[76] Without clear, effectively enforced sustainability criteria that include protection of rights, investments in modern biofuel production will add further such cases.

States have a legal duty to progressively realise economic and increasingly social rights, as well as meet obligations under multilateral environmental agreements. Human rights advocates have adopted environmental norms, such as sustainable development, to further advance human rights, especially economic, social and cultural rights.[77] Environmental lawyers also recognise the potential of using human rights to achieve environmental law objectives.[78] As the following section demonstrates, a convergence, via a number of different pathways, between these two legal fields is resulting in a more integrated normative framing of sustainable development internationally. This is becoming manifest in regard to developing sustainability criteria for biofuels, although there remains a long way to go before it is fully achieved.

Biofuels and sustainability: Evolving an integrated approach

States, transnational corporations, international organisations and some non-governmental organisations (NGOs) have cooperated to foster voluntary international sustainable biofuels guidelines rather than legally binding regulatory approaches.[79] International cooperation between states to promote biofuels began in 2005 with the Group of 8+5 launching the Global Bioenergy Partnership (GBEP).[80] The GBEP's objective is to promote the

75 Report of the Special Rapporteur on the Right to Food, Olivier De Schutter – *Addendum, Large-Scale Land Acquisitions and Leases: A Set of Minimum Principles and Measures to Address the Human Rights Challenge*, UN Doc A/HRC/13/33/Add.2 (28 December 2009) para. 4 available <www2.ohchr.org/english/issues/food/docs/ BriefingNote landgrab.pdf> accessed 5 February 2017

76 Figures from Report of the Special Rapporteur on the Right to Food, Olivier De Schutter, UN Doc A/65/281 (11 August 2010) para 5 available <www.srfood.org/en/documents> accessed 5 February 2017

77 Linda Leib, *Human Rights and the Environment: Philosophical, Theoretical and Legal Perspectives* (Martinus Nijhoff, Leiden 2011)

78 Alan Boyle, 'Human Rights or Environmental Rights – A Reassessment' (2006) 18 *Fordham Environmental Law Review* 471–494

79 Nicole Scarlat and Jean Dallemand, 'Recent Developments of Biofuels/Bioenergy Sustainability Certification: A Global Overview' (2011) 39 3 *Energy Policy* 1630–1646

80 Argentina, Brazil, Canada, China, Colombia, Fiji, France, Germany, Ghana, Italy, Japan, Mauritania, Mexico, Netherlands, Paraguay, Russian Federation, Spain, Sudan, Sweden, Switzerland, United Republic of Tanzania, United Kingdom and United States of America

'continued development and commercialisation of renewable energy' and supports 'wider, cost-effective, biomass and biofuels deployment, particularly in developing countries where [traditional] biomass is prevalent'. In November 2011 the partner states and observers endorsed the Global Bioenergy Partnership Sustainability Indicators for Bioenergy. There are 24 sustainability indicators for all bioenergy, with cross-cutting social, environmental and economic methodological criteria.[81]

Although drawing on existing voluntary biofuel certification schemes, for example the Roundtable on Sustainable Biofuels and the Roundtable on Sustainable Palm Oil, as a template, the GBEP sustainability indicators do not feature directions, thresholds or limits and do not constitute a standard; nor are they legally binding on GBEP partners.[82] The indicators are only a voluntary guide for GBEP partners to evaluate bioenergy development at the domestic level. Also the GBEP emphasises that domestic regulation should not 'limit trade in bioenergy in a manner inconsistent with multilateral trade obligations'.[83] This continues a pattern, begun in the early 1990s, where international trade law principles are interpreted in such a way as to have a 'chilling effect' on legally binding national or regional regulation to advance sustainable development.[84] So it is imperative to explore other avenues adopted to advance sustainability standards by governments. Despite these limitations, the GBEP Sustainability Indicators for Bioenergy are recognised as providing a normative platform for a more integrated approach to advancing sustainable biofuel production. In 2013 the FAO Committee on World Food Security (an observer on the GBEP) issued policy recommendations that 'encouraged public and private sectors to support the integration of sustainable biofuel production into agricultural and forestry policies, according to each country's specificities'. It cited both the Voluntary Guidelines on the Responsible Governance of Tenure of Land, Fisheries and Forests in the Context of National Food Security (VGGT) and the GBEP sustainability indicators.[85]

In 2012 the UN Committee on World Food Security endorsed the VGGT.[86] These complemented other international voluntary initiatives

81 See the Global Bioenergy Partnership Sustainability Indicators for Bioenergy (November 2011) available <www.globalbioenergy.org> accessed 5 February 2017

82 Mairon G. Bastos, 'Biofuel Governance and International Legal Principles: Is It Equitable and Sustainable' (2009) 10 *Melbourne Journal of International Law* 470

83 The Global Bioenergy Partnership Sustainability Indicators for Bioenergy (n 81)

84 Emily Barrett Lydgate, 'Biofuels, Sustainability, and Trade-Related Regulatory Chill' (2012) *Journal of International Economic Law* 1–24; Aaron Cosbey and Petros C. Mavroidis, 'Heavy Fuel: Trade and Environment in the GATT/WTO Case Law' (2014) 23 3 *Review of European, Comparative & International Environmental Law* 288–301

85 The Global Bioenergy Partnership Sustainability Indicators for Bioenergy (n 81)

86 FAO, *Voluntary Guidelines on the Responsible Governance of Tenure of Land, Fisheries and Forests* (FAO, 2012). On political support see e.g. UN General Assembly Resolution No. 67/228 of 21 December 2012 UN Doc A/RES/67/228 para 31 available <www.un.org/en/ga/search/view_doc.asp?symbol=A/RES/67/228)> accessed 5

designed to hold transnational enterprises to account[87] such as those of the Organisation for Economic Co-operation and Development (OECD),[88] the UN Global Compact[89] and the UN Guiding Principles on Business and Human Rights.[90] The VGGT are intended to contribute to achieving sustainable livelihoods, social stability, housing security, rural development, environmental protection and sustainable social and economic development, especially for vulnerable and marginalised peoples.[91] Despite limitations, the VGGT constitute a major step forward in international efforts to tackle land management and governance issues.[92] The VGGT offer opportunities for actors, both state and non-state, to influence law and policy relating to bioenergy investments. For example, several VGGT provisions explicitly call for law reform.[93] The VGGT call on states to safeguard customary and unrecorded rights in land allocation processes;[94] to protect the land rights of indigenous peoples;[95] and to acknowledge informal tenure.[96] They also provide guidance on land-based investments, calling for respect for all legitimate tenure rights in investment processes as well as for transparency, social and environmental impact assessments, benefit sharing, community consultation and – where indigenous peoples are involved – free, prior and informed consent.[97] The VGGT explicitly recognise the connection with human rights law.[98] Given this, the VGGT can be an important addition that

February 2017; *G20 Leaders' Declaration* (Los Cabos, 19 June 2012) para 58 available <www.whitehouse.gov/the-press-office/2012/06/19/g20-leaders-declaration> accessed 5 February 2017; and *The Future We Want – Outcome Document of the Rio+20 Conference* (Rio de Janeiro, 22 June 2012) para 115 available <www.uncsd2012.org/content/documents/727The%20Future%20We%20Want%2019%20June%201230pm.pdf> accessed 5 February 2017

87 Stefanie Ricarda Roos, 'UN Guiding Principles on Business and Human Rights' (2013) *Encyclopedia of Corporate Social Responsibility* 2592–2601

88 *OECD Guidelines for Multinational Enterprises, Annex to Declaration on International Investment and Multinational Enterprises* (1976) revised version 2011 available <www.oecd.org/corporate/mne/1922428.pdf> accessed 5 February 2017

89 The UN Global Compact Principles (2000) available <www.unglobalcompact.org/> accessed 5 February 2017

90 Guiding Principles on Business and Human Rights: Implementing the United Nations 'Protect, Respect and Remedy' Framework, 17/4 A/HRC/17/31 (16 June 2011), available <www.ohchr.org/Documents/Issues/Business/A-HRC-17-31_AEV.pdf> accessed 5 February 2017

91 *Voluntary Guidelines on the Responsible Governance of Tenure of Land, Fisheries and Forests in the Context of National Food Security* (VGGT) (FAO, 2014), available <www.fao.org/cfs/cfs-home/activities/vggt/en/> accessed 5 February 2017

92 Cotula (n 55)

93 VGGT (n 91) paras 4.4 and 5.3, calling for the protection of legitimate tenure rights not currently protected by national law

94 VGGT (n 91) section 7

95 VGGT (n 91) section 9

96 VGGT (n 91) section 10

97 VGGT (n 91) section 12

98 VGGT (n 91) paras 3.2

advances existing voluntary initiatives into progressive law reform to achieve sustainable biofuel production.

Greater integration of social, environmental and economic elements is increasingly understood as necessary for achieving sustainable development.[99] This is most evident in the 2015 Sustainable Development Goals (SDGs). The SDGs could provide a framework to achieve greater integration on biofuels sustainability criteria. States committed to ensure 'access to affordable, reliable, sustainable and modern energy for all' by 2030.[100] However the SDGs' integrated format means that to meet SDG 7 targets, the climate change mitigation target (SDG 13) needs to be met without degrading terrestrial ecosystems (SDG 15) and at the same time as ending poverty (SDG 1), ensuring access to clean water (SDG 6) and nutritious food (SDG 2). Finally any new large-scale energy source needs to promote responsible production and consumption (SDG 12).

The SDGs have become a touchstone for biofuel advocates internationally, both for state and non-state actors. The World Energy Council claims biofuels can meet low-carbon energy demand and increase ecosystem functions resilience whilst contributing to sustainable green economic growth as required under the SDGs.[101] In May 2015, when announcing its intention to speed up the development and deployment of sustainable biofuels, the Roundtable on Sustainable Biomaterials (RSB), an observer of the Global Environmental Change Program, specifically noted this would contribute to the SDG of doubling the global use of renewable energy and ensuring universal energy access by 2030.[102]

However moving from individual goals that recognise substantive and procedural human rights, as well as many global environmental concerns, to designing integrated and effective regulatory sustainability mechanisms for biofuels remains a challenge. This is in part due to existing embedded, multilevel and sectoral governance structures. The European Union (EU), which has claimed that its certification scheme for the Renewable Energy Directive ensures that EU biofuels 'meet the highest environmental standards' and is the 'most stringent in the world', is an example of how governance structures can be an obstacle to an integrated approach to sustainable biofuels

99 Karen Morrow, 'Rio+20, the Green Economy and Re-orienting Sustainable Development' (2012) 14 4 *Environmental Law Review* 279–297

100 Transforming our world: the 2030 Agenda for Sustainable Development A/RES/70/1 (25 September 2015) Goal 7 available <www.un.org/sustainabledevelopment/sustainable-development-goals/> accessed 5 February 2017

101 World Energy Resources (n 1)

102 Meghan Sapp, *New Global Bioenergy Initiative Launched under Sustainable Energy for All*, FAO Biofuels Digest (21 May 2015), available <www.biofuelsdigest.com/bdigest/2015/05/21/new-global-bioenergy-initiative-launched-under-sustainable-energy-for-all/> accessed 5 February 2017

standards.[103] The EU has selectively applied sustainability criteria to biofuels with an eye to international political priorities at the time.

Biofuels and the European Union

The EU, like many states, only began the process to establish sustainability criteria for biofuels, both from within the EU as well as imports, once directives were in place driving an increase in demand. Biofuel consumption rose in the EU primarily due to the introduction of several directives to reduce GHGs after signing the UN Kyoto Protocol in 1997.[104] The EU could no longer meet the rising demand with domestic supply. In 2008, 25 per cent of biofuels in the EU were imported.[105] The EU directives resulted in increases in imports of both bioliquid (from Asia and Africa) and biomass feedstock (Russia and North America).[106] The European Commission is expected to propose new policies for renewable energy and biomass early in 2017 that are likely to increase demand still further.[107] Each feedstock requires different sustainability criteria.

The EU Renewable Energy Directive (RED) is the main driver for increased bioliquids demand in the region. RED Article 3(4) requires that the share of energy from renewable sources in all forms of transport use in 2020 be at least 10 per cent of the final consumption.[108] The RED sustainability criteria for bioliquids require that they should not be sourced from land with high biodiversity value,[109] that certain agro-environmental practices be adhered to and that feedstocks should not be sourced from land with a 'high carbon stock'.[110] Article 17(2) sets a GHG emissions reduction threshold,[111] and Article 19 provides the methodology for calculating biofuels' GHG impact.[112] The methodology is derived from the much-criticised 2006

103 Evgenia Pavlovskaia, 'Legal Analysis of the European Union Sustainability Criteria for Biofuels' (2014) 3 1 *Journal of Sustainable Development Law and Policy* 4–21 6

104 The Directives include the 2001 Large Plant Combustion Directive, the 2006 EU Biofuels Directive, the 2009 Renewable Energy Directive (RED 2009), the 2010 Industrial Emissions Directive – see Pavlovskaia (n 103)

105 Brack (n 28)

106 Ibid

107 Communication on the Energy Union, COM (2015) 80 final; the current EU renewable energy policy does not include volume limits or sustainability criteria for the use of biomass (as opposed to biofuels) for heating and electricity

108 RED 2009 (n 104) 3(4)

109 RED 2009 (n 104) 'Land with high biodiversity value' refers to primary forest and other wooded land, according to Art 17(3)(a)

110 RED 2009 (n 104) Art 17(6)

111 RED 2009 (n 104) Art 17(2)

112 Annex V of the Renewable Energy Directive and Commission Decision 2010/335/EU on Guidelines for calculating land carbon stocks for the purposes of Annex V to Directive 2009/28/EC (notification under document [2010] 3751), OJ 2010 L 151/19

IPCC guidelines.[113] The sustainability criteria apply to domestic as well as imported biofuels, ensuring that they are in compliance with World Trade Organization non-discrimination requirements.[114]

The sustainability criteria set out in Article 17 only apply to bioliquids, not biomass which is increasingly being used as an alternative fuel for coal-fired power stations.[115] The exclusion of biomass conflicts with the EU's Forest Strategy as well as international environmental law obligations. The European Commission in its own Forest Strategy has recognised, in relation to biomass alone, that if member states were to use biomass according to their renewable energy plans, by 2020 the amount of wood used for energy alone would be equivalent to today's total EU wood harvest.[116] By omitting biomass from its consideration of sustainability criteria, the EU was purposefully selective in the biofuels it included. International pressure at the time when bioliquids sustainability criteria were negotiated focused on the threat first-generation biofuels posed to the human right to food and the international cooperation needed for all states to fulfill this right. Biomass, usually a second-generation biofuel, and therefore not associated with competition for agricultural land, did not receive the same level of scrutiny. However the direct and indirect land-use changes threaten biodiversity and ecosystem functions, as well as lead to further pressure on forest-dependent peoples. The renewed interest in including bioenergy carbon capture and storage within climate change mitigation land sector policies will raise further concern over impacts and sustainability criteria development for biomass, especially given the limitations of the LULUCF accounting guidelines to adequately account for emissions from all land-use activities.[117]

Although RED states that '[b]iofuel production should be sustainable', the Directive itself does not explain precisely what sustainably produced biofuels are.[118] The lack of detail is in part due to European administrative law. The EU operates under a principle of subsidiarity whereby directives are implemented and enforced by member states.[119] As such RED Article 18 places the obligation on member states to require economic operators to show that the sustainability criteria have been met. RED Article 18 permits

113 The most basic accounting methods rely on aggregate default data which are highly uncertain – they are 'not well established or are highly variable from region to region, or within very small subregions within a given country'. As a result, global average values, which 'can be used for first order calculations or for comparison … probably do not provide a basis for a credible final inventory. National experts in forestry and related fields should be consulted to determine the most appropriate values for use in national inventories': Eggleston and others (n 27)

114 RED 2009 (n 104) Art 17(1)

115 Ibid

116 EU Forest Strategy, COM (2013) 659 final

117 Eggleston and others (n 27)

118 RED 2009 (n 104) Art 17(1)

119 Treaty on the Functioning of the European Union 2007 Article 3

three distinct methods for member states to meet the compliance framework of the sustainability criteria: a national system, voluntary certification schemes and international agreements. To ensure that existing biofuel sustainability voluntary schemes, international guidelines and member states national systems are equivalent, comparable and fit for purpose in meeting the RED sustainability criteria they will need to be thoroughly scrutinised. RED Article 18(4) authorises the Commission to decide on voluntary national or international schemes setting standards for the production of biofuel products that 'contain accurate data' for the purposes of demonstrating compliance with the sustainability criteria, however it remains within the member states' authority whether to incorporate the Commission's guidance.[120] There is a risk of the obligations imposed by the sustainability criteria not being duly applied in practice. This, in turn, could create a sustainability criteria smokescreen, with the framework seeming effective but in reality lagging behind as inconsistencies between member states implementation differ.[121] Only effective reporting and transparency requirements will lead to equitable implementation across the EU.

The EU framework for sustainable biofuels has the potential to address interlinked challenges identified in this chapter but this would only be possible if suitable sustainable regulatory approaches are chosen, implemented and enforced.[122] At present this is not the case. Concerns over the effectiveness of the sustainability scheme are still pertinent.[123] A report on economic land concessions by the UN special rapporteur on the situation of human rights in Cambodia reveavled that sugar produced on agribusiness plantations for export to the EU was contributing to land appropriation. Lobbying by NGOs and lawyers led to supportive resolutions by the European Parliament as well as the launch of a joint investigation by the Cambodian and EU authorities to assess displacement claims.[124] This is now being presented for consideration as a case before the International Criminal Court, and has prompted the broadening of the terms of human rights violation to include land grabs.[125]

120 RED 2009 (n 104) Art 18(5) – schemes must meet adequate standards of 'reliability, transparency and independent auditing' to be accepted

121 Seita Romppanen, 'Regulating Better Biofuels for the European Union' (2012) 21 *European Energy and Environmental Law Review* 133–138 123

122 Seita Romppanen, 'The EU's Biofuels: Certified as Sustainable' (2012) *Renewable Energy Law and Policy Review* 173

123 Seita Romppanen (n 121)

124 Resolution of the European Parliament of 26 October 2012 on the Situation in Cambodia, para 6 available <www.europarl.europa.eu/meetdocs/2009_2014/documents/dase/dv/1129_13_epres_cambodia_10oct12_/1129_13_epres_cambodia_10oct12_en.pdf> accessed 5 February 2017; and Clean Sugar Campaign, 'Clean Sugar Campaign Public Statement: Commencement of Cambodian 'Blood Sugar' Reparations Process a Crucial Step Towards Justice' (7 December 2014), available <http://farmlandgrab.org/post/view/24305> accessed 5 February 2017

125 Global Witness (n 68)

Conclusion

Increased modern biofuels demand driven by both climate change mitigation policies and energy security concerns, mainly amongst developed and emerging economies, is resulting in negative social, environmental and economic impacts. Investment in biofuels predominately takes the form of public or private foreign direct investment in producer countries, mainly least-developed countries. The consequence is that the poor, rural people and minority groups, including indigenous peoples, in these host countries, most experience negative impacts. Addressing the threats that biofuels pose to realising human rights, indigenous peoples' rights and achieving environmental law objectives, including on climate change, has placed biofuel sustainability on the international law agenda.

An integrated approach to achieving sustainable development is now endorsed by states, most notably with the adoption of the 2015 UN SDGs. An integrated approach to developing sustainability criteria for biofuels production, processing and trade is certainly emerging. At the international level biofuels guidelines such as the GBEP offer a normative framework for countries to design sustainability regulations. The GBEP draws on existing industry sustainability standards, yet it also emphasises legal obligations under international environmental, human rights and indigenous peoples' rights law. Moreover the VGGT guidelines further strengthen the normative foundations to develop integrated biofuels sustainability regulation. With the International Criminal Court broadening its mandate to include land grabs as potentially causing human rights violations, the momentum to deliver effective sustainability regulation has increased for states as well as investors.

Two key drivers behind increased biofuel demand are climate change mitigation policies and energy security. These continue to incentivise investment in the sector at a rapid pace. Turning voluntary biofuel sustainability guidelines into effective regulation that covers all production, processing and trade along the transnational supply chain will take time. As the EU case study illustrates, integrated administrative governance structures are required, as well as the political will to prioritise producer countries peoples' rights and environments above national emission reduction targets and unsustainable energy security strategies. To achieve these, far-reaching political, economic and social reforms are needed. Currently such changes are not on the horizon. Existing efforts to translate sustainability guidelines into regulation on biofuels will not be integrated fully and consequently they will be less effective. Continued focus on technical legal aspects of biofuel production obscures a larger truth, which is that the driving force behind its increasing demand is in and of itself unsustainable. It is also unjust, inequitable and contributes to transnational injustice under the guise of delivering a sustainable transition to a low-carbon world. A fully integrated approach to designing biofuels sustainability regulation would lead to this conclusion – the road to which is short and straightforward.

Part IV

Conflict, corruption and liability

Foreword

Benjamin J. Richardson

Growing evidence of the upheavals of the Anthropocene has done little to moderate humanity's appetite for natural resources, from Canadian oil sands to Congolese minerals. Any interruptions to the commodities boom of the twenty-first century have come not from concerns about resource depletion and ecological impacts but due to tempered market demand in the wake of the Global Financial Crisis. With its underlying values of free trade and economic growth, international law generally enables rather than restricts investment in natural resources. Environmental law, whether domestic or international, has done little to mitigate the plundering of nature's wealth except for high conservation areas that are usually (but not always) off-limits.

The main functions of legal governance of natural resources have been to control access and levy royalties and rents. Although access to resources located in the territory of a country is subject to its regulatory powers, international law limits the prerogatives of host states in order to protect the interests of foreign investors. But often the interests of host states and investors are closely aligned, not only in advancing public welfare but also to its detriment. Particularly prevalent in developing countries, the latter outcome has been branded the 'resource curse', an epithet that refers to how rapacious political elites collude with economic investors to exploit a country's natural resources for their own benefit at the expense of society generally. Too often, such development displaces indigenous and local communities while contaminating the environment with toxic pollution.

These trends have not gone unchallenged, as advocates for human rights and environmental responsibility have pushed for better legal regulation as well as new forms of non-state governance. The Extractive Industries Transparency Initiative, for instance, promotes public awareness of how states manage their oil, gas and mineral resources with the hope that greater transparency can reduce corruption and mismanagement of such resources. Another global initiative to tackle misguided natural resources development is the Principles for Responsible Agricultural Investment that Respects Rights, Livelihoods and Resources, inaugurated in 2010. It sets standards for financial investors in the farming sector to reduce land grabbing and other depredations on host communities. The Climate Principles are another governance gesture attempting to fill gaps and lacunae in international and domestic law in regulating investment in fossil fuels.

Thus, research on international investment law in the resources sector involves important issues about 'sovereign rights', 'benefit sharing', 'community consent' and 'environmental responsibility' that touch on both traditional legal instruments and new governance codes. There is as yet no universal formula for resolving these challenges, and the need remains for greater empirical knowledge and experimentation with potential solutions.

The analysis in this book, edited by respected academics Shawkat Alam, Jahid Hossain Bhuiyan and Jona Razzaque, thus tackles one of the most daunting fields of global governance for environmental law practitioners and scholars. Their work offers a much-needed contribution to prevailing legal and policy discourse. Sustainable use and conservation of natural resources is a global imperative in order to avoid climate change and other catastrophic planetary threats. This important volume brings together an array of international scholars to assess the implications of global investment law for the regulation of natural resources and the impact of a suite of changing dynamics from carbon trading to corporate social responsibility. Readers will find its pages both a valuable critique and rich palette of ideas for better governance of the resources economy.

17 Natural resources, conflict and investment

Conflict minerals in the Democratic Republic of Congo and the challenges to sustainable investment

Onita Das

Introduction

Humankind has always used and exploited natural resources[1] but in many cases, the exploitation is unsustainable. For society to continue to have intra- and inter-generational access to natural resources i.e., that both the current and the future generations have fair access to earth's resources, the way in which these resources are exploited and consumed has to change. Rising demand for natural resources globally increases their exploitation and for many resource-rich nations, the unsustainable or illegal exploitation of resources has also caused or fuelled conflict.[2] This in turn causes harm to the environment, livelihoods and wellbeing of the population affected – which is inimical to sustainable development.

The concept of sustainable development generally refers to development or the process of improving the quality of life of the present generation without compromising the needs and quality of life of future generations.[3] To achieve the overarching objective of sustainable development, sustainable investment in natural resources plays a key role. Unsustainable investment in natural resources has in some circumstances contributed to inequitable distribution of wealth, corruption, human rights abuses and even financed or fuelled conflict.[4] Sustainable investment, by contrast, which incorporates the

1 'Natural resources are actual or potential sources of wealth that occur in a natural state, such as timber, water, fertile land, wildlife, minerals, metals, stones, and hydrocarbons'. See United Nations Environment Programme, *From Conflict to Peacebuilding: The Role of Natural Resources and the Environment* (UNEP, 2009) 7

2 The terms conflict and armed conflict are used interchangeably throughout the chapter

3 See e.g., Sustainable Development Commission, 'What Is Sustainable Development?' <www.sd-commission.org.uk/pages/what-is-sustainable-development.html> accessed 25 April 2016

4 UN Security Council, 'Natural Resource Wealth Fails to Translate into "Equivalent" Benefits for People, Fuelling Conflict, Instability, Deputy-Secretary General Tells Security Council' (Press Release, SC/11037, 19 June 2013)

consideration of environmental, social and governance (ESG) factors,[5] can contribute to the effective management of natural resources for the benefit of the state concerned and its population, and to achieving sustainable development.

To explore the adequacy of sustainable investment in natural resources, the Democratic Republic of Congo (DRC) is used as a case study, primarily because it is a country rich in natural resources, including tin, tantalum, tungsten and gold, as well as minerals also known as 'conflict minerals'[6] which have fuelled armed conflict in the region for decades.[7] Therefore, this chapter first explores the link between natural resources and conflict; second, determines the role of investment in conflict minerals; third, reviews the limits of the legal framework governing conflict minerals; and finally, argues for a more integrated approach of the current international legal framework i.e., that sustainable development principles can be used to fill the gaps in existing law, to ensure more sustainable investment in minerals from conflict-affected regions, which in turn could contribute towards mitigating resources-related conflict and achieve sustainable development.

The link between natural resources and armed conflict

The complex nexus between natural resources and conflict is illustrated by the 'resource curse',[8] which refers to the link between abundant natural resources and poor and inequitable economic development, weak governance, corruption as well as the associated political, social and environmental deterioration, which can lead to increased risk of conflict.[9] An abundance of a particular natural resource can lead to competition over control and inequitable distribution of that resource and thus, cause conflict. This includes conflict that can arise when states or groups within a state or

5 'Sustainable investment', also known as 'socially responsible investment' or 'responsible investment', is an investment approach that expressly recognises the relevance of ESG factors to the investor and a healthy market, and that 'the generation of long-term sustainable returns is dependent on stable, well-functioning and well governed social, environmental and economic systems'. Principles for Responsible Investment (PRI), 'Introducing Responsible Investment' <www.unpri.org/introducing-responsible-investment/> accessed 31 August 2015

6 'Conflict minerals are minerals mined in conditions of armed conflict and human rights abuses, which are sold or traded by armed groups'. See UK Foreign and Commonwealth Office (FCO), 'Guidance: Conflict Minerals' (FCO, 19 June 2013) <www.gov.uk/conflict-minerals> accessed 7 August 2015

7 See generally Peter Eichstaedt, *Consuming the Congo: War and Conflict Minerals in the World's Deadliest Place* (Lawrence Hill, 2011)

8 The term was first coined by Auty. See Richard M. Auty, *Sustaining Development in Mineral Economies: The Resources Curse Thesis* (Routledge 1993)

9 See Paul Collier, 'The Political Economy of Natural Resources' (2010) 77 *Social Research* 1105

region,[10] compete to control access over 'high-value' resources at the expense of a significant portion of the population.[11]

While natural resources are never the sole cause of an armed conflict, conflict over natural resources is often part of, or exacerbates, a larger struggle over political, economic or social issues within a society. This can range from ineffective governance that lacks adaptive capacity to handle political, socio-economic and environmental pressures; a weak economic structure that leads to an inequitable distribution of wealth and high dependence on natural resources; to social instability where the population is fragmented through pre-existing cultural clashes.[12] These factors contribute to a weakened society which creates an atmosphere that can cause resource-related conflict. This is evident in the DRC which 'has been characterised by weak governance, corruption, lawlessness and impunity'.[13]

DRC, armed conflict and minerals

The DRC is a country within the Great Lakes Region (GLR), rich in natural resources (minerals), particularly in the eastern provinces and plagued by intermittent armed conflict over the last four decades.[14] In the background of such conflict, the DRC has been in chaos for decades, suffering from social and economic fragmentation resulting from human and natural resources exploitation, corruption and mismanagement of resources, including serious human rights violations.[15] Fifteen years ago, the UN Security Council (UNSC) first raised the link between armed conflicts in the DRC and illegal mineral extraction, noting with concern 'reports of the illegal exploitation of the country's assets and the potential consequences of these actions on security conditions and the continuation of hostilities'.[16] Furthermore, evidence

10 See e.g., Sierra Leone: diamonds fuelling conflict by Revolutionary United Front (RUF) and financing Liberian warlord Charles Taylor; Angola: diamonds fuelling conflict by União Nacional para a Independência Total de Angola (UNITA) and oil revenues fuelling the Angolan government's war efforts. See UNEP (n 1) 10

11 Hilary Benn, 'Trade and Security in an Interconnected World' in Felix Dodds and Tim Pippard (eds), *Human and Environmental Security: An Agenda for Change* (Earthscan, 2005) 95

12 See e.g., Onita Das, *Environmental Protection, Security and Armed Conflict: A Sustainable Perspective* (Edward Elgar, 2013) 70–77 (on factors causing environmentally related conflict); UNEP (n 1) 5

13 Ken Matthysen and Andrés Z Montejano, *'Conflict Minerals' Initiatives in DR Congo: Perceptions of Local Mining Communities* (International Peace Information Service, 2013) 6

14 See 'Democratic Republic of Congo country profile–Overview' *BBC News* (Africa, 10 August 2016) <www.bbc.co.uk/news/world-africa-13283212> accessed 11 June 2015

15 Belachew Gebrewold, *Anatomy of Violence: Understanding the Systems of Conflict and Violence in Africa* (Ashgate, 2013) 89–93

16 SC Res 1291, UN SCOR, 55th sess, 4104th mtg, UN Doc S/RES/1291 (24 February 2000)

emerged in subsequent years indicating that illegal exploitation of DRC's minerals has played a key role in fuelling its conflicts.[17]

The DRC's mineral wealth is huge. It is estimated that DRC has about 65–80 per cent of the world's coltan reserves (ore from which tantalum is extracted), 49 per cent of its cobalt reserves and 3 per cent of its copper reserves.[18] The DRC also produces 6–8 per cent of the world's tin, 2–4 per cent of the world's tungsten and around 1 per cent of the global gold production.[19] The DRC's gold and diamond deposits are still reportedly under explored.[20] These mineral reserves of tin, tantalum, tungsten and gold in particular (also known as '3TG') have been fought over violently by various state and non-state actors over the years – from non-state armed groups such as the Democratic Forces for the Liberation of Rwanda (FDLR), to rogue brigades within the Armed Forces of the DRC (FARDC) and the Congolese national army. Numerous reports indicate these factions are being heavily involved in the control, operation and trade of such conflict minerals.[21] These sought-after natural resources, instead of being used to improve the lives of millions of Congolese by contributing to the development of the country and raising the standard of living, are instead being used to finance armed groups and prolong violent conflict.[22]

The role of investment in conflict minerals

The DRC example illustrates the link between natural resources and conflict. However, instead of triggering or exacerbating conflict, natural resources or in this case valuable minerals, when responsibly managed, 'play an important and positive role in enhancing growth and stability'.[23] In essence, natural resources can be used for the benefit of the population, in terms of improving livelihoods and developing the country. However, for natural resources to be managed effectively and to prevent further conflict, sustainable investment plays a key role.

17 See e.g., Louise Arimatsu and Hemi Mistry, 'Conflict Minerals: A Search for a Normative Framework' (International Law Programme Paper 2012/01, Chatham House 2012) 9; Ruben De Koning, *Conflict Minerals in the Democratic Republic of Congo: Aligning Trade and Security Interventions* (SIPRI, 2011)

18 FCO (n 6)

19 Ibid

20 Ibid

21 Ibid. See also Enough Project and Grassroots Reconciliation Group, 'A Comprehensive Approach to Congo's Conflict Minerals' (Enough Project 2009) <www.enoughproject.org/files/Comprehensive-Approach.pdf> accessed 20 January 2017

22 Annyssa Bellal (ed), *The War Report: Armed Conflict in 2014* (Oxford University Press, 2015) 154–169 (review of DRC conflicts)

23 United States Agency for International Development (USAID), *Minerals and Conflict: A Toolkit for Intervention* (USAID, 2005) 2–3

At a global level, various technologies commonly part of our daily life – from mobile phones, laptops, flat screen televisions to various industries (e.g., automotive, aerospace, electronic), incorporate crucial components that require 3TG minerals. With increasing demand in consumer products using 3TG minerals, supply rises in response. Supply increases in the extractive industries in areas where these minerals are found, complementing the demand by companies investing in such minerals in order to produce and supply their sought-after products. This of course has led to investment in conflict minerals over many years.[24] As De Koning points out, '[i]nternational demand for these resources has allowed—and even encouraged—non-state groups to finance continued armed violence'.[25] Thus, many companies worldwide have had a part to play in the unsustainable investment in conflict minerals.[26]

Companies can, knowingly or unknowingly, invest and trade in conflict minerals through the supply chain. There are many stages of the supply chain which bear the risk of being contaminated with conflict minerals. Contamination may occur at the initial stages – mining or trading in the eastern provinces of DRC, in a neighbouring country or further along the supply chain. Companies investing in 3TG minerals or using such minerals as part of their products, are at risk of using conflict minerals – 'whether at the 'upstream' stage of the supply chain (i.e., from mine to smelter) or at the 'downstream' stage (i.e., from smelter to end user)'.[27] Simply put, upstream stakeholders extract, trade and process the minerals before they are 'used in downstream manufacturing products, including in the electronic, automotive, aerospace, defence, software, pharmaceutical and other industries'.[28] This illustrates the major role played by investment (directly or indirectly) in the mining, production and trading stages of minerals from conflict-affected regions. Investing in conflict minerals lines the pockets of armed groups and finances the ongoing conflicts in the volatile eastern region of DRC.[29] Companies thus have a responsibility to ensure that their investments 'are not inadvertently helping fuel atrocities'.[30]

It is also worth noting, however, that 16 per cent of the Congolese population (approximately 10 million people) are 'directly or indirectly dependent on the small-scale mining industry'[31] and in conflict-affected parts of eastern DRC, artisanal (small-scale, independent) mining remains a major mode of production. Approximately 80–90 per cent of DRC mineral production is

24 See Sasha Lezhnev and Alex Hellmuth, 'Taking Conflict Out of Consumer Gadgets: Company Rankings on Conflict Minerals 2012' (Enough Project 2012) 2
25 De Koning (n 17) Preface
26 Lezhnev and Hellmuth (n 24)
27 FCO (n 6)
28 Ibid
29 Enough Project (n 21) 1
30 Ibid 1
31 Arimatsu and Mistry (n 17) 7 (citing EITI)

conducted 'by between 1 and 2 million artisanal miners in the DRC who, in turn, support a larger community of 4–12 million people'.[32] Sustainable investment thus includes not only investing in conflict-free minerals but also ensuring that such investment brings opportunities and prosperity to the Congolese people. The DRC example highlights the complex interconnections between global consumer demand, globalisation in trade, the manufacturing process and conflict. The question is, how can companies ensure that their investment in 3TG minerals is conflict free and sustainable?

Prior to reviewing the legal framework governing conflict minerals, the following section explores the concept of sustainable development and its substantive principles.

Sustainable development principles and relevance to conflict minerals

Sustainable development is an evolving concept,[33] having developed from the 1972 Stockholm Conference on the Human Environment[34] to the recent UN Sustainable Development Summit in September 2015.[35] It is a widely accepted concept,[36] being cited and used globally as an objective to achieve or as a guideline to govern both domestic and international issues. The concept of sustainable development requires that for development to be sustainable, the three pillars of economic, social and environmental interests must be integrated.[37] As seen above, underlying socio-economic and political problems within a society as well as unsustainable investment in conflict minerals, can contribute to resource conflict – becoming the very antitheses of sustainable development. As Grynspan points out: '[n]atural resources necessarily play a central role in promoting sustainable development if we understand it as meeting the needs of this generation – without compromising the ability of future generations to meet theirs'.[38] Thus, sustainable development should be the benchmark to adhere to or goal to achieve when investing in resources in conflict-prone areas.

32 FCO (n 6) (citing World Bank Promines Project Appraisal)

33 See e.g., Nico Schrijver, *The Evolution of Sustainable Development in International Law: Inception, Meaning and Status* (Martinus Nijhoff, 2008)

34 *Report of the UN Conference on the Human Environment*, UN Doc A/CONF.48/14/Rev.1 (5–16 June 1972)

35 UN Sustainable Development Summit 2015, 25–27 September 2015, New York (adoption of post-2015 development agenda)

36 Markus W. Gehring and Marie-Claire Cordonier Segger (eds), *Sustainable Development in World Trade Law* (Kluwer Law International, 2005) 4

37 See e.g., World Bank, *Inclusive Green Growth: The Pathway to Sustainable Development* (World Bank, 2012) 2

38 Statement by Rebecca Grynspan at the 'Opening of the 67th UN General Assembly side event on "The Role of Natural Resources in Promoting Sustainable Development"' UN New York, 28 September 2012 <www.undp.org/content/undp/en/home/presscenter/speeches/2012/09/28/rebeca-grynspan-the-role-of-natural-resources-in-promoting-sustainable-development-.html> accessed 20 January 2017

Scholars have varying views on the components or principles that make up the concept of sustainable development. Sands, for example, argues that as a principle of international law, sustainable development requires recognition of inter- and intra-generational equity, sustainable use of natural resources, common but differentiated environmental responsibilities and the integration of environmental decision-making.[39] Magraw and Hawke indicate four components of sustainable development: inter-generational equity, intra-generational equity, environmental protection and the integration of economic, social and environmental interests.[40] The 2002 New Delhi Declaration of Principles of International Law Relating to Sustainable Development[41] (New Delhi Declaration) formulated seven core principles that come under the overarching concept of sustainable development, included amongst them: the duty of states to ensure sustainable use of natural resources, equity and the eradication of poverty, participation and access to information and justice, and good governance.

It is argued that the New Delhi Declaration still remains one of the high watermarks in the general development of the concept of sustainable development as it provides a framework of principles which could be used as a set of guidelines with which to pursue sustainable development.[42] The relevant principles within the structure of the concept provided by the Declaration thus provide the framework for the present discussion. As the concern here is to ensure sustainable investment in minerals and to prevent armed conflict fuelled by conflict minerals, this chapter makes reference only to those principles which are most pertinent to the present topic: equity, public participation and good governance.

The principle of equity 'refers to both *inter-generational equity* (the right of future generations to enjoy a fair level of common patrimony) and *intra-generational equity* (the right of all peoples within the current generation of fair access to the current generation's entitlement to the Earth's natural resources)'.[43] This principle calls for equitable utilisation of resources amongst the present generation as well as taking into account the rights of future generations in relation to those resources. At present this principle is not yet entrenched within customary international law 'due in part to difficulties in

39 Philippe Sands, 'Environmental Protection in the Twenty-First Century: Sustainable Development and International Law', in Richard L. Revesz, Philippe Sands and Richard B. Stewart (eds), *Environmental Law, the Economy and Sustainable Development* (Cambridge University Press, 2000) 369–379

40 Daniel Barstow Magraw and Lisa D. Hawke, 'Sustainable Development', in Daniel Bodansky, Jutta Brunée and Ellen Hey (eds), *Oxford Handbook of International Environmental Law* (Oxford University Press, 2007) 613–638

41 International Law Association (ILA), 'New Delhi Declaration of Principles of International Law Relating to Sustainable Development, 2 April 2002' (2002) 2 *International Environmental Agreements: Politics, Law and Economics* 211, Preamble

42 Ibid

43 Ibid principle 2.1

identifying with certainty the needs of future generations, and the lack of consensus between States on the obligation to ensure distributional justice between States'.[44] Regardless of its normative status, the equity principle is increasingly reflected in international instruments[45] and judicial decisions[46] relevant to sustainable development. This is evidence of not only the international community's growing recognition of the equity principle, but also that this principle is an important objective or guidance tool for states and the international community in their strive for sustainable development.[47]

Two other mutually reinforcing sustainable development principles that are relevant to achieving sustainable investment in minerals are the principles of participation and good governance. The participation principle requires states to ensure that their individual citizens have: 'access to "appropriate, comprehensible and timely" information concerning sustainable development that is held by public authorities, and the opportunity to participate in decision-making processes, as well as effective access to judicial and administrative proceedings, including redress and remedy'.[48] This principle works two ways – not only does public participation assist the relevant authorities in making better decisions by having access to wider 'potential sources of relevant information',[49] it also provides the public the opportunity to be involved in the decision-making process which 'potentially enhances public trust in government decision making … and serves to co-ordinate and reconcile various strategies of achieving public interest objectives'.[50] This principle is reflected in various international instruments[51] but at present is still an emerging norm.[52]

44 Marie-Claire Cordonier Segger and Ashfaq Khalfan, *Sustainable Development and Law: Principles and Practices & Prospects* (Oxford University Press, 2004) 132

45 See e.g., *Rio Declaration on Environment and Development*, UN Doc A/CONF.151/26/REV.1 (12 August 1992) Arts 3 and 5 (Rio Declaration); UN Framework Convention on Climate Change (1992) 31 ILM 851 (UNFCCC) Preamble and Art 3(1); UN Convention to Combat Desertification in those Countries Experiencing Serious Drought and/or Desertification, particularly in Africa (1994) 33 ILM 1328 (UNCCD) Art 2(1); UN Convention on Biological Diversity (1992) 31 ILM 822 (UNCBD) Preamble and Art 15(7)

46 See e.g., *Minors Oposa v Secretary of the Department of Environment and Natural Resources (DENR)* (Supreme Court of the Philippines, 30 July 1993) reported in (1994) 33 ILM 173, 185; *Nuclear Tests (New Zealand v France) (Order on Request for Examination in Accordance with Paragraph 63 of the Court's Judgment of 20 December 1974)* [1995] ICJ Rep 288, 341 (Judge Weeramantry); *Legality of the Threat or Use of Nuclear Weapons (Advisory Opinion)* [1996] ICJ Rep 266, 241 para 29 (ICJ recognised that 'quality of life' in relation to the environment also affected 'generations unborn')

47 Schrijver (n 33) 175–178.

48 Marie-Claire Cordonier Segger, 'The Role of International Forums in the Advancement of Sustainable Development' (2009) 10 *Sustainable Development Law & Policy* 4, 16

49 Jona Razzaque, *Public Interest Environmental Litigation in India, Pakistan and Bangladesh* (Kluwer Law International, 2004) 402

50 Ibid (footnotes omitted)

51 See e.g., Rio Declaration principle 10; UNFCCC Art 6; UNCBD Arts 13 and 14(1)

52 Cordonier Segger and Khalfan (n 44) 156

The principle of good governance requires the application of a range of widely accepted principles such as the rule of law, transparency, accountability, effective management of public resources, corruption control, citizen participation and equity. As aptly set out as a priority in the 2002 Johannesburg Plan of Implementation (JPOI):

> Good governance within each country and at the international level is essential for sustainable development. At the domestic level, sound environmental, social and economic policies, democratic institutions responsive to the needs of the people, the rule of law, anti-corruption measures, gender equality and an enabling environment for investment are the basis for sustainable development.[53]

The international community has begun incorporating good governance, or elements of it, into policies and treaties in the last decade.[54] Although the concept of good governance is not part of customary international law, it operates as a policy or action-guiding tool.[55]

Notwithstanding their legal status, these principles (equity, participation and good governance) have gained some degree of international recognition and are an important part of the concept of sustainable development, providing helpful objectives in order to achieve it. These principles and the concept of sustainable development continue to be reflected in the international arena as evidenced by the international community's adoption of the UN Sustainable Development Goals (SDGs) in 2015 which is the intended blueprint and agenda to achieve sustainable development in the next 15 years.[56]

The SDGs consist of 17 goals and 169 targets covering a range of issues of global importance: from ending poverty, achieving gender equality, climate action, ensuring responsible consumption, to promoting peace – seeking to integrate and balance the three dimensions (environmental, social and economic) of sustainable development.[57] While none of the SDG goals specifically cover natural resources relevant to armed conflict, there are goals

53 Para 4

54 See e.g., *Partnership Agreement between the Members of the African, Caribbean and Pacific Group of States of the One Part, and the European Community and its Member States, of the Other Part* [2000] OJ L317/3 (entered into force 1 April 2003); *United Nations Convention against Corruption*, opened for signature 9 December 2003, 2439 UNTS 41 (entered into force 14 December 2005)

55 Nupur Choudhury and C.E. Skarstedt, 'The Principle of Good Governance' (2005) CISDL Draft Legal Working Paper, 21 <www.scribd.com/document/297124916/CISDL-P5-Governance> accessed 20 January 2017

56 The SDGs are built on the Millennium Development Goals. See *Transforming Our World: The 2030 Agenda for Sustainable Development*, GA Res 70/1, UN GAOR, 70th sess, 4th plen mtg, Agenda Items 15 and 16, UN Doc A/RES/70/1 (21 October 2015)

57 United Nations, 'Sustainable Development Goals' <https://sustainabledevelopment.un.org/?menu=1300> accessed 11 May 2016 (UN SDGs)

and targets relevant to preventing natural resources conflict-related situations indirectly. For example, goal and targets extending from: equitable rights to economic resources including natural resources (1.4), build and develop sustainable infrastructure to support economic development and human wellbeing (9), reduce inequality within and among countries (10), ensure sustainable consumption and production patterns (12), and finally (SDG 16): promoting 'peaceful and inclusive societies for sustainable development, provide access to justice for all and build effective, accountable and inclusive institutions at all levels'.[58] These SDGs and targets not only provide some guided targets to achieving sustainable development globally, but also incorporate elements of the sustainable development principles of equity, good governance and participation.

While the DRC case study highlights the challenges to sustainable development inherent in a resource-conflict situation, the sustainable development principles (equity, participation and good governance) could significantly contribute to preventing or mitigating resource conflict and promoting peace. In the context of conflict minerals or natural resources conflict in general, such sustainable development principles could be used to promote sustainable investment in conflict-free minerals and contribute to the overarching aim of sustainable development in conflict-prone areas. In the context of the DRC in particular, this would mean, for example, that companies investing in 3TG minerals would use these sustainable development principles and targets as guidance for corporate behaviour. This must occur in conjunction with regulatory compliance to ensure sustainable investment in conflict-free minerals and to contribute to sustainable development for the benefit of the Congolese artisanal miners and their dependants.

Exploring the integration of sustainable development principles with norms relating to conflict minerals is discussed below. Prior to that, the next section briefly reviews the existing legal framework that regulates trade and investment in conflict minerals and whether sustainable development principles are adequately reflected.

Normative legal framework governing international investment in conflict minerals and the applicability of sustainable development principles

External actors to the DRC have introduced various measures related to the mineral sector, not because of the lack of domestic law but because of the state's failure to enforce existing laws, illustrating a distinct lack of good and effective governance at national level:[59] from dysfunctional awards of mining

58 Ibid
59 Arimatsu and Mistry (n 17) 28

rights, questionable due diligence, weak monitoring and penalisation for non-compliance by the relevant DRC authorities, to the low success rate of prosecution of military personnel for pillage which has been criminalised under the DRC's Code of Military Justice (1972).[60] Moreover, the 2002 Mining Code, while being the main legal instrument governing mining activities in the DRC, 'has simply had no influence in many of the mine sites in the eastern provinces controlled by the armed forces'.[61] As Arimatsu and Mistry also point out, '[d]espite the existence of a domestic legal framework, the extractive-sector regime remains deeply flawed at all levels as a consequence of non-enforcement or arbitrary decision making'.[62] In addition, due to the major role played by external actors (foreign companies investing in DRC minerals), this chapter focuses on the international legal framework regulating investment in conflict minerals.

International legal framework

In 2000, the UNSC established the Panel of Experts (PoE) on the Illegal Exploitation of the Natural Resources and other Forms of Wealth of the Democratic Republic of the Congo to collate information and analyse the economic and resource relationships to the continuing conflict.[63] In its 2002 Report, the PoE 'named and shamed' international corporations indirectly benefiting from illegal resource exploitation in the DRC.[64] Unfortunately, evidence in support of such allegations failed to pass scrutiny and 'the named companies threatened the UN with lawsuits'.[65] The PoE had to review its list based on more robust evidence and gave its last report in 2003.[66] Despite its shortfalls, the PoE's reports did pave the way for future initiatives – for example, according to Arimatsu and Mistry, the PoE's Second Report prompted the Organisation for Economic Co-operation and Development's (OECD) involvement in the minerals debate.[67]

In 2010, the UN Group of Experts (GoE) on the DRC formulated the UN Due Diligence Guidelines ('UNDD'), a voluntary five-step due diligence concept required by companies investing in minerals from 'red flag' locations

60 See e.g., DRC Military Penal Code (2002) Arts 435 (as amended in 1980), 436, 63 and 65

61 Arimatsu and Mistry (n 17) 28–29. See also Extractive Industries Transparency Initiative (EITI) 'Report 2010' (EITI 2010) 16–18

62 Arimatsu and Mistry (n 17) 28

63 *Statement of the President of the Security Council*, UN SCOR, 4151st mtg UN Doc S/PRST/2000/20 (2 June 2000)

64 See *Final Report of the Panel of Experts on the Illegal Exploitation of Natural Resources and Other Forms of Wealth of the Democratic Republic of Congo*, UN SCOR, S/2002/1146 (16 October 2002) annex III

65 Arimatsu and Mistry (n 17) 10

66 Ibid 11

67 Ibid 9–11 (review of the PoE on DRC), 14

to mitigate the risk of providing support for conflict in the eastern parts of the DRC.[68] The five steps are: strengthening company management systems; identifying and assessing risks in supply chains; designing and implementing a strategy to respond to identified risks; ensuring independent third-party audits; and publicly disclosing supply-chain due diligence and findings.[69] While the UNDD is not legally binding, the UNSC's binding Resolution 1952 did endorse the guidelines. However, the language used by the UNSC was not obligatory, merely calling upon states to take appropriate steps to 'raise awareness' and 'to urge importers, processing industries and consumers of Congolese minerals products to exercise due diligence' by applying the guidelines.[70] Nevertheless, the UNDD does have some legal effect as the resolution authorises the UN Sanctions Committee for the DRC[71] to impose targeted sanctions against companies not exercising due diligence and therefore, imposing indirect pressure on all companies concerned to comply with the guidelines.[72] These guidelines, therefore, do go some way to promoting transparency and accountability in the mineral trade chain, contributing to sustainable consumption and production patterns.

Like the GoE, the OECD also encourages transparent, accountable, sustainable consumption and production patterns by incorporating the five UNDD steps into its own multi-stakeholder initiated 2011 Due Diligence Guidelines for Responsible Supply Chains from Conflict-Affected and High-Risk Areas ('OECD Guidelines').[73] The OECD Guidelines are voluntary non-binding risk-based management recommendations for responsible supply chains of 3TGs worldwide to help companies respect human rights and avoid contributing to conflict through their mineral purchasing practices. The OECD's five-step due diligence framework corresponds to and broadens the UNDD steps above.[74] The OECD Guidelines are for all companies potentially sourcing minerals or metals from any conflict-affected and high-risk area. Thus, the global reach of the OECD Guidelines is greater in comparison than the UNDD as their scope is not confined to the DRC or neighbouring countries.

68 UN Due Diligence Guidelines for the Responsible Supply Chain of Minerals from Red Flag Locations to Mitigate the Risk of Providing Direct or Indirect Support for Conflict in the Eastern Part of the Democratic Republic of the Congo <www.un.org/sc/suborg/sites/www.un.org.sc.suborg/files/due_diligence_guidelines.pdf> accessed 20 January 2017

69 Ibid

70 SC Res 1952, UN SCOR, 65th sess, 6432nd mtg, UN Doc S/RES/1952 (29 November 2010) para 8

71 SC Res 1533, UN SCOR 59th sess, 4926th mtg, UN Doc S/RES/1533 (12 March 2004) para 8 (authorising the Sanctions Committee)

72 SC Res 1952, UN SCOR, 65th sess, 6432nd mtg, UN Doc S/RES/1952 (29 November 2010) para 9

73 OECD, 'OECD Due Diligence Guidance for Responsible Supply Chains of Minerals from Conflict-Affected and High-Risk Areas' (2nd edn, OECD 2013)

74 Ibid 31–113

In addition, as Arimatsu and Mistry note, the OECD is the first to recognise that artisanal or small-scale producing enterprises may not have the same capacity as bigger enterprises to incorporate the guidance, providing that the OECD guidance can be scaled 'to the size of the company's activities or supply chain relationships'.[75] However, the Guidelines clarify that the definition of upstream companies only applies to artisanal and small-scale producing enterprises and not individuals or informal working groups of artisanal miners.[76] This of course excludes the millions of individual and informal artisanal miners in the DRC. While the OECD Guidelines recognise artisanal and small-scale mineral producers embrace to some extent the principles of equity and participation, their exclusion of the millions of individual and informal miners also contributes to inequity and poor participation in the mineral industry – still posing a challenge to sustainable development for the DRC and a significant number of its population.

Other voluntary international guidance and standards initiatives in this field include the 2010 UN Global Compact Guidance on Responsible Business in Conflict-Affected and High-Risk Areas ('UNGC')[77] and the Extractive Industries Transparency Initiative (EITI).[78] The UNCG, providing more general guidance not limited to severing the mineral–conflict link, aims to help companies implement responsible business practices in conflict-affected and high-risk areas in line with the Global Compact Ten Principles.[79] Due to its general scope, the UNCG 'reaches a wider audience than the OECD, it fills a gap that would otherwise exist'.[80] However, as Arimatsu and Mistry further note, 'the overlaps between its recommendations and those of the OECD's risk creating confusion among companies that are subject to both regimes, although neither is mandatory'.[81] The EITI is a voluntary multi-stakeholder initiative that promotes transparency and accountability in natural resources management (oil, gas, metals and minerals).[82] While its main objective is not to de-link the mineral–conflict trade, the requirement by the EITI standard[83] for subscribing countries to fully disclose all information on government revenues, company payments and other key elements around resources extraction, enables citizens to hold their government and companies accountable for the origins and use of such revenues. This contributes to reducing corruption, improving natural resource management

75 Ibid 14
76 Ibid 31 (footnote 1)
77 UN Global Compact, 'Guidance on Responsible Business in Conflict-Affected and High Risk Areas: A Resource for Companies and Investors' (UN Global Compact/PRI 2010).
78 See EITI <https://eiti.org/eiti> accessed 12 May 2016
79 UN Global Compact, 'The Ten Principles of the UN Global Compact' <www.unglobalcompact.org/what-is-gc/mission/principles> accessed 4 September 2015
80 Arimatsu and Mistry (n 17) 23
81 Ibid
82 EITI (n 78)
83 EITI, 'The EITI Standard' (EITI International Secretariat, 1 January 2015)

and consequently, mitigating conflict and achieving sustainable development.[84]

Regional and national responses

The International Conference for the Great Lakes Region ('ICGLR') is an inter-governmental organisation of 12 countries[85] created to re-establish and promote sustainable peace and development in the region. In 2006, the ICGLR agreed on the Pact on Security, Stability and Development for the Great Lakes Region which includes the legally binding Protocol against the Illegal Exploitation of Natural Resources.[86] This Protocol outlines the actions required by state parties to curb the illegal exploitation of natural resources, including its central tool: the Regional Initiative against the Illegal Exploitation of Natural Resources (RINR) which was launched in September 2009.[87] The RINR's main aim is to sever the link between illicit mineral revenues and rebel financing and 'translate the Great Lakes region's rich mineral resources from a source of conflict into a catalyst for development'.[88]

The core element of the RINR is the Regional Certification Mechanism (RCM), a regional tracking and certification system for 3TGs[89] which includes the requirement for mineral tracking (from mine to export, member states chain of custody, to regional tracking).[90] Export certification became mandatory in December 2012 but 'the system is not yet fully operational'.[91] While the DRC integrated the RCM into its domestic legislation in 2012,[92] there are problems in implementation. According to UNSC reports:

> On natural resources, the GoE notes delays in the implementation of the regional certification mechanism due to structural weaknesses in the ICGLR secretariat and lack of political will among its members. The lack

84 EITI, 'Benefits from Implementing EITI' <https://eiti.org/eiti/benefits> accessed 4 September 2015. See also V. Haufler, 'Disclosure as Governance: The Extractive Industries Transparency Initiative and Resource Management in the Developing World' (2010) 10(3) *Global Environmental Politics* 53–73 (on EITI's successes and weaknesses)

85 Angola, Burundi, Central African Republic, Republic of Congo, DRC, Kenya, Uganda, Rwanda, Republic of South Sudan, Sudan, Tanzania and Zambia

86 ICGLR, 'The Pact' <www.icglr.org/index.php/en/the-pact> accessed 6 September 2015

87 ICGLR, 'RINR' <www.icglr.org/index.php/en/rinr> accessed 6 September 2015

88 UN Economic Commission for Africa, 'Special Report on the ICLGR Regional Initiative against the Illegal Exploitation of Natural Resource (RINR) and other Certification Mechanisms in the Great Lakes Region: Lessons Learned and Best Practices' (UN Economic Commission for Africa 2013) 12

89 See ICGLR, 'Briefing Note on the ICGLR Regional Certification Mechanism' (ICGLR/Partnership Africa Canada, June 2012)

90 See ICGLR, 'ICGLR Regional Certification Mechanism (RCM) – Certification Manual' <www.oecd.org/investment/mne/49111368.pdf> accessed 6 September 2015

91 G. Grieger, 'Minerals from Conflict Areas: Existing and New Responsible-Sourcing Initiatives' (European Parliamentary Research Service Briefing 2014) 2

92 Ibid 2

of implementation of the DRC's mine-validation system outside of the Kivus encourages the continuation of smuggling through neighbouring states.[93]

While the RINR initiative is intended to promote transparency, accountability, development and peace in the region, the difficulties facing its implementation demonstrate that a lack of regional and domestic good governance or effective infrastructure are obstacles to implementing any initiative.

In addition to regional responses to the conflict minerals issue, the US Congress in 2010 adopted the Dodd-Frank Wall Street Reform and Consumer Protection Act (Dodd-Frank Act),[94] where its Section 1502 is the first domestic legislation to tackle conflict minerals. This Act requires disclosure from all companies sourcing 3TG minerals[95] from the DRC and its neighbouring countries[96] that report to the US Security and Exchange Commission (SEC). SEC's final rules provide a three-step procedure: companies must determine if the conflict minerals law applies to them; if applicable, companies must establish the origin of minerals used and disclose them; and if revealed that the minerals were sourced from the DRC or neighbouring countries, a Conflict Minerals Report must be filed, which must include the due diligence steps taken and be independently audited.[97] The report must also describe or label minerals sourced and products manufactured that are not 'DRC conflict free'.[98] Additionally, Section 1502 requires companies to disclose on their website whether they are sourcing minerals or manufacturing products labelled 'DRC conflict free' or 'not DRC conflict free'.[99]

The Act has been subject to criticism. Clark argues that 'the "conflict minerals" provisions of Dodd-Frank Act do *not* prevent or otherwise restrict companies from using conflict minerals from mines in DRC; rather, the Act "merely requires companies to disclose information regarding their minerals' origins and chain of custody"'.[100] This may not be such an issue, as being

93 UNSC Report, 'August 2014 Monthly Forecast: Democratic Republic of Congo' <www.securitycouncilreport.org/monthly-forecast/2015-07/democratic_republic_of_the_congo_8.php> accessed 6 September 2015

94 Pub L 111-203, 124 Sta.1376 (July 21, 2010)

95 Section 1502(e)(4) defines conflict minerals

96 Section 150(e)(1) defines adjoining country

97 Grieger (n 91) 3

98 SEC, 'Conflict Minerals: Final Rule' 1. <www.sec.gov/rules/final/2012/34-67716.pdf> accessed 7 September 2015 (added Section 13p to the Securities Exchange Act 1934)

99 Ibid 2

100 R.D. Clark, 'The Control of Conflict Minerals in Africa and a Preliminary Assessment of the Dodd-Frank Wall Street Reform and Consumer Act' in N. South and A. Brisman (eds), *Routledge International Handbook of Green Criminology* (Routledge 2013) 221 (footnote omitted)

unable to label products as conflict free can cause reputational risks for companies,[101] thereby indirectly contributing to sustainable consumption and production of 3TGs. Moreover, coupled with the complex and costly due diligence process of the Act, including 'the scarcity of traceability and certification schemes on the ground to perform supply-chain due diligence',[102] this has induced many US-listed companies to avoid sourcing minerals from the region altogether – causing a de facto embargo. While arguably effective in reducing the demand for conflict minerals, ultimately this also halts any legitimate trade in minerals, which for a country heavily dependent on such resources, causes great hardship – not only increasing inequity amongst the population but also hindering any opportunity for sustainable development.

While there has been no equivalent EU-level law for EU companies, in 2015 the EU Parliament voted for a mandatory due diligence system for the whole supply chain ('all Union importers') of 3TG minerals originating from all conflict-affected and high-risk areas.[103] The proposed EU regulation is more demanding and wider in scope in comparison to the Dodd-Frank Act, applying to all EU upstream and related downstream companies and its geographical scope extending to 'all conflict affected and high risk areas' globally.[104] Initial concerns are similar to the issues resulting from the Dodd-Frank Act – from high costs in implementing the regulations particularly for smaller companies, to the negative impact on the legitimate trade in minerals from conflict and high-risk locations, where costly and burdensome procedures may cause companies to source minerals elsewhere.[105] It remains to be seen what the text of the final regulation will consist of and what its impacts will be.

Limits of the law and integrating sustainable development

Global initiatives aimed at ending both the conflict minerals trade and the financial source of armed rebels in the DRC have had some successes.[106] There are for example, reports of positive changes in larger mines in eastern DRC[107] and there have been reports of improved security as a result.[108]

101 Grieger (n 91) 4

102 Ibid

103 'Conflict minerals: MEPs ask for mandatory certification of EU importers' *European Parliament News* (20 May 2015) <www.europarl.europa.eu/news/en/news-room/content/20150513IPR55318/html/Conflict-minerals-MEPs-ask-for-mandatory-certification-of-EU-importers> accessed 7 September 2015

104 See e.g., C. Barbière, 'Parliament votes for tougher conflict minerals regulation' *EurActiv.fr* (France, 21 May 2015) <www.euractiv.com/sections/development-policy/parliament-votes-binding-conflict-minerals-regulation-314741> accessed 7 September 2015

105 Ibid

106 See F. Bafilemba, et al., 'From Congress to Congo: Turning the Tide on Conflict Minerals, Closing Loopholes, Empowering Miners' (Enough Project, August 2012)

107 Matthysen and Montejano (n 13) 35

108 Ibid 35 and 41

However, some unintended consequences have also materialised, highlighting some lessons for future initiatives applicable to any conflict mineral country globally. The challenges to and suggested integration of relevant sustainable development principles are explored below.

Transparency and traceability

While there have been achievements with transparency and traceability of conflict minerals as a result of international legislative efforts, there have also been problems. Both the UNDD and OECD Guidelines have had some success in increasing accountability and transparency for the supply chain, thus mitigating the risk in investing in conflict minerals,[109] contributing to sustainable investment and preventing the finance of conflict. However, the resulting sustainability is limited to the relationship between the investor and consumer, while minimising or having 'zero' contact with conflict minerals. Although this contributes to conflict prevention which is half the battle, the Guidelines leave no room for taking into account the impact on the everyday Congolese involved in the mineral mining, trade and production.

Similarly, the Dodd-Frank Act did partially achieve its aim to sever the mineral–conflict link and while laudable, its unintended consequences were controversial. Like the UNDD and OECD Guidelines, the Act succeeded in the first half of the complex mineral–conflict issue in that it curbed the trade in conflict minerals and stopped the financing of armed groups. However, the Act failed to take into account the impact of its legislation on the ground.[110] In adhering to the Dodd-Frank Act, many companies avoided using minerals from the DRC altogether effectively creating a 'de facto embargo'.[111] The embargo had a serious effect on the eastern DRC as approximately 90 per cent of export revenue stems from the mineral trade, resulting in a decline in mineral prices, significant job losses and increasing poverty.[112]

Poor domestic policy choices, such as the mining ban imposed by President Kabila in the eastern provinces in 2010, further compounded the negative effects of international and US legislation.[113] Although the intention was to mitigate the illicit exploitation of minerals, the ban had the opposite effect in that rebel factions took the opportunity to gain control over the banned mines.[114] In addition, in a fragile, volatile area like eastern DRC, where alternative employment is few and far between,[115] the loss of mining

109 Arimatsu and Mistry (n 17) 22

110 P.H. Schultz, 'The Controversial New Disclosure Requirement in Dodd-Frank' in P.H. Schultz (ed), *Perspectives on Dodd-Frank and Finance* (MIT Press 2014) 219

111 Ibid

112 A. Atta-Asamoah and N. Githaiga, 'Addressing the "Conflict Minerals" Crisis in the Great Lakes Region' Institute for Security Studies (Policy Brief No. 35, September 2012) 35

113 Arimatsu and Mistry (n 17) 29

114 Ibid

115 Matthysen and Montejano (n 13) 6

jobs meant that many were forced to turn to mineral smuggling and joining armed factions.[116] The ban illustrates a top-down approach to law and a disengagement with the population on the ground, demonstrating a need for a more participatory approach in order to contribute to better governance on the conflict minerals issue. Overall, these impacts not only counter effect the aim of these international initiatives by increasing inequity and contributing to the vicious cycle of illicit mineral trade and conflict, but also massively hinder sustainable development.

Regional initiatives such as the ICGLR have also faced problems, primarily a result of weak domestic infrastructure and a lack of political will. As Matthysen and Montejano point out, '[d]espite the ICGLR's assets, such as local ownership, its comprehensive approach and recognition of the regional dimension of conflict minerals, it has been lacking in vigour'.[117] While it has the much-needed element of public participation at national and regional levels, the ICGLR initiatives suffer from ineffective governance at the implementation stage. The weaknesses in the GLR states, including the DRC, in their inability to effectively implement the certification schemes has not only delayed efforts in promoting transparency and traceability of the supply chain, but has also made it difficult for companies investing in minerals from the DRC to comply with international and national due diligence standards and legislation.[118] First, a lack of certification has not helped the delinking of the mineral–conflict chain. Second, this has resulted in many companies avoiding investing in the DRC due to difficulties in tracing the origins of minerals sourced which subsequently have led to business and mine closures in the DRC, resulting in a loss of livelihoods.[119]

Some of the negative consequences of the legislative efforts have highlighted the problems of ineffective governance and not taking a holistic approach or integrating public participation into decision-making. These consequences have changed the debate focused on conflict minerals. 'It's not just about conflict-free. What's important is promoting responsible sourcing of minerals *from* conflict areas, despite the challenges. Whole-scale disengagement with artisanal miners almost always has harsh consequences for miners' livelihoods'.[120] Therefore, any attempt to deal with the issue of conflict minerals has to be holistic, aiming for not only sustainable investment but also sustainable consumption and production (SG12). Sustainable investment includes not only investing in conflict-free minerals, contributing to peace and security in any conflict mineral country, but also taking into

116 Grieger (n 91) 4
117 Matthysen and Montejano (n 13) 38
118 See UNSC 2014 Report (n 93)
119 See e.g., S. Geenan, *African Artisanal Mining from the Inside Out* (Routledge 2015) 183.
120 T. Gillard and R. Nieuwenkamp, 'Responsible Gold Also Means Supporting Livelihoods of Artisanal Miners' *OECD Insights* (24 March 2015) <http://oecdinsights.org/2015/03/24/responsible-gold-also-means-supporting-livelihoods-of-artisanal-miners/> accessed 7 September 2015

account the sustainable development of the affected population. Thus the sustainable development principles, together with existing legislation, could assist companies to invest in conflict-free minerals.

Due diligence and public participation

While the due diligence and certification initiatives do address the conflict minerals problem, the success of any international initiative requires the backing and commitment of the conflict mineral state and its population.[121] For example, critics note that the Dodd-Frank Act was passed with little African participation, therefore 'imposing an outside solution'.[122] The problems incurred by the international initiatives have brought to light the necessity for all stakeholders, particularly authorities of the state concerned and the people on the ground most affected (such as miners), to participate in the process in order to achieve effective implementation. This is vital to provide an opportunity to demonstrate the importance of the public participation principle. The formulation of new initiatives requires local stakeholder participation, particularly to ensure that any due diligence requirements are feasible and do not adversely impact the very people they were meant to protect. The DRC case study demonstrates that the international community and companies investing in minerals must not only get local stakeholders' views in creating and implementing initiatives, but should also assist them in complying with the complex and costly legislative initiatives.

Companies should take note that one of the stumbling blocks in their ability to comply with due diligence in mineral traceability is the lack of mineral certification mechanisms on the ground. In the DRC example, this was largely due to the GLR states and the DRC in particular, lacking the governmental capacity or political will to do so – from lack of resources (poor technical know-how, insufficient funding and insufficient personnel) to corruption. According to Matthysen and Montejano, '[t]he participation of Congolese public services in the implementation of initiatives linked to the mining sector will not be effective if the structural corruption is not seriously addressed'.[123] Improving governance and capacity in conflict-prone resource dependent countries will require significant international support, including from companies themselves. In line with good governance, SDGs 9 (sustainable infrastructure) and 16 (effective, accountable and inclusive institutions), external actors cannot expect fragile conflict-affected countries to implement and comply with complex international regulations themselves, without giving them the assistance necessary to do so.

121 Matthysen and Montejano (n 13) 37
122 Grieger (n 91) 4
123 Matthysen and Montejano (n 13) 40

Equity

In accordance with SDGs 1.4 (equitable rights to resources) and 10 (reduce inequality within and among countries), the objective of the principle of equity, for example, should be integrated within any existing legislation and guidelines on conflict minerals. Despite the burdensome costs and administrative issues that follow such initiatives, instead of pulling out of conflict mineral countries or regions, companies should recognise that sustainable investment in minerals includes sourcing conflict-free minerals, as well as aiming for sustainable development for the people of nations that are directly or indirectly dependent on the mineral mining industry.[124] Discounting the equity principle means that poverty levels of an already vulnerable population will be exacerbated, once again leading to an inequitable distribution of income and natural resources. Such inequity contributes to an atmosphere for future conflict and is an affront to intrinsic values of participation and good governance.

Implementation and enforcement

Another aim of these international efforts is to formalise the DRC's artisanal mining sector, which in its unregulated form paves the way for illicit trafficking and rebel funding. The formalisation of the artisanal mining sector is necessary for the implementation and enforcement of legislation. As per SDG 16 (effective, accountable and inclusive institutions at all levels), formalisation of unregulated mining sectors could contribute to improved implementation and enforcement of conflict mineral legislation. While formalisation of artisanal mining sectors contributes to good governance, prior to achieving this, effective governance[125] by local authorities is needed in order to increase their control over the informal artisanal mining sector.[126] Formalisation, however, is difficult without participation of all stakeholders (from artisanal miners to local authorities). In addition, stakeholders will require support and capacity building to be able to formalise and comply with the legislation schemes.

With regard to the DRC for instance, attempting to formally transform a sector involving 500,000–2 million people is not easy.[127] However, such transformation would be difficult in any conflict-prone vulnerable state. External support is much needed here. As Matthysen and Montejano argue,

124 M. Nest, *Coltan* (Polity Press, 2011) 1977

125 For local authorities to attain effective governance, measures such as capacity building (training) on achieving good governance, anti-corruption measures (including increasing transparency and accountability), improved communication with the central government and private mining sector, to encouraging better engagement with local communities (including miners), need to be in place

126 Matthysen and Montejano (n 13) 38

127 Ibid

'a well implemented formalisation process would increase the chances of success for initiatives addressing the conflict minerals issue' and also 'help to address issues linked to artisanal mining, such as underdevelopment, poverty, labour condition, environmental degradation, insecurity and conflict financing'.[128] Addressing such social, environmental and economic challenges would significantly contribute to sustainable investment in conflict-free minerals and assist in the achievement of sustainable development in the DRC, particularly its vulnerable eastern provinces.

Conclusion

There is no doubt that the global push for 'conflict minerals' has thrown up new challenges in the extractive industries, particularly in the eastern DRC. The unintended consequences of international initiatives demonstrate that the issue of trade in conflict minerals cannot be tackled in isolation by legislation aimed at severing the minerals–conflict link, particularly as natural resources are never the sole cause of conflicts. The various negative impacts and the underlying complexities of the mineral conflict situation in the DRC and other conflict areas mean that a more holistic approach must be taken by the international community and companies investing in minerals sourced from conflict-prone areas.

This chapter thus argues for integrating salient principles of sustainable development, in particular the principles of equity, participation and good governance, together with existing legislation. Such an approach could mean a more comprehensive approach to sustainable investment in conflict-free minerals, which in addition to curbing the mineral–conflict link and contributing to conflict prevention, aims to mitigate the socio-economic consequences on the people as a result of conflict mineral initiatives – ultimately supporting the millions dependent on the mineral sector in vulnerable conflict-prone societies to achieve sustainable development.

128 Ibid 39

18 Corruption, investment and natural resources

Adam Simpson

Introduction

International natural resources law, as with all international law, is difficult to enforce and operates within a framework of international agreements that rely for their efficacy on the widespread acceptance of, and adherence to, international norms. Corrupt practices within the natural resources sector undermine these norms, and therefore also the international agreements and law that they sustain. Corrupt decisions by public officials are made for private, rather than public, benefit so they can have a corrosive effect on development, but they are also less likely to result in the sustainable exploitation of resources as short-term private gain is prioritised over long-term use.

In the developing countries of the South investment in the natural resource sector has a more significant impact on the economy as a whole than wealthier countries with more diverse economies.[1] In many parts of the South corruption and natural resource extraction are intimately intertwined. There are, however, few places in the world where they do not co-exist in a close symbiotic relationship – the opportunity for large revenues from point sources requiring limited industrial expertise means the allocation of, for example, forestry or mining licences, like real estate development, is highly susceptible to corrupt influences – although the level, type and extent of the corruption varies significantly across geographical, political and economic spaces.[2]

In recent years the notion of transparency has been touted as a key governance cure for these corrupt practices. While transparency can address some issues relating to corruption its impact on broader governance issues is somewhat limited in its scope: it cannot, for example, address issues of societal resource allocation. Focusing too much on transparency can consume the limited resources that are available to developing countries and their state

1 Hans-Jürgen Burchardt and Kristina Dietz, '(Neo-)extractivism – A New Challenge for Development Theory from Latin America' (2014) 35 *Third World Quarterly* 468

2 Hazel M. McFerson, 'Governance and Hyper-Corruption in Resource-Rich African Countries' (2009) 30 *Third World Quarterly* 1529

bureaucracies. For civil society, the emphasis on transparency can also shift attention away from other fundamental questions regarding resource exploitation and exploring policies that can deliver equitable development.

Nevertheless, it is also the case that without transparency of revenue flows between governments and corporations, corruption is much easier. If civil society and the public in general are unable to track revenue flows from natural resource exploitation, it is much simpler for corrupt corporations to make payments to corrupt government officials in order to receive favourable treatment.[3]

Transparency is therefore now seen as a key element in the worldwide fight against corruption. As a result, there have been several legal frameworks established to promote transparency in the global natural resource sectors. The two main tools backed by enforceable legal penalties are Section 1504 of the US Dodd-Frank Wall Street Reform and Consumer Protection Act of 2010[4] and the EU Accounting (and Transparency) Directives of 2013.[5] These approaches have demonstrated the importance of national or regional innovations, but also the problems associated with employing legislative measures, particularly in the US where legal challenges by the petroleum industry resulted in the initial requirements of Section 1504 being struck down.[6]

The third significant innovation in transparency within the natural resources sector is the Extractive Industries Transparency Initiative (EITI), a voluntary international agreement that seeks to challenge corrupt practices in the natural resources sector, primarily mining, oil and gas.[7] Since its emergence in 2003, led primarily by the UK government and a coalition of non-governmental organisations (NGOs) including Global Witness and Publish What You Pay (PWYP), the EITI has become a key tool for anti-corruption campaigners within the natural resources sector in the South, where corruption is most prevalent and destructive. It has reinforced an emerging global norm of transparency in natural resource expenditure and revenue that may provide an avenue for addressing deep-seated corrupt practices. Within states it provides a platform for civil society to engage directly with government and industry on an equal footing through the Multi-Stakeholder Group (MSG), a process that governments must accept as part

3 Ibid

4 Pub L No. 111-203, 124 Stat 1376

5 Directive 2013/34/EU of the European Parliament and of the Council of 26 June 2013 on the annual financial statements, consolidated financial statements and related reports of certain types of undertakings, amending Directive 2006/43/EC of the European Parliament and of the Council and repealing Council Directives 78/660/EEC and 83/349/EEC [2013] OJ L182/19

6 Michael V. Seitzinger and Kathleen Ann Ruane, 'Conflict Minerals and Resource Extraction: Dodd-Frank, SEC Regulations, and Legal Challenges' (7-5700, R43639, Congressional Research Service 2015)

7 EITI International Secretariat, *The EITI Standard 2016* (2016)

of EITI membership. It therefore indicates an implicit confidence in the role of civil society in undermining or preventing corruption.

One of the aims of the EITI is to establish transparency norms within extractive industries that undermine corrupt practices, which are then adopted within other areas of governance. A recent adopter of the EITI is Myanmar, a country with rich natural resources that since 2011 has undertaken a gradual, but radical, shift away from military rule.[8] The EITI process was initiated under the military-backed government of President Thein Sein (2011–2016). The new, more democratic, National League for Democracy (NLD) government, which took power in April 2016, has committed to the transparency principles of the EITI within natural resource governance and, given its historical links to the pro-democracy movement, it is more likely than its predecessor to implement them. In October 2016, the NLD-dominated parliament passed the Myanmar Investment Law,[9] which combined the existing Foreign Investment Law[10] and the Myanmar Citizens Investment Law.[11] It made some attempt to decentralise the approvals process for foreign investment to state and regional governments but natural resource projects still required centralised approval through the Myanmar Investment Commission. The investment rules attached to the law, which came into effect on 1 April 2017, opened natural resource industries to greater scrutiny by civil society (*The Irrawaddy*, 25 May 2017).

Despite the optimism over the EITI, its ability to actually reduce corruption in the natural resources sector is still open to debate. Since Myanmar's political and economic reform process ended its isolation from the West in 2011, it has experienced a flood of foreign investment within its natural resources sector. At the same time, joining the EITI has become emblematic of its newfound acceptance of international norms. It is therefore a key case study for assessing the implementation of the EITI and associated transparency norms in fragile and developing states. This chapter therefore uses Myanmar to explore the impact of corruption in the natural resources sector and assesses the role of the EITI in alleviating this problem.

Corruption and natural resources

Corruption occurs when people in public office breach the 'impartiality principle', whereby everyone should be treated more or less equally by the state.[12] This principle is generally breached when a public official gives unmerited

8 Adam Simpson, Nicholas Farrelly and Ian Holliday (eds), *Routledge Handbook of Contemporary Myanmar* (Routledge 2018)

9 The Myanmar Investment Law, Pyidaungsu Hluttaw Law No. 40/2016, 18 October

10 The Foreign Investment Law, The Pyidaungsu Hluttaw Law No. 21/2012, 2 November

11 Myanmar Citizens Investment Law, The Pyidaungsu Hluttaw Law No. 18/2013, 29 July

12 Oskar Kurer, 'Corruption: An Alternative Approach to its Definition and Measurement' (2005) 53 *Political Studies* 222

favourable treatment, for instance by granting a mining licence or lease to exceed production quotas in exchange for some sort of private financial benefit. The financial benefit is usually a 'kickback': a direct cash payment or a profit-sharing interest in the business. As natural resources are often the most significant component of the economy for developing countries, corruption in this sector can have a highly debilitating effect on economic growth, equitable development and effective governance.

Corruption is more likely to occur in societies with unequal power and resource distributions, which reinforce in-group trust within privileged circles but reduces it between these circles and less favoured citizens, resulting in an 'inequality–mistrust–corruption' trap.[13] Likewise, when the public perceives that the government is making genuine efforts to reduce corruption they are more likely to fight corruption themselves.[14] Perceptions are therefore clearly important in actually increasing or reducing corruption, which accounts for why the NGO Transparency International established its influential Corruption Perceptions Index.[15] Nevertheless, Alina Mungiu-Pippidi argues that in most country contexts, corruption is intrinsic to governance rather than an aberration, reinforcing the immensity of the task in trying to reduce it.[16]

Corruption relating to natural resources differs amongst types of natural resources and the society within which they are exploited. Dependency on natural resource exports can increase corruption, but in some cases it can actually decrease it. According to one study, fuel exports tend to increase corruption while non-fuel mineral exports tend to increase corruption only in developing countries, and particularly in those that export high-value mineral commodities such as diamonds and gold; in wealthier countries, non-fuel mineral exports actually reduces corruption.[17]

In the forestry sector, corruption and resource dependency result in increased deforestation.[18] Attempts by international organisations to promote forestry governance norms in developing countries in Southeast Asia have depended to a large extent on their endorsement and adoption by local politicians and vested interests. Widespread corruption, particularly in

13 Philippe Le Billon, 'Natural Resources and Corruption in Post-War Transitions: Matters of Trust' (2014) 35 *Third World Quarterly* 770

14 Caryn Peiffer and Linda Alvarez, 'Who Will Be the "Principled-Principals"? Perceptions of Corruption and Willingness to Engage in Anticorruption Activism' (2015) 29 *Governance* 351

15 Transparency International, *Corruption Perceptions Index 2015* (2016)

16 Alina Mungiu-Pippidi, *The Quest for Good Governance: How Societies Develop Control of Corruption* (Cambridge University Press 2015)

17 Andrea Petermann, Juan Ignacio Guzmán and John E. Tilton, 'Mining and Corruption' (2007) 32 *Resources Policy* 91

18 Edward B. Barbier, Richard Damania and Daniel Léonard, 'Corruption, Trade and Resource Conversion' (2005) 50 *Journal of Environmental Economics and Management* 276

the palm oil business, has perpetuated unsustainable deforestation for land conversion that has resulted in the visible governance failure of the annual regional haze.[19]

Post-conflict countries, which are often poor to begin with, are particularly susceptible to corruption in their natural resource sector due to disrupted and resource-poor bureaucracies governing highly profitable industries, which can undermine transitions to peace.[20] In all these instances of corruption it is often argued that transparency within the natural resource sector will result in better governance and therefore better development outcomes.

Transparency and evolving governance in the EITI

The main global approach to promote transparency in the natural resources sector is the EITI. It is primarily focused on the mining, oil and gas extractive industries but it is gradually evolving to include other natural resources including fisheries and hydropower. The EITI is advertised as a 'global Standard to promote open and accountable management of natural resources'.[21] It is voluntary for a country to join the EITI but once it does then, in principle, it becomes mandatory for all extractive industry operators within that country to participate, subject to the scope of the industries covered in the EITI and minimum revenue requirements. Countries implementing the EITI disclose information on tax payments, licences, contracts and production from natural resource extraction in an annual EITI Report, which is compiled by an Independent Administrator, allowing civil society and community groups to track the revenue from natural resources from production to the government accounts.

The EITI emerged in the early 2000s as part of a shift in global governance towards revenue transparency.[22] While the focus remains on transparency, an EITI Standard was launched at the EITI Global Conference in 2013 to improve related governance aspects, such as civil society participation, and at the conference in February 2016 in Lima, Peru, a new EITI Standard 2016 was adopted.[23] The new Standard changed the assessment

19 Stephen McCarthy, 'Norm Diffusion and the Limits to Forestry Governance Reform in Southeast Asia's New Democracies' (2014) 27 *The Pacific Review* 755; Shahar Hameiri and Lee Jones, *Governing Borderless Threats: Non-Traditional Security and the Politics of State Transformation* (Cambridge University Press 2015); Helena Varkkey, *The Haze Problem in Southeast Asia: Palm Oil and Patronage* (Routledge 2016)

20 Le Billon (n 13)

21 EITI International Secretariat, *The EITI Standard 2016* (2016)

22 Virginia Haufler, 'Disclosure as Governance: The Extractive Industries Transparency Initiative and Resource Management in the Developing World' (2010) 10 *Global Environmental Politics* 53; James Van Alstine, 'Transparency in Resource Governance: The Pitfalls and Potential of "New Oil" in Sub-Saharan Africa' (2014) 14 *Global Environmental Politics* 20

23 EITI International Secretariat, *The EITI Standard 2016* (2016)

nomenclature for countries from 'Candidate' or 'Compliant' status to a more nuanced four-level assessment based on a country's progress for each requirement and their overall implementation of the EITI Standard: satisfactory, meaningful, inadequate or no progress. At the conference Fredrik Reinfeldt, the former Swedish prime minister, was elected the new EITI chair, replacing Clare Short, who was chair during Myanmar's initial application phase. As of January 2017, 51 countries were implementing the EITI.[24]

EITI Reports are published by independent consultants, who ensure that the income received by the government has been accurately reconciled against the payments made by companies to the government. If the figure that the government reports is less than that of the companies, it may indicate corruption within the government. This reconciliation therefore only deals with reported payments. It is still possible for informal payments to occur but Western companies in particular face increasing scrutiny and pressure by shareholders and governments over transparency and potential corrupt practices, which ensures unaccounted informal payments are minimised.[25] The first EITI Report is due within 18 months of being accepted as an EITI implementing country. An EITI validation process occurs within 30 months of becoming an EITI implementing country, usually after the second Report, and assesses the progress that the country has made towards fulfilling the EITI requirements.

Once countries such as Myanmar join the EITI, all foreign and domestic companies engaging in the extractive sector, above a certain revenue threshold, are required to report their payments to the government. Legislation in the US and the EU already requires companies to do the same, although the courts have struck down key elements of the US legislation. Section 1504 (the Cardin-Lugar Transparency Amendment) of the Dodd-Frank Wall Street Reform and Consumer Protection Act of 2010 made the US a leader in transparency in the extractives sector. It required US corporations in the extractive industries to disclose payments made to governments of the countries in which they operate. Unfortunately, the fossil fuel industry stymied this progress with the American Petroleum Institute and related corporations, particularly Exxon Mobil, attacking the legislation through the courts.[26] The rule was vacated by a US district court in 2013, which resulted

24 EITI International Secretariat, EITI (2017) <https://eiti.org/> accessed 19 January 2017

25 Klaus E. Meyer and Htwe Htwe Thein, 'Business under Adverse Home Country Institutions: The Case of International Sanctions against Myanmar' (2013) 49 *Journal of World Business* 156

26 Alice Ross, 'Dodd-Frank's Bid to Clean Up Extractive Industries Stymied by Oil Business' *The Guardian* (London, 27 July 2015) <www.theguardian.com/global-development/2015/jul/22/dodd-frank-act-section-1504-natural-resources-extractive- industries-oil-api-sec> accessed 22 September 2016

in the US Securities and Exchange Commission (SEC) needing to rewrite its rationale for the legislation.[27] In June 2016 the SEC approved its new final rule, which came into effect in September 2016, although only payment data from the 2017–2018 financial year onwards was required to be released.[28] Nevertheless, transparency civil society groups such as PWYP considered it a significant step forward for transparency in the extractive sectors.[29]

In 2013 the EU went further than Section 1504 with new disclosure requirements for the extractive industry and loggers of primary forests in its EU Accounting (and Transparency) Directives (Country by Country Reporting).[30] It required that companies disclose the payments they make to governments on a country-by-country basis and, where appropriate, on project-by-project basis. Unlike the Dodd-Frank legislation, which only covered listed companies in the mining and oil and gas industries, the EU requirements covered both unlisted companies and forestry companies. Although the EU directives lagged behind the US legislation, the legal challenge by the petroleum industry in the US ensured that most EU companies were required to start their reporting much earlier than those in the US, starting from the 2015–2016 financial year.[31]

These measures complement the EITI by providing legally enforceable mechanisms for transparency in home countries but they only cover EU and US companies, which has partially been the cause of the vociferous opposition by some fossil fuel companies.[32] The EITI, by contrast, is applied to all companies operating within a member country and therefore provides a nominal level playing field in each country with, for example, Asian, Russian and Latin American corporations subject to similar requirements as EU and US-based corporations. These types of binding corporate regulations are generally more effective than non-binding voluntary initiatives, particularly in terms of stimulating state development in developing countries.[33] This is particularly important in many countries implementing the EITI, which are generally characterised by weak administrative capacity and often have

27 *American Petroleum Institute v SEC*, 953 F Supp 2d 5 (D DC, 2013)

28 Securities and Exchange Commission, Disclosure of Payments by Resource Extraction Issuers, Final Rule, 17 CFR Parts 240 and 249b, Release No. 34-78167; File No. S7-25-15, RIN 3235-AL53, June 2016

29 Publish What You Pay, 'News: It's Official – the SEC rule has been published in the US' (1 August 2016) <www.publishwhatyoupay.org/pwyp-news/its-official-the-sec-rule-has-been-published-in-the-us> accessed 22 September 2016

30 Dir 2013/34/EU [2013] OJ L182/19

31 Securities and Exchange Commission, Disclosure of Payments by Resource Extraction Issuers, Final Rule

32 Penalties for non-adherence vary: in relation to the EU Accounting Directive, Article 51 states that 'Member States shall provide for penalties applicable to infringements of the national provisions adopted in accordance with this Directive …'

33 Thomas McInerney, 'Putting Regulation before Responsibility: Towards Binding Norms of Corporate Social Responsibility' (2007) 40 *Cornell International Law Journal* 171

limited experience with the democratic practices required by civil society participation.

Civil society engagement is a central component of the key management process of the EITI, the MSG. The MSG has been at the centre of the EITI project since its inception and is the decision-making body for implementation in each country. The key structural element of the MSG is the equal voting rights between government, industry and civil society, which is often a novel arrangement in the EITI implementing countries of the South. The MSG is convened by the in-country secretariat and overseen by the international EITI Board and Secretariat. Representatives are drawn from business groups and government ministries and also from local NGOs and environmental groups who focus on the extractive industries; international NGOs may act as advisers to local civil society but cannot sit on the MSG. The numbers of representatives are often similar, but more importantly, the voting rights for each sector are equal.

Despite civil society participation, the traditional focus primarily on revenue transparency in the EITI has ensured it has been somewhat limited as a governance tool. Indeed, it is the narrow focus that has made it relatively attractive to corporations and governments. It is not intended to contribute to debates over the distribution or ownership of resources, the levels or type of environmental protection or the use of government funds resulting from resource extraction. A depoliticised focus on transparency at the expense of accountability and social and political processes has been criticised for resulting in limitations in policy development.[34]

Despite this novel approach to implementation, scholarly assessment of the EITI has been inconclusive, but not particularly favourable. Indeed, numerous studies on the EITI suggest that implementation in its early days had a limited effect on natural resource governance more generally due to its particularly limited remit.[35] However, even though countries often join the

34 Deval Desai and Michael Jarvis, 'Governance and Accountability in Extractive Industries: Theory and Practice at the World Bank' (2012) 30 *Journal of Energy & Natural Resources Law* 101; Ken MacLean, 'Counter-Accounting with Invisible Data: The Struggle for Transparency in Myanmar's Energy Sector' (2014) 37 *PoLAR: Political and Legal Anthropology Review* 10

35 Ivar Kolstad and Arne Wiig, 'Is Transparency the Key to Reducing Corruption in Resource-Rich Countries?' (2009) 37 *World Development* 521; Liliane C. Mouan, 'Exploring the Potential Benefits of Asian Participation in the Extractive Industries Transparency Initiative: The Case of China' (2010) 19 *Business Strategy and the Environment* 367; Susan Ariel Aaronson, 'Limited Partnership: Business, Government, Civil Society, and the Public in the Extractive Industries Transparency Initiative (EITI)' (2011) 31 *Public Administration and Development* 50; Van Alstine (n 22); Annie Sturesson and Thomas Zobel, 'The Extractive Industries Transparency Initiative (EITI) in Uganda: Who Will Take the Lead when the Government Falters?' (2015) 2 *The Extractive Industries and Society* 33; Benjamin Sovacool and Nathan Andrews, 'Does Transparency Matter? Evaluating the Governance Impacts of the Extractive Industries Transparency Initiative (EITI) in Azerbaijan and Liberia' (2015) 45 *Resources Policy* 183

EITI to gain international acceptance and increased aid, there is some evidence that it reduces corruption because the multi-stakeholder institutions improve accountability.[36] In the most significant recent quantitative analysis on the efficacy of the EITI, Sovacool and others use data from the World Bank to test how EITI countries performed over the first decade of the EITI relating to eight distinct metrics covering accountability, political stability, government effectiveness, regulatory quality, rule of law, corruption, foreign direct investment and growth in per capita gross domestic product (GDP).[37] They found that for most metrics EITI countries do not perform better during EITI compliance than before EITI compliance, and that in most metrics they do not outperform other countries. They suggest four possible explanations behind the relative weakness of the EITI: a limited mandate, its voluntary nature, stakeholder resistance and dependence on strong civil society.

To address the limitations apparent in the first decade of EITI implementation, the EITI Board and Secretariat have made significant attempts at broadening its reach. Although it started as a very simple revenue transparency instrument for tracking payments to governments, it is gradually evolving into a more substantial governance tool. While the focus remains on ‘transparency’, an EITI Standard was launched at the EITI Global Conference in April 2013 to improve governance aspects such as civil society participation.[38] This civil society participation was then refined further in the EITI Standard 2016 through EITI Requirement 1.3 on civil society engagement in the MSG, subsection (a) of which states ‘civil society must be fully, actively and effectively engaged in the EITI process’.[39] A protocol on ‘Participation of civil society’, which provides an assessment framework for the provisions related to civil society, was also approved by the EITI Board in January 2015 and adopted in the 2016 Standard.

The EITI Board has attempted to ensure that civil society participation in the decision-making process is genuine through the assessments in its validation reports. Due to concerns over a government crackdown on civil society, Azerbaijan, the first country to be validated against the EITI Standard 2013, also became the first country to be downgraded by the Board from compliant to candidate status in April 2015.[40] It avoided

36 Liz David-Barrett and Ken Okamura, *The Transparency Paradox: Why Do Corrupt Countries Join EITI?* (2013) <https://eiti.org/sites/default/files/documents/The-Transparency-Paradox.-Why-do-Corrupt-Countries-Join-EITI1.pdf> accessed 19 January 2017

37 Benjamin K. Sovacool and others, ‘Energy Governance, Transnational Rules, and the Resource Curse: Exploring the Effectiveness of the Extractive Industries Transparency Initiative (EITI)’ (2016) 83 *World Development* 179

38 EITI International Secretariat, *The EITI Standard* (2013). See EITI Requirement 6

39 EITI International Secretariat, *The EITI Standard 2016*; EITI International Secretariat, *EITI 2016 Progress Report: From Reports to Results* (2016)

40 EITI, ‘Azerbaijan’ (2017) <https://eiti.org/azerbaijan> accessed 19 January 2017

suspension by acquiescing to some EITI requests and in a further validation, the first by a country against the EITI Standard 2016, it was found by the EITI Board to have made 'meaningful progress', although they scheduled a third validation to address ongoing concerns on civil society engagement. Given that international approval for member governments is one of the key benefits of the EITI the rebuke by the Board, followed by the threat of suspension, may well act as a stimulus for governments to ensure that the civil society provisions in the Standard are upheld.

While transparency in government revenues was the key initial goal of the EITI, transparency in determining who actually owns a company and who benefits from the private natural resource revenues has become increasingly important to addressing corruption. A World Bank review of 213 major corruption cases in 80 countries between 1980 and 2010 revealed that over 70 per cent involved the use of corporate vehicles to conceal the real owners.[41] The emerging global Beneficial Ownership movement to address this issue is driven by civil society groups such as the PWYP and the Financial Transparency Coalition, whose member groups include the Centre for Budget and Governance Accountability, Christian Aid, Global Witness, Tax Justice Network and Transparency International.[42]

To highlight the 'beneficial owners' of companies the EITI Standard 2013 recommended the establishment of public registers, which could be analysed by civil society actors, and commissioned a Beneficial Ownership pilot study.[43] The 2016 Standard has gone one step further and made it a compulsory requirement that the beneficial owners of companies that have bid for, invested in or operate extractive assets will have to be disclosed in EITI Reports from 1 January 2020.[44]

These are key improvements to reducing corruption in the extractive industries with the beneficial ownership provisions in particular likely to improve policy making and governance through greater scrutiny of the actual beneficiaries of natural resource extraction. These provisions are likely to be particularly difficult to implement in Myanmar. Until 2011 the entire operation of its government under military rule was impervious to outside examination. While some progress has been made, much of its natural resources sector is still highly opaque and requires significant reform to adhere to international governance norms.

41 Emile van der Does de Willebois and others, *The Puppet Masters: How the Corrupt Use Legal Structures to Hide Stolen Assets and What to Do About It* (World Bank Publications, 2011) 117; see also J.C. Sharman, 'Testing the Global Financial Transparency Regime' (2011) 55 *International Studies Quarterly* 981

42 Financial Transparency Coalition, 'Financial Transparency Coalition' (2017) <https://financialtransparency.org/> accessed 19 January 2017

43 EITI International Secretariat, *The EITI Standard* (2013)

44 EITI International Secretariat, *The EITI Standard 2016* (2016)

Natural resource governance in Myanmar

Much of Myanmar's natural resource governance is limited, opaque and corrupt.[45] Some industries are better governed than others – natural gas is increasingly transparent and open to investment by international corporations, while much of the jade industry remains hidden – but there has been a general improvement in environmental governance across the board since direct military rule ended in 2011.[46] Nevertheless, remnants of deep military–state involvement in the drug trade,[47] forestry,[48] rubber[49] and particularly jade,[50] have ensured that well-connected vested interests continue to oppose governance reforms aimed at reducing corruption. Like many other sectors of the economy, the jade industry in Myanmar is run by an oligopoly of military-owned corporations and associated cronies.[51] This dominance creates impediments to removing corruption within the natural resources sector, which is particularly problematic given Myanmar's structural position as a producer and exporter of raw commodities.[52]

Corruption is clearly endemic in Myanmar. In Transparency International's Corruptions Perception Index 2015 Myanmar was perceived as one of the most corrupt countries in the world, ranked 147 out of 168 countries.[53] This corruption is particularly embedded within the natural resources sector. In the inaugural Resource Governance Index in 2013, which preceded Myanmar joining the EITI, Myanmar ranked last out of 58 resource-rich countries in terms of the quality of governance in the extractive

45 Gillian Cornish and Vlado Vivoda, 'Myanmar's Extractive Industries: An Institutional and Regulatory Assessment' (2016) 3 *Extractive Industries and Society* 1075; Adam Simpson, 'The Environment – Energy Security Nexus: Critical Analysis of an Energy "Love Triangle" in Southeast Asia' (2007) 28 *Third World Quarterly* 539

46 Adam Simpson, 'The Environment in Myanmar: Evolving Governance under a Regime in Transition' in Philip Hirsch (ed), *Routledge Handbook of the Environment in Southeast Asia* (Routledge 2017)

47 Patrick Meehan, 'Drugs, Insurgency and State-Building in Burma: Why the Drugs Trade Is Central to Burma's Changing Political Order' (2011) 42 *Journal of Southeast Asian Studies* 376

48 McCarthy (n 19)

49 Kevin Woods, 'Ceasefire Capitalism: Military–Private Partnerships, Resource Concessions and Military–State Building in the Burma–China Borderlands' (2011) 38 *The Journal of Peasant Studies* 747

50 Global Witness, *Lords of Jade* (2015) <www.globalwitness.org/reports/lords-jade/> accessed 19 January 2017

51 Lee Jones, 'The Political Economy of Myanmar's Transition' (2014) 44 *Journal of Contemporary Asia* 144; Michele Ford, Michael Gillan and Htwe Htwe Thein, 'From Cronyism to Oligarchy? Privatisation and Business Elites in Myanmar' (2016) 46 *Journal of Contemporary Asia* 18

52 Lee Jones, 'Political Economy' in Adam Simpson, Nicholas Farrelly and Ian Holliday (eds), *Routledge Handbook of Contemporary Myanmar* (Routledge 2018)

53 Transparency International, *Corruption Perceptions Index 2015*

sector.[54] As a report on the extractives industry in Myanmar noted, '[p]reviously, many grievances with the extractive industries sector were resolved by fiat or use of force, rather than through policy-making, mediation or dialogue'.[55] In addition, all levels of government and bureaucracy in Myanmar have extremely limited capacity and resources: although there is a concerted effort underway to digitalise the information, much of the government data remains on paper. Due to conflict and corruption there is a significant black economy that is not captured when measuring the official economy. These factors have resulted in the resources sector being particularly opaque with government data unreliable. Statistics by international agencies have been more reliable, but, as in other conflict zones, only when they can be determined externally, such as deforestation by Geographic Information System (GIS) mapping.[56]

Myanmar's ethnic diversity and history of conflict and authoritarianism have resulted in complex political and economic systems with overlapping and contested authority structures.[57] Many of Myanmar's natural resources are situated in ethnic minority areas, which has resulted in civil society opposition and exacerbated long-term civil conflicts.[58] Forestry and mining are particularly prone to exacerbating corruption and conflict because of their concentration in ethnic areas and their revenue raising capabilities. A comparative study on natural resources and conflict was unable to find a demonstrable statistical link between conflicts and exploitable forest resources across all the cases they examined, but Myanmar was the clearest case where it did exist.[59]

Mining is included in Myanmar's EITI while in July 2015 Myanmar signed a memorandum of understanding (MoU) on an EU Forest Law Enforcement, Governance and Trade (FLEGT) Voluntary Partnership Agreement.[60] There are some concerns in ethnic areas that FLEGT will

54 Natural Resource Governance Institute, *The 2013 Resource Governance Index: A Measure of Transparency and Accountability in the Oil, Gas and Mining Sector* (2013)

55 Adam Smith International, *Institutional and Regulatory Assessment of the Extractive Industries in Myanmar* (2015) 9

56 Ernst Céline and others, 'National Forest Cover Change in Congo Basin: Deforestation, Reforestation, Degradation and Regeneration for the Years 1990, 2000 and 2005' (2013) 19 *Global Change Biology* 1173

57 Kim Joliffe, *Ethnic Armed Conflict and Territorial Administration in Myanmar* (The Asia Foundation, 2015)

58 Adam Simpson, 'Challenging Hydropower Development in Myanmar (Burma): Cross-Border Activism under a Regime in Transition' (2013) 26 *The Pacific Review* 129; Simpson, Farrelly and Holliday (eds), *Routledge Handbook of Contemporary Myanmar* (n 8)

59 Siri Aas Rustad and Helga Malmin Binningsbø, 'A Price Worth Fighting For? Natural Resources and Conflict Recurrence' (2012) 49 *Journal of Peace Research* 531

60 'Timber traders move to meet EU standards' (*Eleven Myanmar*, 1 October 2015) <www.elevenmyanmar.com/business/timber-traders-move-meet-eu-standards> accessed 22 September 2016

reinforce centralised control of forest resources in ethnic areas, and that this may also happen under the EITI,[61] but some form of improved governance is necessary. According to the Global Forest Resources Assessment 2015,[62] Myanmar had the third largest area of annual deforestation – after Brazil and Indonesia – between 2010 and 2015, losing 546,000 hectares, or 1.7 per cent of the country, of forest per annum. The forested area has decreased from 60 per cent of the country in 1990 to 47.7 per cent in 2012.[63] Despite an export ban on logs from 1 April 2014 discrepancies in figures between the Myanmar government and its trading partners indicate that the corrupt and illegal export of logs continues.[64] This is consistent with research demonstrating that military-connected companies in the border regions often receive agricultural concessions as a cover for logging operations that appear to be the primary objective.[65]

The tracking of activity in the jade and gemstones industry, which is included in the EITI, is unable to be undertaken externally by satellite and is very unreliable, being subject to corruption at many levels. Officially all gemstones and jade produced in Myanmar must be sold at the government's annual Myanmar Gems Emporium, and the government insisted that this was the figure to be used in the EITI.[66] In the 2015 Emporium, gemstone sales were US$1.26 billion, down from a record $3.4 billion the previous year, with jade accounting for about 90 per cent of the total sales.[67] According to Myanmar's Central Statistical Organization, jade exports were approximately $1 billion, or 10 per cent of the total, in the financial year April 2013–March 2014, with around the same amount in 2014–2015.[68]

61 Interview with ethnic activist (Yangon, Myanmar, 21 January 2015)

62 Food and Agriculture Organization, *Global Forest Resources Assessment 2015* (2015) 15

63 World Bank, *Forest Area* (2016) <http://data.worldbank.org/indicator/ AG.LND.FRST.ZS> accessed 19 January 2017

64 According to the government, after the ban came into effect Myanmar received US$44 million from timber exports in the 2014–2015 fiscal year compared with $900 million the year before. These figures are not borne out by figures from its six major trading partners' which indicate Myanmar's log exports were only slightly down to $1.3 million from $1.5 million the year before with timber trade increasing from $622 million to $677 million in the same periods: NCRA, *Myanmar Business Update* (2015) <www.newcrossroadsasia.com/docs/Volume%2037.pdf> accessed 19 January 2017

65 Kevin Woods, *Commercial Agriculture Expansion in Myanmar: Links to Deforestation, Conversion Timber, and Land Conflicts* (Forest Trends and UK Aid, 2015) <http://forest-trends.org/releases/uploads/Conversion_Timber_in_Myanmar.pdf> accessed 19 January 2017

66 Interview with MEITI International Consultant (Yangon, Myanmar, 21 January 2015)

67 *Reuters*, 'Myanmar gems sales slump as conflict stems jade supply' (9 July 2015) <www.reuters.com/article/2015/07/09/myanmar-jade-idUSL3N0ZP2DH20150709> accessed 19 January 2017

68 Moore Stephens, *Myanmar Extractive Industries Transparency Initiative: Scoping Study for the First EITI Report – For the Period April 2013–March 2014* (2015) 15; Central Statistical Organization, 'Central Statistical Organization' (Ministry of National Planning and Economic Development, 2015) <www.csostat.gov.mm/> accessed 20 November

According to Chinese customs data provided to the UN's Comtrade database, however, China imported $12.3 billion of gemstones from Myanmar in 2014, with most of the trade being jade.[69] While almost all of Myanmar's jade is ultimately exported to China, the discrepancy between these figures indicates that there is far more jade being mined and exported than the government admits. The Chinese figures also only include official exports; it is also reasonable to assume that there are significant flows of gemstones in the black economy not being accounted for in these figures.

Furthermore, a report by Global Witness employs two separate estimates of the jade sector – one based on the aforementioned Chinese data – with both methods concluding that the value of the amount of jade mined in 2014 was worth over $30 billion,[70] which is almost half Myanmar's total estimated 2014 GDP of $64 billion.[71] Both estimates are based on official production data that take no account of the jade production kept entirely off the books, which is likely to be significant. This uncertainty and unreliability ensure that the figures used in the EITI for gemstones are likely to be a small fraction of what the industry actually produces and highlights a severe limitation of the EITI process. Nevertheless, it represents a substantial improvement in the transparency of natural resource governance in Myanmar.

The EITI also represented, for the Thein Sein government, Myanmar's re-emergence into the international community after five decades of relative isolation. The thaw in relations with Western countries in particular allowed international financial institutions and many international organisations to work with the Myanmar government for the first time since the late 1980s.[72] Aid agencies such as Australian AID and the UK Department for International Development (DfID) rapidly expanded their aid programmes in Myanmar and, having bypassed the state for much of the previous two decades, began working directly with it to provide international expertise in environmental and natural resource governance. As the Western sanctions regime dissolved, the presidential commitment to join the EITI in 2012 became emblematic of this increased engagement, with Myanmar open to investment from Western companies for the first time since the 1990s. In this climate it was crucial that civil society participation was mandated within the stakeholder components of the EITI to ensure community concerns were adequately reflected within natural resource governance.

69 NCRA, *A $12bn Jade and Gem Industry Rides to the Kyat's Rescue* (2015)

70 Global Witness, *Jade: Myanmar's 'Big State Secret'* (2015) <www.globalwitness.org/reports/myanmarjade/> accessed 19 January 2017

71 World Bank, *Myanmar* (2016) <www.worldbank.org/en/country/myanmar> accessed 15 June 2016

72 Adam Simpson and Susan Park, 'The Asian Development Bank as a Global Risk Regulator in Myanmar' (2013) 34 *Third World Quarterly* 1858

The EITI MSG and Reports

The key components of the EITI implementation process are the formation and operation of the MSG and the EITI Reports. Given the authoritarian and militarised history of Myanmar, the equal voting power of representatives of business, industry and civil society within the MSG was always going to be a challenging format for the Thein Sein government to accept. In addition to the government's traditional animosity towards civil society, ethnic representation issues caused conflict between the civil society representatives of the MSG and the foreign governments and international organisations that tried to promote Muslim representation in the process. This was particularly pertinent for the Rohingya and other Muslims who make up one third of Rakhine State. One of the ethnic Rakhine representatives of the MSG eventually made his feelings clear: 'if you include *Kala* [a derogatory term for the Rohingya] I'll walk out'.[73]

The Myanmar Development Resources Institute's Centre for Economic and Social Development (MDRI-CESD) was given the task of establishing the Myanmar EITI (MEITI) secretariat and forming the MSG, which, after a lengthy process to determine the representatives, met for the first time in February 2014. Myanmar's EITI candidature application was eventually submitted in May 2014 and it was formally accepted as a candidate country in July of that year.[74] MEITI then had 18 months to prepare the groundwork for the first EITI Report, which was due in January 2016, during the transition period from Thein Sein's government to that of the NLD.

Despite the limitations of the EITI in Myanmar there exist inflated expectations in relation to what the EITI can actually achieve. Expectations were raised from the extensive media coverage the EITI received, which occurred concurrently with the emergence of a free media in the country from 2013. While in some countries the EITI has not been widely publicised,[75] in Myanmar, as in Liberia,[76] it received widespread coverage, resulting in some parts of society viewing it as a panacea for corrupt or incompetent natural resource governance. In reality the scope of the EITI is far narrower.

Part of the optimism in Myanmar may have been the key role of both democracy and environmental activists representing civil society in the EITI through the MSG. The key structural component of the MSG is the equal voting rights between government, industry and civil society. In most countries where the EITI is being implemented, this horizontal distribution of authority is rare, if not unique; certainly in Myanmar after five decades of

73 Interview with Deputy Leader MEITI (Yangon, Myanmar, 3 February 2015)

74 MEITI, *MEITI Candidacy Application Form* (2014)

75 Aaronson (n 35)

76 Eddie Rich and T. Negbalee Warner, 'Addressing the Roots of Liberia's Conflict through the Extractive Industries Transparency Initiative' in Päivi Lujala and Siri Aas Rustad (eds), *High-Value Natural Resources and Peacebuilding* (Earthscan, 2012)

military rule this process provided a particularly challenging format for the new quasi-civilian government of President Thein Sein once it committed to joining the EITI in 2012.

Although historically suppressed by military rule, civil society quickly organised itself for the MSG by forming a peak organisation, the Myanmar Alliance for Transparency and Accountability (MATA). MATA drew its membership from natural resource civil society organisations (CSOs) from across the country after a diverse gathering of 150 CSO representatives in Yangon elected nine representatives for the MSG.[77] Throughout Myanmar's EITI accession process, CSOs, particularly the local groups that comprise the MSG membership, have been endeavouring to broaden the role of the MSG beyond 'transparency', and even corruption, issues to deal with any related natural resource governance concerns. This became evident in January 2015 when CSOs called an emergency MSG meeting in January 2015 over the shooting of a protester at the Letpadaung Copper Mine in December 2014.[78] Due to disagreements over the shooting and its relevance to the EITI MSG, both the government and civil society threatened to withdraw from the entire EITI process although, according to an MSG CSO representative, the CSOs were split, with 'personalities' causing ruptures in the decision-making processes.[79] CSOs were essentially attempting to deploy the EITI as a human rights grievance mechanism, which the MEITI international consultant argued reflected a 'lack of understanding' of what the EITI was for.[80] Yet the EITI is one of the few channels where the government has been forced to sit down with CSOs and listen to their grievances, resulting in the CSOs leveraging their internationally mandated influence to expand the range of issues to be considered through the EITI.[81]

Nevertheless, corruption reduction through transparency remains at the core of the EITI and this is primarily to be achieved by the reconciliation of revenue data in the annual EITI Report by international consultants, which is used in the validation process to assess the country's level of progress in satisfying the EITI requirements. The sectors to be assessed in Myanmar's first EITI Report, released in January 2016,[82] were set out in the Scoping

77 Interview with Coordinator: Myanmar Alliance for Transparency and Accountability (MATA) (Yangon, Myanmar, 30 January 2015)

78 Fortify Rights and International Human Rights Clinic, *Crackdown at Letpadan: Excessive Use of Force and Violations of the Rights to Freedom of Peaceful Assembly and Expression in Letpadan, Bago Region, Myanmar* (2015)

79 Interview with MSG civil society representative (Yangon, Myanmar, 21 January 2015)

80 Ibid

81 Adam Simpson, 'The Extractive Industries Transparency Initiative: New Openings for Civil Society in Myanmar' in M. Crouch (ed), *The Business of Transition: Law Reform, and Development and Economics in Myanmar* (Cambridge University Press 2017)

82 Moore Stephens, *Myanmar Extractive Industries Transparency Initiative: EITI Report for the Period April 2013–March 2014: Oil Gas and Mining Sectors* (2015)

Report prepared by the consultancy Moore Stephens.[83] The only sectors to be included in the reconciliation were oil and gas (including transportation), which was relatively achievable due to the existence of large contracts and the investments of international business, and the mining sector (including gems and jade), which, with its diverse scales, multitude of stakeholders and deep integration with the economies of the ethnic minority-controlled areas, presented a different set of challenges.

Natural gas is the largest and most transparent contributor to official export earnings, accounting for 29 per cent of earnings in 2013–2014 ($3.3 billion), with a 50 per cent increase in production for 2014–2015 contributing 41 per cent of export earnings ($5.2 billion).[84] Due to this transparency it is also likely to be the least corrupt sector considered in the report. According to the MEITI international consultant, the government argued that gems or jade should be excluded from the EITI process,[85] but the benefits of an internationally moderated process meant that the international actors, including the EITI Secretariat and Board, ensured that these core sectors for the EITI, and ones that are also riven by corruption, were included.

Hydroelectricity was omitted from the first Report but it was agreed that a schedule would be incorporated into the Report to include it at a later date. The EITI has not traditionally encompassed hydroelectricity but it has been included by countries such as Albania. In Myanmar the prospect of numerous large dams in ethnic areas on the Thanlwin (Salween) and Ayerawady (Irrawaddy) Rivers made this a priority for some ethnic CSOs.[86] Other CSOs wanted either forestry or fisheries included: forestry was excluded because the FLEGT process has set up a parallel internationally mediated governance regime and fisheries were considered non-core for the initial EITI Report. The Scoping Report recommended hydropower and fisheries be included in future EITI Reports.[87]

Some of the limitations to the reconciliation process were set out in the Scoping Report by Moore Stephens: they did not obtain the statement of revenues collected from the extractive sector from the Internal Revenue and Custom Departments; they did not obtain a comprehensive list of military holding companies and their related subsidiaries; and they did not obtain the list of operators in the gems and jade sectors from the Ministry of Mines.[88] Added to this that records were mostly kept on paper and it was clear that

83 Moore Stephens, *Myanmar Extractive Industries Transparency Initiative: Scoping Study for the First EITI Report: For the Period April 2013–March 2014* (2015)

84 Central Statistical Organization, 'Central Statistical Organization'

85 Interview with MEITI International Consultant (Yangon, Myanmar, 21 January 2015)

86 Simpson, 'Challenging Hydropower Development in Myanmar (Burma): Cross-Border Activism under a Regime in Transition' (n 58)

87 Moore Stephens, *Myanmar Extractive Industries Transparency Initiative: Scoping Study for the First EITI Report: For the Period April 2013–March 2014*

88 Ibid

the reconciliation in the gemstones industry in particular was partial at best. The lack of disaggregated company data, and other associated data limitations, meant that it was difficult to assess the government revenue from a particular company or site, such as the Letpadaung Mine.

In the final report Moore Stephens highlighted the lack of legal support for the EITI. They noted that 'the EITI reporting obligations are not covered by any other Law organising the process of collection in the current Legislation' and recommended developing a legal framework including an EITI law that could be harmonised with existing legislation with provisions relating to 'reporting obligations for extractive companies and government entities alike, while specifying the level of disaggregation of the data to be submitted'.[89] MATA, the main civil society group on the MSG, has also pushed for an overarching EITI law,[90] while the manager of the Extractives Programme in the Myanmar Centre for Responsible Business indicated that union-level legislation would provide more support for both CSO and MEITI representatives at township level.[91] He indicated that many of the CSO representatives from the MSG are not from NGOs registered with the government; they therefore receive curt treatment from township-level authorities, most of which have lived their entire lives within an authoritarian military structure that precluded civil society engagement. In contrast, the Myanmar manager of NRGI, an organisation with extensive multi-country experience on the EITI, argued that an EITI law is not necessary for successful implementation of the EITI; not every country does it.[92] Despite several months of relative inaction on the EITI under the new government throughout 2016, support for the EITI from the NLD is likely to eventuate, whether legislative or administrative. Regardless of the form of the support, strong leadership from within the new government supporting the EITI is seen as a more important determinant of the efficacy of the EITI as an anti-corruption tool within the natural resources sector by the senior technical and policy analyst at MEITI.[93] No one is criticising the NLD-led government for inactivity on the EITI yet; as he noted, the people of Myanmar feel that, for the first time, 'this is our government'.

89 Moore Stephens, *Myanmar Extractive Industries Transparency Initiative: EITI Report for the Period April 2013–March 2014: Oil, Gas and Mining Sectors*

90 Interview with Coordinator: Myanmar Alliance for Transparency and Accountability (MATA) (Yangon, Myanmar, 30 January 2015)

91 Interview with Manager: Extractives Programme: Myanmar Centre for Responsible Business (Yangon, Myanmar, 7 September 2016)

92 Interview with Myanmar Manager: Natural Resource Governance Institute (Yangon, Myanmar, 6 September 2016)

93 Interview with EITI Senior Technical and Policy Analyst: MEITI, Centre for Economic and Social Development, Myanmar Development Resource Institute (Yangon, Myanmar, 5 September 2016)

Conclusion

Corruption in the natural resources sector has a corrosive effect on economic and social development in the South. Countries in the South, such as Myanmar, are poor and most in need of development, but they are also the ones that suffer from the most corruption. Investment in Myanmar's natural resources sector has increased significantly since the political and economic reform process was initiated in 2011. Nevertheless, international investment has been largely focused on the natural gas industry while local companies, which are often military owned, together with ethnic militias, dominate the gemstones and forestry industries. This contrast is reflected in the levels of transparency and corruption in the respective industries: the gas industry is relatively open and free of corruption while the gemstone and forestry industries are highly opaque and corrupt.

There is no objective way to measure corruption within the jade and gemstone industry, its opacity prevents such investigation, but rigorous analysis by NGOs, particularly Global Witness, suggests that only a very small fraction of the jade industry is captured in state revenues or statistics. This suggests that there is widespread corruption within the industry, at the very least to avoid the payment of government taxes, levies and royalties. Some leakage of this activity is probably due to a lack of capacity within various government bodies and agencies or a lack of access to areas due to ethnic conflict, but much of it must also be due to corrupt officials at various levels of government receiving private payments in return for wilful blindness to extractive activities that would otherwise attract larger government payments. This corruption reduces the prospects for the sustainable exploitation of natural resources by removing the public good consideration from decision-making.

The EITI is one attempt to overcome this corruption in the extractive industries by increasing transparency in the sector. Although Myanmar is yet to be validated against the EITI Standard 2016 and the first Report was clearly full of holes, particularly in relation to the jade industry, it has clearly made some progress in satisfying the requirements relating to transparency and civil society engagement. The new NLD government has an enormous task ahead of it to capture the economic activity of the industry in both its revenue stream and its statistics. A legal support framework for the EITI requirements, which is yet to be established, would certainly go some way to formalising transparency norms. Attempts at reducing corruption by implementing the EITI face the same hurdles that impede other attempts at effective governance in Myanmar, resulting from its history of authoritarianism, military rule and civil conflict. Through the MSG, however, the EITI provides a model of civil society engagement that, if replicated by the new NLD government in other aspects of its resource governance, could help undermine corruption across the natural resources sector.

19 Criminal liability for exploitation of natural resources

Michael Faure

Introduction

This chapter will focus on the role of the criminal law in conserving and preserving natural resources at different levels of governance. The crucial question will be to what extent the criminal law in a variety of jurisdictions and at the international level is indeed able to provide an adequate protection to natural resources.[1]

In order to analyse the way in which the criminal law awards its protection, a theoretical approach will be followed. Starting from the theory on a model environmental criminal law, it will be shown that generally an environmental criminal law system needs abstract endangerment, concrete endangerment and autonomous crimes. The questions of the extent to which those can play a role in the protection of natural resources and how ideally a criminal law aiming at the protection of natural resources should be shaped will then be addressed. Assuming that violators may be rational in their behaviour (e.g. deforestation or illegal hunting), the question arises of whether the sanctions provided can accurately deter violations of natural resources law. In addition, the question also arises of whether liability should/is merely allocated to individual violators or whether there is also an important role for corporate criminal liability. The question of an ideal criminal law protecting natural resources will not only be addressed in the abstract, but also applied to specific crimes e.g. related to the protection of waters or forests (illegal logging) or wildlife (illegal hunting).

In addition to addressing the issue from a theoretical perspective, we will next analyse the extent to which specific legal rules that can be found at the international, regional and national level provide adequate protection to these natural resources. In that respect attention will be paid to the

1 See generally on the relationship between investment regimes and the protection of natural resources, Elena Blanco and Jona Razzaque, *Globalisation and Natural Resources Law. Challenges, Key Issues and Perspectives* (Edward Elgar, 2011); and Julia Swart, 'Natural Resources and the Environment: Implications for Economic Development and International Relations' (DPhil thesis, Erasmus University Rotterdam, Tinbergen Institute, 2012)

Convention on International Trade in Endangered Species (CITES) (of 1973),[2] and also to the European Directive on the protection of the environment through criminal law.[3] Next a further critical analysis follows, paying attention to the literature addressing the implementation deficit and specific problems in combatting specifically illegal hunting and deforestation. This leads to the following structure: after an introduction a theory how to protect natural resources via the criminal law will be provided and examples of criminal sanctions in a variety of jurisdictions at different layers of government will be provided as well. Critical issues related to implementation and enforcement will be discussed. The final section concludes.

How to protect natural resources via the criminal law?

Theoretical foundations

There is a substantial amount of economic, legal and criminological literature that has generally addressed the question how the legislator can use the criminal law to provide protection to the environment. To an important extent that literature is also relevant in answering the question how natural resources can be protected by using the criminal law. This chapter will use an economic approach to environmental criminal law as well as a legal theoretical approach. An alternative approach of green criminology, which would also indirectly be valuable, remains further undiscussed within this chapter.[4] The economic approach to environmental crime is inter alia interesting since it considers environmental crime from a classic deterrence-based approach, as can be found in the early works of Gary Becker.[5] The classic idea that criminal law should be applied in such a way as to increase the cost of crime and therefore deter criminality has also been applied to the domain of environmental crime.[6] A basic premise of this economic model is that offenders are rational calculators who weigh the benefits of crime against the prospective costs and who hence could be deterred (also from wildlife crime) through an appropriate probability of detection and sanctioning. Obviously, important questions can be asked

2 See <www.cites.org>, last visited on 3.2.2017

3 Directive on the protection of the environment through criminal law 2008/99/EC, OJ L328 of 6.12.2008

4 See on green criminology inter alia Michael J. Lynch and Paul B. Stretsky, 'The Meaning of Green: Contrasting Criminological Perspectives' (2003) 2 *Theoretical Criminology* 217, 217–238; and see Michael J. Lynch and Paul B. Stretsky, *Exploring Green Criminology. Toward a Green Criminological Revolution* (Ashgate, 2014)

5 See inter alia Gary S. Becker, 'Irrational Behavior and Economic Theory' (1962) *Journal of Political Economy* 1, 1–13 and Gary S. Becker, 'Crime and Punishment: An Economic Approach' (1968) *Journal of Political Economy* 169, 169–217

6 See inter alia Michael G. Faure, 'Environmental Crimes' in Nuno Garoupa (ed.), *Criminal Law and Economics* (vol. 3, Edward Elgar, 2009) 320–345

with respect to the rationality of many offenders and hence with respect to the effectiveness of the deterrence approach.[7] Although also in the economic analysis other perspectives than the deterrence approach are now employed, it still serves as a useful starting point.

In addition, we will address German legal dogmatics that have stressed that the goal of the criminal law is to protect particular legal values and interests. The goal of environmental (or natural resources) law would therefore be to protect natural resources.[8] The value of this approach is that it is able to show how different types of criminal provisions provide a different type of protection to the environment, thus enabling a critical reflection on the effectiveness of various criminal provisions in the protection of natural resources.

We argue that a variety of different provisions is necessary to protect natural resources against harm.[9] An adequate protection of those natural resources through the criminal law therefore requires a combination of different types of provisions, consisting of the penalising of the abstract endangerment and the concrete endangerment of the natural resources as well as an independent crime for when the violation has serious consequences.

Abstract endangerment

The notion of abstract endangerment refers to the fact that, within this model, the criminal provision usually does not punish damage to natural resources directly. In this model, the criminal law is a supplement to a system of administrative decisions[10] concerning the amount and quality of emissions into the environment. Indeed, most systems of environmental law are based on administrative statutes regulating the conditions under which the administrative authorities can allow environmental pollution. Crucial within these administrative statutes are the so-called emission standards or emission limit values that fix the amount of a certain compound that can be emitted into the environment. These type of standards usually aim at so-called point source pollution, but the natural environment can obviously also be endangered through so-called diffuse pollution as well. Administrative regulations now increasingly also focus on pollution coming from so-called diffuse sources. However, within this model the task of the criminal law is to back up prior administrative decisions. Obviously these are also relevant in relation

7 See inter alia Angus Nurse, 'Repainting the Thin Green Line: The Enforcement of UK Wildlife Law' (2012) *The Internet Journal of Criminology* 11, 11–13

8 Compare Günter Heine, 'Allemagne. Crimes against the Environment' (1994) *International Review of Penal Law* 731, 731–759

9 This part of the chapter builds further on Susan F. Mandiberg and Michael G. Faure, 'A Graduated Punishment Approach to Environmental Crimes: Beyond Vindication of Administrative Authority in the United States and Europe' (2009) 34 *Columbia Journal of Environmental Law* 447, 447–511

10 Those administrative decisions can for example be a permit or licence, but also specific conditions included in such a permit

to the resource sector. Many legal systems will for example submit the cutting of trees to prior administrative permissions.

It is important to stress that environmental criminal law has usually started with these kinds of provisions, where the criminal law follows prior administrative decisions and punishes abstract endangerment of environmental values. Traditionally criminal law applies in these kinds of cases as soon as the administrative provision (for example, in the form of an administrative obligation in a licence) has been violated, whether or not this causes harm to the environment. In some legal systems these abstract endangerments, for instance violations of permit conditions, are not even primarily punished under criminal law, but, for instance, by means of fines under administrative penal law.

Concrete endangerment

Concrete endangerment refers to the fact that, that in this case, some kind of an endangerment of natural resources by posing a concrete threat to the environment is a prerequisite for criminal liability.[11] But in this case, a mere abstract danger that, for example, the illegal operation of a plant might cause danger to the environment is too abstract and therefore insufficient for criminal liability. Usually at least an emission is required.[12] This can indeed lead to a concrete danger for the environment, although usually the provisions falling under this model do not require that actual harm needs to be proven as well. Usually a threat of harm is sufficient.

In addition to this requirement of causing a concrete danger to the environment, these provisions only lead to criminal liability if a second condition is met, namely that this emission takes place illegally. In a model of absolute administrative dependence all that needs to be shown is that the act violated administrative rules. In this case, in addition the emission or pollution that can cause a threat of harm needs to be proven. However, as long as the administrative rules are followed, usually no criminal liability will follow since the act will not be considered unlawful. This is the major difference with the subsequent model, to be discussed below, in which criminal liability can occur even if administrative requirements were formally met. Indeed, even if there is no administrative regulatory framework that has been violated, criminal liability can apply in this case since the emission can still be

11 Theodorus J.B. Buiting, *Strafrecht en milieu* (Gouda Quint, 1998) 28–29; Leo E.M. Hendriks and J. Wöretshofer, *Milieustrafrecht* (WEJ Tjeenk Willink, 1995) 38; and Cornélie Waling, *Het materiële milieustrafrecht* (Gouda Quint, 1990) 23

12 See, for example, Section 324 of the German Criminal Code which punishes anyone 'who pollutes water or otherwise detrimentally changes its qualities without authorisation' ('wer unbefugt ein Gewässer verunreinigt oder sonst dessen Eigenschaften nachteilig verändert'): Michael Faure and Günter Heine, *Environmental Criminal Law in the European Union. Documentation of the Main Provisions with Introductions* (Max Planck Institute for Foreign and International Criminal Law, 2000) 147

illegal. In such circumstances, no criminal liability would occur under a traditional model of abstract endangerment, merely aiming at the enforcement of prior administrative decisions.

Independent crime for serious harm to natural resources

A third type of criminal provision directly punishes some cases of very serious harms to natural resources. It can be that the model also punishes emissions, but it could equally refer to consequences of a more serious nature, such as the long-term pollution of a wetland, killing of endangered species, etc. The main difference between this model and the others discussed so far is that the linkage between criminal law and prior administrative decisions can now be left aside totally. Under this type of provision, serious harm to natural resources can be punished even if the defendant has complied with the conditions of his licence. The notion behind it is that the administrative regulation never allows this specific risk or harm. These are therefore provisions where the veil of the famous dependency of the administrative law is pierced.[13] The major difference between this and the two previous models is that hence unlawfulness is no longer required.

Combination

At the policy level, the strength and weaknesses of the various models show that an effective environmental criminal law really needs a combination of these various types of provisions. The penalisation of abstract endangerment is absolutely useful and necessary. However, the weakness of these provisions is that they apply even if no ecological harm or danger exists. Moreover, they cannot provide an adequate protection if there is no violation of existing administrative rules because of the too-strong relationship with administrative law and the too-high dependency on administrative decisions.[14] In that respect the provisions merely penalising the non-respect of administrative obligations (which remain necessary) need to be complemented with provisions aiming at the concrete endangerment of the environment. This can be done by penalising unlawful emissions. However, in this case the conditions

13 An example is constituted by Section 330a of the German Criminal Code which punishes 'anyone who diffuses or releases substances containing or producing poisons, thereby causing a risk of death or severe damage to another's health or a risk of damage to the health of a large number of people' ('Wer Stoffe, die Gifte enthalten oder hervorbringen können, verbreitet oder freisetzt und dadurch die Gefahr des Todes oder einer schweren Gesundheitsschädigung eines anderen Menschen oder die Gefahr einer Gesundheitsschädigung einer großen Zahl von Menschen verursacht'): Faure and Heine (n 10) 153

14 Michael Faure and Marjolein Visser, 'How to Punish Environmental Pollution? Some Reflections on Various Models of Criminalization of Environmental Harm' (1995) 4 *European Journal of Crime, Criminal Law and Criminal Justice* 316, 358

of an administrative licence will still release a polluter from criminal liability. But the protection granted to the environment by the judge is already far more autonomous since it is not limited to the penalisation of the non-respect of administrative obligations. Finally, the system needs to be complemented with an independent crime which is applicable to serious harm to natural resources,[15] if a concrete danger to human life or health exists. Only in this case, the interdependence of environmental criminal law and administrative law is entirely abandoned.

This criminalisation model, which has largely been developed for the type of point source pollution by emissions, can easily be transposed to the case of natural resources as well: often natural resources are protected through systems relying on prior administrative decisions. Violating those decisions (e.g. building a house in a protected wetland) could of course endanger the particular natural resource. Many of the natural resources crimes will not be of an abstract, but rather of a concrete nature. For example, illegal fishing, illegal hunting, wildlife crimes and deforestation do not merely cause an abstract but real danger to the natural resources and in some cases (where game has been illegally killed) it is not merely an endangerment, but real damage to the natural resource. As we will illustrate below, also in natural resources law the protection mechanism is often based on prior administrative decisions: hunting, fishing, deforestation are all activities that are not absolutely prohibited. The law hence allows an infringement against those natural resources on the condition that the administrative decisions are complied with. Also the way in which the criminal law protects natural resources is hence strongly dependent upon prior administrative decisions. However, also in this domain there may be absolute prohibitions. In some cases, these absolute prohibitions are again first decided upon in administrative law, for example when the decision is made that a particular species is absolutely protected (for which hence no licence to hunt or trade can be obtained) or an absolute protection to, for example, a wetland would be granted through a prior administrative regulation (as a result of which there is no possibility at all to justify an infringement by granting an administrative permit). An absolute protection is granted through prior administrative/regulatory decisions and not so much through an independent protection granted through the criminal law. However, there may be cases of gross environmental harm, seriously harming natural resources that would (hypothetically) not have been prohibited yet *ex ante* through regulatory decisions. This could, for example, be the case when a permit would hypothetically have been granted against the rules. If that were the case there could be room for an independent protection granted through the criminal law. But the difficulty in those cases always remains whether it is possible to

15 Those are the type of provisions discussed in the subsection 'Independent crime for serious harm to natural resources' above

describe the conditions for criminal responsibility with sufficient clarity and precision, as required by the *lex certa* principle.[16]

Examples and critical analysis

As we already mentioned in the introduction, the type of regulations and criminal provisions we are focusing on in this contribution are those that in a relatively wide sense protect the natural resources. In the literature focusing on 'wildlife' law and crime, various attempts towards definitions have been made and usually wildlife crime is distinguished from poaching involving species of gamebirds or animals that were specially bred for game shooting.[17] In the latter case the animals are rather considered as property and the loss is therefore mainly considered for the economic value of the animals. The question arises as to what extent some of the models of protection that were discussed from a theoretical perspective in the previous section can also be found in the concrete legislation in which the criminal law is employed to protect natural resources. I will use a selection of different examples, some focusing on natural reserves and wetlands, others typically on wildlife crimes, but others also on forestry. The main interest is to provide a few examples of the techniques used by different criminal legislators to provide protection to natural resources.

These types of provisions can also be found at different levels. First, one example from the international level will be discussed, more particularly CITES; next, examples from the European level will be provided.

International level: CITES

CITES[18] was signed in 1973 and entered into force in 1975. It lists particular species of wild flora and fauna of which the conservation is threatened through international trade. Depending upon the specific list on which the species is listed, the level of protection will be higher or lower. Implementation and enforcement take place at the national level. CITES, moreover, is regularly adapted as a result of resolutions and decisions that can be taken by the Conference of the Parties (COP).[19]

16 See further on the *lex certa* principle and its importance as regulatory tool: Michael G. Faure, Morag Goodwin and Franziska Weber, 'The Regulator's Dilemma: Caught between the Need for Flexibility & the Demands of Foreseeability. Reassessing the Lex Certa Principle' (2014) 24 *Albany Law Journal of Science & Technology* 283, 283–364

17 See inter alia Kristie R. Blevins and Terry D. Edwards, 'Wildlife Crime' in J. Mitchell Miller (ed.), *21st Century Criminology: A Reference Handbook* (SAGE Publications, 2009) 557, 557–564

18 See for a detailed analysis Valsamis Mitsilegas and others, *Analysis of International Legal Instruments Relevant to Fighting Environmental Crime. Study in the Framework of the EFFACE Project* (Queen Mary University of London, 2015) <www.efface.eu>, last visited on 3.2.2017. See also <www.cites.org>, last visited on 3.2.2017

19 See <https://cites.org/eng/cop/index.php>, last visited on 31.05.2016

The protection awarded to particular species hence depends crucially on whether they are listed in particular appendices. When particular species (such as, for example, most timber) are not listed in any of the appendices, the protection and enforcement mechanisms under CITES are not available.[20] In that sense one can argue, in the light of the theoretical framework presented above, that CITES has also an administrative dependent structure: the protection mechanisms provided via CITES cannot work unless a particular species has first been listed on specific appendices.[21] Moreover, the importance of administrative documents is also made clear via Article VI of CITES which refers to permits and certificates.[22] Depending upon the intensity of the protection awarded (which again depends upon the listing of the species in particular appendices), a species usually is not subject to an absolute prohibition of trade, but to specific permits and certificates. There is hence no absolute or autonomous protection of a particular species, but rather a regulation of the trade.

Enforcement of CITES (and hence the determination of sanctions) takes place at the national level. Article VIII of CITES determines the measures to be taken by the parties. It inter alia holds:

> The parties shall take appropriate measures to enforce the provisions of the present convention and to prohibit trade in specimens in violation thereof. These shall include measures:
> a) To penalise trade in, or possession of, such specimens, or both; and
> b) To provide for the confiscation or return to the state of export of such specimens.[23]

At its 11th meeting the COP decided that '[p]arties should advocate sanctions for infringements that are appropriate to their nature and gravity'.[24] With respect to sanctioning it is further important that a toolkit for dealing with wildlife and forest offences has been developed by the international consortium on combatting wildlife crime. The goal of this toolkit is to support the national states to comply with these provisions.[25]

Article VIII (4) of CITES mentions that:

> Where a living specimen is confiscated as a result of measures referred to in paragraph 1 of this article:

20 See Mitsilegas and others (n 16)
21 Mitsilegas and others (n 16)
22 Mitsilegas and others (n 16)
23 Art VIII(1) of CITES
24 Mitsilegas and others (n 16) 32
25 International Consortium on Combatting Wildlife Crime, *Wildlife and Forest Crime Analytical Toolkit: Revised Edition* (2012), see <www.unodc.org/documents/Wildlife/Toolkit_e.pdf>, last visited on 3.2.2017

a) The specimen shall be entrusted to a management authority of the state of confiscation;
b) The management authority shall, after consultation with the state of export, return the specimen to that state at the expense of that state, or to a rescue centre at such other place as the management authority deems appropriate and consistent with the purposes of the present convention; and
c) The management authority may obtain the advice of a scientific authority, or may, whenever it considers it desirable, consult the secretariat in order to facilitate the decision under subparagraph (b) of this paragraph, including the choice of a rescue centre or other place.[26]

This shows that CITES explicitly refers to the importance of complementary sanctions, in line with what was mentioned above: confiscated animals should in principle return to the state of origin. It is, however, reported that this often gives rise to conflicts between the state of confiscation and the state of export as a result of which animals are not always returned and in some cases are simply killed because the state of export does not have an appropriate rescue centre.[27]

This brief look at CITES hence shows a few important aspects concerning the way in which international instruments are used to protect nature via the criminal law. A first point is that also at international level, at least in CITES, administrative dependence remains important: an autonomous or independent protection is not awarded. The protection of the specific species is dependent upon the decision of the parties to include the species in particular appendices. Moreover, even when that is the case, there is no absolute protection, but a mere regulation of trade, subject to particular certificates and permits. Of course those certification and permitting procedures do, as such, have the welfare of the species as goal[28] but if those administrative conditions are met, the trade is in principle allowed. There are hence no absolute prohibitions. Violation of the CITES rules (trade without complying with the administrative obligations) could hence constitute a concrete endangerment of the species.

26 Art VIII(4) of CITES. See <www.cites.org>, last visited on 3.2.2017

27 See on this respect Ragnhild Sollund and Jennifer Maher, *The Legal Wildlife Trade: A Case Study Report on the Illegal Wildlife Trade in the United Kingdom, Norway, Columbia and Brazil. A Study Compiled as Part of the EFFACE Project* (2015), available at <www.efface.eu>, last visited on 3.2.2017

28 For example concerning the species included in appendix I (those are those that are on the basis of Art II(1) threatened with extinction or may be affected by trade) export is only allowed when specific conditions are met. The scientific authority of the state of export must *inter alia* have decided that such export will not be detrimental to the survival of the species (Art III(2)(a) of CITES)

A second element is that the sanctioning system as such is not regulated by CITES. For combatting trade in violation of CITES, the convention is hence dependent on implementation and enforcement at the national state level.

A third important element is that the implementing documents do not only refer to the importance of dissuasive penalties, but also to complementary sanctions, more particularly the return of a species that was illegally traded to the state of export. However, as we will discuss below,[29] there is quite a bit of literature indicating that notwithstanding the principle aim of the CITES framework to protect the species via an effective enforcement mechanism, in practice many problems and violations may still occur.

European level

Convention on the Protection of the Environment through Criminal Law

It is interesting to mention that the model theory of environmental criminal law, discussed above,[30] also had an influence at the legislative level. On 4 November 1998 the Council of Europe adopted a Convention on the Protection of the Environment through Criminal Law.[31] In this Convention, the various signatory states agreed to adopt specific provisions to protect the environment in their criminal law. It hence contains minimum provisions on environmental criminal law. Interestingly, many of the ideas presented above can be found in this convention, more particularly the three types of provisions mentioned above.

The core is – not surprisingly – a concrete endangerment crime which can be found in Article 2. This Article provides a long list of behaviours that the signatory states will criminalise on the basis of their national law. Article 2(1b) refers to:

> The unlawful discharge, emission or introduction of a quantity of substances or ionising radiation into air, soil or water, which causes or is likely to cause their lasting deterioration or death or serious injury to any person or substantial damage to protected monuments, other protected objects, property, animals or plants.

Here one recognises clearly the concrete endangerment crime. It is the unlawful emission which is penalised. This provision goes, as was mentioned above, much further than provisions which would merely aim at penalising

29 See subsection 'Low priority, lacking capacity and law sanctions' below

30 See subsection 'Theoretical foundations' above

31 The text has inter alia been published in Faure and Heine (n 10), also available at <www.coe.fr/eng/legaltxt/172ehtm>, last visited on 3.2.2017

the non-respect of administrative obligations. Note, moreover, that this Article refers to 'animals or plants', which hence has a potential to aim at the protection of nature as well. Note, however, that there is a relatively high threshold by requiring that there would be 'substantial damage' to animals or plants.[32]

The Convention also goes a step further and has in Article 2.1(a) also an independent crime aiming at serious pollution: 'The discharge, emission or introduction of a quantity of substances or ionising radiation into air, soil or water, which: – causes death or serious injury to any person, – or creates a significant risk of causing death or serious injury to any person'.[33]

Note that in this particular case, when the emission has these serious consequences of creating death, serious injury or a significant risk of death or serious injury, the unlawfulness requirement is abandoned. This is hence a truly independent crime, in the sense that this provision applies irrespective of the violation of administrative obligations. The idea is apparently that emissions that cause death/serious injury or create a significant risk of such damage can never be justified under administrative law.

It is interesting to note that protection awarded here is rather to human interests than to the environment. One could therefore hold that the provision has an anthropocentric rather than an ecocentric focus. However, when an emission is that serious that it causes death or serious injury to any person, this will undoubtedly cause damage to nature as well. In that sense such an autonomous crime may contribute to the protection of nature as well, although for that protection to intervene human interests have to be primarily endangered.

The Council of Europe Convention also has the traditional abstract endangerment provisions, but they – logically – occupy a less important place in the Convention. More particularly Article 4 refers inter alia to: 'f. the unlawful causing of changes detrimental to natural components of a national park, nature reserve, water conservation area or other protected areas; g. the unlawful possession, taking, damaging, killing or trading of or in protected wild flora and fauna species'.[34] These two provisions clearly focus on the protection of nature, national parks, but also wild flora and fauna species. Note, however, that in this particular case it holds: 'Each party shall adopt such appropriate measures as may be necessary to establish as criminal offences or administrative offences, liable to sanctions or other measures under its domestic law'.[35] The drafters of the Convention clearly recognise

32 See Art 2(1)(b) of the Council of Europe Convention on the Protection of the Environment through Criminal Law

33 See Art 2(1)(a) of the Council of Europe Convention on the Protection of the Environment through Criminal Law

34 See Art 4 of the Council of Europe Convention on the Protection of the Environment through Criminal Law

35 See Art 4 of the Council of Europe Convention on the Protection of the Environment through Criminal Law

that in the case of abstract endangerment, ecological values are not endangered in the same way as with a concrete endangerment. In this case member states can rely on administrative offences.

Although this Council of Europe Convention has not yet entered into force, it is an instrument that truly demonstrates a new attitude towards environmental criminal law. If environmental criminal law really wants to play an important role in supporting sustainable development, it should not limit itself to sanctioning administrative obligations, but criminal law should grant a more direct protection to ecological values. This has been realised in the Council of Europe Convention, which also refers to unlawful emissions and even recognises truly independent crimes in the case of pollution which has serious consequences.

Environmental Crime Directive

It is equally interesting to see what type of provisions mentioned above are used in Directive 2008/99/EC on the protection of the environment through criminal law.[36] Article 3, which lists the conduct that should constitute a criminal offence, when unlawful and committed intentionally or at least with serious negligence, refers to a few provisions which explicitly focus on the endangerment of nature:

> f. the killing, destruction, possession or taking of specimens of protected wild fauna or flora species, except for cases where the conduct concerns a negligible quantity of such specimens and has a negligible impact on the conservation status of the species;
> g. trading in specimens of protected wild fauna or flora species or parts or derivatives thereof, except for cases where the conduct concerns a negligible quantity of such specimens and has a negligible impact on the conservation status of the species;
> h. any conduct which causes the significant deterioration of a habitat within a protected site.[37]

It is striking that with respect to nature, the Directive does not merely focus on the endangerment of particular species, but rather on a behaviour or conduct, such as killing or destruction, which refers to reaching a particular result. In those cases ('killing, destruction of protected wild fauna or flora species'),[38] the threshold for the protection awarded through the criminal law is apparently quite high. The mere (abstract or concrete) endangerment does not suffice, but the protected value really has to be infringed before the

36 [2008] OJ L328/28
37 Ibid Art 3
38 Ibid Art 3(f)

criminal law intervenes. In other cases, more particularly provision (g) referring to trade, it is more the concrete endangerment which is punished. A trade as such does create a danger for the protected species, but does not require an infringement, i.e. a particular result. In one case, more particularly provision (h), the result is required as a condition for criminal liability, i.e. the conduct should have 'caused' the significant deterioration of a habitat. The disadvantage of those provisions, requiring causation, is that it may in practice be very hard for the prosecution to show that it was a specific conduct which 'caused' the deterioration.

It is, moreover, also striking that the provisions use a lot of rather vague notions. Provisions (f) and (g) both exclude criminal liability when the conduct 'concerns a negligible quantity of such specimens and has a negligible impact on the conservation status of the species', whereas (h) to the contrary requires the 'significant' deterioration of a habitat.[39] Obviously national legislators in the member states cannot simply transpose these provisions into the criminal law, as this would violate the *lex certa* principle in criminal law, which requires that the criminal behaviour is described by the legislator with sufficient precision.[40]

Further it should be mentioned that other provisions in Article 3 aim rather at abstract or concrete endangerment (such as the operation of a plant in which a dangerous activity is carried out in (d)), but a condition is that the particular conduct would 'cause or is likely to cause death or serious injury to any person or substantial damage to the quality of air, the quality of soil or the quality of water, or to animals or plants'.[41] Hence, even though the threshold for criminal liability is relatively high, again animals or plants are included as protected interests.

Implementation and enforcement deficit

So far we have mainly focused on the question how criminal liability for resource exploitation can be shaped in legislation. However, a totally different story is obviously how this legislation is enforced in practice. There is a broad literature arguing that specifically in the area of nature protection, there is an important implementation and enforcement deficit. It is, inter alia, one of the criticisms with respect to the effectiveness of CITES.[42]

39 Ibid Art 3

40 See further on this, Michael G. Faure, 'Vague Notions in Environmental Criminal Law' (2010) 18 *Environmental Liability* 119, 119–133; and Michael G. Faure, 'Vague Notions in Environmental Criminal Law' (2010) 18 *Environmental Liability* 163, 163–170

41 Dir 2008/99/EC [2008] OJ L328/28, Art 3(d)

42 See in that respect more particularly the fascinating dissertation by van Uhm, who presents several case studies with respect to wildlife crime: Daan P. van Uhm, 'Uncovering the Illegal Wildlife Trade. Inside the World of Poachers, Smugglers and Traders' (DPhil thesis, Utrecht University, 2016)

It may be clear that within the trade-off between the protection of investments and economic interests on the one hand and the protection of nature and wildlife on the other, enforcement plays a crucial role. The result of this trade-off may be laid down in various regulations such as CITES, but obviously the effectiveness of those regulations will crucially depend upon enforcement. Effective enforcement is on the one hand of great importance for legitimate business interests in order to protect their investments from unfair competition (from those who would act illegally). On the other hand investors benefitting from natural resources may equally lobby against effective enforcement or in other ways try to jeopardise the effective enforcement of regulations aiming at the protection of natural resources, in order to protect their business interests.

Low priority, lack of capacity and law sanctions

There is a large number of studies especially dedicated to the enforcement of CITES, but also to other national legislation focusing on nature protection. As the discussion below will illustrate, the usual tenet of this literature is that the implementation in practice of legislation in many countries remains ineffective as a result of a variety of reasons. Some refer to a lack of capacity or low investments by national governments in capacity building and staff; others refer to the relatively low sanctions, compared to the huge benefits that could be gained with wildlife crime. In the EU context, attention is especially given to the fact that the implementation and enforcement of CITES are a national matter and hence beyond the scope of either CITES or the EU. Finally, poor collaboration between the authorities at various levels is also indicated as one of the sources of an enforcement deficit. We will discuss in a bit more detail some of this literature, often based on detailed case studies concerning specific cases of wildlife crime.

A point obviously often mentioned in the literature is that there may be a lack of resources for investigation and a lack of specialist wildlife knowledge, especially for wildlife crime, even in so-called developed countries.[43] But also other case studies argue that the effectiveness, for example of the implementation and enforcement of CITES, will to a large extent depend upon priorities, political interest and available resources.[44] A case study noticed that even though trafficking in endangered species is identified as a serious crime in both the UK and Norway it is in fact poorly prioritised. This seemed to be the case in Brazil and Colombia as well.[45] Low prioritisation of wildlife crime was already mentioned as a problem in a 1994 study by Traffic Europe, not only for developing countries, but for Europe too.[46]

43 See in this respect, for example, Nurse (n 5) 6

44 See Sollund and Maher (n 24) 33

45 Ibid

46 Traffic Europe, *The Implementation and Enforcement of CITES in the European Union* (1994)

Interestingly, on the positive side, it is mentioned that NGOs can play an important role in the enforcement of wildlife crime. In some legal systems, like in the UK, they can themselves, via private enforcement, bring public actions.[47] In other legal systems NGOs can obviously play an important role as gatekeepers and watchdogs, informing the authorities and thus partially providing a counterweight for the lack of resources and prioritisation on the side of the authorities.

High gains

A second important issue often mentioned in the literature is that the probability of detection may be relatively low and the gains from criminality quite high. This is especially mentioned as far as wildlife trafficking is concerned. The profits from animal trafficking may far outweigh the potential risk in terms of prison sanctions or fines.[48] An important part of wildlife crime is also caused by the huge profits that especially rhino horn can provide in Asian countries.[49] The potentially high gains that may, not only with wildlife crime, but also with illegal logging, be gained may obviously constitute an important motivation for this type of criminality. Sanctions may not always provide a serious deterrent, especially taking into account the low probability of detection which follows from the low prioritisation mentioned earlier.

Weakness of domestic enforcement

Another issue frequently mentioned in the literature is that as far as the enforcement of international conventions, such as CITES (but also others), is concerned the conventions are obviously dependent upon the implementation and enforcement at the national member state level.[50] Also in the EU, where CITES has been supported with a regulation,[51] the problem remains that implementation is a matter of national legislation and hence also of prioritisation within the member states.[52] This is for example illustrated by an issue often mentioned in the literature with respect to complementary sanctions. The ideal model of CITES is that confiscated species should be returned to the state of export.[53] The state of consultation may consult with

47 Nurse (n 5) 4

48 Sollund and Maher (n 24) 34

49 See on that issue in detail Julie Cheung, 'Implementation and Enforcement of CITES: An Assessment of Tiger and Rhinoceros Conservation Policy in Asia' (1995) 5 *Pacific Rim Law & Policy Journal* 125, 125–159

50 See inter alia Mitsilegas and others (n 16) 31–35

51 See inter alia Council Regulation 338/79 of 9 December 1996 on the protection of species of wild fauna and flora by regulating trade therein [1997] OJ L61/1 which has subsequently been regularly amended by other regulations

52 See Traffic Europe (n 37) 26–27

53 See Mitsilegas and others (n 16) 35–38

the CITES secretariat, but the CITES secretariat has no power to decide the final destination of confiscated animals.[54] An especially serious problem is that in some member states, even such as Norway, confiscated animals are routinely killed for the reason that they lack rescue facilities to deal properly with the animals.[55]

Importance of cooperation and networking

Crimes against nature, whether one considers illegal logging, illegal hunting or wildlife crime, all involve transboundary trade and that therefore necessarily also requires cooperation between states. With respect to illegal fishing, it was recently established that the source of the failure of states to respond to the growing illegal, unreported and unregulated fishing crisis is a lack of effective governance by both vertical and horizontal government networks.[56] Most of the case studies reporting on serious wildlife crime usually indicate that the criminality was facilitated by a lack of cooperation between enforcement authorities.[57] This is undoubtedly important within the context of CITES.[58] Precisely since implementation is a national matter, '[t]he efficacy of CITES ultimately hangs on the international cooperation of states, which is vital to the protection and conservation of the tiger, rhinoceros and other threatened or endangered species'.[59] Obviously there are already many initiatives that have been taken to further collaboration between authorities in this domain. This is, inter alia, the case with respect to CITES[60] and there is generally an important stimulating factor with respect to collaboration in the area of environmental crime, being the International Network on Environmental Compliance and Enforcement (INECE). Networking and collaboration may indeed be especially crucial for combatting crime against nature.[61]

54 Ibid 38

55 See Sollund and Maher (n 24) 35

56 See Anastasia Telesetksy, 'Laundering Fish in the Global Undercurrents: Illegal, Unreported, and Unregulated Fishing and Transnational Organized Crime' (2015) 41 *Ecology Law Quarterly* 939

57 Sollund and Maher (n 24) 33–36

58 See for a recent criminological study on tackling wildlife smuggling via the customs authorities Chang-Ryung Han and Hans Nelen, 'Decoupling Policy and Practice in the Fight against Wildlife Smuggling' (2015) 57 *British Journal of Criminology* 132–151

59 Cheung (n 40) 159

60 See, for example, the collaboration between Interpol, the United Office on Drugs and Crime (UNODC) and the World Customs Organization (WCO) with respect to the international consortium on conducting wildlife crime. See Shirleen C.S. Joo and Wouter J. Veening, *Actors and Institutions, Relevant to Fighting Environmental Crime. Study in the Framework of the EFFACE Research Project* (The Hague: Institute for Environmental Security, 2014) available at <www.efface.eu>, last visited on 3.2.2017

61 See further on the necessity and advantages of environmental networking Michael Faure, Peter De Smedt and An Stas (eds), *Environmental Enforcement Networks. Concepts, Implementation and Effectiveness* (Edward Elgar, 2015)

Concluding remarks

The goal of this chapter was to focus on one particular legal instrument that may play a crucial role in the protection of natural resources, being the criminal law. The chapter tried to analyse both from a theoretical as well as from a practical perspective how criminal law should protect natural resources and, moreover, how this is in reality done in practice. The use of the criminal law to protect natural resources raises a number of interesting questions with respect to the relationship between investments in natural resources on the one hand and nature protection on the other. This leads to a trade-off, resulting in a balancing process whereby the criminal law needs to provide an adequate protection to natural resources without jeopardising legitimate business interests in investment decisions.

It was argued that from a theoretical perspective an ideal criminal law should protect the natural environment through a combination of provisions punishing the abstract and concrete endangerment of the environment, but that for serious harm to natural resources also an autonomous protection (i.e. not linked to the administrative law) should be provided. It was equally argued that the protection of natural resources may require different sanctions than the traditional fine and imprisonment. The most important aspect of the remedy system is that the natural environment is restored again and that future harm is prevented. Sanctions should hence also focus on that goal.

Examples of the protection of the environment at international and regional levels were provided, showing that a variety of different types of provisions can indeed be found. It remains, however, striking that most of the time the criminal law can only award its protection as a backup for prior administrative decisions. An autonomous protection awarded by the criminal law for gross infringements against the natural environment is still rare.

Finally, I equally addressed the practical problems with respect to the implementation and enforcement of the criminal law aiming at the protection of the natural environment. As with environmental criminal law generally, natural resources law seems in many countries to suffer from being given low priority, from a lack of capacity (of enforcement agencies) and from low sanctions. That raises questions concerning the effectiveness of the sanctioning system. Since much of the crime against natural resources (more particularly wildlife crime) is often transboundary, the importance of international cooperation and networking was equally stressed.

Although it was shown in this chapter that theoretically the criminal law could be used to provide an adequate protection to natural resources, it was equally argued that there are serious limitations in the way in which the criminal law can provide this protection. Those limitations have to do with difficulties in the adequate formulation of the criminal provisions, but also with difficulties in implementation and enforcement. It is therefore important to realise that other instruments will undoubtedly be far more important in the protection of natural resources. Given its limited ability to provide this adequate protection, the criminal law will always remain an instrument of last resort.

Index

Made in the USA
Coppell, TX
17 August 2022

81643128R00273